AF327345

The Prints of
LeROY NEIMAN

The Prints of LeROY NEIMAN

A Catalogue Raisonné
of Serigraphs, Lithographs,
and Etchings

Knoedler Publishing, Inc.,
Publishers, New York
1980

Editor: Dr. Maury Leibovitz

Editorial Consultant: F. Lanier Graham

Designer: Cam Newell

Library of Congress Cataloging in Publication Data

The Prints of LeRoy Neiman: a catalogue raisonne
of serigraphs, lithographs, and etchings.

Library of Congress Catalogue Card Number: 80-81484

ISBN #0-937608-00-9   Printed in Japan.

Contents

Key to the Catalogue

This catalogue of limited editions has been divided into three sections: serigraphs, lithographs, and etchings. The items in each section have been arranged in chronological order according to the date of release. Dimensions of the image size are given in inches, and then centimeters, with height preceding width. The titles for each piece are definitive, and should be used to replace previously published variations.

Since 1976 all of the serigraphs have been printed on especially made Arches paper, manufactured at the Arches Mill in France, with the artist's signature watermark.

Acknowledgements

We wish to express our thanks to Alfred Frankenstein, one of the most respected art critics and art historians in America, for writing the preface to this book. He has written fifteen books and monographs on American art, among them the definitive book on William Harnett, *After the Hunt,* and two books published by Abrams, *William Sidney Mount,* and *Karel Appel.*

We are also indebted to Lanier Graham, formerly Chief Curator of The Fine Arts Museums of San Francisco, for his comprehensive and insightful text to this book.

We would like to express a special thanks to Cam Newell who has served as the art director as well as directing the research into the detailed and complex areas of identifying and dating all the editions.

Knoedler Publishing, Inc. has been the exclusive publisher of LeRoy Neiman's serigraphs, lithographs and etchings from 1975 to the present.

For the period 1971–1975, the major publishers were: Circle Gallery, Ltd., Lublin Graphics, Inc., Felicie Inc., Orangerie, Inc., F.K.H. Editions, Inc., Merrill Chase, Community Academy Arts, Mayfair Inc., Mogul Graphics, Bernard Slepak, Richard Phillips, and Nabis Fine Arts, Inc.

While the publisher has made every effort to accurately compile and describe all the prints of LeRoy Neiman, we are unable to take responsibility for the final accuracy of every entry because of the complexity of the material.

In particular, I would like to thank the skilled photographic team of George Roos, Jay Lubinsky for his mechanicals, and Jack Murphy for his valued assistance in compiling the information needed for this book.

Dr. Maury Leibovitz
Editor

Preface

During most of the history of American art, genre painting (the painting of life's daily events) has been part of the "truth to nature" cult. This literal rendering of what we can see around us offered leeway for caricature and exaggeration. But William Blake's "firm and determinate outline" was always in command. LeRoy Neiman, on the other hand, is a modern artist. His is an esthetic of a later generation. As Ananda Coomaraswamy once put it, the modern artist does not imitate the outward appearance of nature, but "nature in her method of working."

Modern artists of the 20th century have been inspired by the conceptual breakthroughs of the Post-Impressionists, Symbolists, Expressionists, and especially the masters of the School of Paris. Now color and form are free to serve as symbols of how nature is working inside each artist.

Neiman is best known and most admired as an artist who specializes in sporting events. Indeed, he is the Official Artist of the 1980 Olympic Games. Building on the work of the many American and European artists who have focused on this field (not only Daumier and Lautrec, but also the American Ashcan School), Neiman has created his own unique sporting idiom. In the area of boxing, for example, it is not merely a matter of images of fighters chopping each other up—George Bellows did that decades ago. With Neiman, the fight enters the substance as well as the subject of the picture. One of his favorite color schemes is a spurting, spattering blood-red being pounded through ice. Throughout his work, there is a consistent mortal combat between the jagged flame of blood-hot red, and the smooth cold plane of thickly frozen ice.

But his palette does not stop there. The range of his expression is such that he also can render an overview of the beach at Cannes with a gentle, softly colored lyricism.

For me, not all of his prints have been of the same quality. His most mature and well-studied work has come in recent years, especially from his study of horses and their environment. For years he has been concentrating on this theme, which has held a magical fascination for artists since the prehistoric cave paintings of France and Spain. He has been working not only from observation, but from the perspective of other artists (historic and contemporary), as well as the rich mythology of wild horses riding through the thundering heavens on hooves of lightning, carving jagged glimpses of the sky's lurid infinity.

In works such as these, he manages to create effects of hugely extended terrestrial space, sometimes as if speed had broken the space barrier and let speed spill as it will. But the ghost of William Blake may be peeking over the edges of those turmoiling clouds. It can't be left merely to spill. The athlete or the rider may leap like the spraying fronds of a Baroque-Mannerist fountain suddenly, and then be off again.

Visual experiences are like that. No abstract system holds the experience together. It is held together by LeRoy Neiman's eye.

Alfred Frankenstein

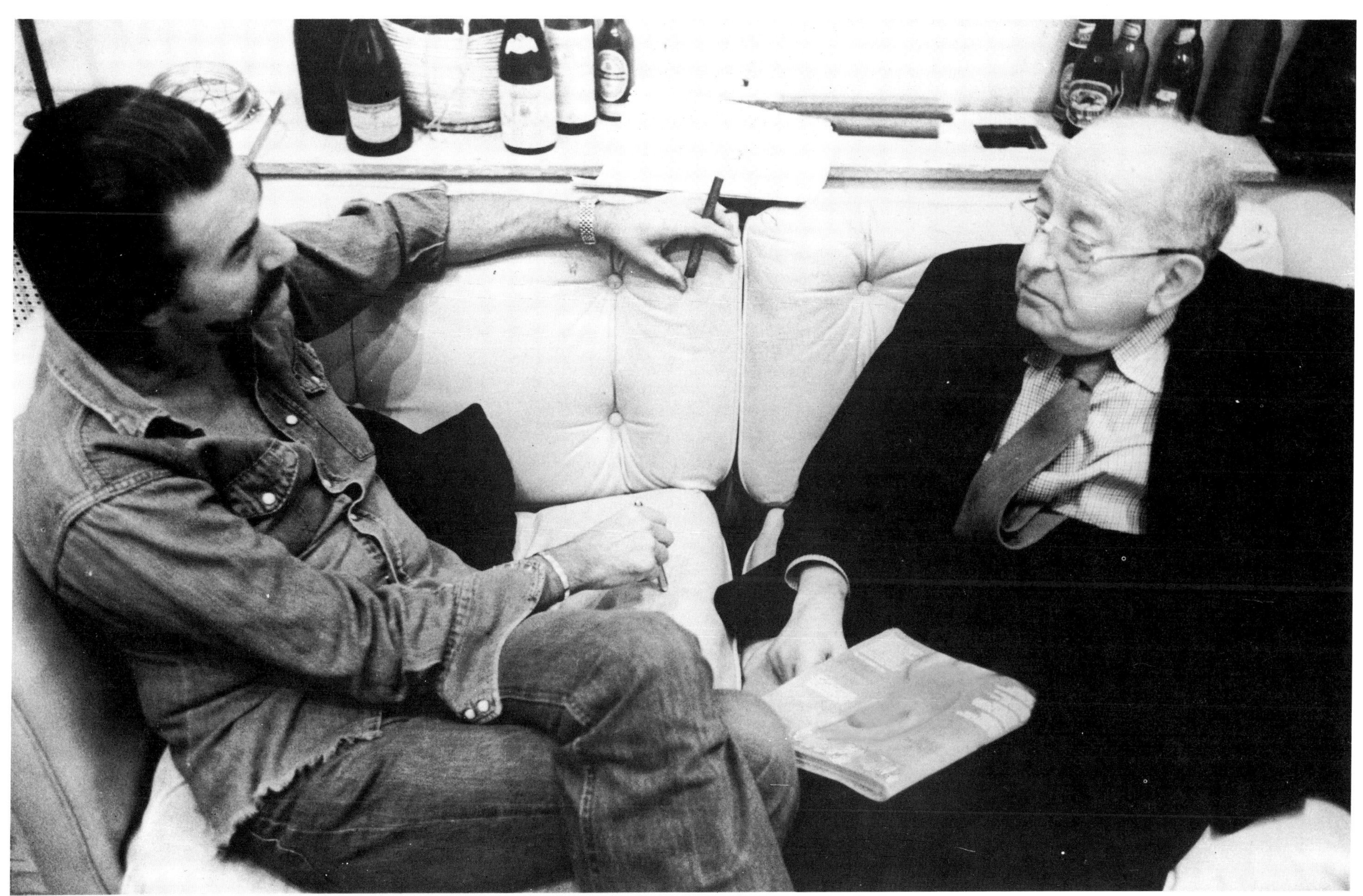

Neiman and Frankenstein in the artist's New York studio, 1979.

*"Should art be abstract? No. Unaffected, simple,
direct. It is like a bridge. What would be the
best bridge? Well, the one which could be reduced
to a thread, a line, without anything left over,
which fulfilled strictly its function of uniting
two separated distances."*
                                    Pablo Picasso (1935)

*"Goya foreshadows all modern art with a response to
the cry…of deep-rooted collective emotions which
modern art has chosen to ignore."*
                                    André Malraux (1946)

*"Communication is what it's all about.
Art is simply the means by which it happens.
It's something that just passes through me
and on to them."*   *LeRoy Neiman (1980)*

THE NEIMAN PHENOMENON:
A General Overview

The art of LeRoy Neiman is unique.
It stands alone, without any real comparison.
It is an art which has become controversial
because Neiman has broken the barriers
of many of the most hallowed assumptions
of modern art history and contemporary criticism.
It is an art that is loved by millions of people
throughout America and around the world.

His remarkable commercial success simply
doesn't fit the modern mythology
that "real artists" should be starving
in an old attic or basement somewhere
impoverished, misunderstood and depressed.
LeRoy Neiman happens to be quite happy,
very well understood, and wealthy.

Is it *proper* for an artist to be so appreciated?
So easily understood? So immediately clear?
Something must be wrong, the critics tell us.
How could this be?

As if this were not enough,
LeRoy Neiman has done some other things
that simply are not supposed to be done,
according to the clearly defined rules of
modern art criticism.

His colors are so intense that
they are "outrageous" to the eyes
of people raised on the cool, relatively subtle
harmonies of the School of Paris masters.

Moreover, he took hold of a very distinguished,
very respected "High Style"
of painting called Action Painting
(because of the action of the painters who
invented this style in the mid 1940's,
especially Pollock, Kline, and de Kooning.)
Then he had the audacity to merge this semi-sacred
painting technique with the "Low Style" of
figurative painting from the so-called
"minor" tradition of Social Realism.

Well, he wasn't supposed to do that.
It goes against everything that the modern
art establishment thinks is correct.
But LeRoy Neiman did it anyway.
And millions of people are over-joyed that he did.
He has brought art into the lives of more people
than most post-war American painters put together.

Surely, something must be wrong somewhere?
But where?
There is another way to ask the question,
of course.
Is it possible that something is
right somewhere?

But let's go on.
Let's forget his style for a minute.
Maybe we will find what's wrong if we
look at his subject-matter.

Many critics have been surprised to find
that Neiman actually believes
in the story-telling importance of figures

responding to real life situations.
Why are they surprised?

Well, there are some people
to whom the painting of human figures
in an effort to portray social situations
is a totally unacceptable practice,
and cannot be considered "art"
no matter how well it is done.
That is not what "real painting" is about.
Such activities are best left to illustrators,
photographers and filmmakers
whose media require figurative imagery.

As an historian, I find it very strange
that this formalist point-of-view
became so widely established
in the contemporary art community
over the last 20 or 30 years.

Not everybody feels this way of course.
But the prejudice has been pervasive.
This attitude has been so widely held
by so many of our leading critics
throughout the East Coast art establishment
over the last generation
that I sometimes wonder
if the structural principles of criticism
are still flexible enough to recognize and deal with
figurative painting in a meaningful way.

How did this anti-figure attitude establish itself?
The evolution of the formalist position in America
is clear, and will be documented in the following essay.
In brief, the story (highly simplified) goes like this.

The most advanced painters since Impressionism
(a hundred years ago)
have not been very interested in the human figure,
or in the rendering of clear, coherent "stories."
The artistically interesting problems became
formal questions of abstract composition
and private symbolism.

So, not many *important* painters of the 20th century
have engaged in narrative (story-telling)
picture painting since way back when Cubism
fragmented, and then shattered
the human figure
until nothing was left
to relate to with our minds and hearts
except the non-figurative elements
of an abstract composition.

So it has been difficult (psychologically) for some critics
to consider figure painters *important*
no matter how good they may be.

The masterpieces of The Modern Tradition
are extremely rich in symbolism,
and deeply powerful in their visual intensity.

Some of these abstract works of art
have such an overwhelming emotional impact
that people have been known to kneel in their presence.
A major canvas by Pollock or Rothko or Motherwell
tends to be regarded with a reverence

that our tribal ancestors reserved
for their most sacred images
of The Tribal Totem.

If art of such intense spiritual quality
can be achieved by non-figurative means,
the critics have tended to say,
"why bother with a pictorial form
that is as antiquated and unnecessary
as the human figure?"

One reason why some artists from Picasso to Neiman
have *insisted* on the use of the human figure
is so that the general public
can understand what they're doing.
One of the tragedies of The Modern Tradition
is that so few people have been able
to understand and appreciate it.

As far as the general public is concerned,
it is as if the most modern of modern art
has become inaccessible,
as if the non-figurative masters
have created a completely private imagery
which (try as they might)
they simply cannot understand.

Studies have been conducted,
and the estimate is that only about 1%
of the American people are able
to understand and appreciate
non-figurative painting.
That means that the vast majority

are completely cut off
from the profound spiritual power
of contemporary American art—
a body of art that is widely considered
the most important in the world today.

It is as if only a small priestly class
knows the meaning
of the secret symbols.
The Tribe has been cut off
from its Totems.

When we take a long look back over
the history of art as a whole,
it is very strange to find a situation in which
most of the people in a society
are disconnected
from the inspiration that is offered
by the most respected artists of the time.

Indeed, there is no reason to believe
that this state-of-affairs
has ever existed before:

Not in the tribal times of our most distant ancestors.
Not in the Middle Ages, or the Renaissance.
Not in 17th and 18th century Europe
when paintings and prints were purchased
by many classes of society.
Not even in 19th century France
when Daumier's work was in the magazines,
and Lautrec's work was on the lamp-posts.

Not in 19th century America
when people bought contemporary
paintings and prints
from our leading artists
by the thousands.
Only in the last several decades
have 99% of urban societies been
disconnected from the vitality
of contemporary art.

This fact is of profound social importance.
There are good reasons to believe that this fact
plays a role in putting millions of people
on the mental health rolls of the U.S. Government.
It is hard for mental health to maintain itself
when there is so little color to eat,
when there is so little access to the magic
that only art is able to provide.

We all have our own window
on aesthetic experience, of course.
No two people have quite the same taste.
Our taste is as unique as our individuality.
Groups, and subgroups, and cultures and subcultures
all have slightly different kinds of aesthetic experience.
But all human beings regularly have intense aesthetic
experiences of one kind or another.
At least until lately,
when entire national societies got out of touch
with the practice of contemporary art.

The brain scientists and social anthropologists
are telling us that one of the reasons why
whole classes of people are sick
is because they are not using the aesthetic side of their
brain—the right hemisphere.
Here is a report from Dr. Colin Blakemore,
Director of Medical Studies at
Cambridge University in England.
His book, *Mechanics of Mind* (1977), has become a
standard reference.
"The left-hemisphere is our intellectual side.
The…left talks, writes, does mathematics,
and thinks in a logical, serial way;
the right recognizes shapes and faces,
appreciates music…and works in a
global, intuitive fashion.
(From the right comes)…spatial perception,
pictorial recognition…intuitive thought
(and) emotional reaction."

This information about how our mind
actually works is not entirely new.
The Double Brain/One Mind concept
has been around, in one form or another
for thousands of years.
But it is only in the last generation
that what the brain scientists considered a theory
was confirmed by experiments
conducted during open skull surgery.

So the scientific fact is that our
cerebral cortex has two hemispheres
which have complementary functions.
The left hemisphere
is what we use when we are using our capacity to
read and write, plan logical plans for the future,
and think about things in particular.
The right hemisphere is what we use when we are
using our capacity to see color, be aesthetic,
be emotional, and have a feeling about things in general.
Each of us has the capacity to be both, of course:
logical and aesthetic, intellectual and intuitive.

The biological system itself is perfectly balanced, as a rule.
As Pogo used to say in the comic strips: "The enemy is us."
Our individual psychologies keep us out-of-balance.
Most personalities tend to lean one way or the other.
The stereotype is that males tend to be one way, and
females another. Our social system as currently
structured reinforces this duality, as is well known.

But this polarized stereotype is not a very healthy
concept, according to the scientific and spiritual
leaders of today.
Mental health and physical health tend to increase
together as we learn to develop our
capacity to use both sides of ourselves at the same time
(in a balanced way), as we learn how to think and feel
simultaneously.

Art is one of the best means known
to develop the right side of our brains.
It is a powerful and painful fact
that people who are out-of-touch
with any form of art
don't have much of a chance to succeed
in their Pursuit of Happiness.
They probably will remain unbalanced
in spite of their Constitutional Rights.

Enough of science and social philosophy.
Let's get back to art—the art of LeRoy Neiman.
This artist and those who respond to his art
are passionately involved with the Pursuit
of Happiness. They will not be denied.
Well, all this is very interesting you might say.
But, so what? What does all this mean?
Let's go back to where it all began.
First let's take a careful look at
the stylistic evolution of the art of the
most popular painter in America,
and then try to figure out
what the Neiman Phenomenon is all about.

F. Lanier Graham

Reflections on the Evolution of Pop Art and Popular Criticism

*"As early as 1855 Charles Baudelaire in his <u>De l'Essence du Rire</u>
sensed that cartoons were somehow becoming a distinctive form of art
parallel to painting and no longer dependent on it…; by the 1890s
perceptive observers were suggesting that art critics should take cartoons
more seriously because advance-guard painters were so obviously
borrowing from them.…*

*And in all fields of artistic activity much the same has
happened. Literature is typical. "I incline to come to the alarming
conclusion," T. S. Eliot wrote in his ponderous way in 1936,*

> *that it is just the literature that we read for "amusement" or
> "purely for pleasure" that may have the greatest…least sus-
> pected…earliest and most insidious influence upon us. Hence
> it is that the influence of popular novelists, and of
> popular plays of contemporary life, requires to be scrutinized.
> [<u>Essays Ancient and Modern</u>, p. 105]*

*John Steinbeck put it much more brutally a few years
later in his 1953 introduction to Al-Capp's <u>World of Li'l
Abner</u>:*

> *How do we know what Literature is? Well, one of the symptoms
> or diagnostics of literature should be, it seems to me, that it is
> read, that it amuses, moves, instructs, changes, and criticizes
> people. And who in the world does that more than Capp? …
> Nobody reports on the doings of Horace Hairlip the sad and
> decadent denizen of [Faulkner's] aristocratic but mouldy
> South. And yet he is discussed in our literary gazettes as though
> he were literature.…I think Capp may very possibly be the best
> writer in the world today.…*

*I would not go so far as that; but it is worth pointing out that of all
writers in the 1930s and -40s the two still most influential and widely
read today (outside of English literature course assignments) are
George Orwell and C. S. Lewis, neither of whom literary critics at the
time paid any attention to.*

*From Alan Gowans, <u>The Unchanging Arts: New Forms for
the Traditional Functions of Art in Society</u> (1971)*

The Art of LeRoy Neiman:
A Stylistic and Sociological Analysis

by F. Lanier Graham

*"Ten years ago, the question, Is painting
dead? was seriously being raised as artist after
artist deserted the illusory world of the canvas . . .
The traditional activity of painting,
especially hand painting with brush
on canvas, as it had been practiced in the West
since oil painting replaced manuscript illumina-
tion and frescoed murals, seemed to offer no
possibility for innovation, no potential for
novelty so startling it could compete with the
popular culture for attention. . . . In the past, of
course, the painter would never have compared his
activity with the practical side of life; but by
the time Senator Javits presented President Kennedy
with an American flag painted by Jasper Johns,
the idea that art was an activity parallel in some
way with politics, business, technology and
entertainment was on the way."*

Barbara Rose
American Painting: The Eighties (1979)

THE EARLY WORK OF LeROY NEIMAN:
Heros, Hopes and Struggles

LeRoy Neiman did not begin life as an artist. He did win a national art prize for his painting of a fish when he was in the 6th grade. But art was an interest that developed gradually as he casually sketched animals for the grocery store windows and designed posters for the dances and football games of his high school in St. Paul, Minnesota.

Most of his time was spent participating in the life around him—the busy life of an impoverished city boy, especially sporting events and movies about sports heroes. And he loved to get into the boxing ring in the basement of his church. During his high school years, the people who ran the Side Show for Ripley's Believe-it-or-Not asked him to touch up the giant canvas that hung out in front of the show depicting the acts and the freaks. As he wandered through the neighborhoods of gangland mobsters, and rode the boxcars to Duluth and Chicago, he saw it all—life in the big city. Like a sponge, his eye drank in the rapidly passing images of horses, cars, and walls full of bullet holes; hobos, whores and movie stars; action, power, speed, and thoughtful reflection; deep dark sadness, and radiant joy…life in the big city.

When World War II erupted, he dropped out of high school and joined the army where he found himself painting highly suggestive wall murals for the troops in the mess hall, as an oasis of semi-sanity from the blood and guts that spilled around him from the invasion of Normandy to the Battle of the Bulge.

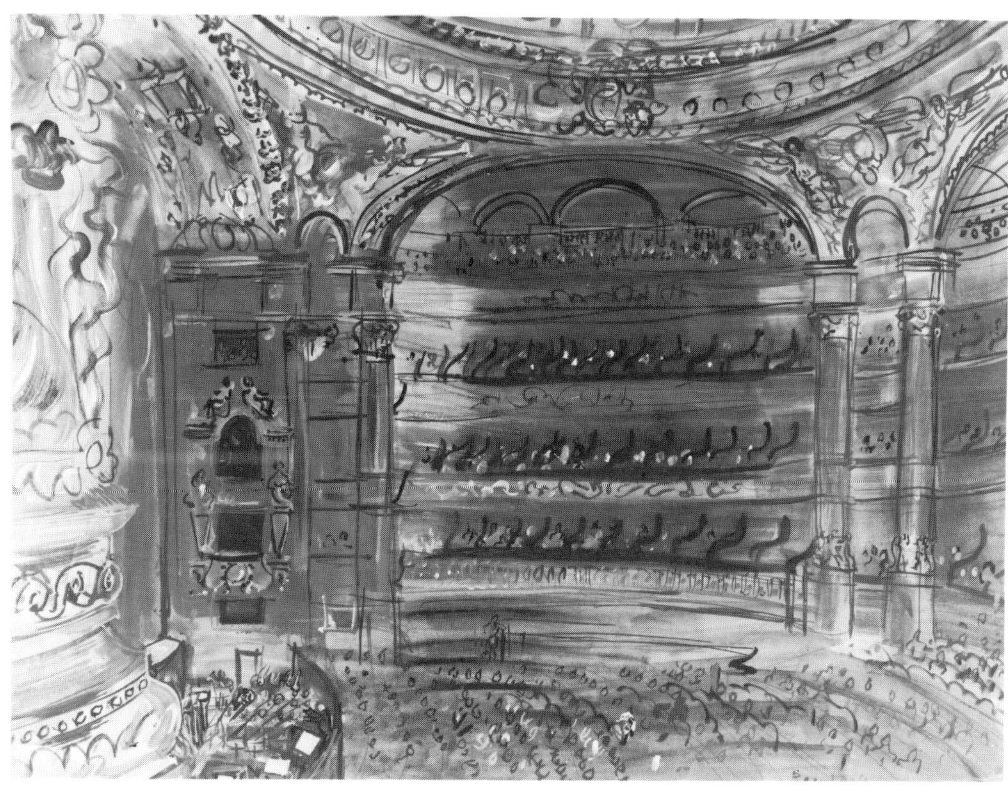

Raoul Dufy, *The Opera, Paris* (ca. 1939), The Phillips
Collection, Washington, D.C.

The officers liked it. The enlisted men liked it. The nurses liked it. Everybody liked it. And Neiman liked doing it. So he decided to become an artist when he returned to his home town in 1946.

His first teacher was a colorist named Clement Haupers who was a leading artist in the city, and taught at the St. Paul Art Center (which is now the Minnesota Muscum of Art). Haupers had studied with André Lhôte at the Académie Montparnasse in Paris. He took Neiman into the country to paint landscapes and drilled him in the mechanics of rendering a convincing three-dimensional image. He also taught him the basic compositional principles of Cézanne. Then he suggested that Neiman go on to study art and art history at the School of the Art Institute of Chicago.

In the fall of 1946, using the GI Bill, he did just that. Here, at the age of 20, Neiman had his first real introduction to the history of art. Until then, all he had actually experienced was American art of the traditional kind that could be found in the portrait gallery of his State Capital or on the streets. Now he could wander through one of the largest and most complete art museums in the world. Most of the major styles of human history were at his fingertips. It was an exhilarating experience, and he was wide open to all of it.

His primary guide to all these mysteries was Boris Anisfeld, a Russian painter who had come to the United States with the Diaghilev Ballet in 1918, and had taught at the Art Institute since 1928. Neiman studied with him for two years. Anisfield was large, strong, fastidious, and (during the 20s) famous. He had catholic tastes, liking both the most ancient and the most modern, and regarded himself as the follower of no one.

He was not so fashionable when Neiman became his student. But he was the sort of teacher to whom students naturally became devoted. The psychological connection between student and master was so close that Anisfeld provided a role model. This is how Neiman remembers it:

"In the beginning I was totally undisciplined. Haupers and Anisfeld were important because they acted like artists, looked like artists, and felt like artists. They taught me the craft of painting, and also the notion of being totally involved with and dedicated to art; you need to know that the artist really exists and is something beyond the picture itself." [1]

His influence on young Neiman was considerable, both as an artist and as a person. Anisfeld was a passionately sensuous man who lived and worked in a world of intense color, and was deeply in love with opera and the dance. His work for Bakst, Diaghilev, and the Metropolitan Opera in New York are rich explosions of color. As a teacher of anatomy, life drawing and painting, he stressed that his students would be free to do anything they wanted, said his daughter, in a recent interview, "once they had discipline and a background in true craftsmanship." [2]

Neiman feels indebted to him primarily for what he taught him about the psychology of color, and the potential of dramatic juxtapositions of color, as well as his attitude towards art and life. Neiman once told me that, "the most important thing this warm and wonderful old Russian mystic told me is that I should paint from the heart. That's where everything should be coming from."[3]

But what comes from the heart must go through something else before it can reach the heart and mind of another. What was the structure of the art into which Neiman wanted to pour his heart? At that point, Neiman did not know what his style would be. He had a lot to choose from, and was busy considering all the possibilities.

Anisfeld was not his only teacher at the Chicago Art Institute, only the most influential. By the early 1950s, all the major art movements were represented on the faculty. At first (in the late 1940s) Neiman was involved with the traditional mainstream of modern urban art especially the American realists. The ethical, sociological orientation of this art was stressed by a faculty made up almost exclusively of East European Jews who had recently migrated to Chicago. Neiman joined this faculty in 1951 teaching drawing and fashion illustration, and stayed for ten years.

In the early 50s, came the explosion of Action Painting, and the arrival of the "Hans Hoffman School" of Abstract Expressionists who perpetuated the lurid color combinations which many non-expressionists find so vulgar. Both kinds of painting had a strong influence on Neiman. The central problem of his work became how to synthesize these two very different ways of seeing and thinking. It was a problem that he would struggle with for years.

Who were the artists whose work was particularly important to Neiman at the time? What were the primary formal influences on him when he was just beginning to find himself?

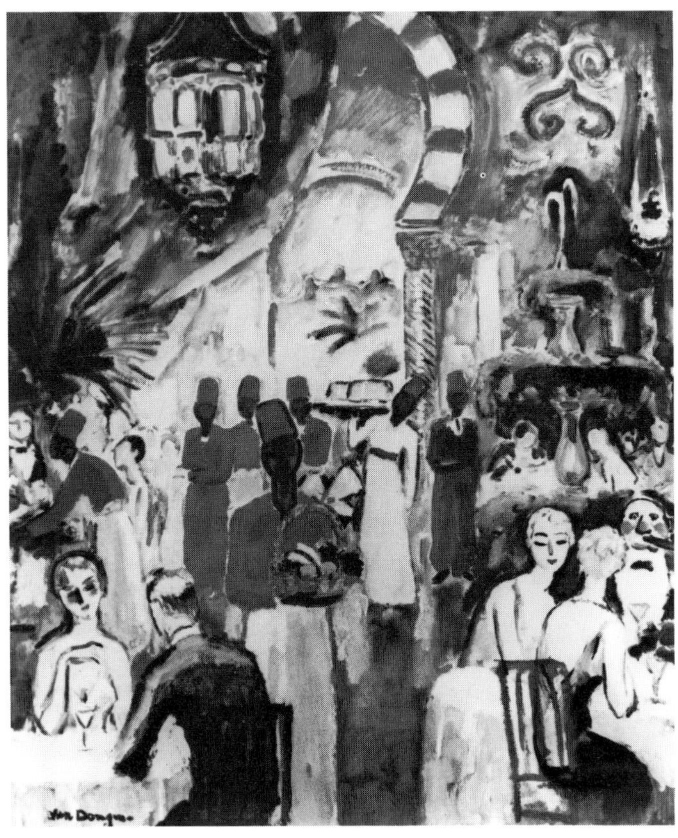

Van Dongen, *Shephard's Hotel Restaurant at Cairo* (1928),
photograph courtesy of Lenoir M. Josey, Inc.

When I asked him this question, in the summer of 1979, this was his first reply: "Leonardo and Rubens for spirit. Tintoretto for space, and Fragonard for brushwork."[4] As we went on to talk about color as line, he spoke of the whole genealogy of Romantic Realists from Goya and Delacroix and Daumier, to the Impressionists, Post-Impressionists, and Fauves, and especially the East European Expressionists Van Dongen and Kokoschka.

At first he was shy to tell people how much he responded to both the cool, clear lyricism of Dufy, *and* the deep, soul-searching intensity of the Expressionists. Usually, it is expected that one likes one or the other. Neiman, who has both of these psychological polarities in himself, liked both.

For color as field, for pure color as an arena in which to act, he is quite conscious of his close relationship with Action Painters, particularly the work of Pollock, Kline, and de Kooning.

For certain kinds of color, Neiman also reached back into his earlier American heritage. Neiman was especially drawn to the subtle overlays of Inness, and the rich Wagnerian color dramas of Moran. He also liked Homer and Sargent and Remington, all of whom rendered energetic bursts of human activity. Eakins he found too silent and too still.

For subject matter, the artists who inspired him most—who validated his desire to render urban life as a whole—were members of the Ashcan School, and those who followed in the mainline American tradition of social realism on the heels of the New York Realists.

Contrary to the belief of many critics, Social Realism is not a "minor" tradition. Art that focuses on the life of people and comments on their daily activities has been the mainstream of American art throughout most of our history. It was the New York Ashcan painters (Henri, Sloan, Glackens, Shinn, and Luks) in the early years of the 20th century, who first painted The Urban Scene in America—the life of the streets and the nightclubs and the boxing rings. This focus on city life was continued by Henri's younger students, George Bellows and Edward Hopper, as well as Reginald Marsh, Raphael Soyer, and Ben Shahn. Mainstreams move slowly. Abstract painting did not start to become "mainstream" until the 1950s, when Neiman already had finished his academic training.

To assimilate all of these influences at once is a very difficult thing to do. But it is what young art students in America are asked to do. In every major metropolitan area of the United States since World War II, this is the way art students are educated. Most of their time is spent in studio work. In a semester or two, they are exposed to the entire history of art.

For young art students who have known only traditional kinds of portraiture and genre painting, being exposed to the whole history of human imagination is a transformative experience. No one is quite the same afterwards. For Neiman, it was as if the Armory Show went off in his head like a firecracker. [5]

As his student years ended, and his teaching years began, he had what he needed to work with: his own solid grounding in the figurative tradition, and the idea that color is free, totally free to do with as he wanted. What did he want to do with all this? What was his purpose? What was his philosophy? Where was he coming from?

He recounts: "If nothing else, the army completely confirmed me as an artist. During this period I made my crucial discovery of the difference between the lifestyles of the officer and the Pfc. This was to become the basis for my later mission in art, to investigate life's social strata from the workingman to the multimillionaire." [6]

He was a good, solid American, was raised on the realism of movies, and comics, and figure painting, and the true life drama of the streets. He is proud of being a "street artist." Representational art was fundamental to his nature. He had no desire to depart from the story-telling potential of figures in action. But he had to find out what to do with all those surges of color that continued to pulsate through his mind.

What did he want to do with all this color? To work with he had the naturalistic color of the American tradition, and the symbolic color of the European tradition. He also had the background of a society that has very little color in its daily life. Until after World War II, American painting is not very colorful, as a rule, when compared with contemporary Europeans. The paintings have color in them. But most are not intensely colorful. The parallel fact is that American cities are not very colorful. In the living spaces, and working spaces of most Americans, there is a pervasive grayness. The only time the average American sees a great deal of color is while shopping or watching T.V. (as Madison Avenue knows very well).

Part of this is due to our Puritan heritage. Since the 17th century, our Puritan ancestors have been opposed to the use of color as something that is sinfully sensuous. Neiman, however, is not a puritan. He loves color—huge quantities of color. He swallowed Expressionist color whole, and decided to try to integrate it with his solid American sense of the human figure.

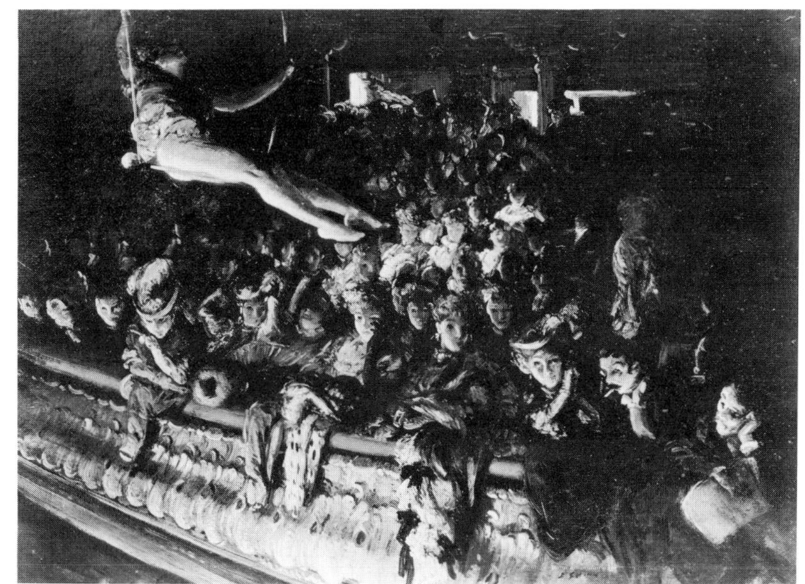

Everett Shinn, *London Hippodrome* (1902), The Art
Institute of Chicago, Friends of American Art Gift

That was an enormous ambition. He did not realize his ambition all at once. It took years. In the meantime, he worked his way through all of the post-cubist figure painters who had the most dynamic visual surfaces before he was able to generate his own idea of how to make colored forms in motion become people in action. Following this time-honored tradition of learning from other artists, Neiman's style in the early 50s is indebted to the mainline Social Realism of Reginald Marsh, and Jack Levine, as well as the jazz-like compositions of Ben Shahn.

As he wrestled with the problem of integrating symbolic coloration with naturalistic figuration in the early 50s, he did it by doing just what he set out to do in the first place—painting the people of the urban world that he knew best. At this point in his life, the slice of city life that he knew best was the night-life of the back streets of the big city: the jazz clubs on Chicago's Southside, the strip joints on Clark Street, Rush Street, and the twinkling lights on those luxurious yachts that moved softly up and down the lake front.

From the window of his modest basement studio, Neiman's eye was fascinated by the neon glitter of the city alive at night—color in motion. When we look at the world through artificial light, something begins to happen to our sense of color. For centuries, all art was done under natural light. The effort was to capture natural color. But in the last few generations, most American painting has been done under artificial light. The result has been the widespread use of curious kinds of artificial color. This expanded range of colors gave Neiman a great deal of freedom to discover just the kind of color symbolism he wanted to use. His regular association with *Playboy Magazine*, from its beginning in 1954, gave him an unlimited opportunity to study "The Good Life" (usually the Night Life) in all the major cities of the world.

More often than not, his oil and acrylic colors are the strangely fluorescent colors of the artificially illuminated night, realistic and expressionistic simultaneously. After years of being immersed in this phosphorescent ocean of

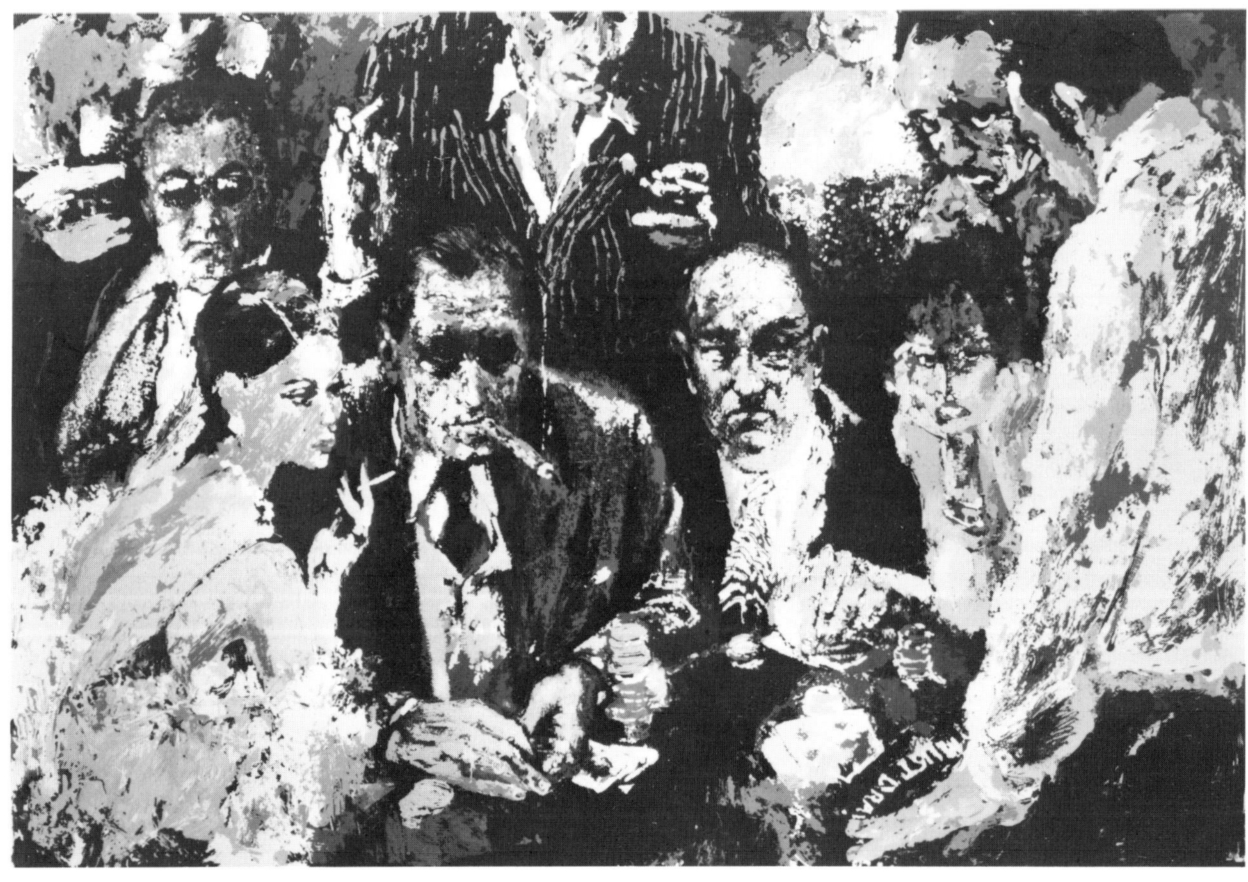

Vegas Blackjack, oil on canvas, 30 x 48″, 1959, collection of Mr. & Mrs. Milton Krishbaum

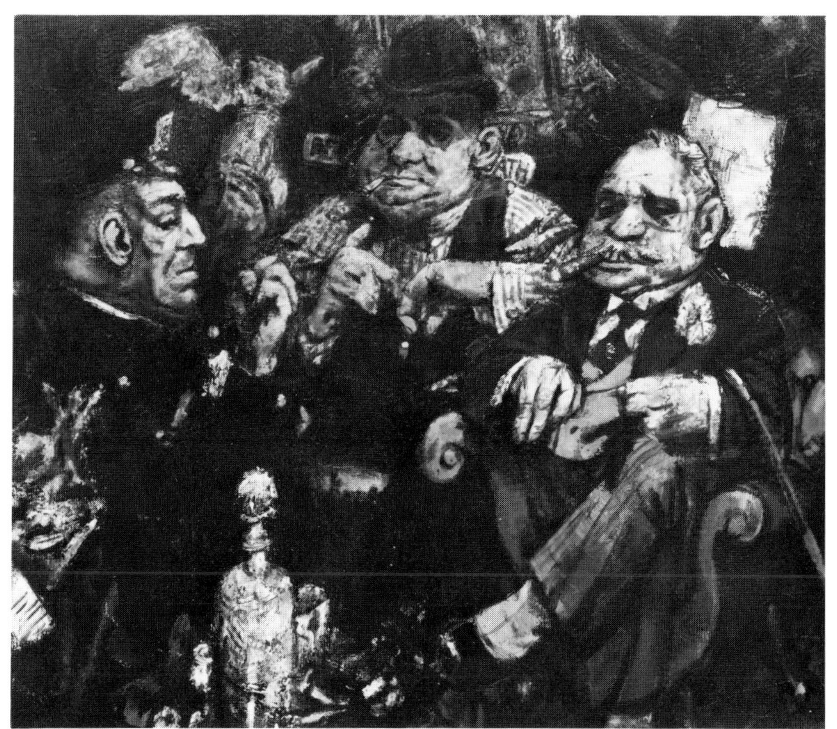

Jack Levine, *The Feast of Pure Reason* (1937), The Museum of Modern Art, New York on extended loan from the United States WPA Art Program

colored light, Neiman finally found a way of using colors in a way that is both naturalistic and symbolic. This was a large part of the marriage he was working for by bringing together two extremely different influences. This is how he explains it:

"I do not depart from the colors borrowed from life. But I use color to emphasize the scent, the spirit, and the feeling of the thing I've experienced. The behavior and interplay of these colors determine the psychological impact of the painting." [7]

Neiman does not paint fantasies as a rule. He paints what he has experienced with his own eyes. Psychologically, he has a hunger for wholeness. His passion is to render the essence of the entire experience. Like most artists since the Renaissance (until a few decades ago), Neiman sets out to capture not simply what he sees, but the whole of the reality that he experiences at a specific time and place.

Throughout this essay, we are taking a careful look at the evolution of the artist's style. But we should be careful not to get caught in the trap that many art historians set for themselves when they forget that, to the artist, the subject is more important than the style in which it is rendered. One does not paint in order to develop a style. Style is the product of a purpose, the after-effect of an effort to communicate.

"For me," says Neiman, "communication is what it's all about. Art is simply the means by which I am able to do it." So he had to find a way of dealing with his subject-matter that would make his message easily available to as many people as possible.

What was his decision? What part of what he sees does he render in his effort to communicate a sense of the whole? What does he actually paint?

What Neiman decided to make his subject-matter is images—public images—the images we all carry around with us when we are out in the world. He never paints private moments, as a rule. He even admits that he can't.

"When I paint, I seriously weigh the public presence of a person—the surface facade. I am less concerned with how people look when they wake up or how they act at home. A person's public presence reflects...efforts at image development." 8

So he genuinely respects the quiet little visual arts of everyone. And he paints what people look like when they cover up their private bodies with clothes and jewels and scents. The image of all this is what he goes for. This is a subtle point. At first it may seem difficult to grasp. But it is very easy to see visually. Many of his critics call him "superficial." There is nothing wrong with using a word like this, if that is what we really mean. There's room for confusion if the word is not used correctly. "Superficial" is a tricky word.

There are "superficial" things about Neiman's work. Some of his early serigraphs, for example, are thinly conceived and hastily executed. As I

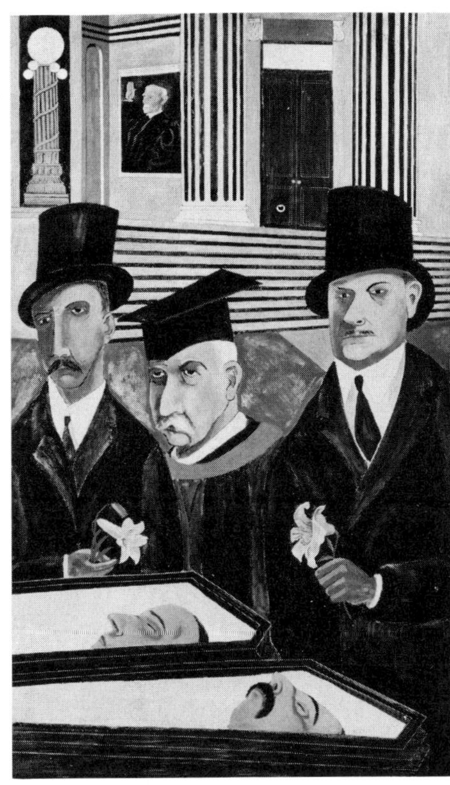

Ben Shahn, *The Passion of Sacco and Vanzetti* (1931-32),
The Whitney Museum of American Art, Gift of
Edith and Milton Lowenthal in memory of
Juliana Force.

studied these early editions I wondered why the bodies are so thin, as if he were painting only the skins of these athletes instead of their whole bodies. Some of his portraits have some of the quality of caricature. Then he explained how he goes for both the actual *look* of people, and the image that is either self-projected or projected onto them by the general public.

Neiman's work in general is specifically *superficial* in a very special sense. Neiman's iconography, his actual subject-matter, is the symbolic *surface* of things, in their relation with each other. His interpretation is, by turns, sympathetic and satirical, but usually his attitude is quite positive.

Everyone has a certain look—a look that usually is quite carefully cultivated consciously or unconsciously. The "image" includes many things: how we cut our hair, how we dress, how we walk, and how our attitudes towards life have a way of carving themselves into the corners of our face. Groups of people also have images. Corporations have images. Nations have images. Our world is very much a world of images now-a-days. Image-building is a multi-billion dollar industry. Our national security depends on projecting a certain image. And so does the everyday psychological functioning of our individual personalities.

Neiman is only concerned with the people part of all this. He could be called an "Environmental Artist", in a certain way. He paints the look of people and their places. Unlike the existential Andrew Wyeth, Neiman almost never paints people alone. He paints people being together in public places. People who hang out in bars tend to look one way. People who attend museum openings tend to look another way. One of the unique achievements of Neiman's mature work is that he has been able to capture just this—the actual *look* of everyday reality in motion. This extremely realistic image is pervaded by colors that symbolically evoke a feeling of the entire physical and psychological environment.

And it works. It does not always work equally well, but it works. In spite of his freely admitted unevenness, his compositions work to such a degree that the public response is seldom casual. Usually the response is passionately

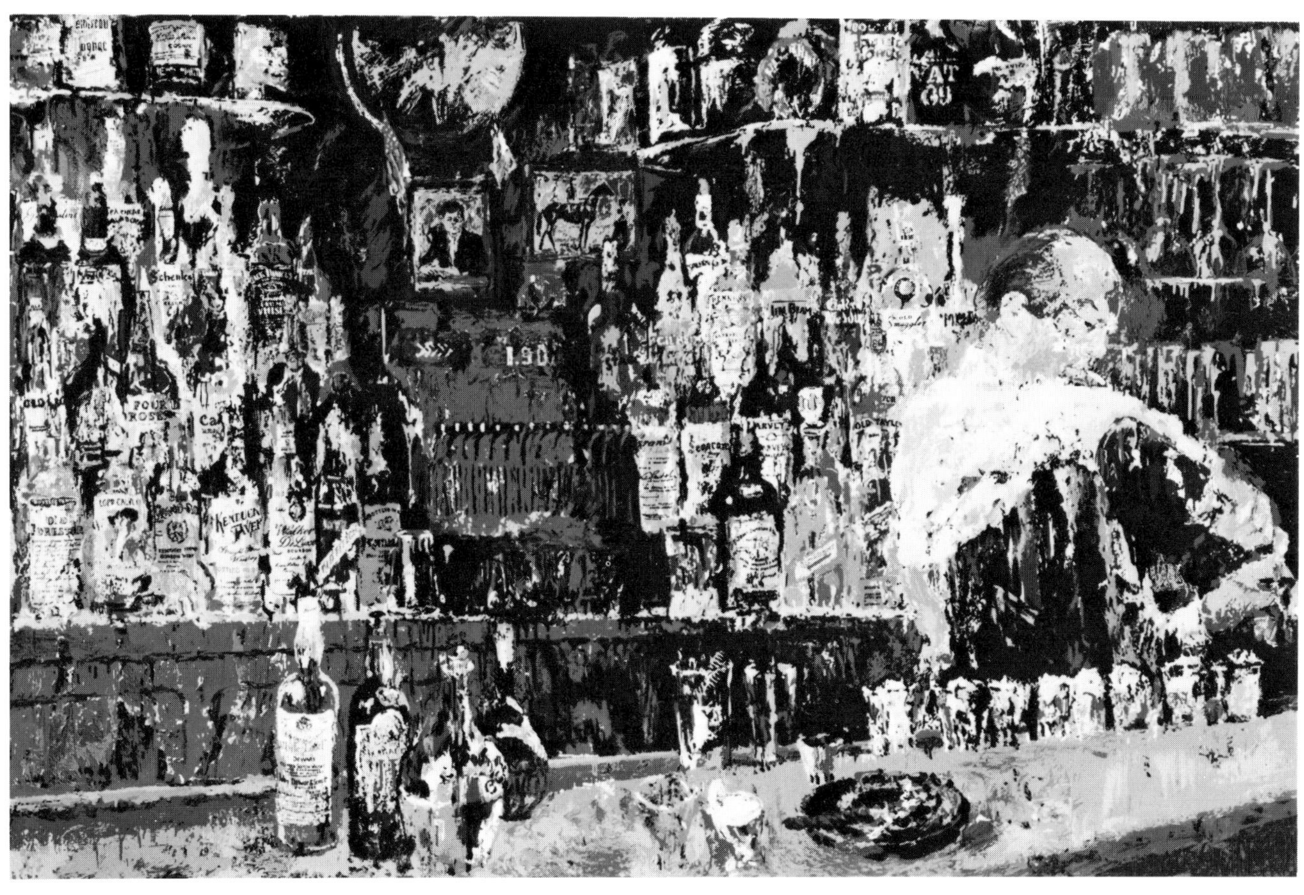

Irish American Bar,
oil on board, 6' x 4', 1959–78,
collection of the artist.

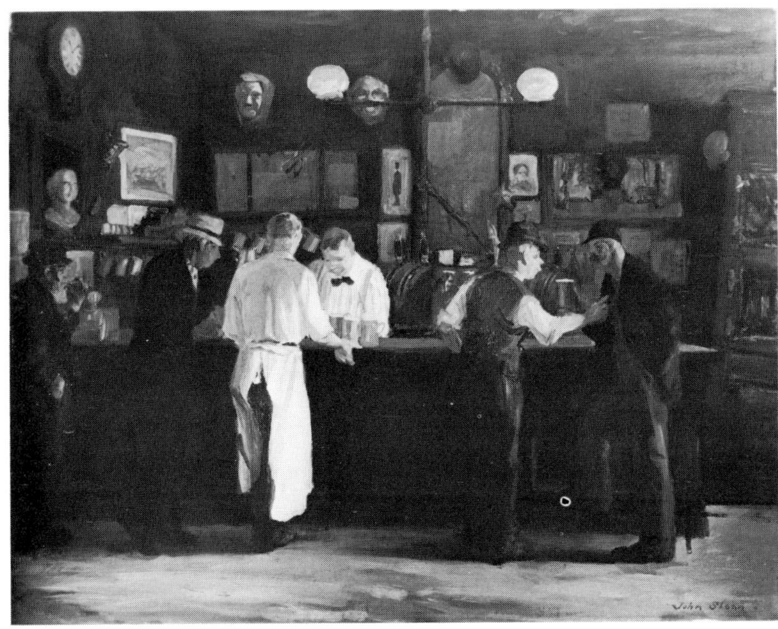

John Sloan, *McSorley's Bar* (1912), The Detroit Institute
of Arts, Gift of the Founders Society

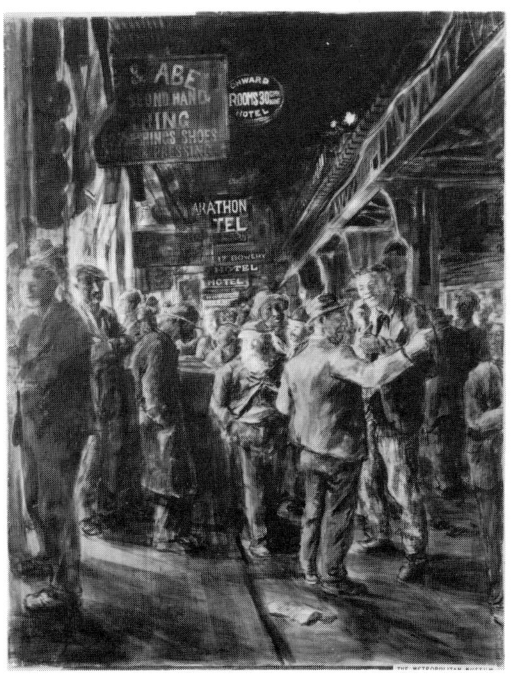

Reginald Marsh, *The Bowery* (1932), The Metropolitan
Museum of Art, Arthur H. Hearn Fund

favorable or passionately unfavorable. It would be instructive to do a sociological survey of who is *pro,* who is *con,* and why. To those who do not like
Neiman's work, it is vulgar subjects that are merely "illustrational" in concept, and grotesque in coloration. His fans, on the other hand, love his
work so much that they fill their homes and offices with many examples.

To his many ardent admirers Neiman captures both the *look* and the *feel*
of the world as they see it working. This is what most people want art to be:
as human as a story, as simply phrased as a poem by Robert Frost, as intense
and colorful as urban life, and as visually moving as a movie. And this is
what Neiman has devoted his life to doing—giving the people what they
want by creating an art that is accessible to everyone.

This moral position about what art should be became quite unfashionable
during the spread of Abstract Expressionism, and did not resurface until
Pop Art in the 1960s. Neiman was ahead of his time. From the point of view
of subject matter, he was a pop artist before Pop Art popped. But the style he
was developing in the 50s to convey popular imagery was something quite
different from the "hard-edge" approach of the classical Pop Artists. He was
committed to Action Painting as the best possible means of communicating
the action of light, the action of people, the action of life.

THE MATURE WORK OF LeROY NEIMAN:
Color, Form, & Action

Action was the third great stylistic problem that Neiman had to solve. But he was not conscious of this fact in his earliest years. He did not become aware of it until it was shocked out of him by his profound confrontation with the work of Jackson Pollock and the other Action Painters in 1953. His discovery of Action Painting was the most important discovery he made after symbolic color of Europe.

Before we look at how he got action into his paintings, let's pause for a moment and look at the physical motions that Neiman himself makes while he is working. Some of these actions are quite traditional. Some are quite unusual. The following quote is from the essay written for the catalogue of Neiman's retrospective exhibition at the Minnesota Museum of Art in 1975 by Malcom Lien:

"Neiman, working in a manner similar to that used by many earlier artists such as the Hudson River School, makes quick sketches and studies on the scene, at the event or spectacle. Whether in Las Vegas or Moscow, he always carries his sketchbook and a number of felt tipped pens, ready to catch the drama of the moment. Later, in his studio he develops and augments these sketches into finished oils, applying his paint rapidly and thickly onto canvas or panels of masonite which he prepares by coating with a thin application of polymer ground. But unlike the Hudson River School painters who composed their works in the quiet and tranquility of silence, Neiman surrounds himself with noise, sounds, and human activity. He describes his unusual working habits as follows: "When I work, I like to have a lot of people around me, a lot of action, sort of keeps the adrenalin going, I get up to a pitch, revved up..." [9]

In other words, Neiman himself is always in motion. The pace of urban life is fast. And Neiman is continuously moving at the high-intensity, neon pace of the Big City. It should not be surprising that he wanted to get all of this "action" into his painting. But how?

It was in 1953 that he was able to build on the clue that Pollock had provided, a clue that would enable Neiman to solve all of his most important formal problems at once: color, form and action.

Pollock painted with intense colors. His paintings are direct, vigorous, intensely powerful in their psychological effect. This is exactly what Neiman wanted in his own work. Even though he had no intention of eliminating the human figure, Neiman wanted to be able to capture the vigorous action of his figures by having vigorous action in his brushstroke.

The physical quality of the paint Pollock used played a large part. What did Pollock use? He used simple ordinary enamel housepaint. The liquidity of this kind of paint is very different from that of traditional paints that are so thick that they must be slowly loaded on the brush and then slowly layered on the canvas. Freely flowing paint makes possible fast-moving strokes. With fast-moving strokes, one can render the impression of fast-moving action.

One day in 1953, the custodian of the apartment house next door was cleaning out the basement of half-used paint cans, and gave him some of this enamel house paint. Neiman started to work immediately on a piece called *Idle Boats*. He got the effect he wanted, and was overjoyed. From that moment forward, Neiman knew he had begun to develop his mature style. In his own words, "that was when I hit my stride!"

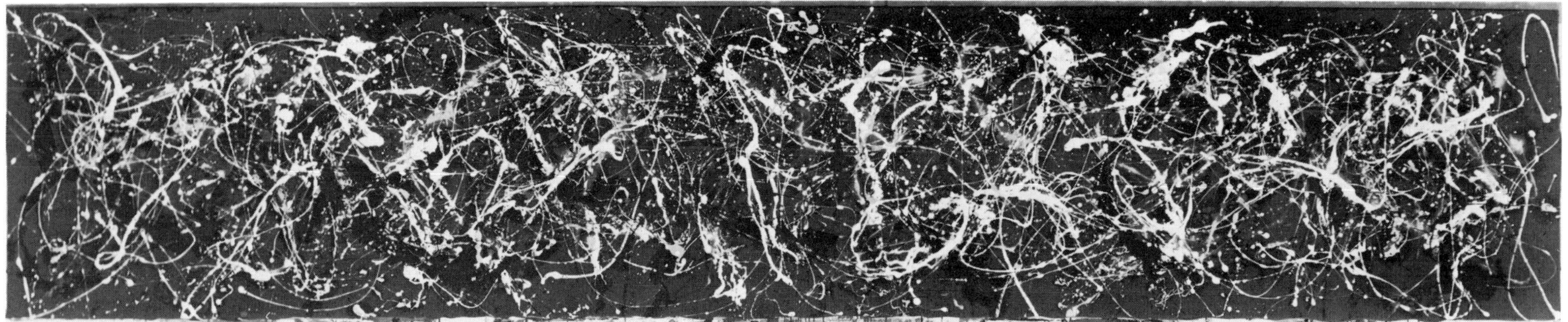

Jackson Pollock, *No. 2, 1949* (1949), Munson-Williams- Proctor Institute

The mature work of LeRoy Neiman had indeed begun. He now had all the elements he needed to create his own synthesis of color, form and motion. But he did not achieve this synthesis all at once. Moving in a direction that no one else was moving towards, he had a great deal of experimenting to do before the alchemy of his art could produce the gold he was after. There were years of groping uncertainty and self-doubt.

During the 1950s his palette remained relatively dark and he continued to make use of a number of compositional formulas that had nourished his work for years. There was little else to help him through his voyage toward an unknown goal. Along the way, he felt entirely free to quote passages from other painters, just as Shakespeare borrowed plots from fellow authors. He can "quote" with uncanny accuracy—an accuracy that infuriates many of his critics, and delights many of his supporters such as Andy Warhol who said in a 1978 interview with *New Times:* "I think he's wonderful. I watched him on the Olympics…every night from start to finish…He was terrific. I'm doing sports figures myself now."[10]

By 1960 the art of LeRoy Neiman could no longer be associated with that of his forerunners. He had become himself. He had become himself both as a person and as a painter. We don't think about it very much in quite this way. But the fact is that artists and the art they create are inseparable in many ways. This is one of the most rigorous aspects of what it means to become an artist. And this is one of the major reasons why few people ever dare to become artists, and why even fewer succeed. It is one of the most difficult challenges a human being can face. In the process, one must be able to become a highly integrated individual. Otherwise, there is no hope of being able to achieve one's own style.

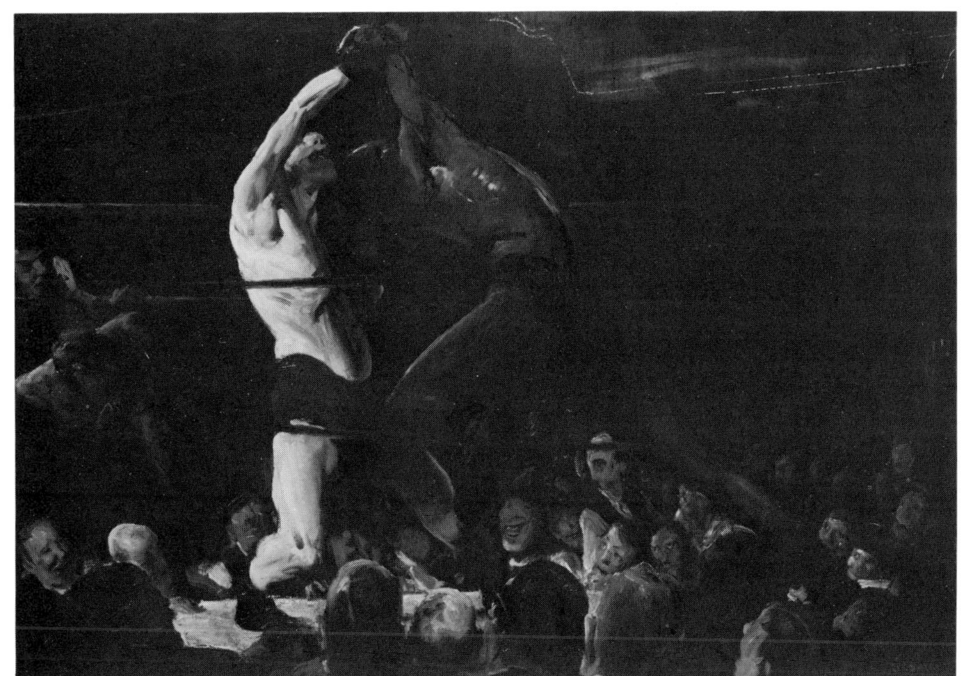

George Bellows, *Both Members of this Club* (1909),
National Gallery of Art, Gift of Chester Dale

Between 1954 and 1959, Neiman managed to shake all of those influences that had played such a large role in his development. He achieved uniqueness. By 1960 he was his own man. In the process of becoming his own man, at the psychological level, he created a radically new kind of style. The results of this style are filled with a new kind of light, much brighter colors, and a robust enthusiasm for portraying the highest points of human achievement in all fields of endeavor, or what Neiman calls "the winners". As a rule, his subjects are the people whom the public most admire—the sports stars, the music stars, the movie stars, the political stars—that glittering galaxy of people who have made it into America's living Hall of Fame.

A representative list of names of people he has portrayed includes: President Carter, Brigitte Bardot, Frank Sinatra, Jack Nicklaus, Mickey Mantle, Louis Armstrong, Muhammed Ali, Beverly Sills, Margaret Mead, Salvador Dali, Dizzy Gillespie, Charlie Parker, Martin Luther King, Sr., Gina Lollobrigida, Art Buchwald, Joe Namath, Mark Spitz, Bobby Fischer, Leopold Stokowski, Duke Ellington, Jack Dempsey, Leonard Bernstein, Diana Ross, Bobby and Ted Kennedy, Reggie Jackson, Pelé, Abdul Jabbar, Mae West, The Beatles.

By the early 1960s, Neiman had started to become a star himself. He and his wife Janet moved to New York City. He began to exhibit at The Hammer Galleries where he has been exhibiting ever since. As his innovative style became more and more appreciated, the prices of his paintings gradually grew from the three-figure level, to the four-figure level, the five-figure level. According to the last issue I saw of *Time Magazine* (31 March 1980), he has now broken through to the six-figure level. In the American art world, that is stardom.

Many attempts have been made to put a name around his style, to classify it. Some have simply labeled him an Impressionist, which is inaccurate even though he employs some of those techniques. Some have called him a Social Realist, which is an accurate statement but one that is incomplete. His work does not resemble any of the Social Realists who preceded him, even though his heart may be in the same place. Many have called him an Expressionist, which is not too far from the mark. It is the Expressionists who acted as a major influence. But again, his work usually does not resemble Van Dongen or Kokoschka except in its deep emotional intensity. Those who have referred to him simply as an Abstract Realist seem to be very close to the target. But that term really doesn't tell us much, except that he is certainly involved with realism and does it in a very abstract way. Those who call him a Pop Artist also are correct as to subject, but not style. Some have gone so far as to call him an Abstract Expressionist.

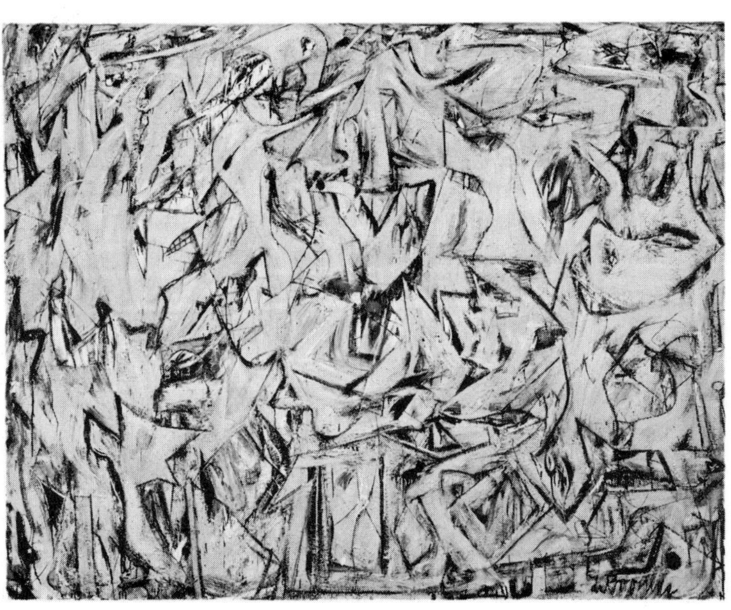

Willem de Kooning. *Excavation* (1950), the
Art Institute of Chicago, Gift of Mr. & Mrs. F. C.
Edgar Kauffman, Jr. and Mr. & Mrs. Noah Goldowsky

This particular attempt to label him is the most provocative of all. It gets us into the heart of the matter. The term "Abstract Expressionist" was coined by Alfred Barr of The Museum of Modern Art, and used by Robert Coates in 1946 to identify the close relationship between what Kandinsky and the others were doing earlier in this century and what Pollock and the others were doing after World War II. Both groups of painters were involved with a kind of Expressionism, but one that is totally abstract—non figurative. So this term is hard to apply to a figurative painter such as Neiman. And yet the action of Action Painting is very much a part of Neiman's art. This is why some critics have been tempted to use the term.

None of these attempts to name his style have worked very well for one simple reason. What LeRoy Neiman has done falls between all the established categories of art-historical and contemporary criticism. It simply does not fit. And that fact is something that upsets people who want things to fit into clear, trustworthy, well-established categories to guide their response to the world.

To be able to understand the exact nature of his stylistic achievement, let's consider how Neiman was thinking at the time of his final breakthrough. Then we will compare how he thinks with how he works.

Many hundreds of articles have been written about Neiman in magazines and newspapers over the years. His scrapbooks are bulging. The first major article on Neiman in a national art magazine appeared in the April 1961 issue of *American Artist.* It was the result of an interview with William Caxton, Jr., a critic who was quite moved by what he called the "sense of immediacy" in Neiman's work. That same spring, Neiman wrote a letter that appeared in the body of the article. It actually is a manifesto which explains very clearly what the artist was trying to do, and how he was doing it. It is the longest and most complete statement the artist has published about his philosophy and the most concise explanation of his technique.

Here is the substance of that document:

"The transformation activity of today's artist stems from our culture which aims more at transfiguring the world than in adapting itself to its environment, or even accepting certain chosen elements of it. This is nothing new in art where there never has been nature imitation. All great art has declined to imitate life and insists on transforming or transcending it."

"In everyday life the impression apparent to the senses when one comes upon a scene for the first time is far different from that experienced through familiarity. When I allow myself the total impact of new surroundings, the initial effect remains, while details become clear, describable and different only upon adjustment. The appearance of shapes and objects immediately or quickly experienced compared with those realized and studied is extraordinary. Here lies the prime objective of my work—this phenomenon of change."

"The spectator looking at a painting of mine must deal with this condition of change. Areas are broken up at close range and fit together only at a distance. Ready recognition of key elements is difficult because of a certain lack of clearness. Important elements are frequently repressed and the unimportant often stressed in order to bring out the main elements in a hidden way. The idea is not to be unclear but to make clarity look like an accident. An averted or shadowed face may contain a chief expression."

"I seek to make the task of the spectator increasingly difficult. I set traps for him. Modeling takes place where emphasis does not lie; accents are subordinated; foreground and background merge up close, and then expand with distance. As one advances on my painting it becomes more abstract, more fluid, and as one moves away it falls into focus and is realistic. By venturing into and penetrating the painting, the spectator discovers for himself new substances and has a prolonged contact. At no two distances will the painting appear the same. This gives the spectator more room for conjecture, and his contribution to the visual image, upon contemplation, adds to its provocative possibilities. These plastic qualities of my painting coincide with the realities of contemporary society and its rapidly moving, shifting and ever-changing panorama. Today's man accepts many casual observations, and oft-times the real truths escape him if he doesn't take the time to look beneath the surface."

Such subjective testimony as the foregoing points up the undercurrent philosophy that prompts Neiman to continually think about his intentions, but it does not preclude his delight in the vicarious experience he constantly extracts from an active fraternity with people in all walks of life. He states: "I love people and like being surrounded by them yet I try to paint life as an objective observer. Even though my rendering is sometimes satirical, I want the receiver of my painting to create his own emotion."

Neiman puts in long hours in his studio often working at his easel from eight in the morning till late at night. He admits to working intermittently on five or six paintings at a time, for when he is interrupted by telephone or callers, his immediate mood is broken, and on resuming his painting he often goes to work on a different panel.

There is nothing puny about Neiman's scale of painted surface, for many of his pictures measure 4 x 6 feet! Instead of canvas he normally paints on large panels of Masonite or Upson board which he surfaces with a thin coating of polymer ground. His large areas of color patterns are painted over this irregular surface with commercial enamels, in both dull and glossy finish. On top of these areas he reverts to glazes of oil to complete his color orchestration—certain passages are heightened in color and others subdued. Generally his method progresses from a transparent film body of middle tones to an overpainting of opaque ones. This may be easily seen in the highlighted areas of the color reproductions. Concerning his procedure the artist reports: "At first the entire surface of a painting is covered with color, then shaped into forms and values. The key and temperature of the painting is generally established at this stage. My preliminary drawings are used as reference, but these are not necessarily followed religiously unless an attitude or gesture is indispensable. More often than not, a color psychologically employed does the better job than a calculated rendering.

"Extremely important in my painting is the use of the same color for both positive and negative purposes. An example of this is a red used for a waiter's jacket, the red foil on a bottle of wine, a tomato in a salad, a lady's lipstick, and a vaporous object such as a cloud of smoke. The same color can be used for a hard or soft object, for a liquid or dry one. This is accomplished by deliberate selection of the adjacent colors, possibly a complement or an opaque if the red is transparent, which permits the same red to be flat, fall back or stand out, highlight, outline and describe whatever is emotionally necessary for its intended function in the picture."

"Understanding the possibilities of one color next to another gives the artist complete control over the psychological impact he is striving to achieve. I believe that the use of color orchestration makes it unnecessary to think about the values (light and dark) in painting, for by working with color intensities in tonal relationships, the darks and lights automatically take care of themselves."

"Inventive color is essential—like a deep, dark orange in shadow and a cool pink in light, or a dark green or dark purple object in light, and light blue objects in shadow—all winding up equal in value. Artificial light will do this sort of thing. The scale of the objects creating the space and the amount of description or detail determine their importance. Perhaps the more cursory-treated area will in the end be the most important. Line can flow through the entire composition changing color and value according to pictorial need."

Finally, Neiman sums up his goal, and one I feel he is presently reaching out to attain in a highly independent and creative fashion, by saying:

"Today's artists, in attempting to execute a convincing painting, representative of subject matter around him, must strive for a quality and excitement that holds up to the powerful and expressive pictures by his contemporaries. The realist has a greater task than ever before…he must be well-grounded in the same basic fundamentals required of artists since the Renaissance…" [11]

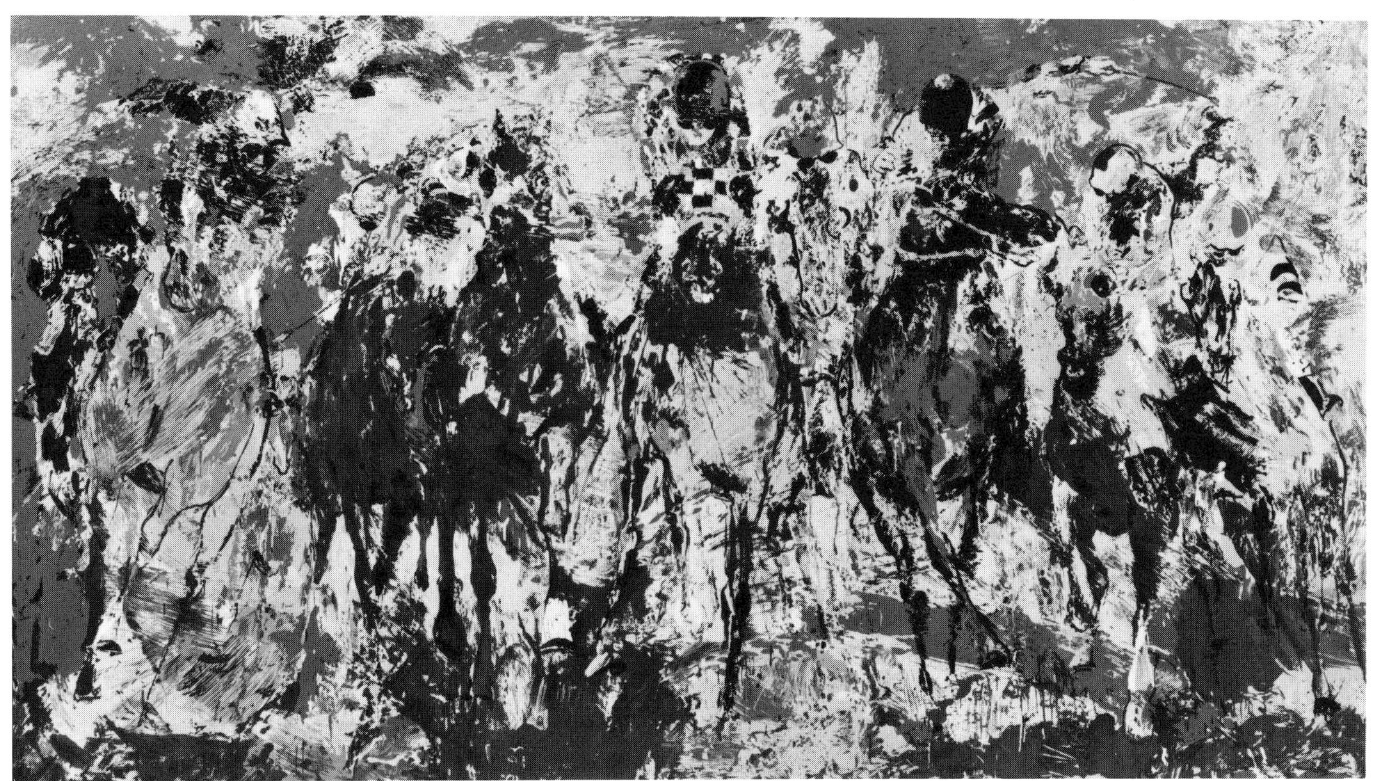

Stretch Stampede, oil and acrylic
on canvas, 9 x 16″, 1975, collection of the
artist.

We could not ask for a more complete statement from a painter-writer
who thinks in words as he paints, and paints actual words almost as often as
he paints people. (He also is the author of two books).[12] His manifesto
reflects a very democratic attitude built on a deep respect for people as
people. It is the same kind of concern that is held by the novelists and play-
wrights for whom Neiman has such respect and feels such kinship: Steinbeck, Dos Passos, Hemingway, Lawrence, Becket, Brecht, and Kafka.
Neiman is both a story-teller and a painter. And story-telling painting
requires realism. What is the vocabulary of Neiman's realism?

The artist informs us that his primary objective as a painter is rendering
the "phenomenon of change". That is a very difficult thing to render. Who
had ever done it? Well, Duchamp and the Futurists did it just before World
War I. But they did it (more often than not) without using images of real
people, only non-recognizable figures, or non-figurative colorations. That's
not hard. Any third or fourth generation Abstract Expressionist can do that.
But how do you do that with real people doing real things in real life?

In short, there was no contemporary visual vocabulary to express what he wanted to express. So, he had to invent one. To invent a new visual vocabulary is an extremely difficult thing to do. How did he do it? By the fusing with what he already has synthesized (color, form, active surface) with the realistic, action-packed rendering of motion itself.

During the 1950s, Neiman succeeded in synthesizing his own sense of figuration with his own sense of symbolic color. He did this by integrating what was meaningful to him about Expressionism and the School of Paris, with the American Social Realism of Bellows, Shahn, and Levine. These were the most recent "Schools of Art" that painted people as people interacting with each other. But it is not until the 1960s that the action-packed seeds planted in him by the Action Painters flowered into full maturity.

Until 1959 his paintings contain a great deal of visual movement. But there is not a great deal of the sensation of actual motion. The aesthetic surfaces are quite active due to his fluid brushwork, but all of the compositional elements are not equally active. After 1959 every element in the composition actually seems to be in motion. All of the colored lines and planes interpenetrate continuously creating a wholistic sensation of dynamic action. To understand the full significance of this extraordinary accomplishment, we must back up and see how action was represented before Neiman.

Action is not a subject that painters focus on in the pre-industrial cities of the western world. Most subjects are rendered standing still. When motion is suggested, it is arrested motion. It is not until the 19th century that action enters the picture.

Before that, artists did portray activity, but only as if we were seeing the single frame of a stop-action movie sequence. The technique of painting permitted little else. So until the second half of the 19th century, and the true beginnings of modern art, we do not have the kinesthetic feeling of activity itself, of motion-in-action. For example, when Eakins painted a man diving off a rock into a pond, the painted form itself is as static as a stuffed pig.

The French led the way in the rendering of the feeling of motion. Delacroix and Daumier started the process by surrounding their figures with vibrating lines suggestive of action. Monet and Renoir developed brushstrokes that retained the spirit of the actual motion of the hand that brought the forms into being. Degas and Lautrec made dramatic distortions in the figure-forms, and their relation to the picture plane, in order to convey a sensation of the experience of people moving.

The Ashcan School was the first group of American painters to deliberately render the sensation of motion: the motion of the ferry boat, the motion of the subway, the motion of people in night clubs, the endless motion of "high intensity" city life.

Between the 1920s and the 1950s, the most active visual surfaces in America were painted by the post-cubist Social Realists such as Shahn, Levine, and Evergood. Then came the Action Painters in the late 40s and early 50s led by Pollock and Kline. They blew the lid off all previous assumptions.

We should keep in mind that they did not create non-figurative abstraction. Painters and sculptors and printmakers have been doing non-figurative compositions since the first decades of the 20th century. What the Action Painters did was create non-figurative compositions that are filled with a deep sense of immediacy, pervaded by a dramatic sensation of motion itself. How did they create canvases that always look as if they were just painted? That feel as if they are moving right before our eyes?

They did it by moving as they painted. Until then painters stood still as they worked, usually moving little more than their fingers, wrists and arms. The Action Painters moved everything, walking around and across the canvas, stroking and/or dripping paint as they moved. Looking back, easel painters can be seen as something that is more cerebral than corporeal. In their traditional stance, painters can easily render the idea of motion. But they rarely can render the feeling of motion itself.

Like the old Zen masters of Japan (whom Pollock and Tobey admired), America's Action Painters were not content with rendering the concept of motion. They wanted the feeling of motion itself. This can be done most effectively if the action of the paint on the surface is the direct result of the body in motion, the action of the body in motion.

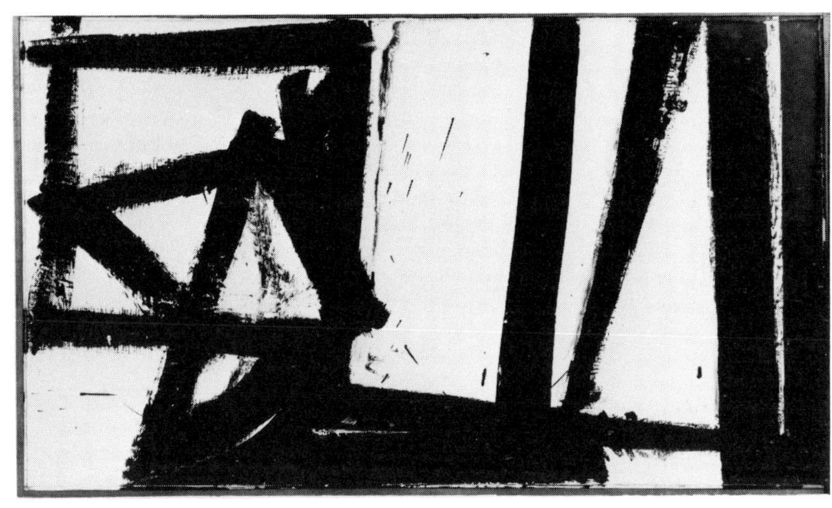

Franz Kline, *Untitled* (1956), The Poindexter Collection, Montana Historical Society

However, as a rule, it was not bodies that they painted. Instead they painted motion itself, the motion of their own internal rhythms. Generally speaking the first generation of the New York School eliminated the figure from its classical place at the center of the artist's iconography. Pollock, Kline, Newman, Motherwell, Still, Rothko wiped the canvas clean of figure forms. Abstract, symbolic forms became their subject-matter. De Kooning is a partial exception to this rule; but only a partial exception. He was much more concerned with the action of the paint than he was with the action of the human figure.

The work of Pollock, Kline, Motherwell, and all the others rapidly earned the deepest respect and highest praise of artists, critics, and historians all around the world during the 1950 s and 1960 s. The profound achievement of this first generation of Action Painters catapulted American painting into the Number One position in the international art world. Until then, much of America's art had been under the influence of Europe. We copied them for centuries. Now, for the first time in history, the rest of the world was copying American art. And New York City became the capital of the modern art movement.

The New York School of Abstract Expressionists moved the forefront of American painting into a very special kind of space and time. By removing any iconographic references to a past we might remember, or a future we might anticipate, the spectator is left with no choice but to experience exactly what is before the eye *Right Now*—a *Right Now* that is filled with the magical vibration of immediacy.

The visual result of Action Painting was a revelation not only to Neiman but also to many painters of the Chicago School. Many of his fellow painters in that region became Abstract Expressionists. Not all of them, however. Realism is very strong in the midwest. The Chicago School was also to foster the New Realism of Oldenburg and Robert Indiana after the first tidal wave of Abstract Expressionism had subsided. But while this tidal wave was cresting, what happened in Chicago happened all over the country. A radically new, nationwide value system emerged firmly in favor of non-figurative art. All of a sudden,   there were thousands of little Pollocks painting from coast to coast, and in every major industrial city of every inhabited continent on earth. A whole aesthetic morality developed, along with a committed international establishment of artists, critics, curators, and dealers. As these assumptions cemented, a wall built up that was (consciously or unconsciously) opposed to figure painting in any form.

But LeRoy Neiman was not among them. His core values were not washed away by all this. He had had the privilege of listening to Ben Shahn talk once. And that was the tradition Neiman identified with. He held solidly to his conviction as to the importance of the human figure. And he was aware that the lesson of Pollock was not to paint like Pollock, but to paint directly from the very heart of where you are coming from, wherever that may be.

Even though the idea of abandoning the human figure never occurred to him, he loved the action of Action Painting. From the very beginning of his career, Neiman's primary interest has been color-in-motion, people-in-motion, the ever-present phenomenon of change. The technique of action-filled, corporeal painting appealed very much to a man who is always in motion.

So Neiman decided to make his figures really move, like they do in the movies, like they do in the *Right Now* of real life. He did this by first mastering the lessons of Action Painting, and then turning them inside out. By a remarkable leap of imagination, he was thus able to fuse traditional Social Realism with the highly animated techniques of Action Painting. After many years of effort, LeRoy Neiman was able to bring a whole tradition of relatively static figure painting into the dynamic world of *Right Now.*

He found a way of making his brush move as fast and as vigorously as an Abstract Expressionist without sacrificing a single ounce of figurative verisimilitude. And he found an extremely dynamic way of making the abstract background and realistic foreground merge and separate simultaneously by alternately fusing and separating the two spaces. In this remarkable synthesis, he was able to make the action within the painting as intense as it actually is in our direct experience. The visual result stimulates a kinesthetic response in our own bodies.

The purpose of this essay has not been to proclaim that "LeRoy Neiman is the greatest painter in America!" I have simply attempted to provide a technical analysis of his style, to indicate what he has contributed to the history of American painting, and to offer a framework for beginning to evaluate the significance of that contribution. History is a record of the ideas, images, and objects that have been meaningful to people. What is no longer meaningful gradually disappears. The whole Renaissance tradition of realistic, figurative sculpture was in danger of disappearing in the 1950s. More than any other single factor, it was the "pop" sculpture of George Segal that kept this tradition alive. History makes her judgments very slowly, after all the little fads have flashed and passed away. But I think Neiman's work is going to last. And when I think about all of those other artists his work has influenced over the last twenty years, I find myself wondering if History might not remember the name of LeRoy Neiman (even before the names of Philip Pearlstein and Alex Katz), as having played a larger role than any other painter in re-vitalizing the native American tradition of figure painting as the vehicle of Social Realism, as the vehicle for imaging our collective reality as a society of human beings.

CONCLUSION: Man, Myth, and Magic

The role of the realist painter has become quite complex since the advent of Abstract Expressionism. In one form or another, Social Realism has been the backbone of American painting for most of our nation's history. Suddenly it was not. For decades now, the majority of our most distinguished critics have convinced the art world that the mainstream of American painting is non-figurative. And most art historians would agree that between the late 1940s and the 1970s it has been non-figurative work that has occupied the hearts and minds of the majority of our most important painters. What the art magazines and the art museums have most consistently celebrated during this period is Action Painting and the Color Field painting from Still, Rothko and Newman, to Frankenthaler, Louis, Noland, Reinhardt, Stella and all the others.

Realism quickly became unfashionable. Social Realism changed media. Photo-journalism took over from painting the social function of portraying our collective reality. The only images we as a people have had of our social being have come to us by means of newspapers, magazines, T.V., and the movies.

When the traditional desire of Americans for realistic images re-emerged in the form of Pop Art in the 1960s, it was generally considered a side-current rather than part of the new mainstream. It was many, many years before The Museum of Modern Art finally, reluctantly decided to exhibit Pop Art. Over time, the remarkable artistic achievements of Rauschenberg, Johns, Oldenburg, and all the others forced the art world to reconsider. The magazines and the museums gradually gave the New Realism more and more respect. During the course of the 1970s, various forms of Super Realism and Photo Realism started to become quite popular, and respectable. Realism is coming back in style, and probably will be even stronger in the reality-oriented 1980s.

So it is not only in the area of style that Neiman has been between categories. The same is true from the point of view of mythology. The modern myth is that "real artists" are poor, struggling, usually misunderstood, frequently in pain, and generally spurned by the general public. Neiman does not fit with any part of this modern myth. Everything seems to be exactly the opposite with him. All the evidence points to him being happy, healthy, well-fed (in fact, wealthy), and very much liked by millions of people who feel they understand him completely. And this is all quite disconcerting to those who believe in the modern myth. On the other hand, he fits quite well with the traditional idea of what an artist should be: one who can be understood by all social classes. No painter has ever appealed to everyone. But the range of Neiman's audience is extremely large, from the taxi-driver to the aristocrat.

Artists have not always been thought of as starved individuals barely staying alive in garrets at the outside edges of society. This modern myth did not start until the 19th century. For the vast majority of human history, the artist has been a highly honored, respected member of society because of the artist's ability to provide magical services—because of the capacity of the artist to visualize those aspects of life that are most meaningful to the society they are serving. More often than not, this has been story-telling of one kind or another, usually stories of mythological heroes and heroines whose values are those of the people.

It was the duty of the traditional artist to perpetuate the Sacred Myths. Keep in mind that the word "Myth" is not being used in the popular sense of being an untruth. Here we are talking about Myth in the traditional sense of being a statement of what are considered eternal truths that work as a binding force of unquestioned assumptions for society as a whole. As Joseph Campbell, the distinguished mythologist, has said, "each of us has private dreams. Myths are the public dreams that all members of a society share."

During the European Middle Ages, for example, when a master painter completed an altarpiece it was an occasion for public rejoicing, as the most sacred images of the community were carried through the streets from the Guildhall to the Cathedral. It was a collective, unifying value-system that the artists and the people were celebrating together. And that's the way things have been in the traditional world for thousands of years, in fact, for more than 99% of human history.

It was not until after the Industrial Revolution, and the political revolutions that followed, that traditional agrarian society fell apart, and had to be constructed all over again. The modern industrialized urban society that was built up in Europe and the United States in the 19th and 20th centuries decided that art and artists were not very important —decorative, yes, but not extremely valuable. And so things have tended to remain until quite recently.

In the language of psychophysiology, modern society became left-brain in its orientation, stressing *"readin', 'ritin' & 'rithmetic"* in the schools in order to produce citizens who are logical, aggressive, and oriented towards the values of our individual reality. In this society much less attention is paid to the right-brain's capacity to be visual, emotionally receptive to aesthetic experience, and oriented towards the values of our collective reality. [13]

The result is a very unbalanced world. Art remains a very low priority in our schools and in our homes. Only a small percentage of society has any direct contact with original works of art. Very few painters are actually able to earn a living by painting. So the problem is much deeper than the bias of East Coast critics. But critics who recognize only one kind of art in a democratic society do not help the social situation as a whole.

Happily, things have improved somewhat since World War II. As Dore Ashton observed in *The New York School: A Cultural Reckoning* (1972), none of the famous Abstract Expressionists were able to earn even a modest living from their work until the 1950s. Today, most of the best known Pop Artists and Color Field painters are earning comfortable incomes. Several have become millionaires. This is a striking sociological fact. Never before in the history of American painting has this much financial recognition been given to living American painters. This has happened because of a combination of good art and good business practices. Now, across the nation, and around the world, there is something that can really be called a Fine Arts Industry, in the same way that there is a Publishing Industry, or a Theatre Industry. And the truly popular artists have begun to command the same kind of incomes as popular writers, movie-stars, and professional athletes.

None of this could be happening if it were not for the fact that the general public has started to demand that there be more art in their lives. The idea that art is important to family life is coming back. The idea that art is important to community life is coming back. The idea that art is important to corporate life is coming back. Art is coming back towards the central place (at the very middle of life) which it has occupied for 99% of human history. The art museums which served only a few thousand people a year two decades ago, now are serving tens of millions of people a year. Indeed, art museums are now a major part of the multi-billion dollar Fine Arts Industry, as business managers start to replace art historians as museum administrators.

Nevertheless, in spite of all this new art world of advertising and merchandizing, no American painter of 60s and 70s has been catapulted into the semi-shamanic status of Popular Hero except LeRoy Neiman. So he must be touching something down deep—a depth that almost seems to be at the "archetypical" level of traditional heroes and heroines, the dwelling place of the Image Maker who also is the Myth Maker.

Each generation has had its own set of heroes and heroines. At the turn of the century, there were those very popular book illustrators from N.C. Wyeth to Maxfield Parrish who were the last to illuminate the heroes and heroines of agrarian mythology. In the 1920s and 1930s, there was Norman Rockwell on the covers of *The Saturday Evening Post* celebrating the values of a recently urbanized nation that was still longing for its agrarian roots. Then came Andrew Wyeth in the 40s and 50s with his haunting realism infused with the kind of penetrating insights into the psychology of individual human beings that usually is found in the writings of our best poets and novelists. Wyeth is as rural and as sophisticated as Steinbeck or Faulkner.

The imaging of social values is important. Unless values are symbolized they cannot be exchanged. Unless values are visualized continuously they cannot be lived by a society of people.

All the artists mentioned in this chapter have been in touch with the people to some degree, or they wouldn't be making so much money. As Alfred Frankenstein reminds us in his preface to this book, artists since the Stone Age have been offering value-laden images to the fellow members of their society. Only by being *connected* could they fulfill their public purpose—to render images of such power that Truth can be illuminated. The same *connection* between the artists and the people continued through the ages of Egypt, Greece and Rome; continued through the Middle Ages, and the Renaissance of Europe; and continued through government-supported Public Works of the 1930s and 40s.

Then, when the human figure suddenly vanished, the psychological connecting link was broken. The American public was left with little to identify with, to empathize with, until a new artist-hero emerged who was able to "tell the stories" they could understand and love.

During the 1970s, America's best-known artist-hero has been LeRoy Neiman. The people he paints are the heroes of the totally urbanized middle classes: The athletes, the musicians and movie stars, and those colorful members of various social classes who are in love with joie-de-vivre and passionately in pursuit of happiness. For the first time in the history of American art, a *city* boy has become an artistic hero to millions. Neiman renders the lives of the people as they would like to be.

So it should not be surprising that Neiman-loving urbanites like neon-flavored "shocking pink," or that the experience of "Neiman Green" is as shrill as a high jazz note. There are the sights and sounds of the city. It would be surprising if there were not a lot of flash and glitter in his palette and in his legend.

The people love what he does with powers they believe are truly magical. And he loves doing it. "For me," says Neiman, "communication is what it's all about. Art is simply the means by which it happens. It's something that just passes through me and on to them." What he is communicating are images of enormous social power—images that embody and reflect the people's collective value-system. And the gratitude of the citizenry has been overwhelming.

The intensity of this popular admiration and respect is a remarkable phenomenon in itself. Neiman is not only the best known artist in America (with the possible exception of Andy Wyeth who also received very little attention from major critics until recently). He also is the first American painter to have risen from poverty to become a multi-millionaire.

His many T.V. appearances, (especially his painting of Olympic events *live* as they happened), in addition to his 25 years of regular monthly contributions to *Playboy,* has made his name a household word from coast to coast, and all around the world. And all this happened without much help from art museums or art magazines. Neiman is a truly popular phenomenon — a grass-roots phenomenon — a Popular Hero with as much fan mail as a Hollywood Super Star.

The American people have always loved the art of the concrete, or what E. P. Richardson calls "the poetry of fact." Neiman has been able to give this to the American people, just those concrete qualities for which they have been thirsting for many years. As Andy Warhol said (in effect) when he painted his satirical images of Abstract Expressionist brushstrokes in the early 60s, "beautiful colors and beautiful brushwork are not enough!"

They are certainly enough for some people, but not enough for most people. As noted in the Introduction, it has been estimated that only about 1% of the American people are able to appreciate non-figurative painting. These are people who see the world very differently from most people. They look at the world, and at art, from an extremely high level of philosophical abstraction.

The vast majority of Americans have absolutely no interest in non-figurative abstractions, no matter how "beautiful" they might be. The basic psychosocial fact at work here is that if a work of art does not have a figure in it, the world at large is psychologically unable to relate to it. A world full of people is what most people see when they look. As Neiman expresses it, "the human eye is universal." They want to see images of the world that correspond with the way their eye actually perceives the world, with the sky up and the earth down and most of us in between.

And this Neiman (quite magically) is able to provide. He is so concrete in his precision that one is able to tell just about what temperature it is, how much smoke is in the room, and how much salt is in the air, whether at ringside, on an Olympic ski-slope, or the sunlit beach of Cannes.

As a committed artist-of-the-people, Neiman has used a wide range of media in order to reach as many people as possible. In addition to painting and sculpture, he has worked with both traditional and contemporary media. His experience includes books, magazines, T.V., and computer graphics, as well as several kinds of techniques that range from etchings and monotypes, to lithographs and silkscreen prints. The serigraphs are organic extensions of his paintings. They have the same *look* and *feel.* Similarly, his etchings are natural extensions of his draftsmanship, and include some of the best work he has done in any media.

This catalogue is dedicated to his accomplishment as a graphic artist. It is a fitting way to begin to record his life's work, since it is by means of his serigraphs that he has been able to offer tangible works of art to the greatest number of people. During the 1970s, Neiman executed over 170 limited editions of serigraphs with an average of 300 prints in each edition. That means that over 50,000 original works of art have been made available to his avid audience.

As the collective eye of the modern art establishment begins to re-focus on realism, it is difficult to overlook Neiman's achievement. And recently, some highly respected critics and artists have begun to take a second look at his work—work that is now in the permanent collections of such institutions as the Baltimore Museum of Fine Art, the Art Institute of Chicago, the Indianapolis Museum of Art, the Minneapolis Institute of Arts, the Minnesota Museum of Art, the Museo de Bellas Artes in Caracas, and the Hermitage in Leningrad.

During all those years when anyone who painted figures was viewed with suspicion by the modern art establishment, Neiman went on only doing his own thing. He was confident of his direction, and supported by enormous public approval. While none of the critics were looking, this pop artist/action painter was able to single-handedly bridge that giant gulf which separated the general public from the most advanced stylistic developments of the 20th century.

The sociological fact is that Neiman did what no other American artist was able to do. He made the profound stylistic innovations of Action Painting available to the general public by providing the psychological bridge of the human image grounded in everyday reality. This is not to overlook the important contributions of other American painters who also were experimenting with the synthesis of Abstract Expressionism and figure painting in the 1950s and 60s, such as Larry Rivers, and the San Francisco School of Park, Bischoff, Oliveira, and Diebenkorn. But the point I am making is quite simply that their work was not able to reach out and touch the hearts of the general public, and Neiman's work does.

The people Neiman reaches are the people he set out to serve in the first place—the General Public of the Big City. By doing exactly what he set out to do, he has helped to re-invigorate figure painting in particular, and Social Realism in general at a time when both were in danger of dying.

Social Realism is coming back to life again. This is a healthy sign. The making and appreciating of the art of our own time is an important way of coming to understand the whole of what it means to be a human being. A society that feels cut off, alienated from its leading artists, is not a healthy society. But Neiman has begun to help society to heal itself by putting art back into the life of the people.

San Francisco, March, 1980

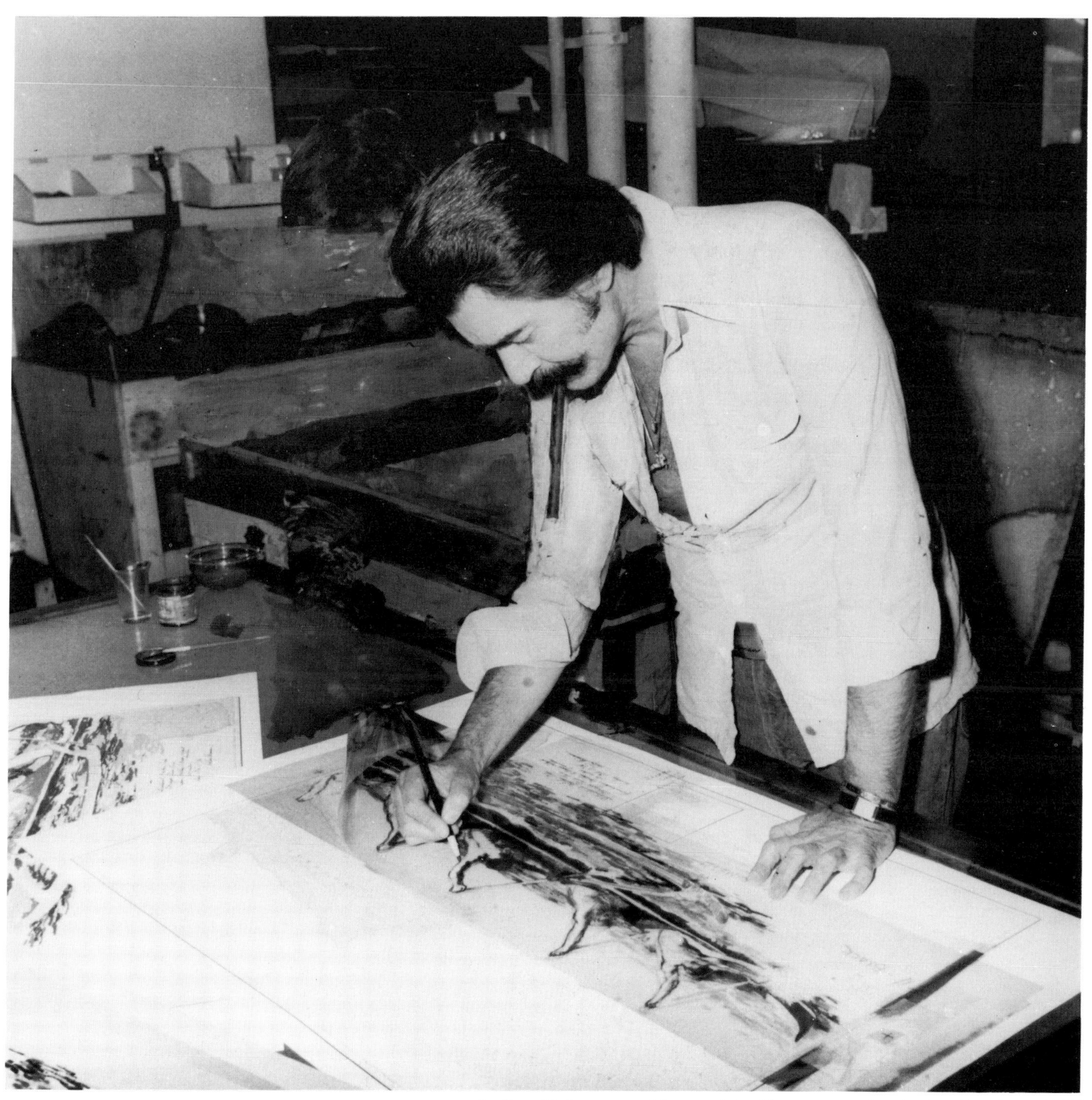

LeRoy Neiman working on his silkscreen at Styria Studios, Inc., 1978

Serigraphs

The Serigraphs

Neiman's serigraphs are organic extensions of his paintings. His earlier experiments with lithographs and monotypes in the 1950s and 1960s prepared him for the serigraphic technique that he began to use in 1970.

Neiman works very closely with the masterprinter and the chromist in the execution of these prints. Often, as many as 36 oil-based colors must be orchestrated into that symphony of tones that is the final work of art. He has worked with a number of different ateliers over the years. Since 1975 he has worked exclusively with Styria Studios, Inc., New York, under the direction of Adi Rischner.

It is a delight to Neiman that the character of the serigraph media enables him to achieve the same dynamic *look* and *feel* that his paintings have. And it is a joy to Neiman collectors that they can actually feel the sensuous texture of the paint as it has been applied to the custom-made, 100% rag, French paper.

It is by means of the serigraphs that Neiman has been able to reach widest possible audience. In the last decade more than 180 serigraphs have been published.

F.L.G.

For a short history of the serigraph by Fritz Eichenberg, see page 355

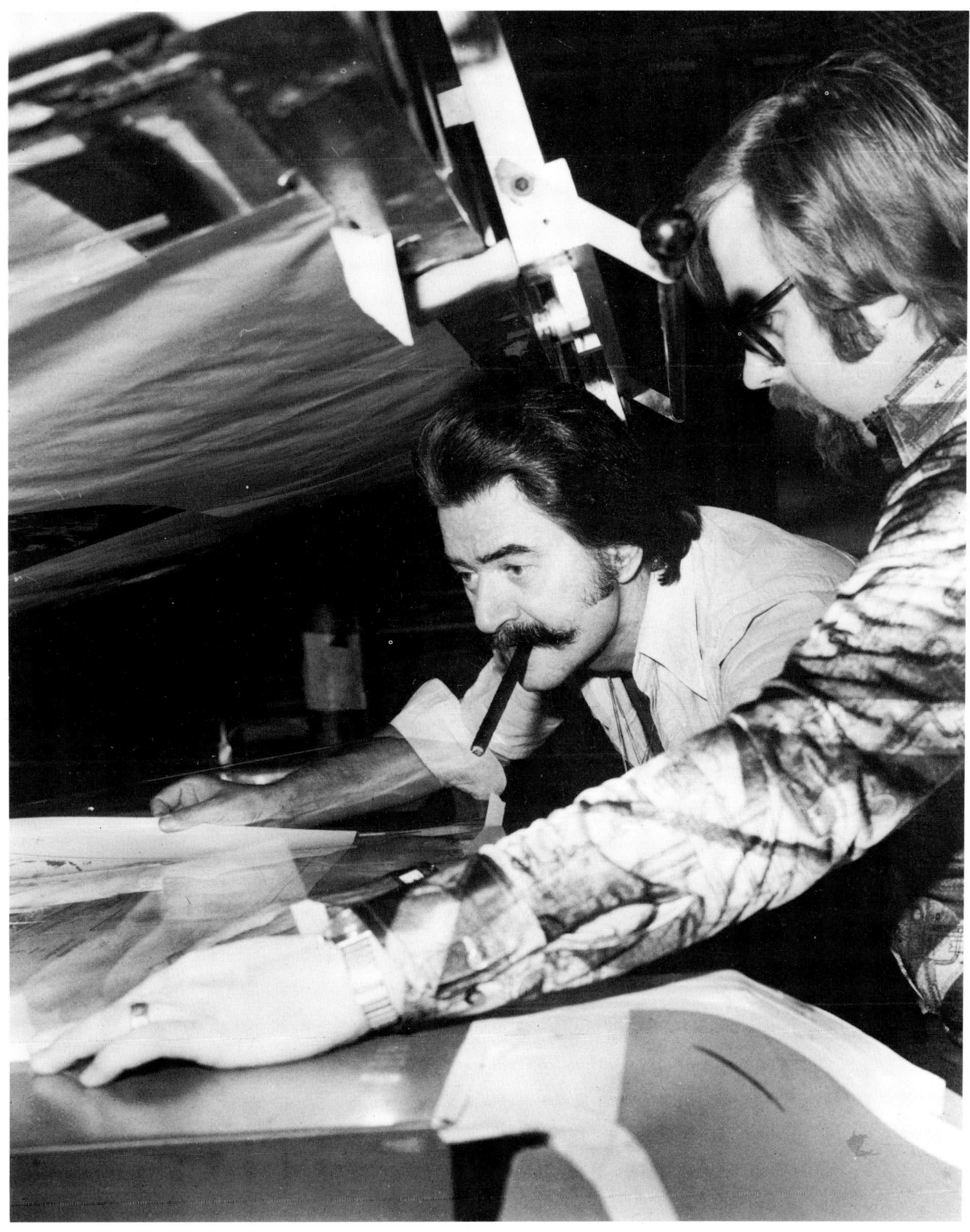

LeRoy Neiman checking color on serigraph at Styria Studios, Inc. with Adi Rischner, director , 1978.

Part I
Serigraphs, 1971–1973

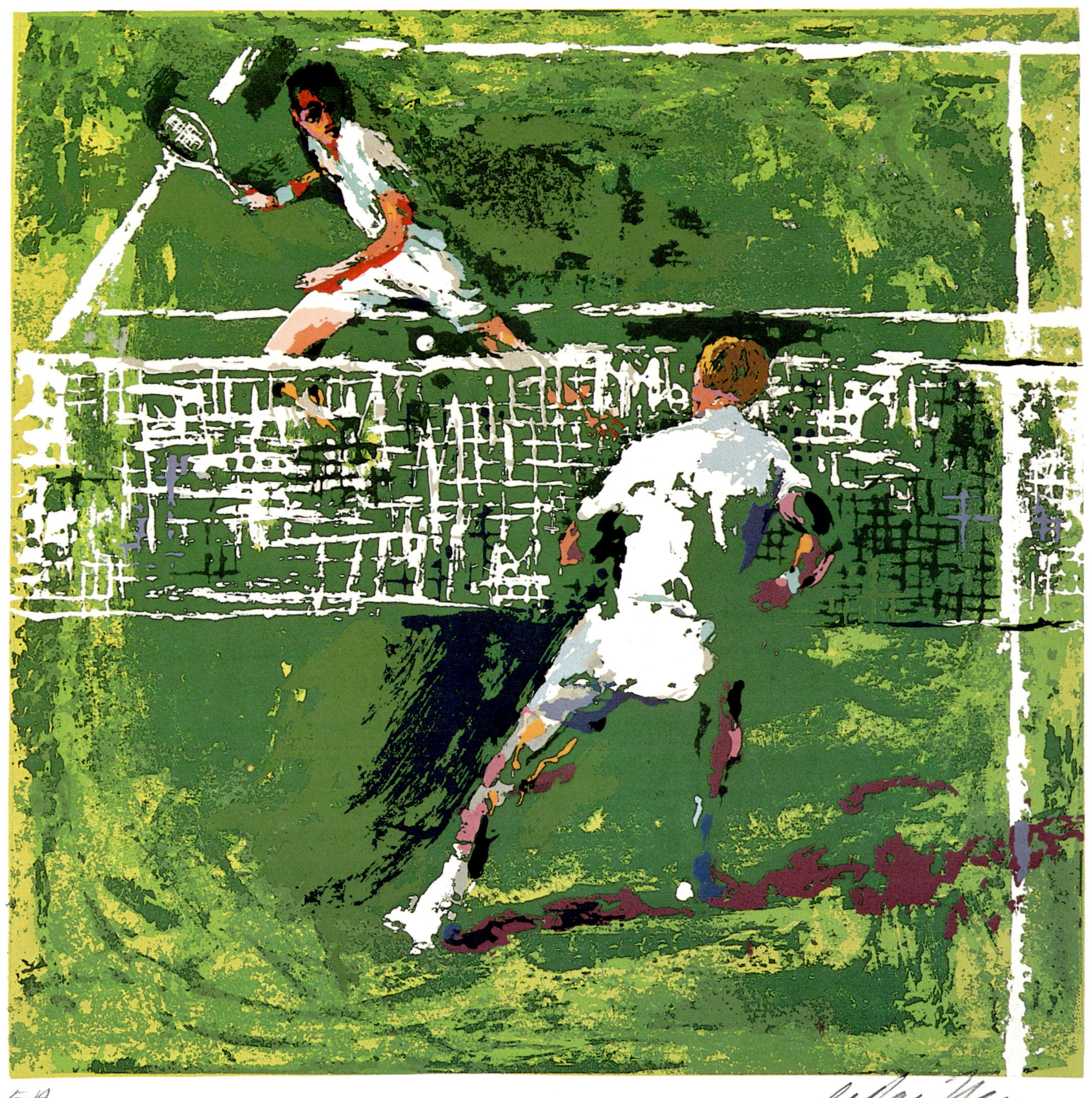# 1 Tennis Players

1971
Serigraph
14 x 14 (35.6 x 35.6 cm)
A limited edition of 300, signed and numbered
by the artist.

2   Pool Room

1971
Serigraph
17⅜ x 20⅞ (44.13 x 53.02 cm)
A limited edition of 350, signed and numbered
by the artist.

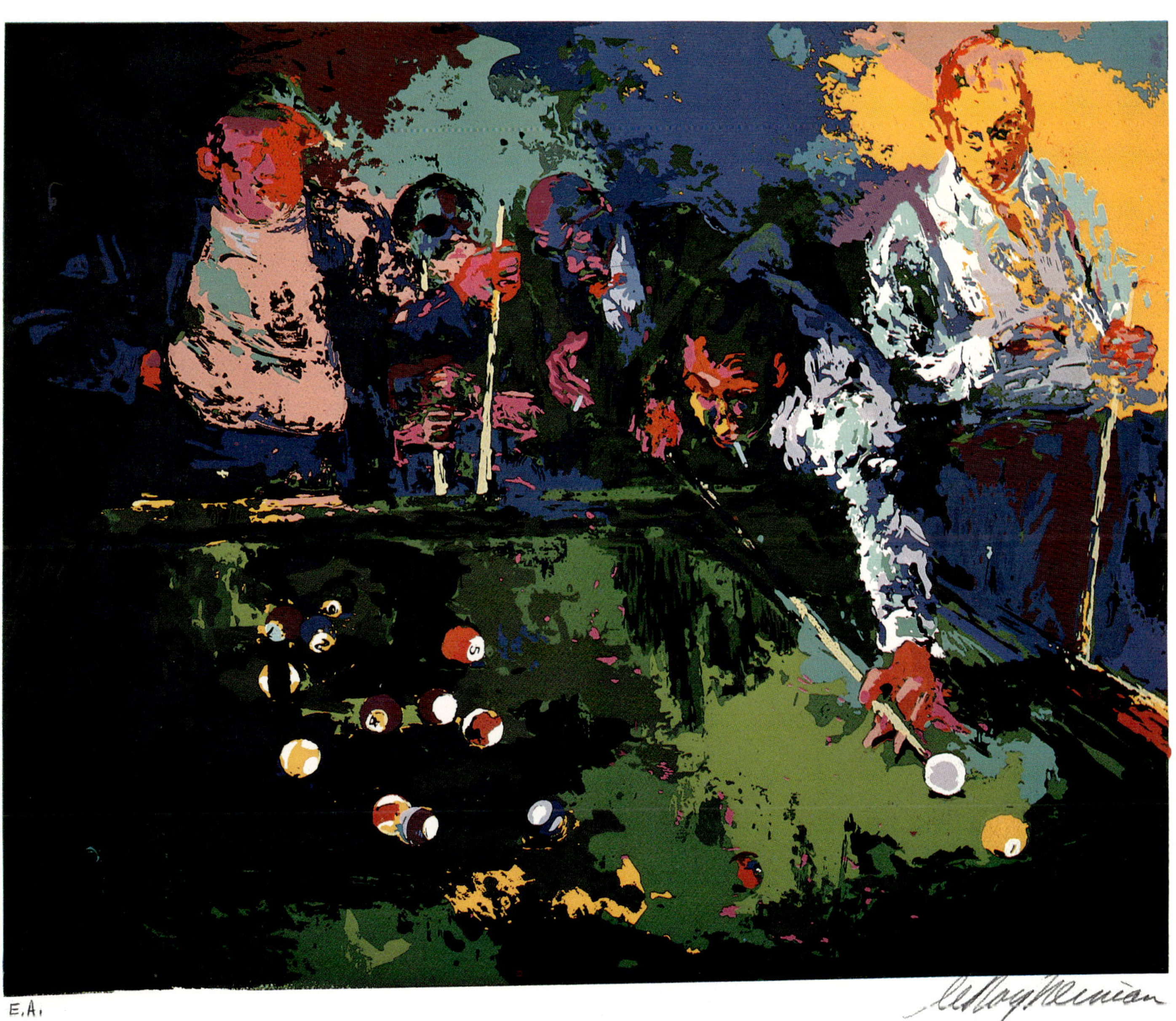

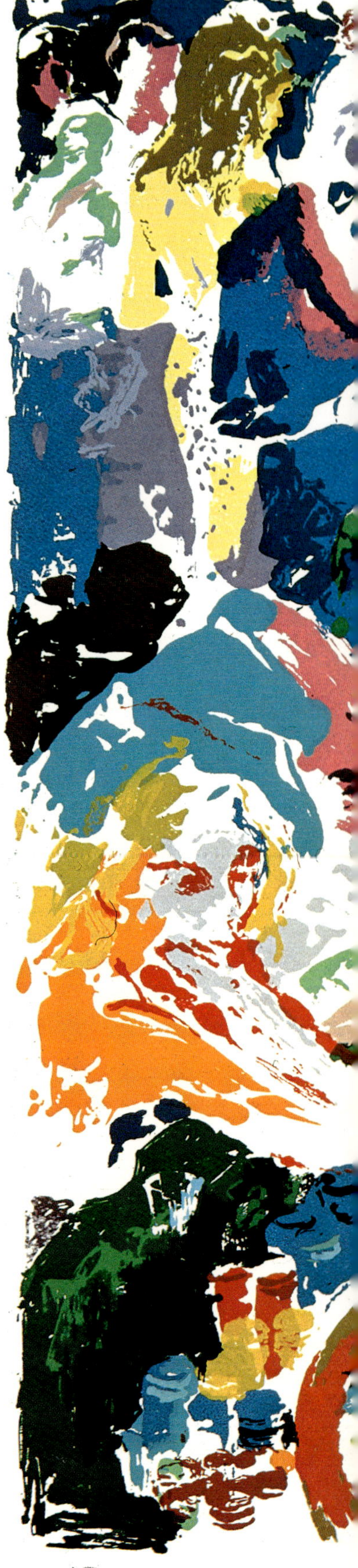

3   Casino

1972
Serigraph
21 x 26 (53.34 x 66.04 cm)
A limited edition of 300, signed and numbered
by the artist.

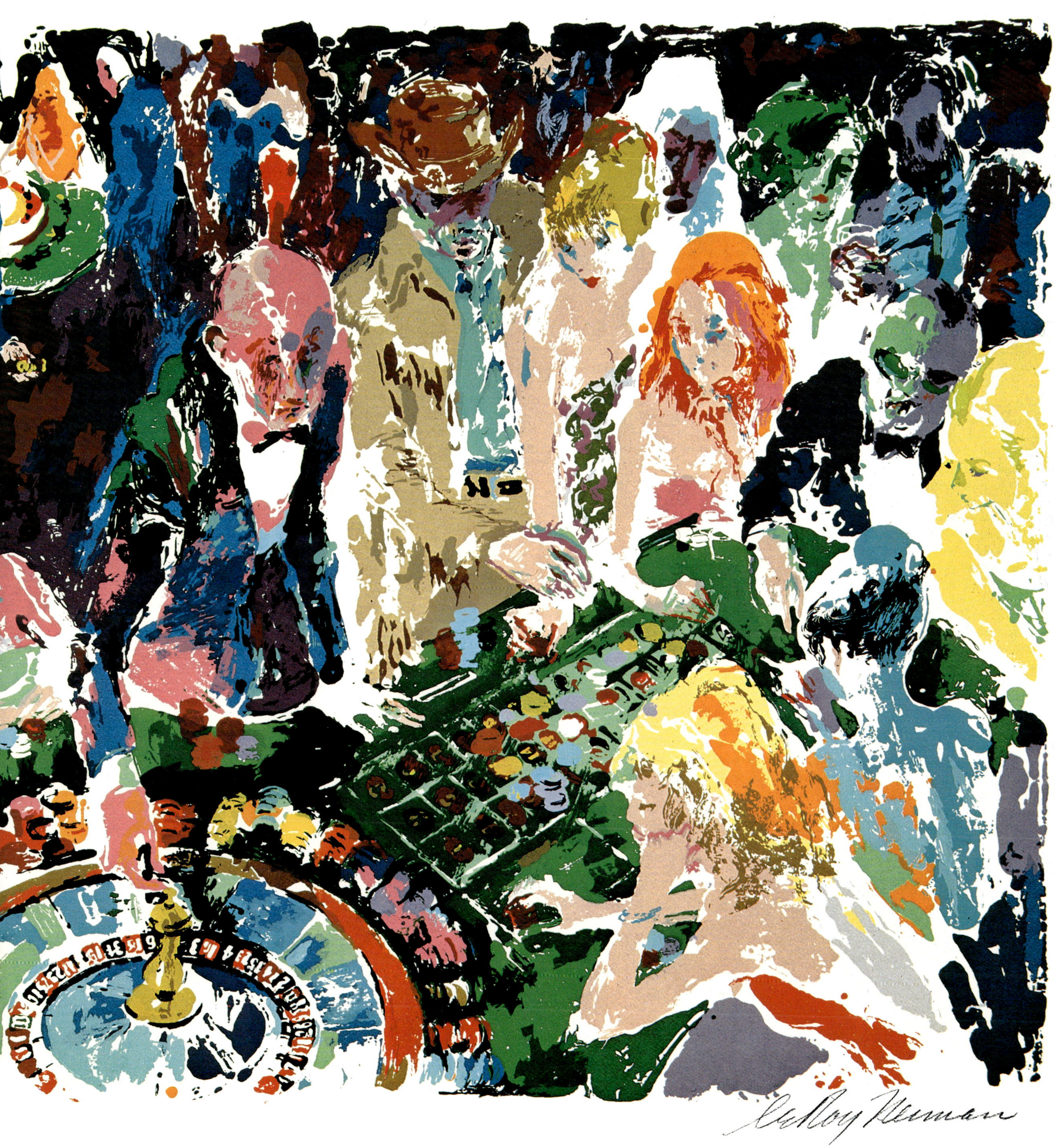

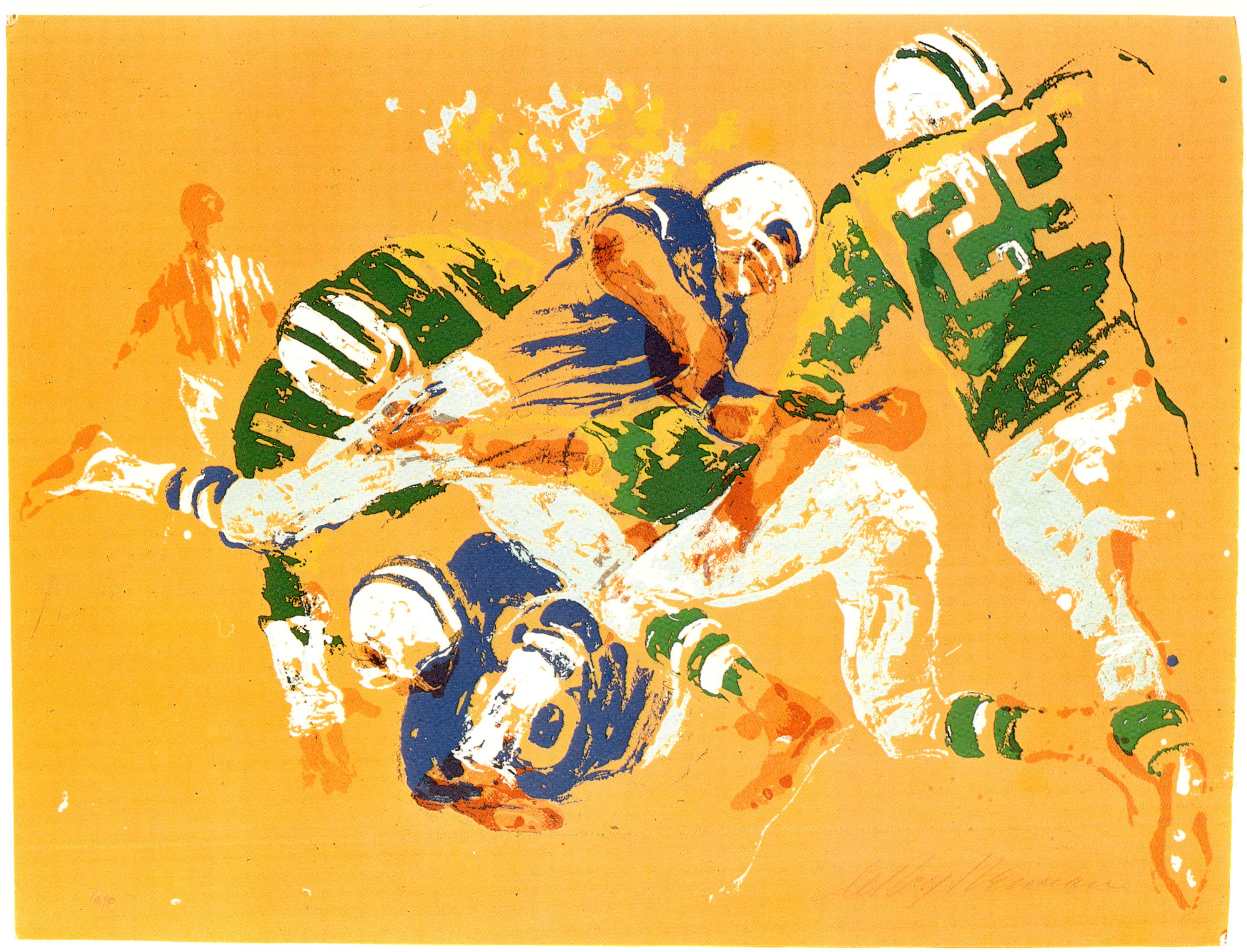

4 Orange Football

1972
Serigraph
20 x 26 (50.8 x 66.04 cm)

A limited edition of 175, signed and numbered
by the artist.

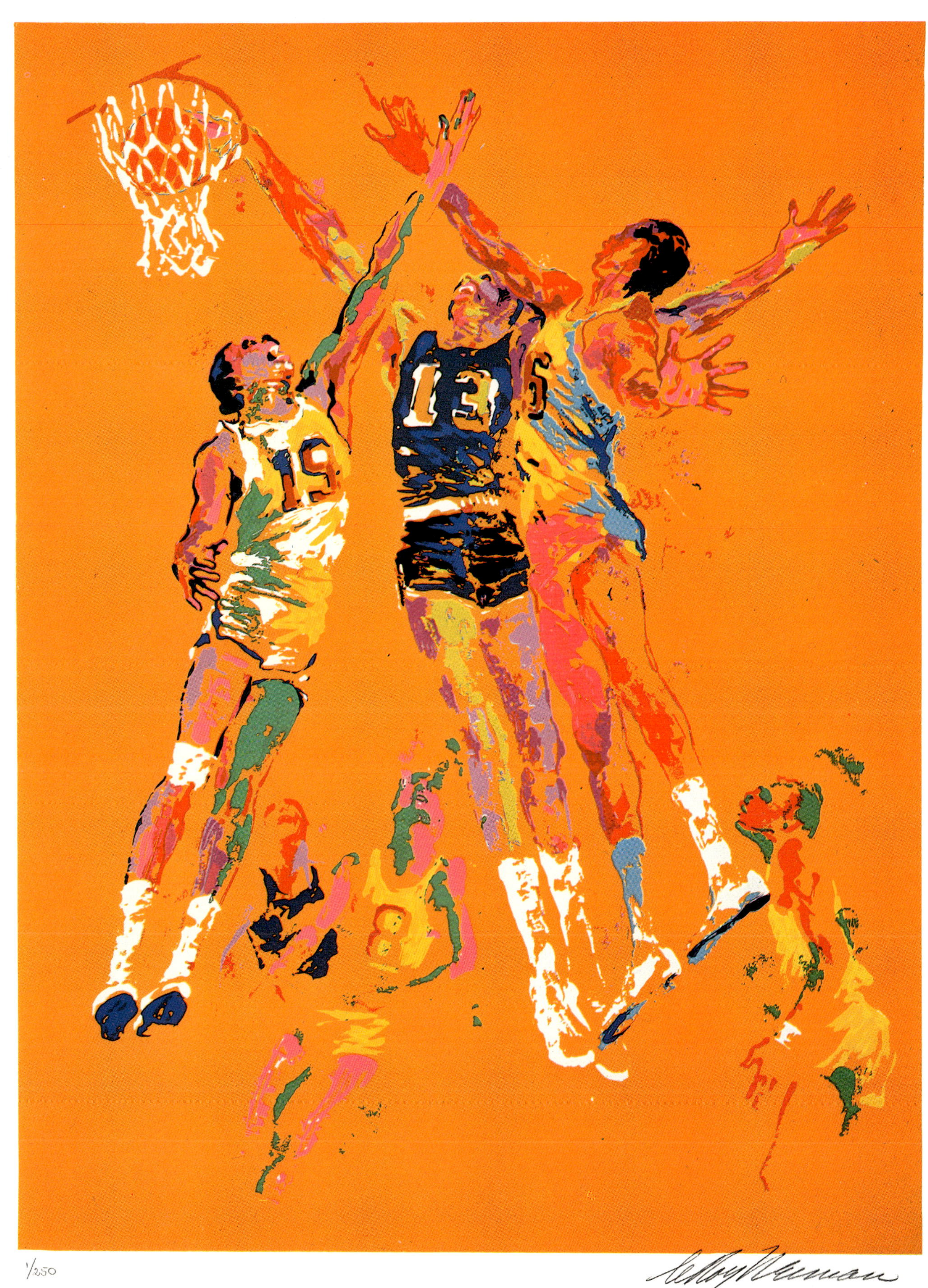

5　Basketball

1972
Serigraph
27¼ x 20 (69.22 x 50.8 cm)
A limited edition of 250, signed and
numbered by the artist.

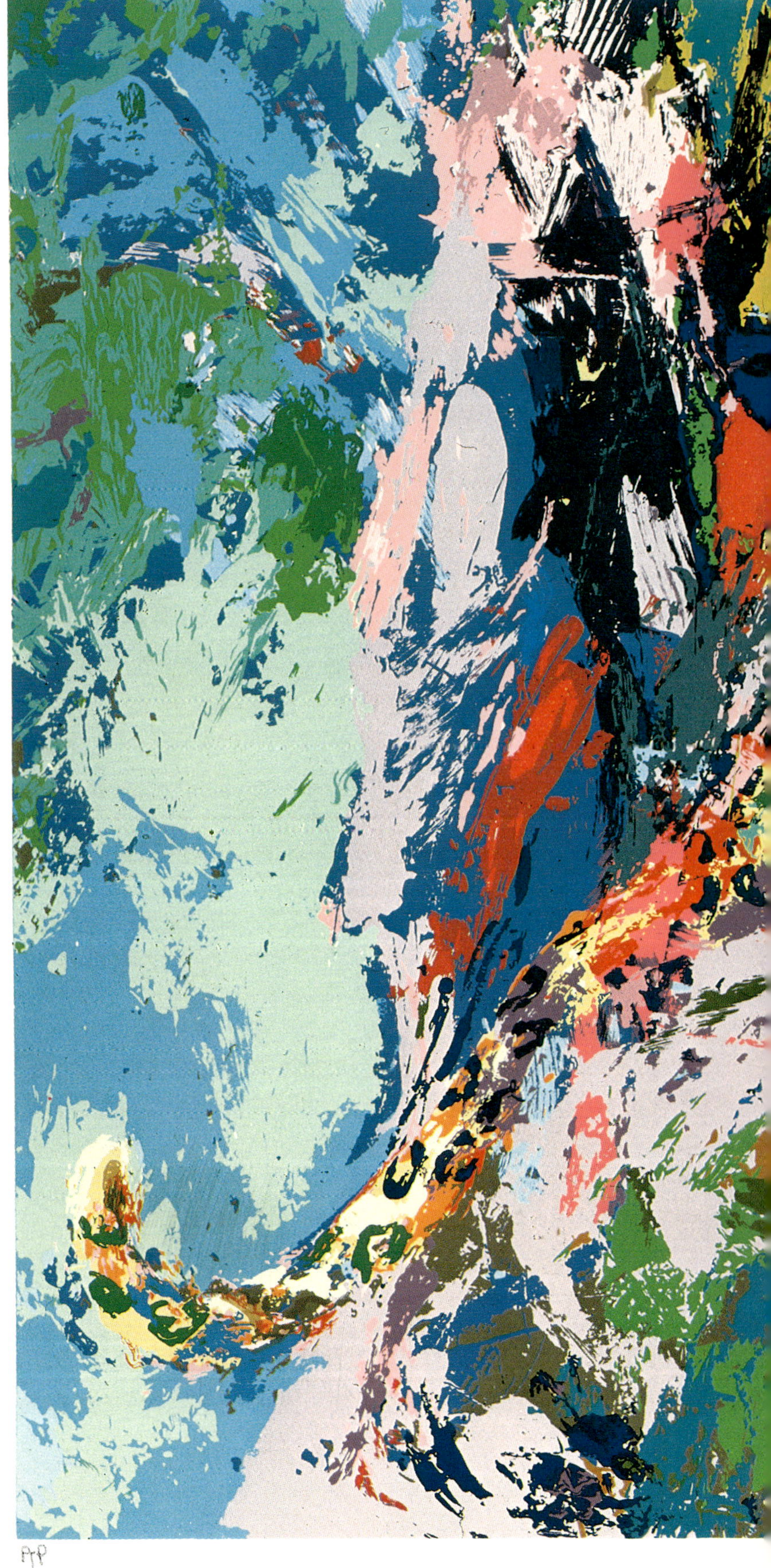

6 Leopard

1972
Serigraph
32½ x 45⅛ (82.55 x 114.62 cm)
A limited edition of 300, signed and numbered
by the artist.

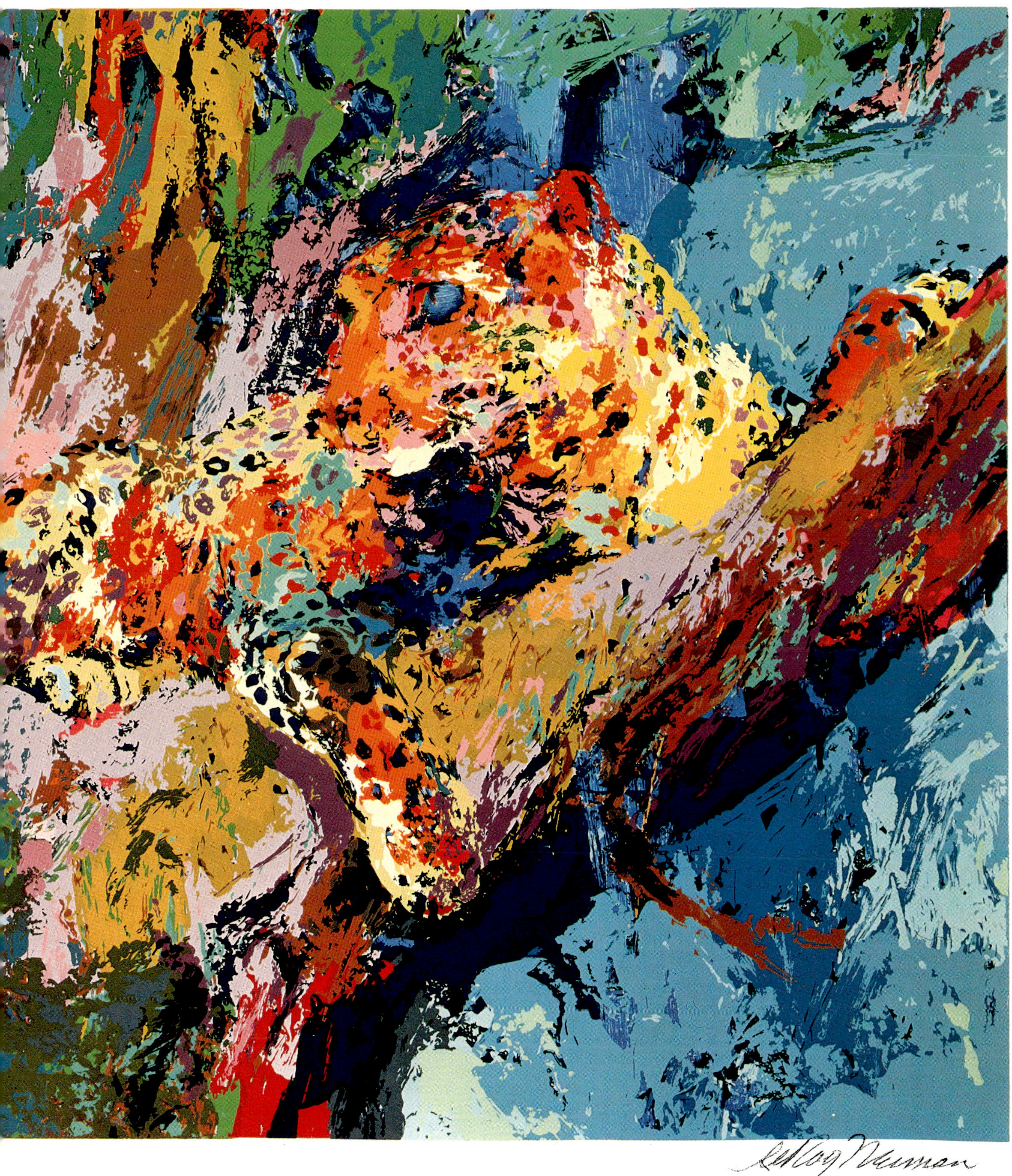

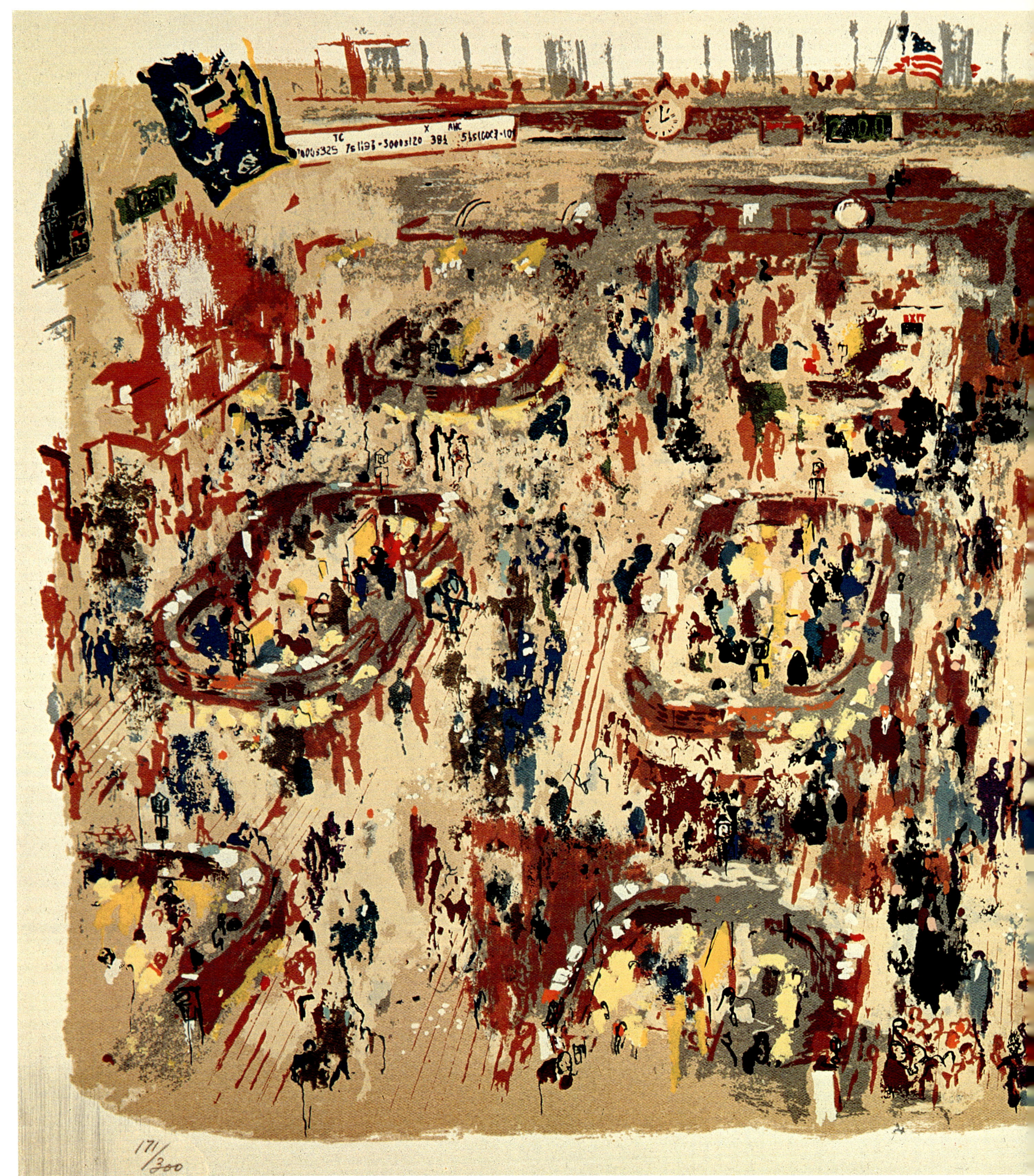

171/300

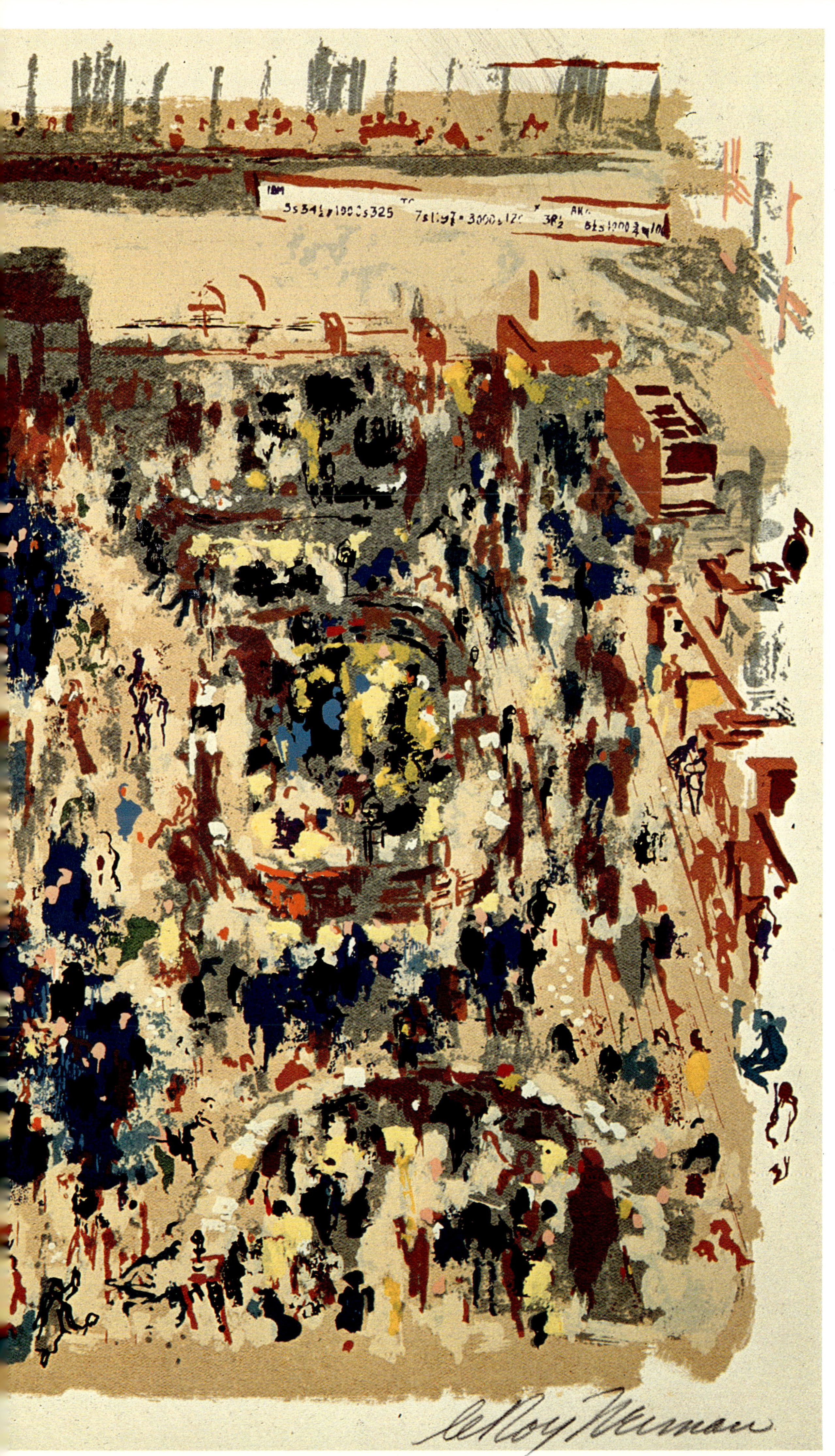

7 Stock Market

1972
Serigraph
25¼ x 37⅜ (64.13 x 94.93 cm)
A limited edition of 300, signed and numbered
by the artist.

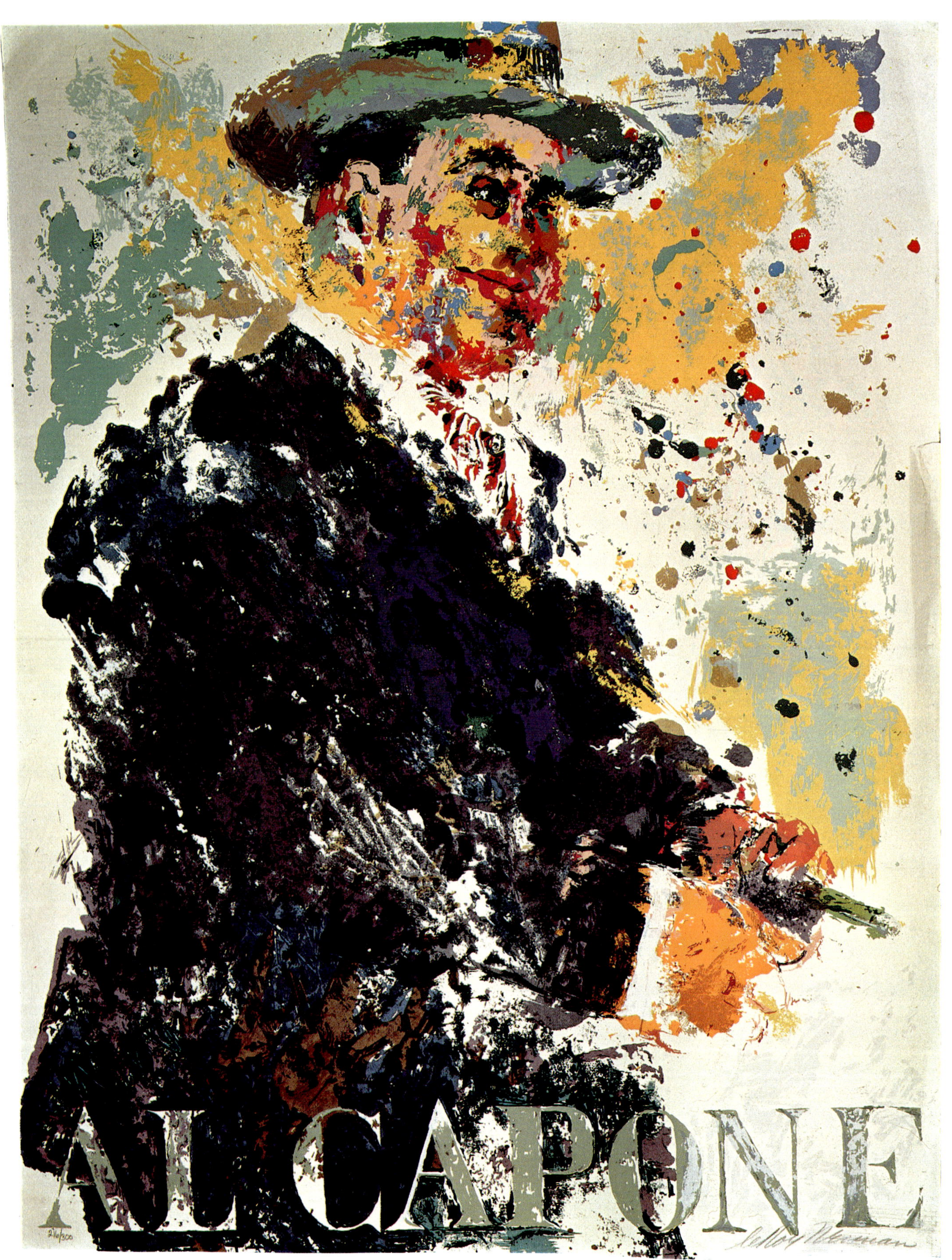

8   Al Capone
1972
Serigraph
39¾ x 30 (100.96 x 76.2 cm)
A limited edition of 300, signed and
numbered by the artist.

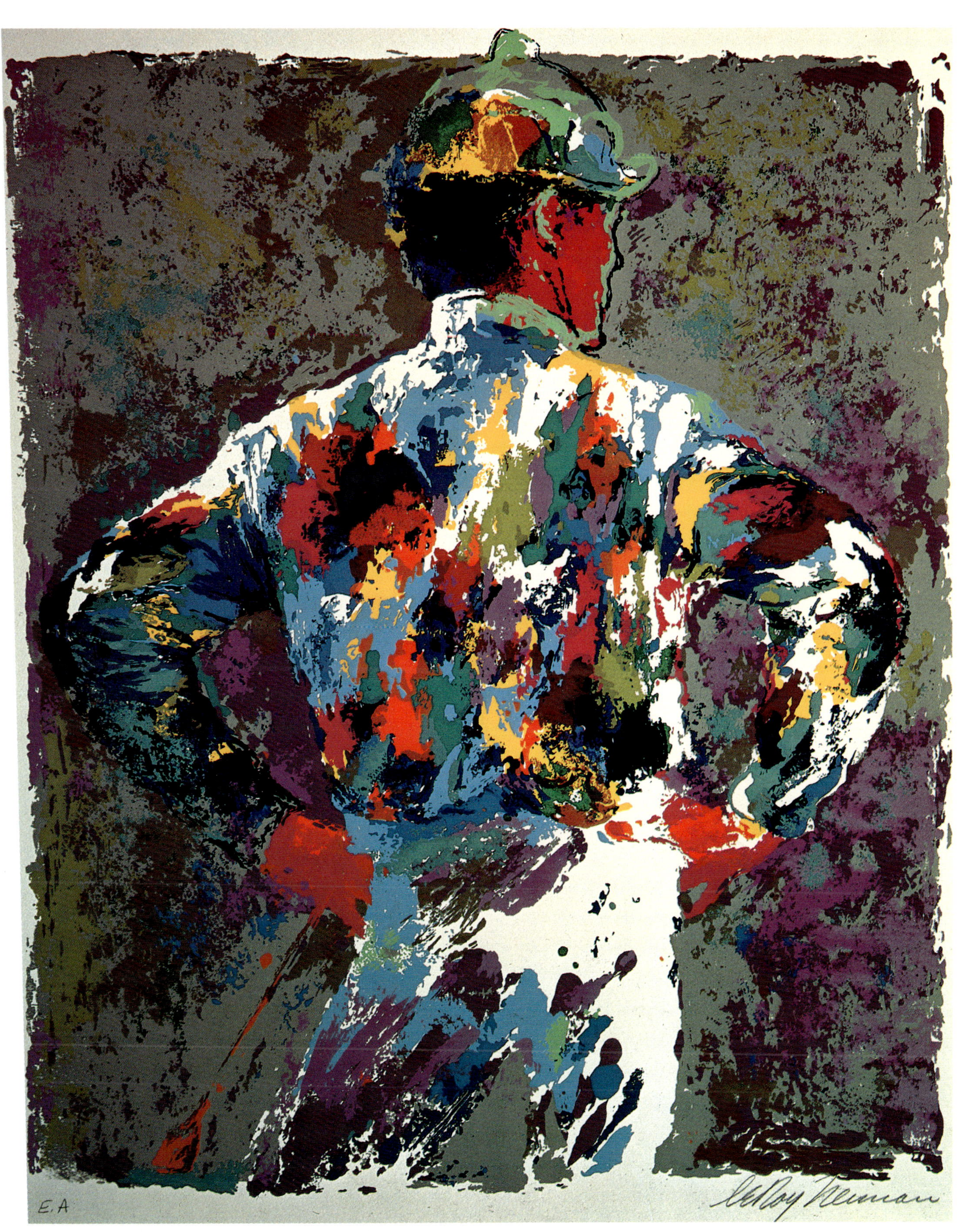

9　Jockey

1972
Serigraph
20⅜ x 16¼ (51.75 x 41.27 cm)
A limited edition of 300, signed and numbered
by the artist.

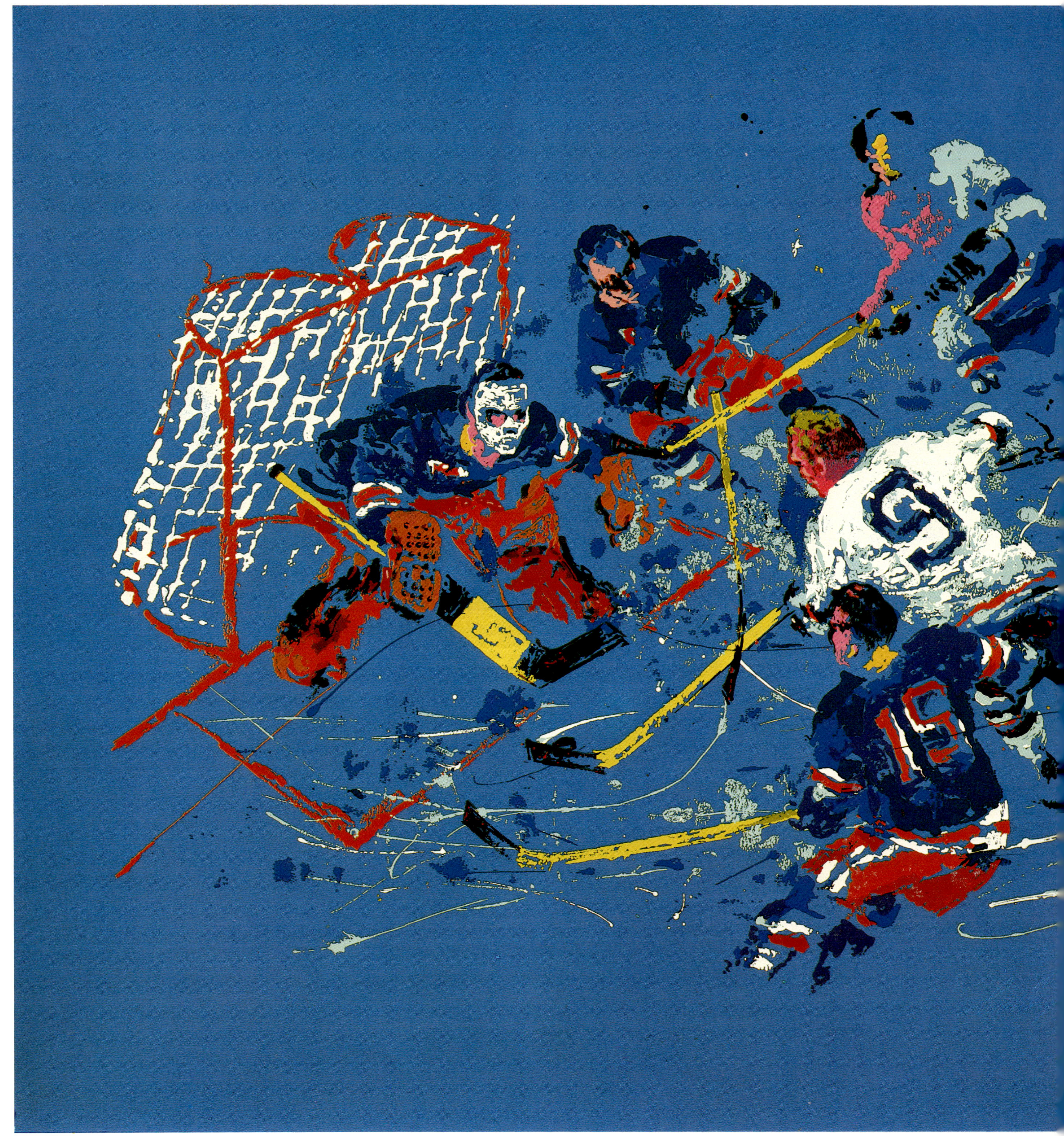

A.P.

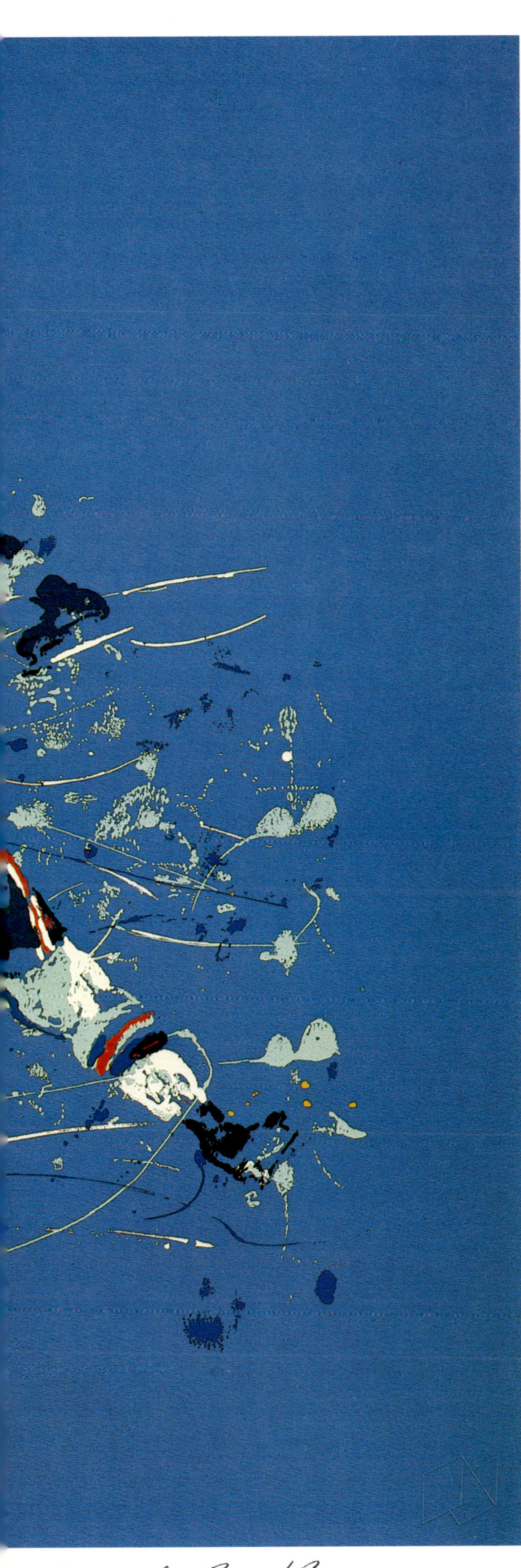

10   Blue Hockey

1972
Serigraph
30½ x 40½ (77.47 x 102.87 cm)
A limited edition of 200, signed and numbered
by the artist.

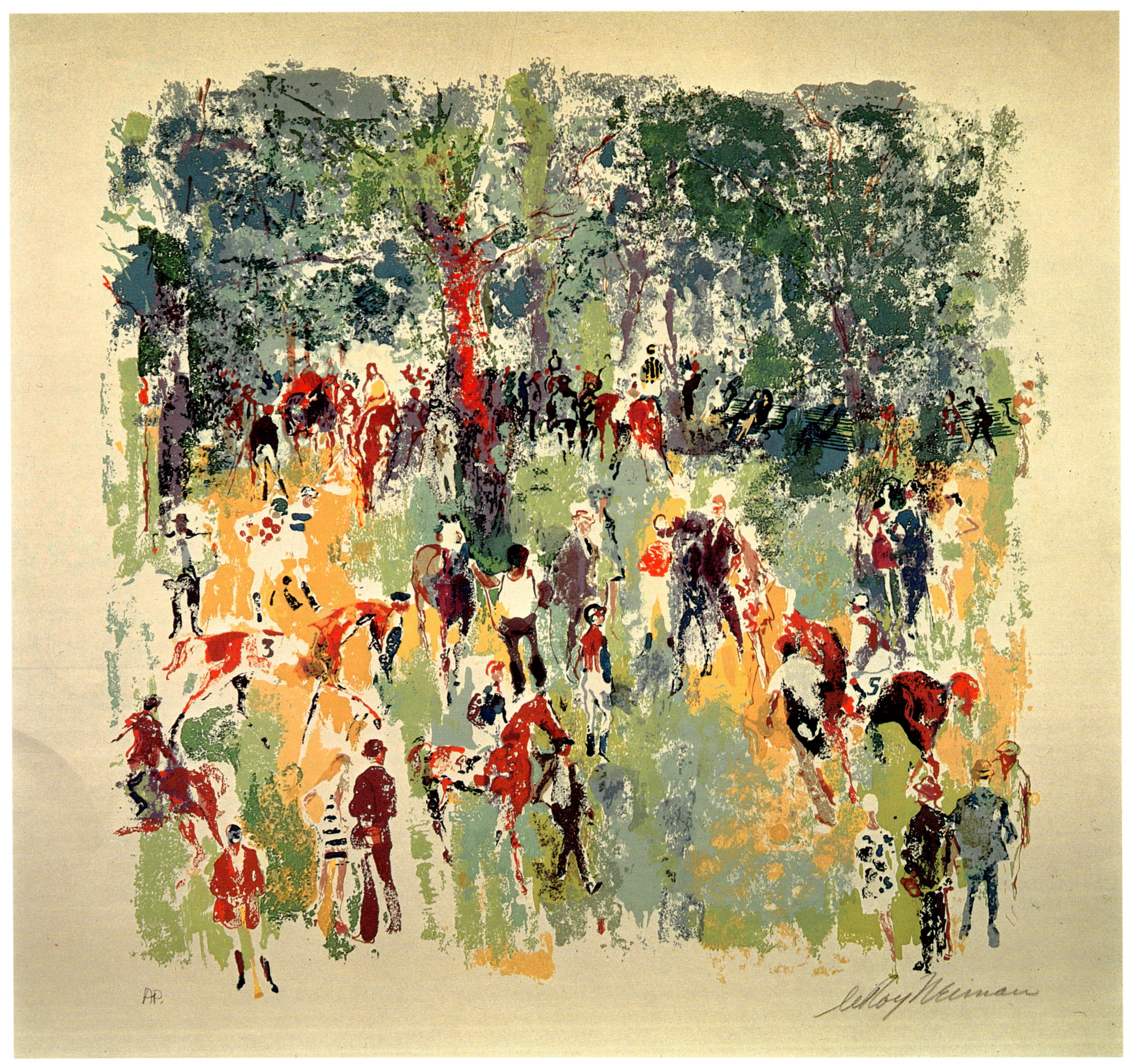

11 Paddock

1972
Serigraph
25 x 25⅜ (63.5 x 64.45 cm)

A limited edition of 300, signed and numbered
by the artist.

12 Four Aces

1972
Serigraph
26 x 17½ (66.04 x 44.45 cm)
A limited edition of 300, signed and
numbered by the artist.

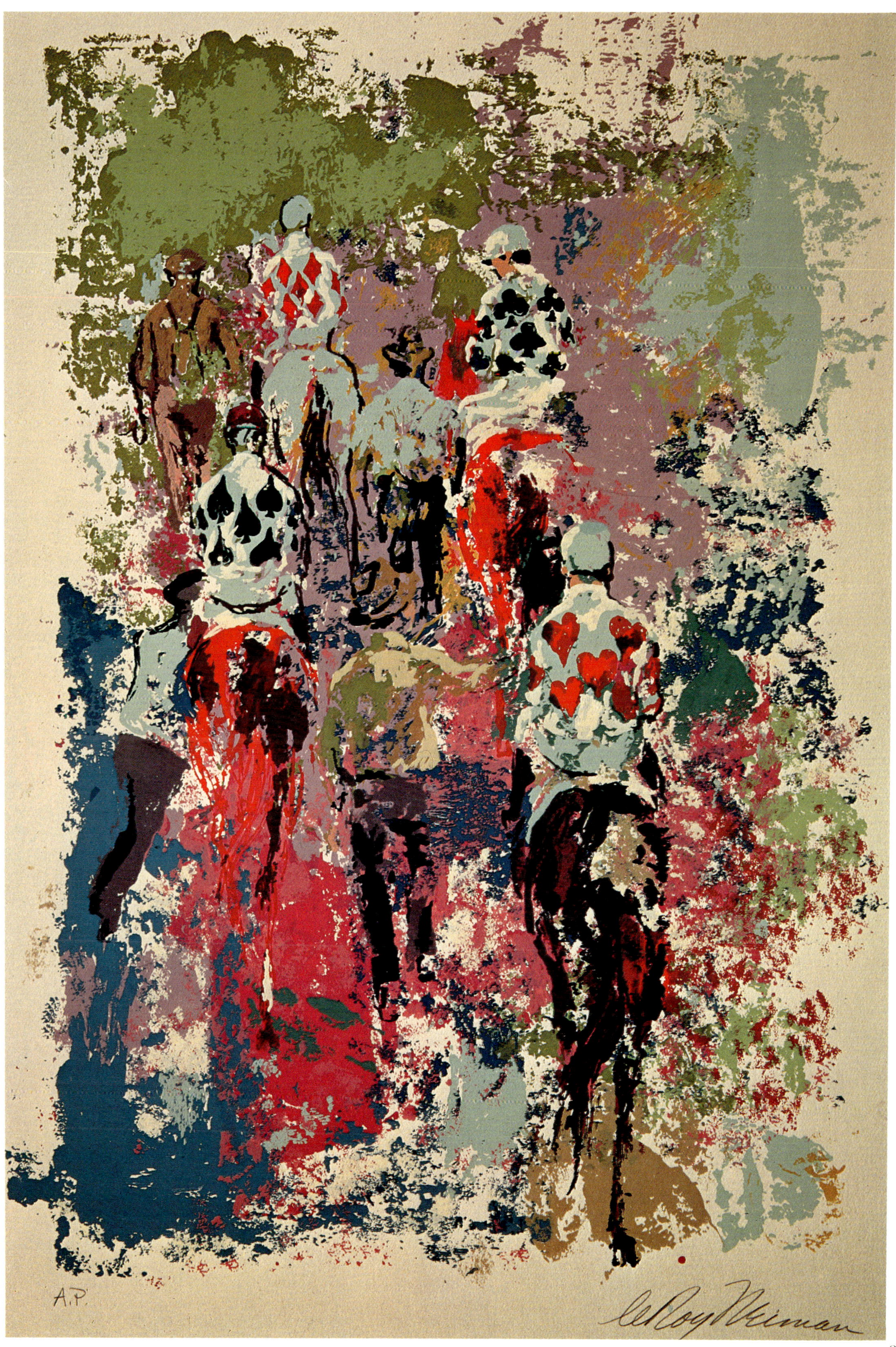

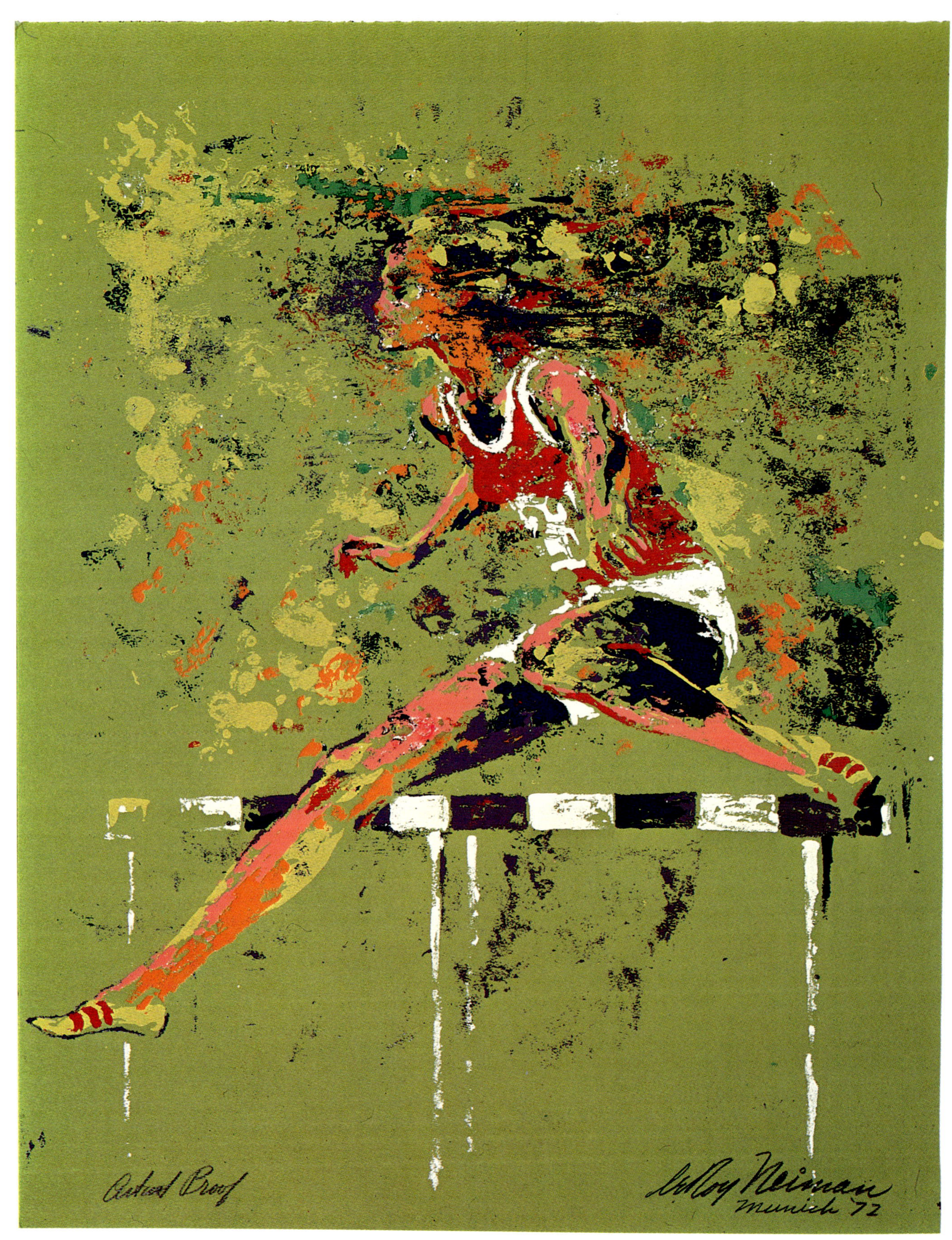

13 Olympic Hurdler
1972
Serigraph
26 x 20 (66.04 x 50.8 cm)
A limited edition of 175, signed and numbered
by the artist.

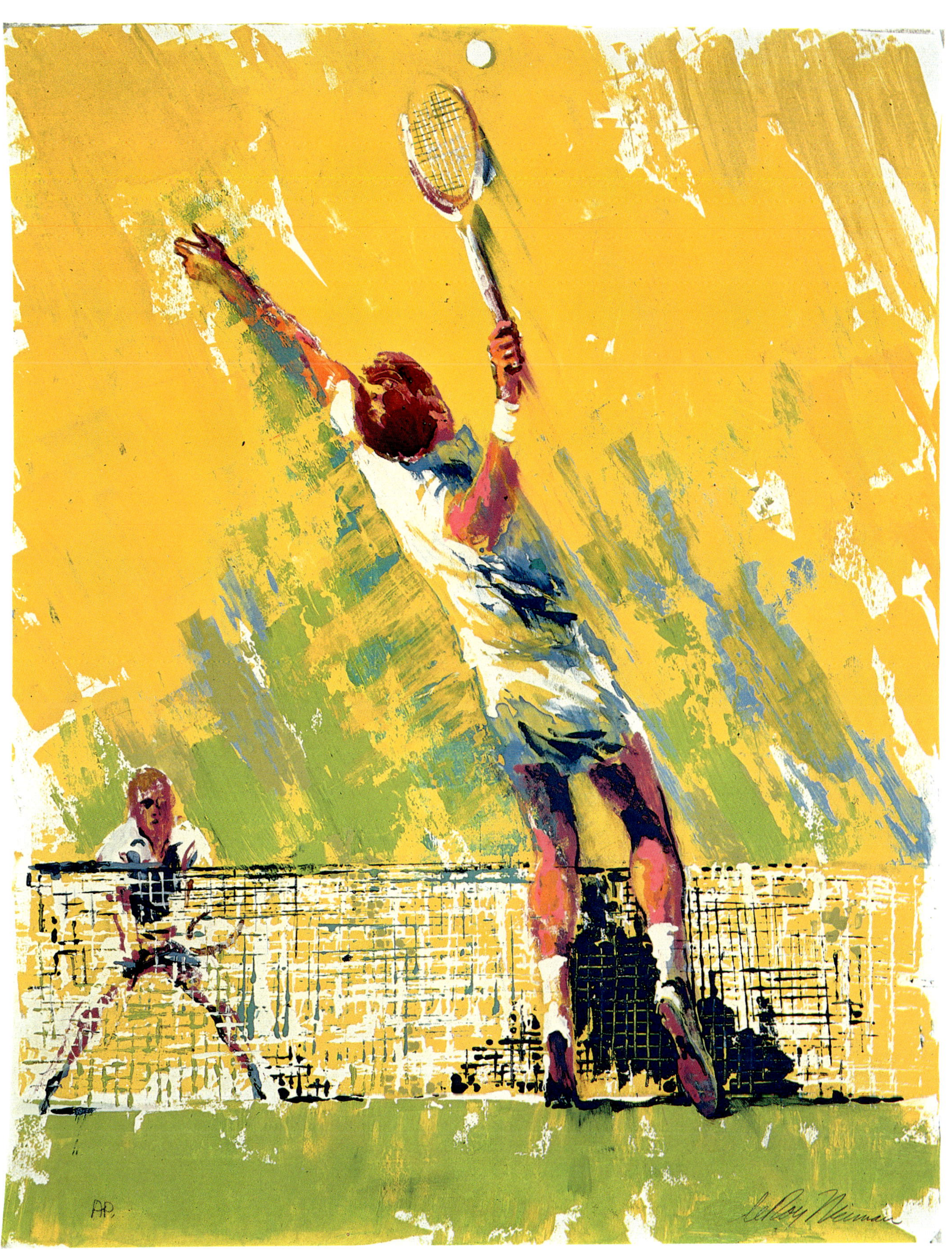

14 Deuce
1972
Serigraph
26 x 19½ (66.04 x 49.53 cm)
A limited edition of 275, signed
and numbered by the artist.

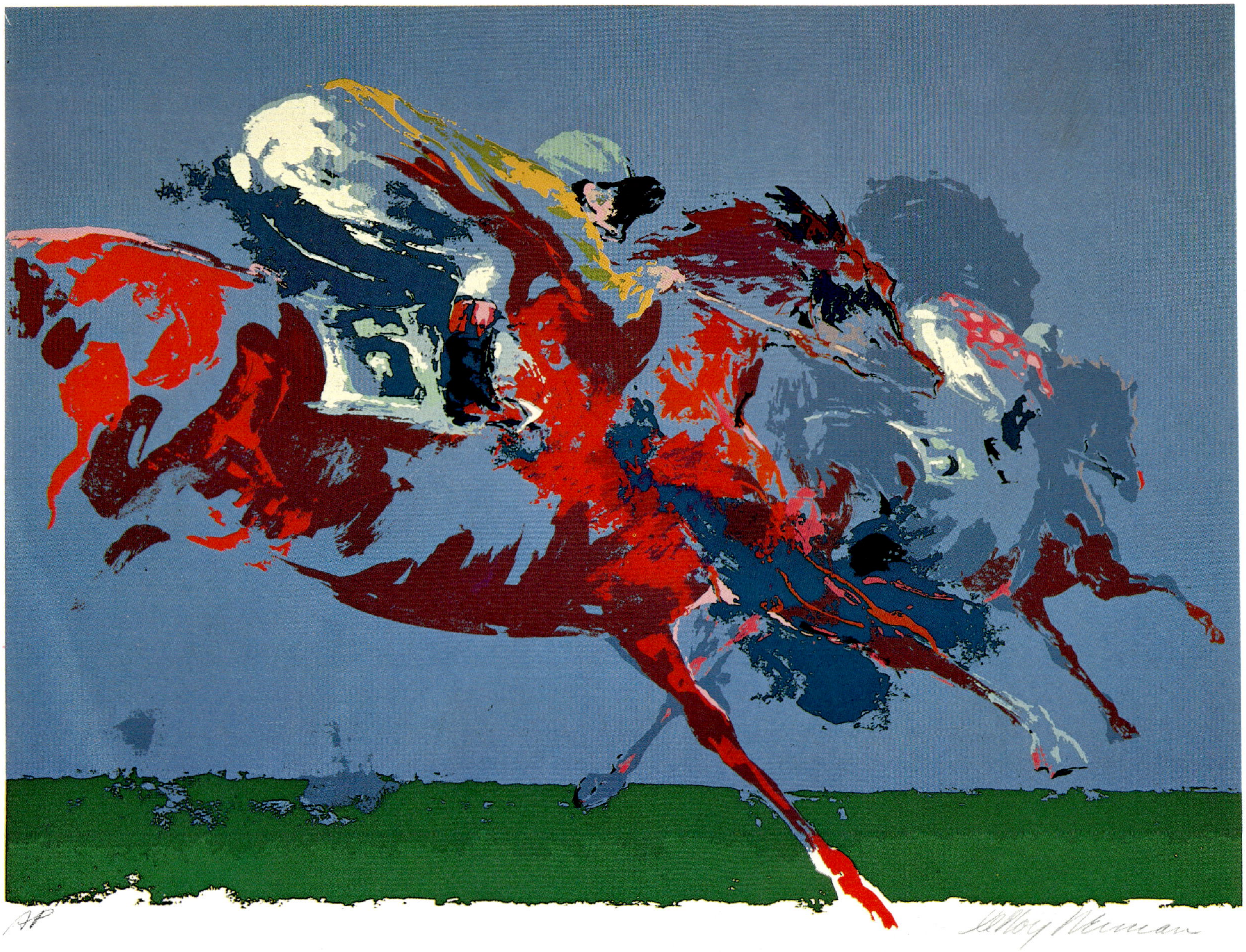

15 In The Stretch

1972
Serigraph
20⅝ x 28 (52.39 x 71.12 cm)
A limited edition of 250, signed and numbered
by the artist.

16 Along the Rail

1972
Serigraph
19⅞ x 16 (50.48 x 40.64 cm)
A limited edition of 200, signed
and numbered by the artist.

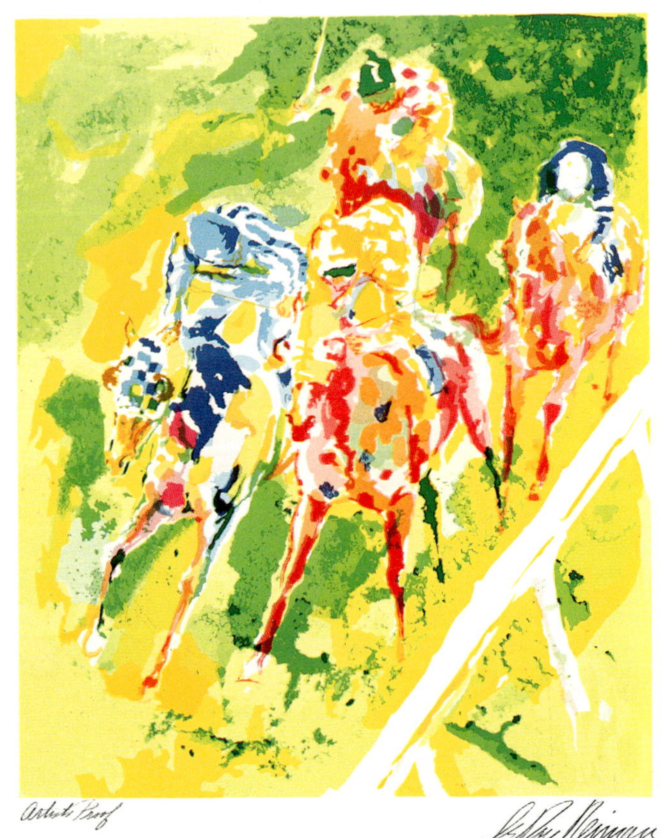

17   The Race

1972
Serigraph
9¾ x 18¼ (24.76 x 46.35 cm)
A limited edition of 300, signed and numbered
by the artist.

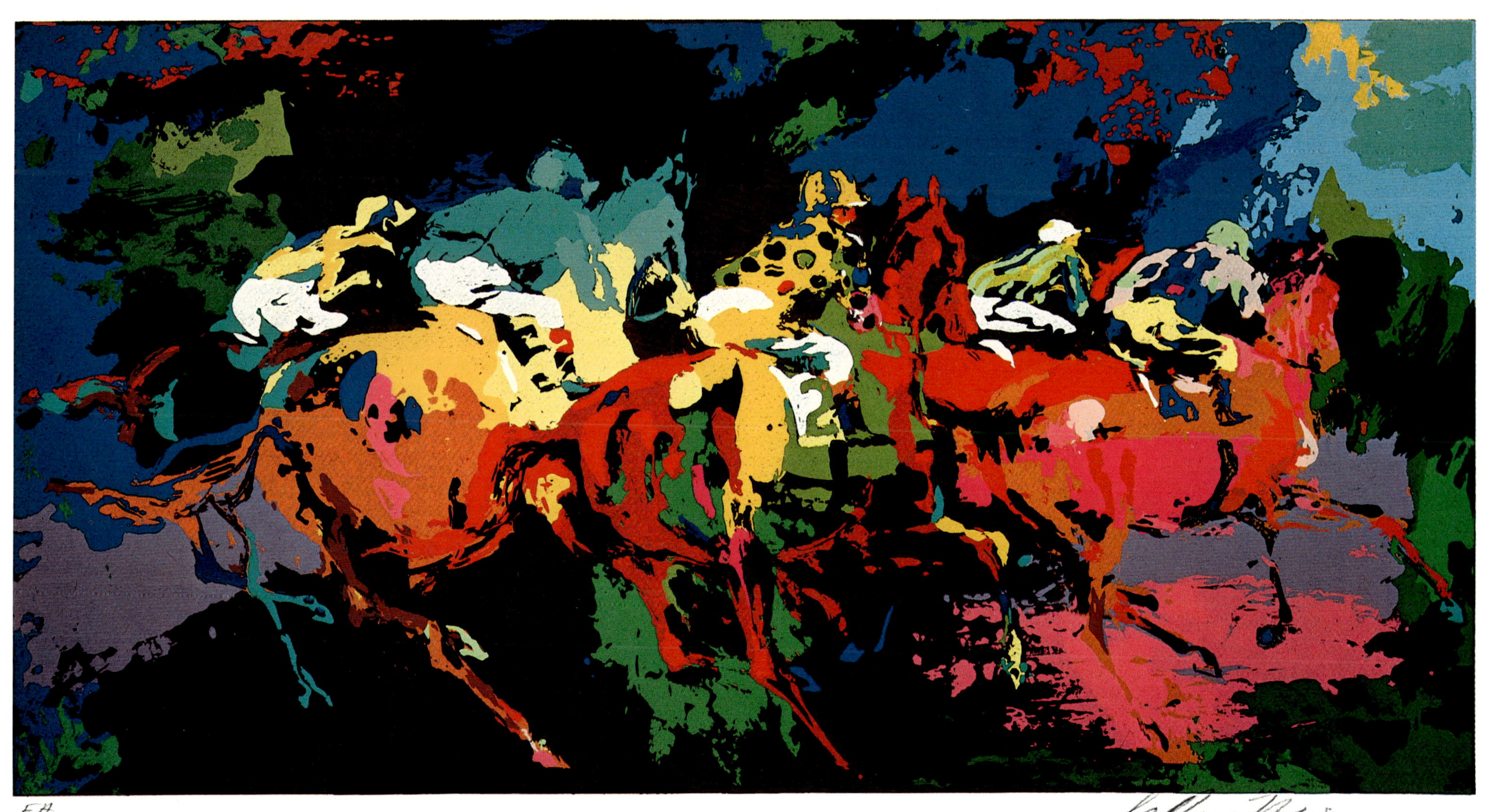

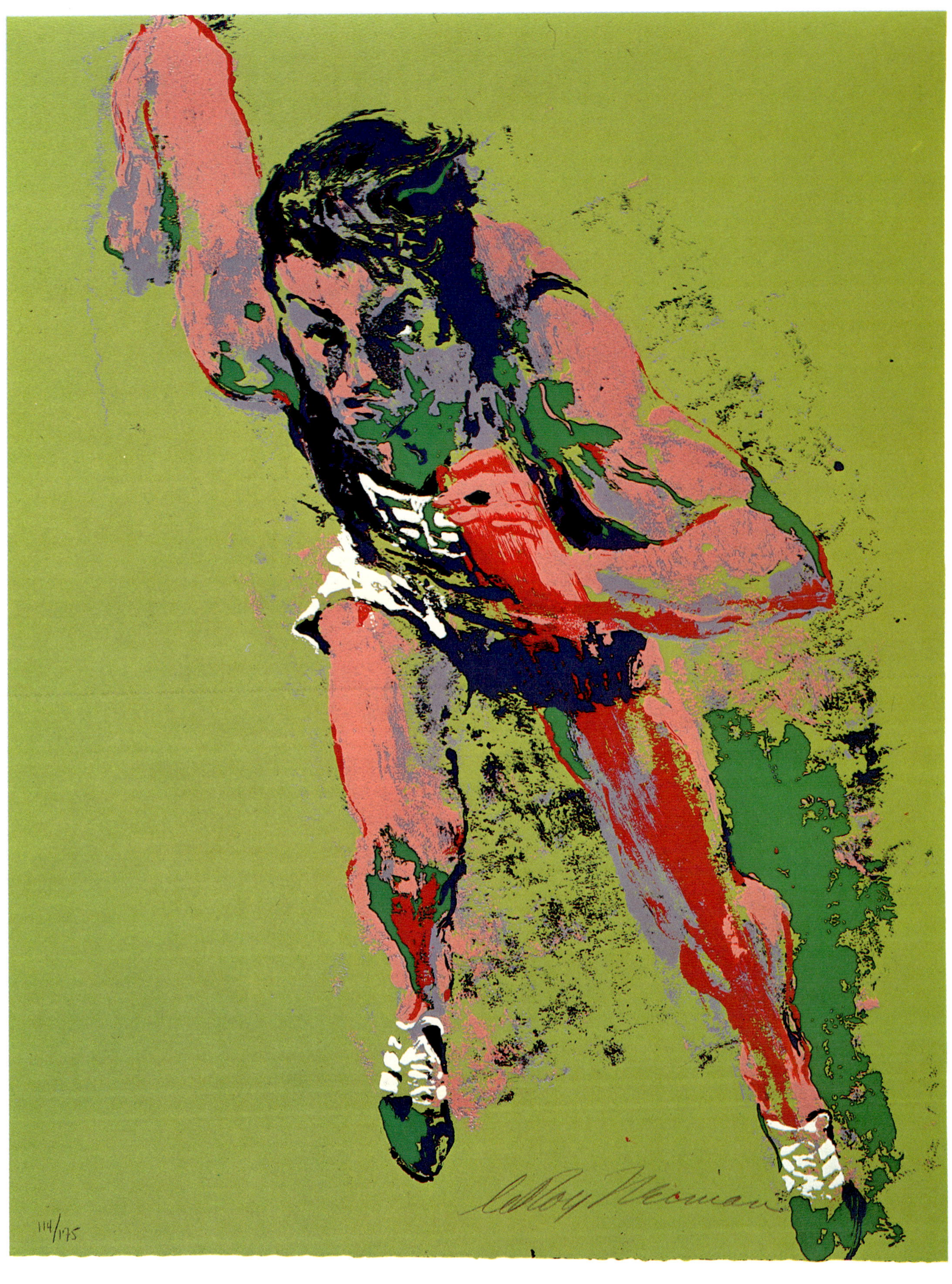

18 Olympic Runner

1972
Serigraph
26 x 20 (66.04 x 50.8 cm)
A limited edition of 175, signed and numbered
by the artist.

19 Olympic Fencers

1972
Serigraph
25⅝ x 40⅛ (65.09 x 101.92 cm)
A limited edition of 175, signed and numbered
by the artist.

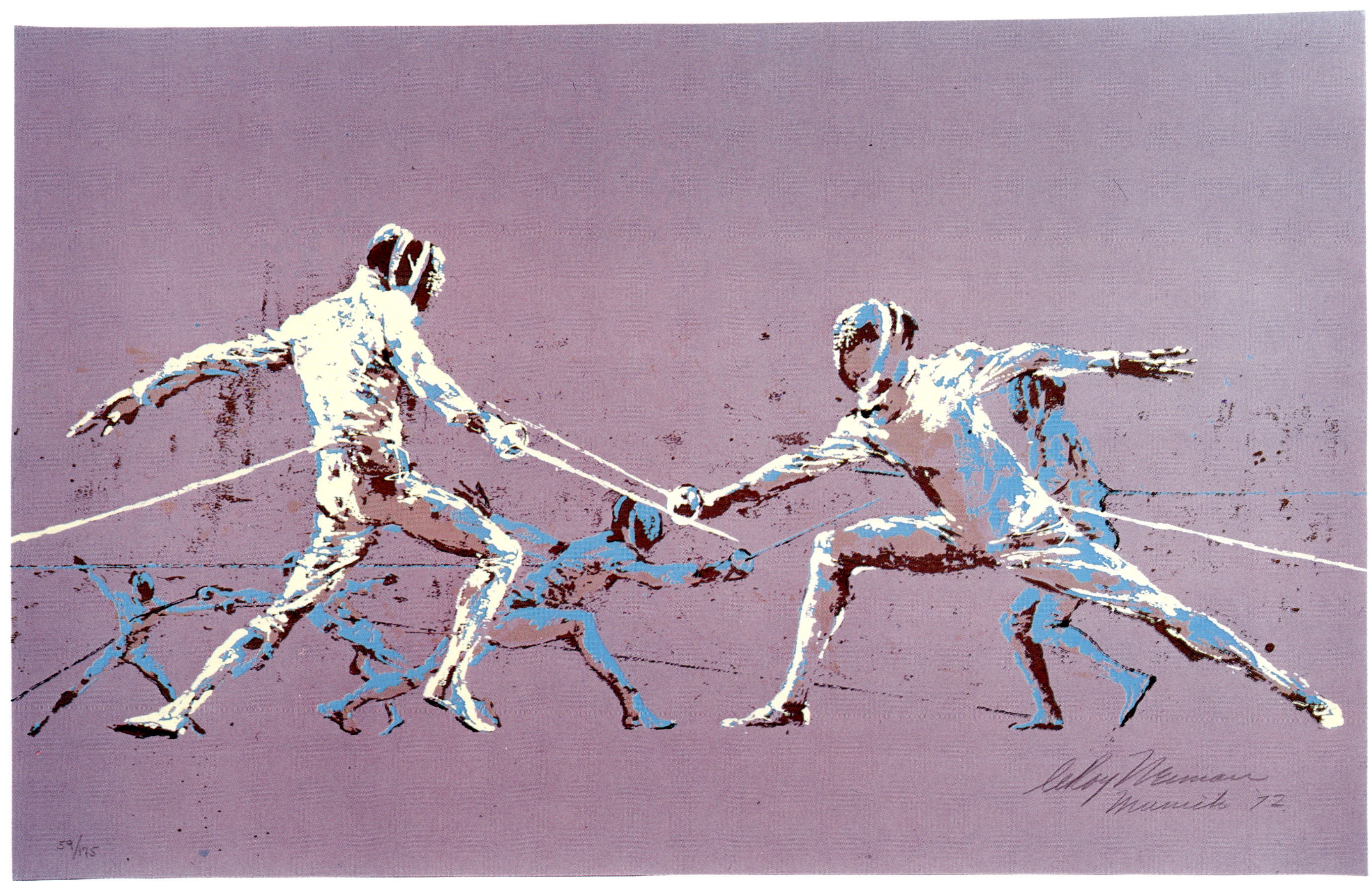

1972–MUNICH SUITE

A limited edition of 150, signed and numbered by the artist.

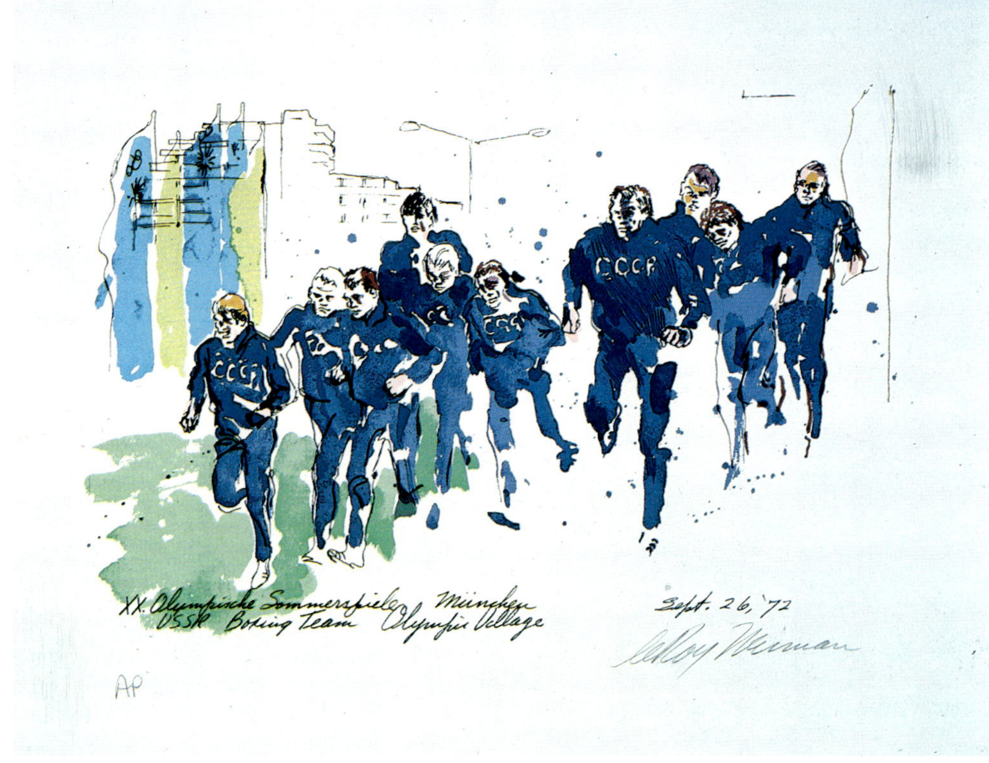

20
Russian Boxing Team
1973
Serigraph
11 x 16 (27.94 x 40.64 cm)

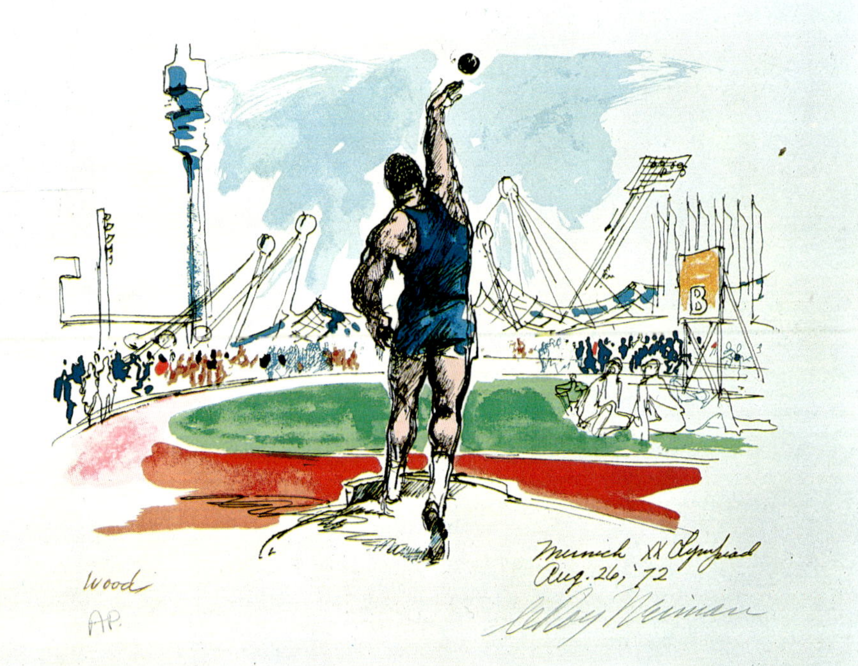

21
Shot Put
1973
Serigraph
11½ x 16 (29.21 x 40.64 cm)

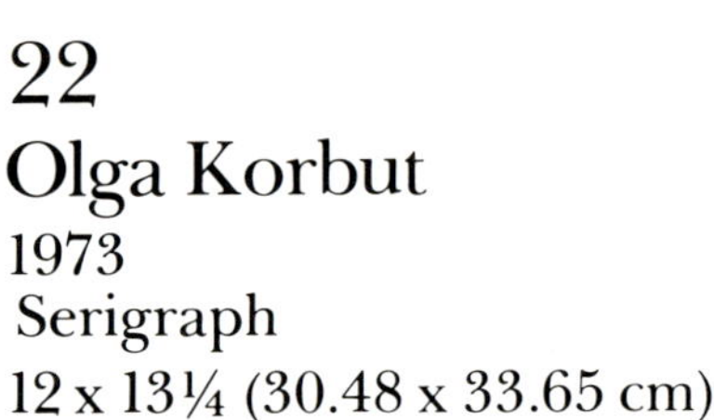

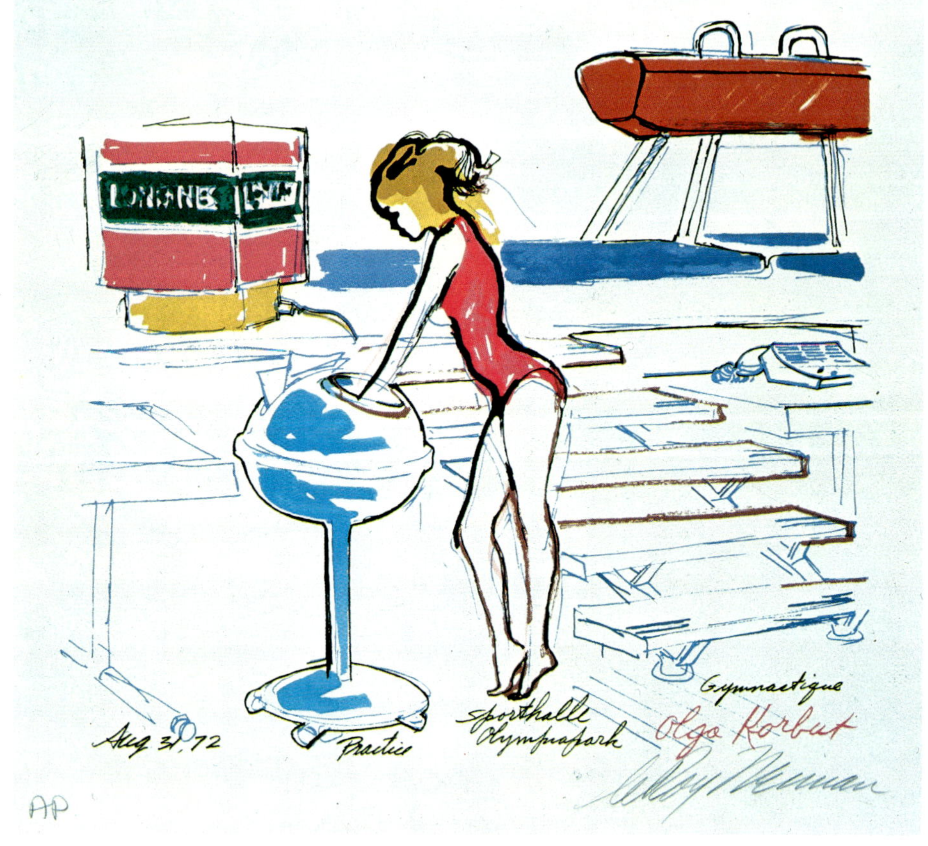

22
Olga Korbut
1973
Serigraph
12 x 13¼ (30.48 x 33.65 cm)

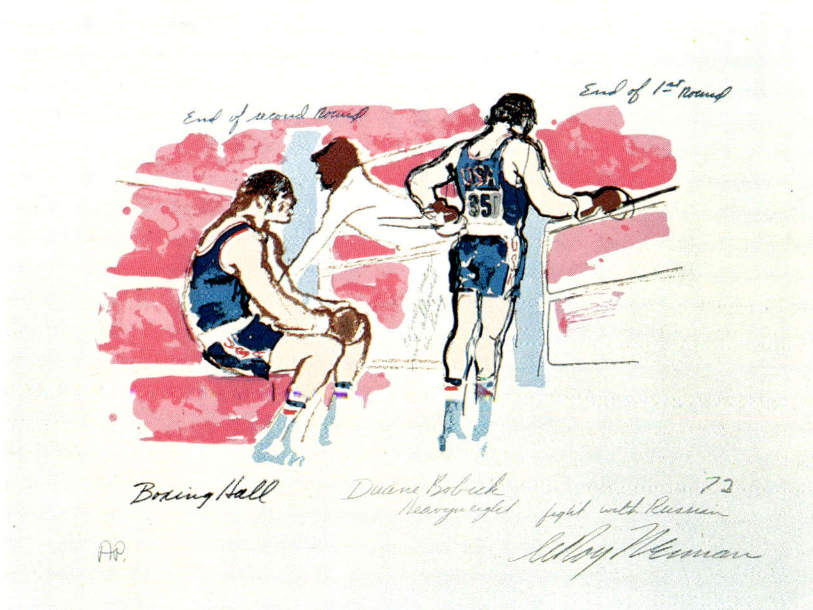

23
Bobick in the Ring
1973
Serigraph
9¼ x 14 (23.50 x 35.56 cm)

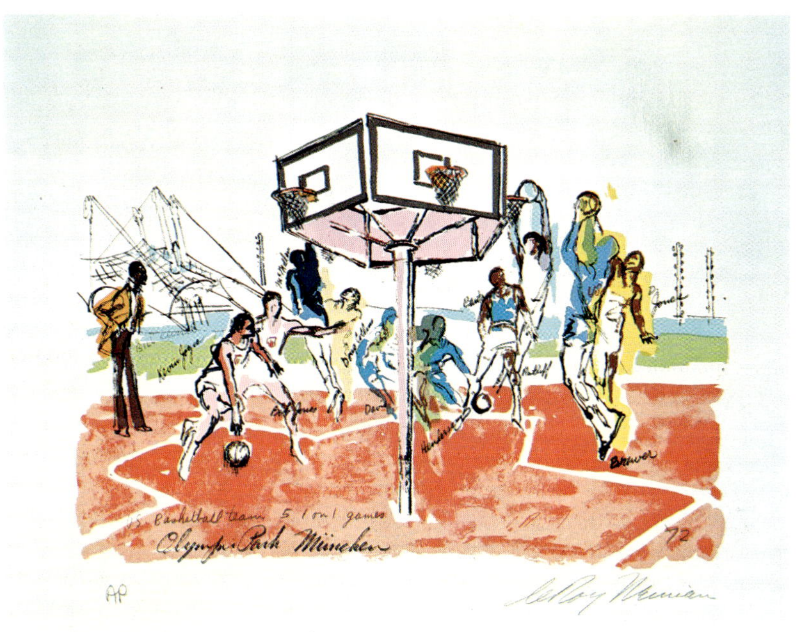

24
Basketball
1973
Serigraph
11¼ x 16 (28.57 x 40.64 cm)

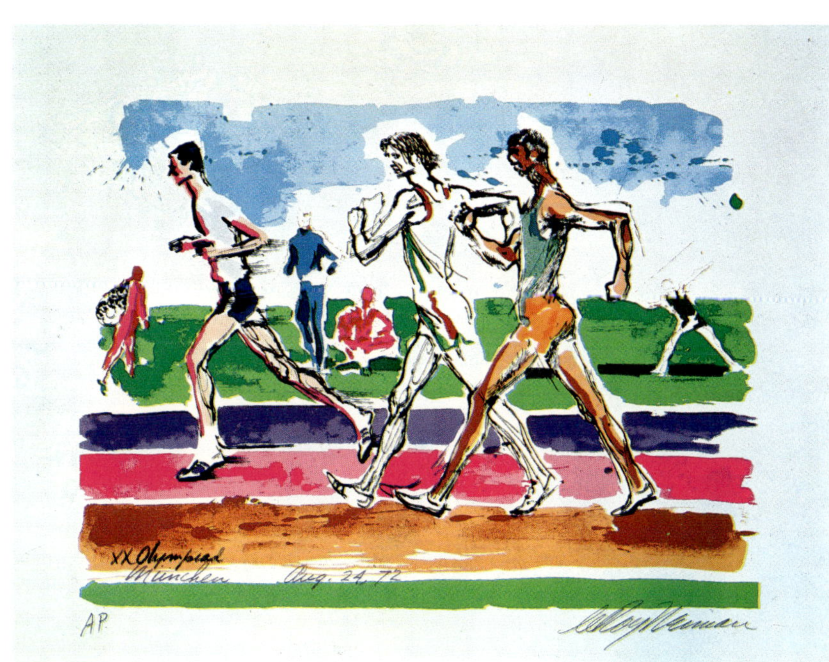

25
Jim Ryan
1973
Serigraph
12 x 16 (30.48 x 40.64 cm)

1972– MUNICH SUITE

A limited edition of 150, signed and numbered by the artist.

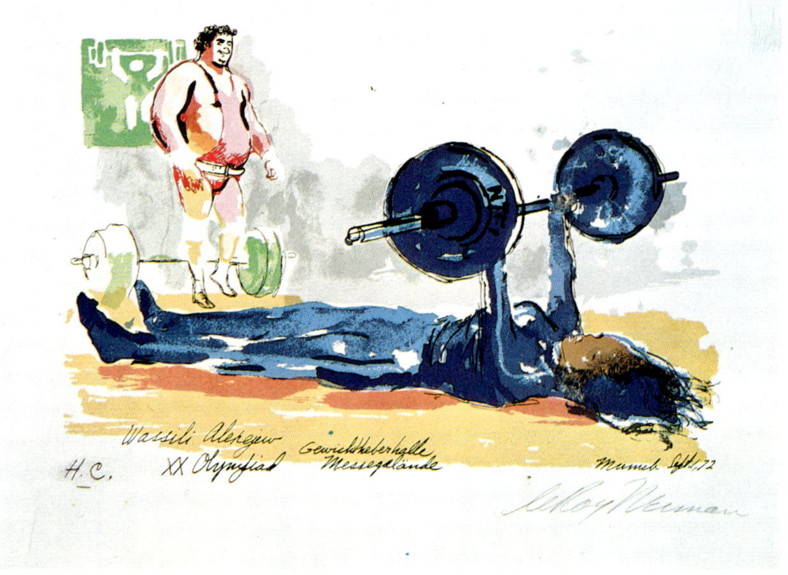

26

Woman Weight Lifter

1973
Serigraph
11¼ x 16 (28.57 x 40.64 cm)

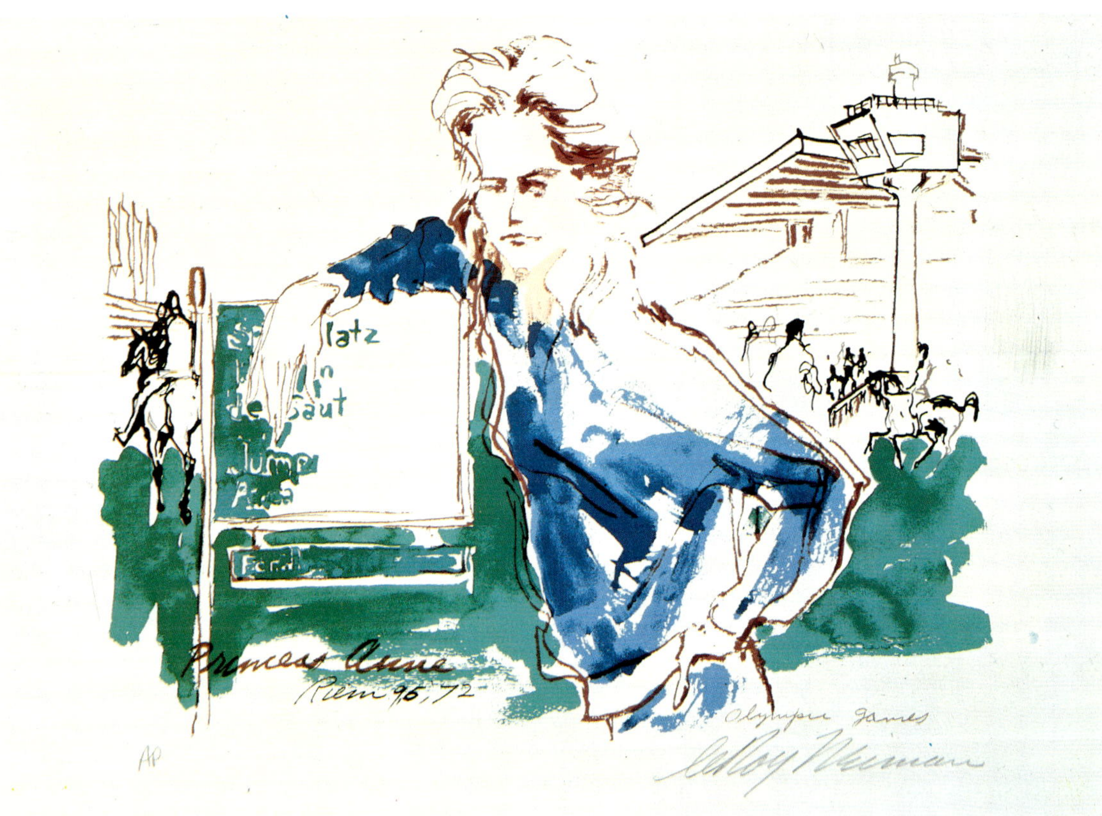

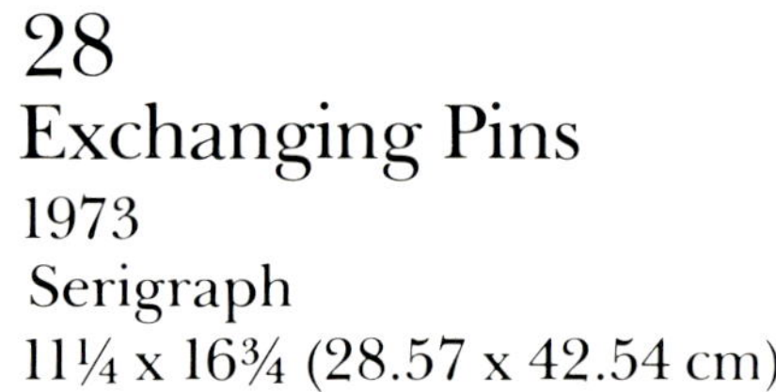

27

Princess Anne

1973
Serigraph
12 x 15¼ (30.48 x 38.73 cm)

28

Exchanging Pins

1973
Serigraph
11¼ x 16¾ (28.57 x 42.54 cm)

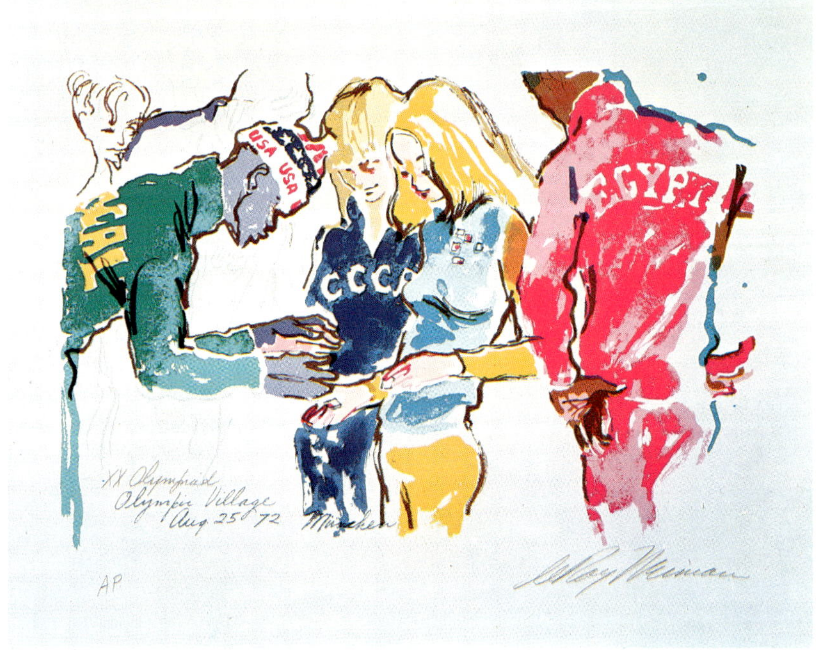

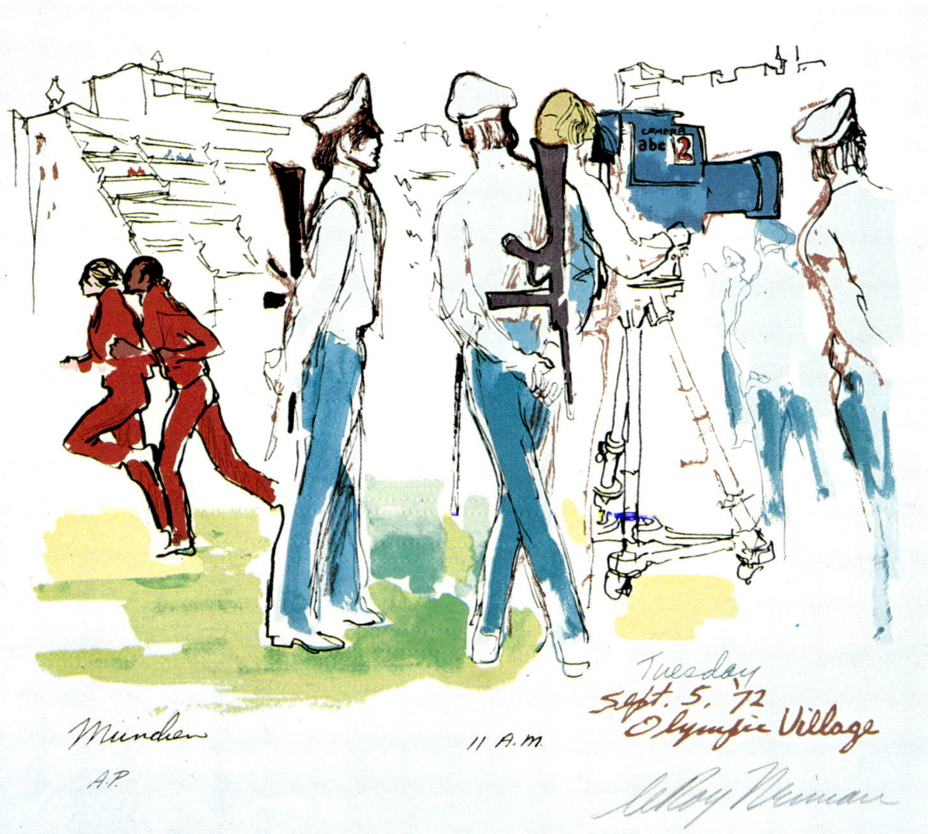

29
September 5th, 11 A.M.
1973
 Serigraph
11¼ x 14¾ (28.57 x 37.46 cm)

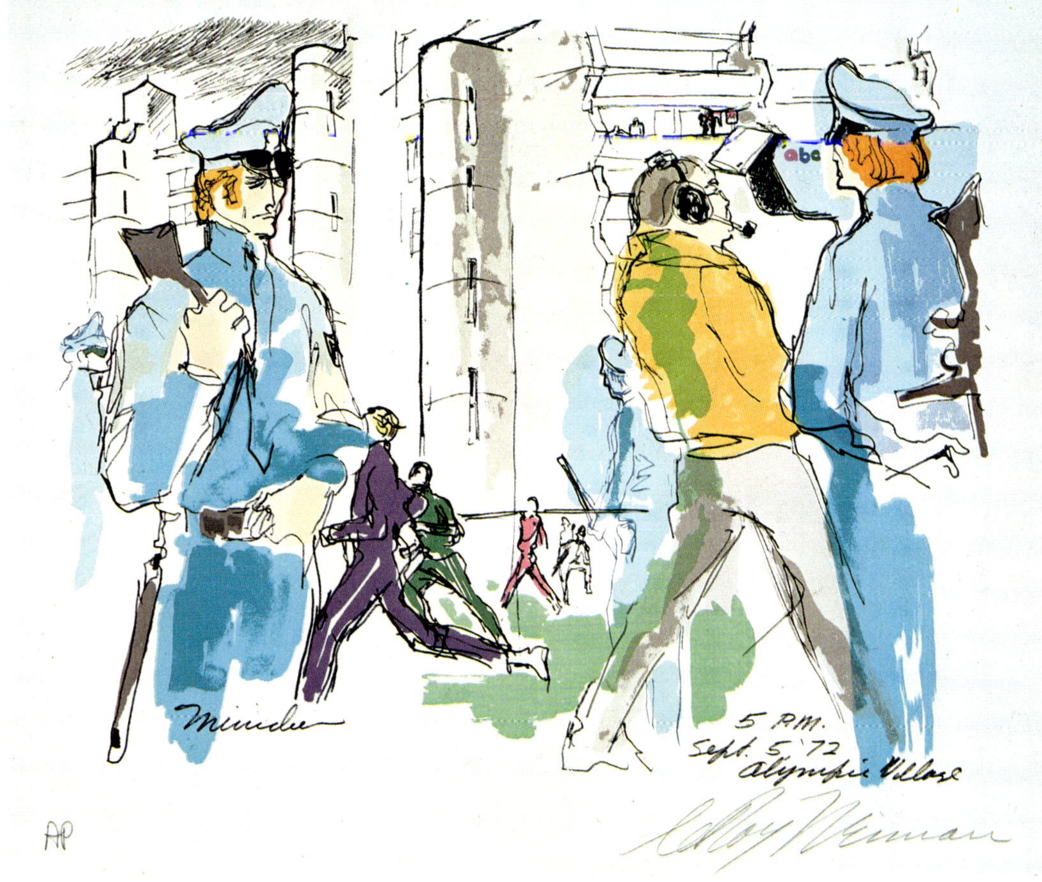

30
September 5th, 5 P.M.
1973
Serigraph
11¼ x 14¾ (28.57 x 37.46 cm)

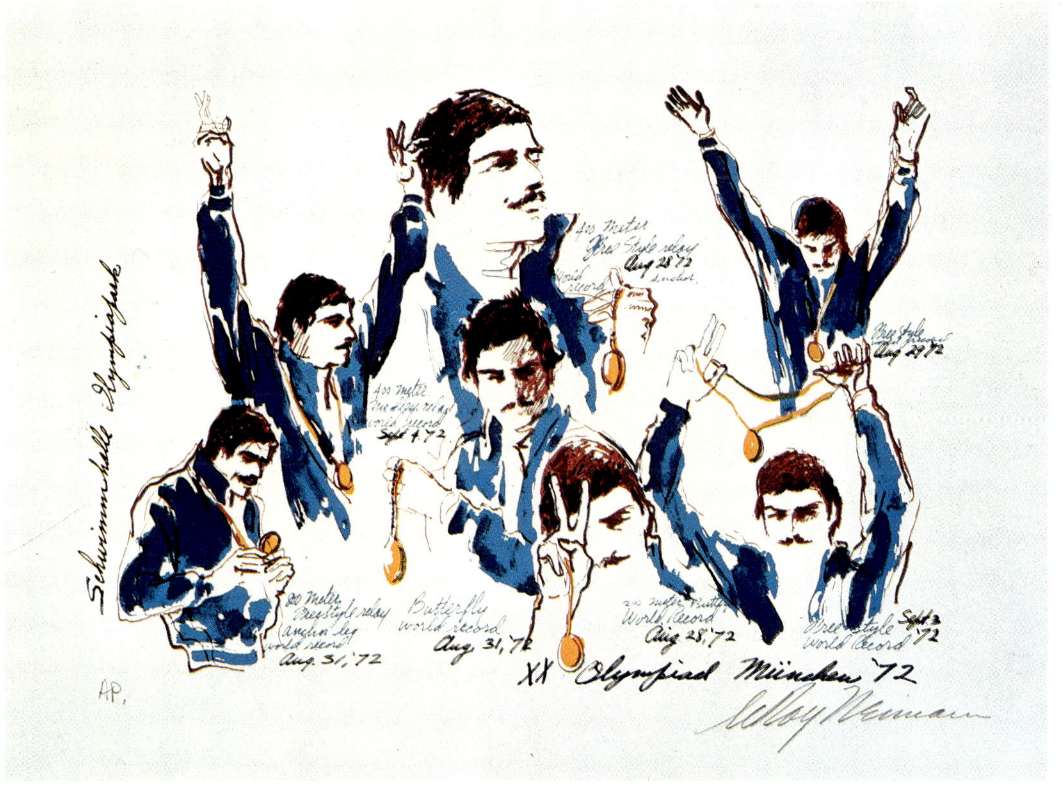

31
Mark Spitz with Medals
1973
Serigraph
10¼ x 15 (26.04 x 38.1 cm)

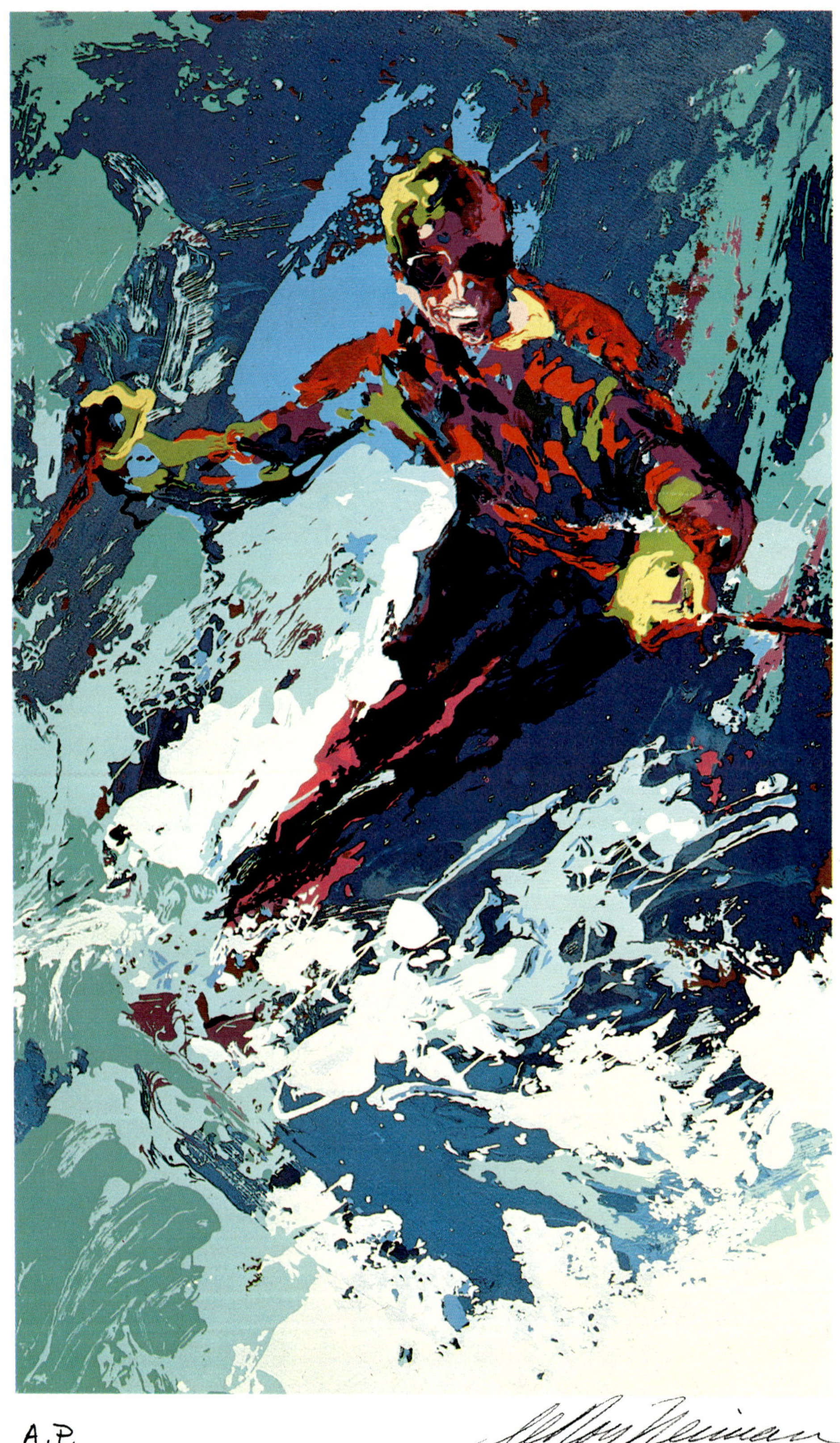

32 Skier

1972
Serigraph
11¾ x 20 (29.85 x 50.8 cm)

A limited edition of 300, signed and numbered
by the artist.

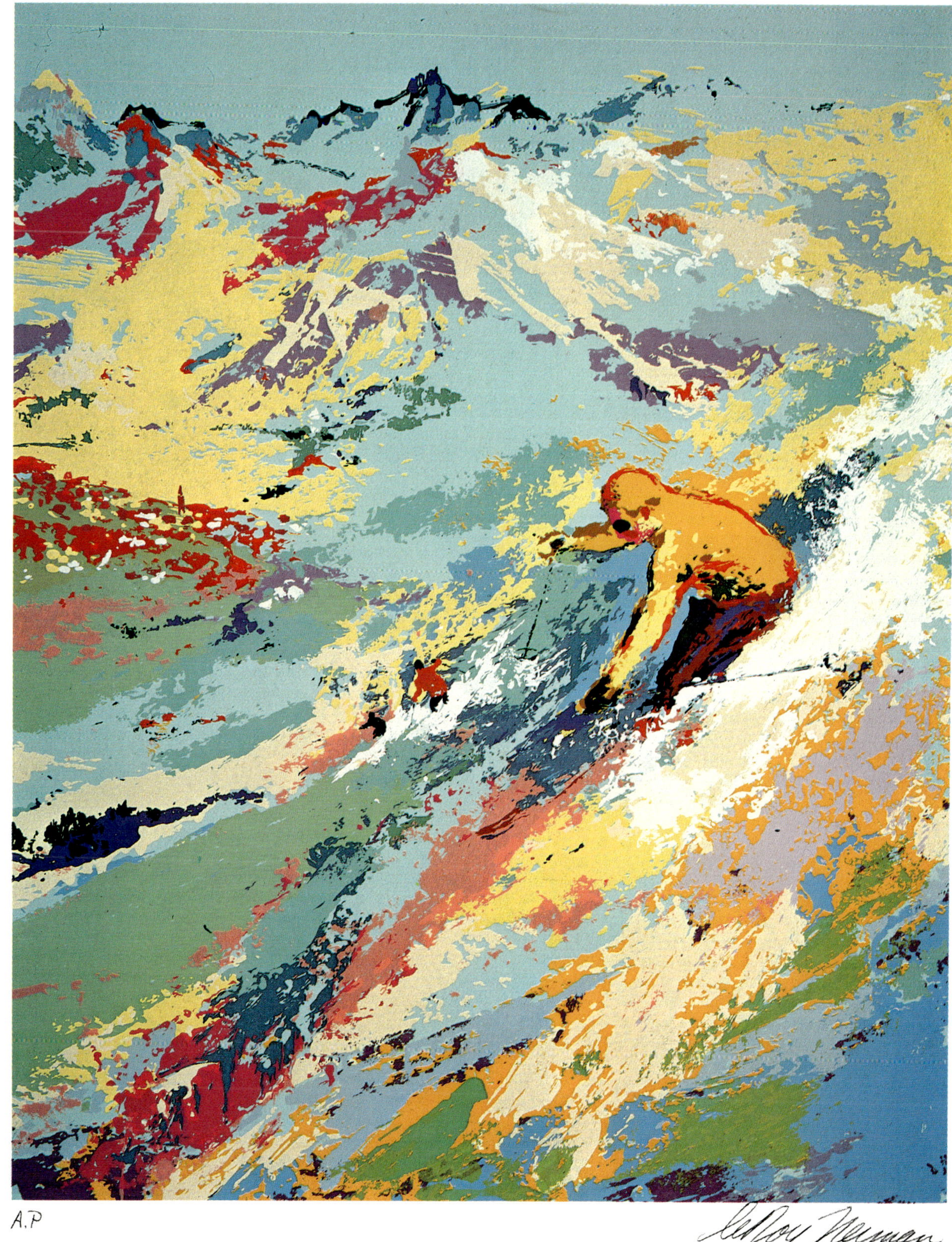

33 Alpine Skiing

1972
Serigraph
24¼ x 19 (61.59 x 48.26 cm)

A limited edition of 300, signed and numbered
by the artist.

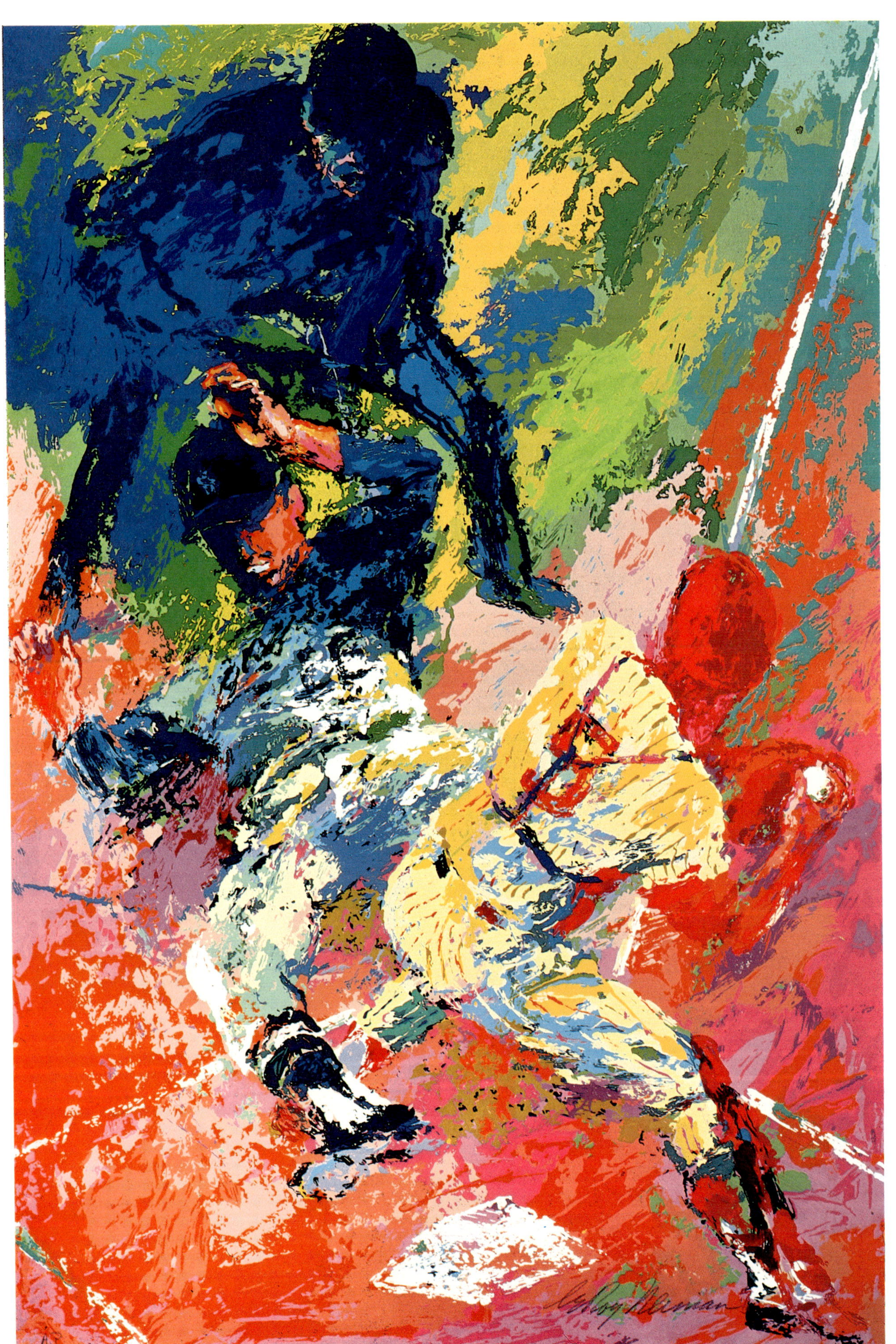

34 Sliding Home
1972
Serigraph
36 x 24 (91.44 x 60.96 cm)
A limited edition of 300, signed and numbered
by the artist.

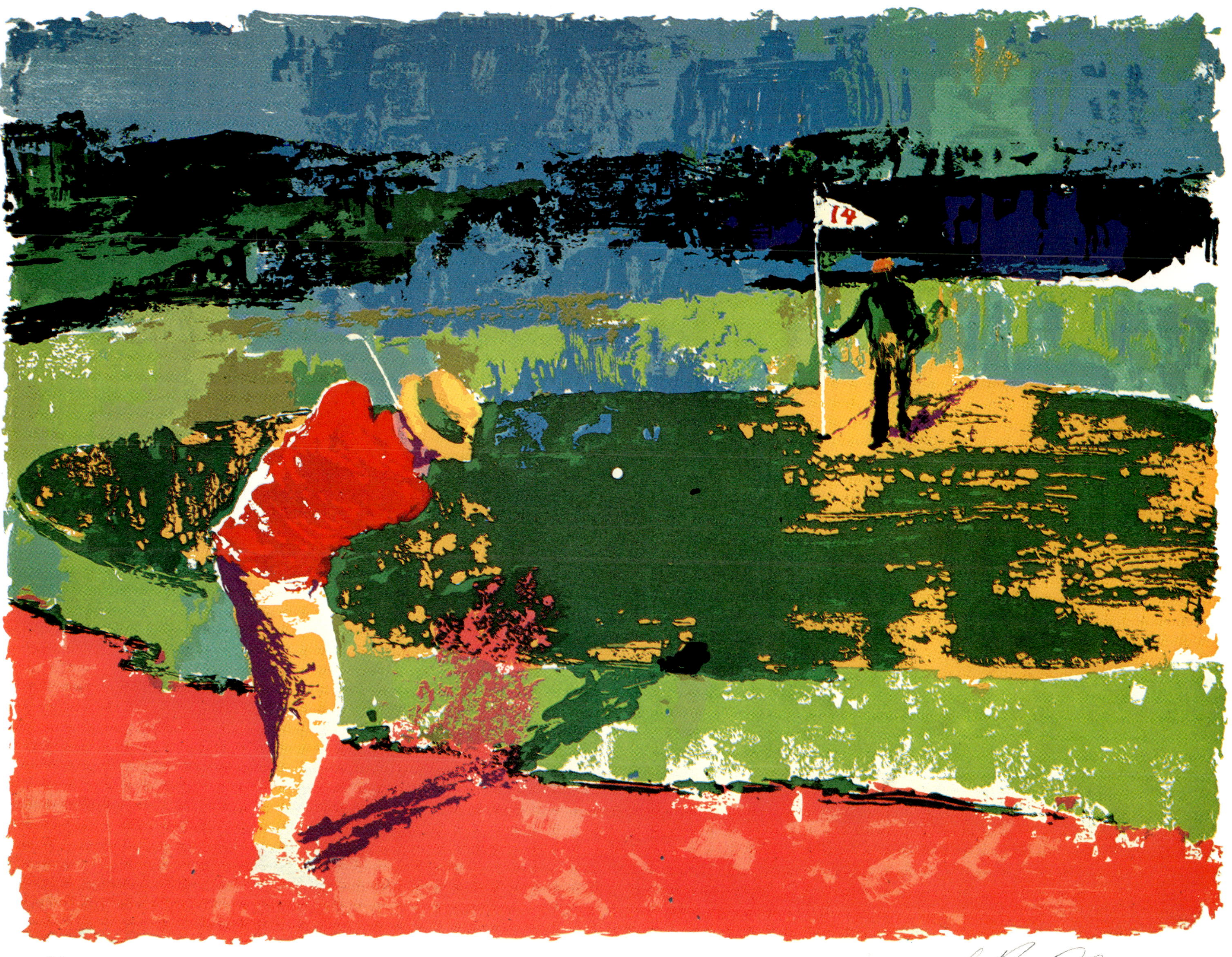

AP.

35 Chipping On

1972
Serigraph
20 x 25¾ (50.8 x 65.41 cm)
A limited edition of 275, signed and numbered
by the artist.

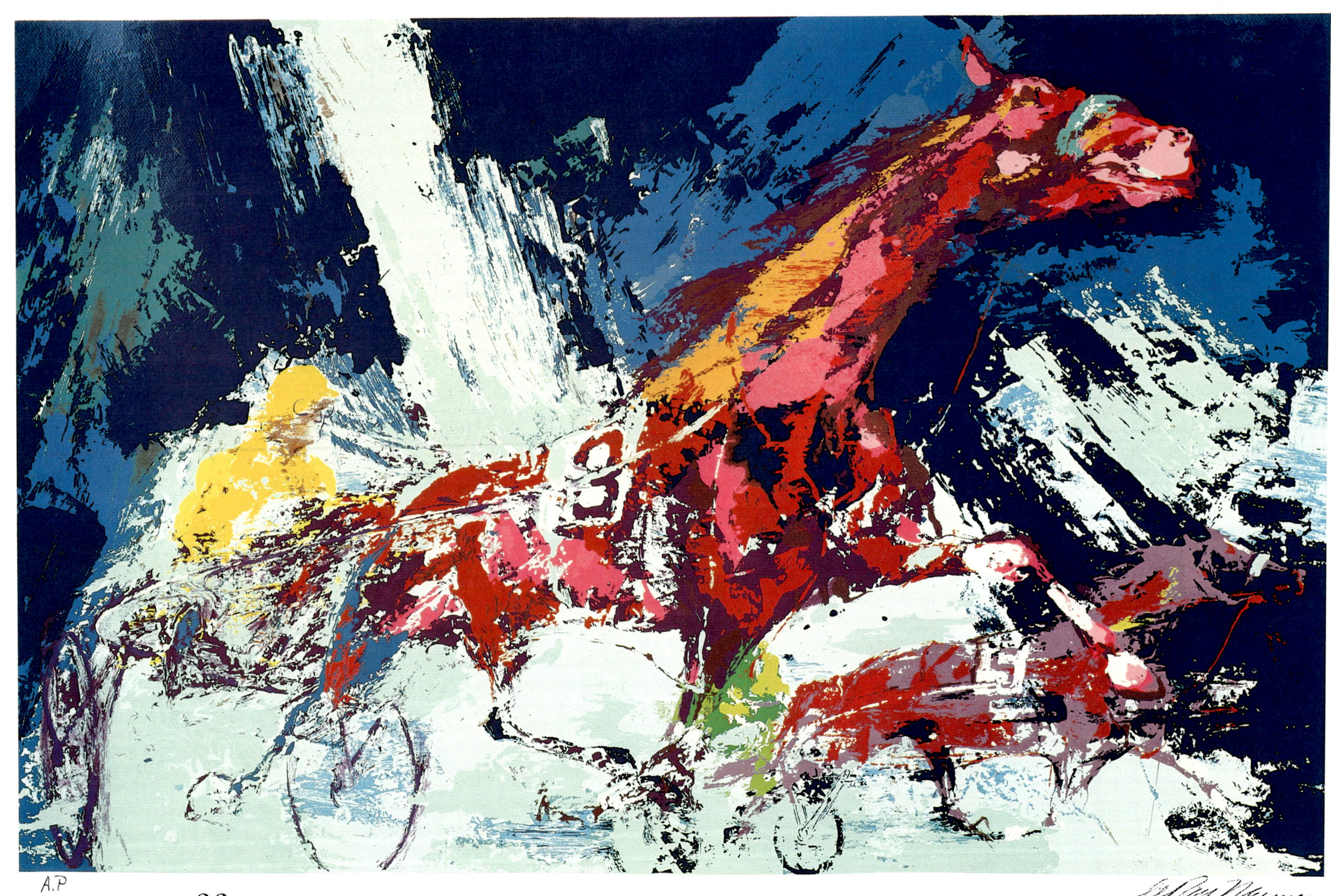

36 Trotters

1973
Serigraph
29 x 44 (73.66 x 112.08 cm)

A limited edition of 300, signed and numbered
by the artist.

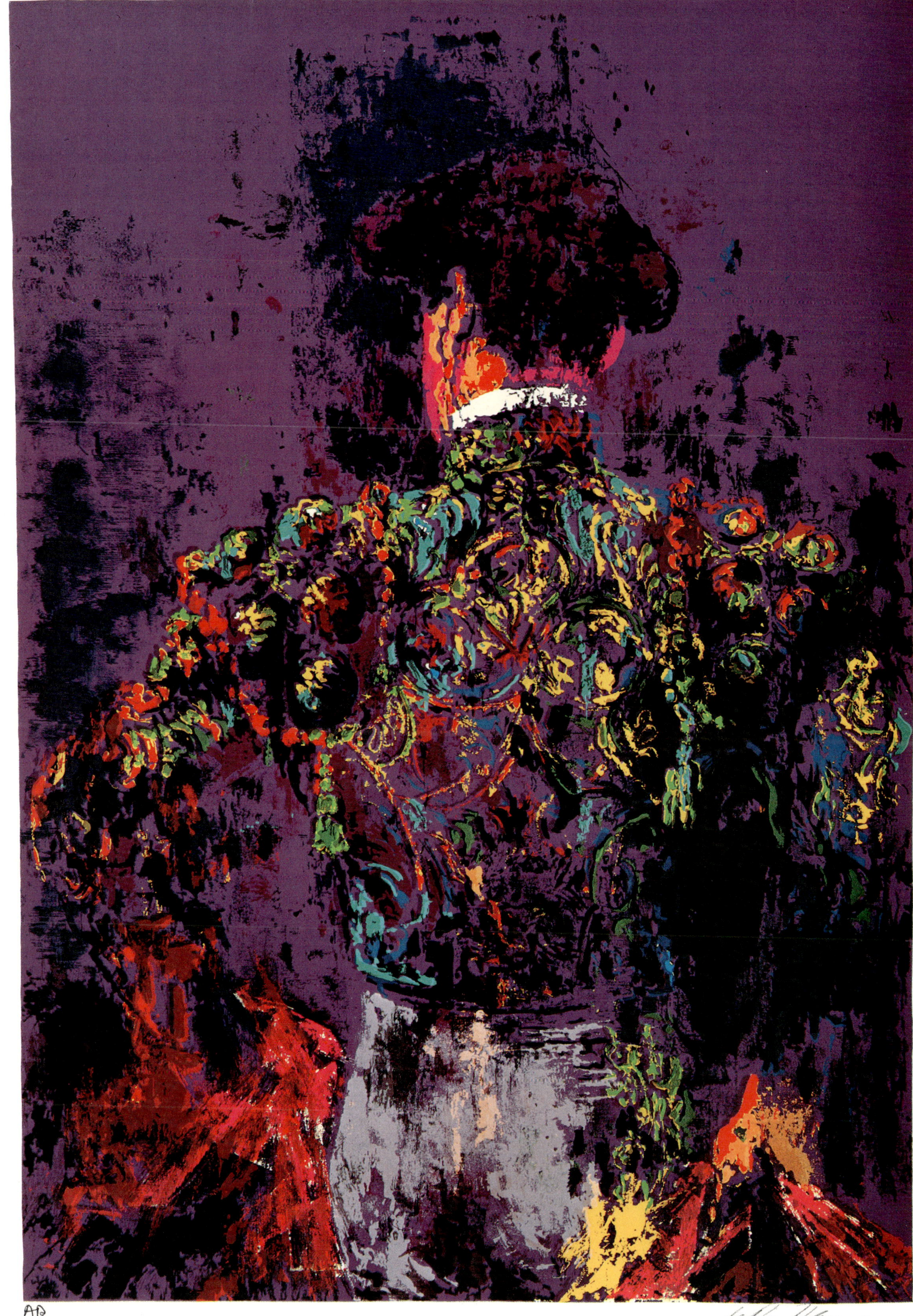

37 Toreador

1973
Serigraph
38 x 26¼ (96.52 x 66.67 cm)
A limited edition of 250, signed
and numbered by the artist.

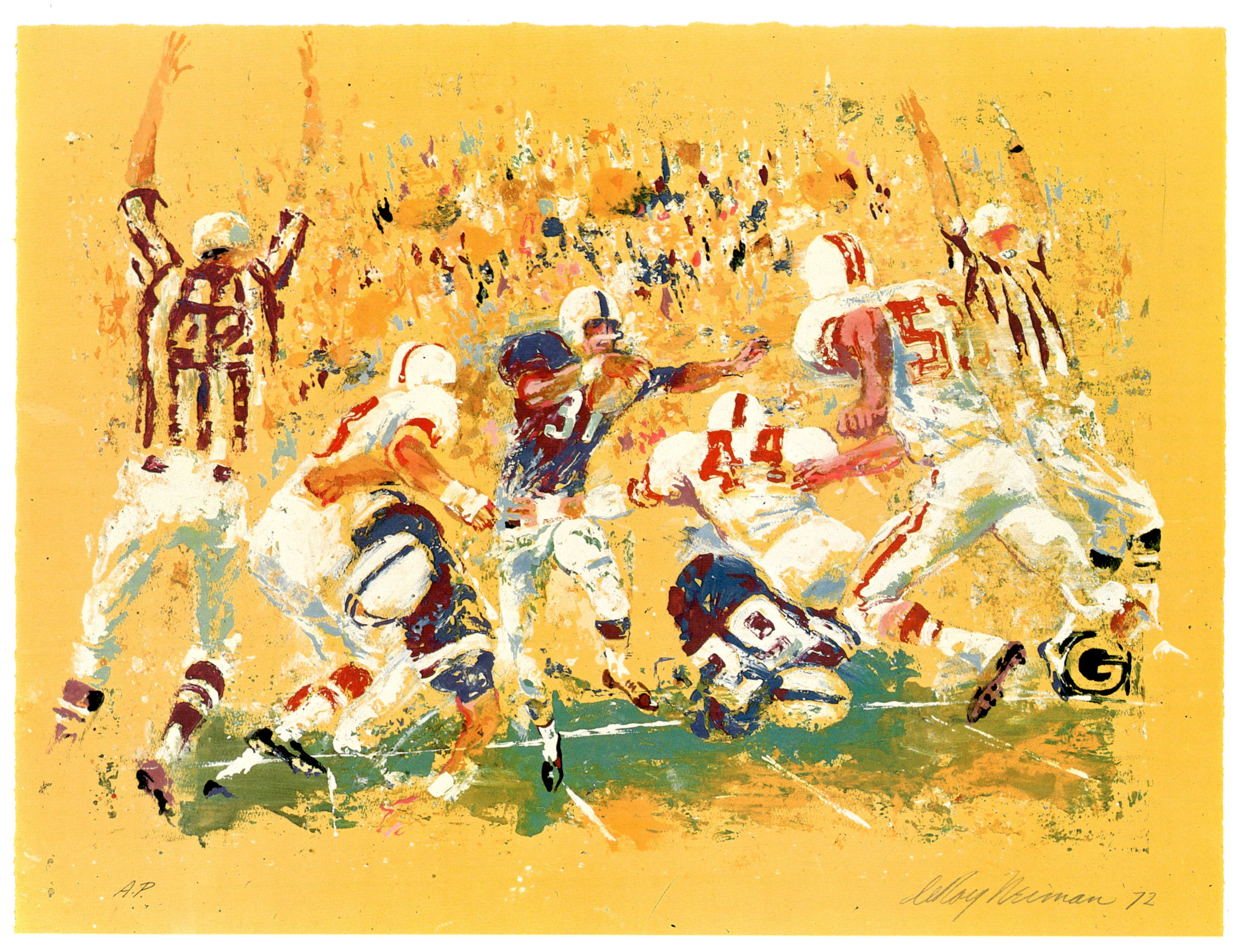

38 Touchdown

1973
Serigraph
19 x 26⅛ (48.26 x 66.36 cm)

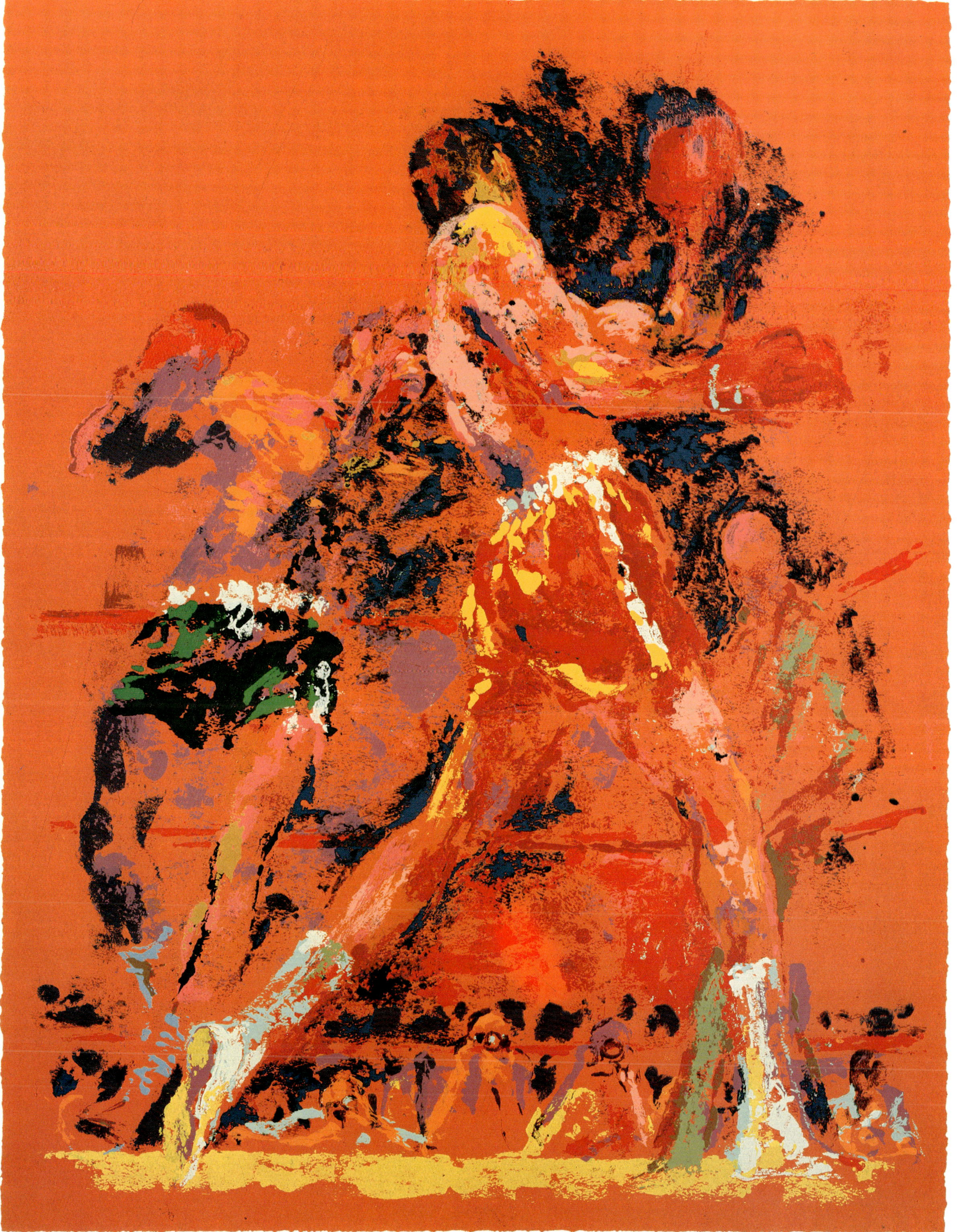

39   Red Boxers

1973
Serigraph
26¼ x 20 (66.67 x 50.8 cm)
A limited edition of 250, signed
and numbered by the artist.

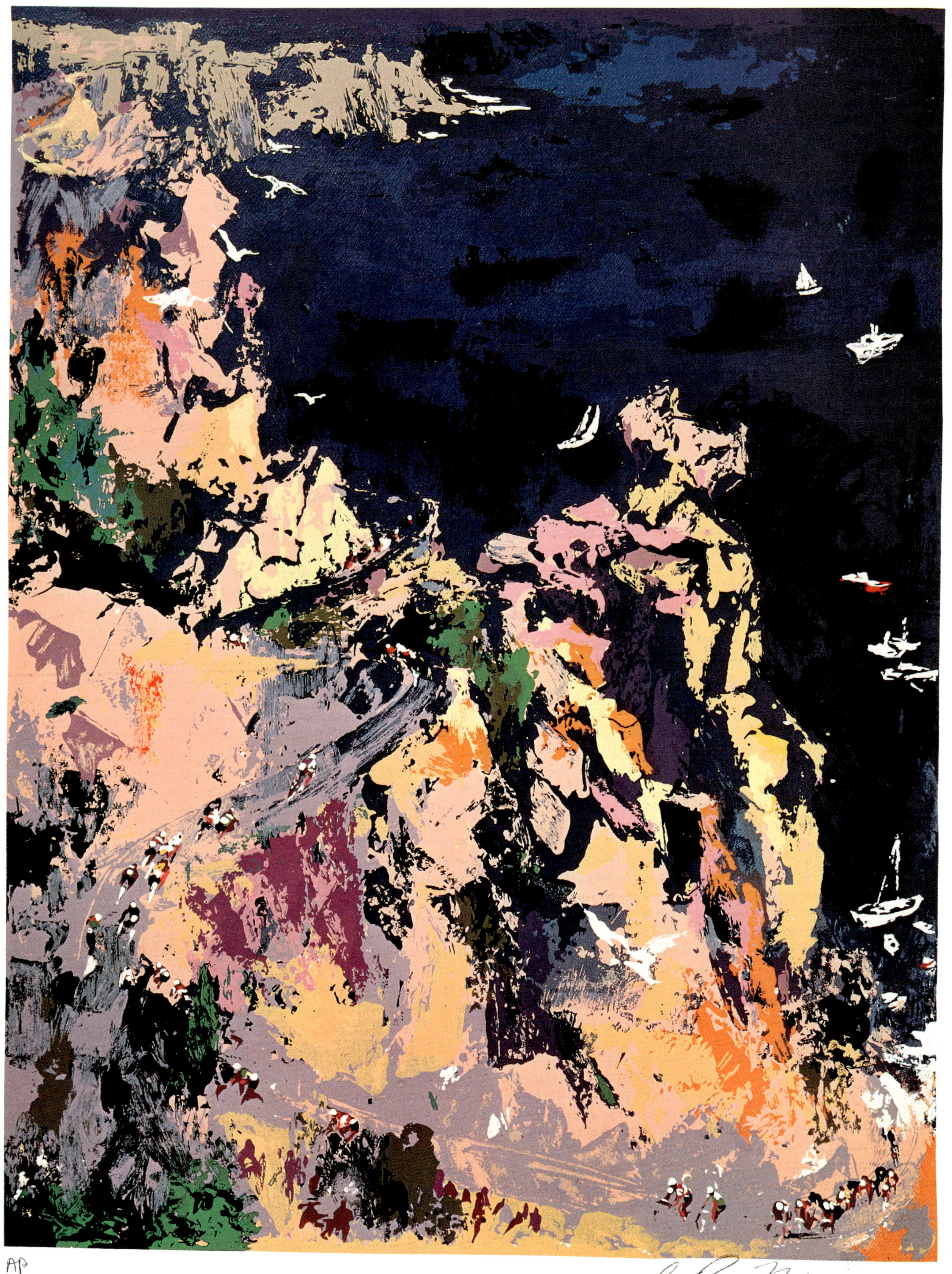

40 Bikes & Boat

1973
Serigraph
28⅛ x 21
(71.44 x 53.34 cm)
A limited edition of 300,
signed and numbered
by the artist.

AP

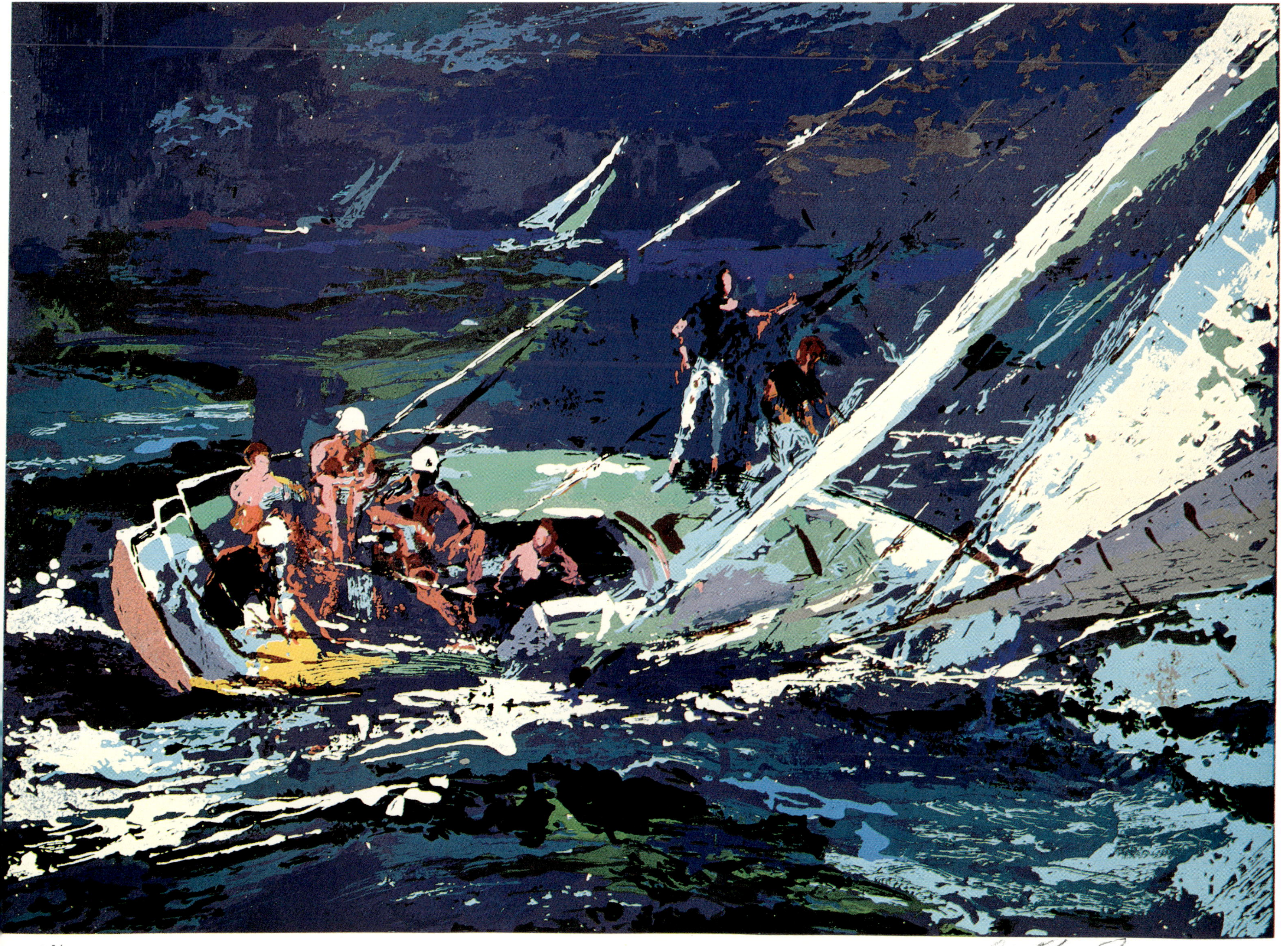

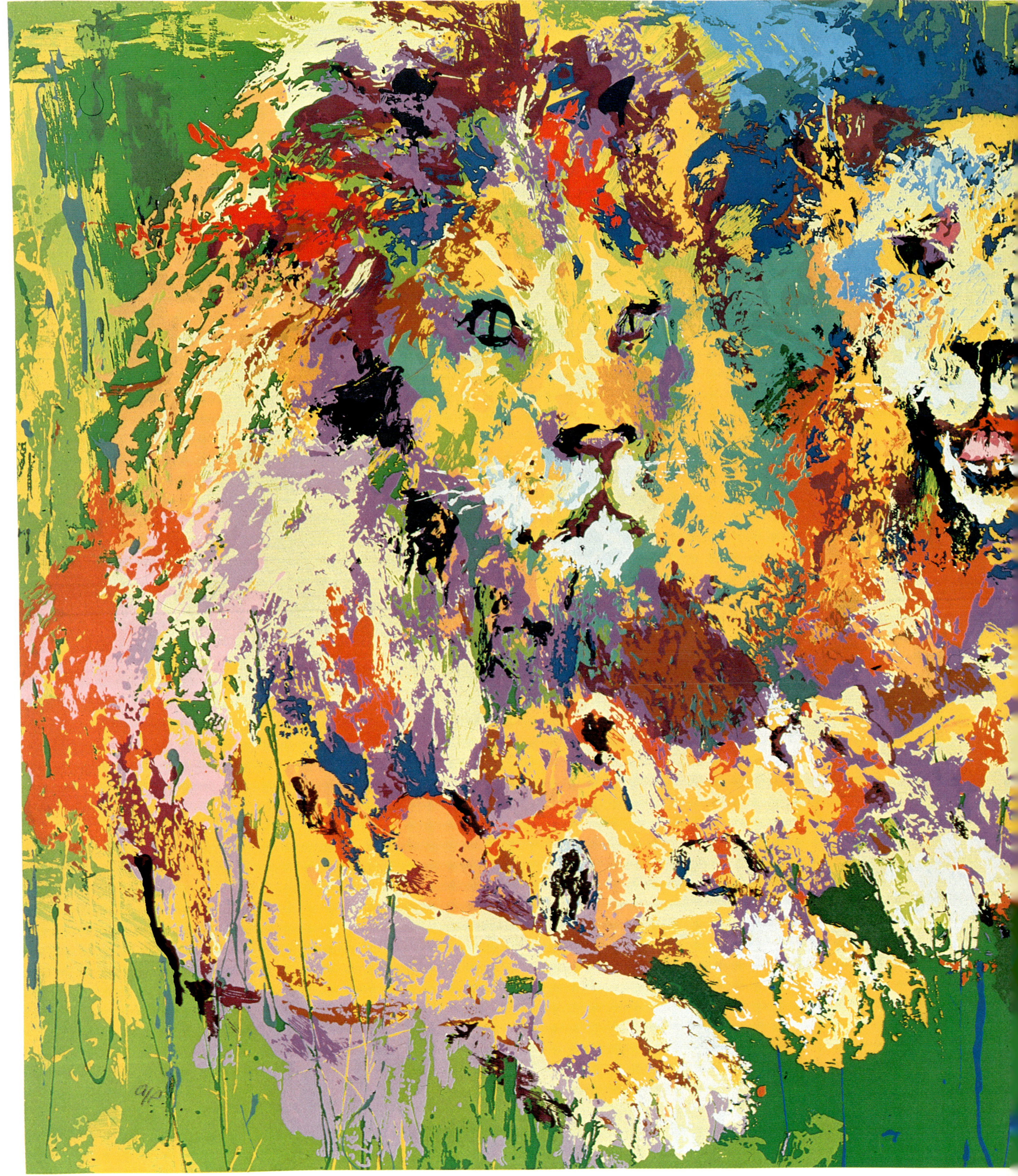

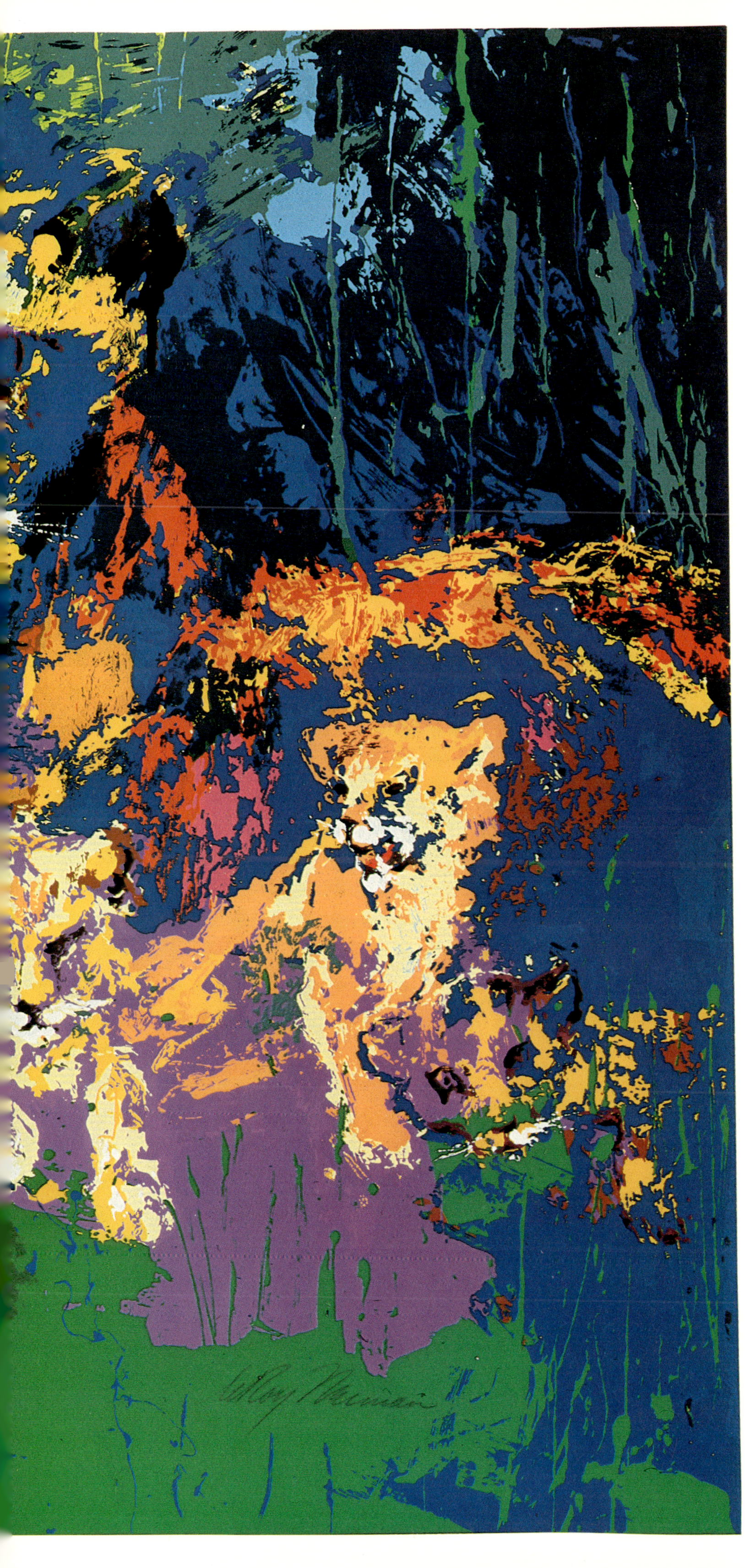

42 Lion's Pride

1973
Serigraph
34 x 46 (86.36 x 117.16 cm)
A limited edition of 300, signed and numbered
by the artist.

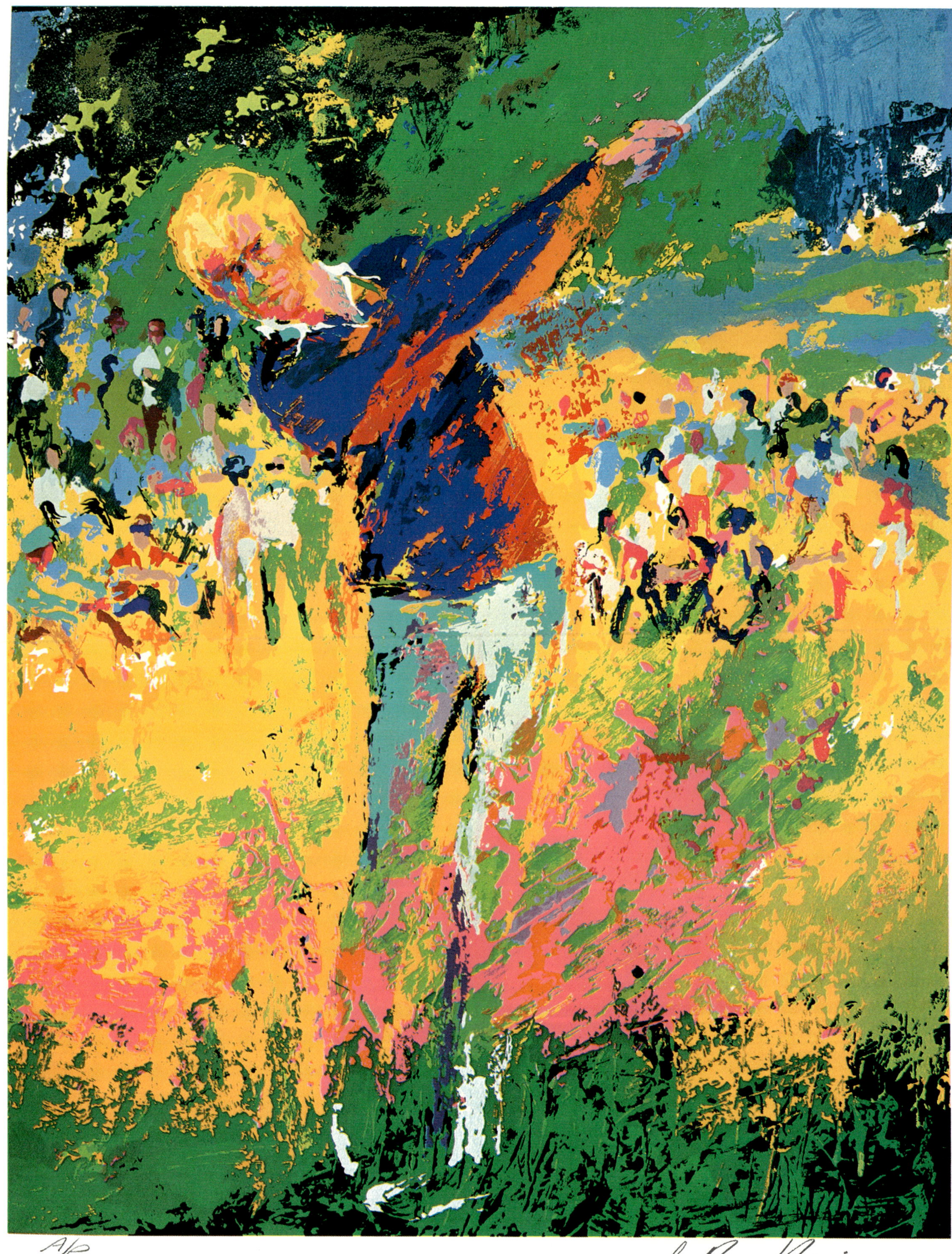

**43   Tee shot
(Jack Nicklaus)**
1973
Serigraph
25¾ x 20 (65.41 x 50.8 cm)
A limited edition of 300, signed and
numbered by the artist.

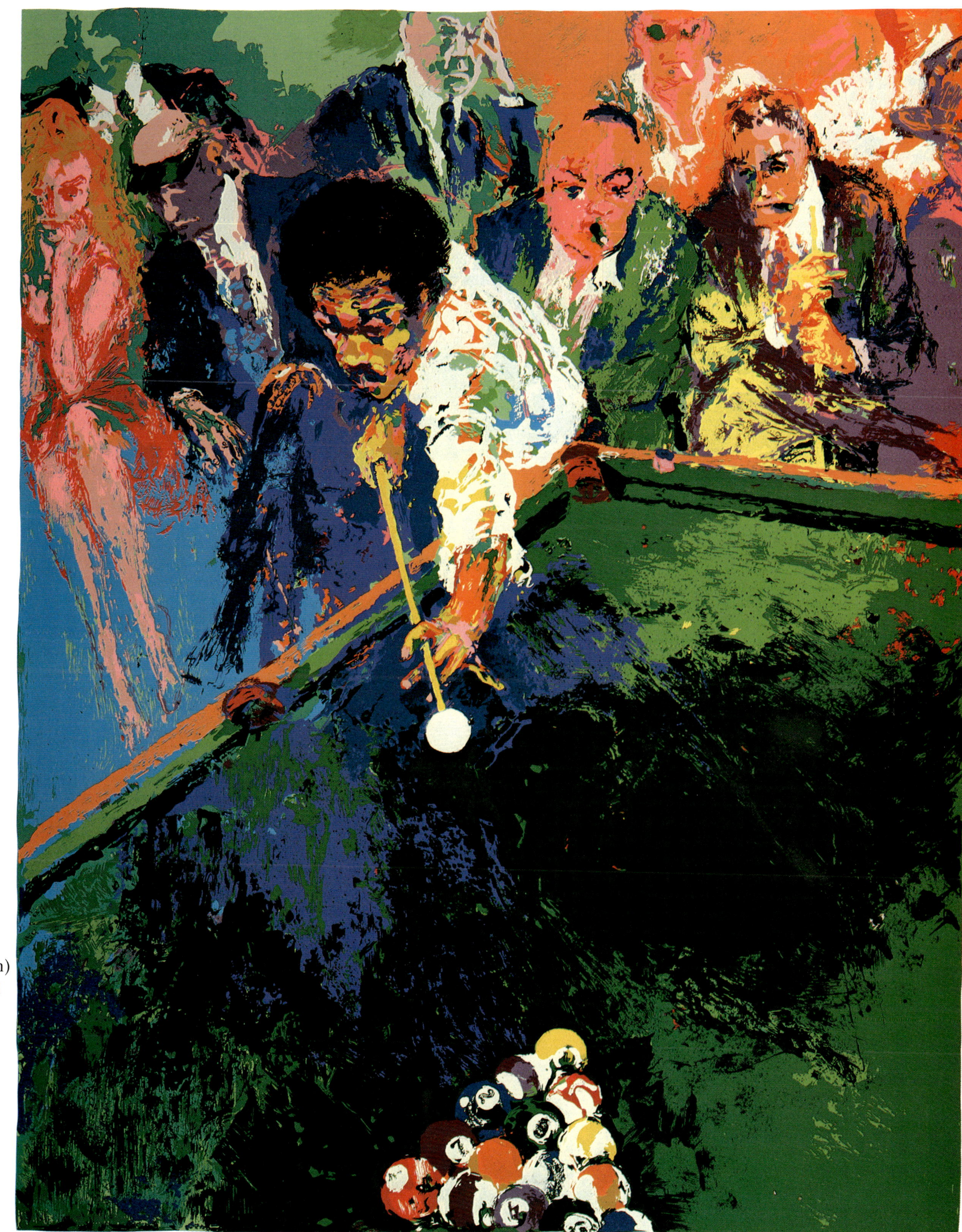

44 Black Break

1973
Serigraph
26 x 20⅛ (66.04 x 51.12 cm)
A limited edition of 300, signed
and numbered by the artist.

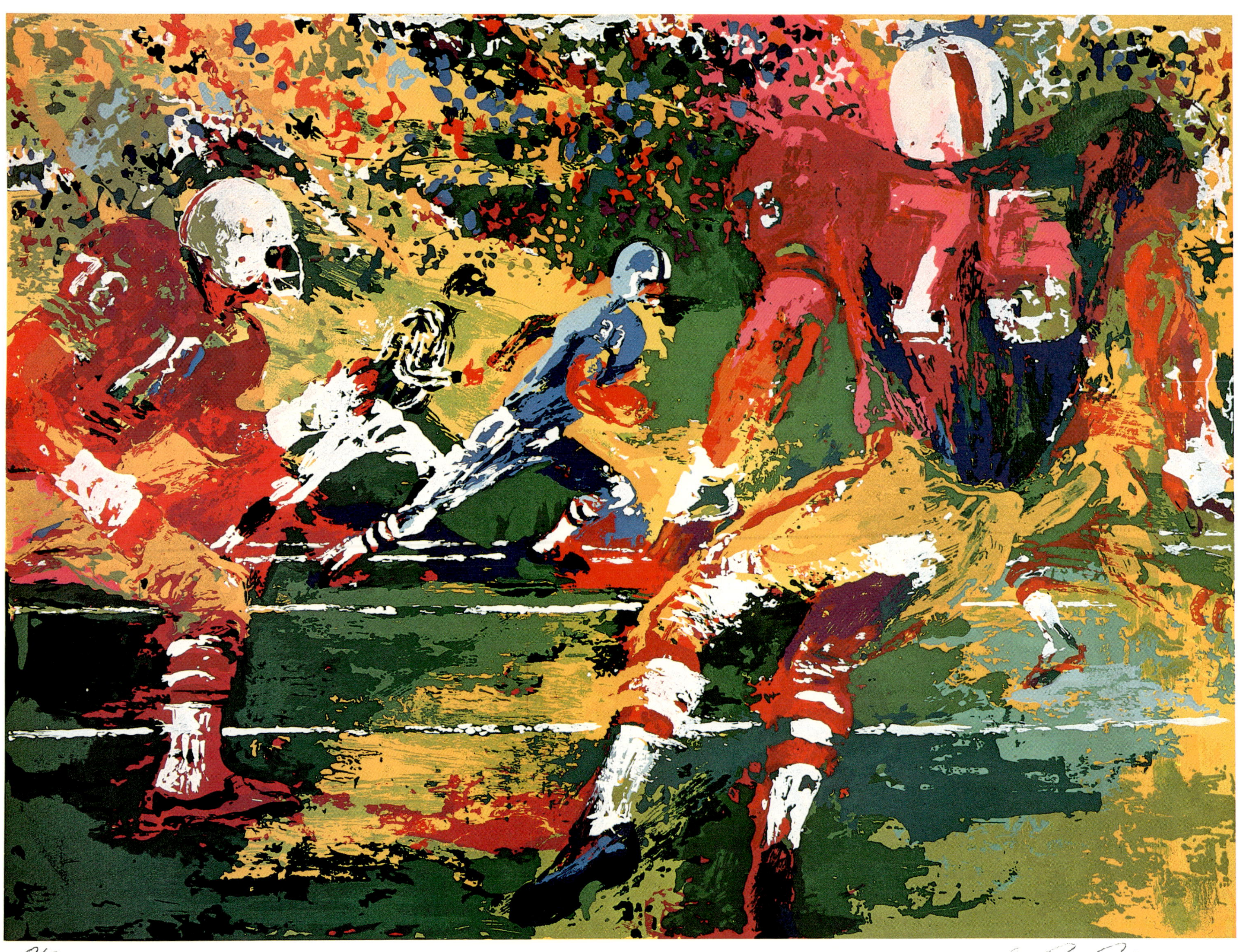

45 Scramble

1973
Serigraph
22 x 32 (55.88 x 81.28 cm)
A limited edition of 300, signed and numbered
by the artist.

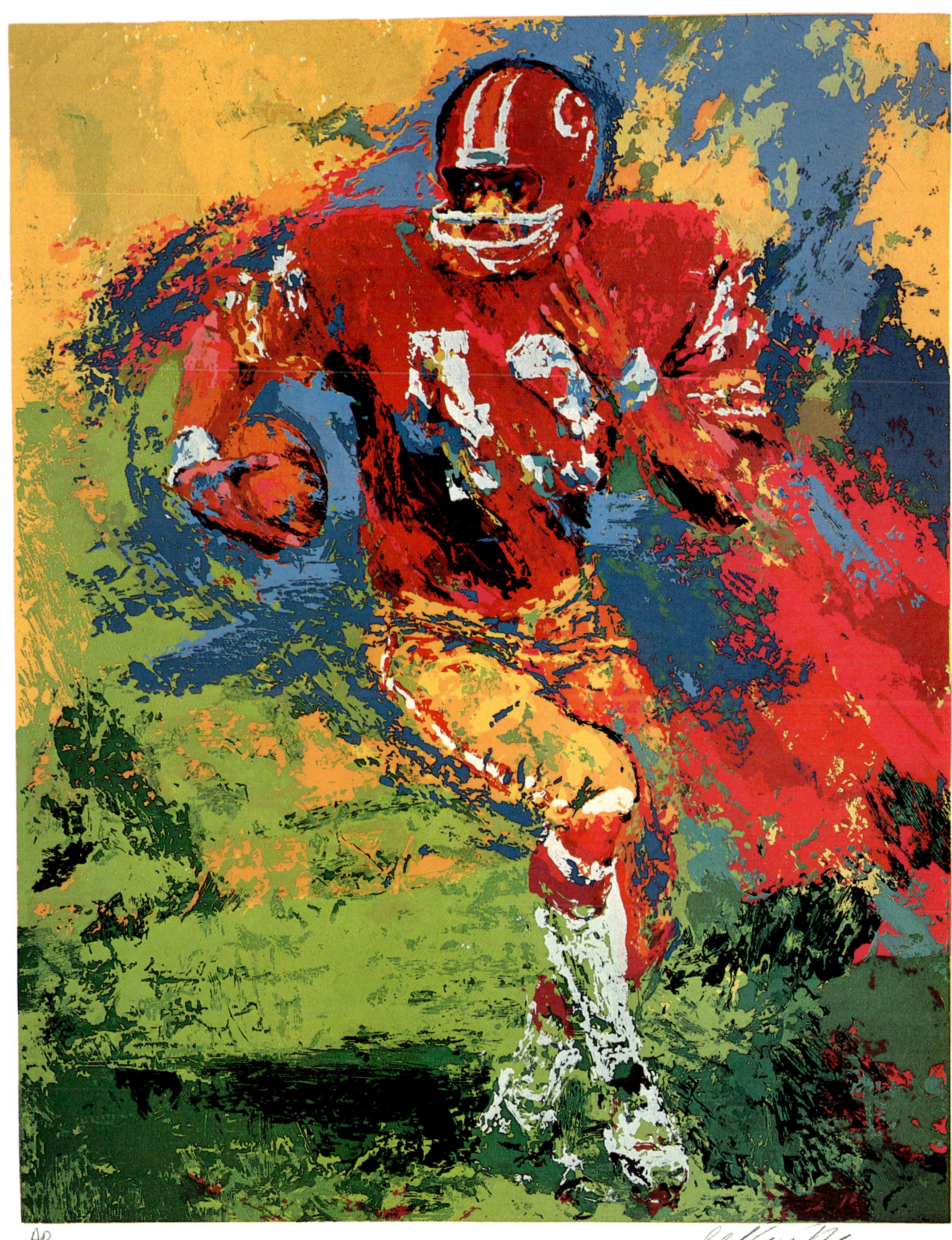

**46 End Around
(Larry Brown)**

1973
Serigraph
25¾ x 20 (65.40 x 50.8 cm)
A limited edition of 300, signed and
numbered by the artist.

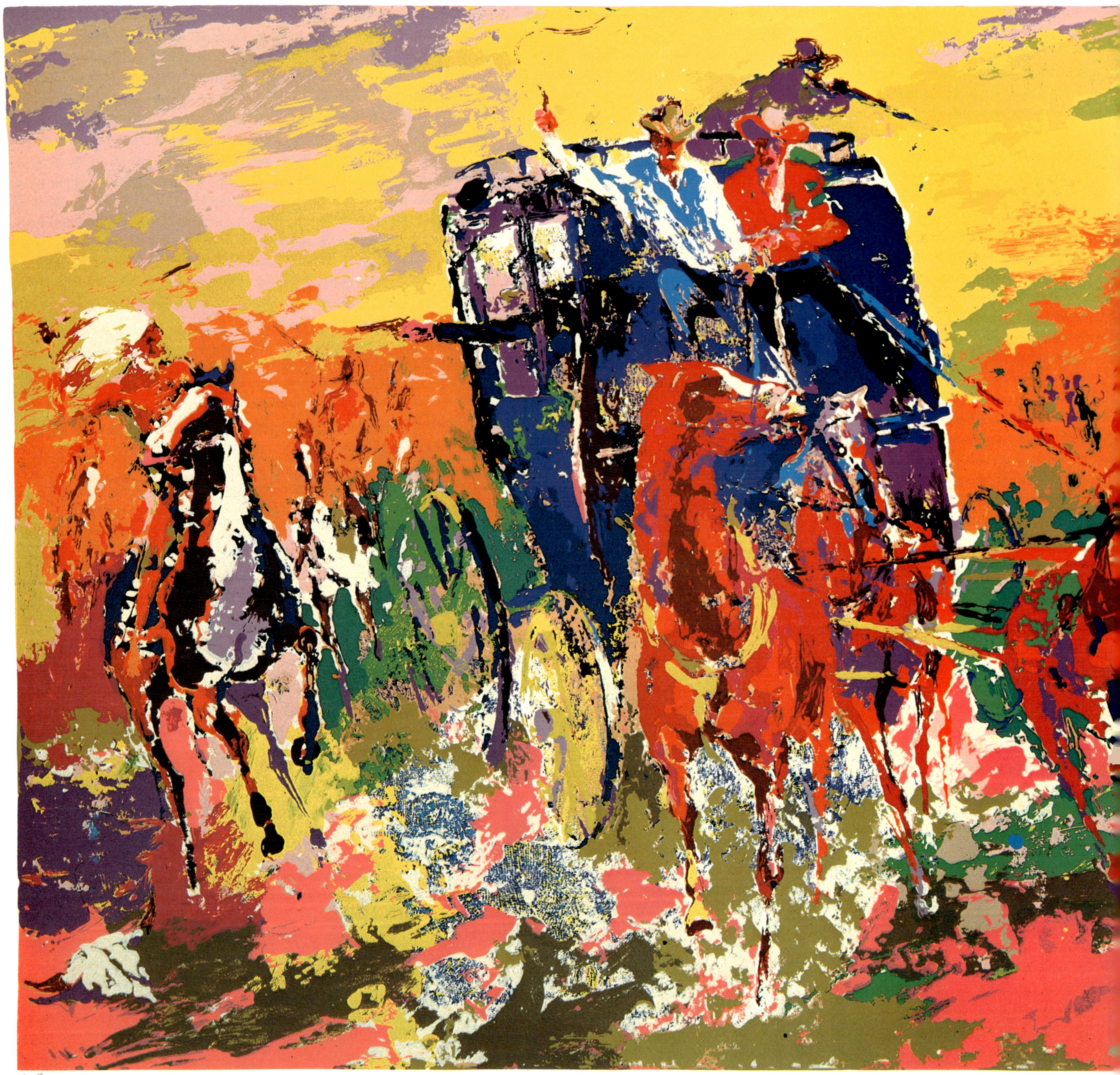

A.P.

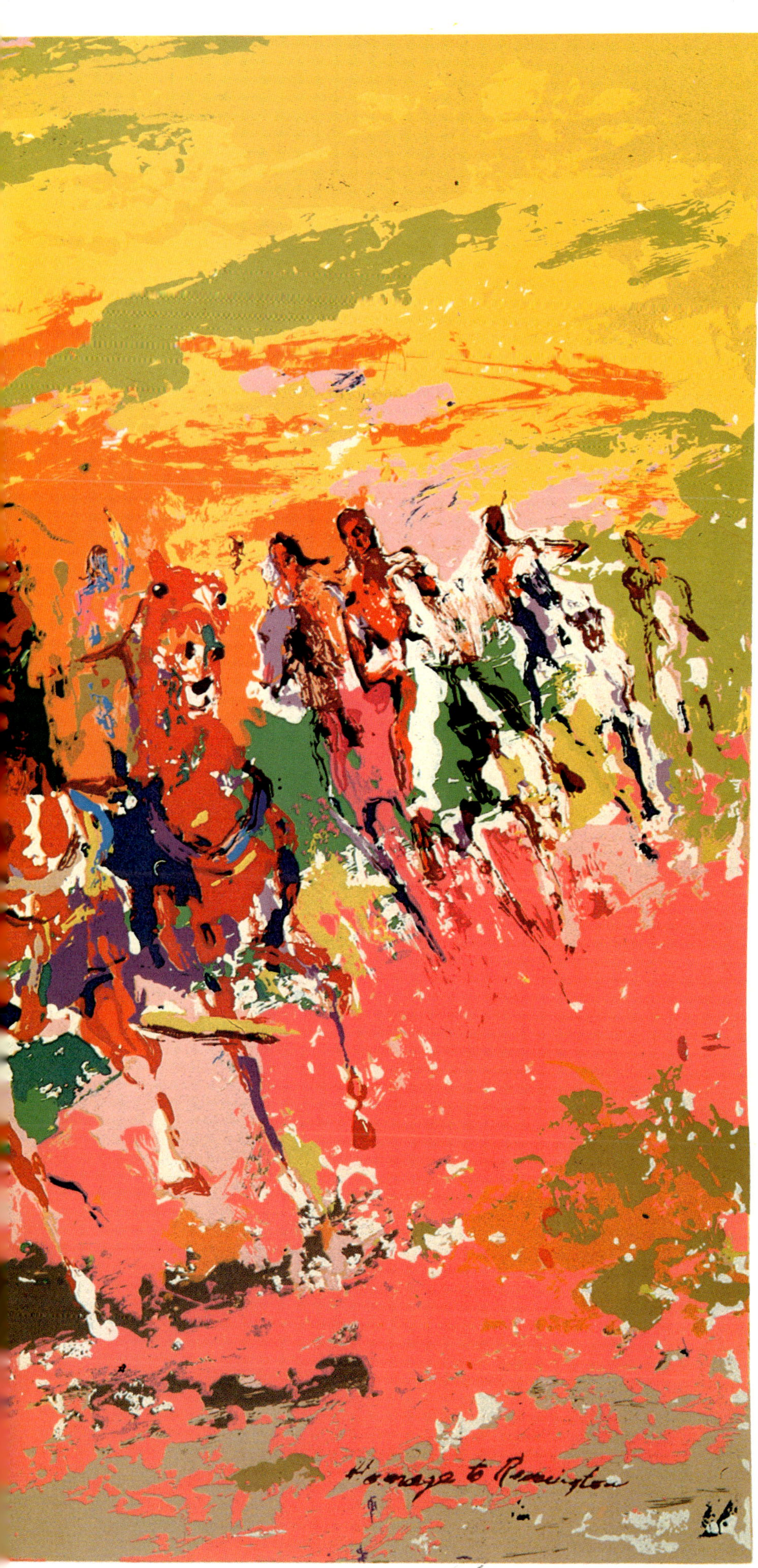

47   Homage to Remington

1973
Serigraph
18 x 28 (45.72 x 71.12)
A limited edition of 300, signed and numbered
by the artist.

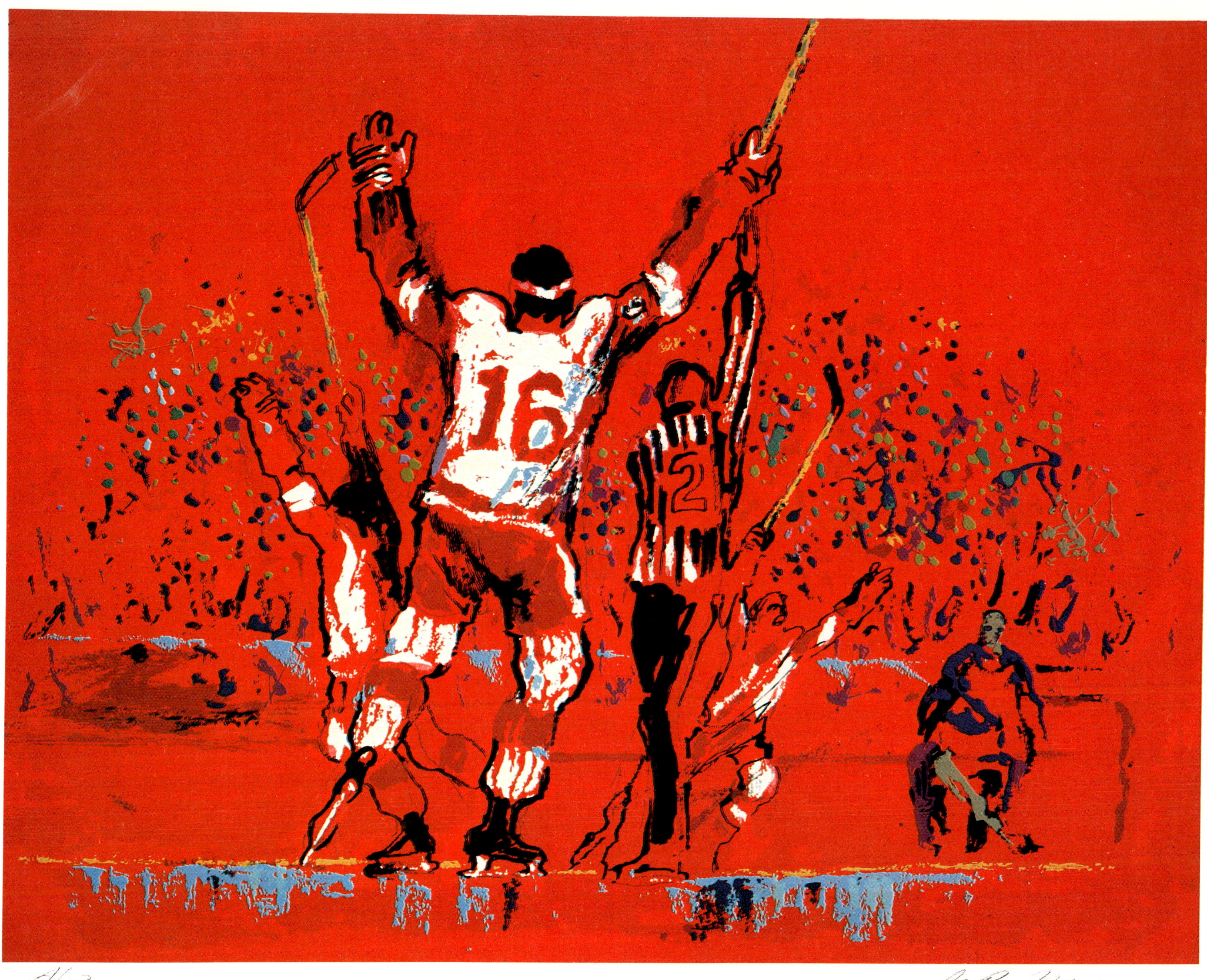

48   Red Goal

1973
Serigraph
19⅞ x 24 (50.48 x 60.96 cm)
A limited edition of 300, signed and numbered
by the artist.

49   Indy Start

1973
Serigraph
28¾ x 22¼ (73.03 x 56.52 cm)
A limited edition of 300, signed and numbered
by the artist.

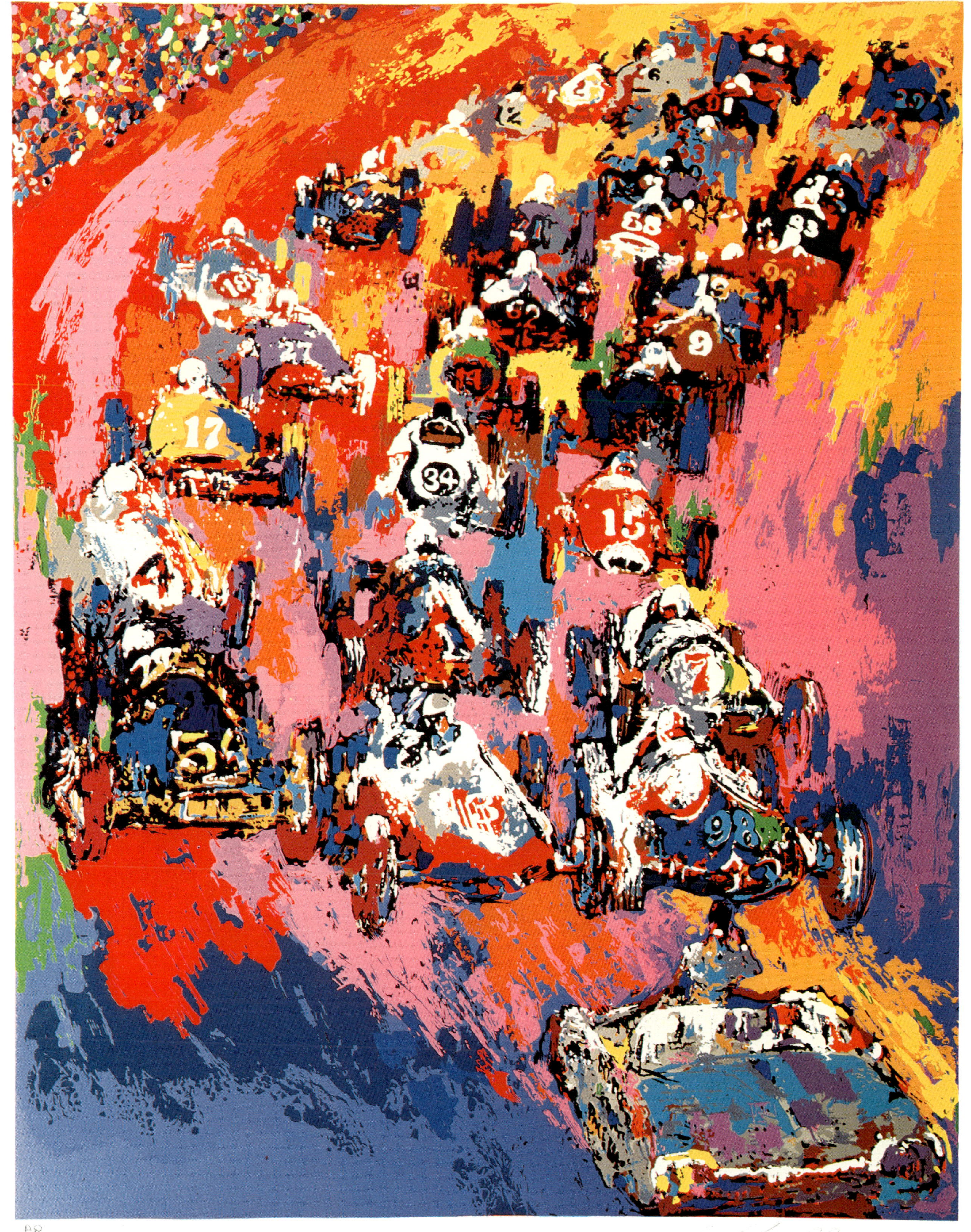

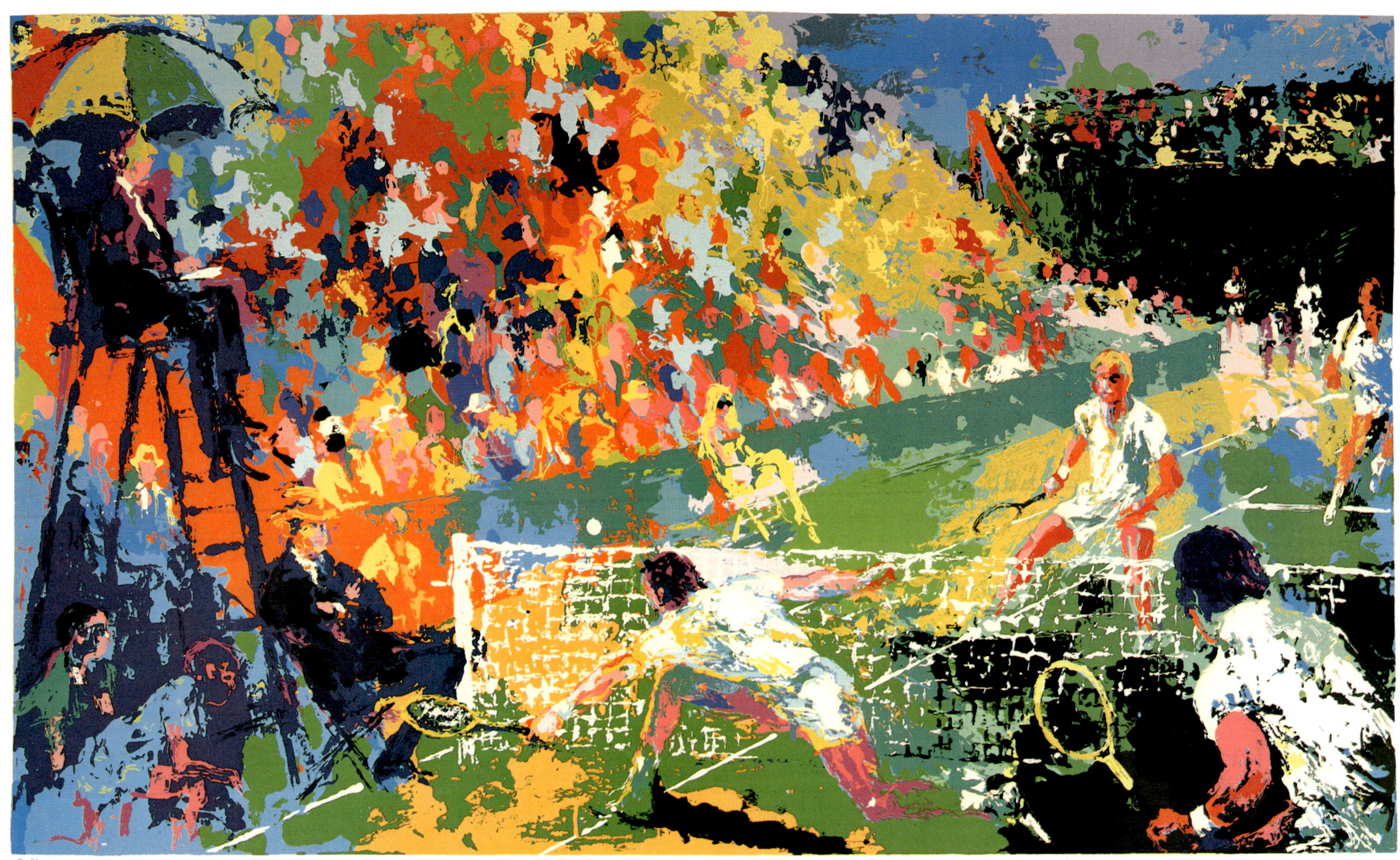

50 Love Story

1973
Serigraph
22 x 36 (55.88 x 91.44 cm)
A limited edition of 300, signed and numbered
by the artist.

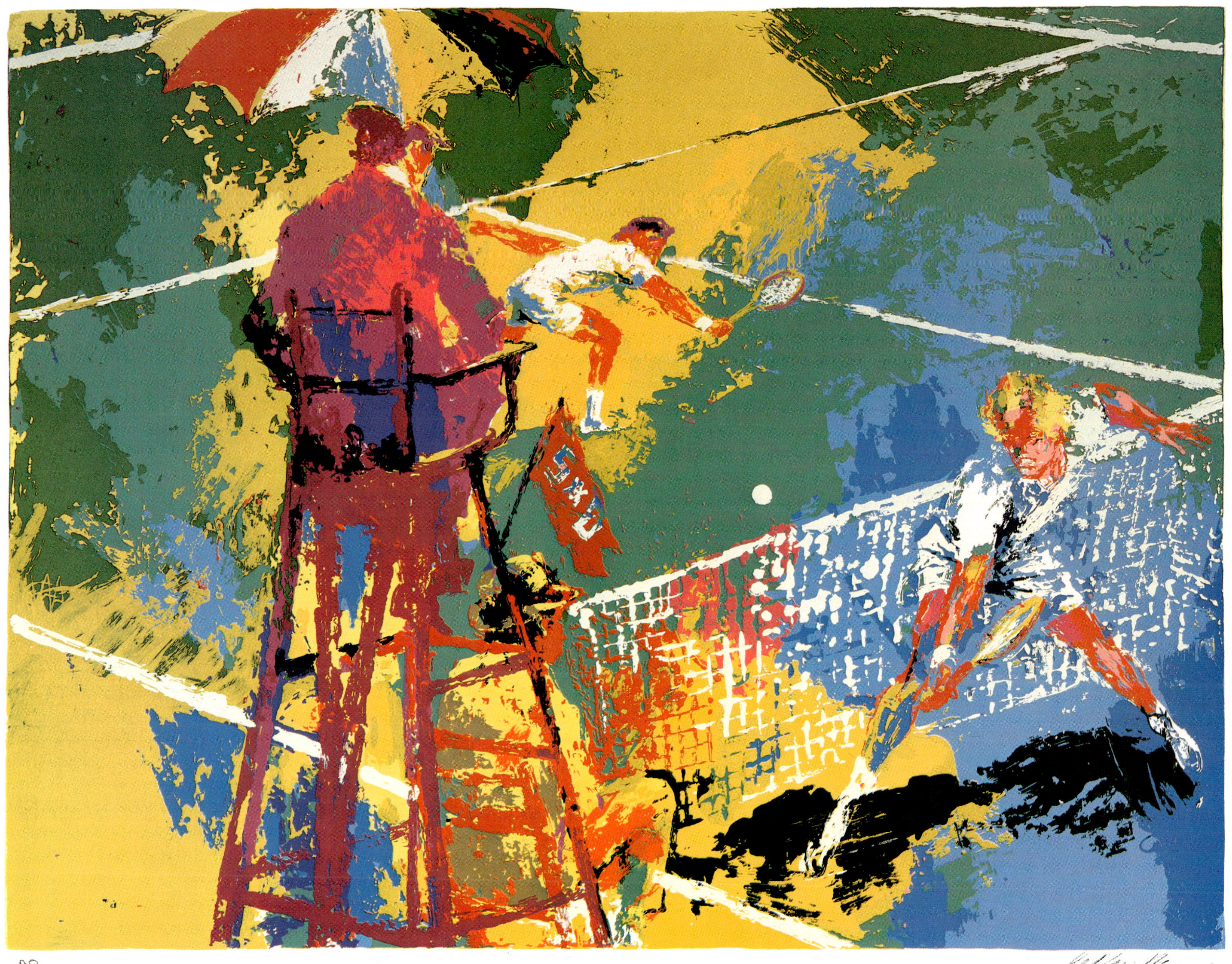

51   Sudden Death

1973
Serigraph
27⅞ x 36⅛ (70.80 x 91.76 cm)
A limited edition of 250, signed and numbered
by the artist.

1973
Serigraph
19⅞ x 35¼ (50.48 x 89.53 cm)
A limited edition of 250, signed and numbered
by the artist.

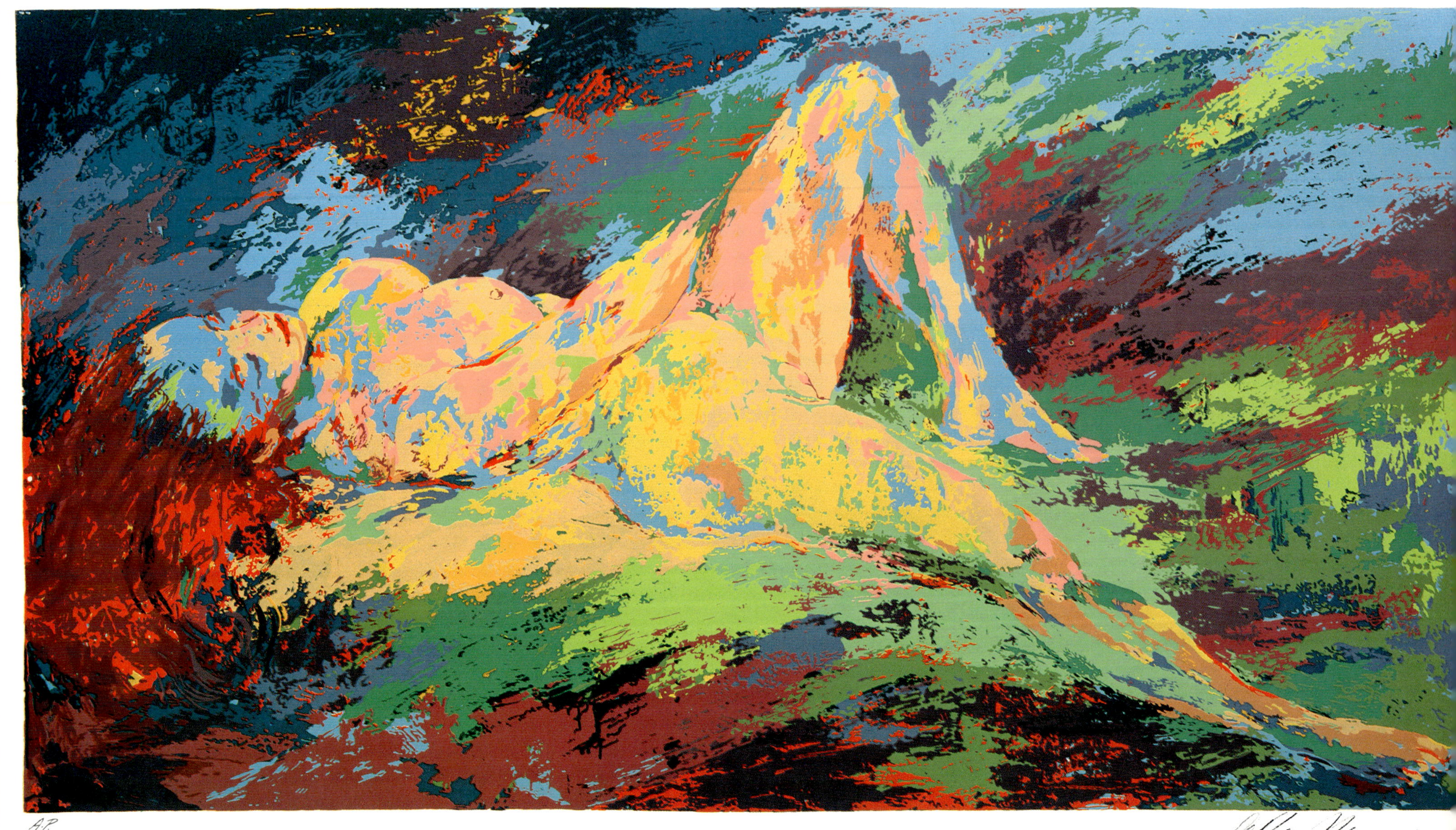

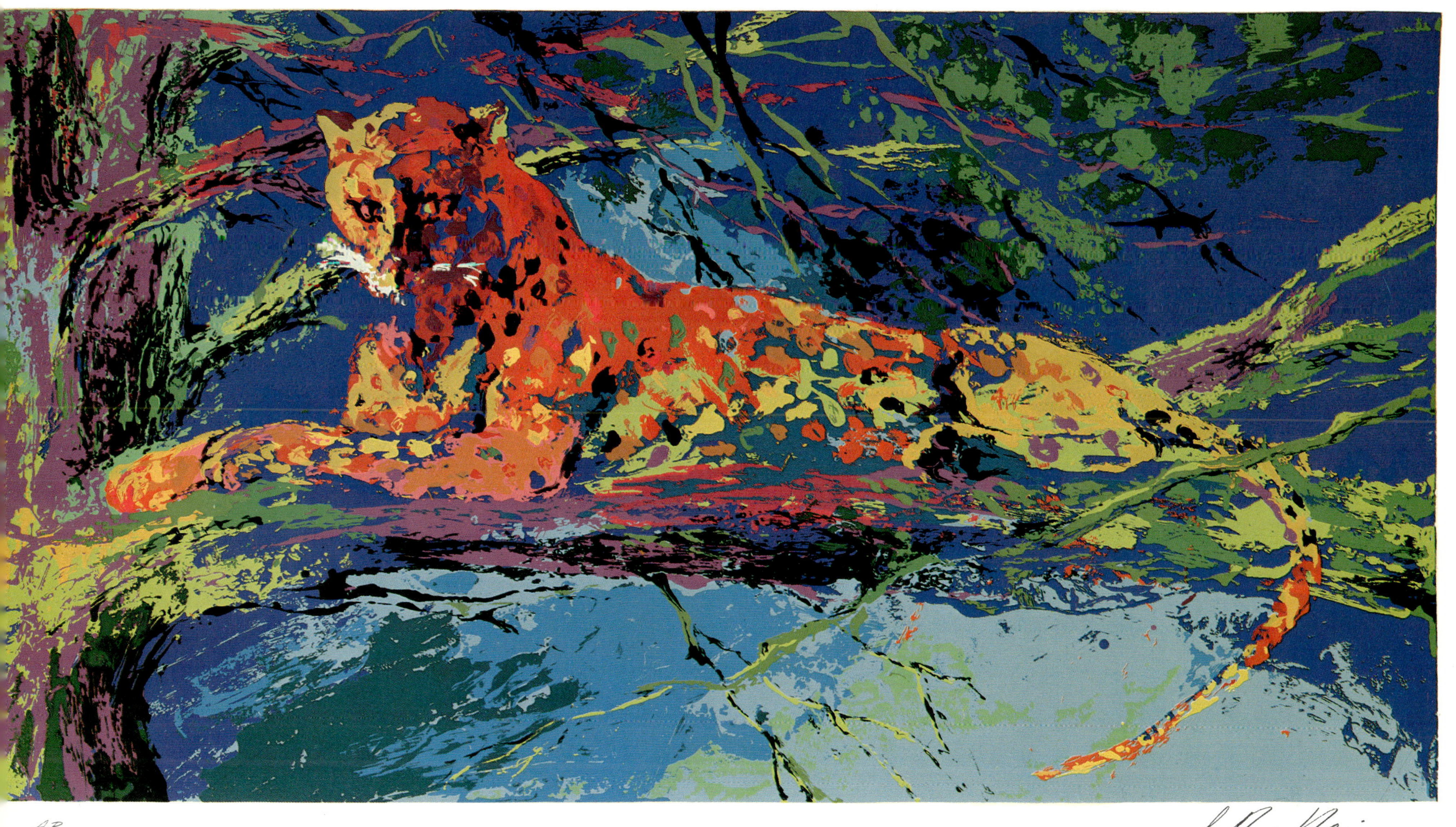

53 Kenya Leopard

1973
Serigraph
20¾ x 38 (52.71 x 96.52 cm)
A limited edition of 300, signed and numbered
by the artist.

54 Ocelot

1973
Serigraph
24 x 34⅛ (60.96 x 86.68 cm)
A limited edition of 250, signed and numbered
by the artist.

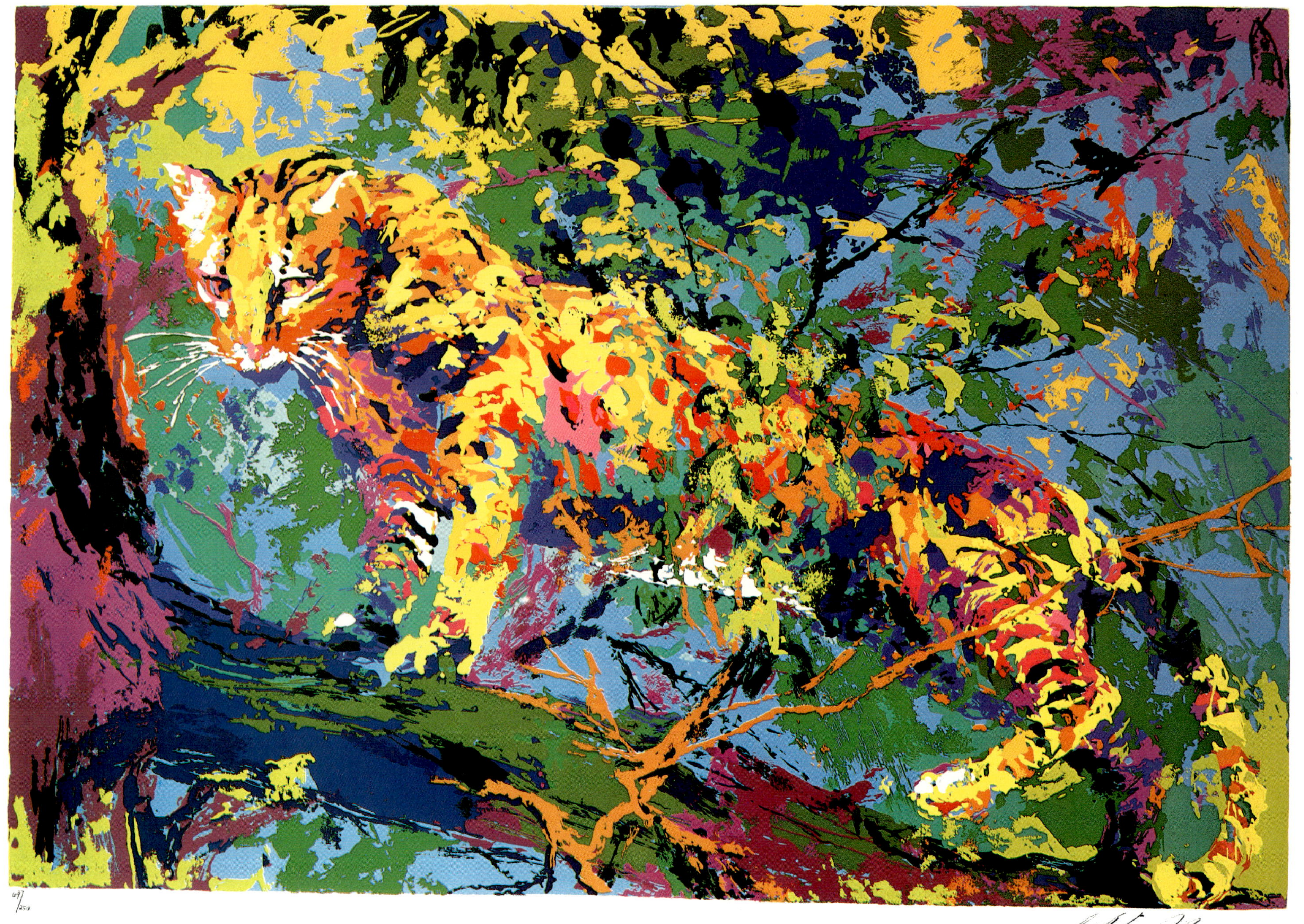

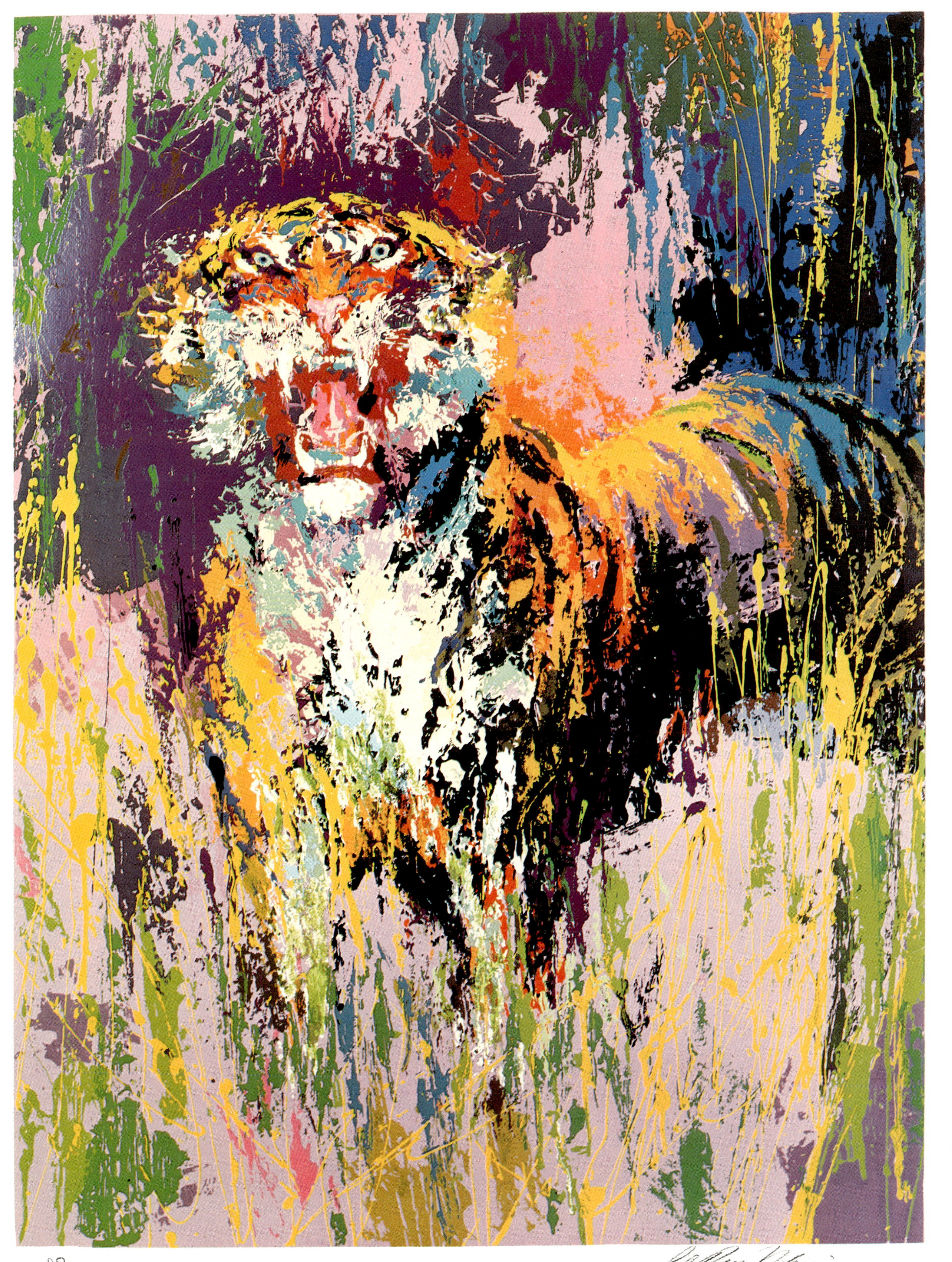

55 Bengal Tiger
1973
Serigraph
42 x 31 (106.68 x 78.74 cm)
A limited edition of 300, signed and
numbered by the artist.

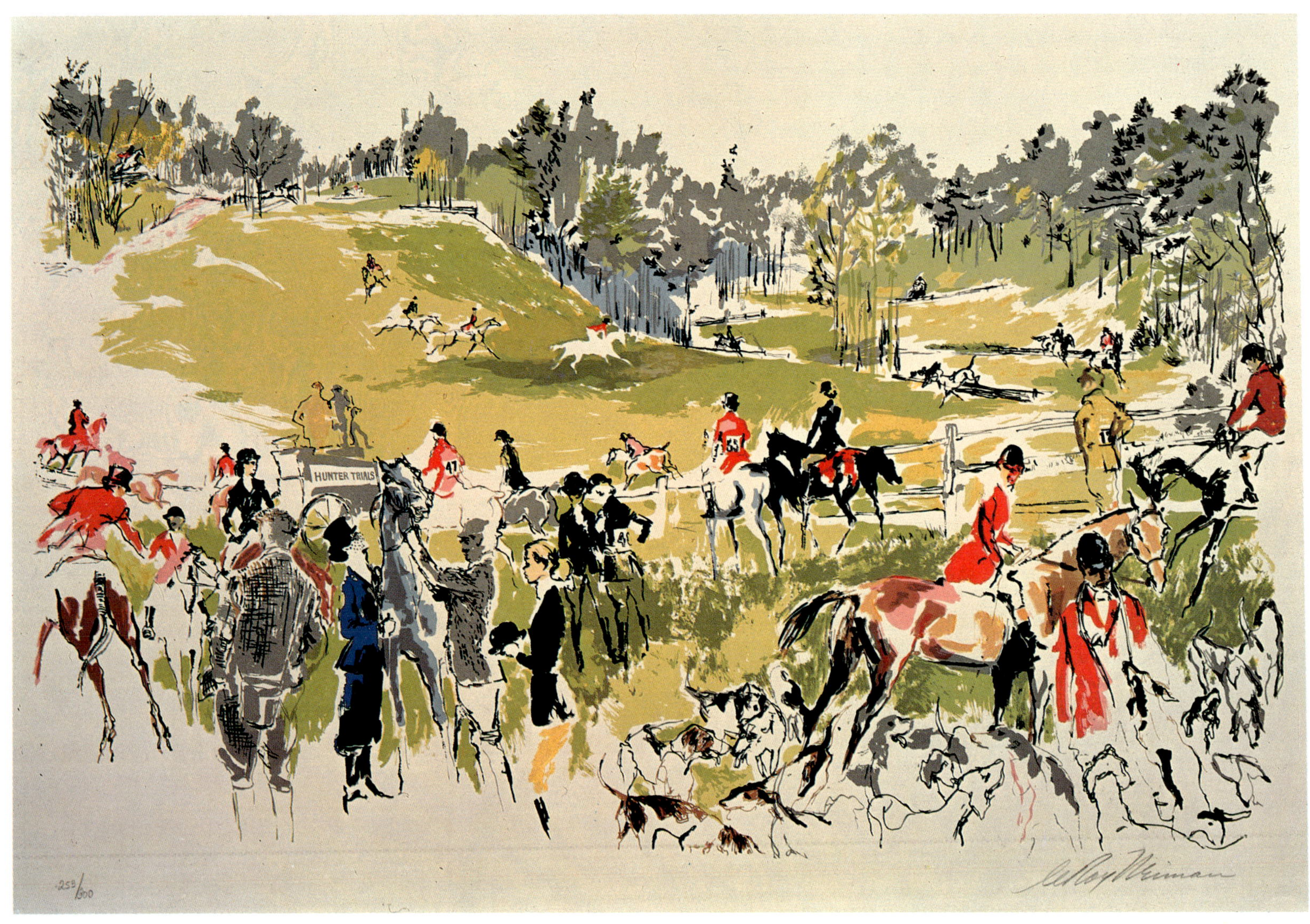

56   Hunter Trials

1973
Serigraph
29½ x 41¼ (74.93 x 104.77 cm)
A limited edition of 300, signed and numbered
by the artist.

57 Racing "1973"

1973
Serigraph
21⅛ x 36¼ (53.66 x 92.08 cm)
A limited edition of 300, signed and numbered
by the artist.

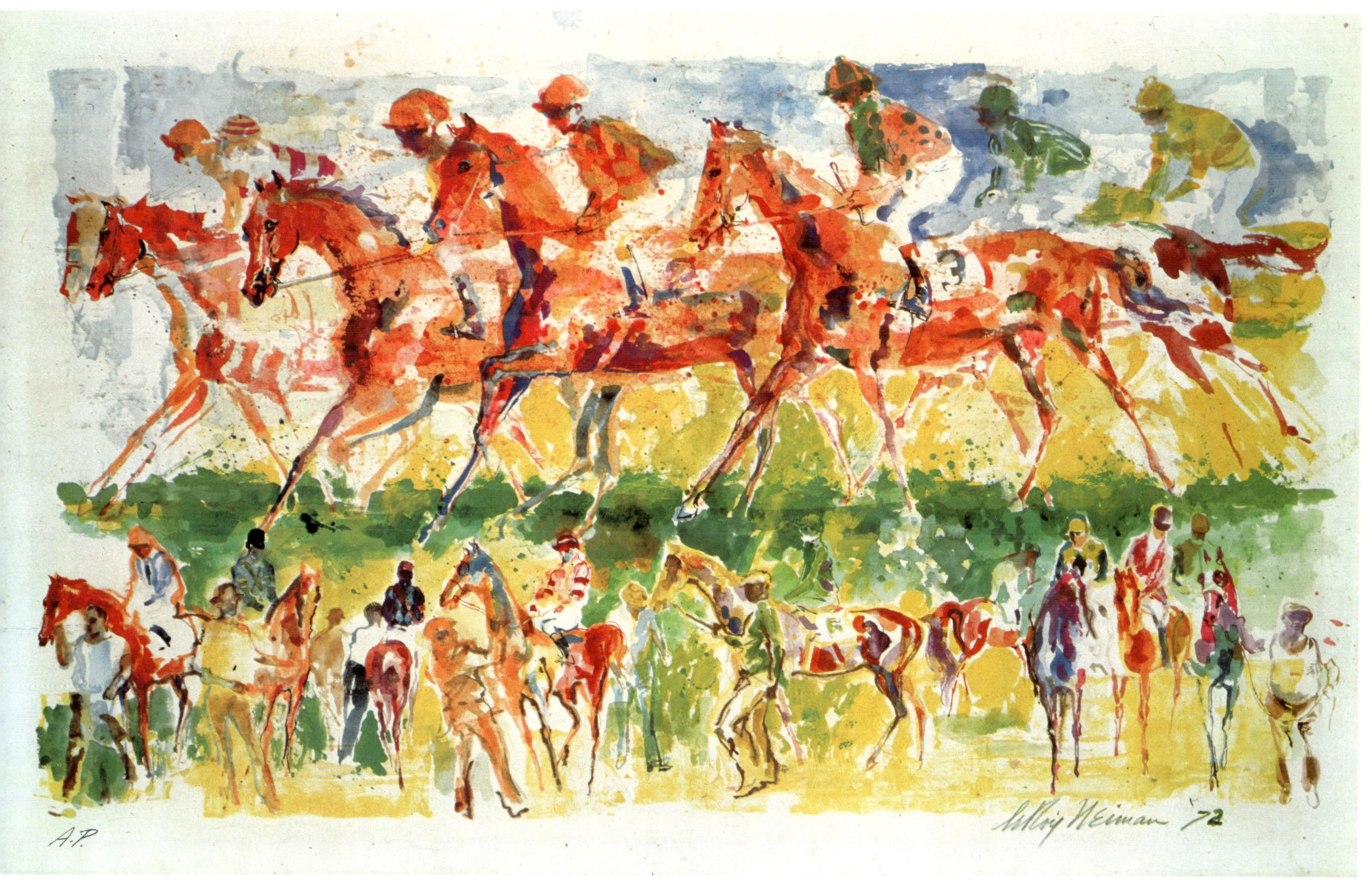

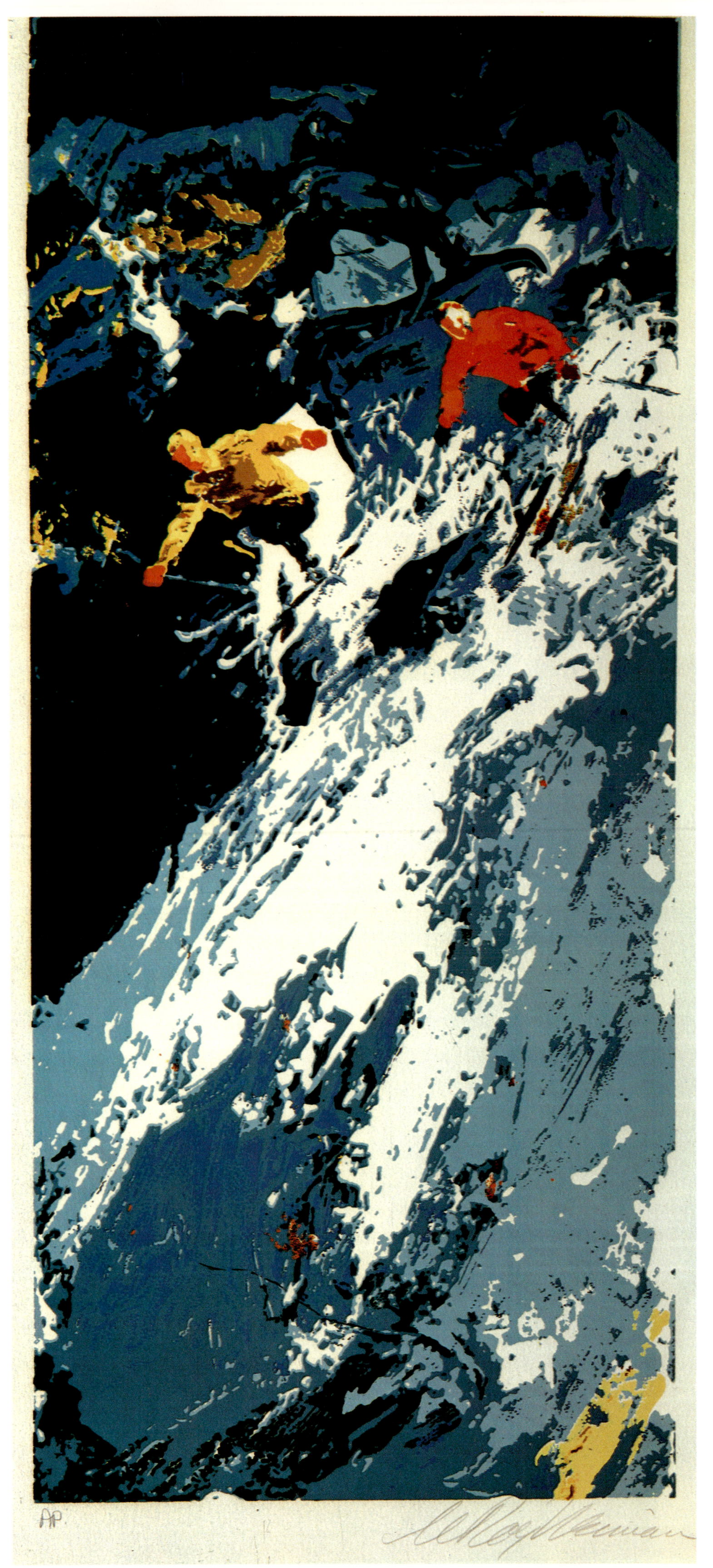

58   Ski Slope

1973
Serigraph
25⅞ x 11¼ (65.72 x 28.57 cm)
A limited edition of 300, signed and numbered
by the artist.

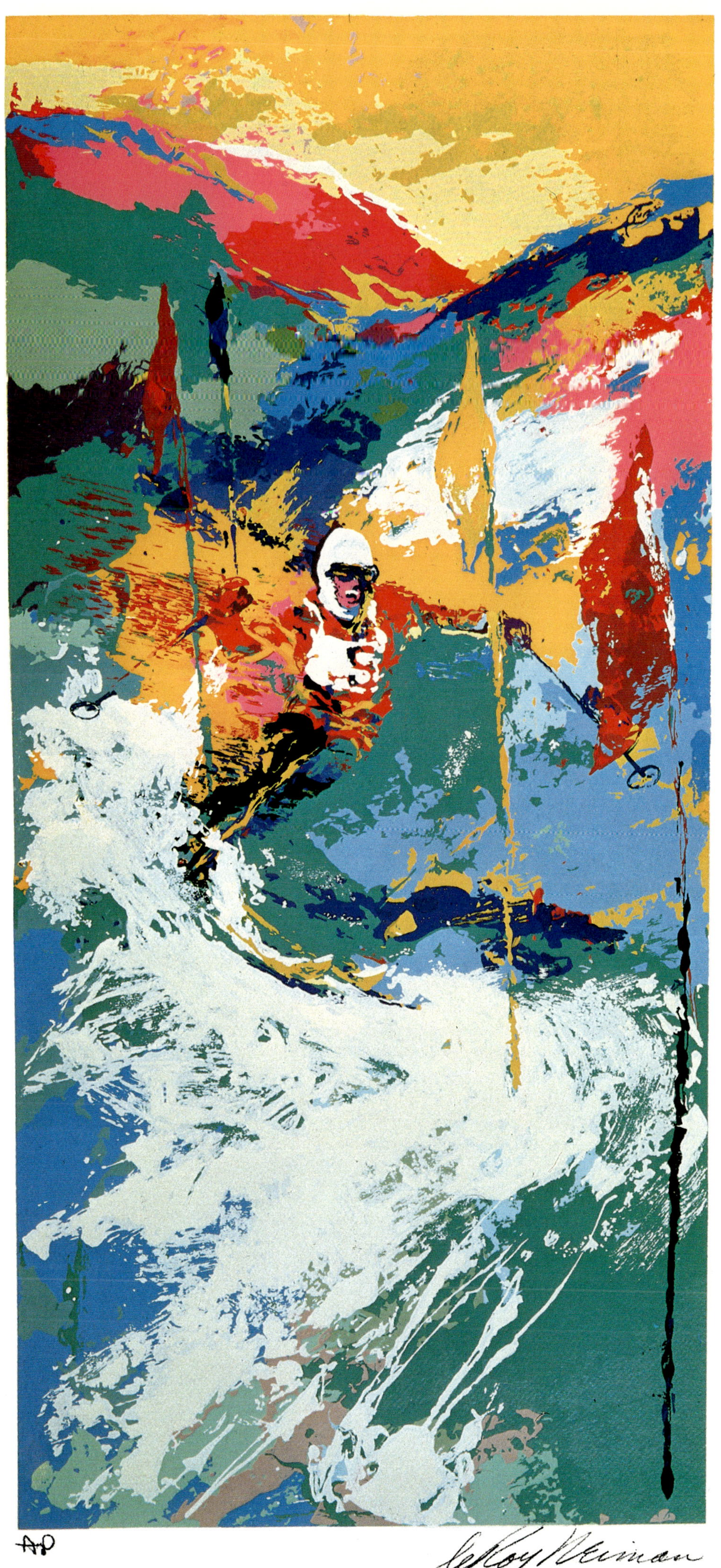

59 Downhill
1973
Serigraph
26 x 12 (66.04 x 30.48 cm)
A limited edition of 300, signed and numbered
by the artist.

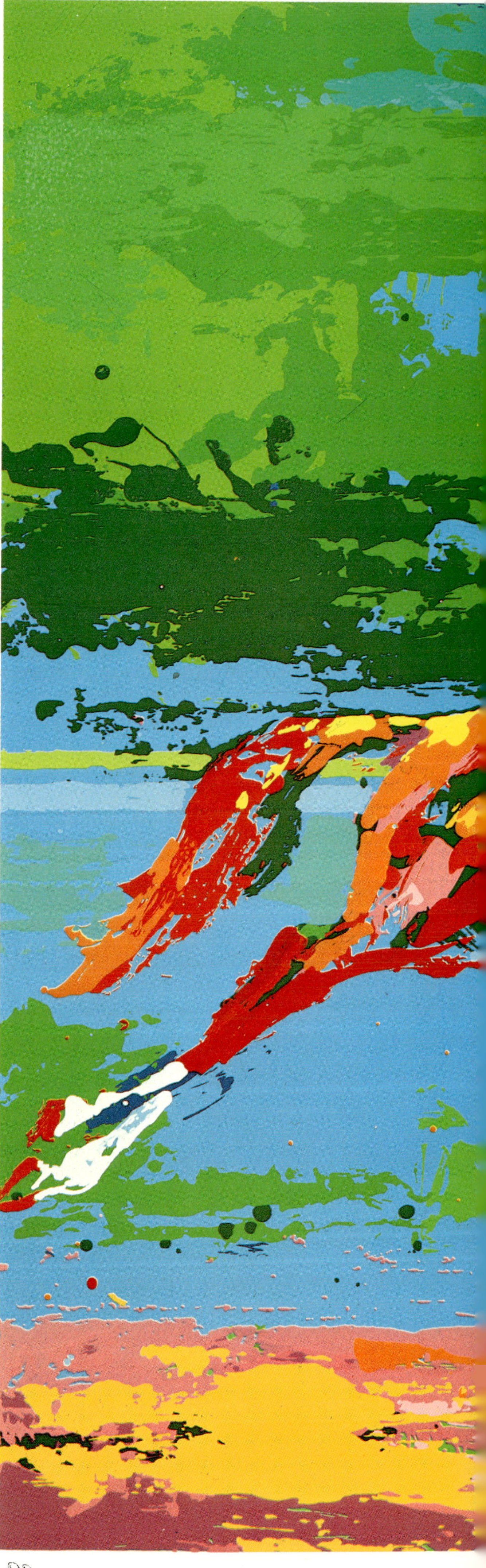

60   Secretariat (Big Red)
1973
Serigraph
20 x 24 (50.8 x 60.96 cm)
A limited edition of 300, signed and numbered
by the artist.

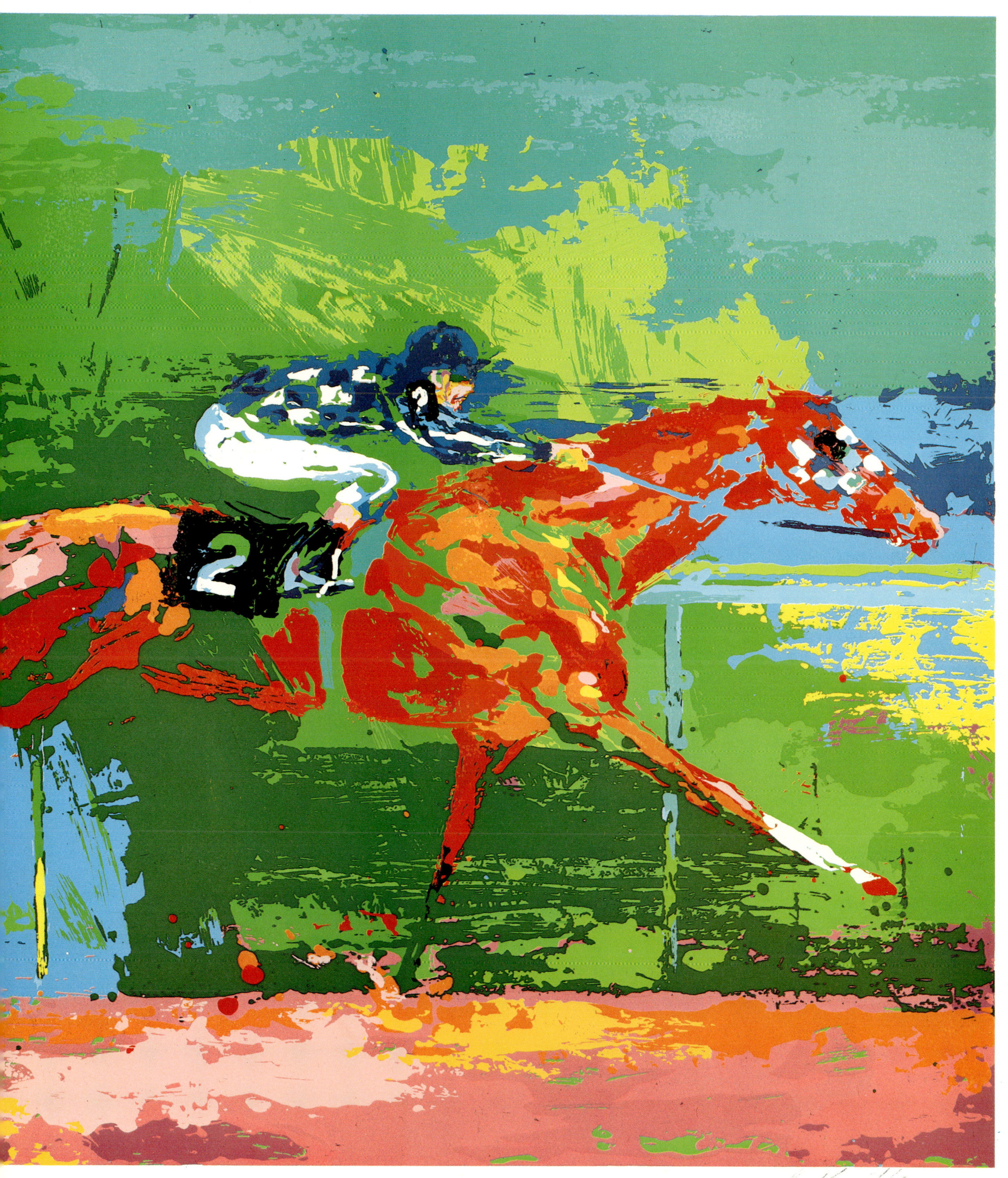

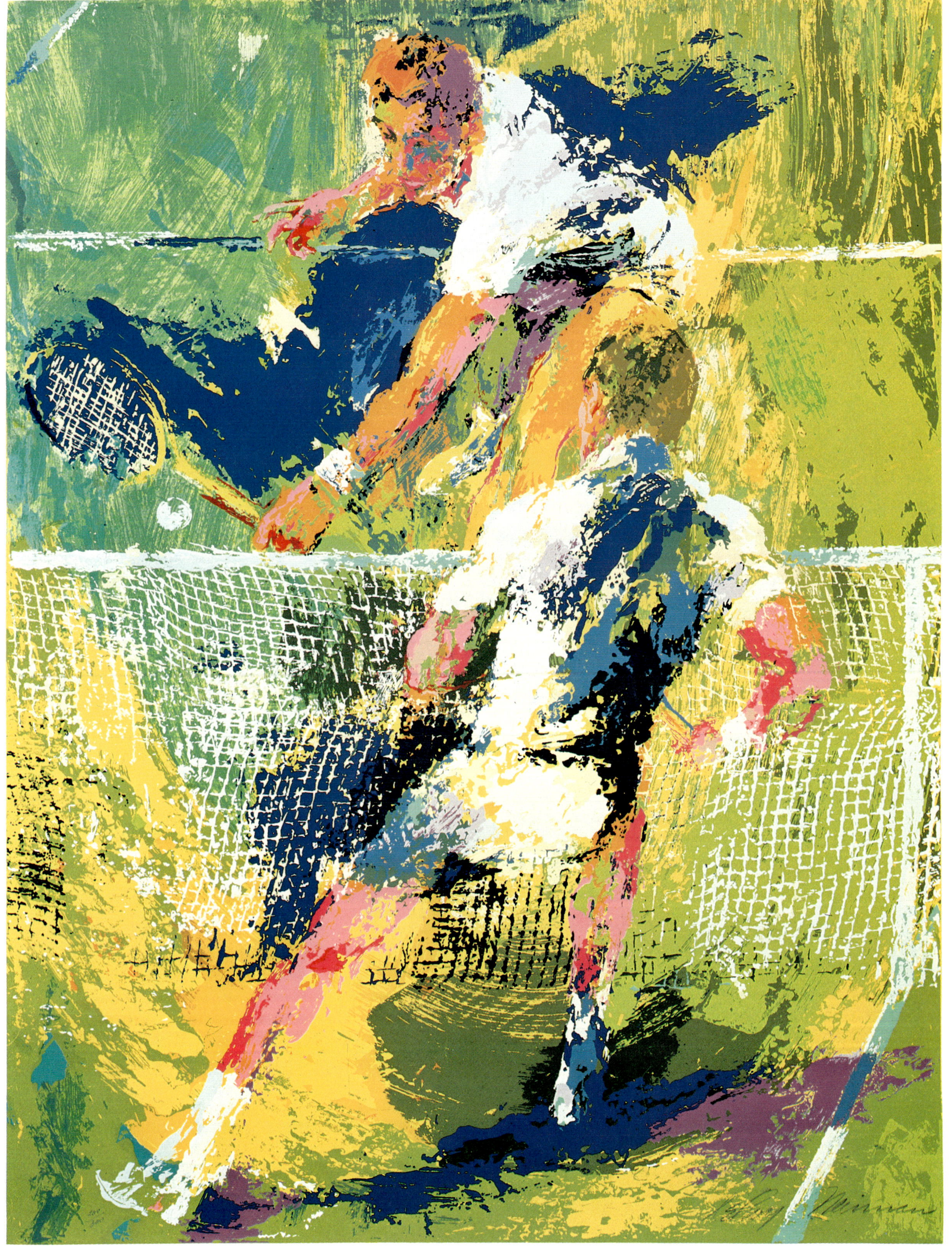

61 Match Point
1973
Serigraph
46 x 34½
(116.84 x 87.63 cm)
A limited edition of 300,
signed and numbered
by the artist.

62   Get Shot
1973
Serigraph
12 x 28⅛ (30.48 x 72.39 cm)
A limited edition of 300, signed and numbered
by the artist.

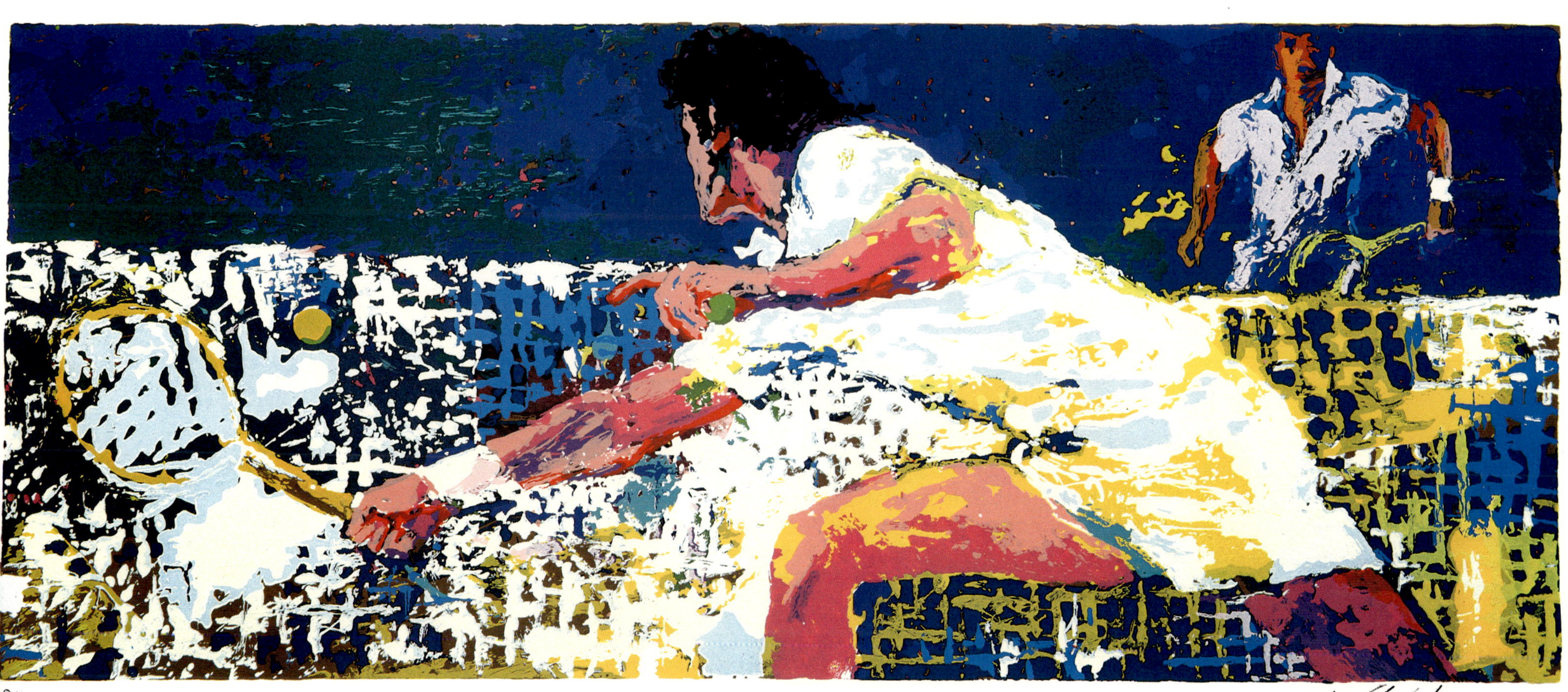

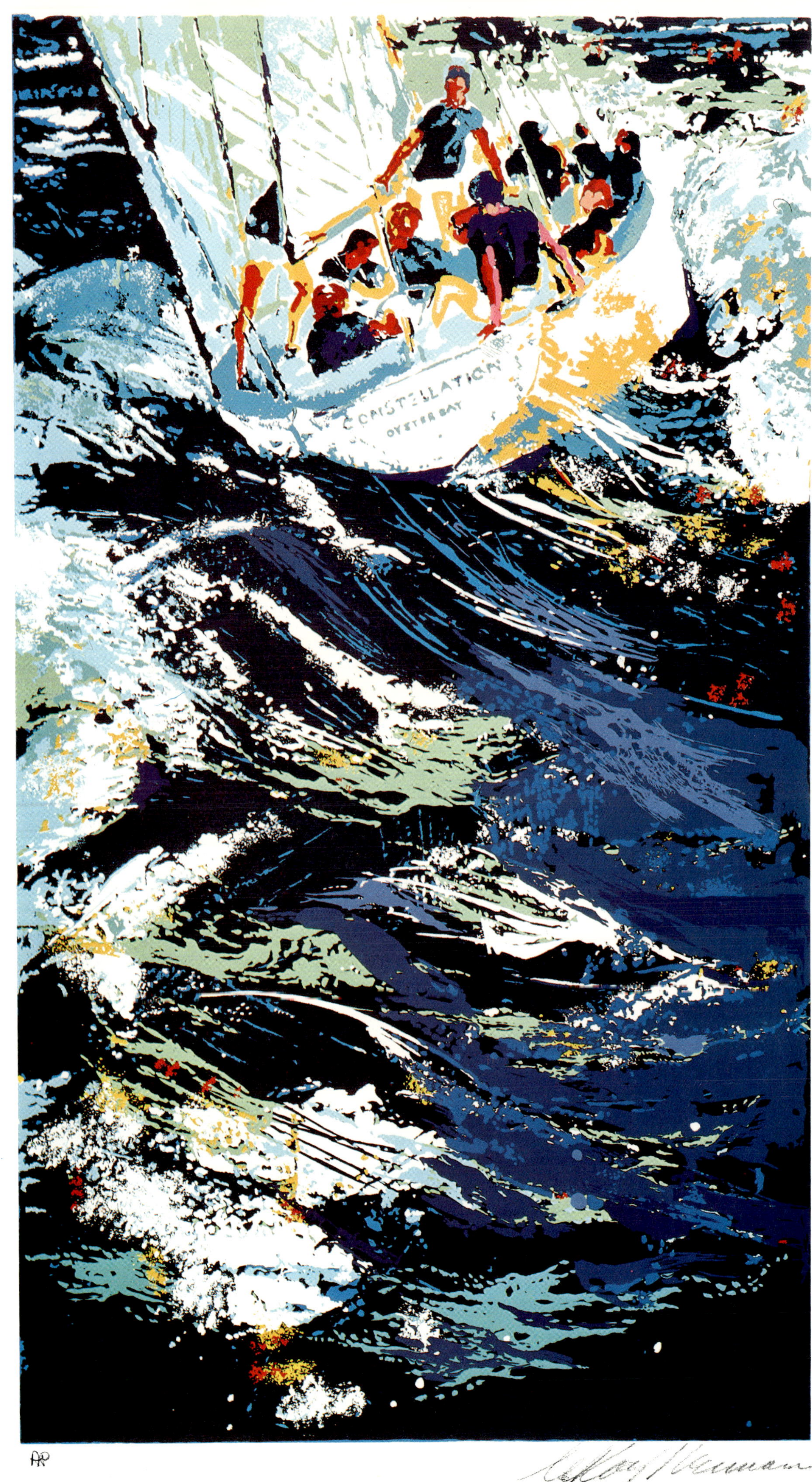

63   Twelve Meter Yacht Race

1973
Serigraph
24⅛ x 13½ (61.28 x 34.29 cm)
A limited edition of 250, signed and numbered
by the artist.

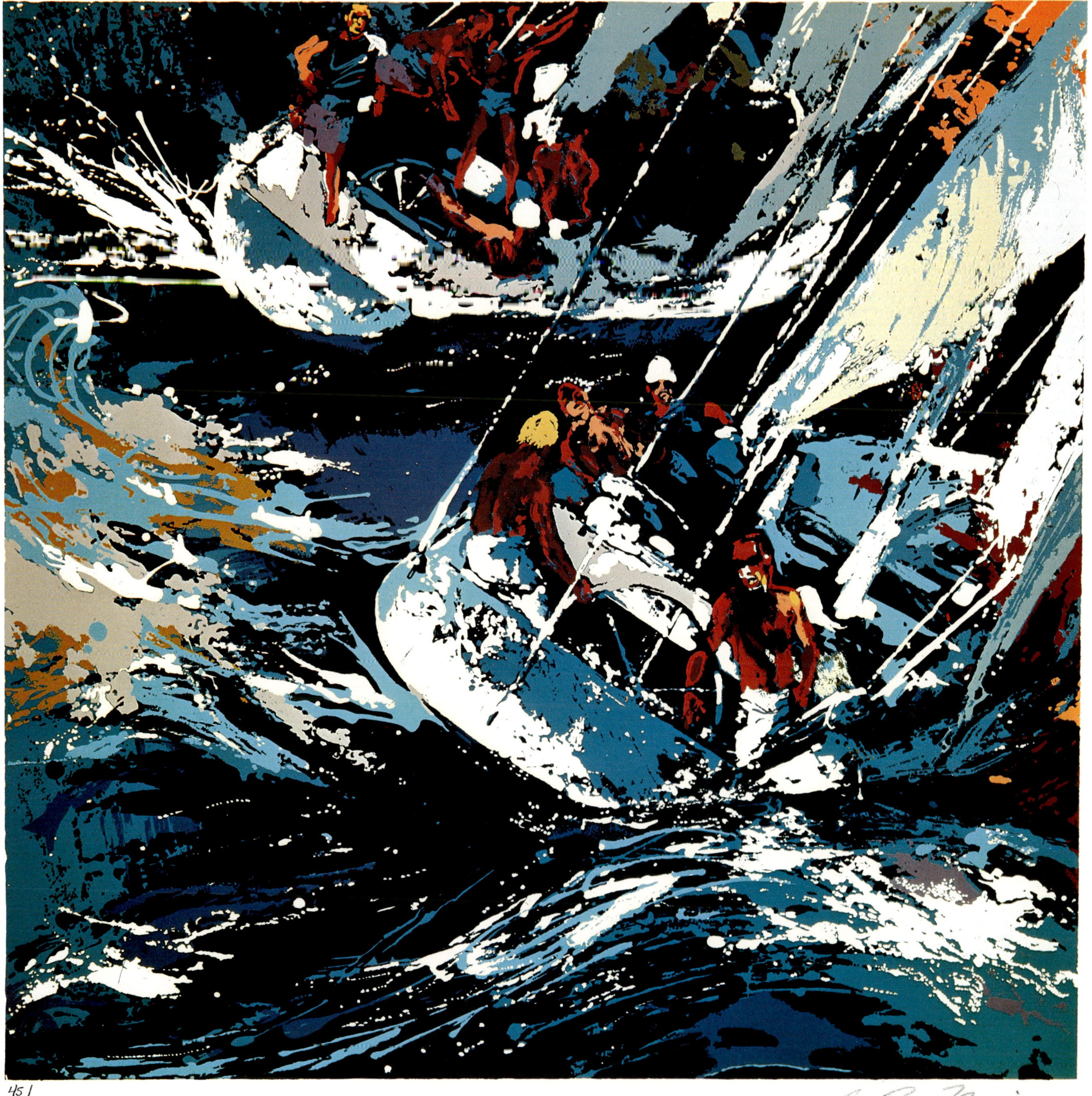

64 Two Twelves

1973
Serigraph
24 x 24 (60.96 x 60.96 cm)
A limited edition of 300, signed and numbered
by the artist.

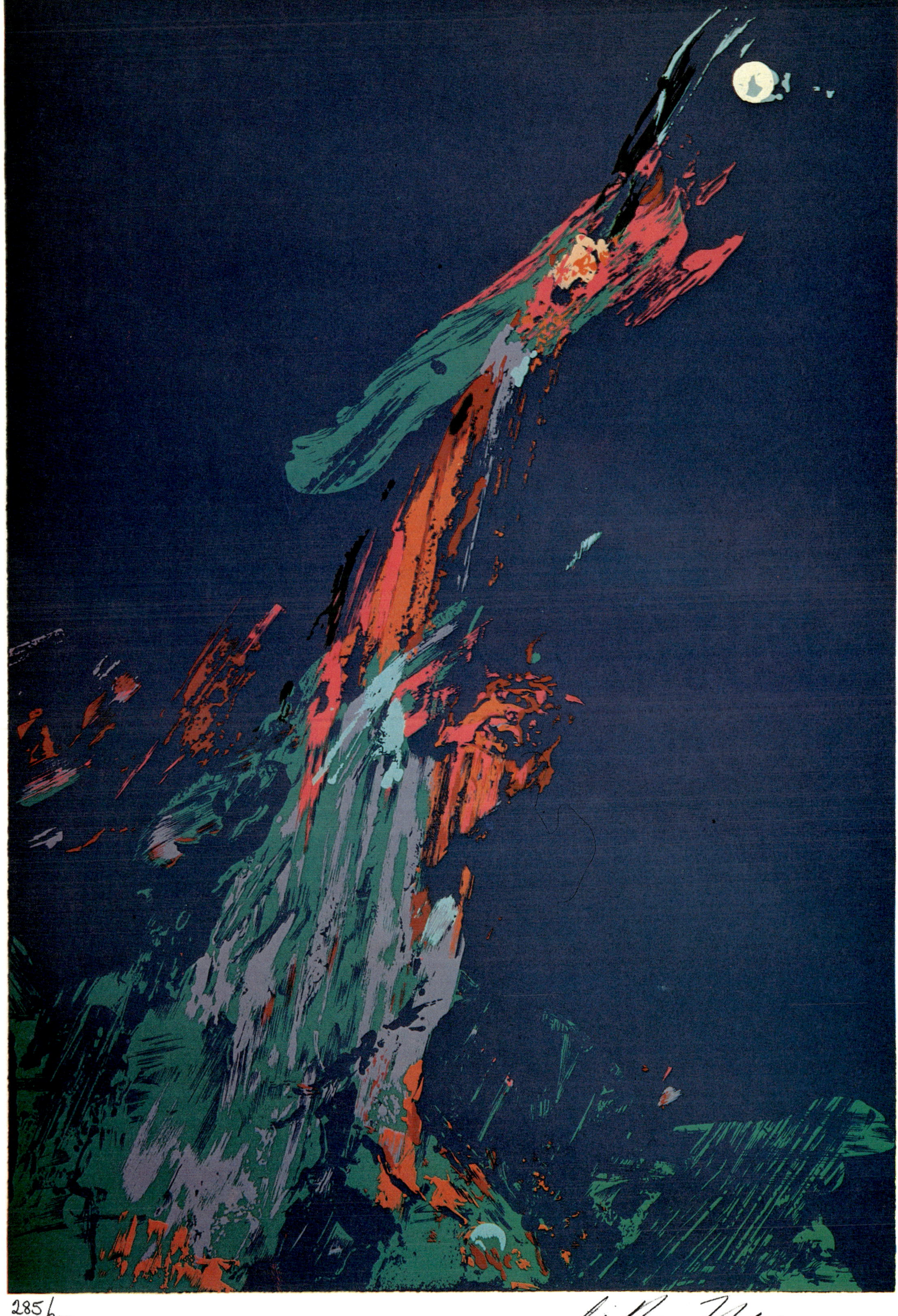

65 Smash
1973
Serigraph
20½ x 14 (52.07 x 35.56 cm)
A limited edition of 300, signed
and numbered by the artist.

285/300

66 Surfer

1973
Serigraph
17½ x 26¼ (44.45 x 66.67 cm)
A limited edition of 300, signed and numbered
by the artist.

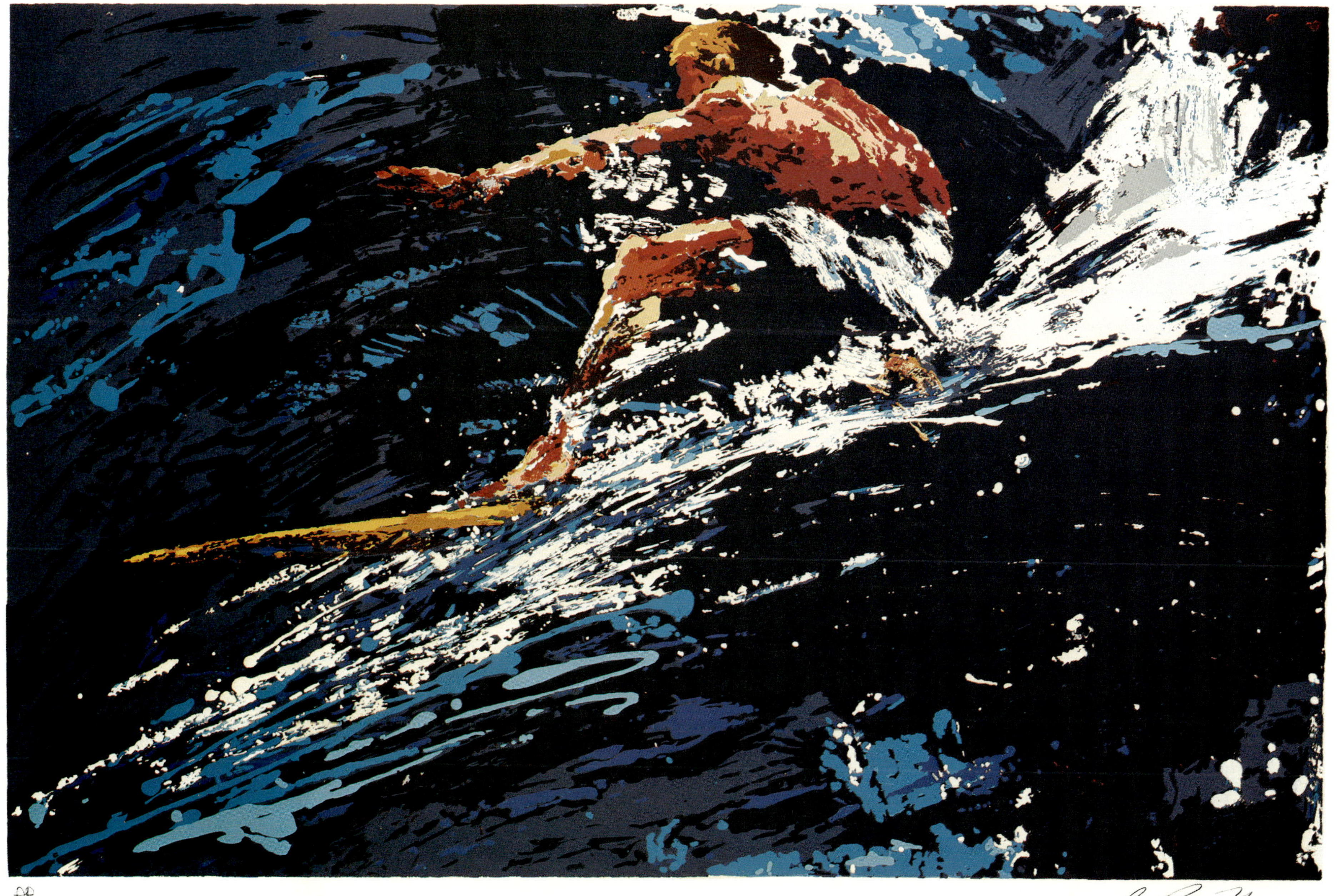

OHIO STATE (BUCKEYE) SUITE

A limited edition of 300, signed and numbered by the artist.

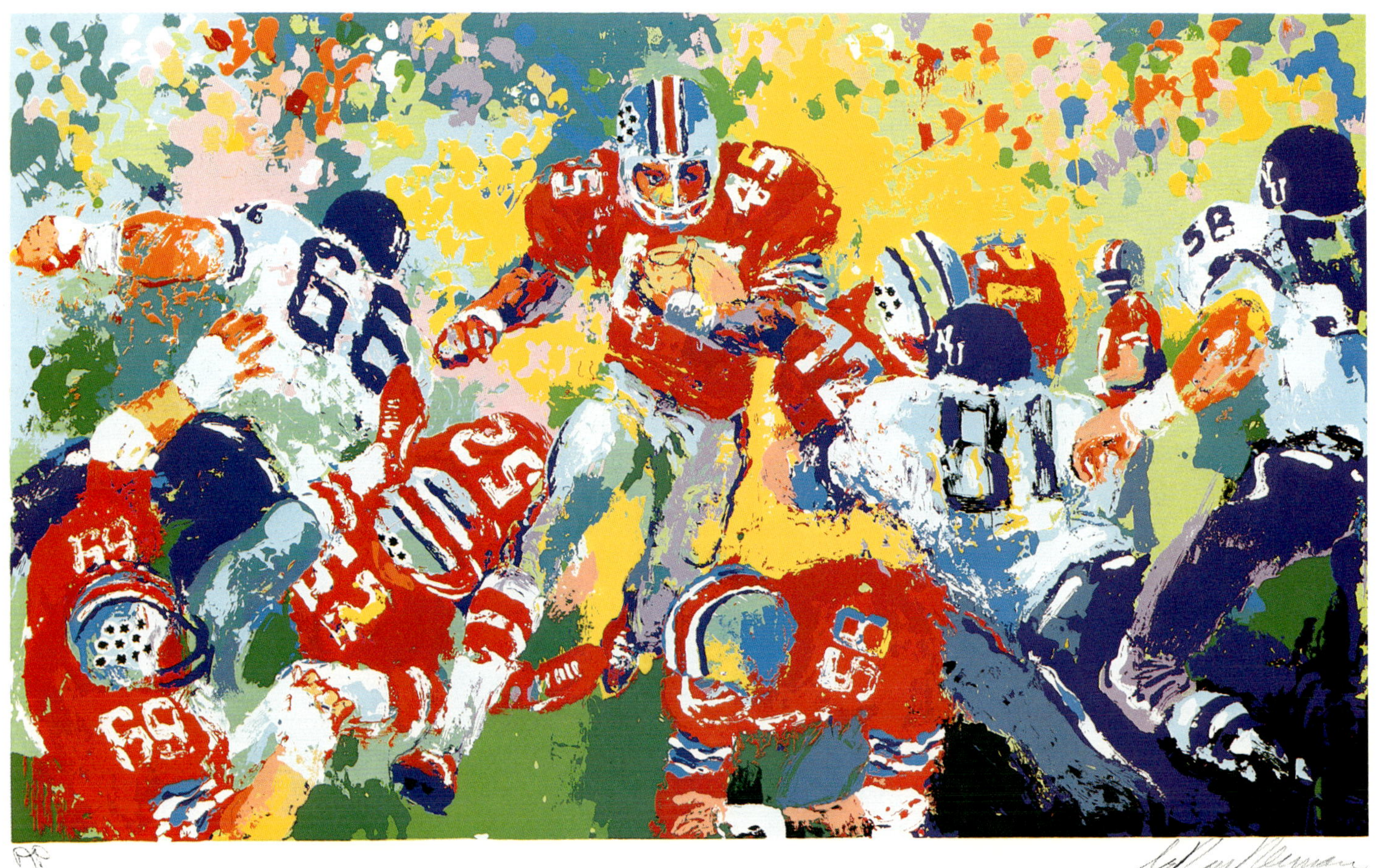

67   Archie

1973
Serigraph
20 x 32¾ (50.8 x 83.18 cm)

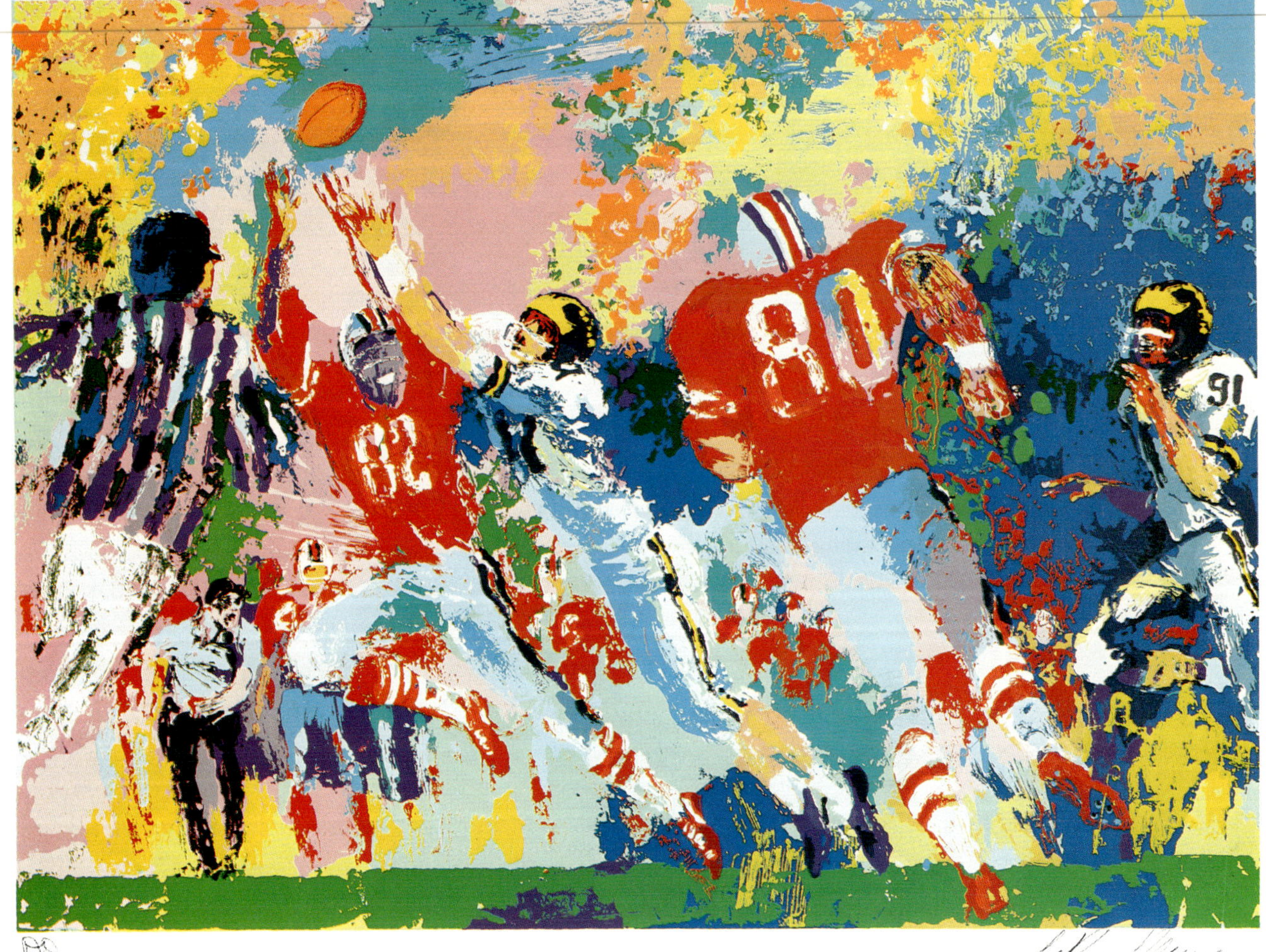

**68   Rivalry
(Michigan & Ohio State)**

1973
Serigraph
21 x 28 (53.34 x 71.12 cm)

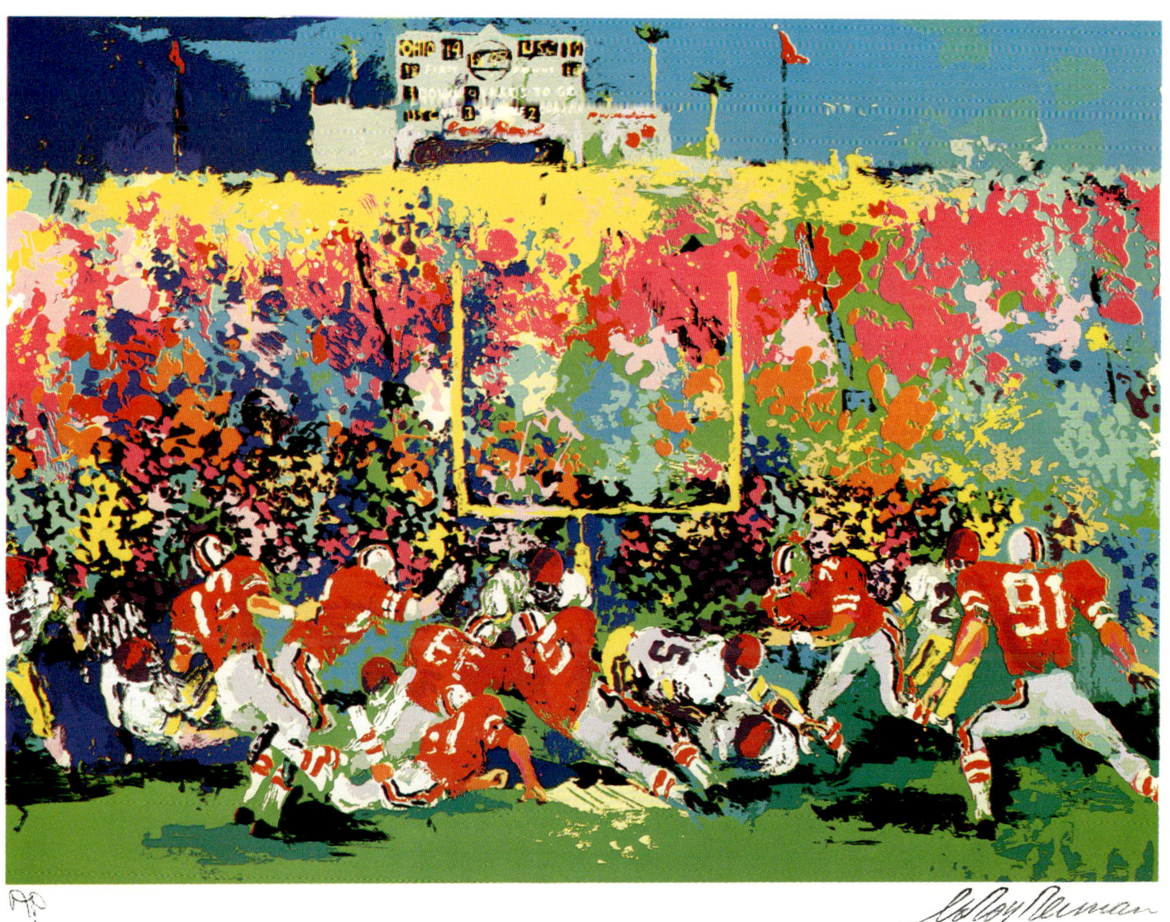

**69   Rose Bowl
(USC & Ohio State)**
1973
Serigraph
21 x 28 (53.34 x 71.12 cm)

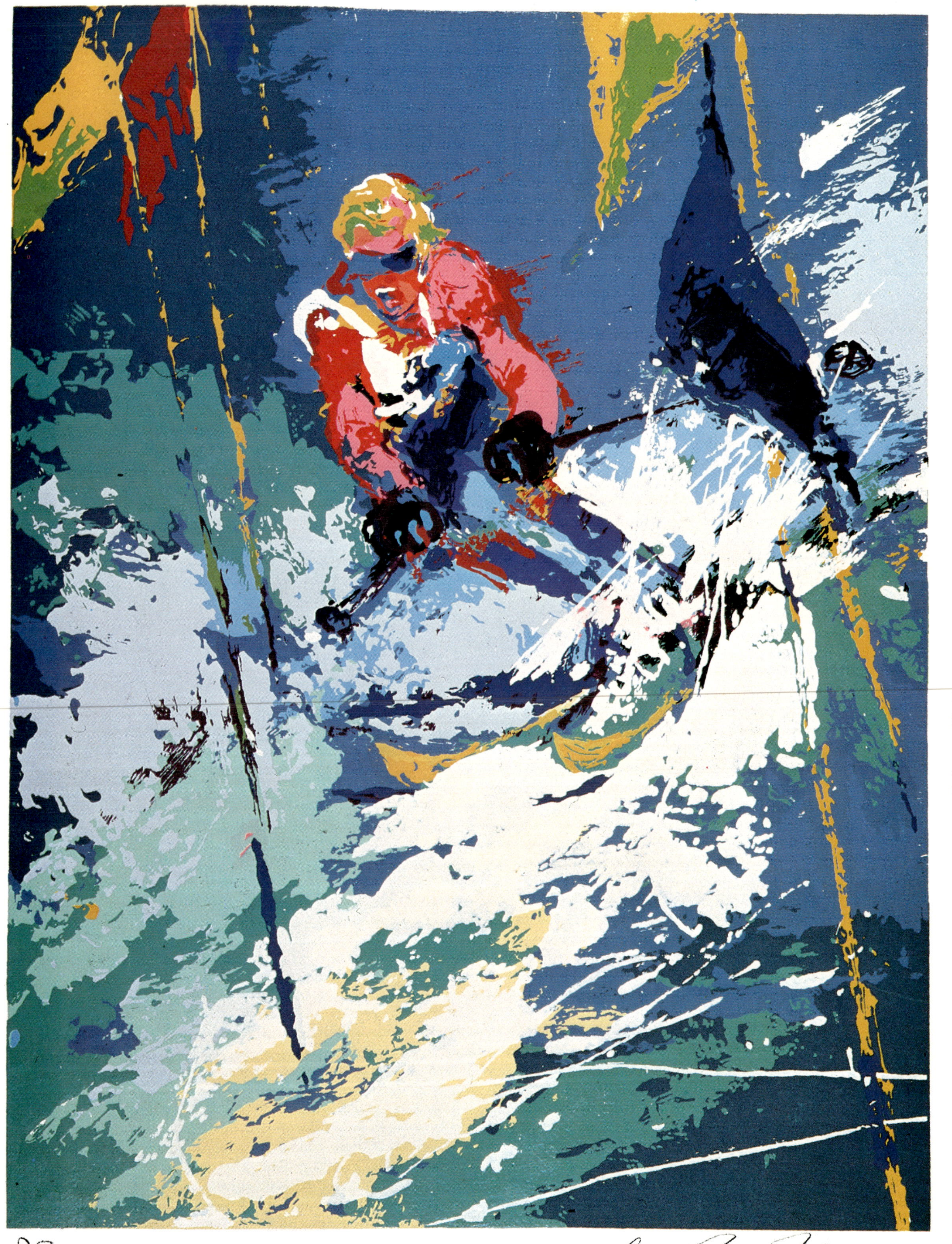

70   Innsbruck
1973
Serigraph
16 x 12 (40.64 x 30.48 cm)
A limited edition of 300, signed and
numbered by the artist.

71   Stan Smith
1973
Serigraph
19½ x 20 (49.53 x 50.8 cm)
A limited edition of 300, signed
and numbered by the artist.

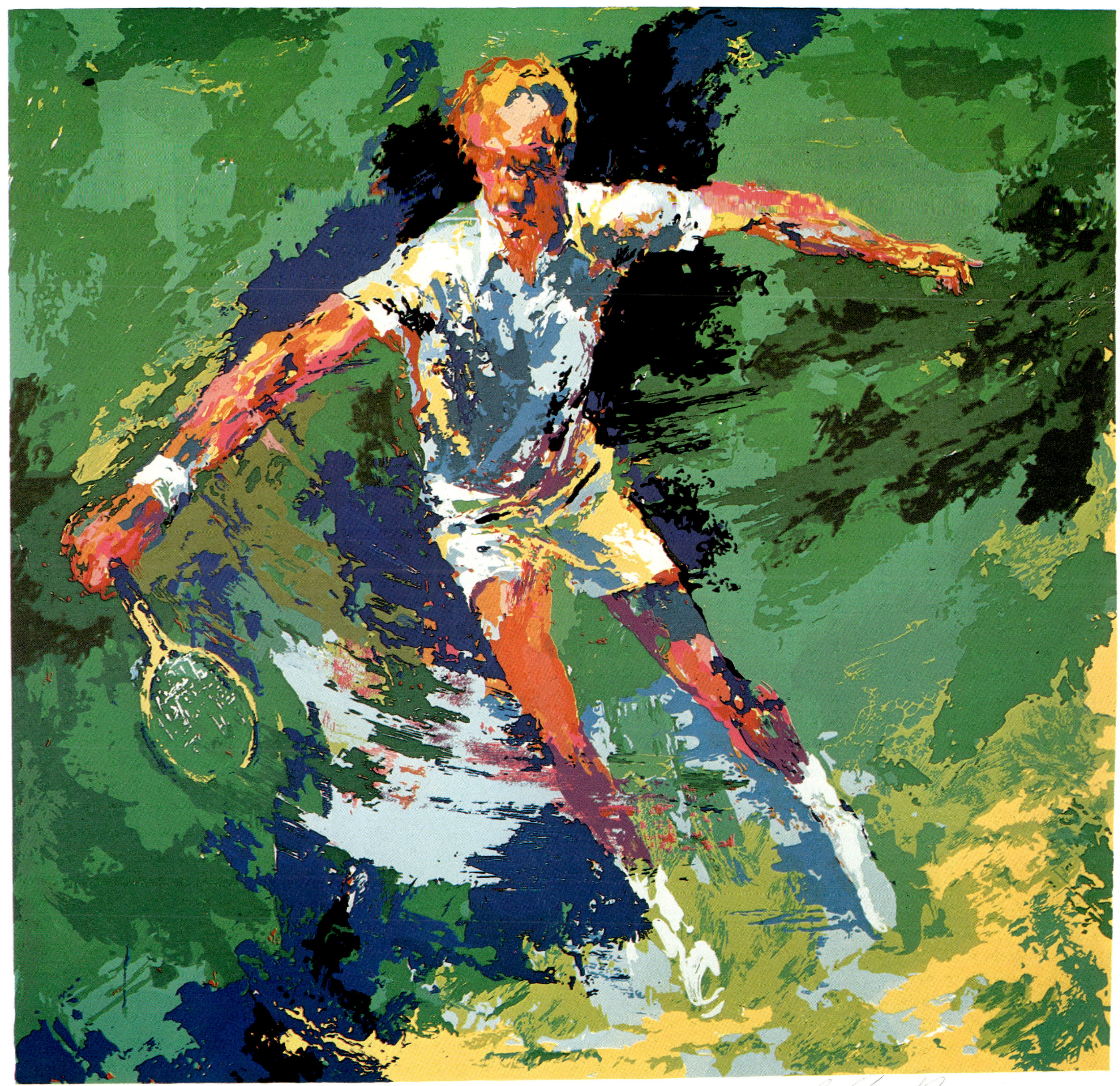

AP

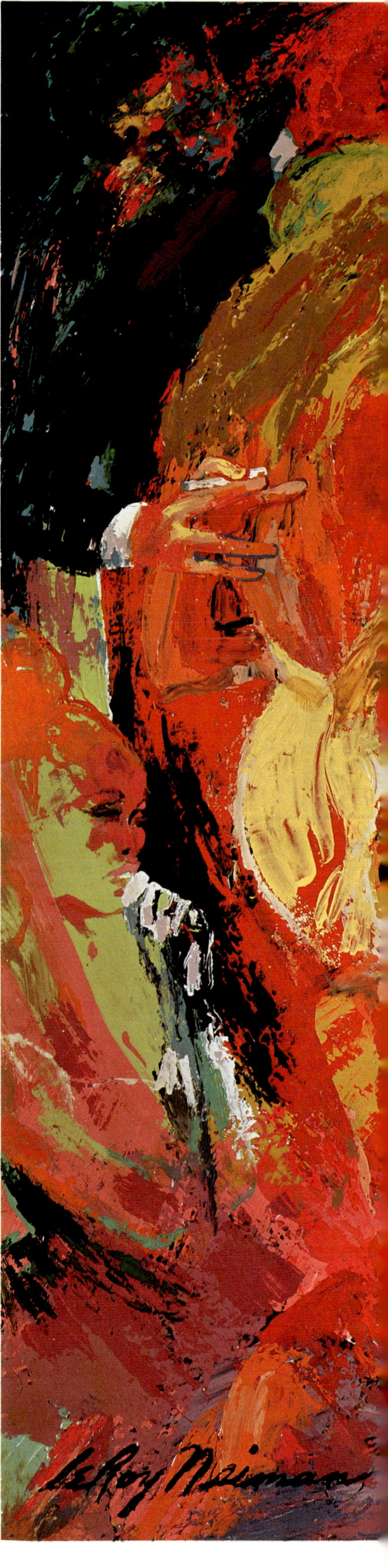

72 Roulette

1973
Serigraph
48 x 60 (121.92 x 152.40 cm)
A limited edition of 40, signed and numbered
by the artist.

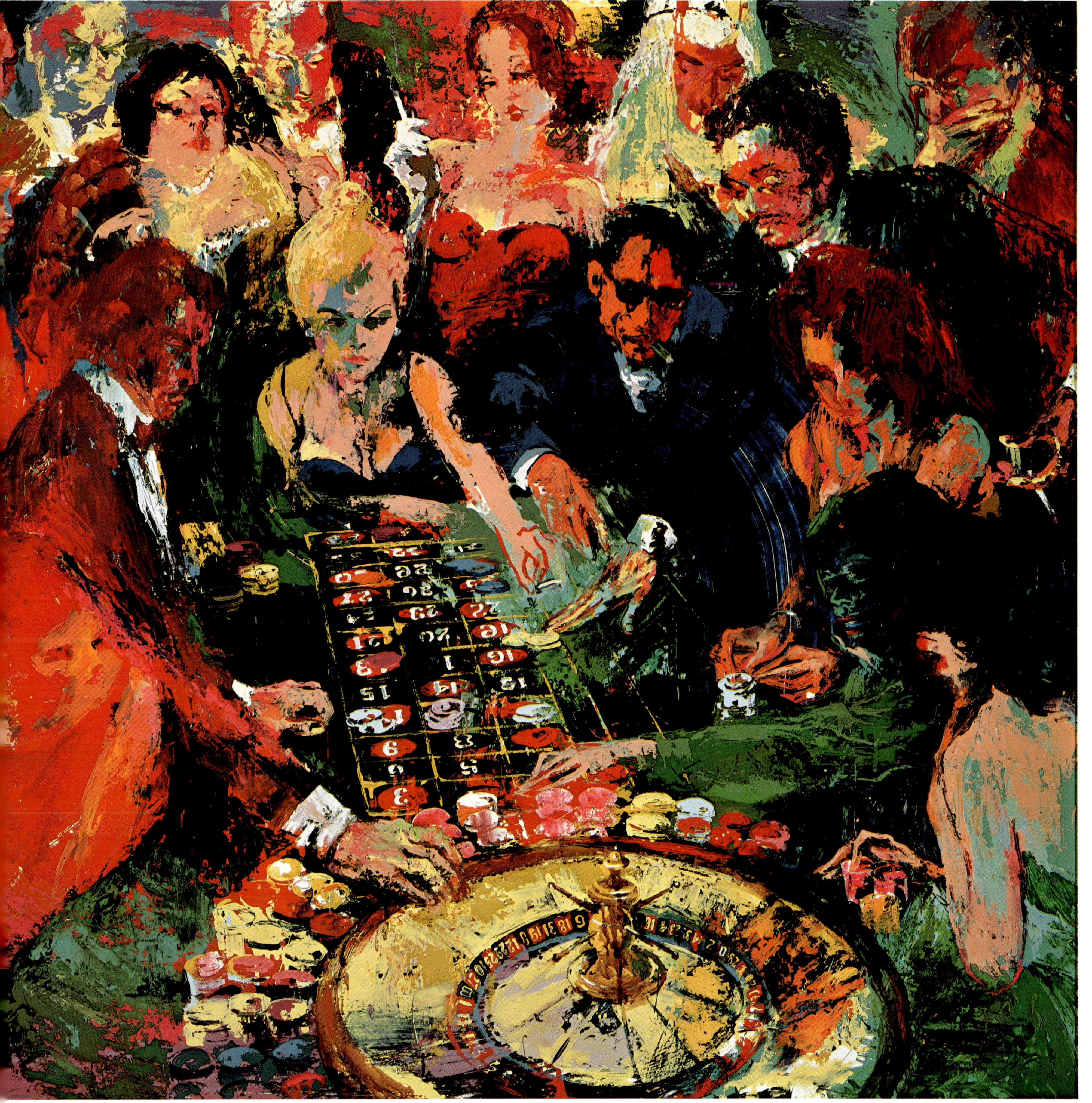

Part II
Serigraphs, 1974–1976

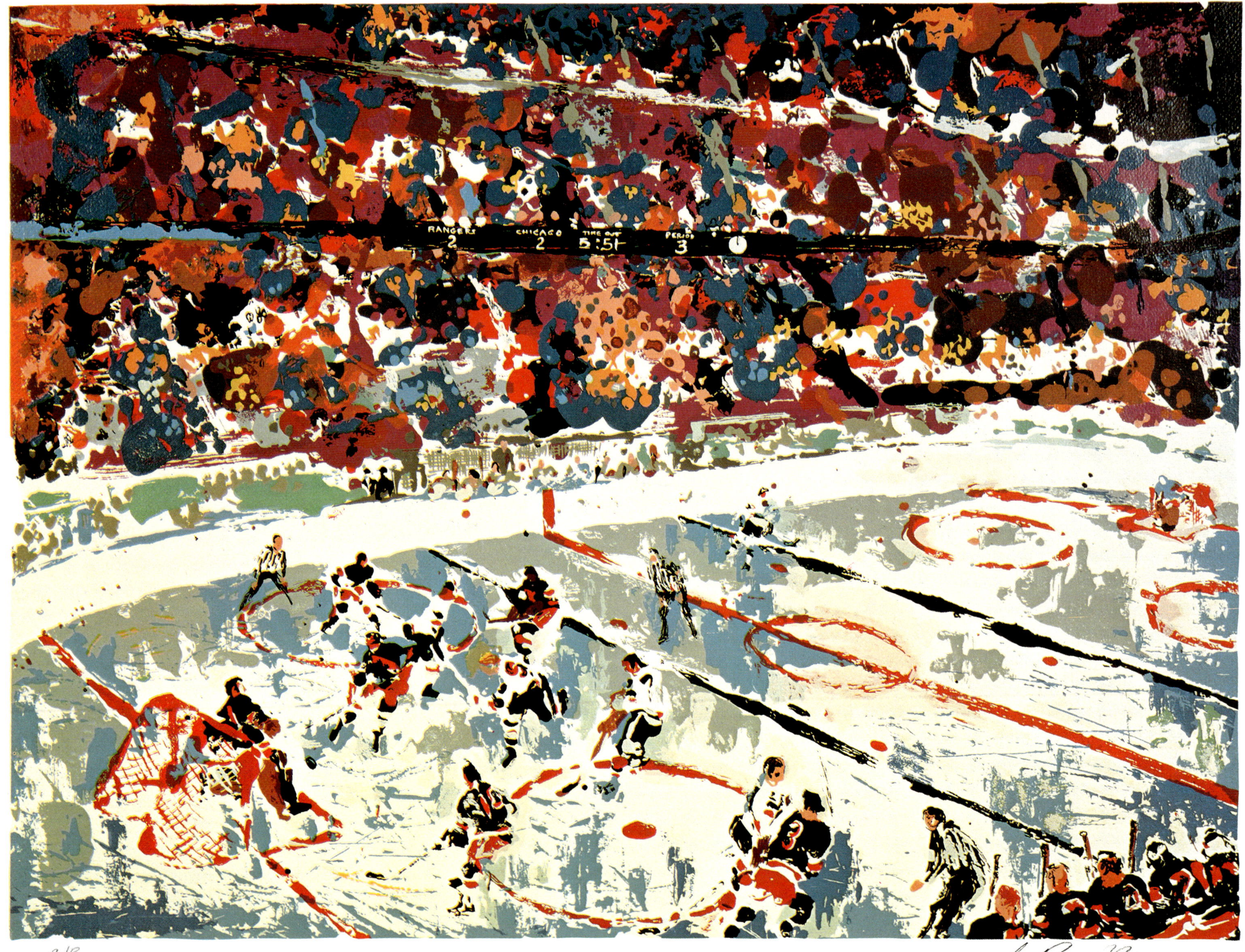

73   Slap Shot

1974
Serigraph
22 x 28½ (55.88 x 72.39 cm)
A limited edition of 300, signed and numbered
by the artist.

74   Ice Men

1974
Serigraph
22½ x 32⅛ (57.15 x 81.60 cm)
A limited edition of 300, signed and numbered
by the artist.

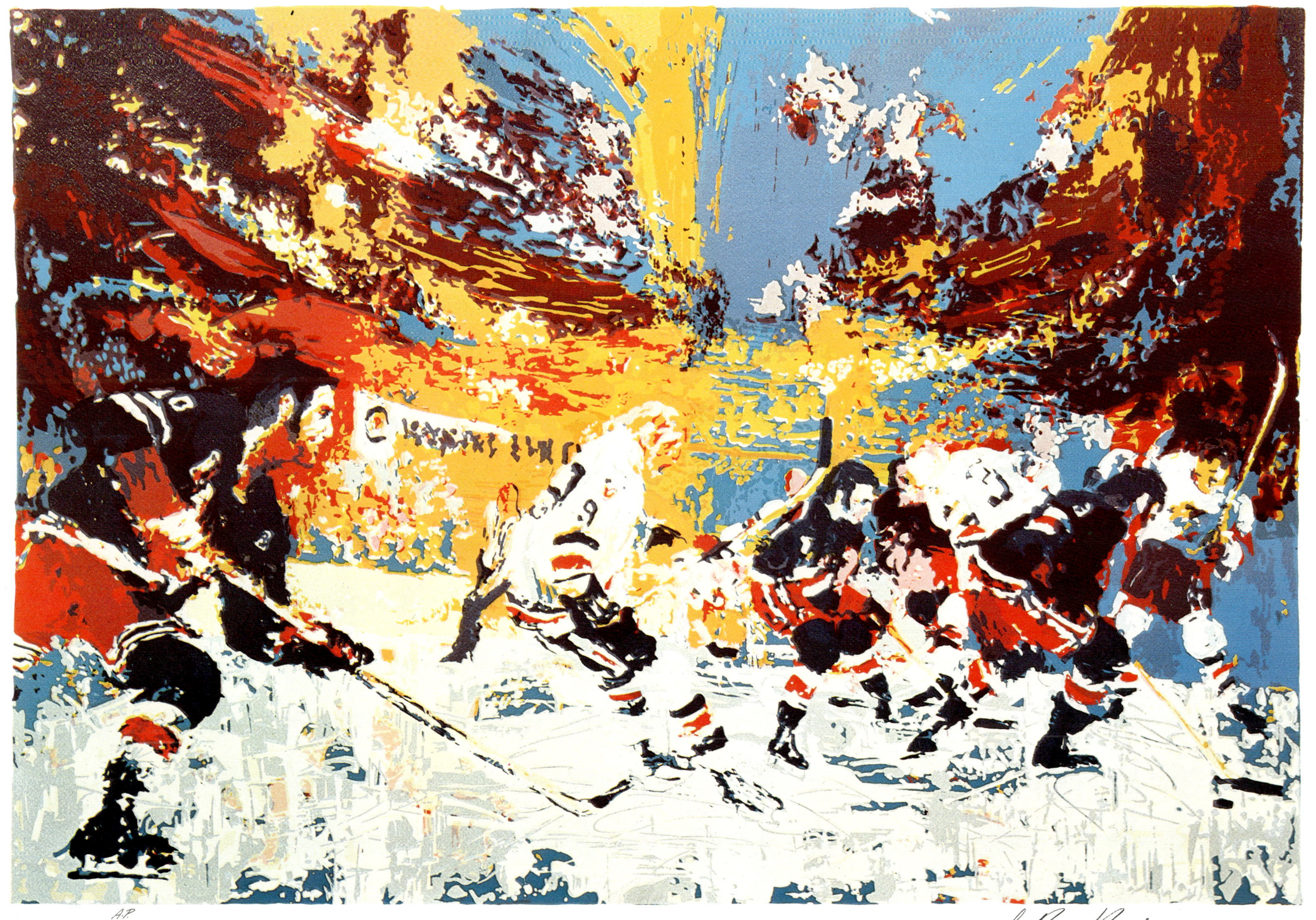

75 Hawaiian Surfers

1974
Serigraph
26 x 40 (66.04 x 101.6 cm)
A limited edition of 300, signed and numbered
by the artist.

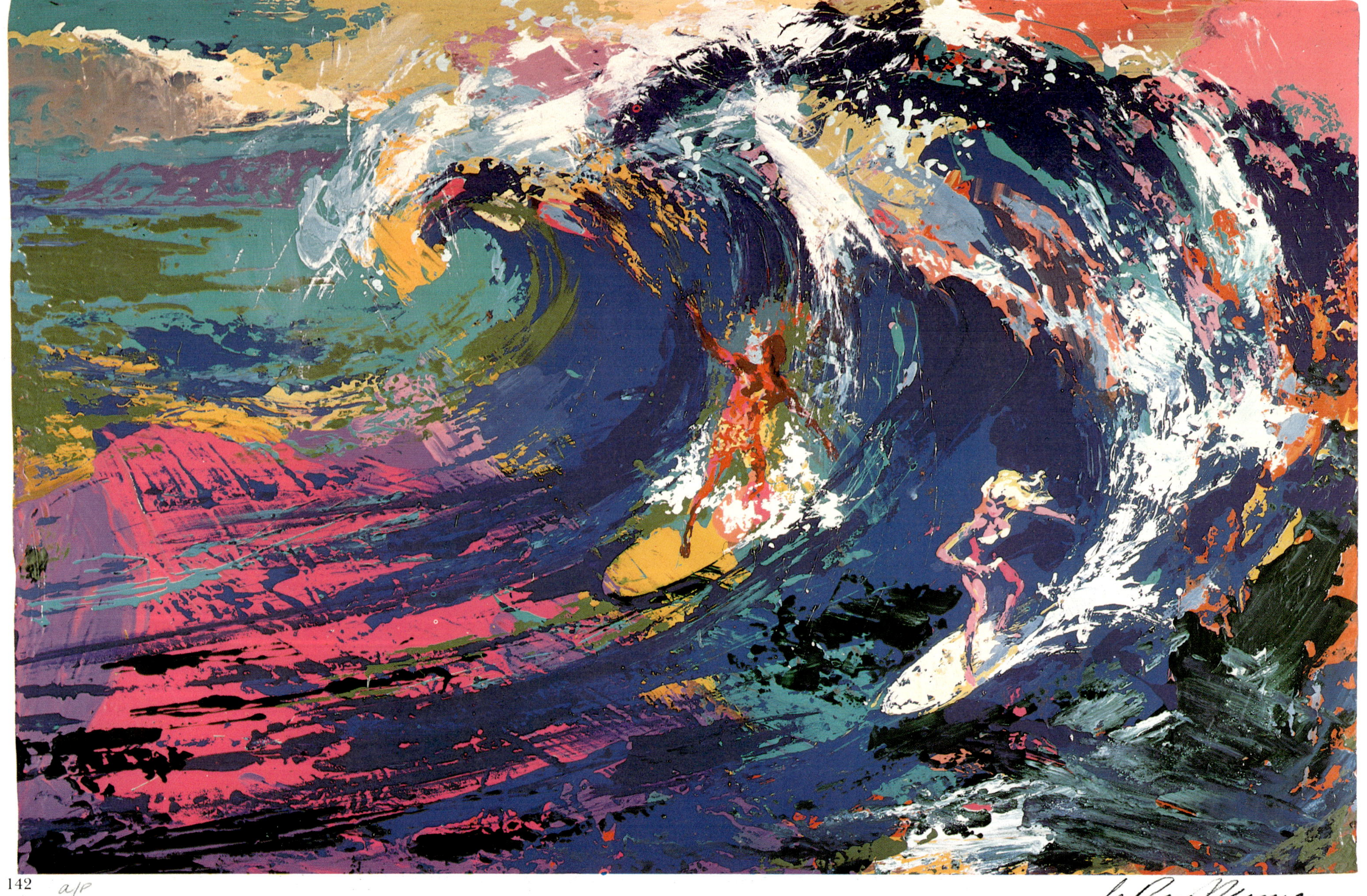

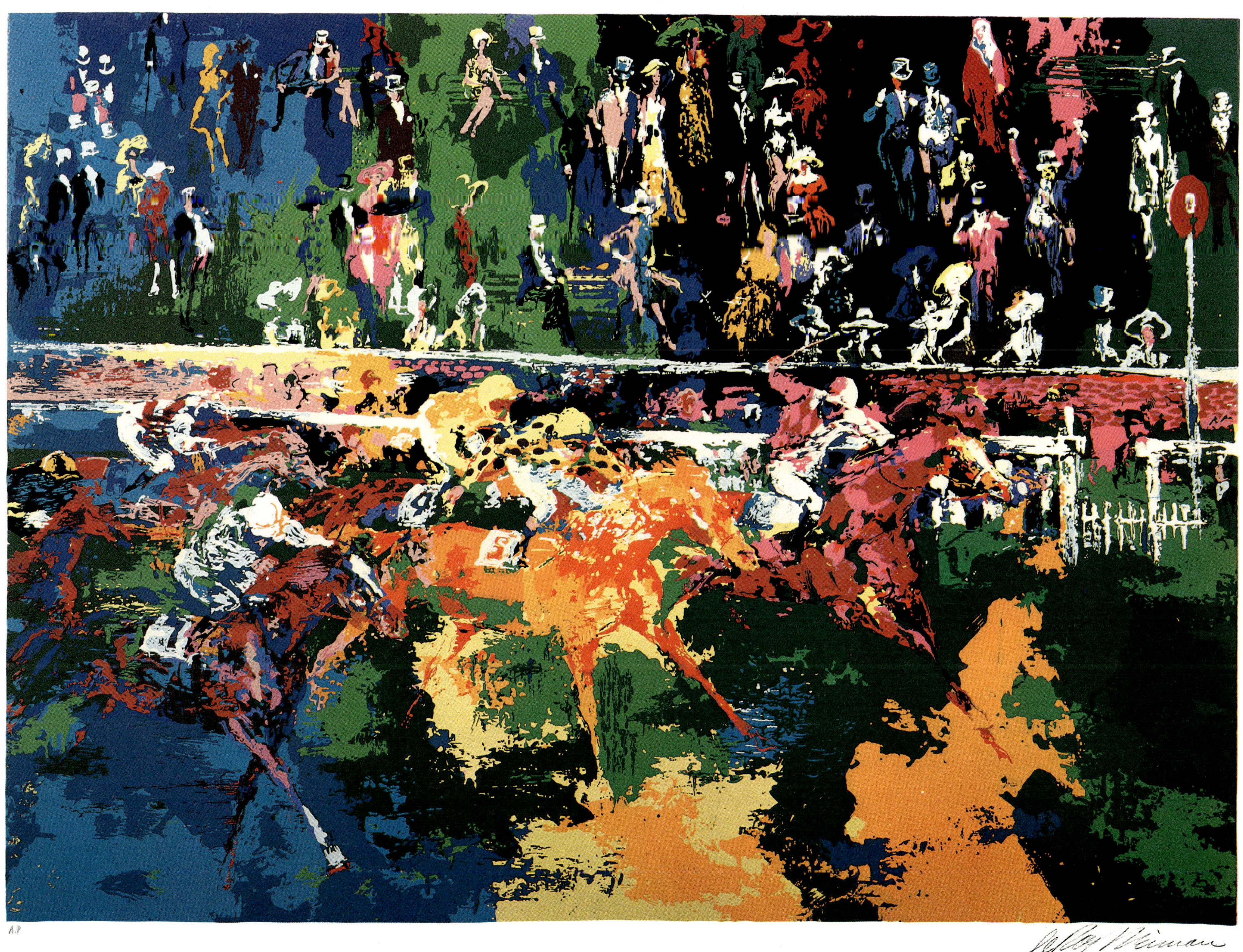

76 Ascot Finish

1974
Serigraph
26 x 34⅞ (66.04 x 88.58 cm)
A limited edition of 300, signed and numbered
by the artist.

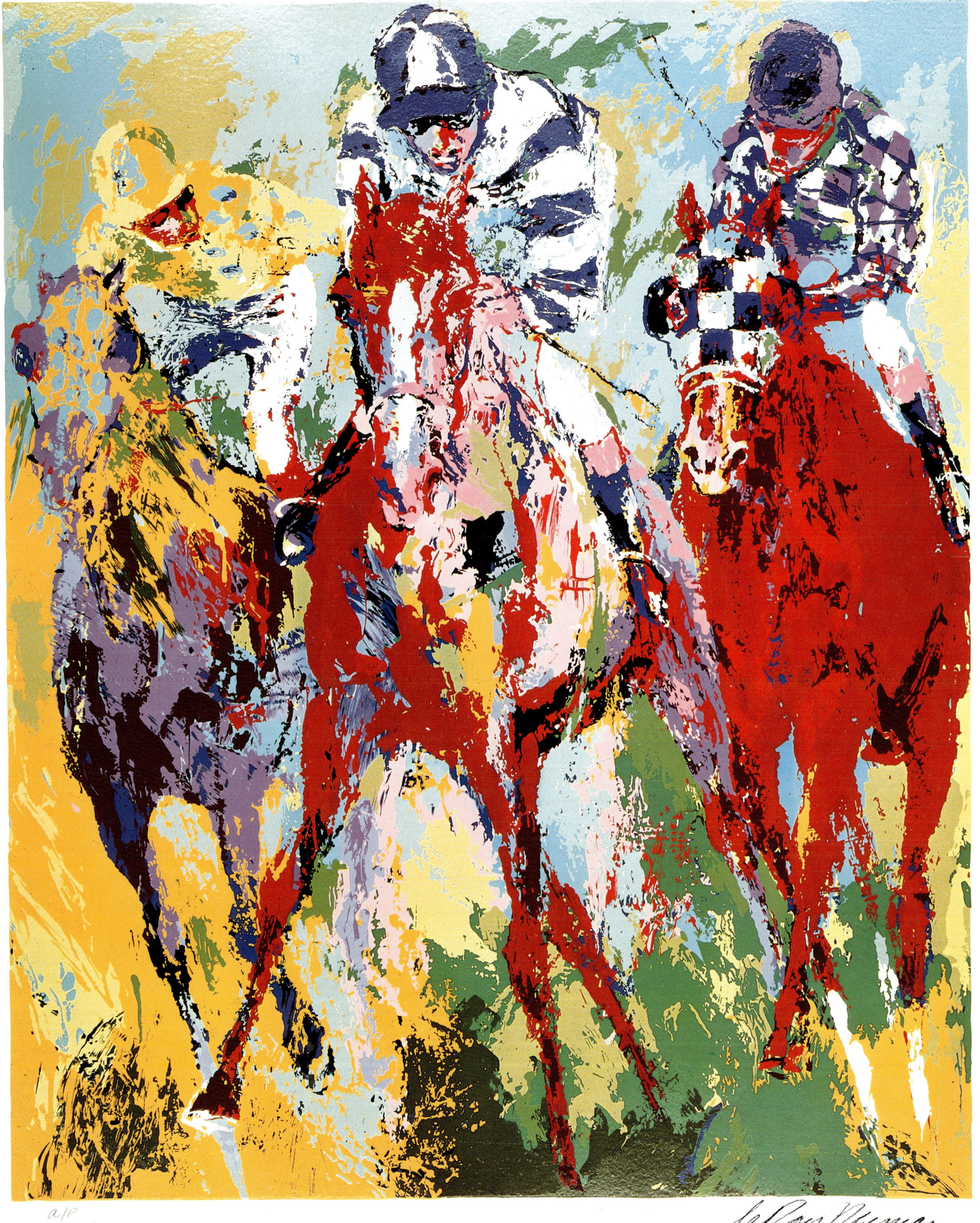

77 The Finish

1974
Serigraph
33 x 26⅜ (83.82 x 66.99 cm)
A limited edition of 300, signed
and numbered by the artist.

1974
Serigraph
20½ x 31½ (52.07 x 80. cm)
A limited edition of 300, signed and numbered
by the artist.

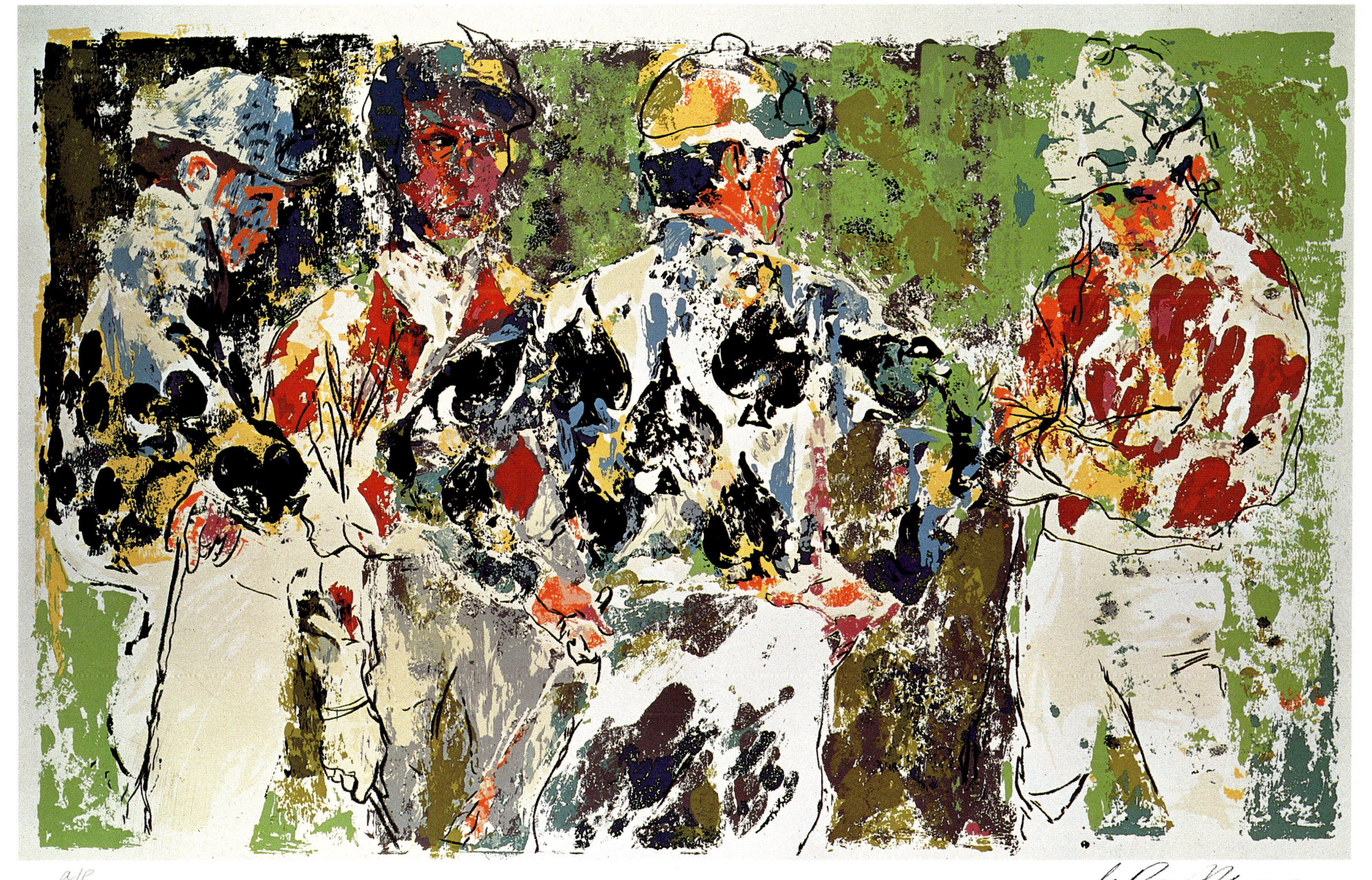

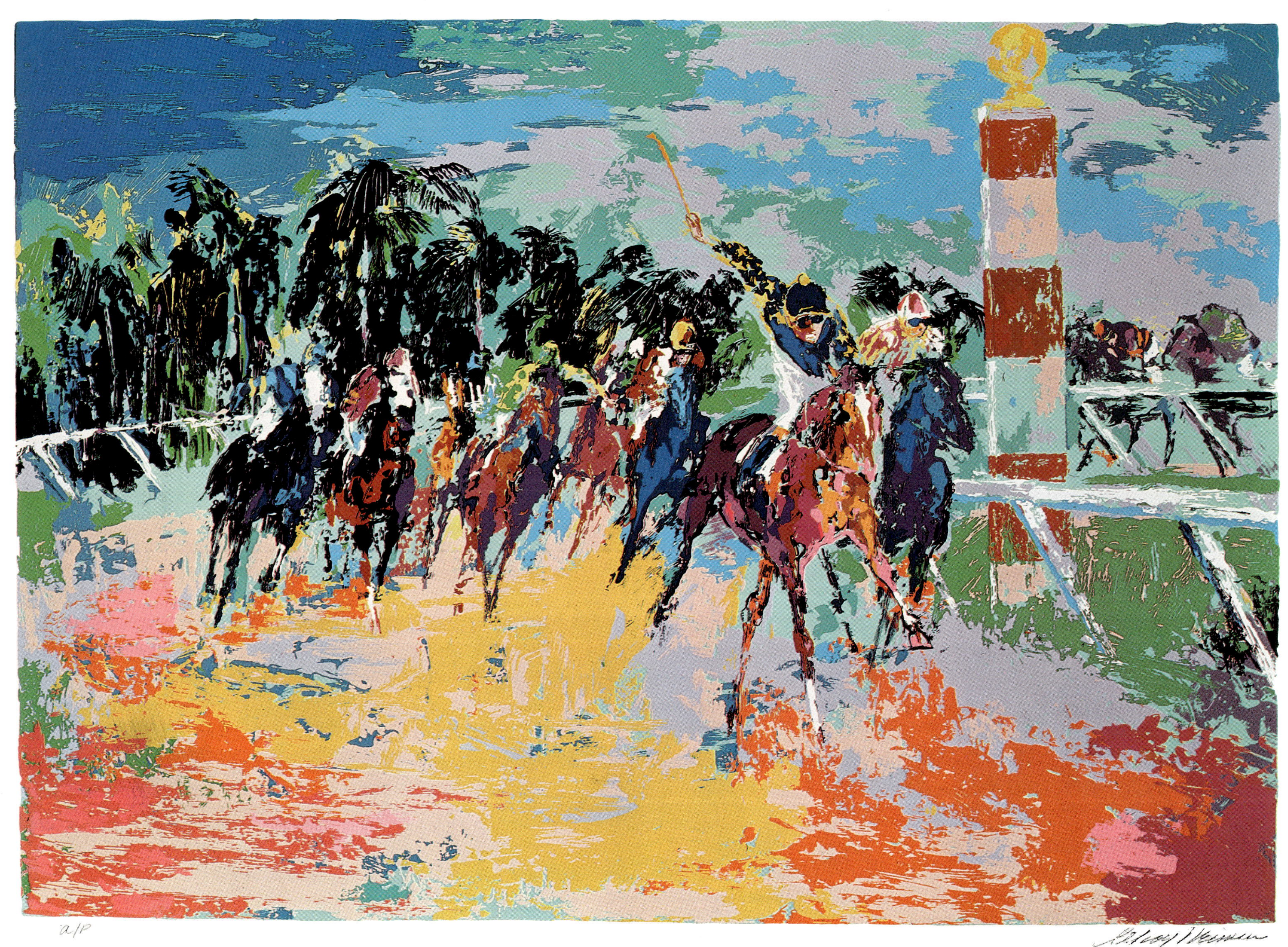

79 Florida Racing

1974
Serigraph
29⅜ x 40¾ (74.61 x 103.50 cm)
A limited edition of 300, signed and numbered
by the artist.

1974
Serigraph
25 x 33¼ (63.54 x 84.45 cm)
A limited edition of 300, signed and numbered
by the artist.

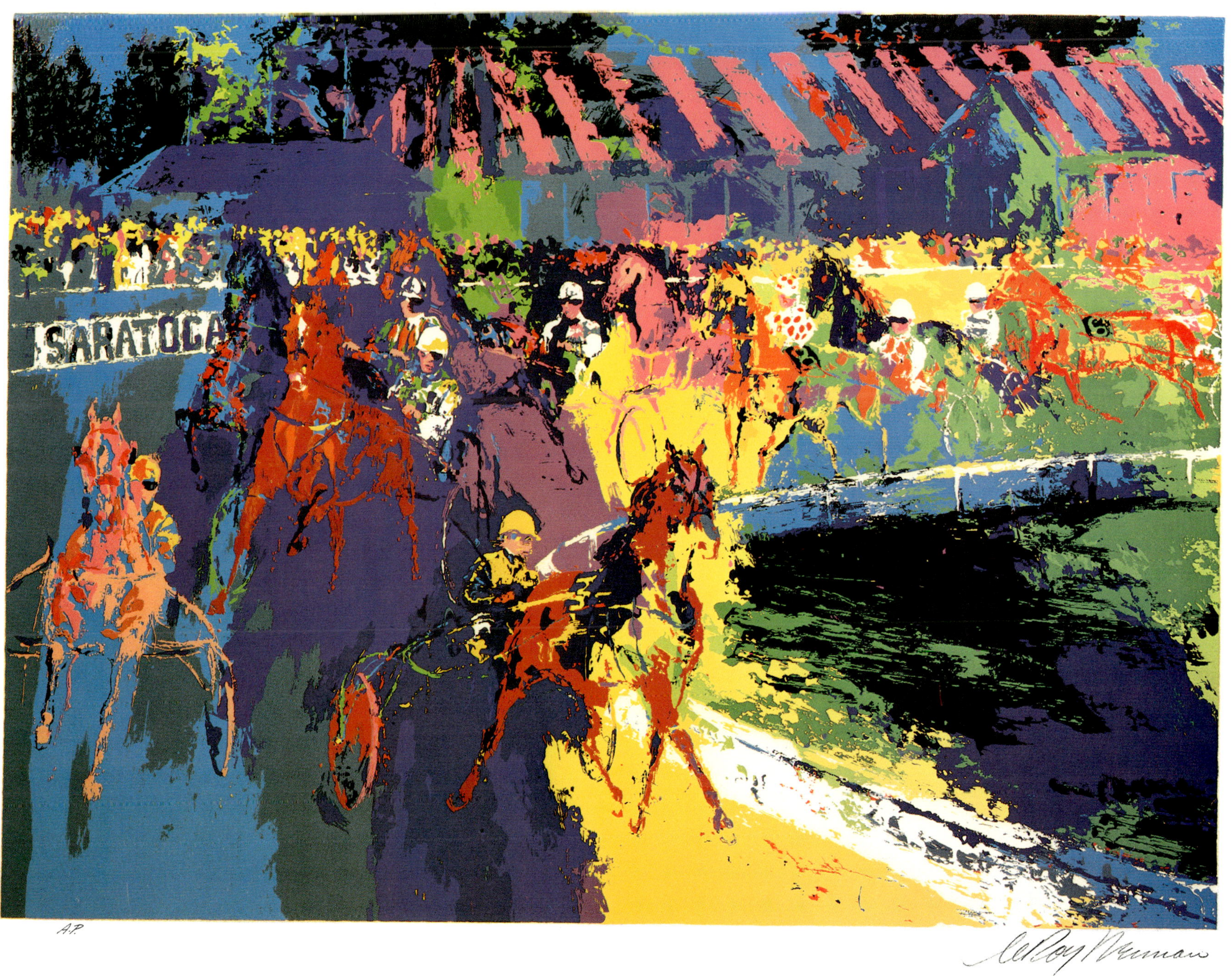

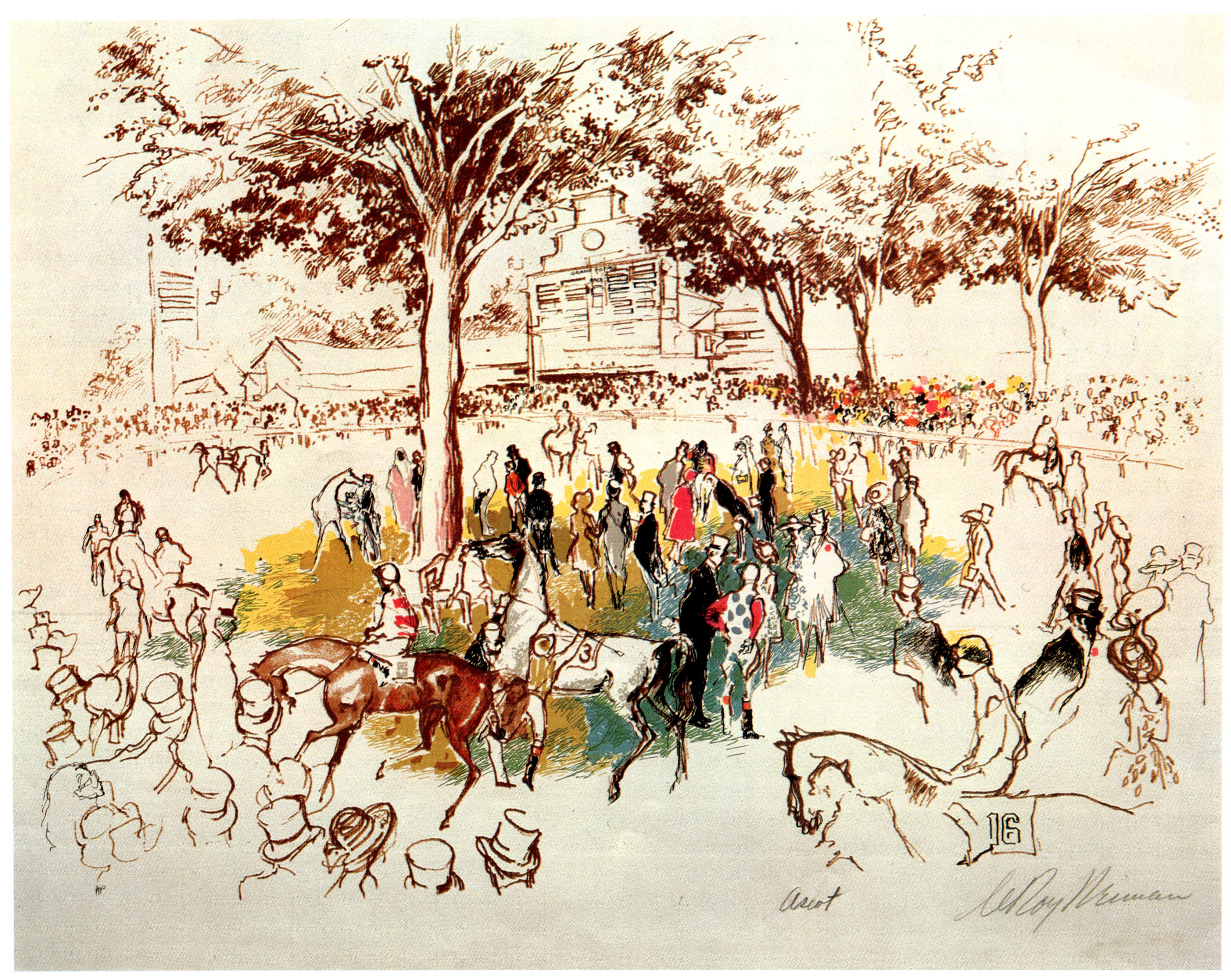

81 Ascot Paddock

1974
Serigraph
21½ x 29½ (54.61 x 74.93 cm)
A limited edition of 300, signed and numbered
by the artist.

82   Fox Hunt

1974
Serigraph
20¼ x 27 (51.45 x 60.58 cm)
A limited edition of 300, signed and numbered
by the artist.

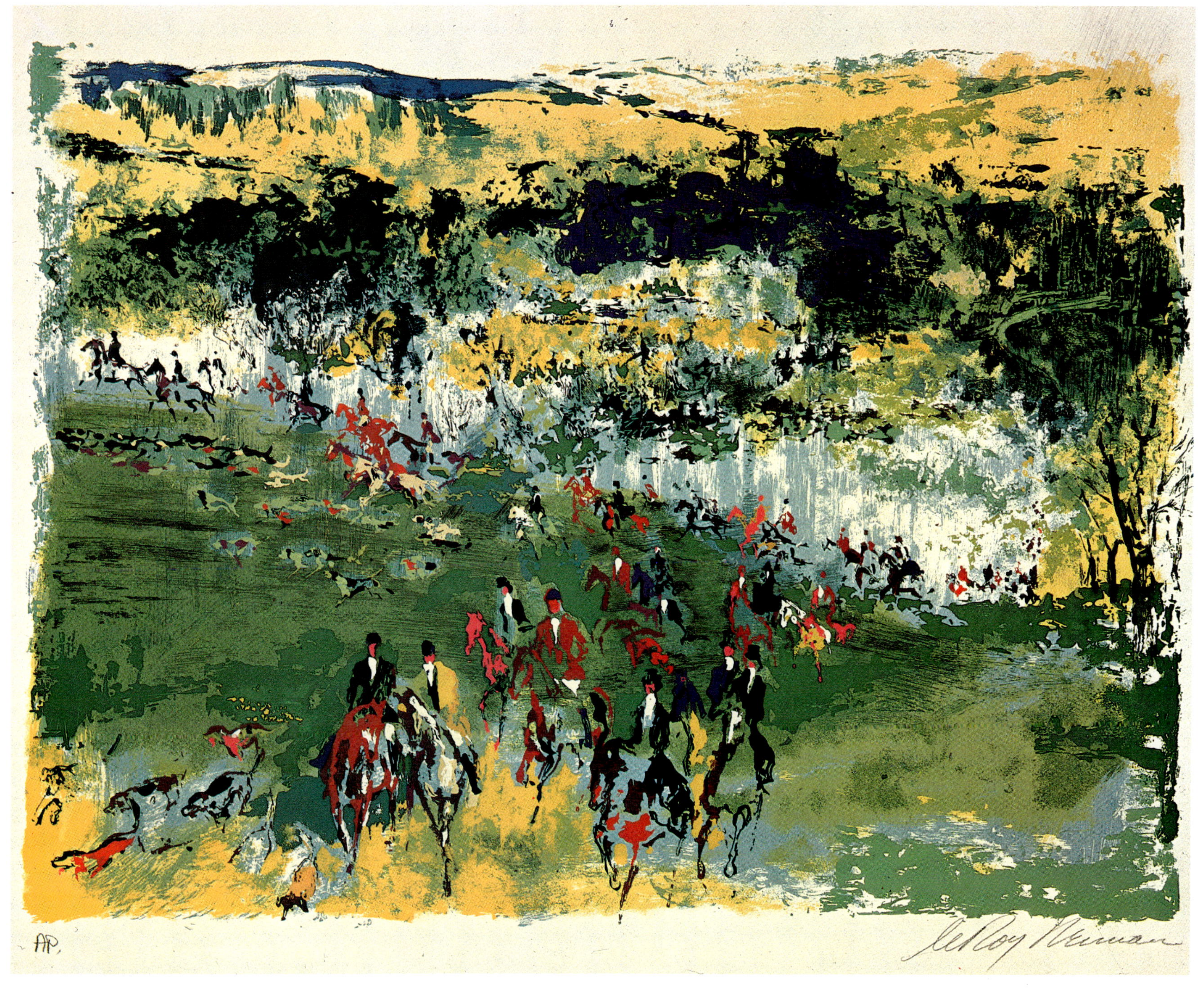

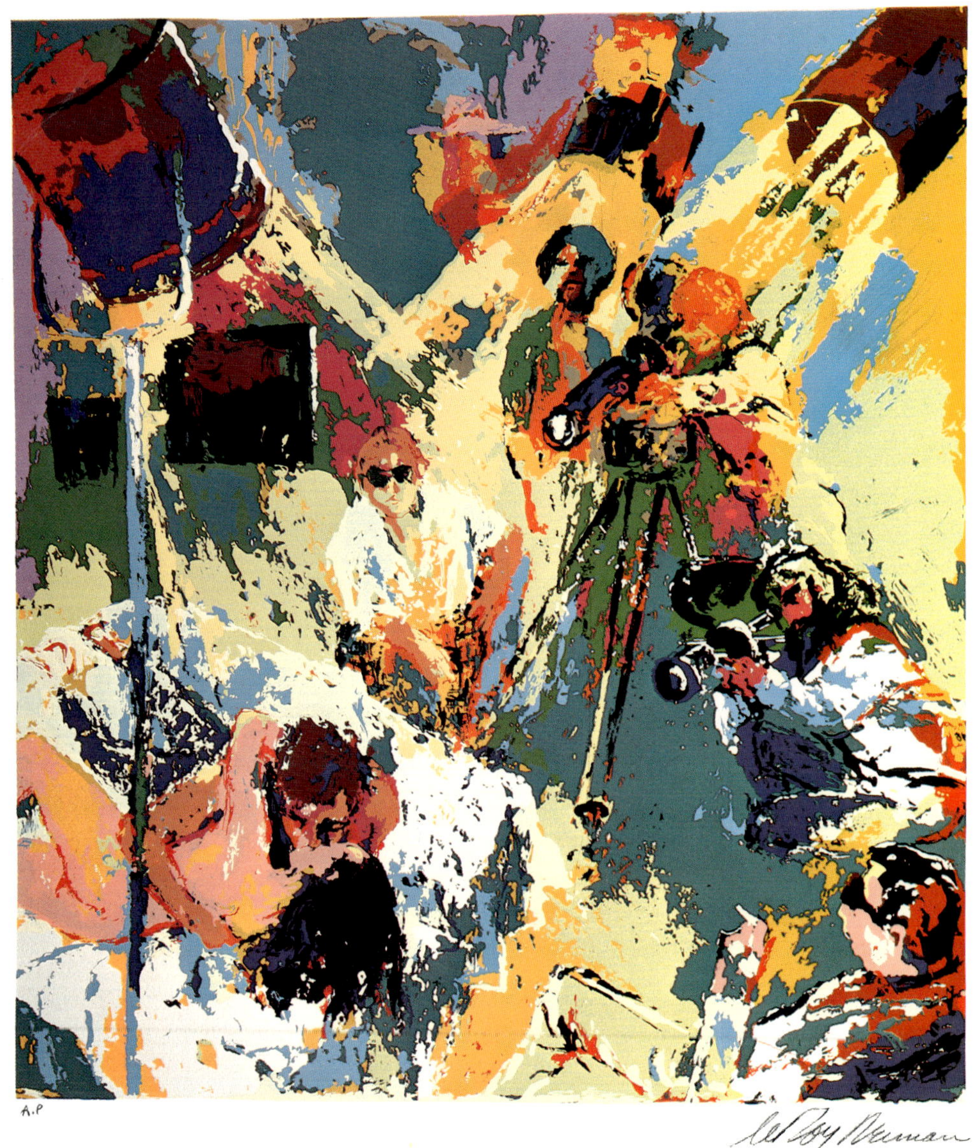

83 X Rated Filmmakers

1974
Serigraph
23 x 20 (58.42 x 50.8 cm)
A limited edition of 300, signed and numbered
by the artist.

84 Red Corrida

1974
Serigraph
18½ x 22½ (46.99 x 57.15 cm)
A limited edition of 300, signed and numbered
by the artist.

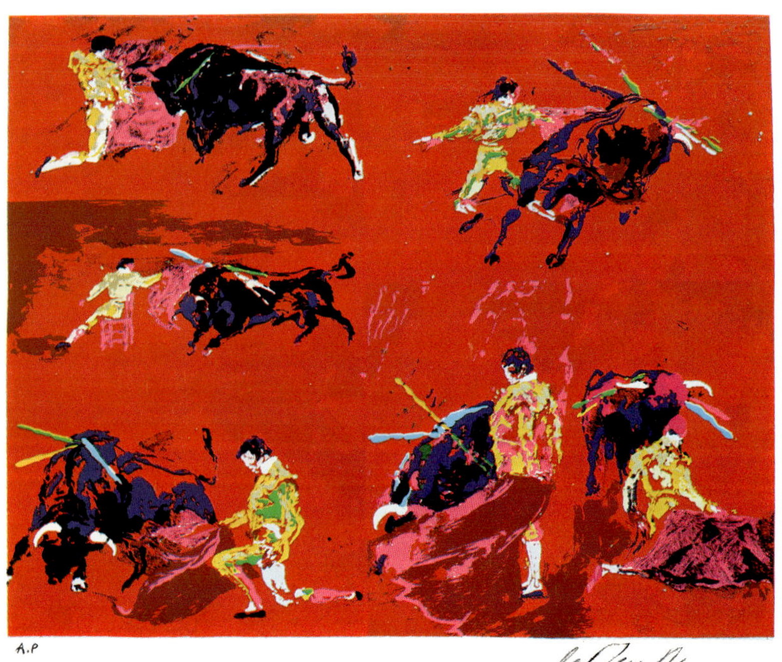

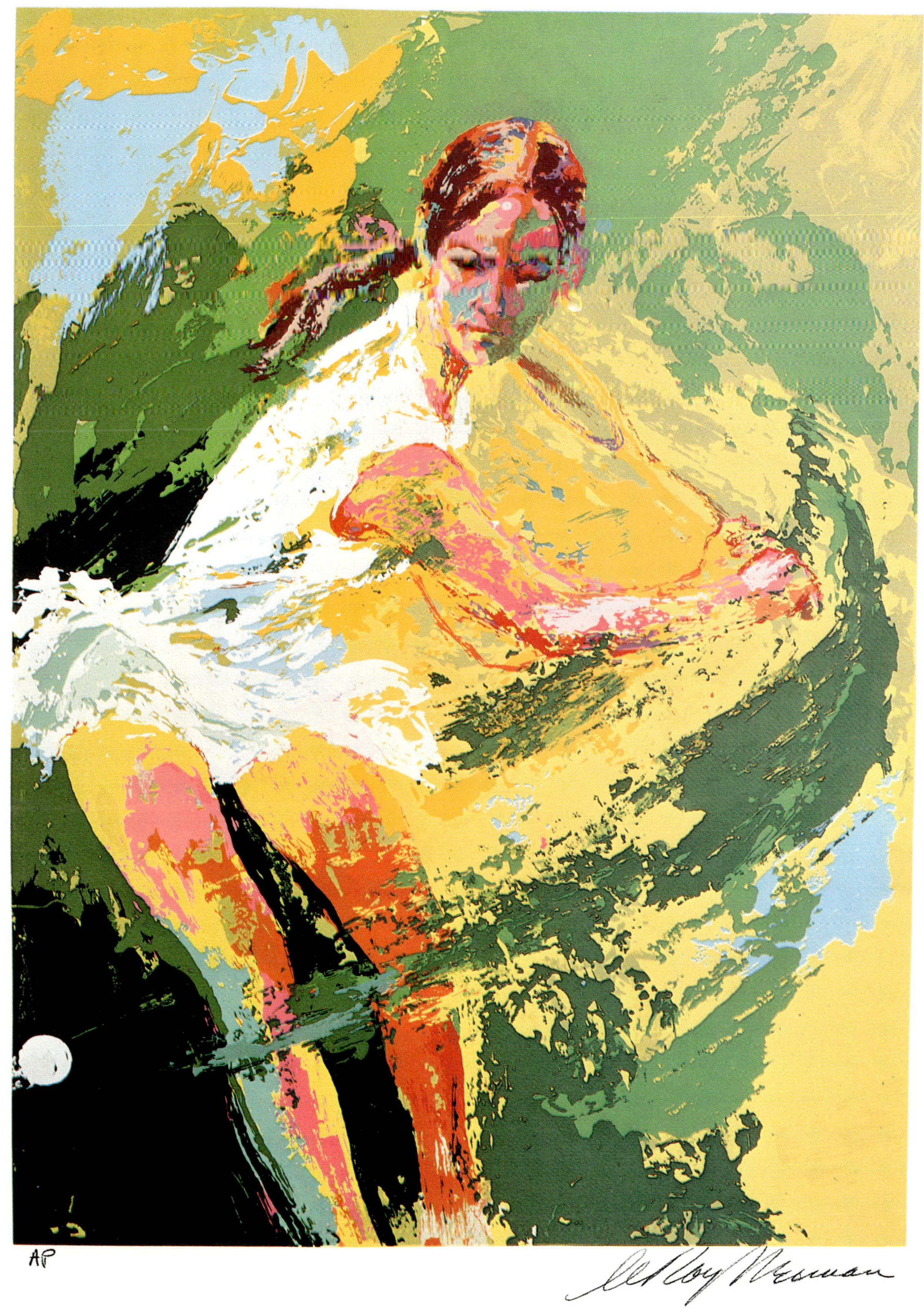

85   Back hand
(Chris Evert)
1974.
Serigraph
24 x 17½ (60.96 x 44.45 cm)

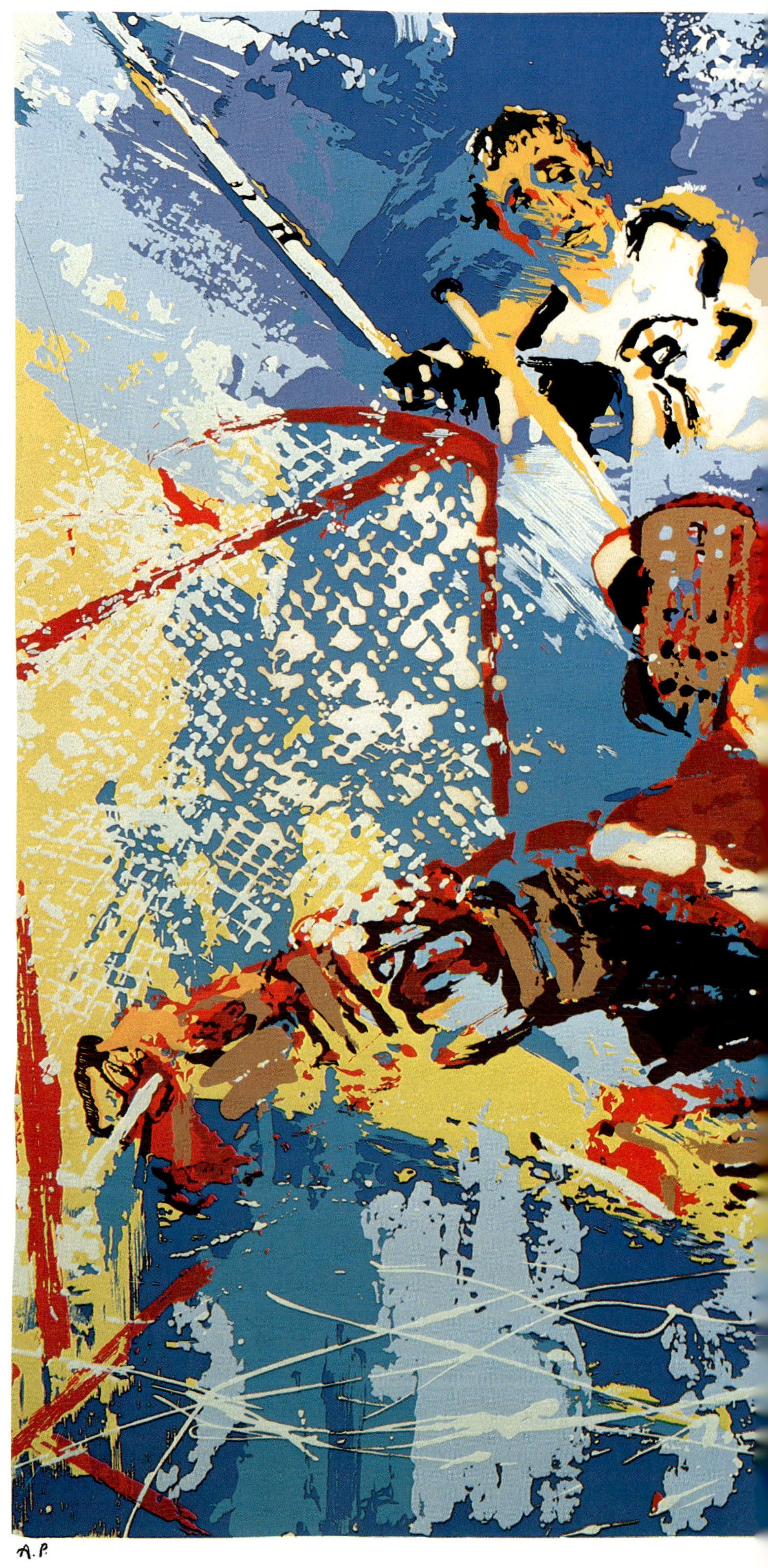

86 Philadelphia Flyers
    (Boston Bruins)
1974
Serigraph
25 x 37½ (63.5 x 95.25 cm)
A limited edition of 300 signed
and numbered by the artist.

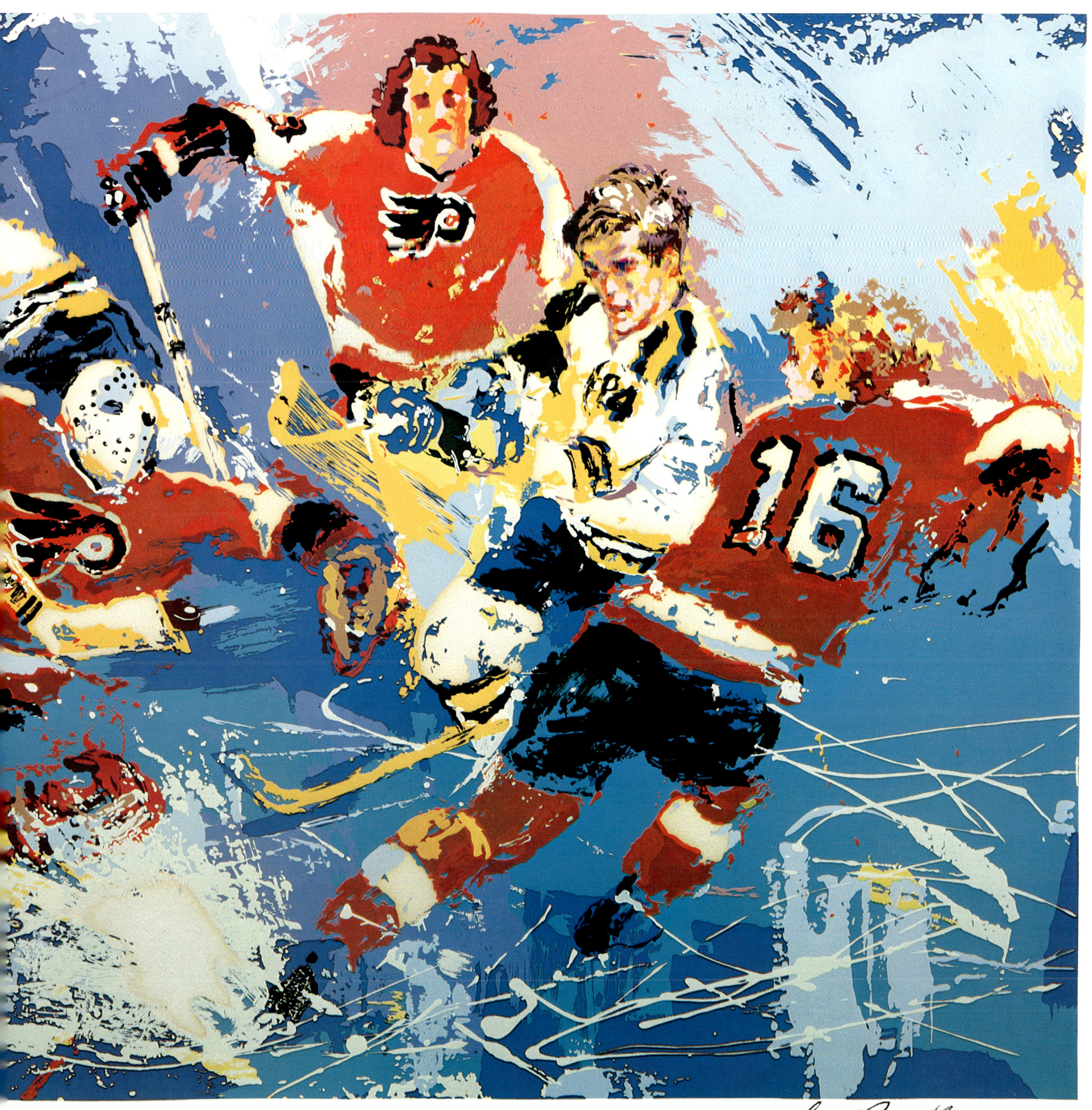

LeRoy Neiman

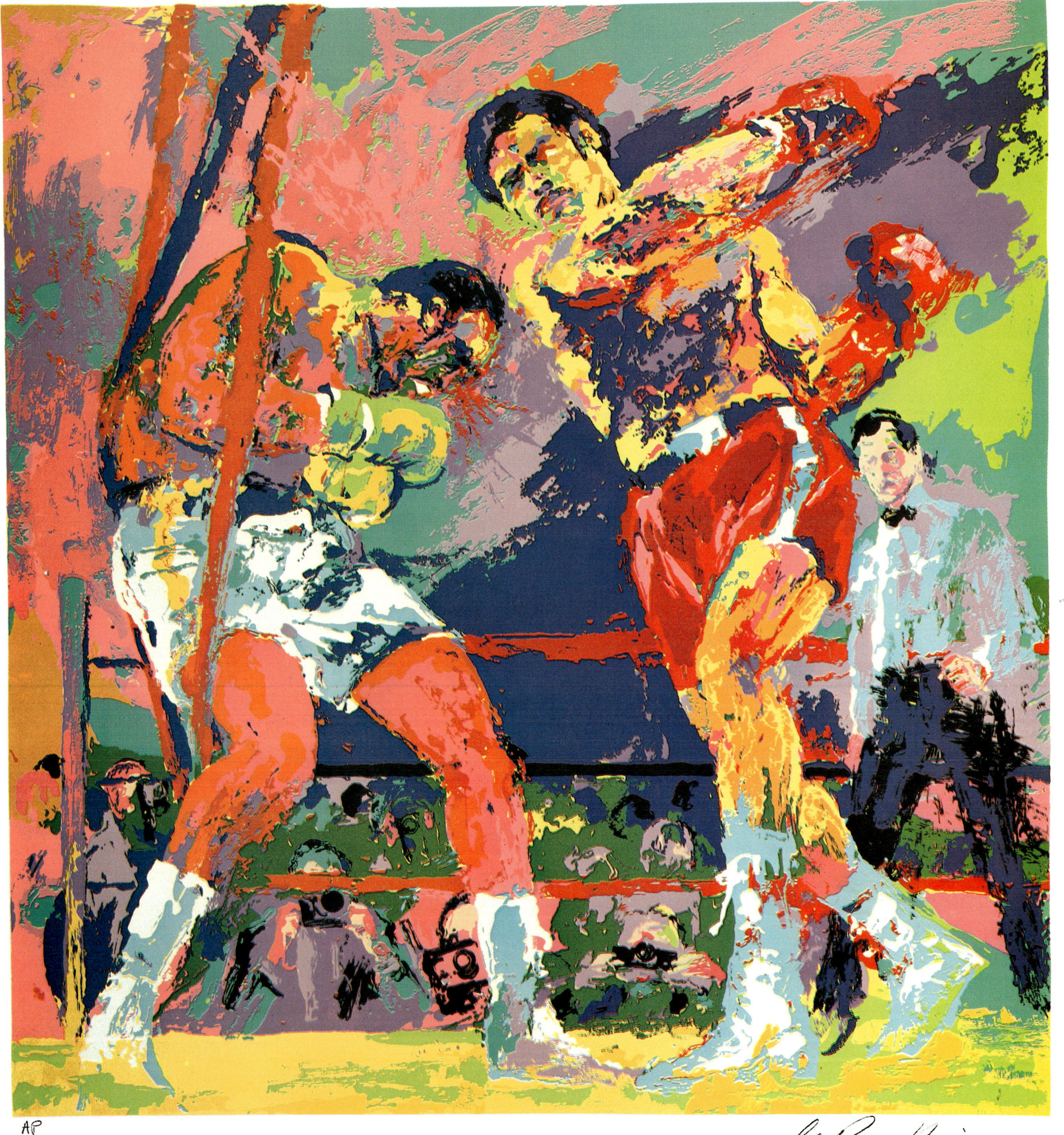

AP

87   Frazier-Forman—Jamaica

1974
Serigraph
21¾ x 20¼ (55.24 x 51.43 cm)
A limited edition of 300, signed and numbered by the artist.

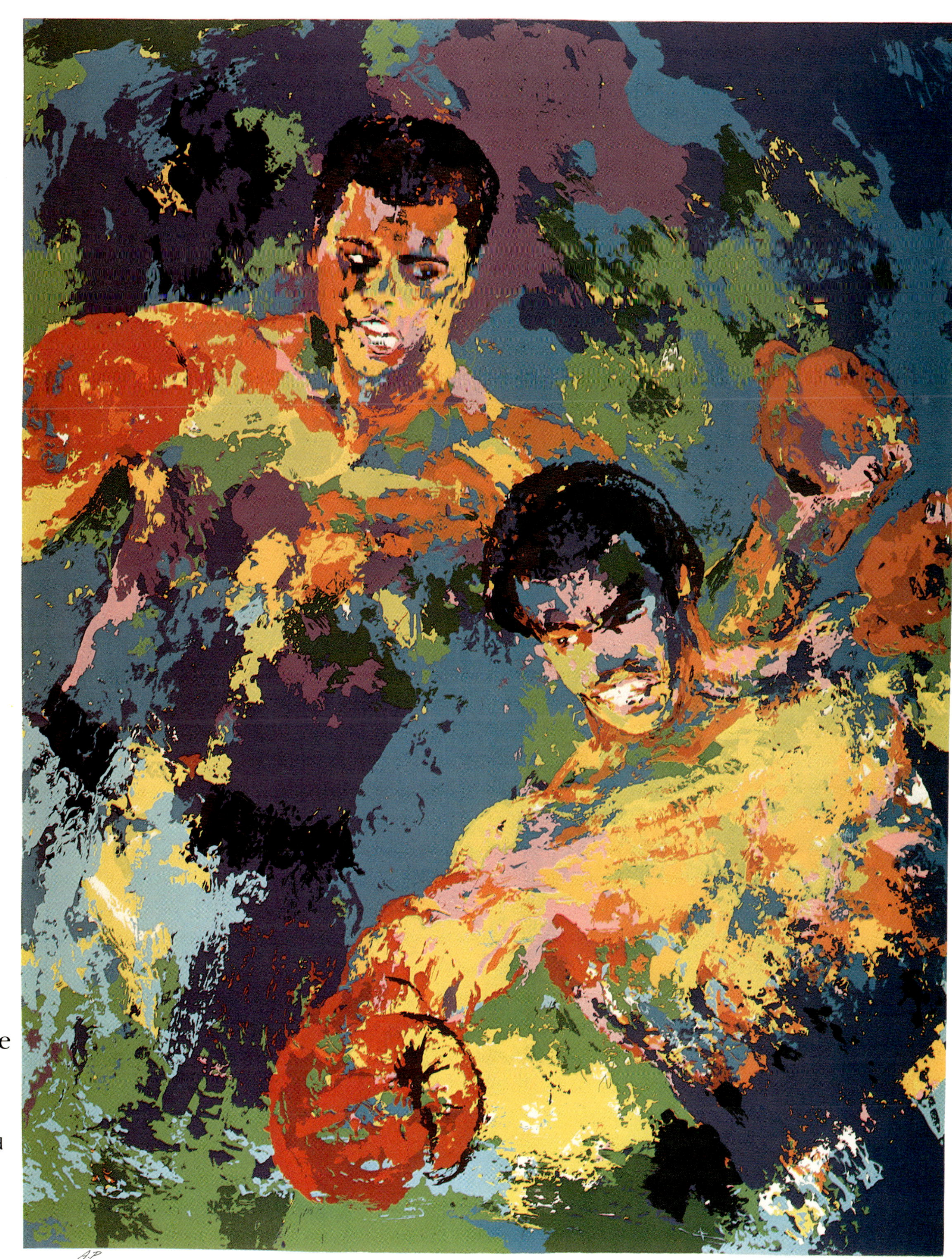

88 Ali-Forman—Zaire
1974
Serigraph
33 x 24⅞ (83.82 x 63.18 cm)
A limited edition of 300, signed and
numbered by the artist.

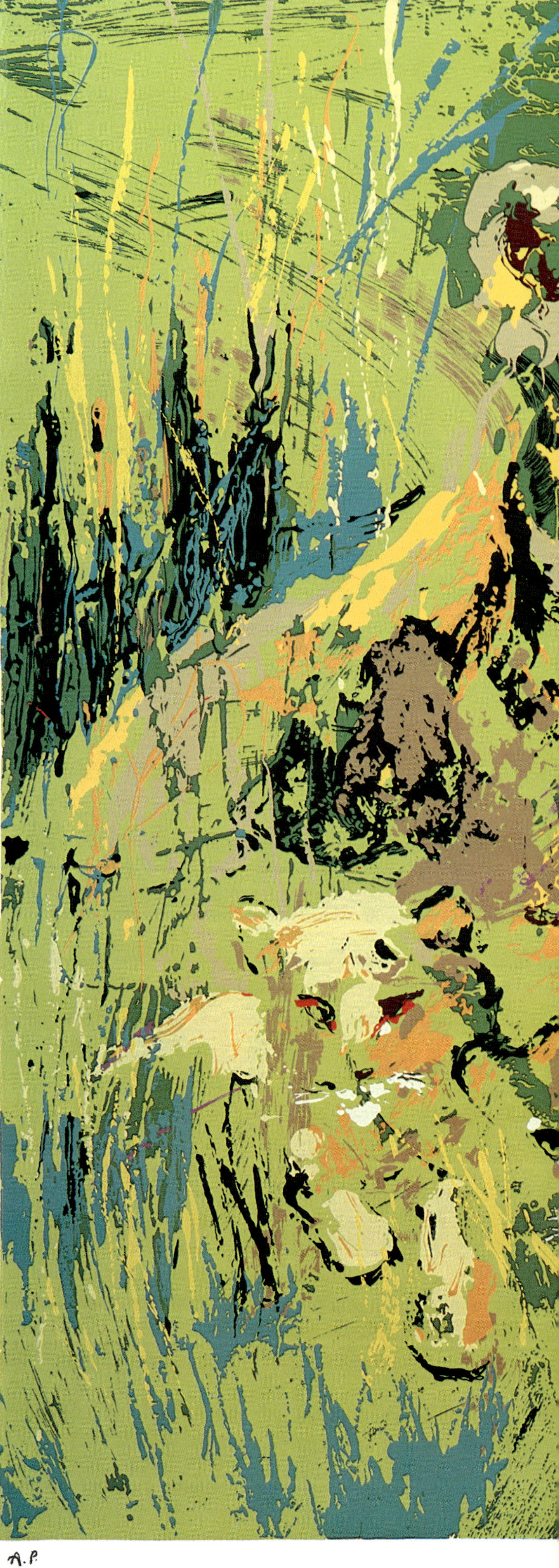

89 Lion Family
1974
Serigraph
29½ x 36⅞ (74.93 x 93.66 cm)
A limited edition of 300, signed and numbered
by the artist.

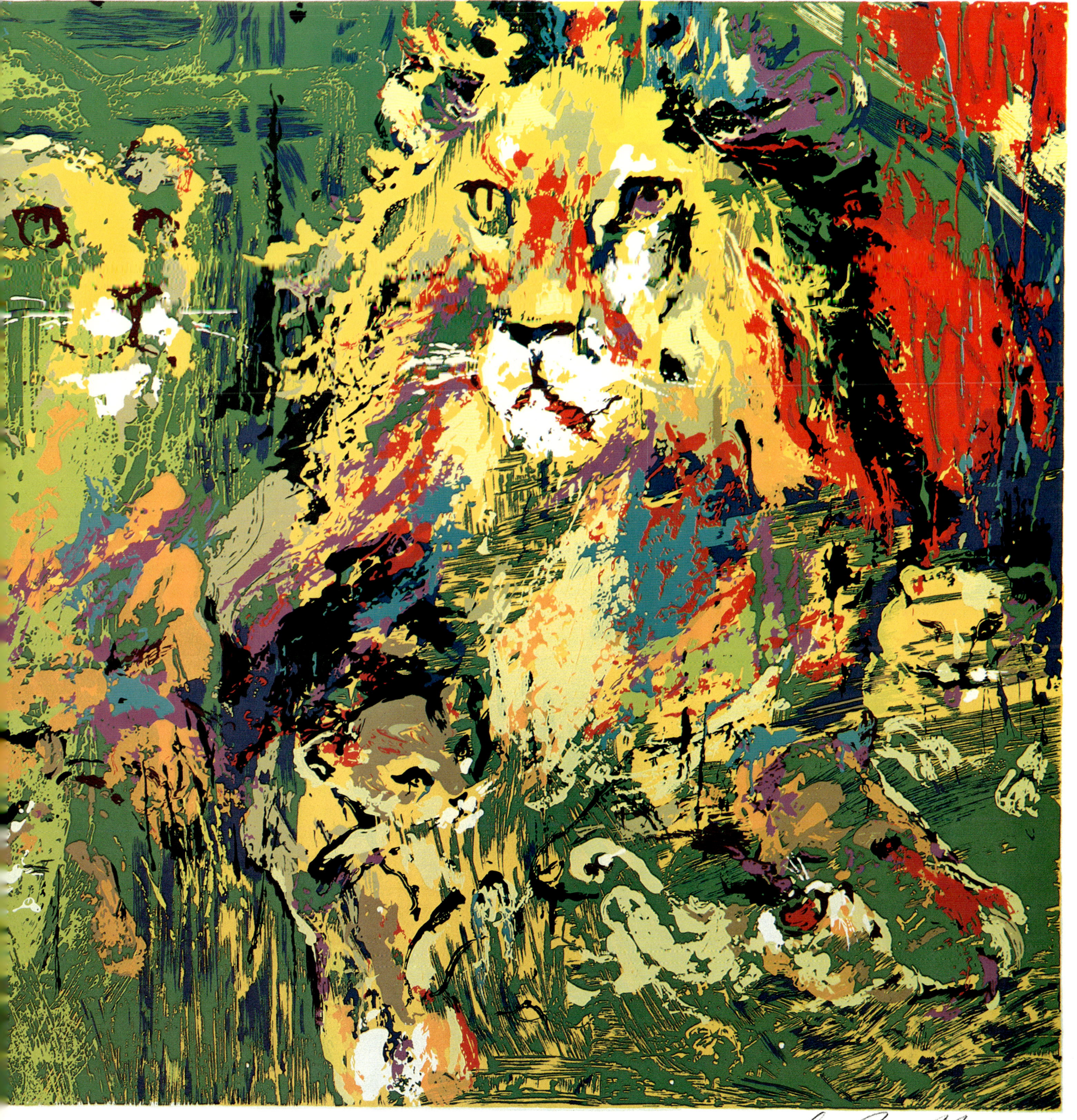

90 Sax Man

1974
Serigraph
31⅞ x 28 (80.96 x 71.12 cm)
A limited edition of 300, signed and numbered
by the artist.

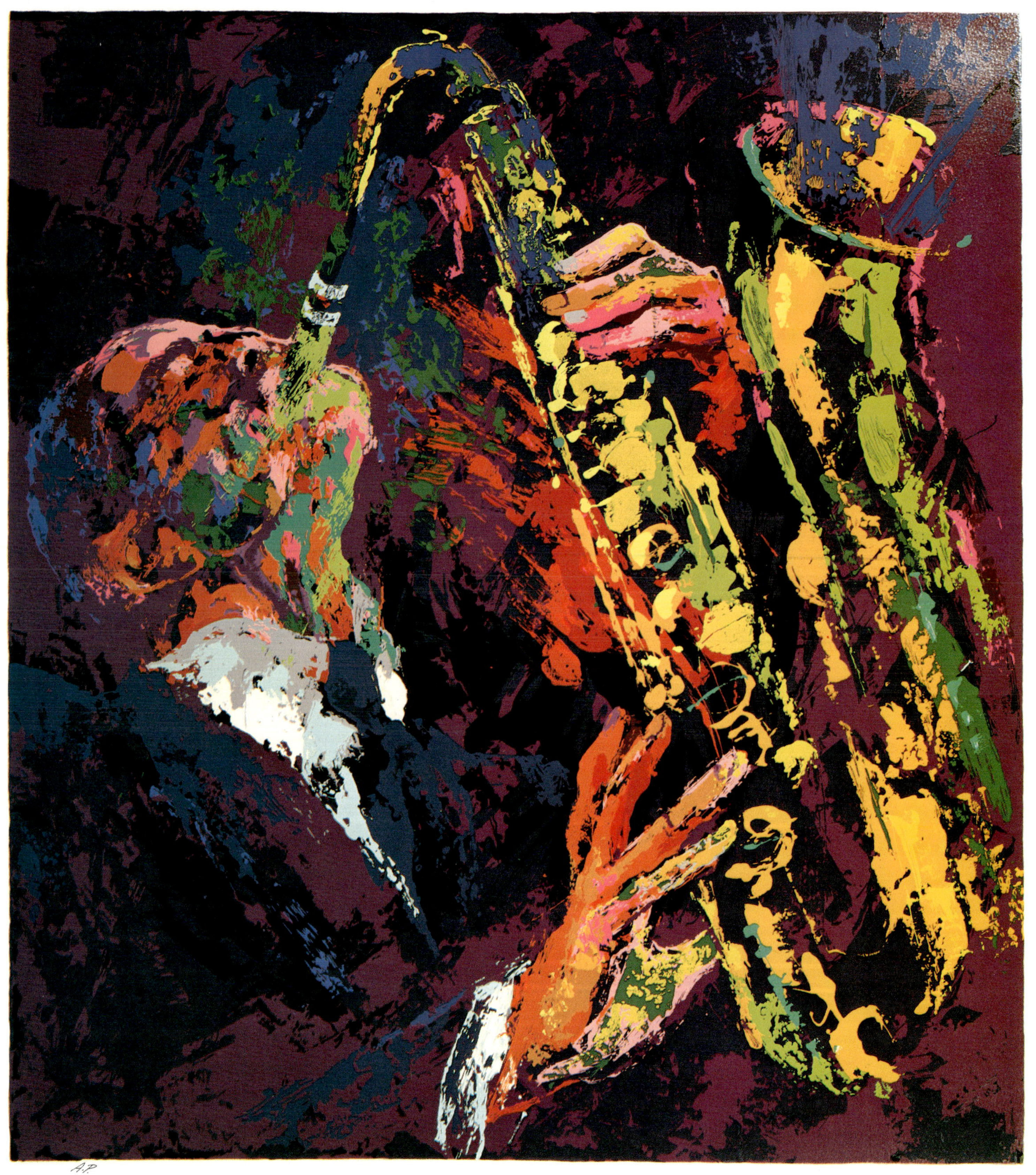

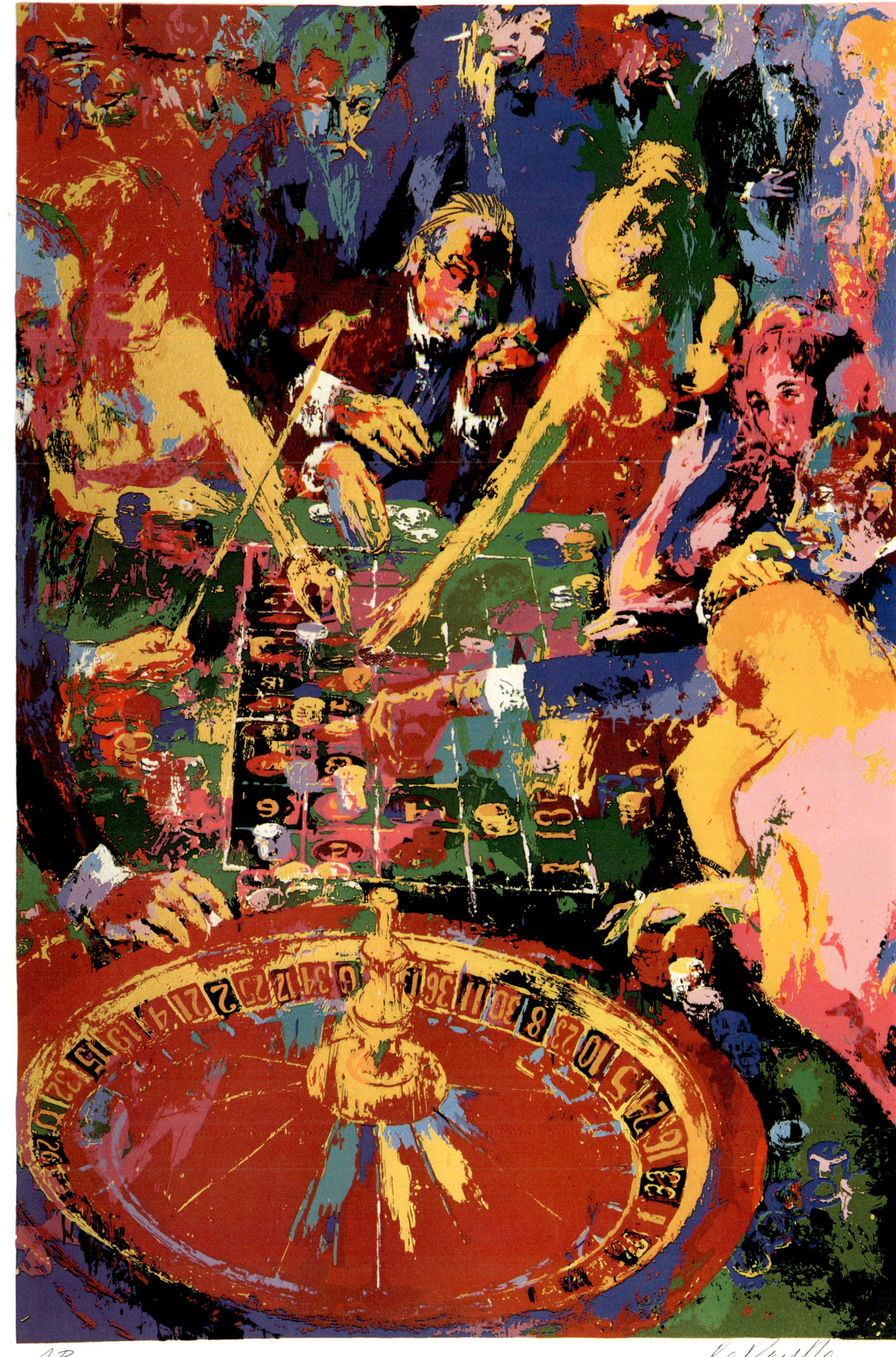

91   The Green Table

1974
Serigraph
39¾ x 26⅛ (100.97 x 66.36)
A limited edition of 300, signed
and numbered by the artist.

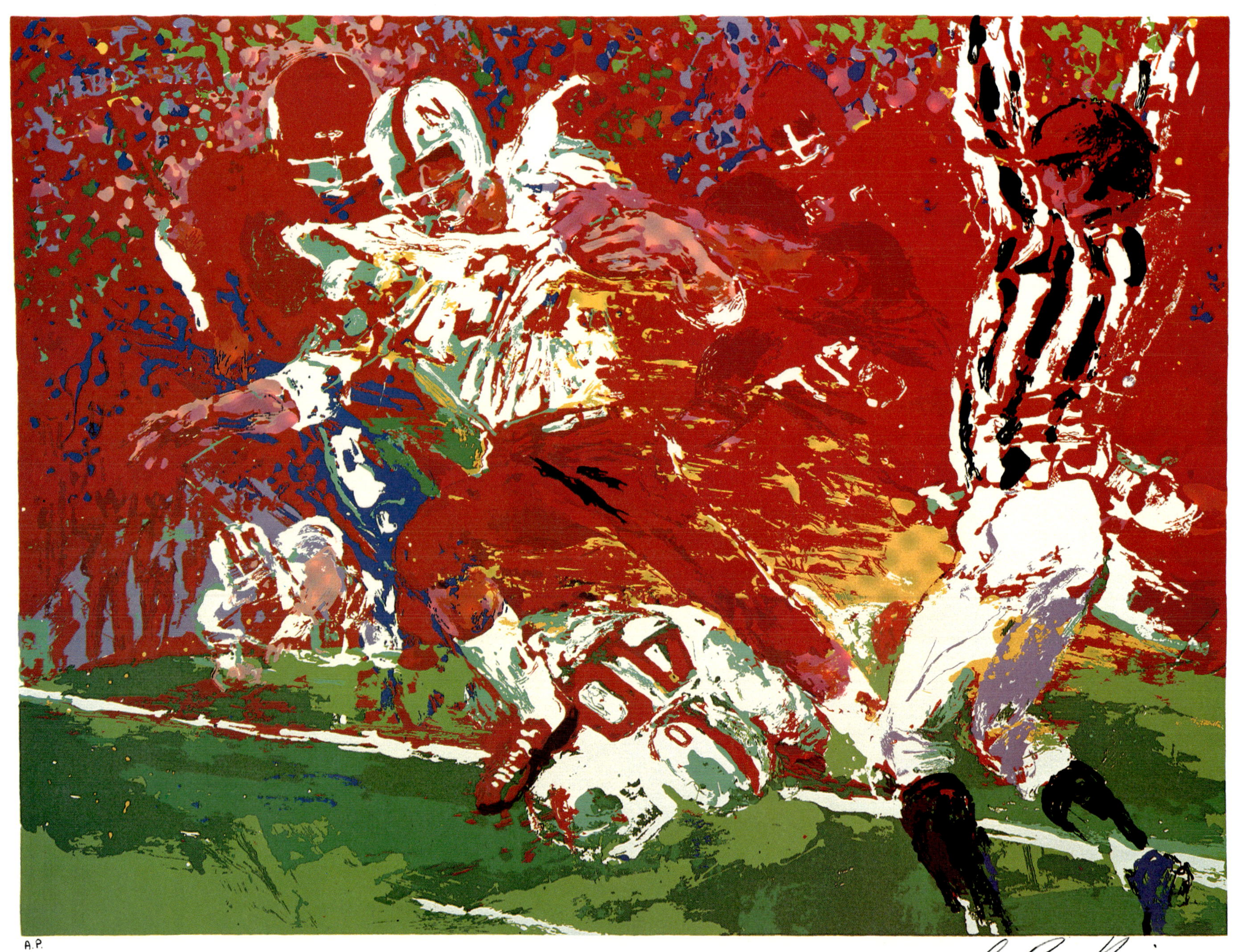

92   Game of the Century
1974
Serigraph
20 x 26 (50.80 x 66.04 cm)

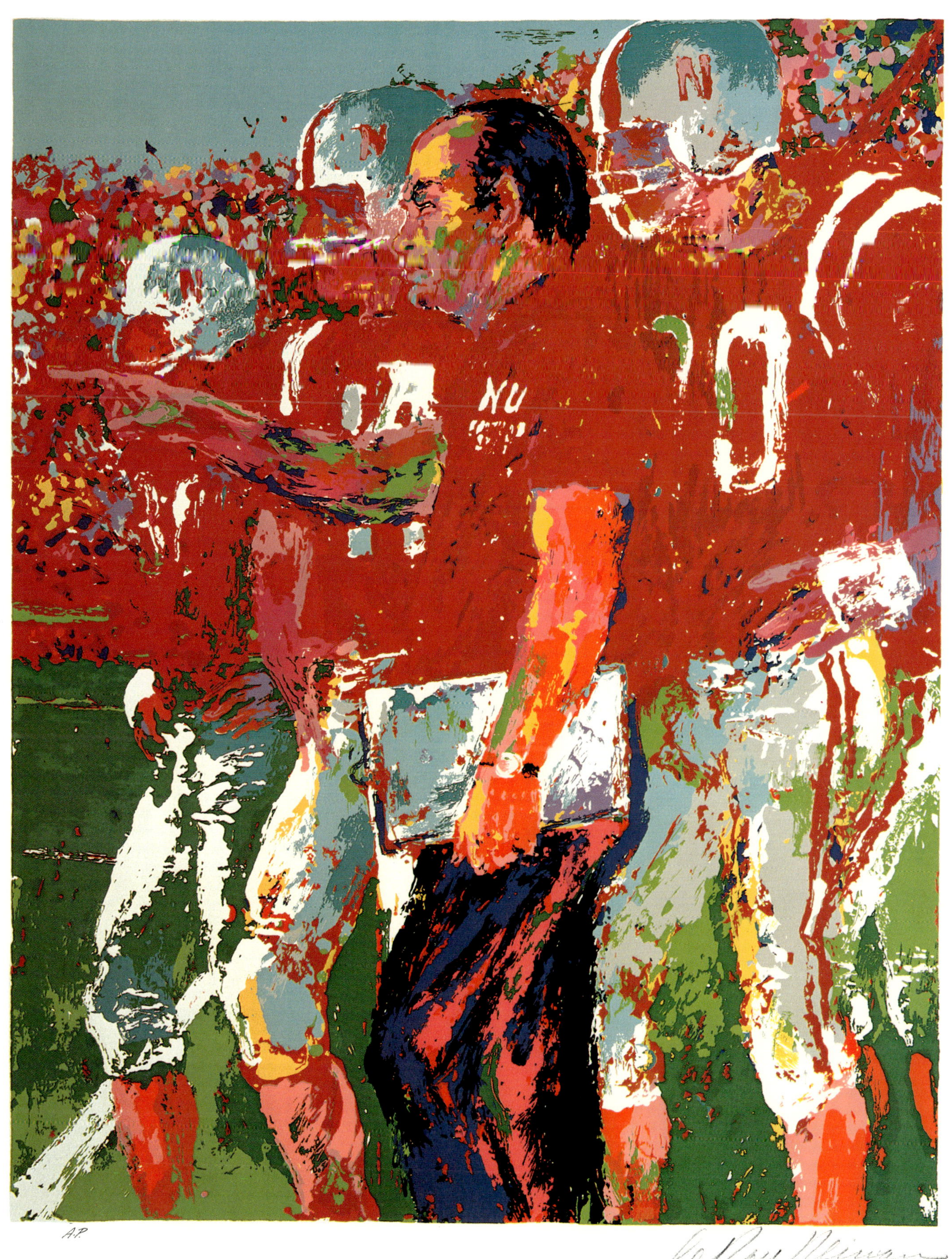

93 Coach Devany

1974
Serigraph
26 x 20 (66.04 x 50.8 cm)

NEBRASKA SUITE

A limited edition of 300, signed and numbered
by the artist.

94   Black Shirts
1974
Serigraph
20 x 26 (50.80 x 66.04 cm)

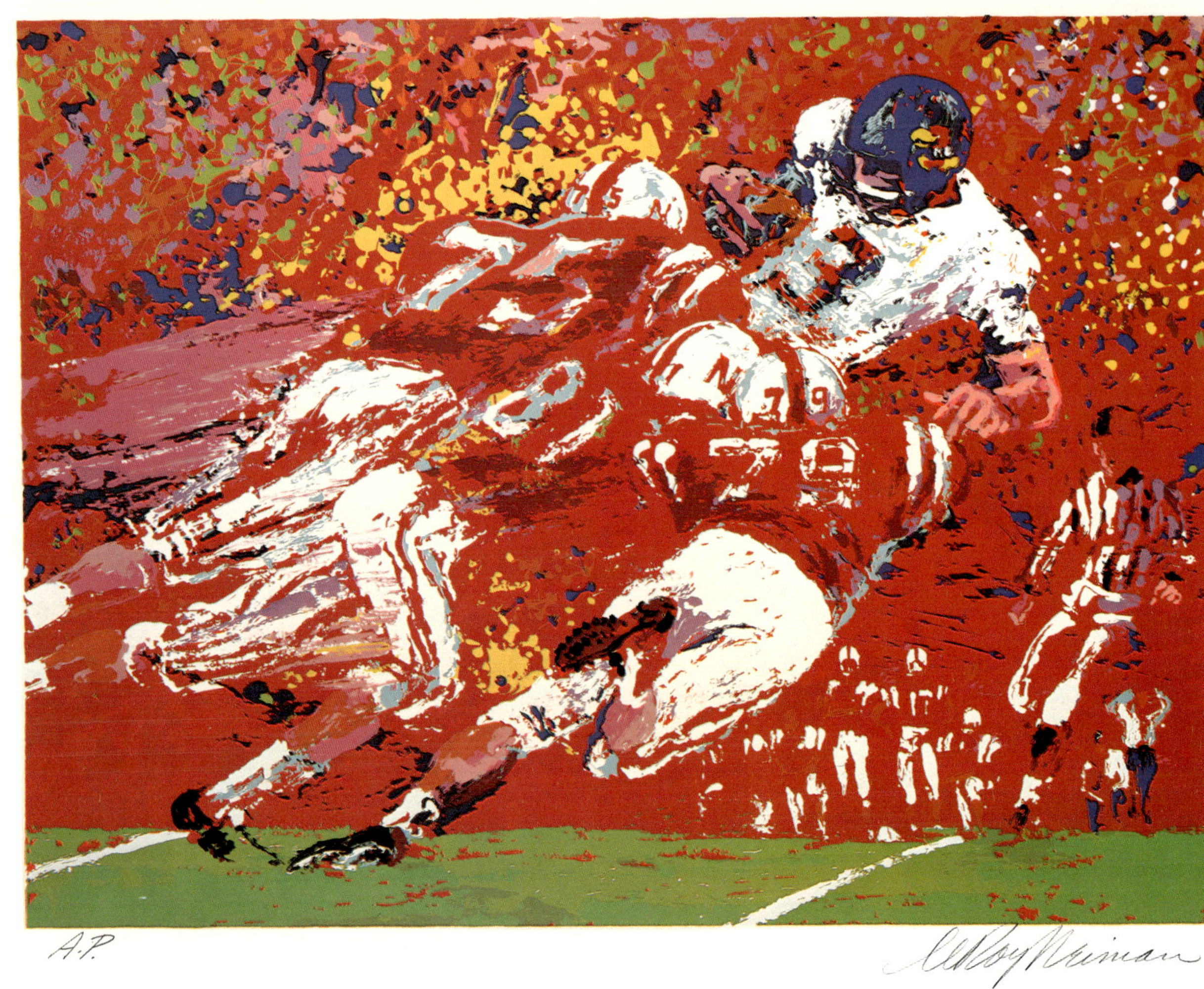

95   National Champions
1974
Serigraph
20 x 26 (50.8 x 66.04 cm)

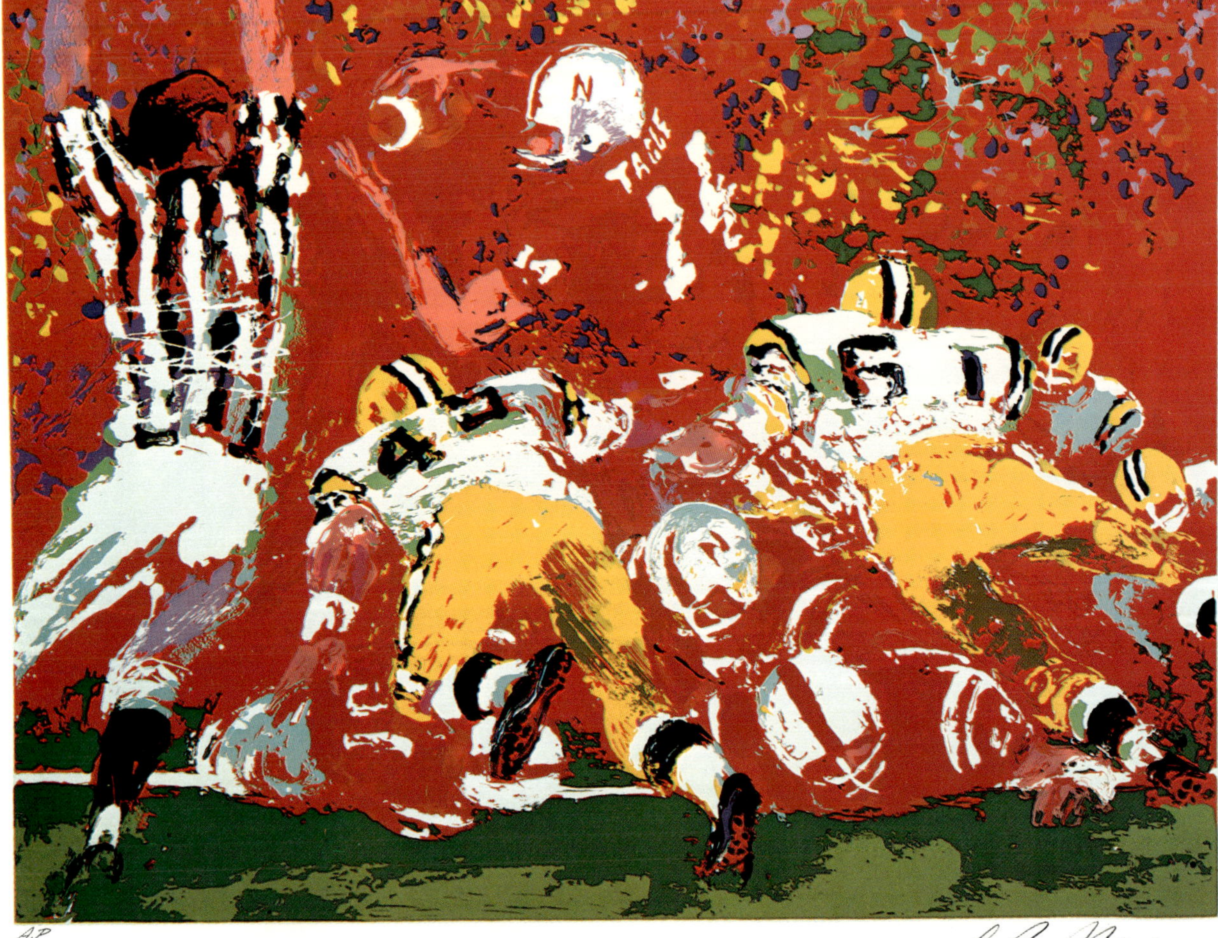

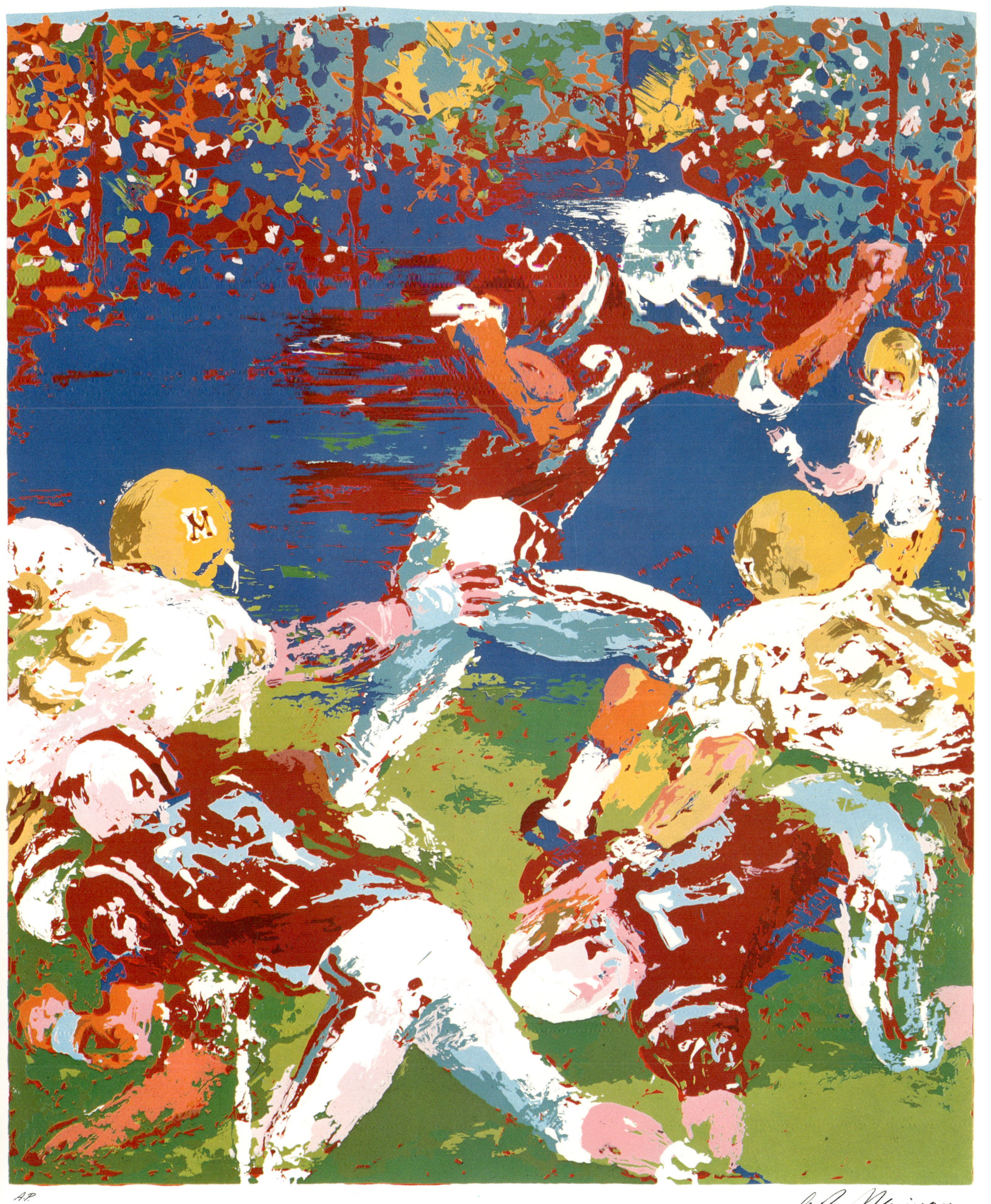

96 Breakaway
1974
Serigraph
26 x 20 (66.04 x 50.8 cm)

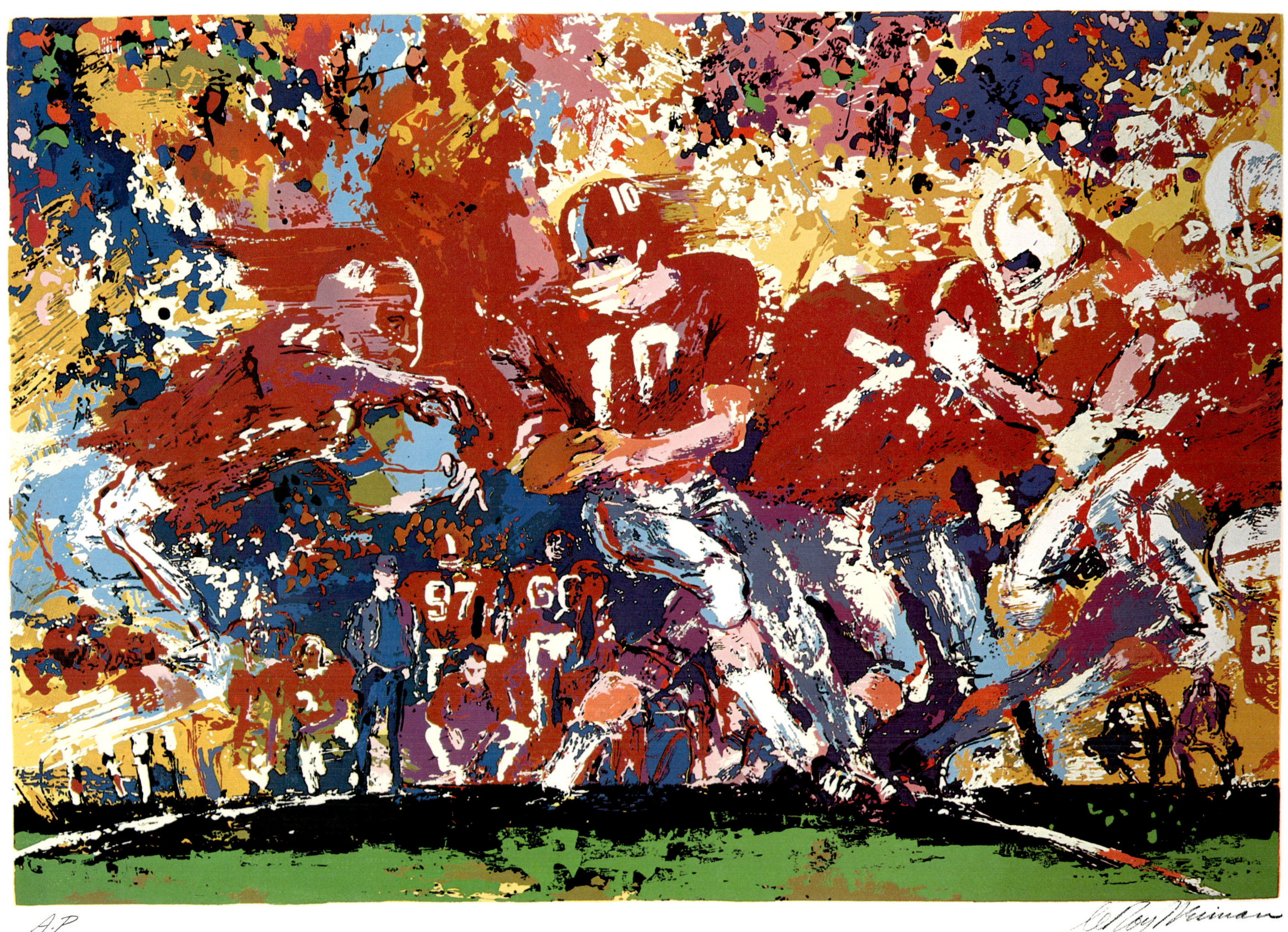

97 Alabama Hand Off

1974
Serigraph
26 x 37 (66.04 x 93.98 cm)
A limited edition of 300, signed and numbered
by the artist.

98 Rushing Back

1974
Serigraph
26⅛ x 39⅛ (66.36 x 99.38 cm)
A limited edition of 300, signed and numbered
by the artist.

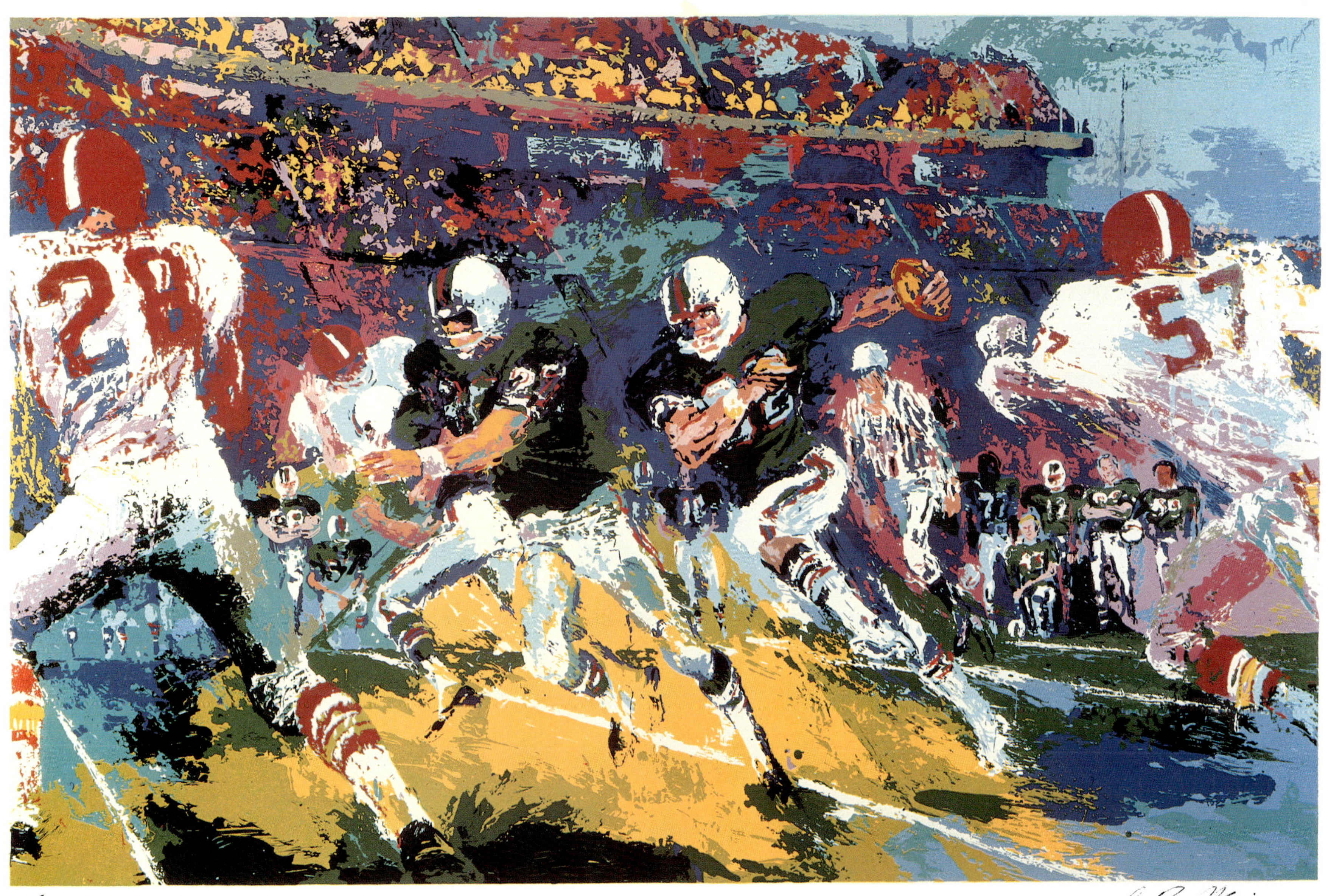

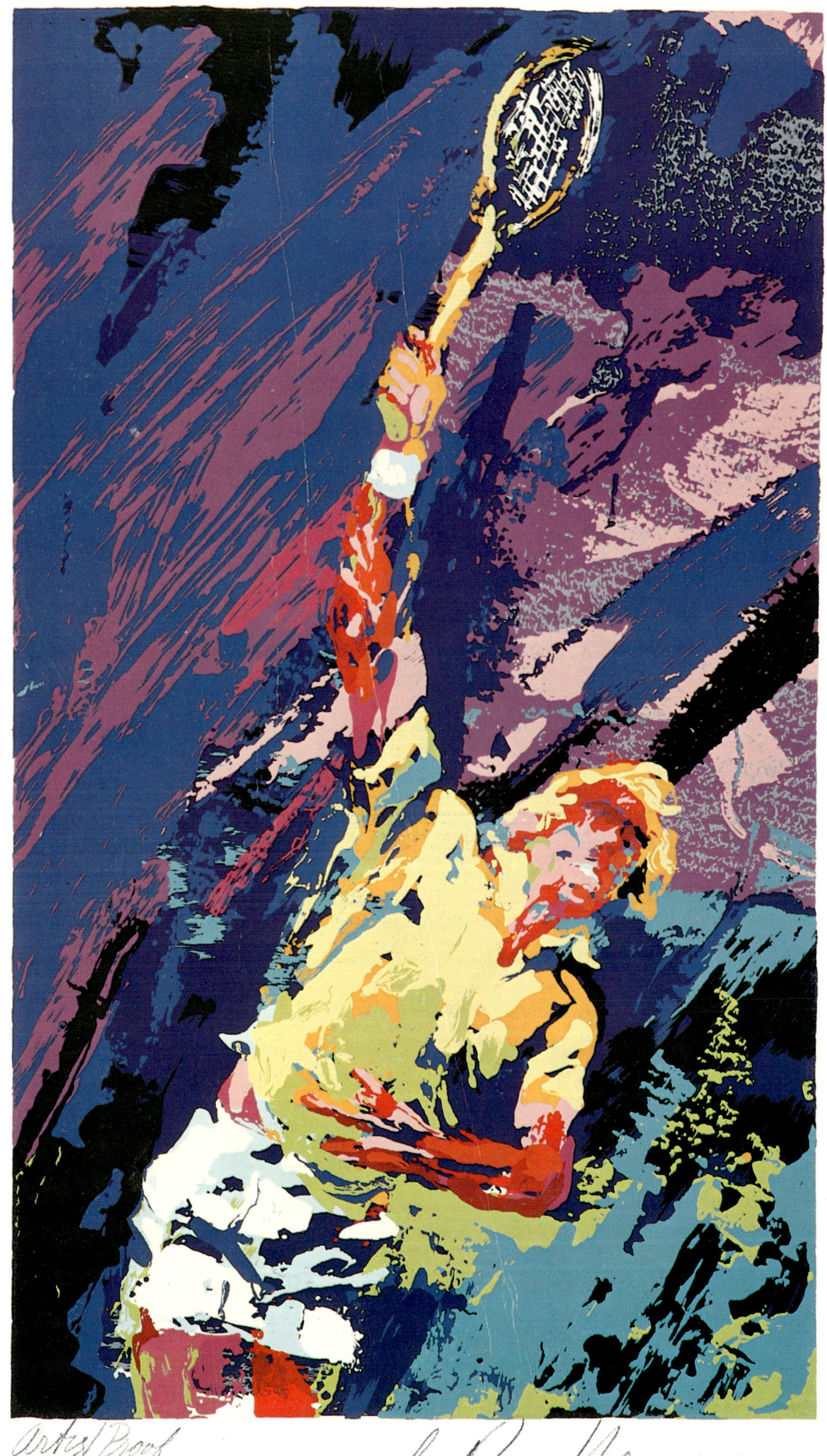

99 Classic Serve

1974
Serigraph
13¾ x 7⅞ (34.92 x 20. cm)
A limited edition of 300, signed and numbered by the artist.

1974
Serigraph
24 x 36 (60.96 x 91.44 cm)
A limited edition of 300, signed and numbered
by the artist.

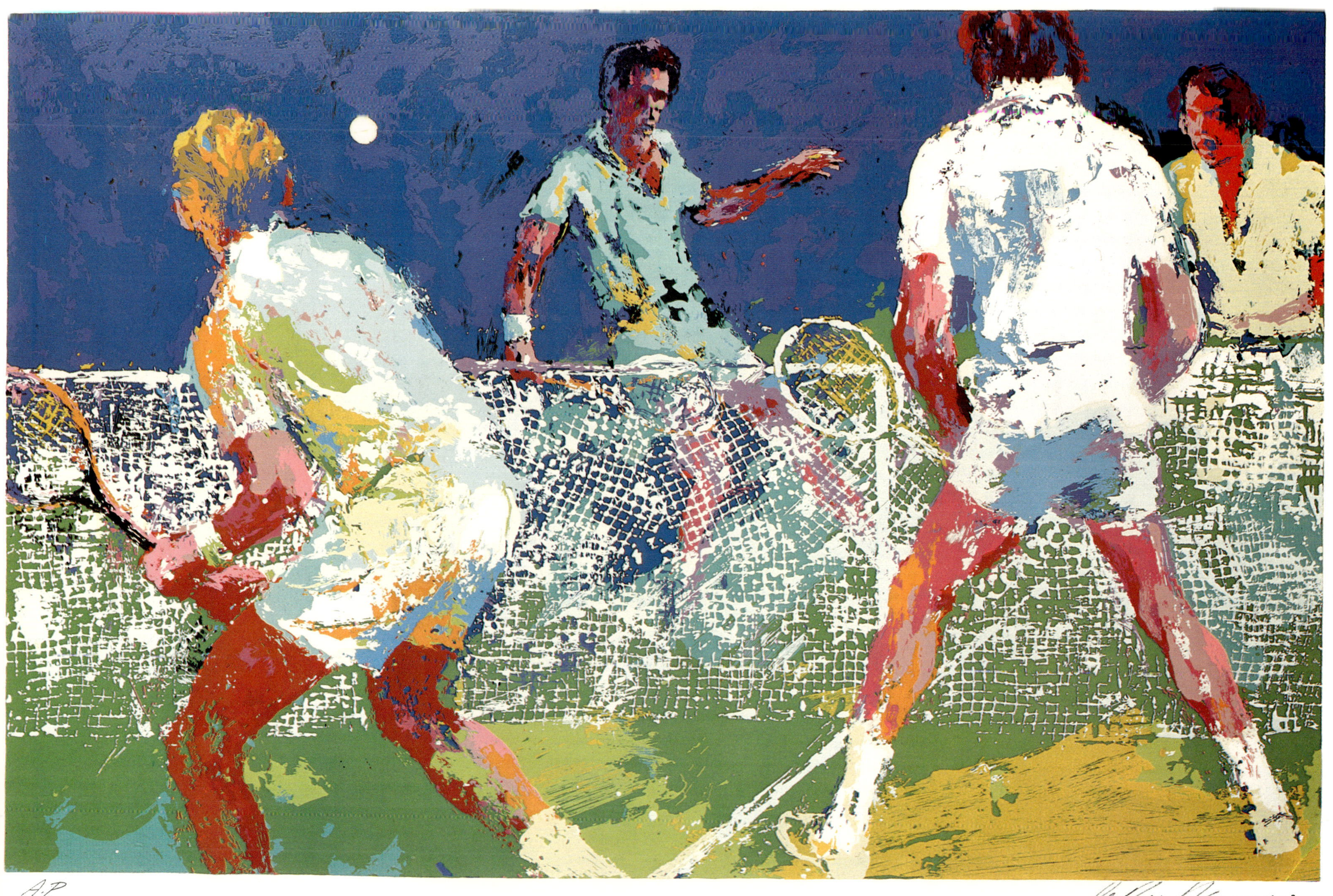

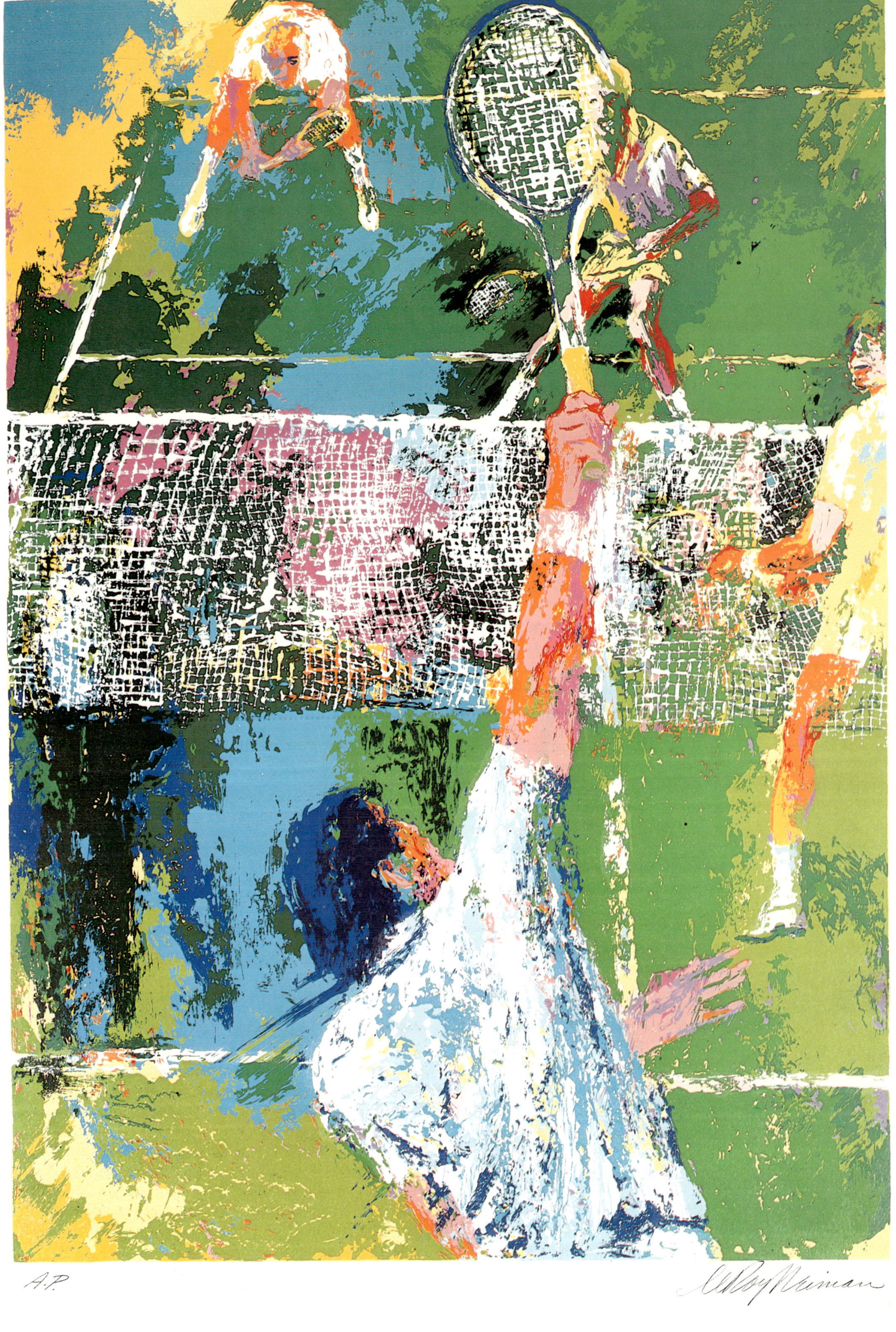

101 The Racketeers

1974
Serigraph
40⅛ x 28 (101.92 x 71.12 cm)
A limited edition of 300, signed and numbered by the artist.

1974
Scrigraph
30½ x 43 (77.47 x 109.22 cm)
A limited edition of 300, signed and numbered
by the artist.

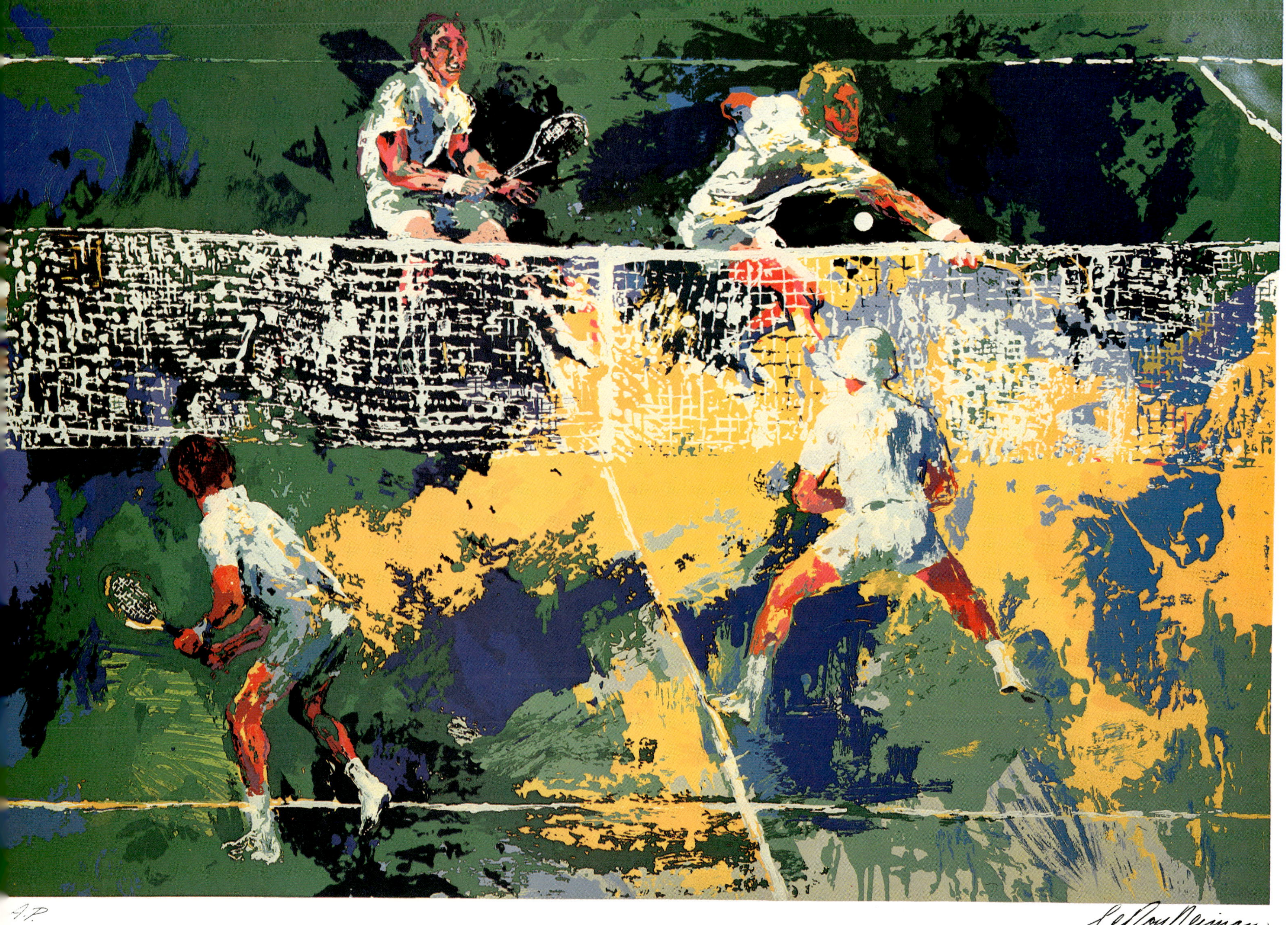

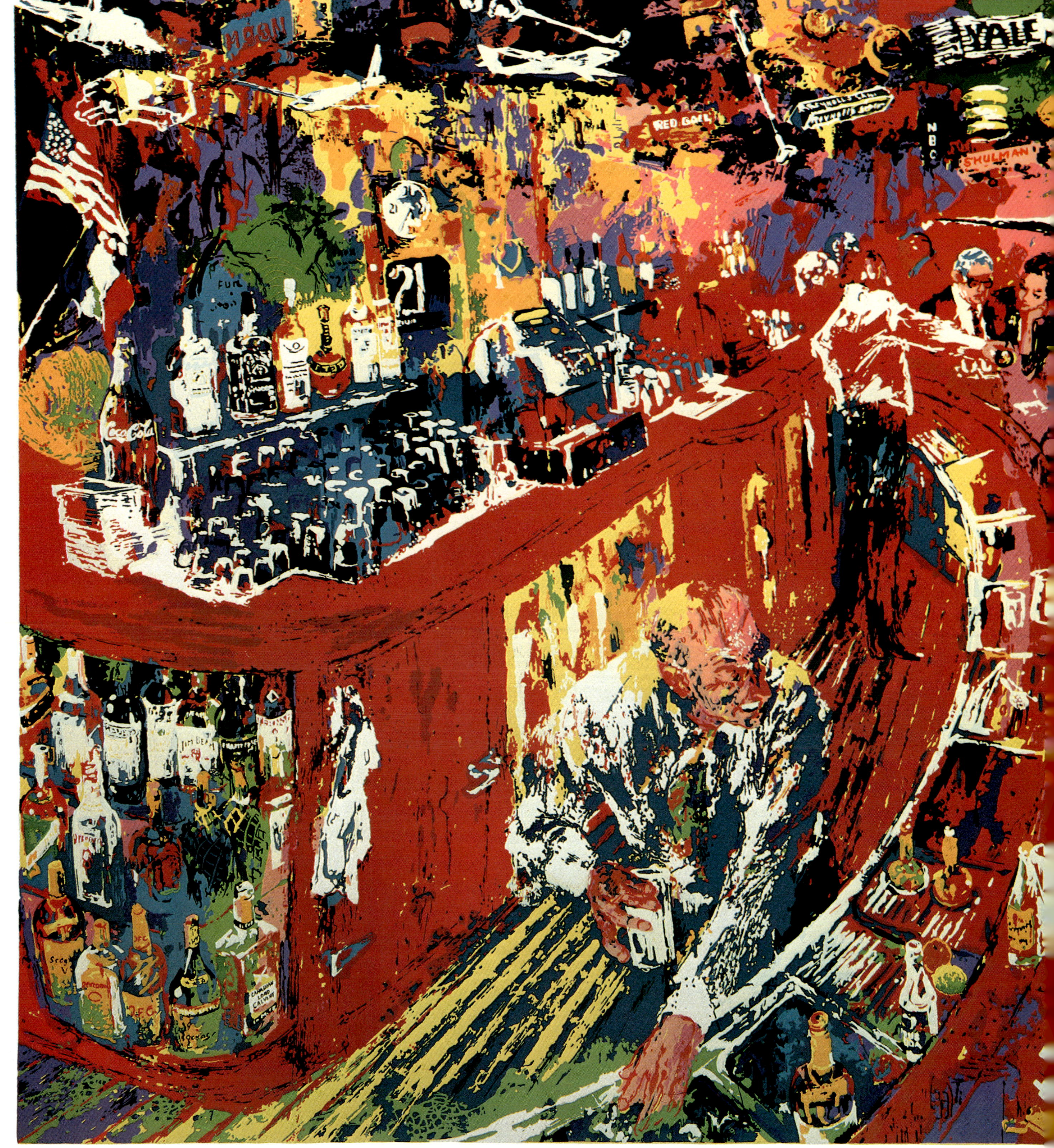

170

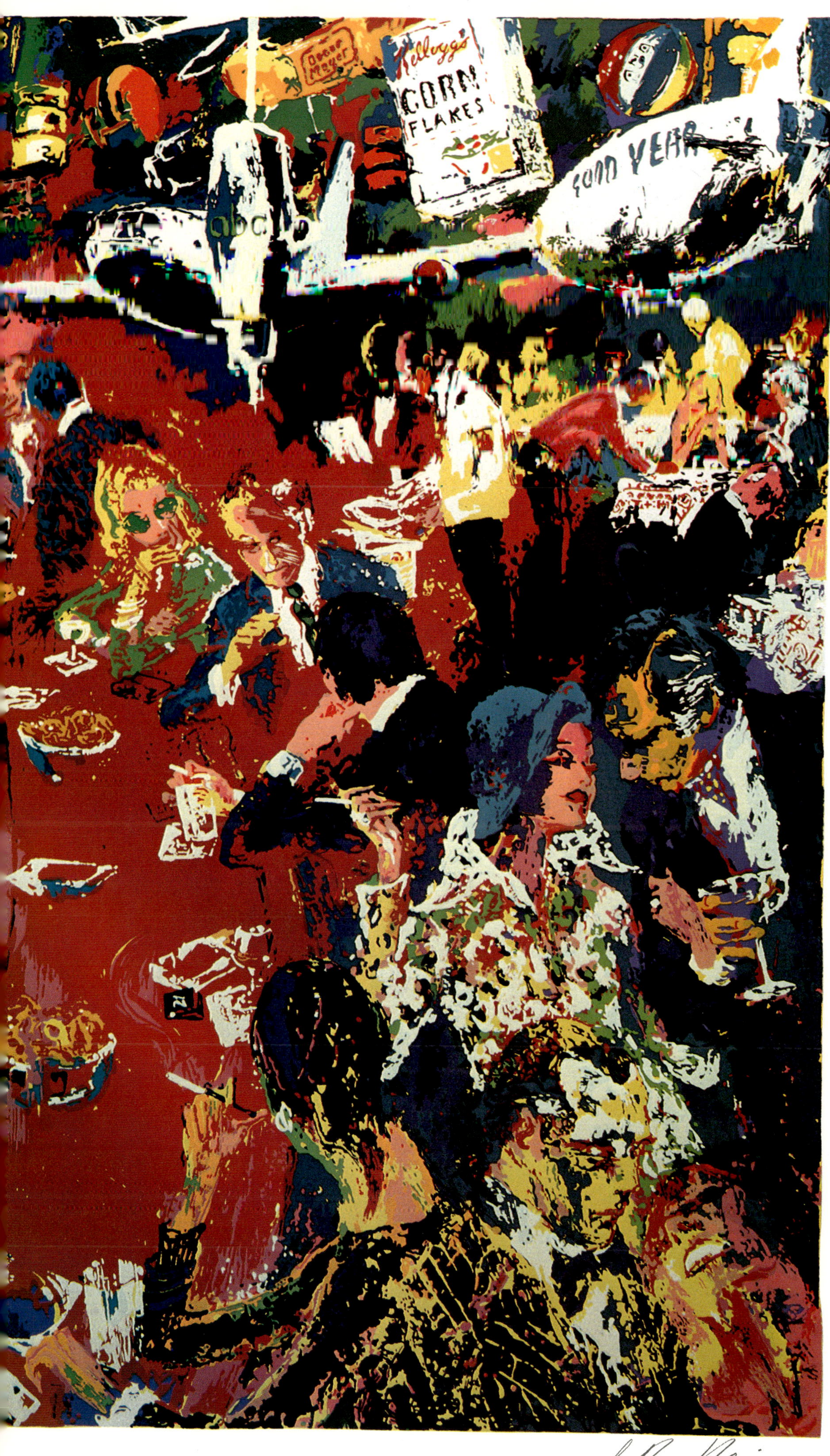

103   The Bar at "21"

1974
Serigraph
25⅞ x 39 (65.72 x 99.06 cm)
A limited edition of 300, signed and numbered
by the artist.

104   Downers

1974
Serigraph
24 x 38 (60.96 x 96.52 cm)
A limited edition of 300, signed and numbered
by the artist.

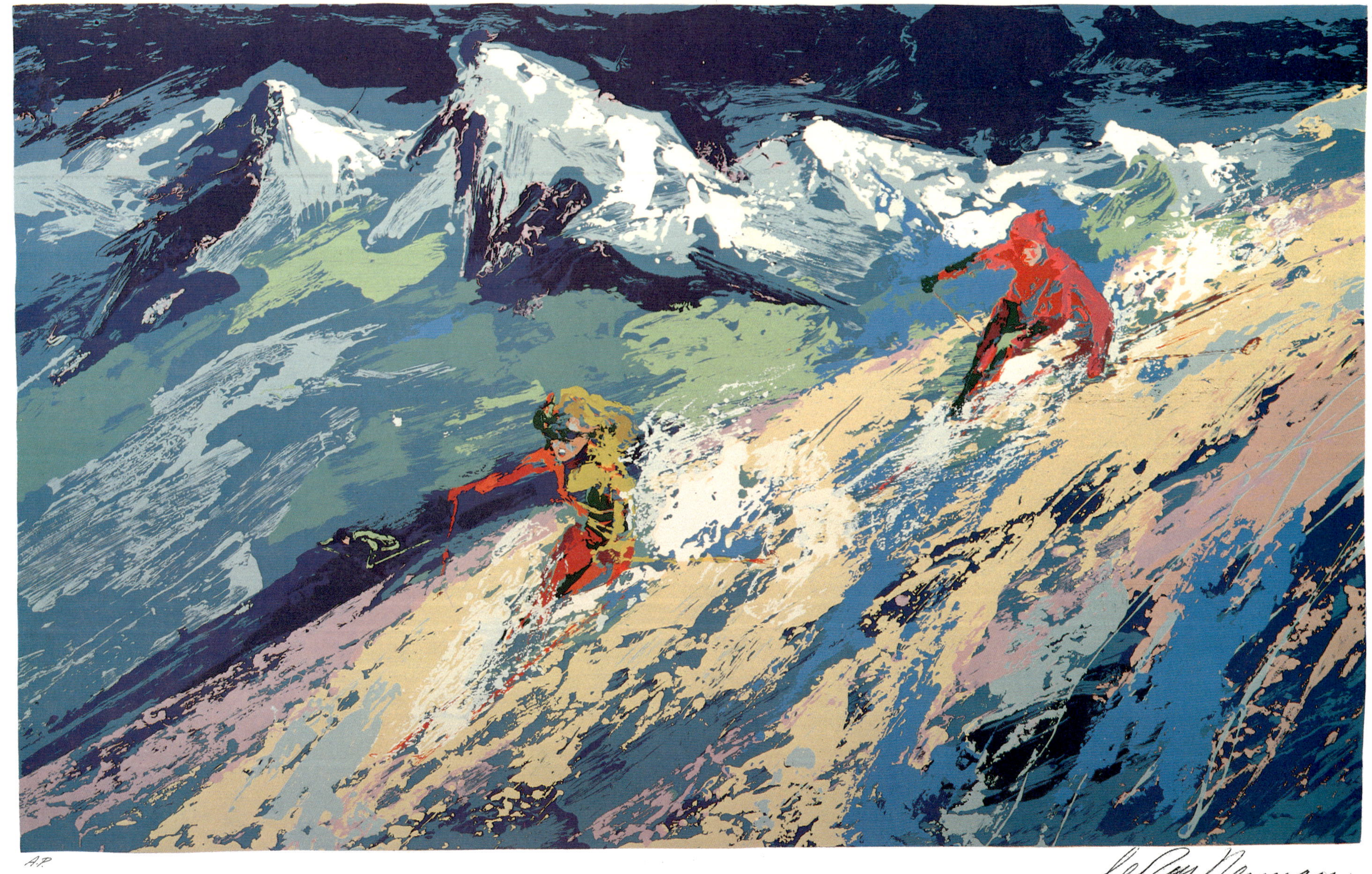

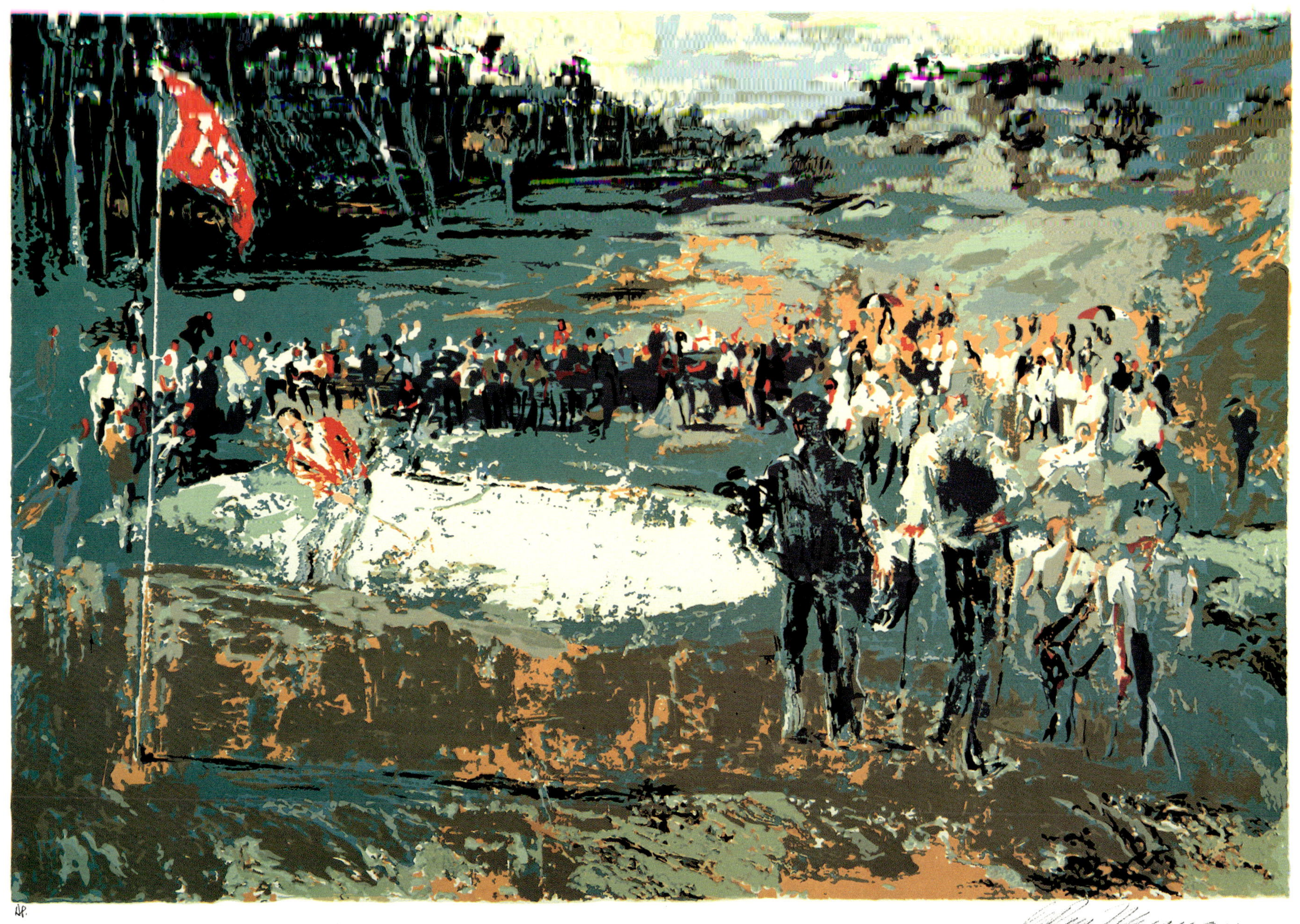

105   Tournament Golf

1974
Serigraph
22½ x 32 (57.15 x 81.28 cm)
A limited edition of 300, signed and numbered
by the artist.

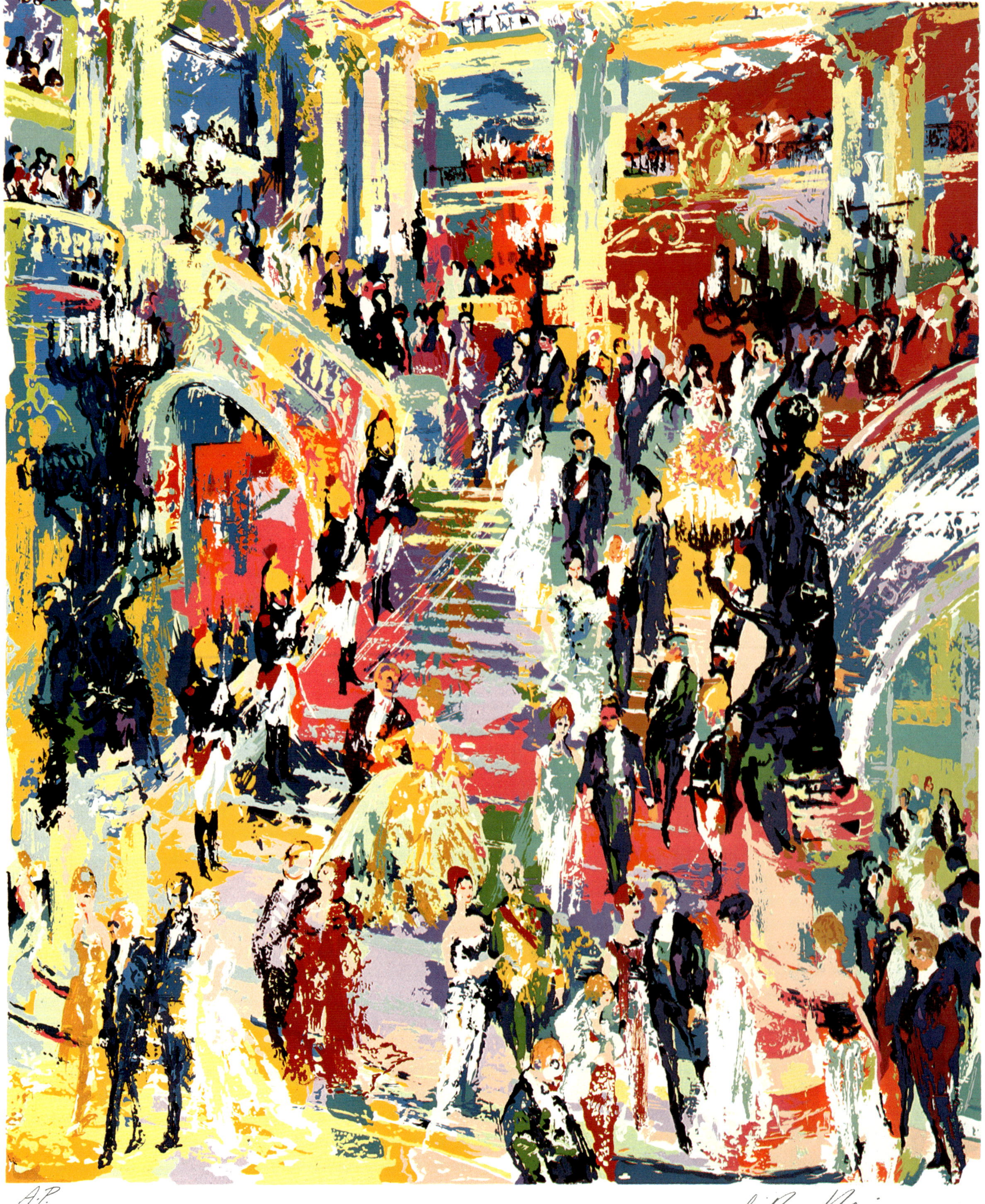

106
Le Grand Escalier
de l'Opera
1975
Serigraph
31½ x 25 (80.01 x 63.5 cm)
A limited edition of 300, signed
and numbered by the artist.

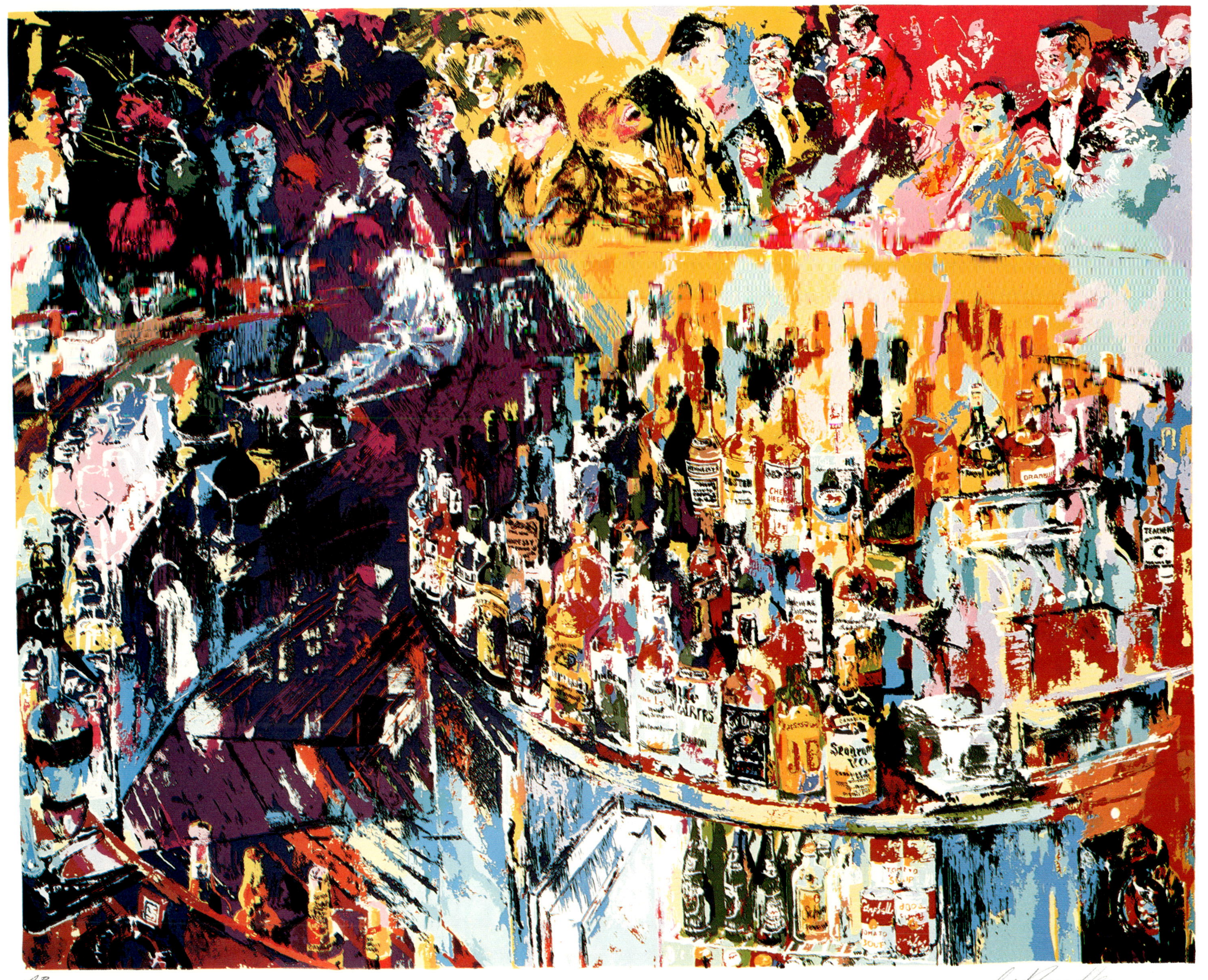

107 Toots Shor Bar

1975
Serigraph
30¾ x 25¼ (78.10 x 64.14 cm)
A limited edition of 300, signed and numbered
by the artist.

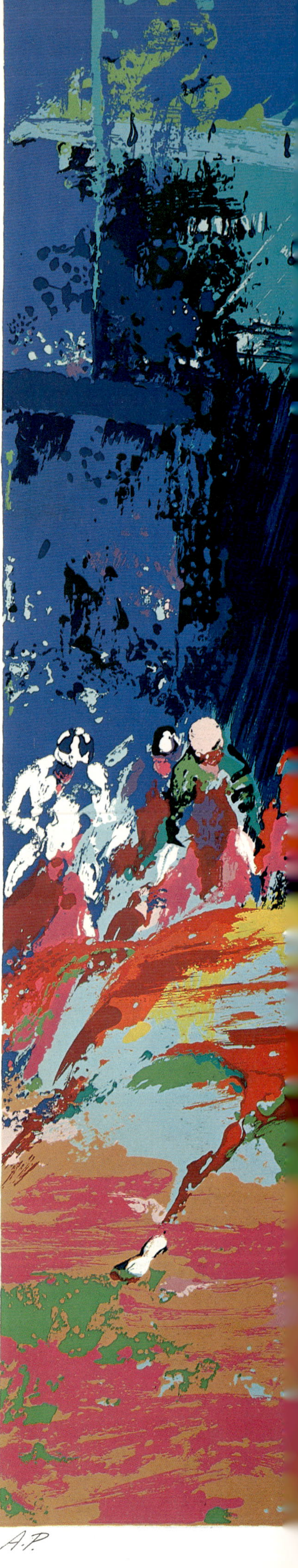

108 Clubhouse Turn

1975
Serigraph
38¾ x 36 (98.43 x 91.44 cm)
A limited edition of 300, signed and numbered
by the artist.

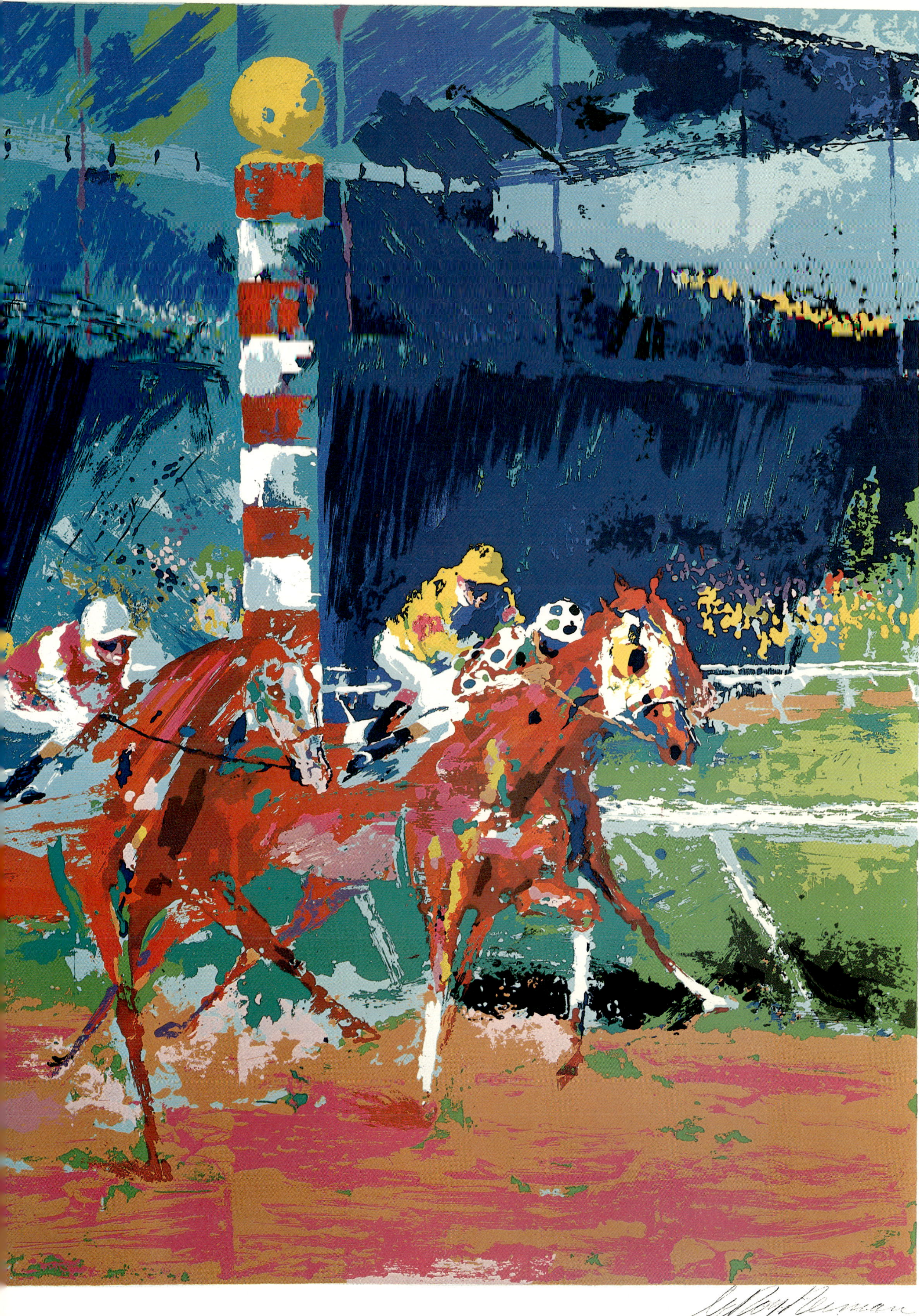

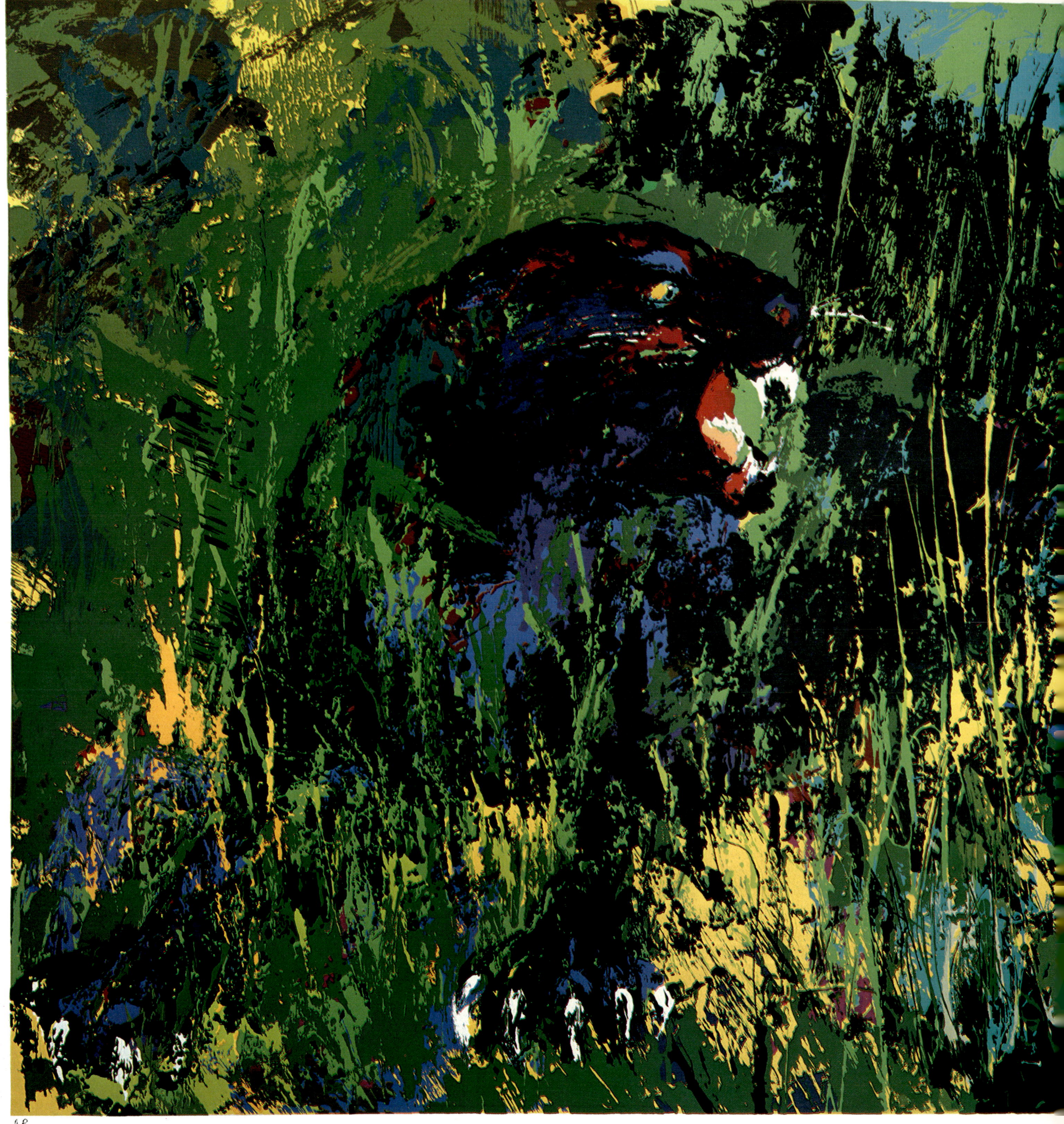

A.P.

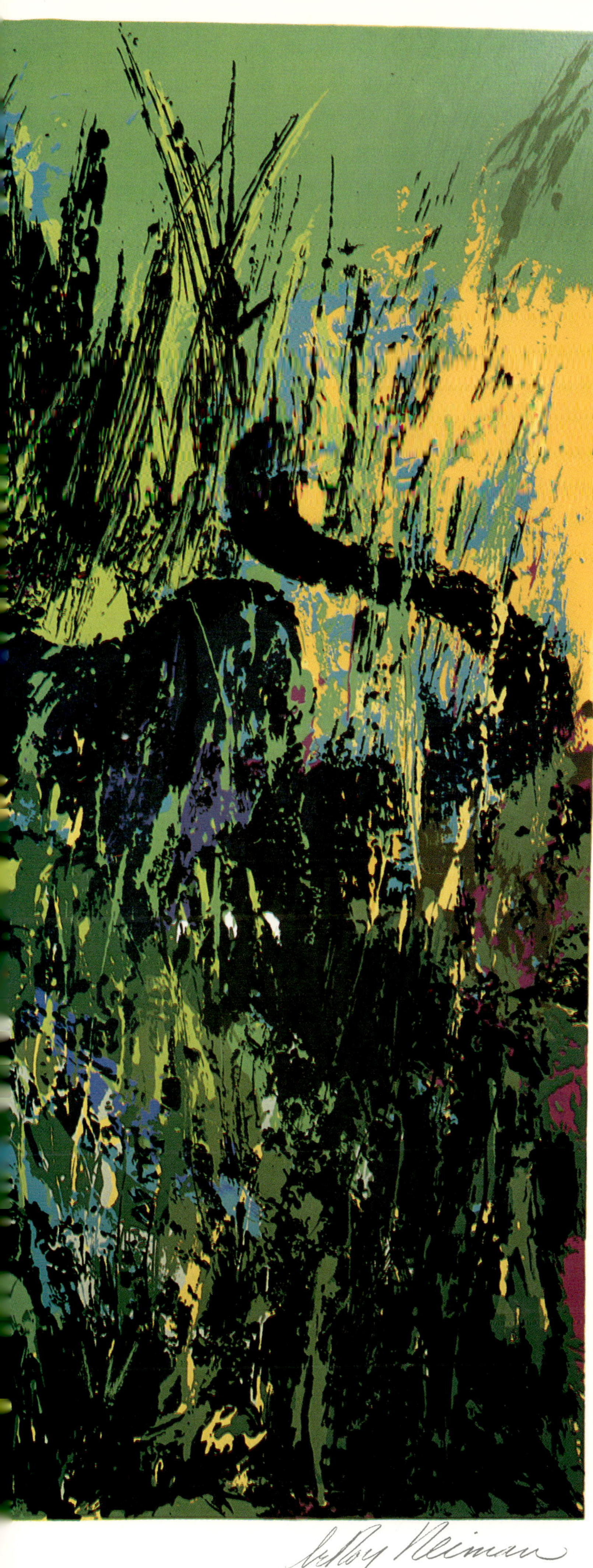

109 Black Panther

1975
Serigraph
28½ x 39 (72.39 x 99.06 cm)
A limited edition of 300, signed and numbered
by the artist.

179

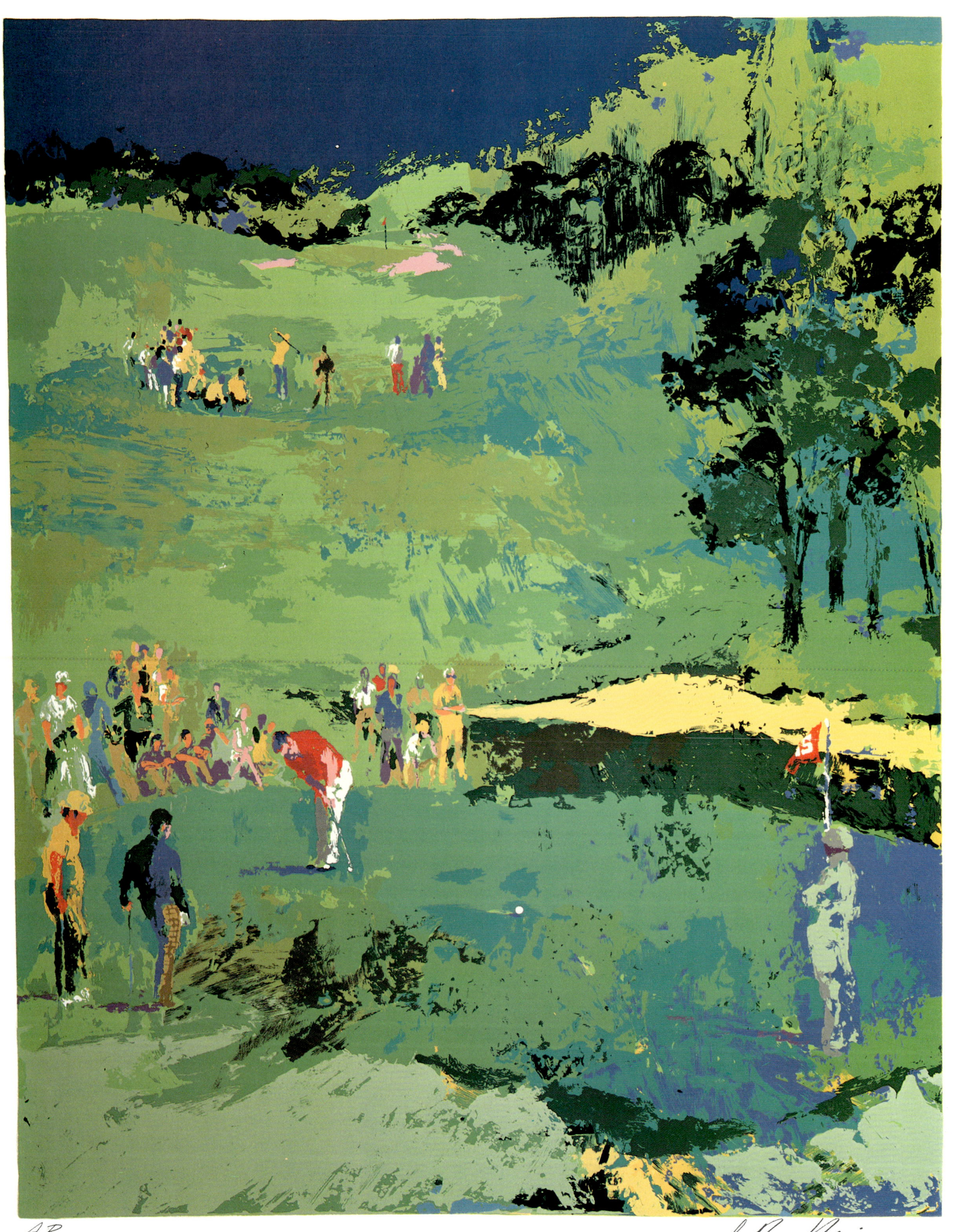

110   Golf Landscape
1976
Serigraph
36 x 28 (91.44 x 71.12 cm)
A limited edition of 300, signed
and numbered by the artist.

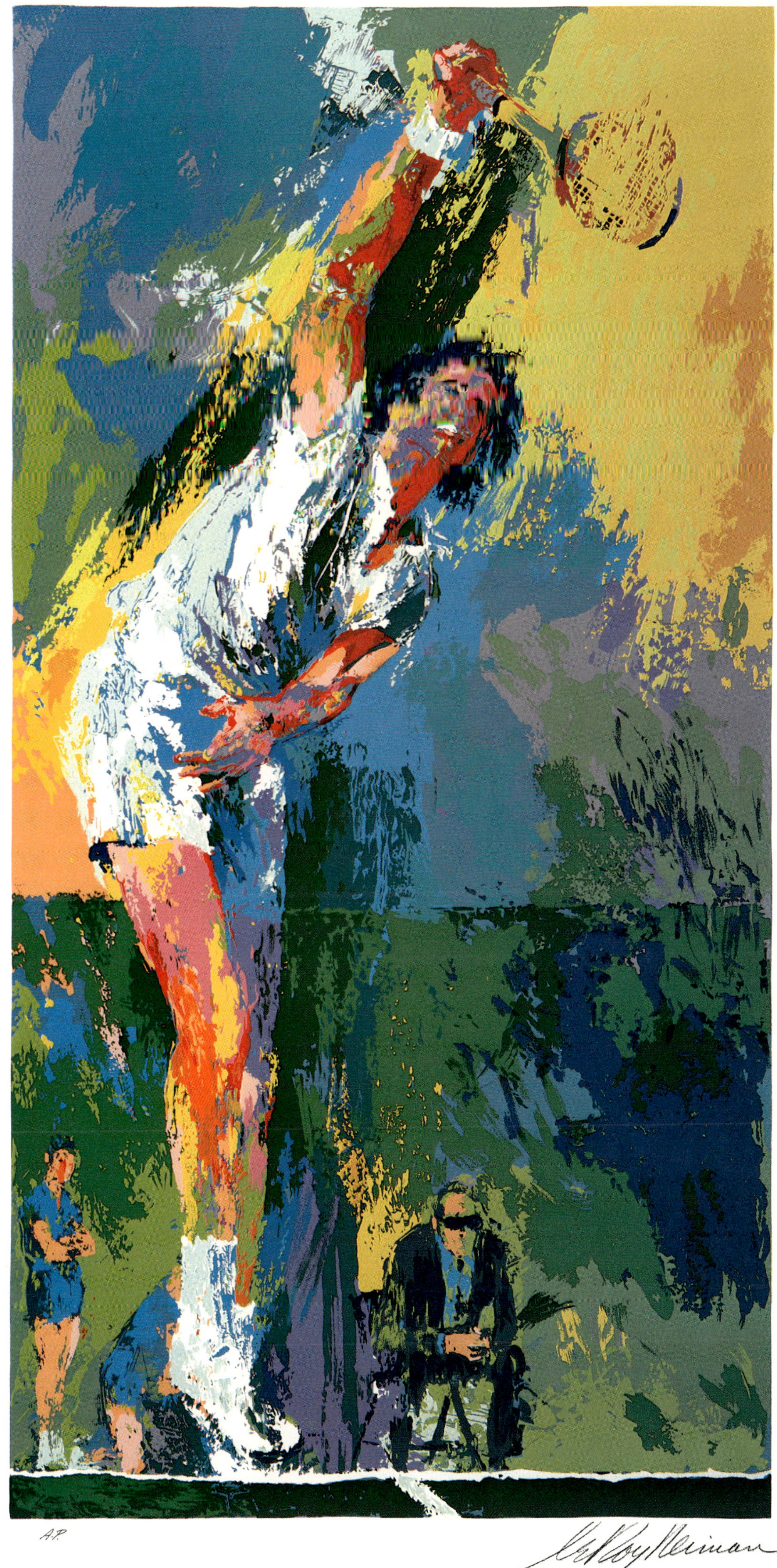

111 Sun Serve
1976
Serigraph
36 x 18 (91.44 x 45.72 cm)
A limited edition of 300, signed and numbered
by the artist.

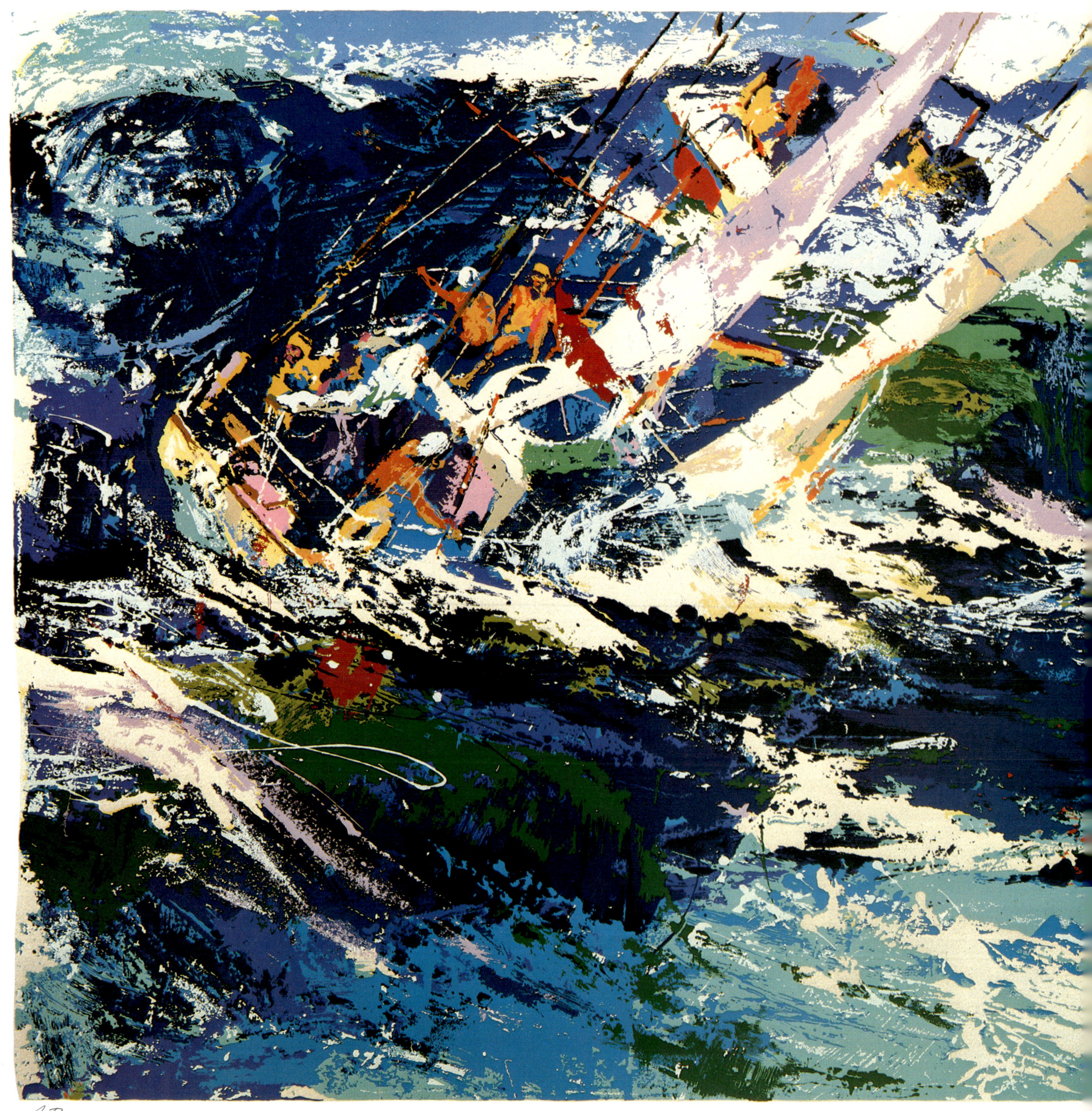

A.P.

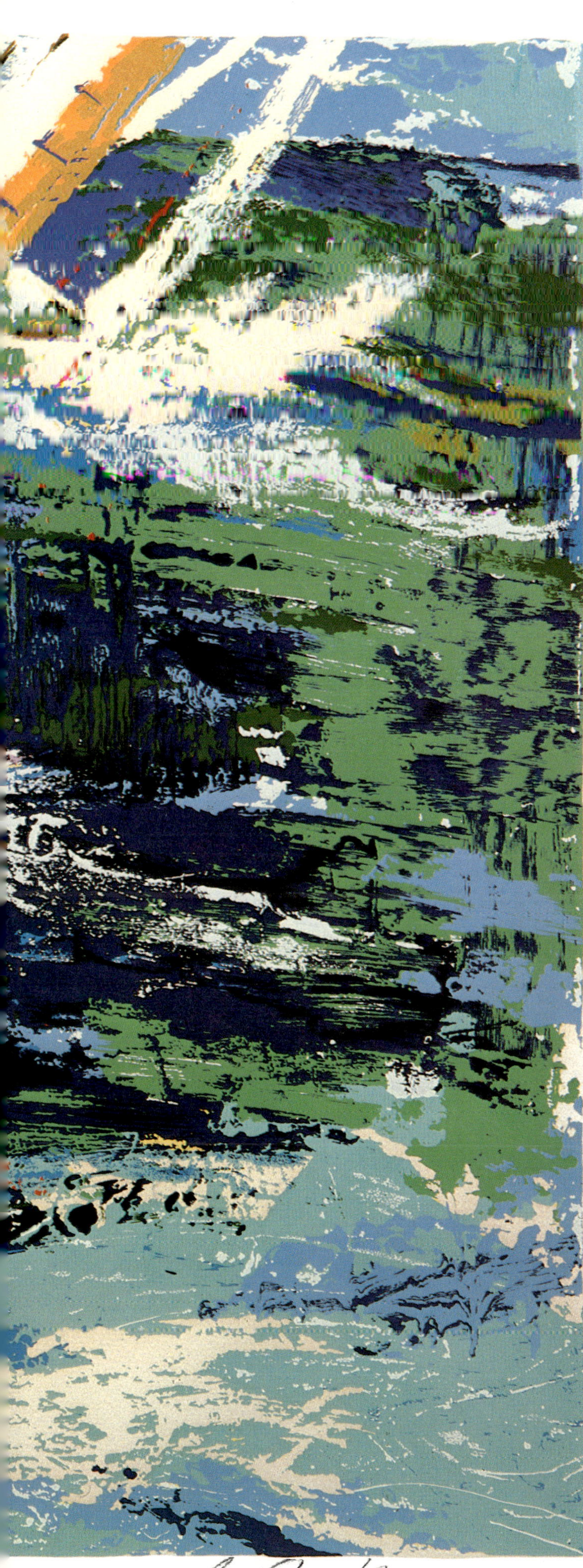

112   High Sea's Sailing
1976
Serigraph
25 x 33½ (63.5 x 85.09 cm)
A limited edition of 300, signed and numbered
by the artist.

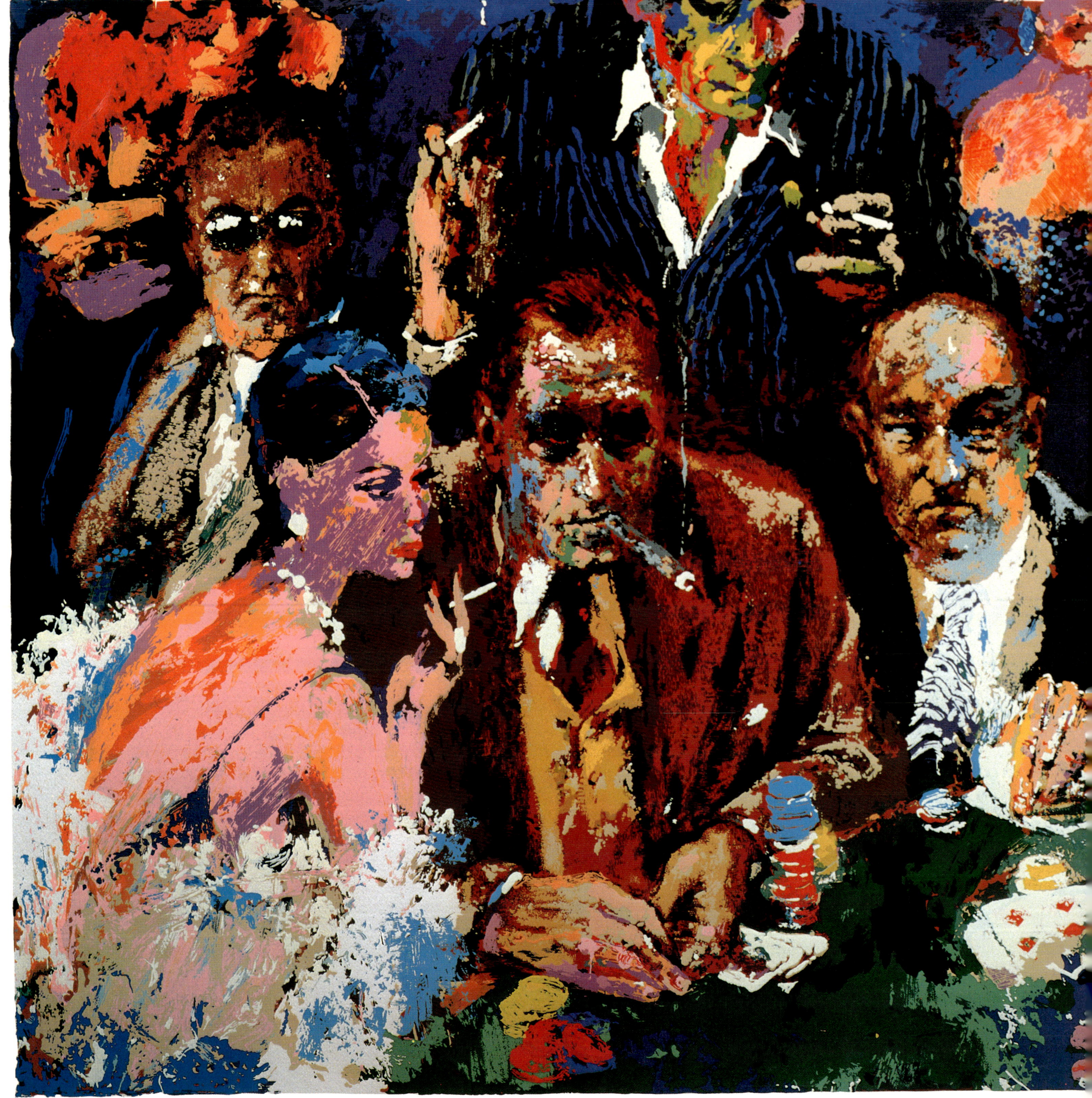
A.P.

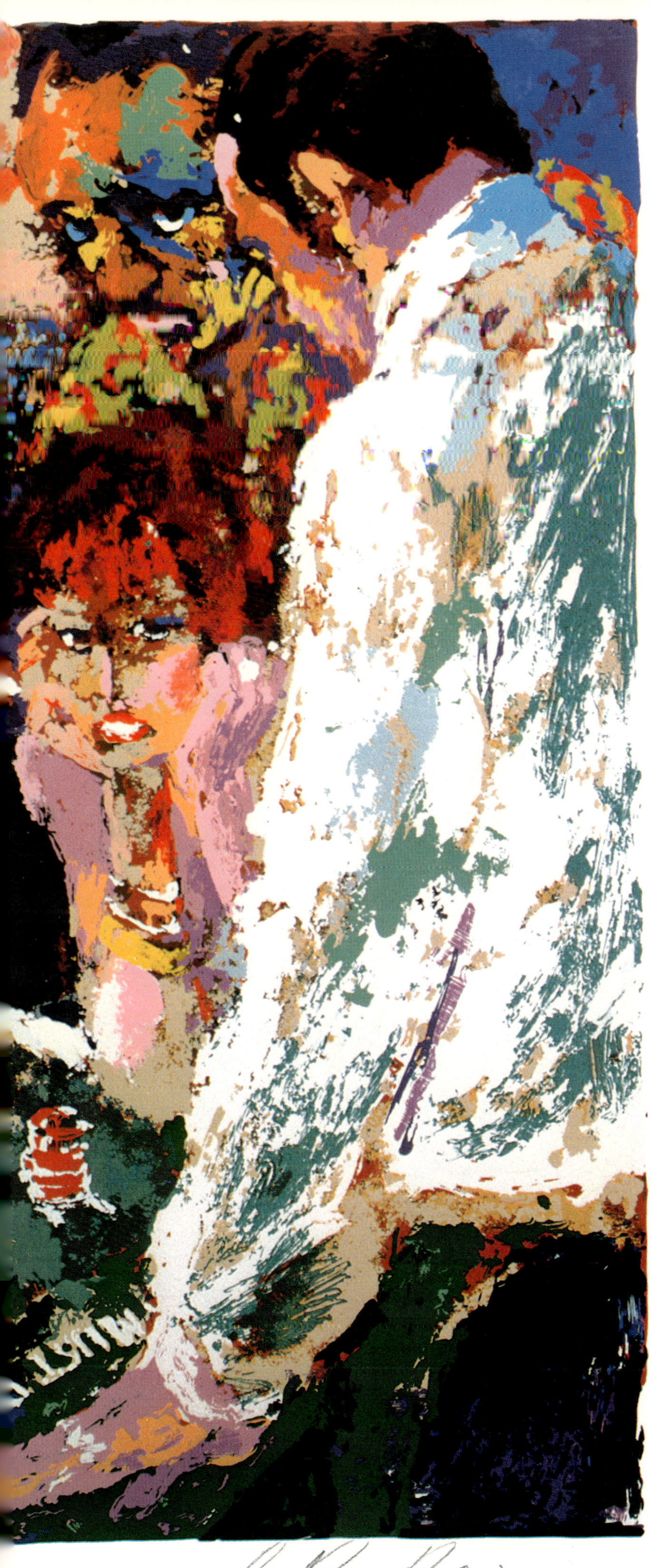

113   Vegas Blackjack

1976
Serigraph
22¼ x 31½ (56.52 x 80.01 cm)
A limited edition of 300, signed and numbered
by the artist.

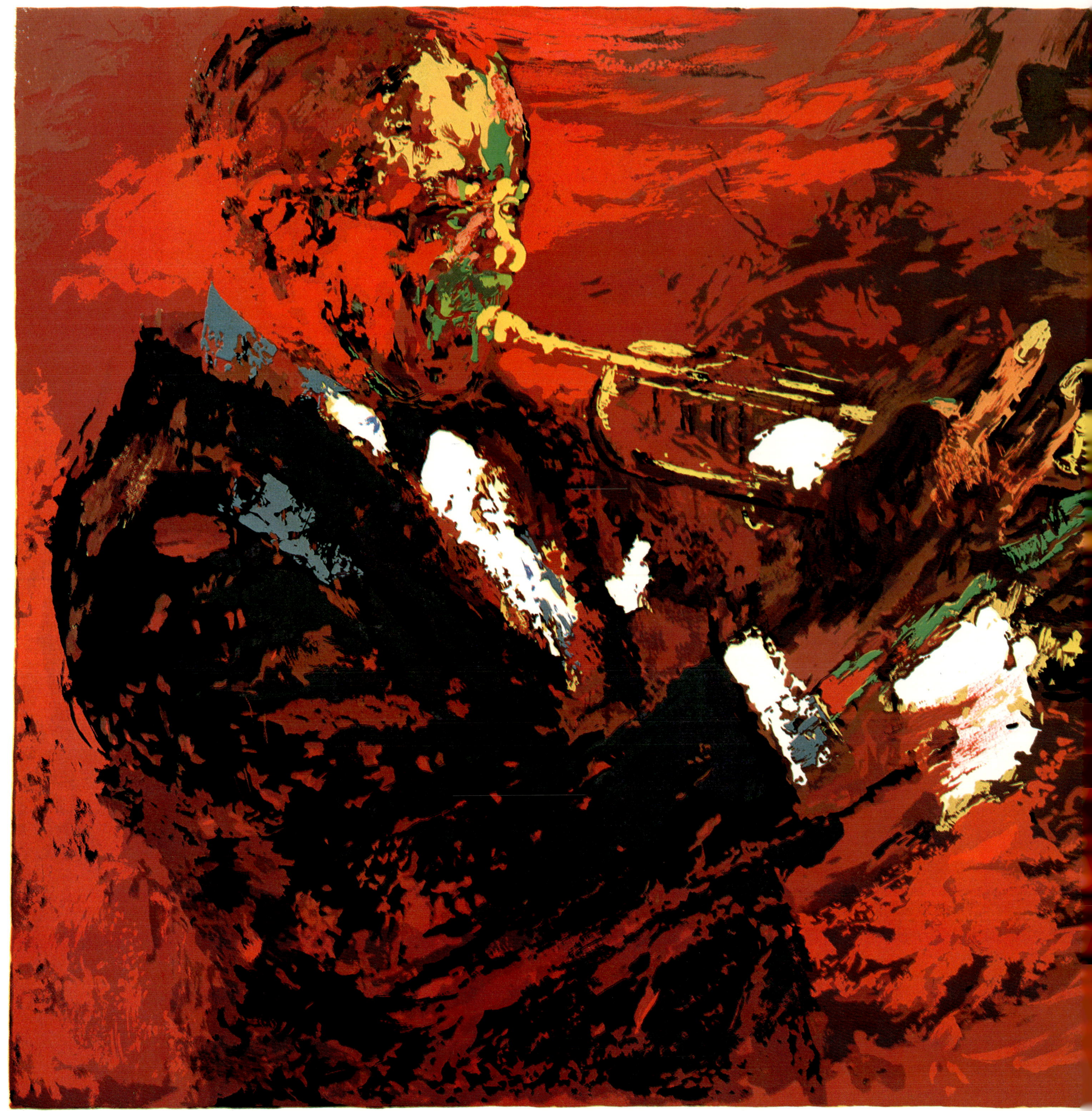

A.P.

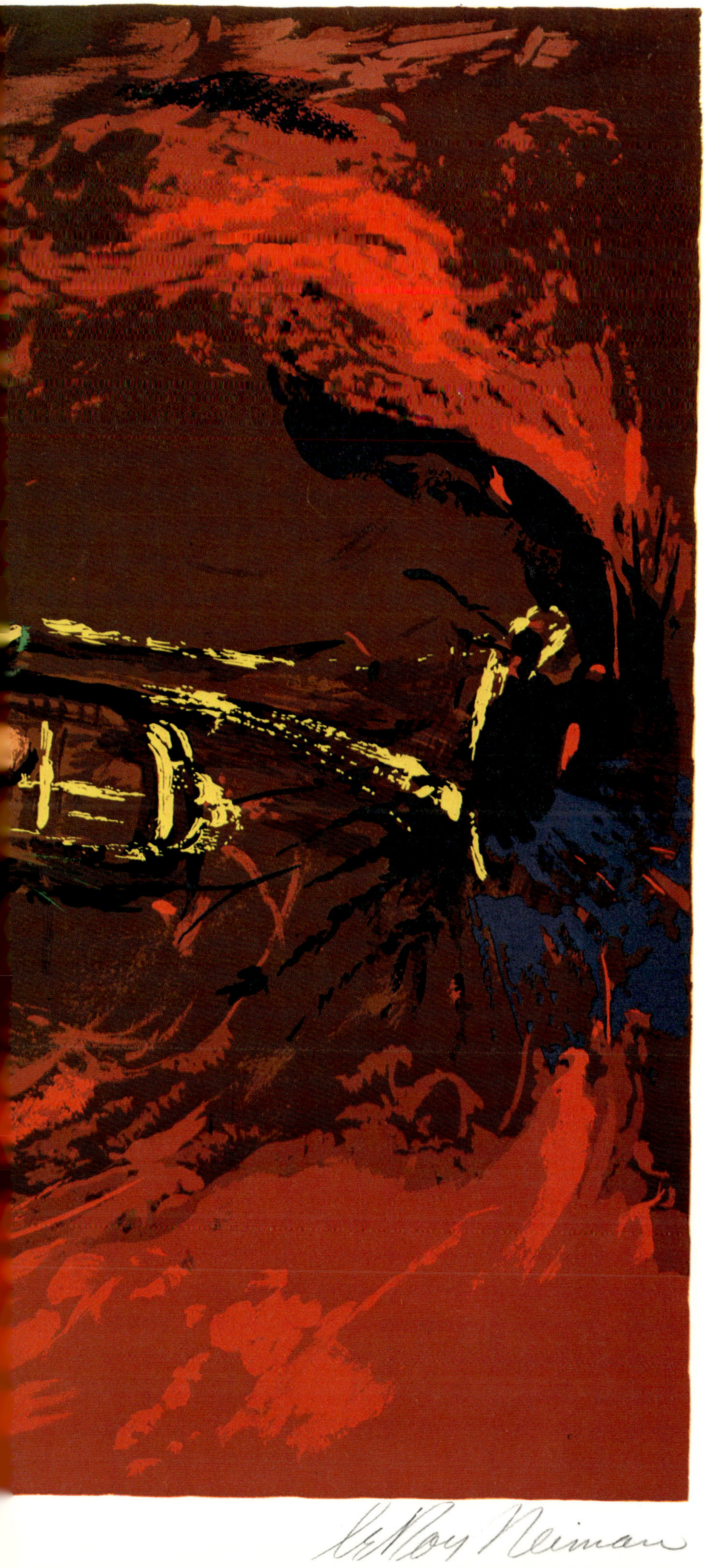

114   Satchmo

1976
Serigraph
25¼ x 38 (64.14 x 96.52 cm)
A limited edition of 300, signed and numbered
by the artist.

115   Abraham Lincoln

1976
Serigraph
18 x 18 (45.72 x 45.72 cm)
A limited edition of 750, signed and numbered by the artist.

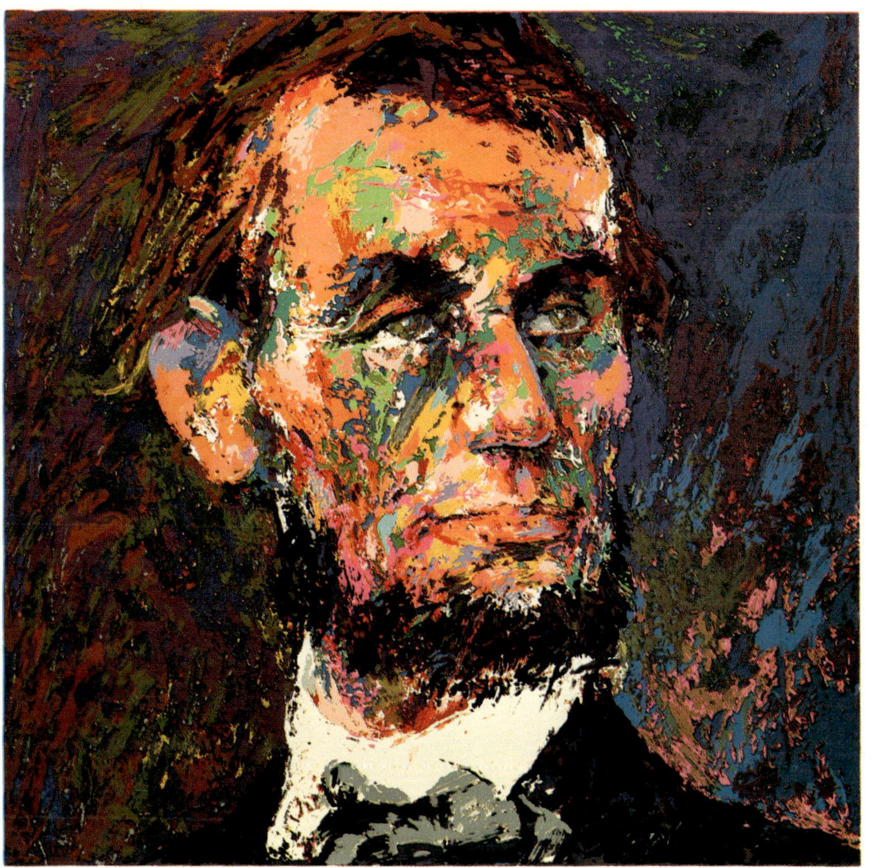

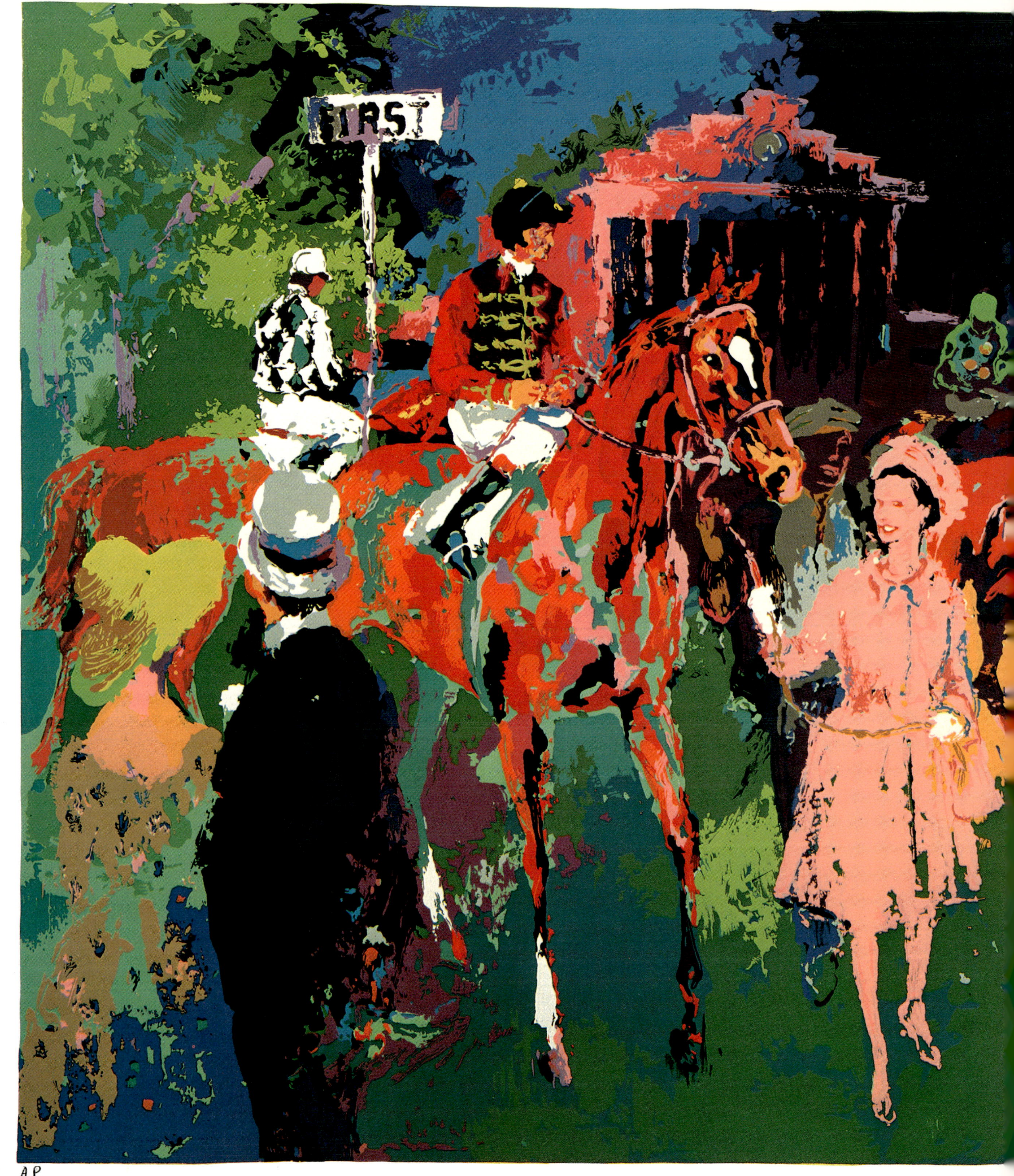
FIRST
A.P.

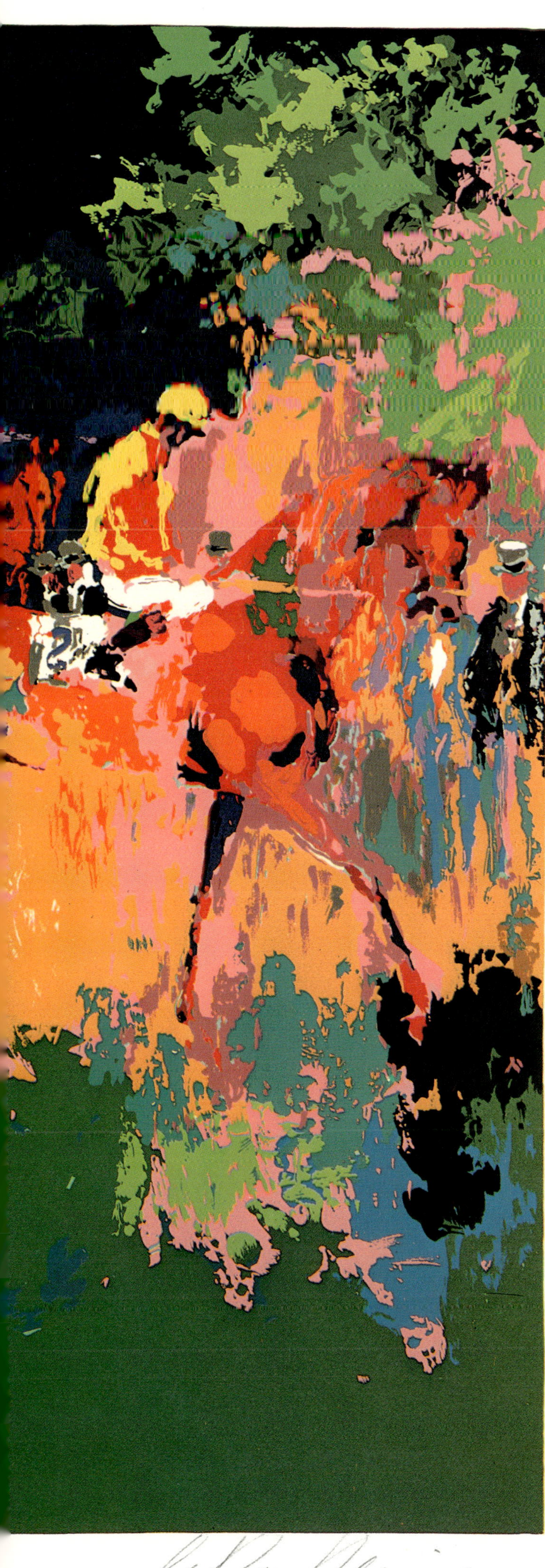

116 Queen at Ascot
1976
Serigraph
24¼ x 30 (61.60 x 76.2 cm)
A limited edition of 300, signed and numbered
by the artist.

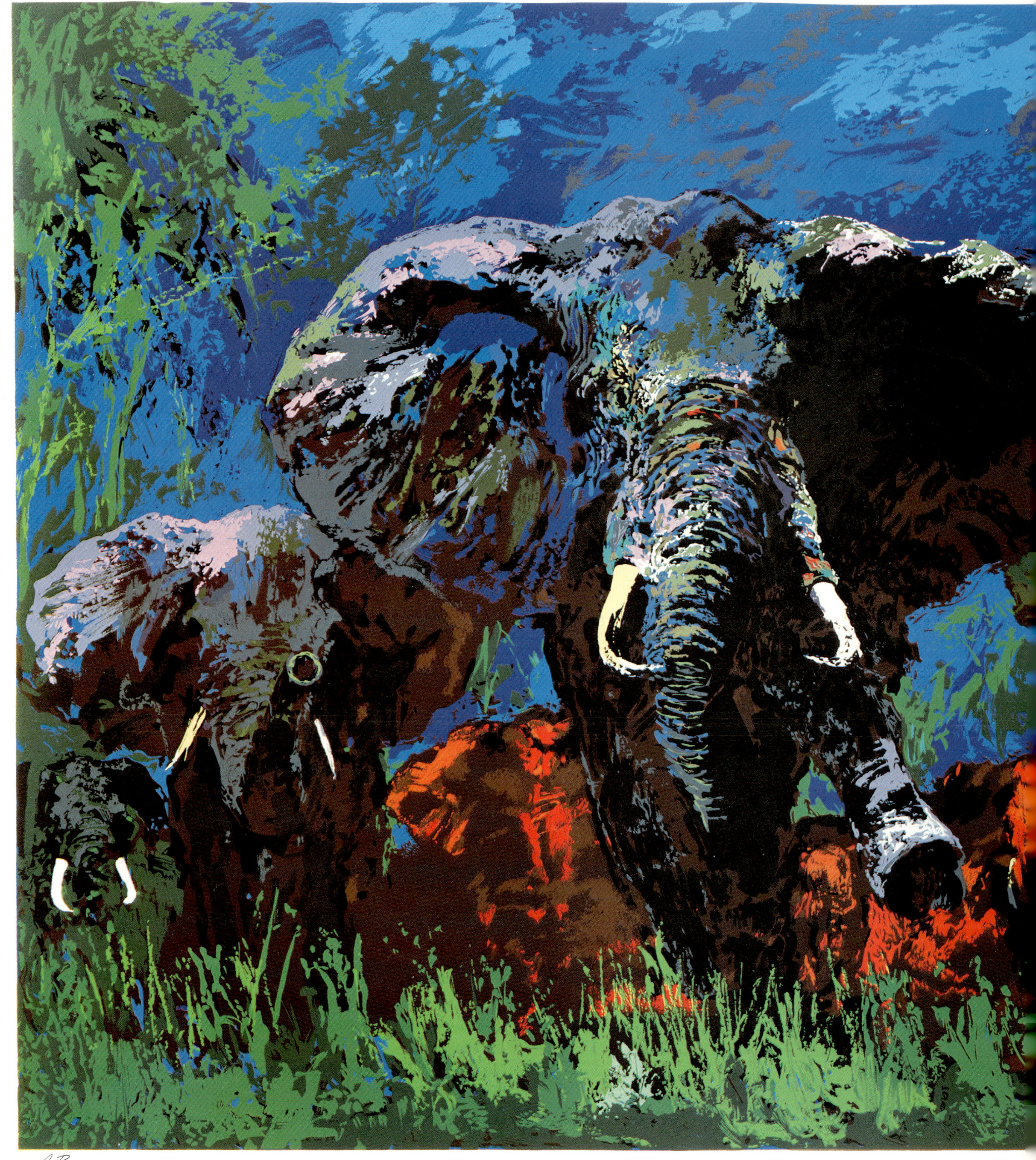

A.P.

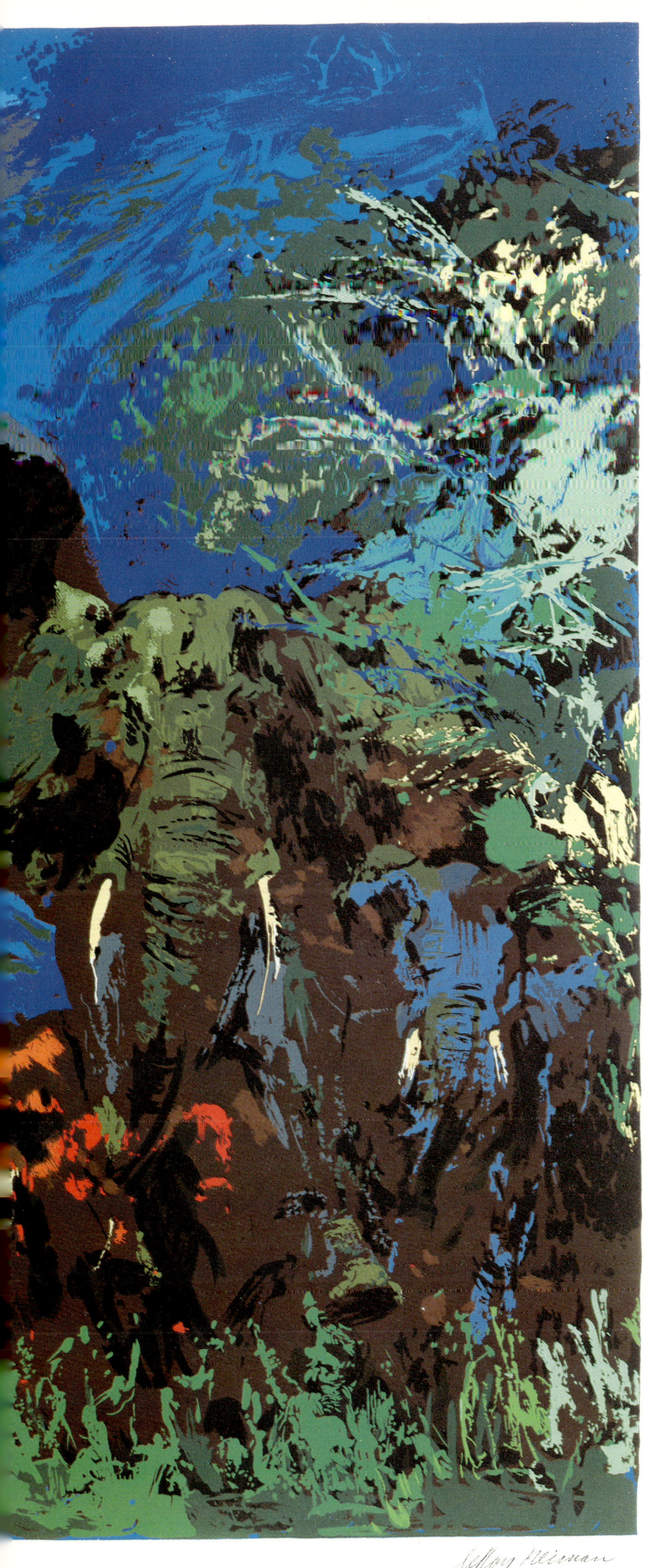

117   Elephant Stampede

1976
Serigraph
30¼ x 40 (76.84 x 101.6 cm)
A limited edition of 300, signed and numbered
by the artist.

118   Cafe Deux Magots

1976
Serigraph
23 x 34 (58.42 x 86.36 cm)
A limited edition of 300, signed and numbered
by the artist.

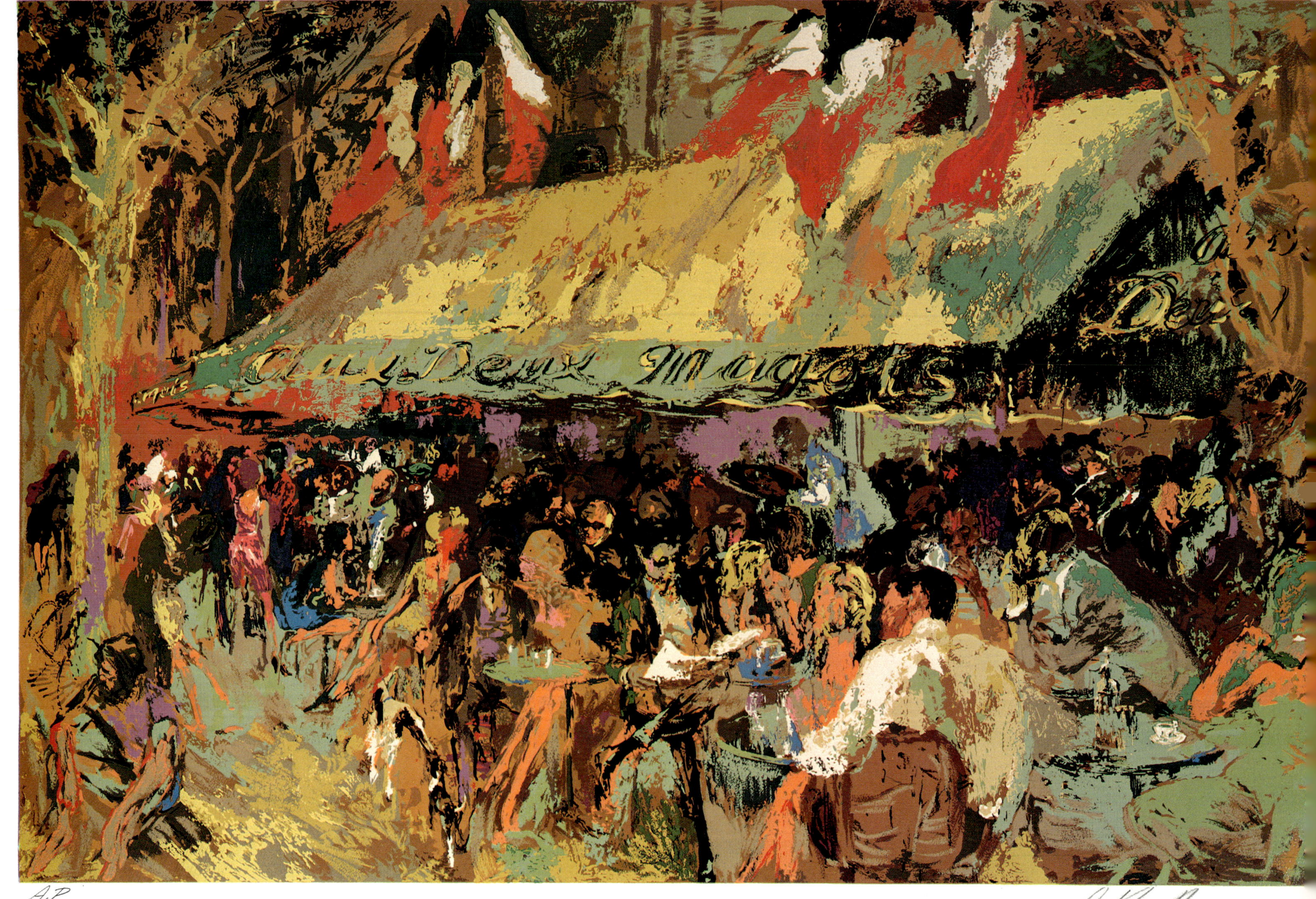

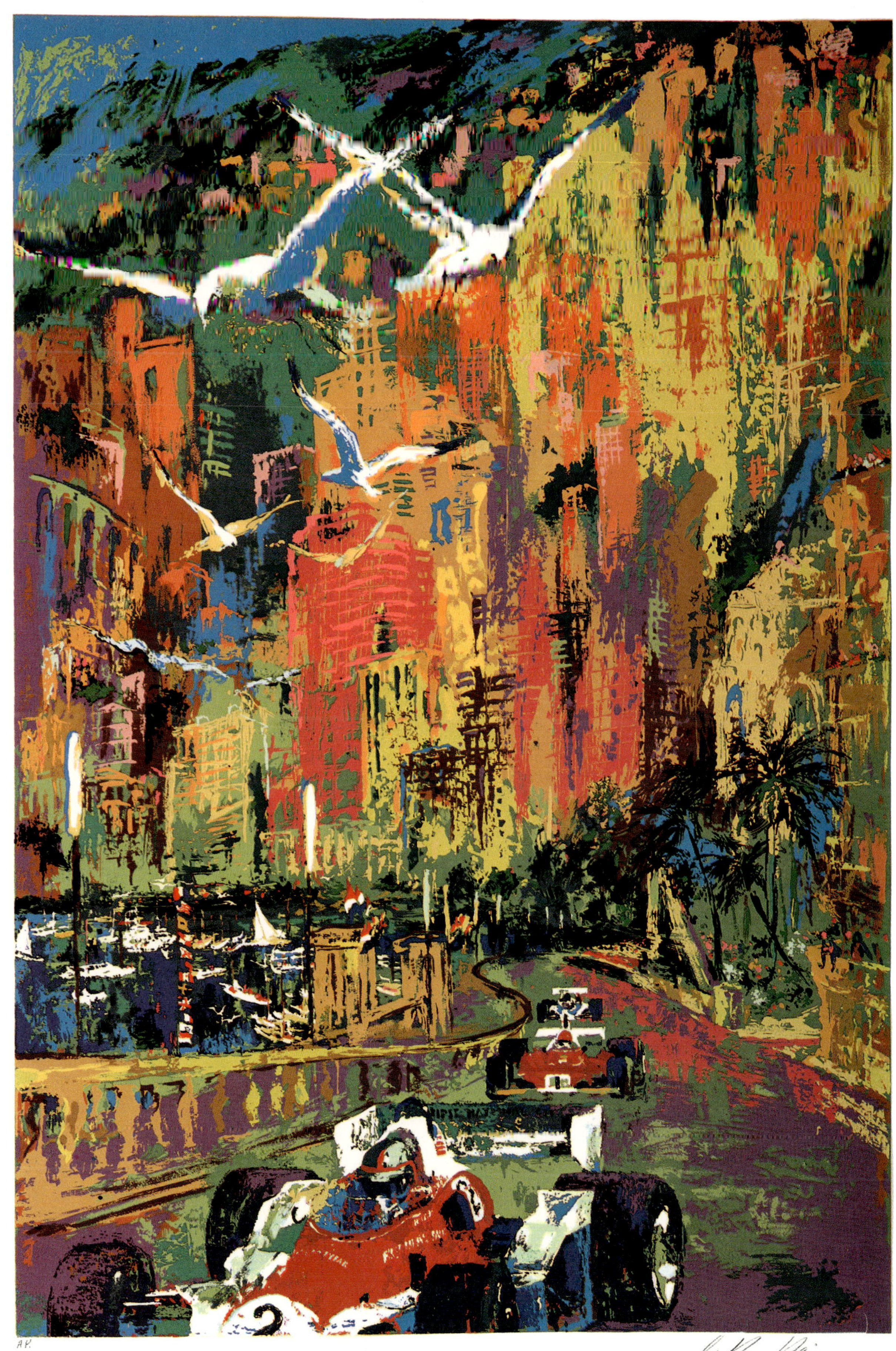

119 Grand Prix de Monaco

1976
Serigraph
36 x 24 (91.44 x 60.96 cm)
A limited edition of 300, signed and numbered
by the artist.

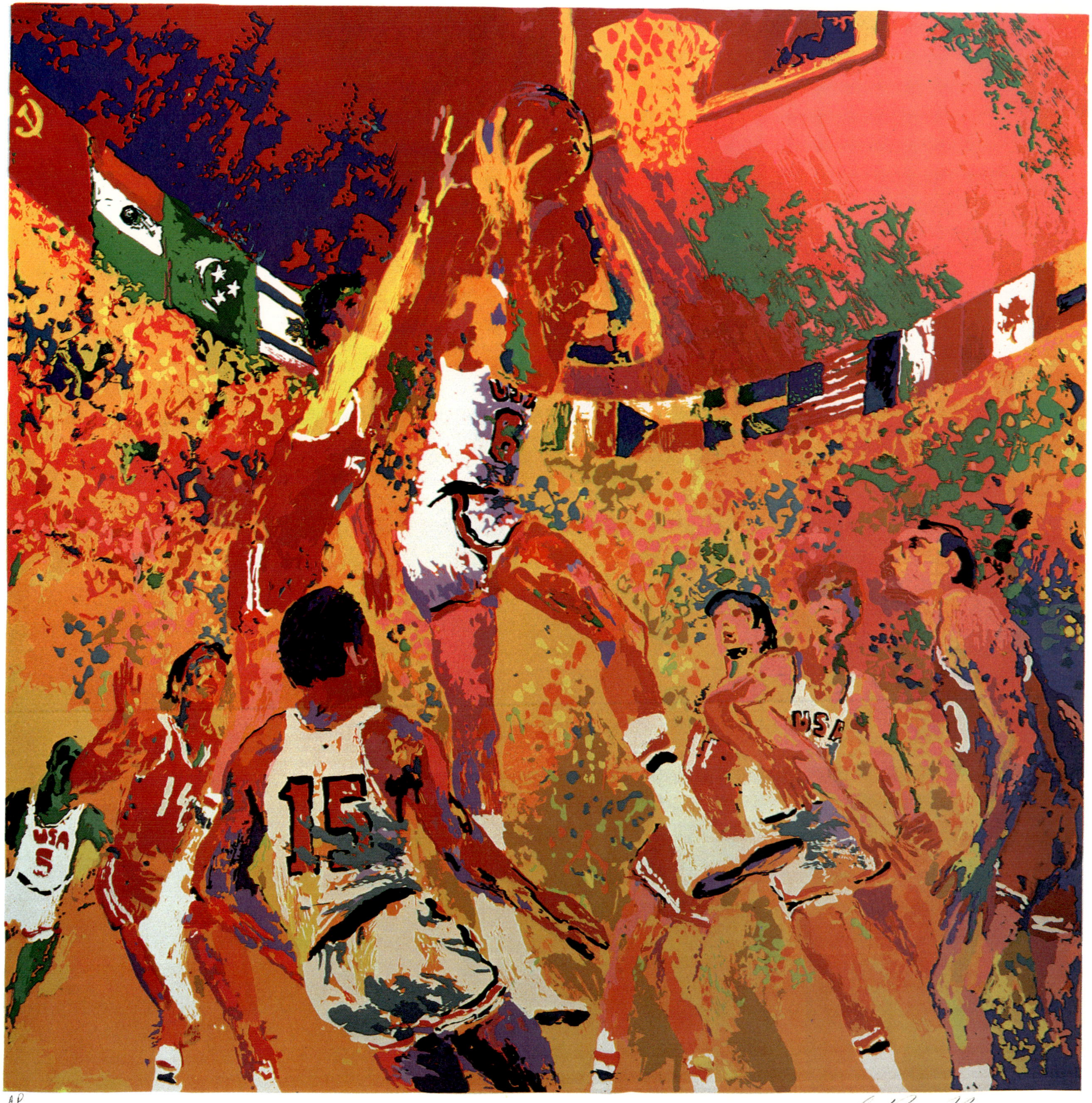

120 Olympic Basketball
1976
Serigraph
26 x 25⅞ (66.04 x 65.72 cm)
A limited edition of 300, signed and numbered
by the artist.

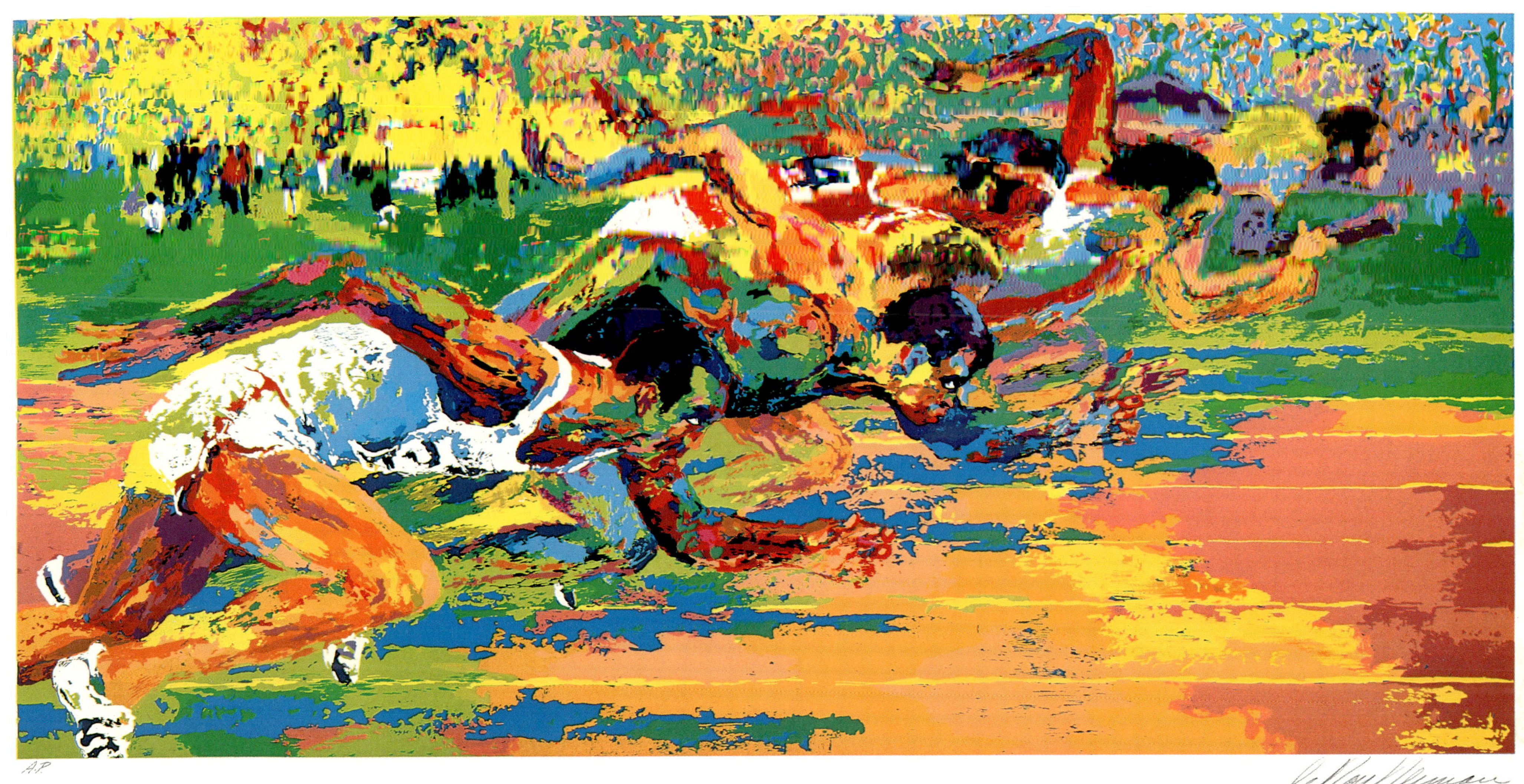

121 Olympic Track

1976
Serigraph
20 x 40 (50.8 x 101.6 cm)
A limited edition of 300, signed and numbered
by the artist.

122   Olympic Swimmers

1976
Serigraph
18 x 36 (45.72 x 91.44 cm)
A limited edition of 300, signed
and numbered by the artist.

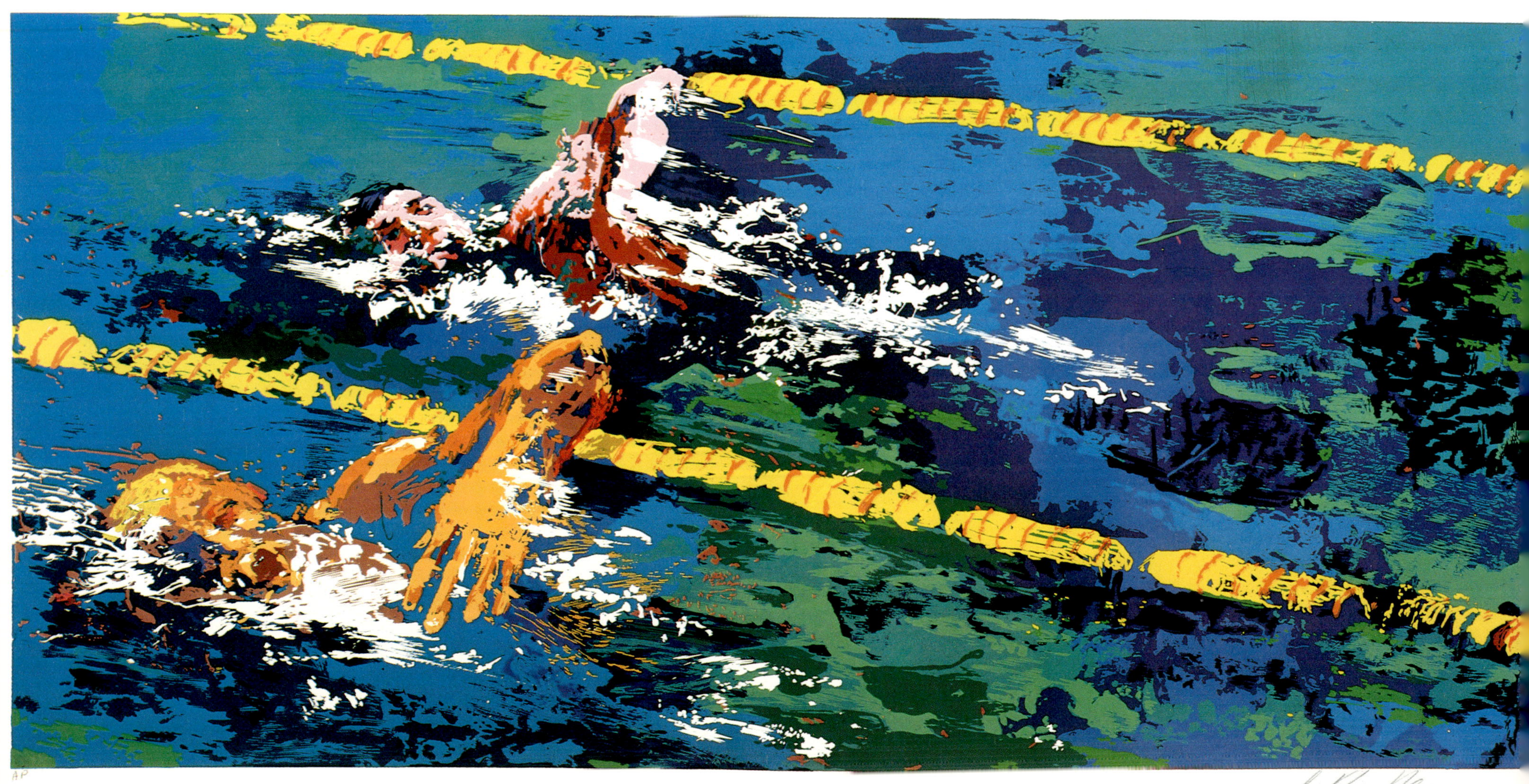

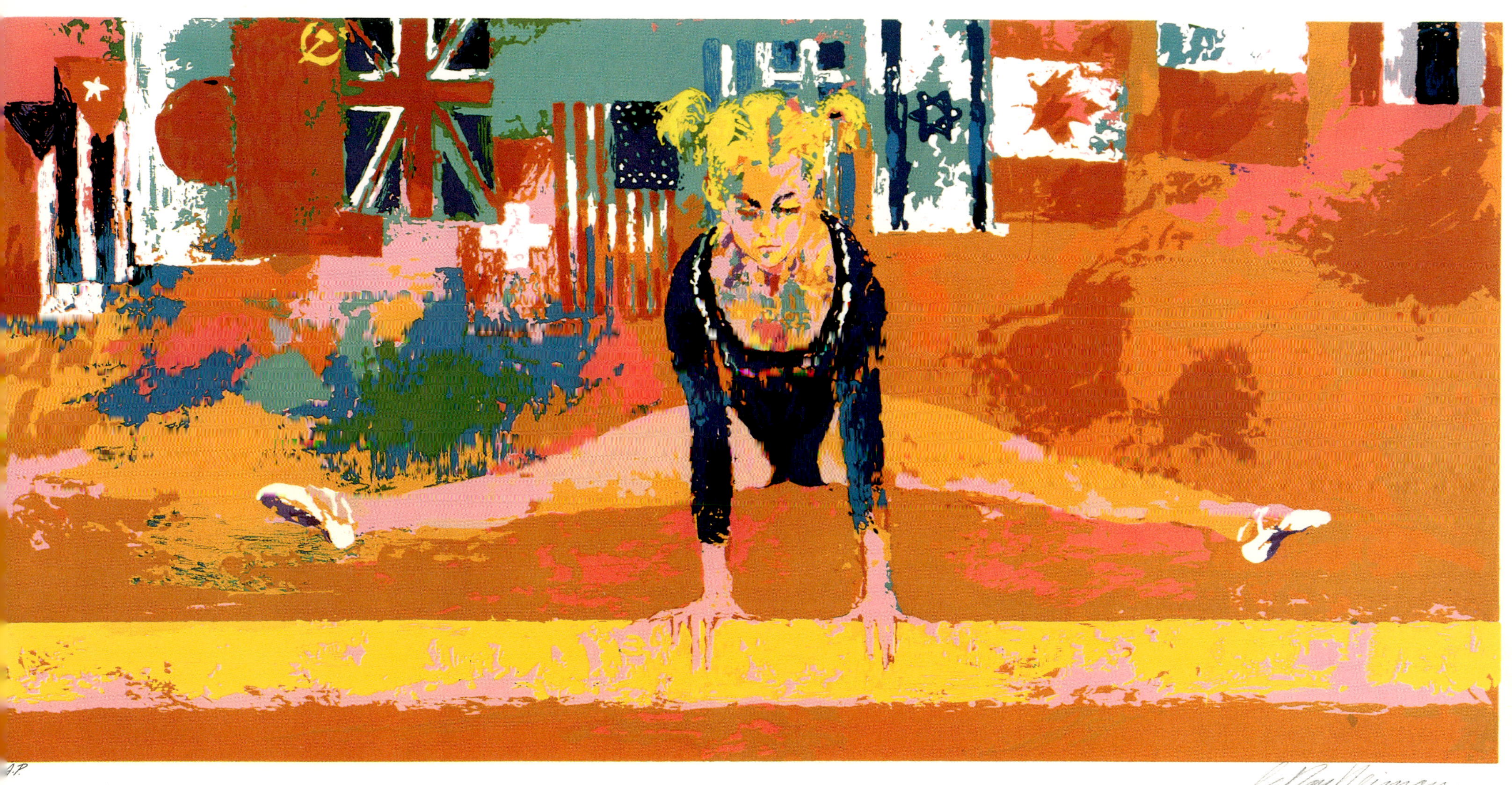

123 Olympic Gymnast
1976
Serigraph
18 x 36 (45.72 x 91.44 cm)
A limited edition of 300, signed
and numbered by the artist.

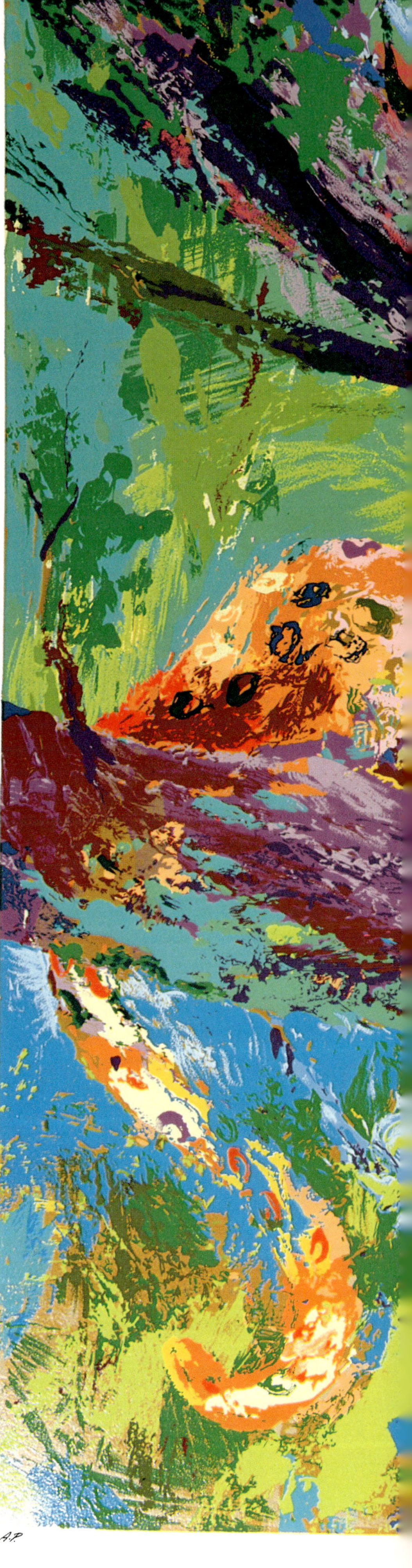

124 Serengeti Leopard
1976
Serigraph
33 x 42 (83.82 x 106.68 cm)
A limited edition of 300, signed and numbered
by the artist.

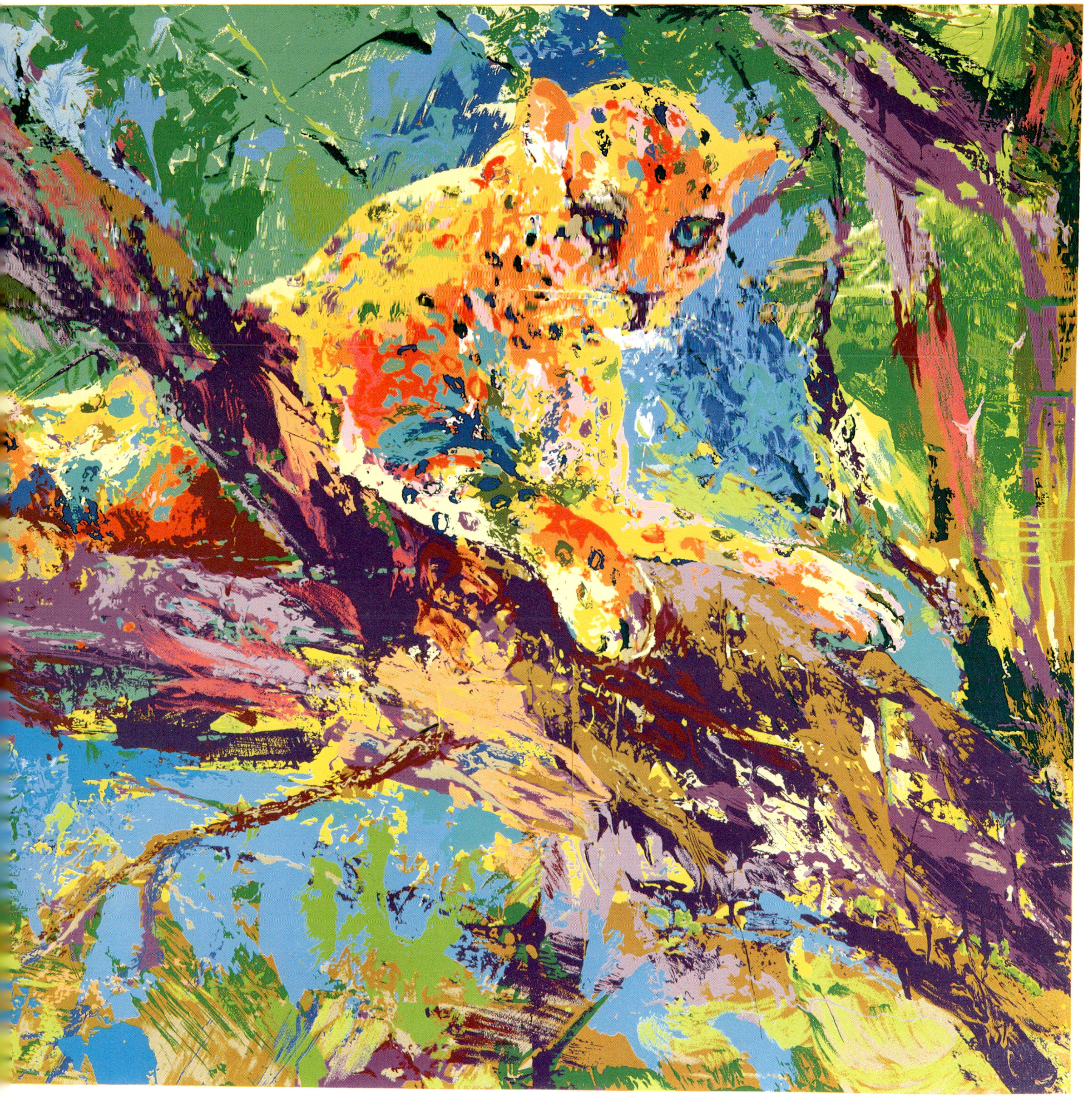

Part III
Serigraphs,
1977–1980

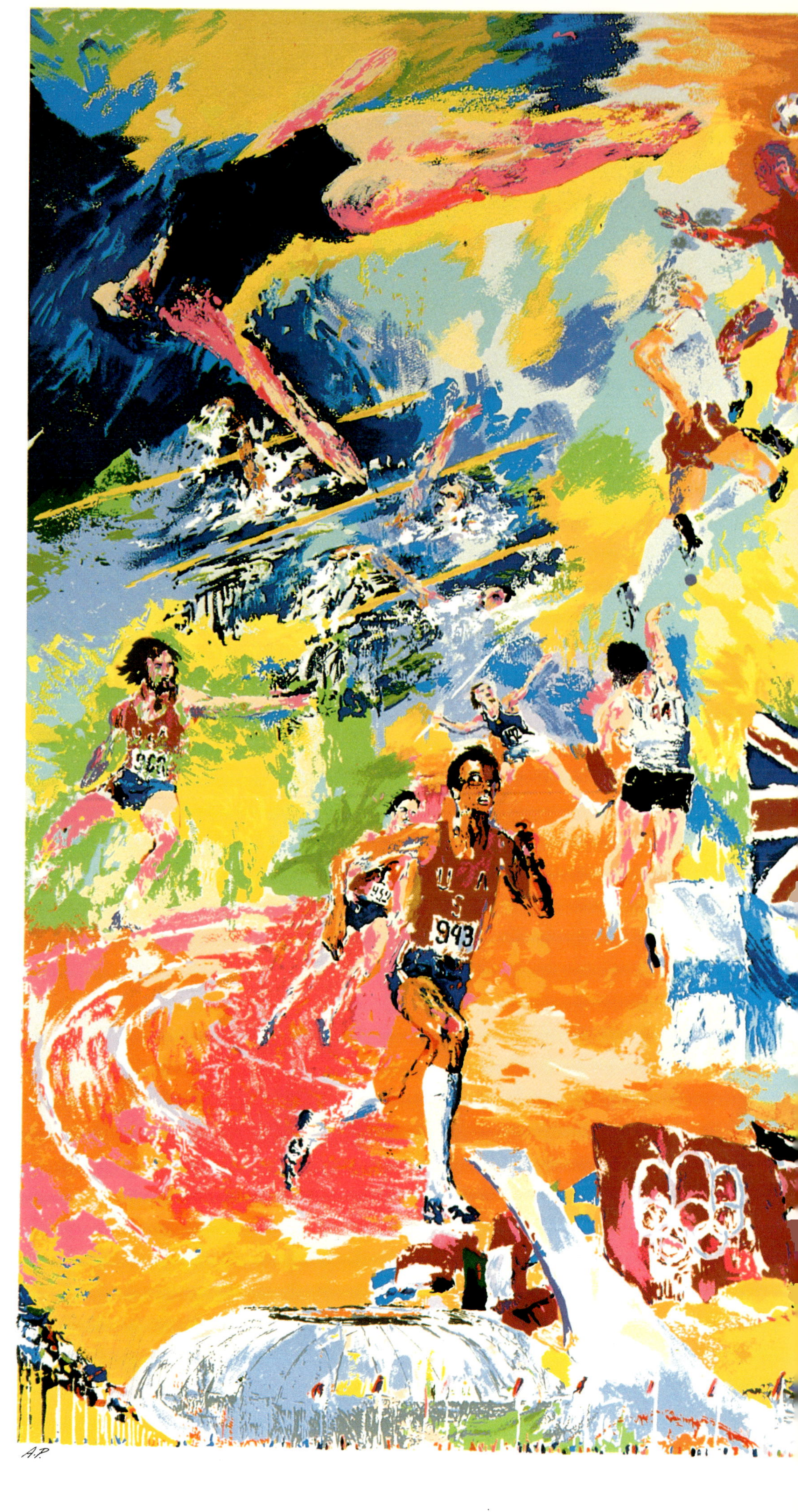

125 Neiman's Montreal '76

1977
Serigraph
31⅜ x 48 (79.69 x 121.92 cm)
A limited edition of 600, h.c.-60, signed and
numbered by the artist.

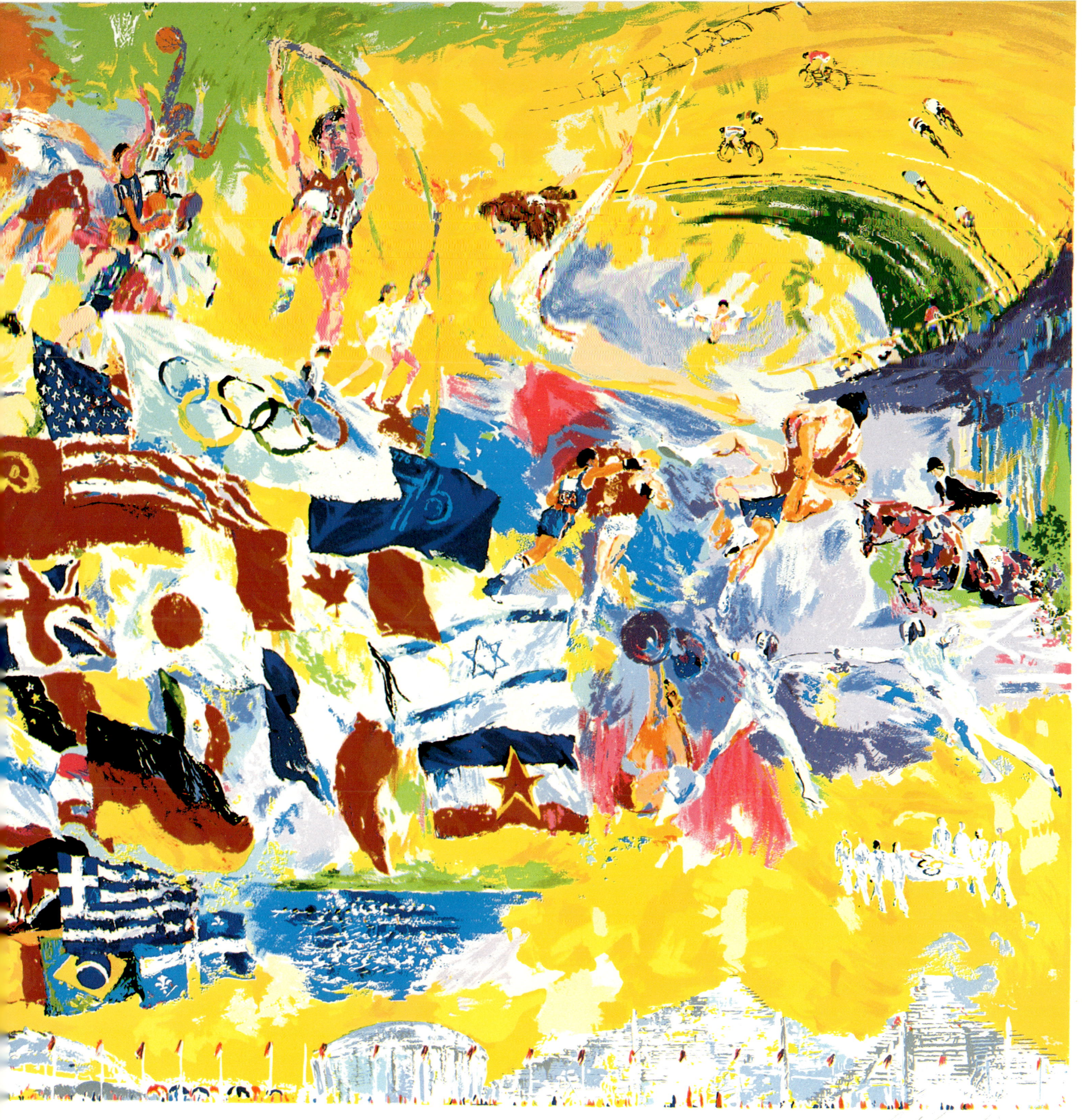

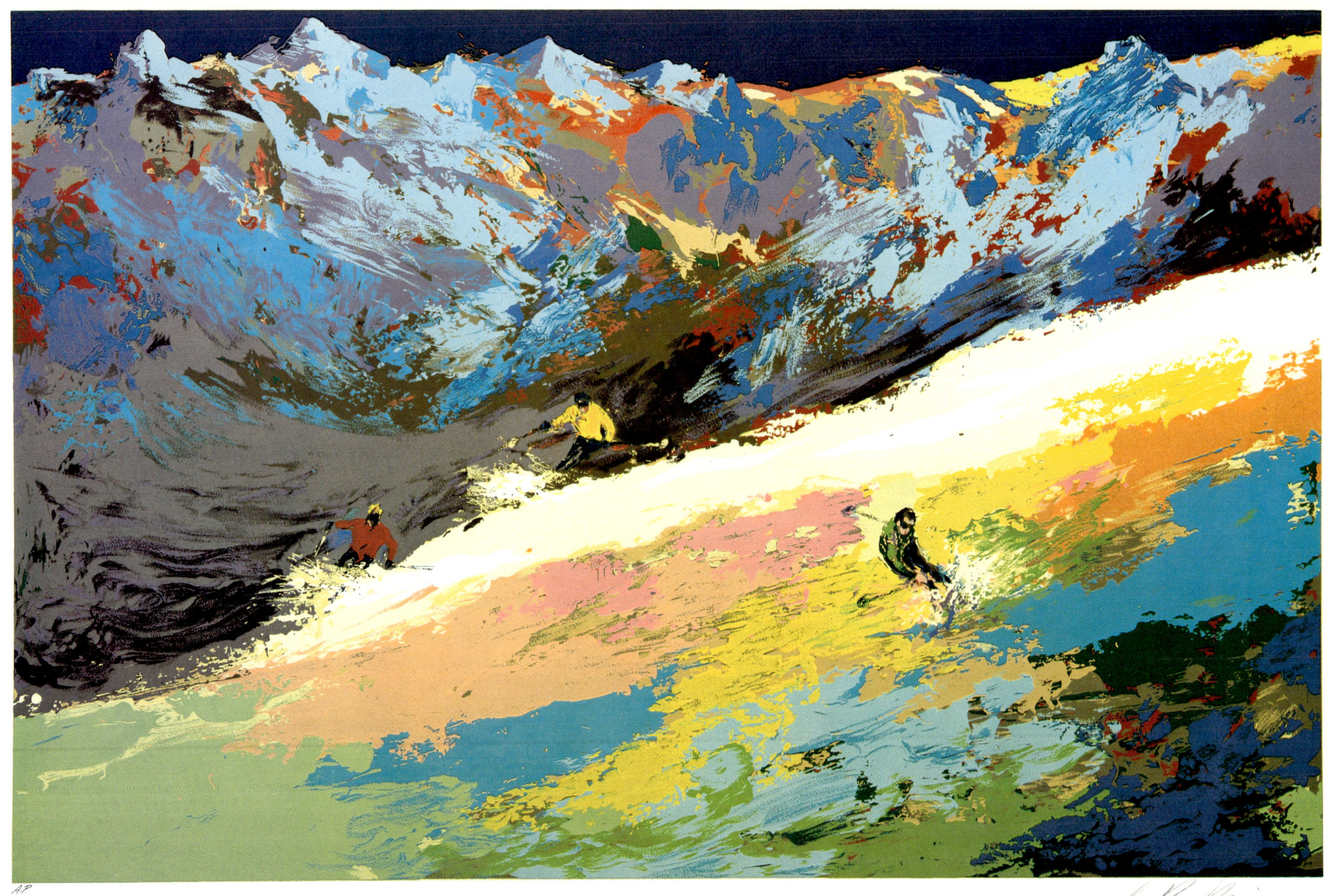

126 High Altitude Skiing

1977
Serigraph
24 x 36 (60.96 x 91.44 cm)
A limited edition of 300, signed and numbered
by the artist.

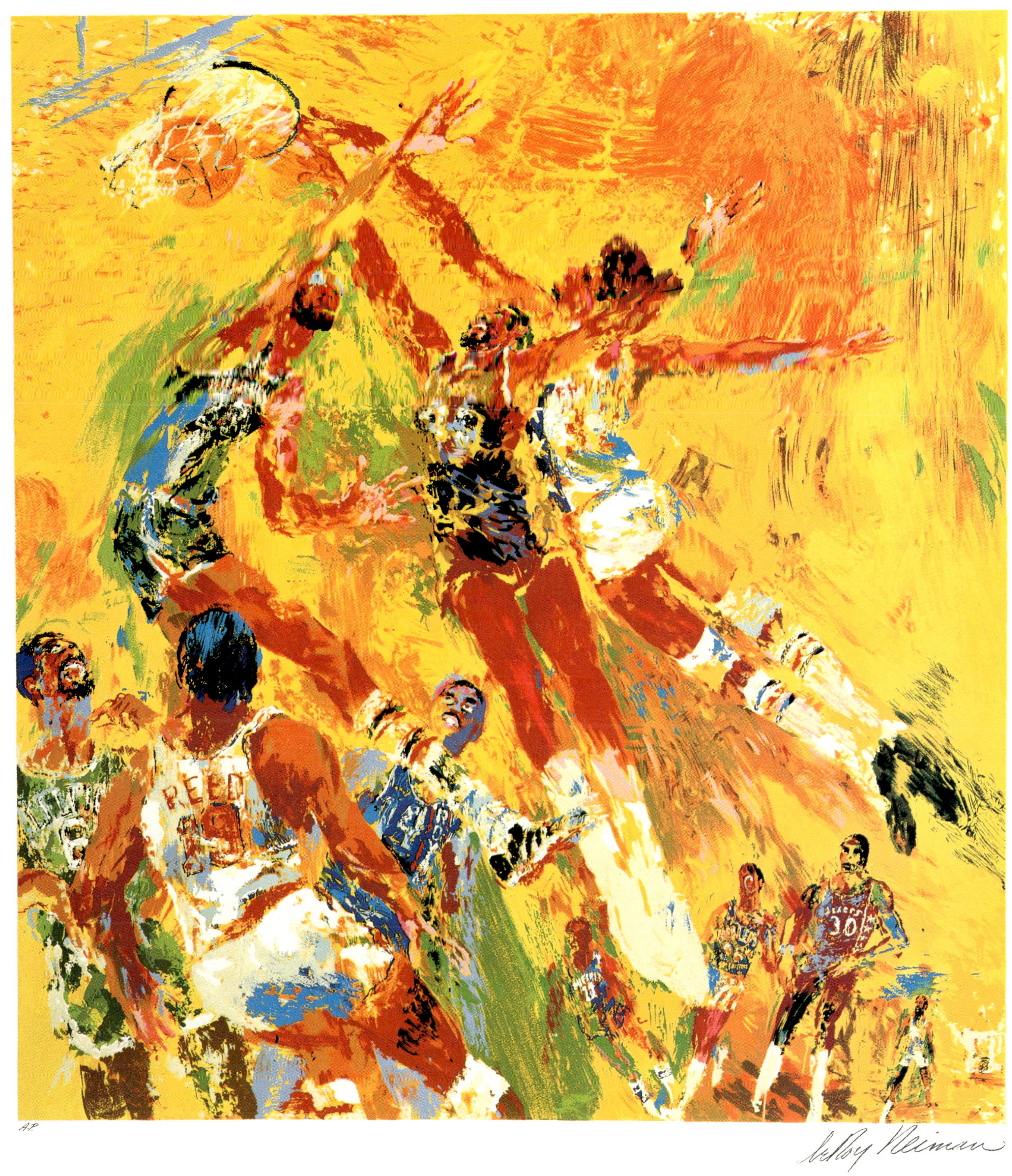

127   Basketball Superstars

1977
Serigraph
31½ x 28 (80.01 x 71.12 cm)
A limited edition of 300, signed and numbered by the artist.

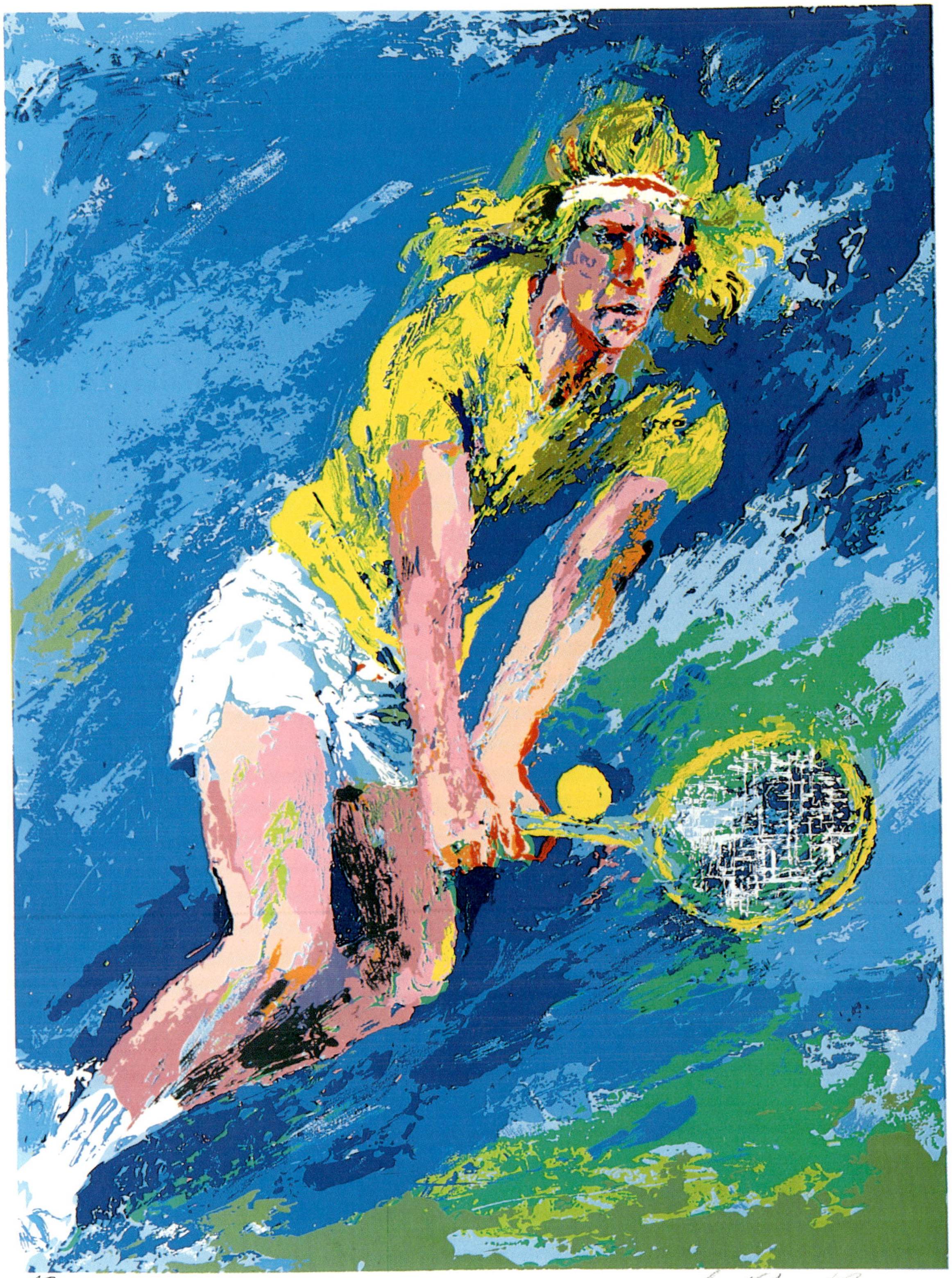

128   Bjorn Borg

1977
Serigraph
23¾ x 17¼ (60.33 x 43.79 cm)
A limited edition of 300, signed and
numbered by the artist.

129   Harlem Jazz Street Scene

1977
Serigraph
39⅞ x 26 (101.28 x 66.04 cm)
A limited edition of 100, signed and numbered
by the artist.

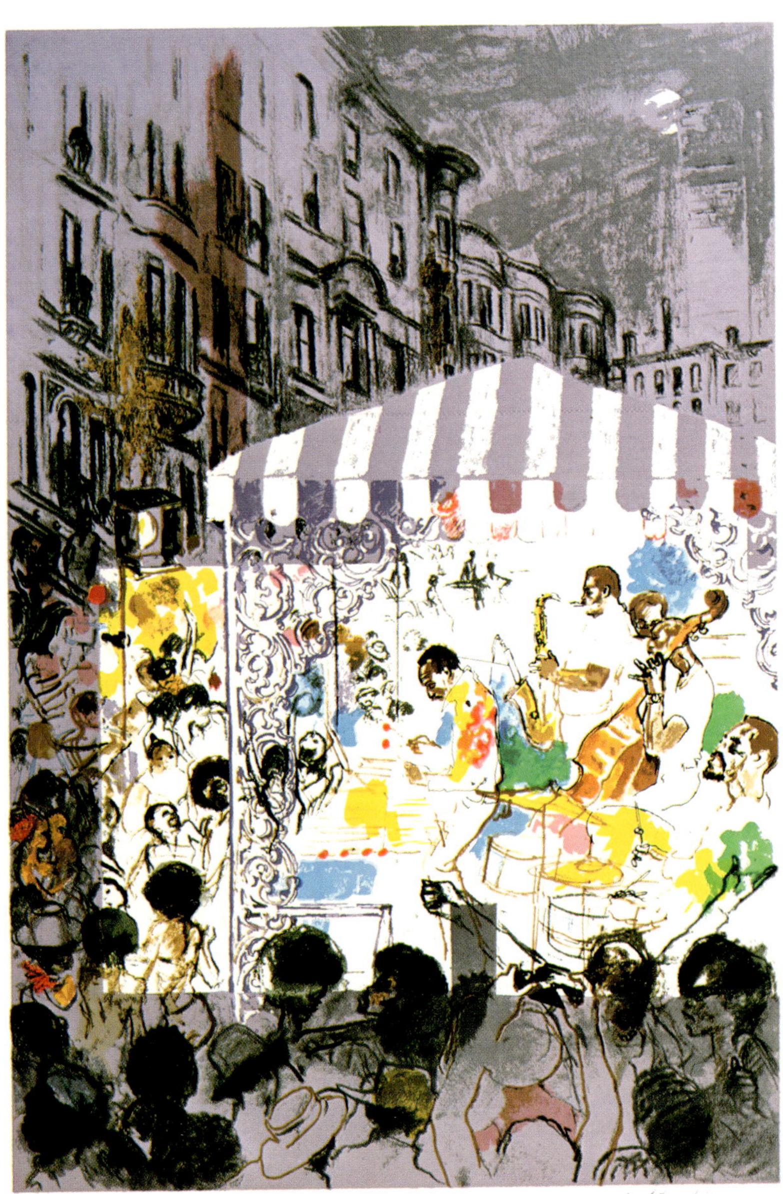

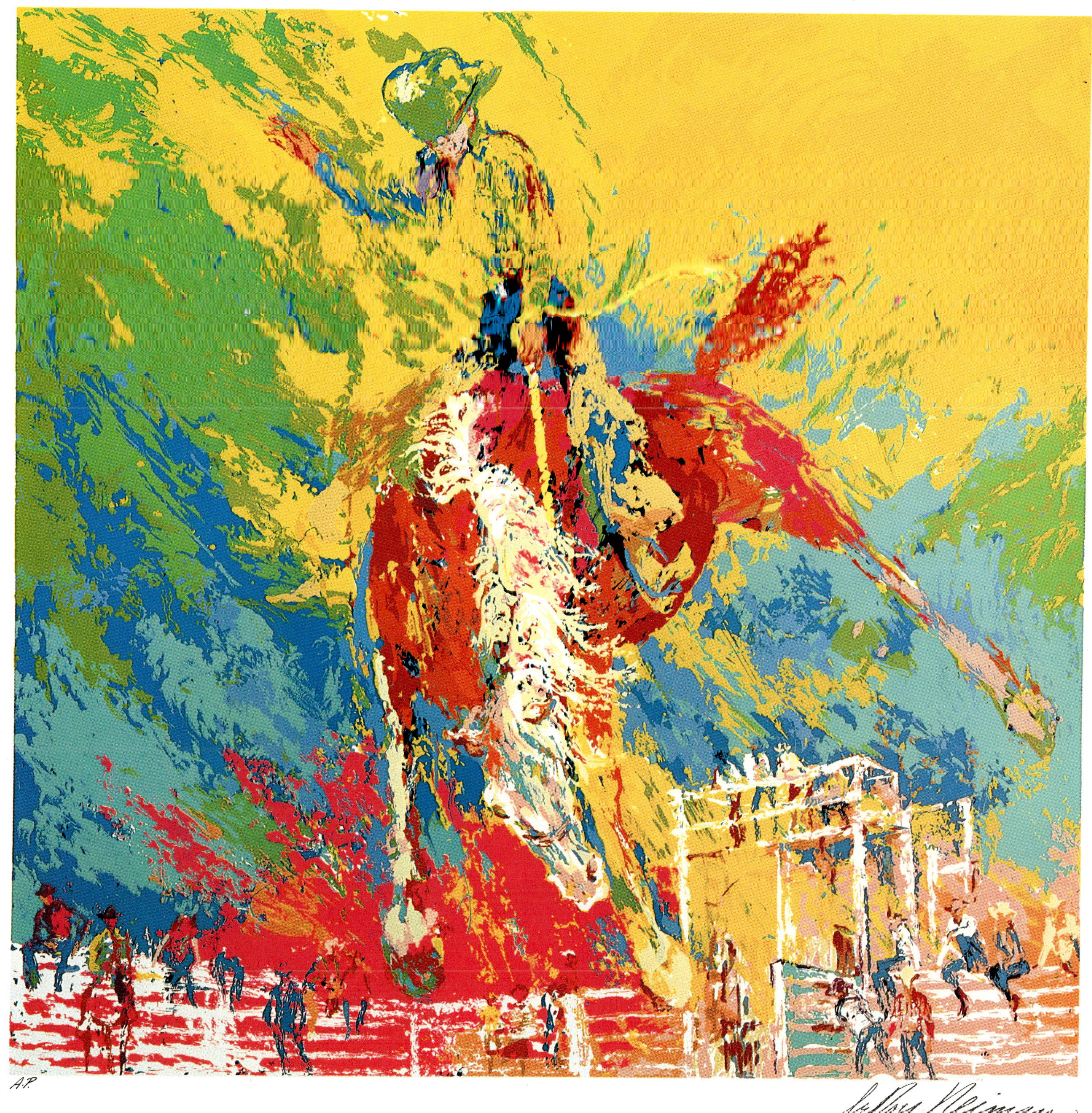

130   Bucking Bronc

1977
Serigraph
31⅛ x 31⅛ (79.06 x 79.06 cm)
A limited edition of 300, signed and numbered
by the artist.

131 Marlin

1977
Serigraph
25½ x 34⅛ (64.77 x 86.67 cm)
A limited edition of 300, signed and numbered
by the artist.

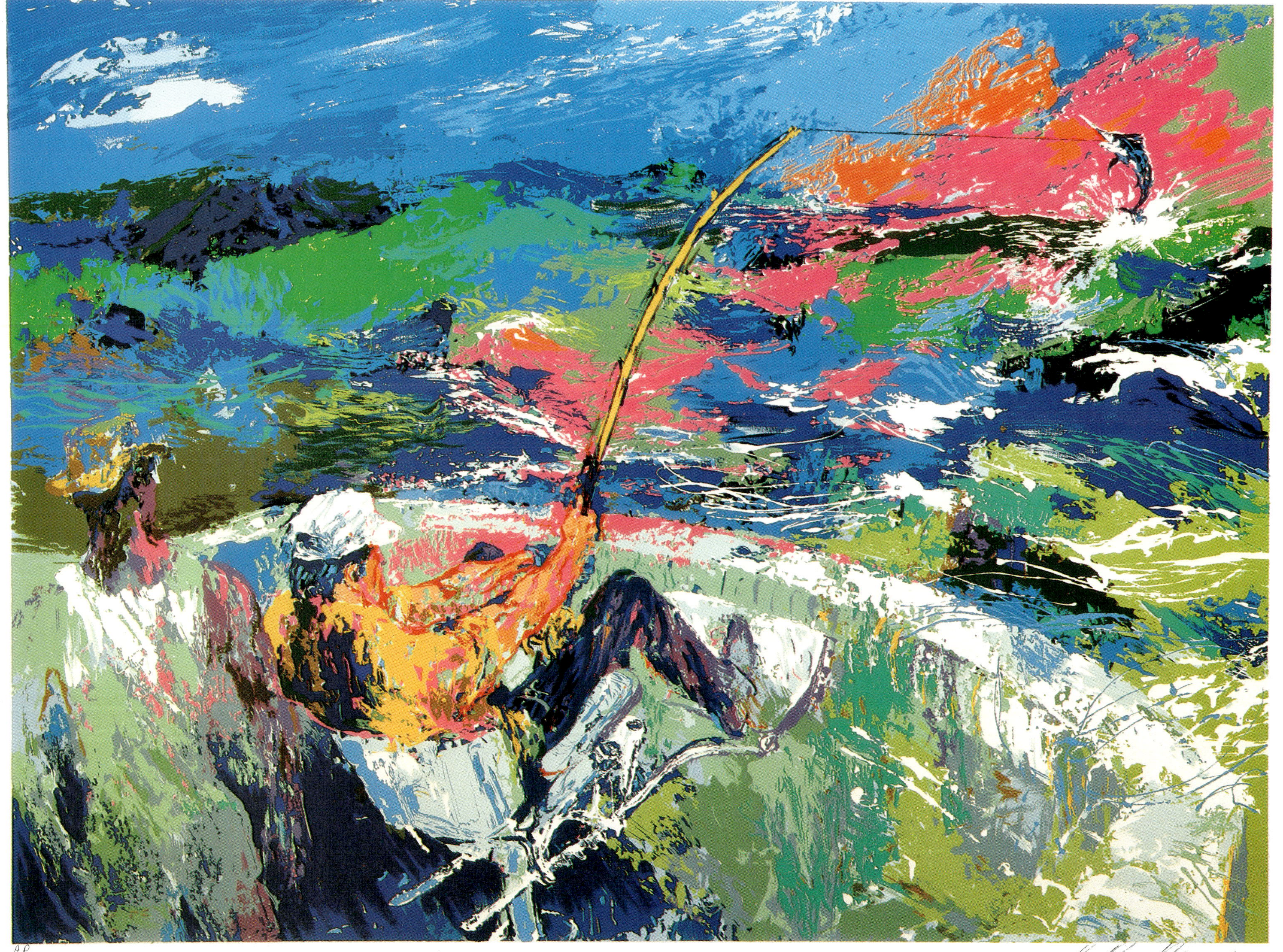

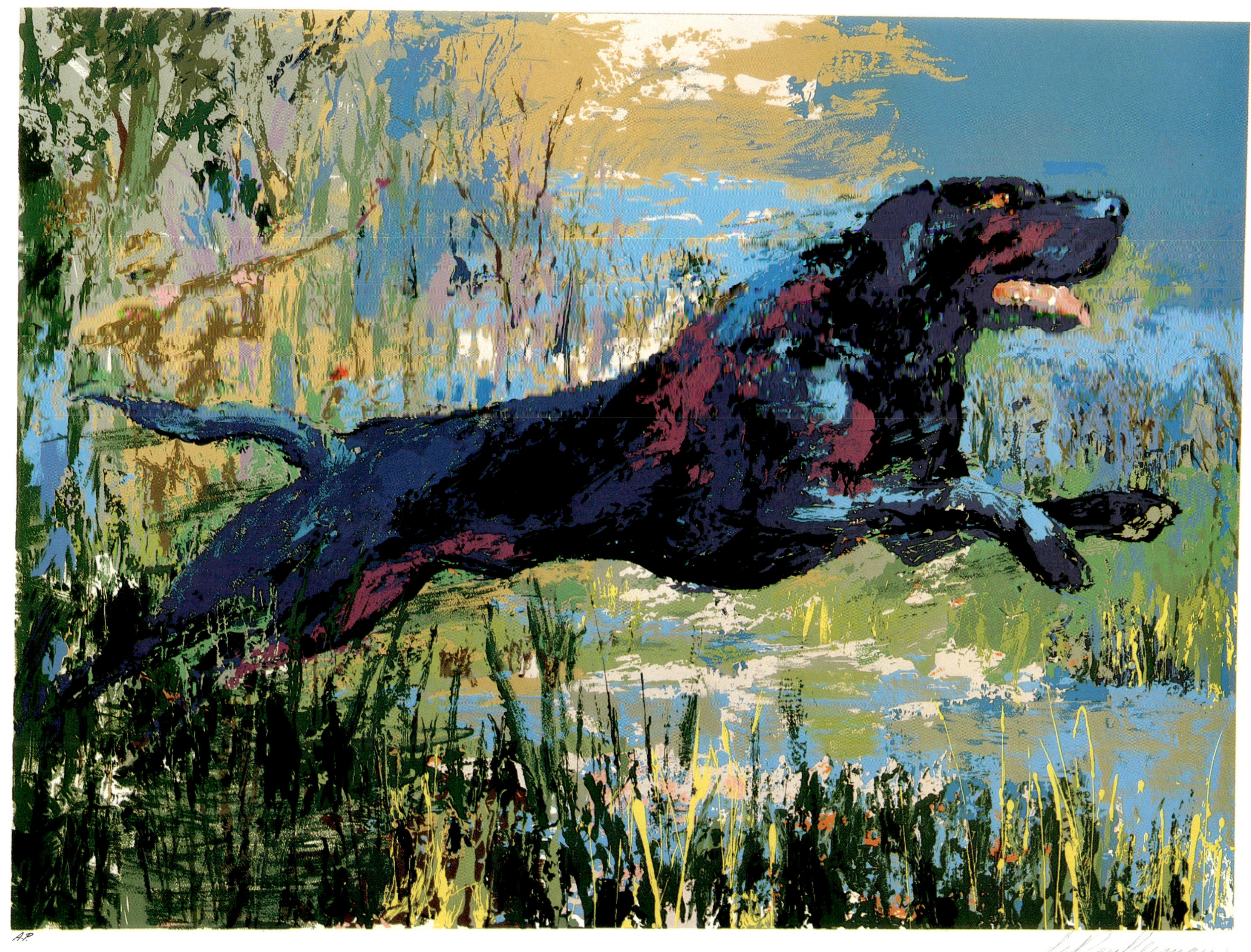

132   Black Labrador

1977
Serigraph
27¼ x 36¼ (69.22 x 92.08 cm)
A limited edition of 300, signed and numbered
by the artist.

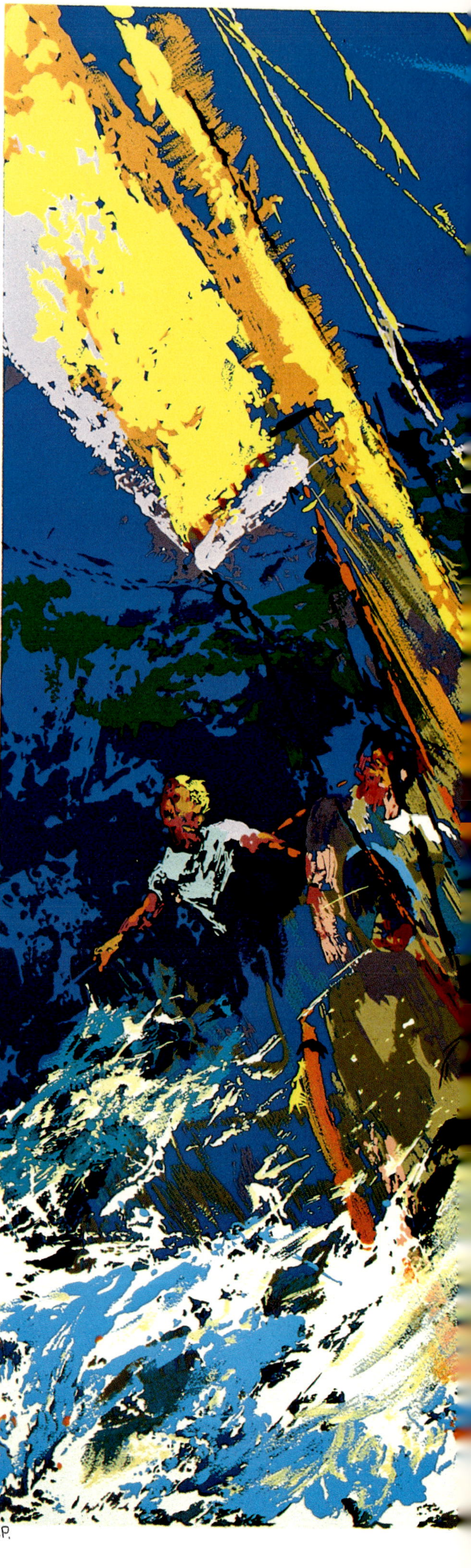

133   Ocean Sailing
1977
Serigraph
26 x 34¾ (66.04 x 88.27 cm)
A limited edition of 300, signed and numbered
by the artist.

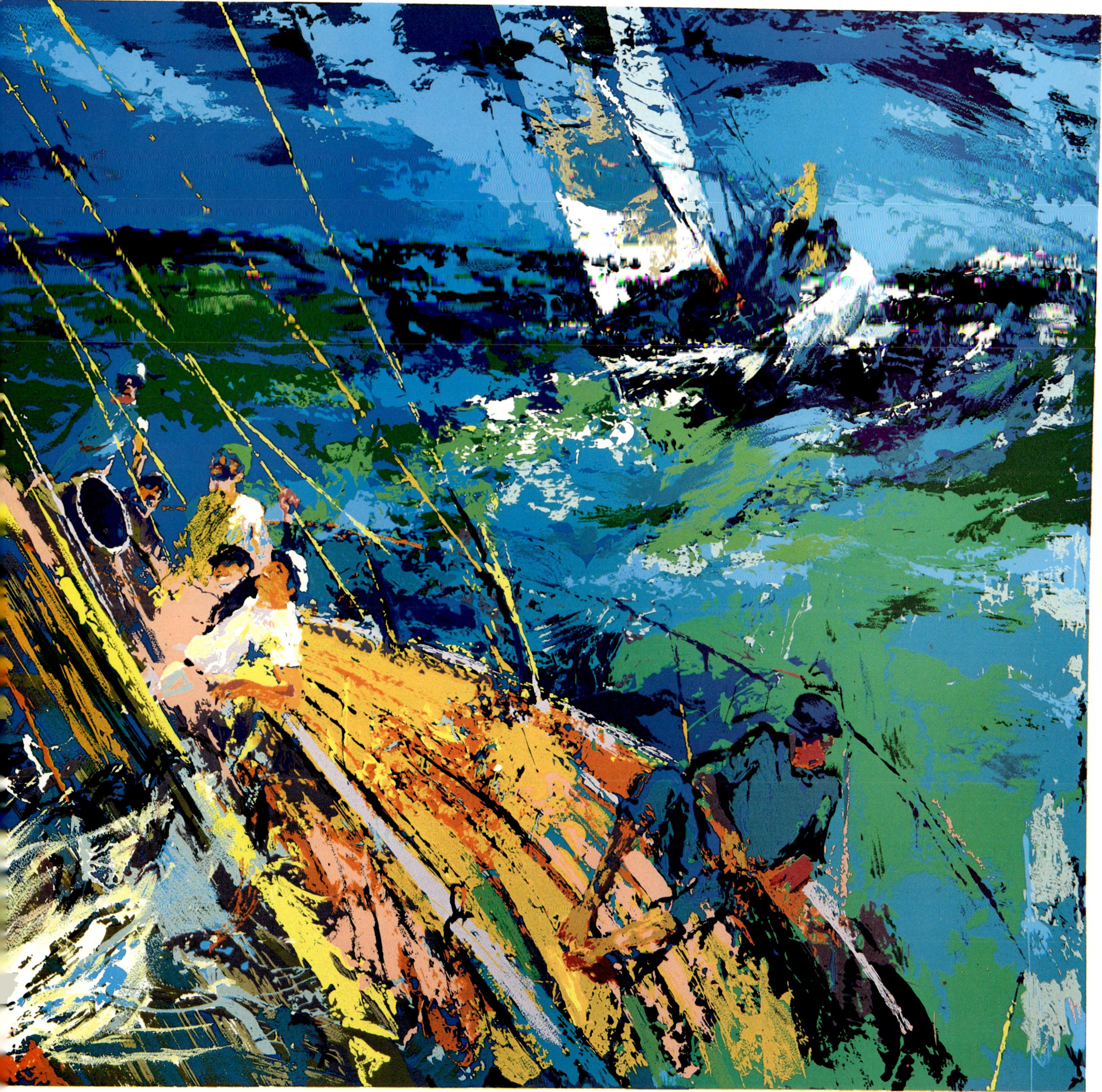

134   Delacroix's Tiger

1977
Serigraph
28⅝ x 38⅛ (72.71 x 96.84 cm)
A limited edition of 300, signed and numbered
by the artist.

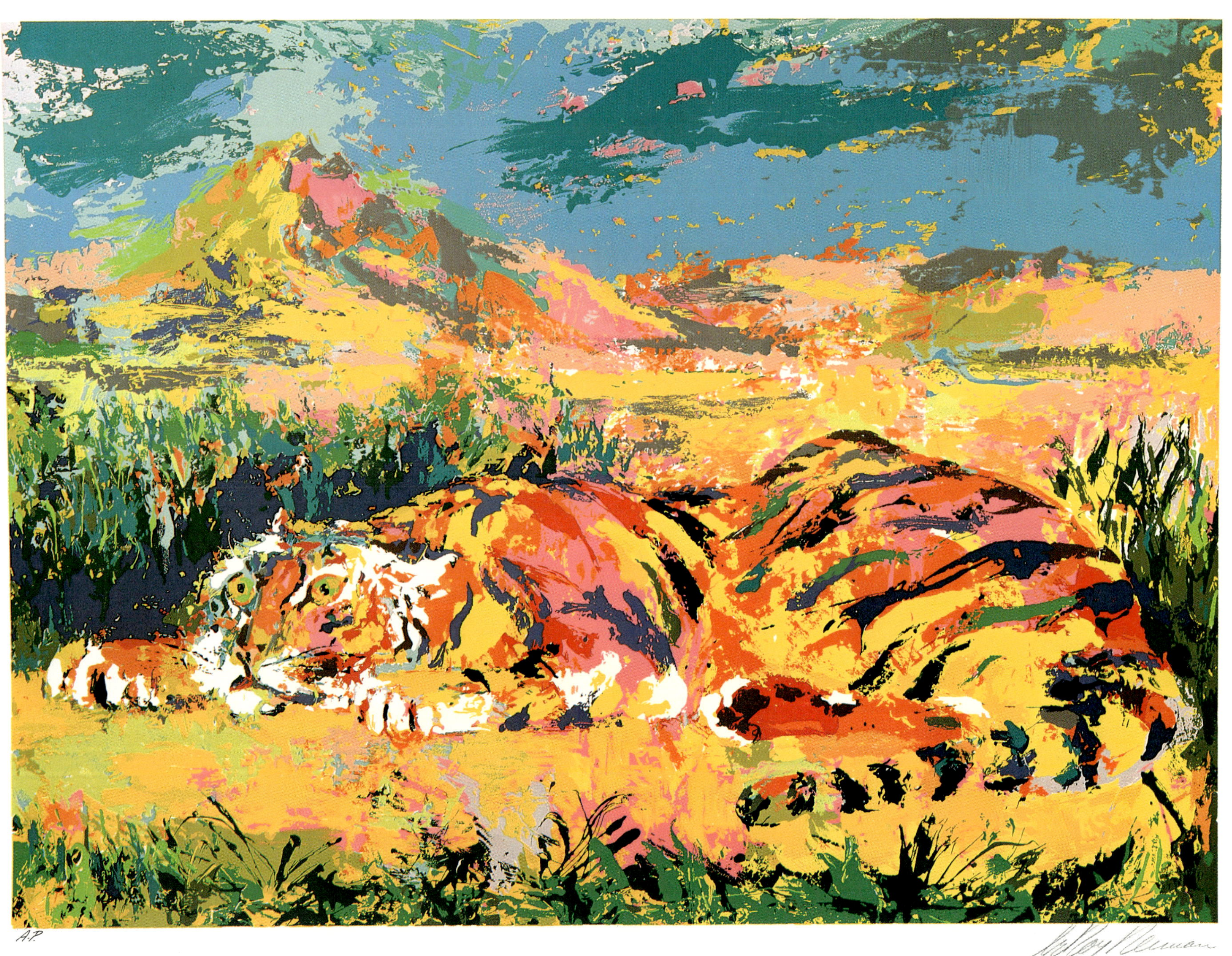

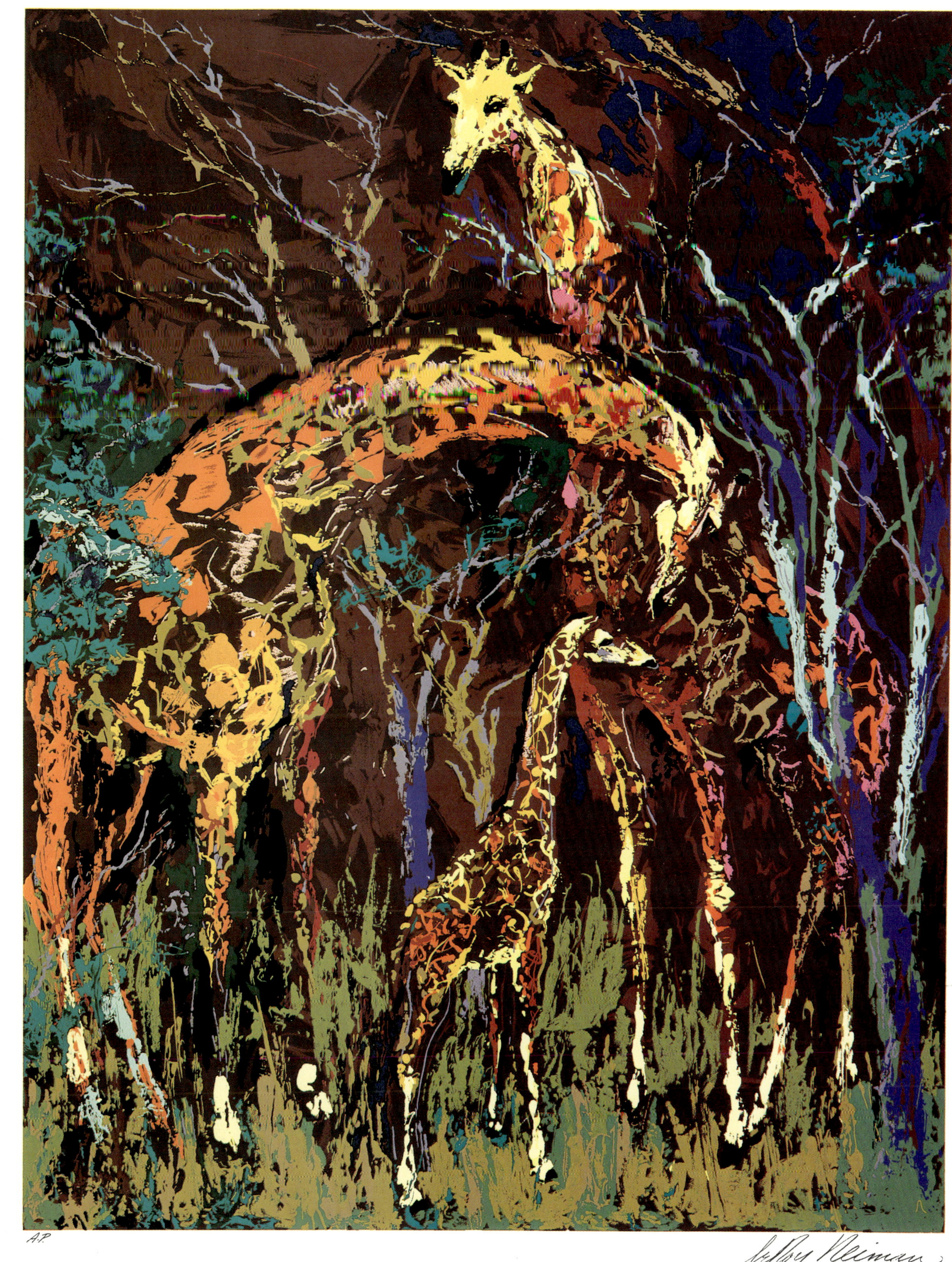

135   Giraffe Family
1977
Serigraph
38¼ x 28¾ (97.16 x 73.03 cm)
A limited edition of 300, signed and
numbered by the artist.

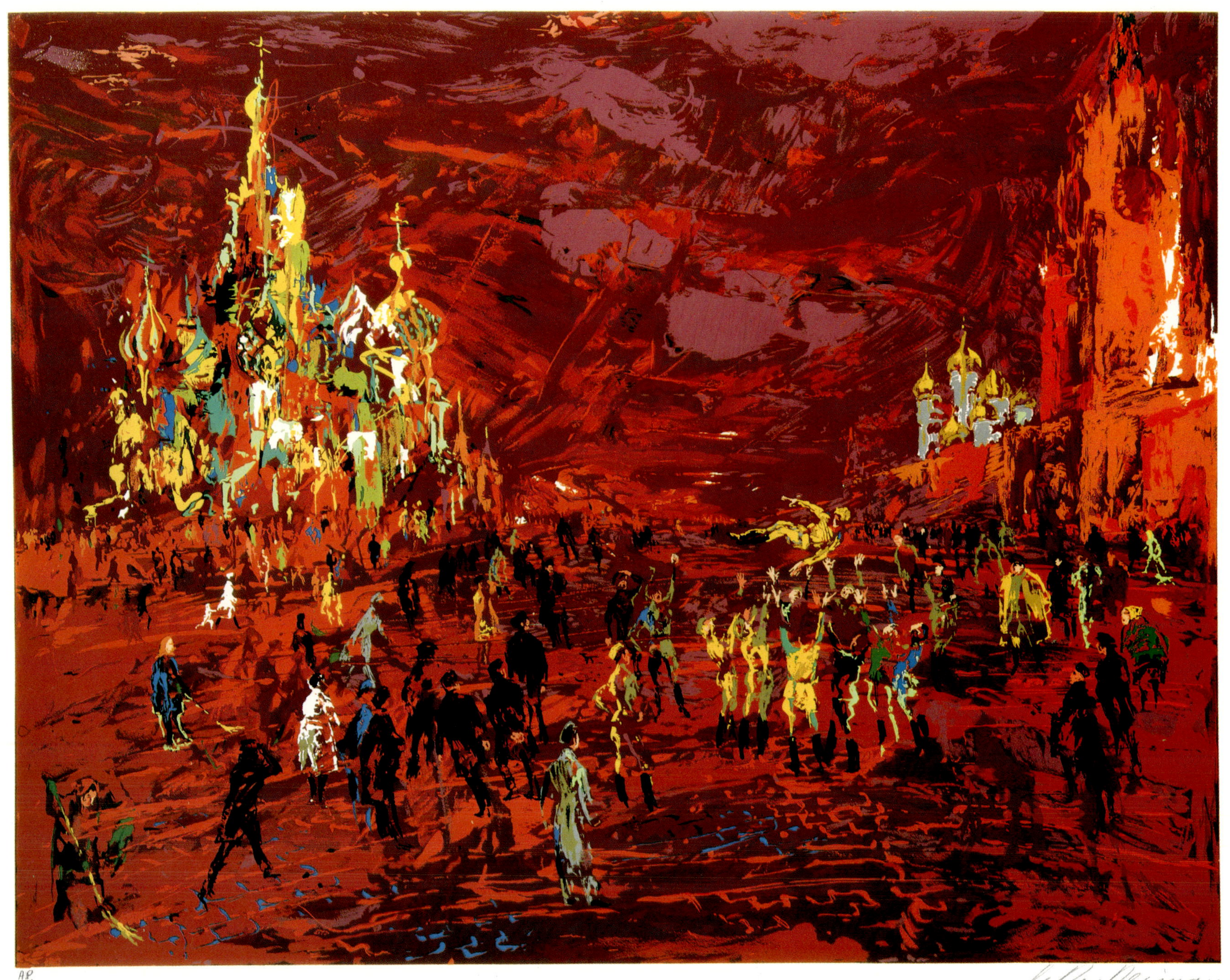

136 Red Square

1977
Serigraph
26 x 32¾ (66.04 x 83.19 cm)
A limited edition of 300, signed and numbered
by the artist.

137   French Connection

1977
Serigraph
23 x 30¾ (58.42 x 78.11 cm)
A limited edition of 300, signed and numbered
by the artist.

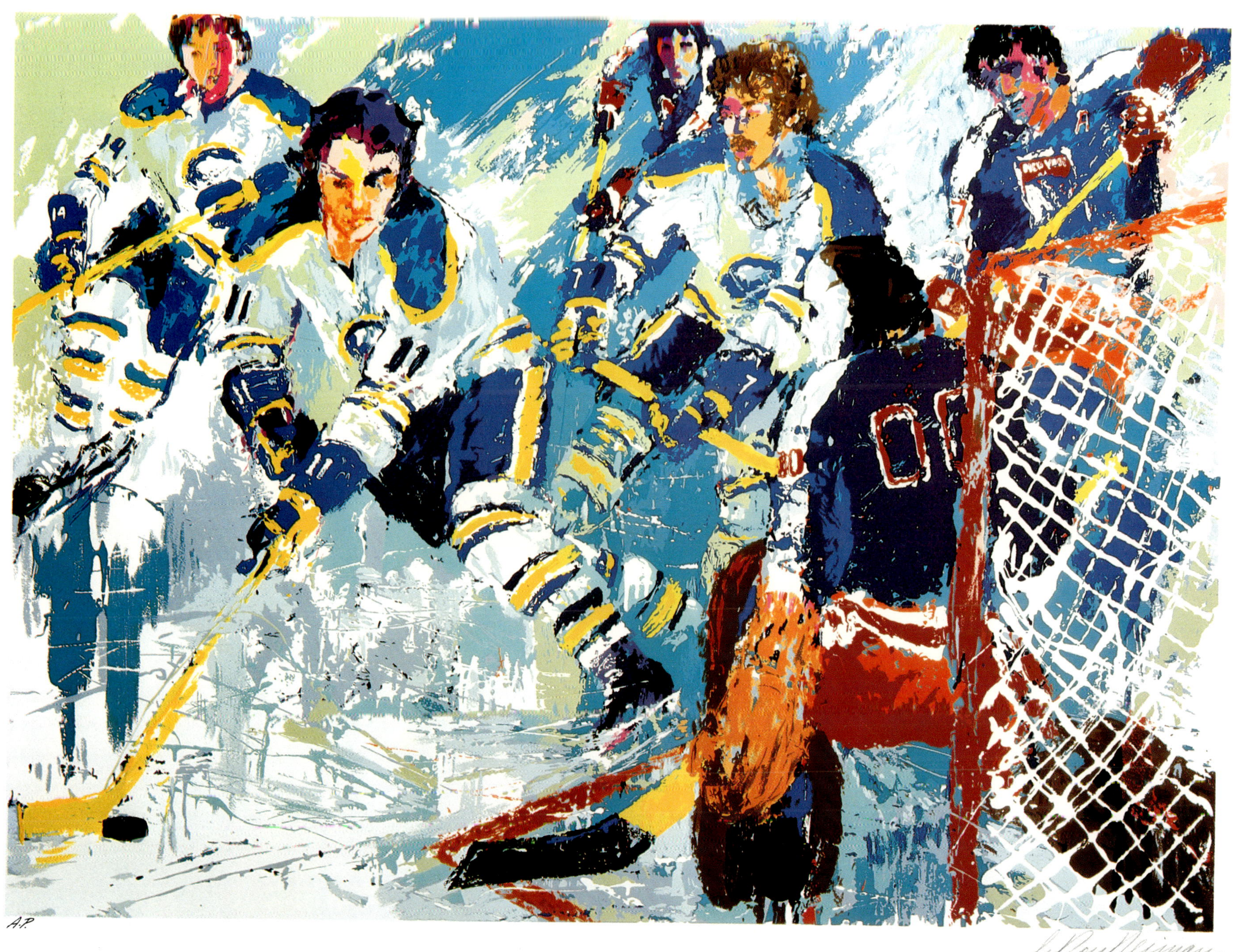

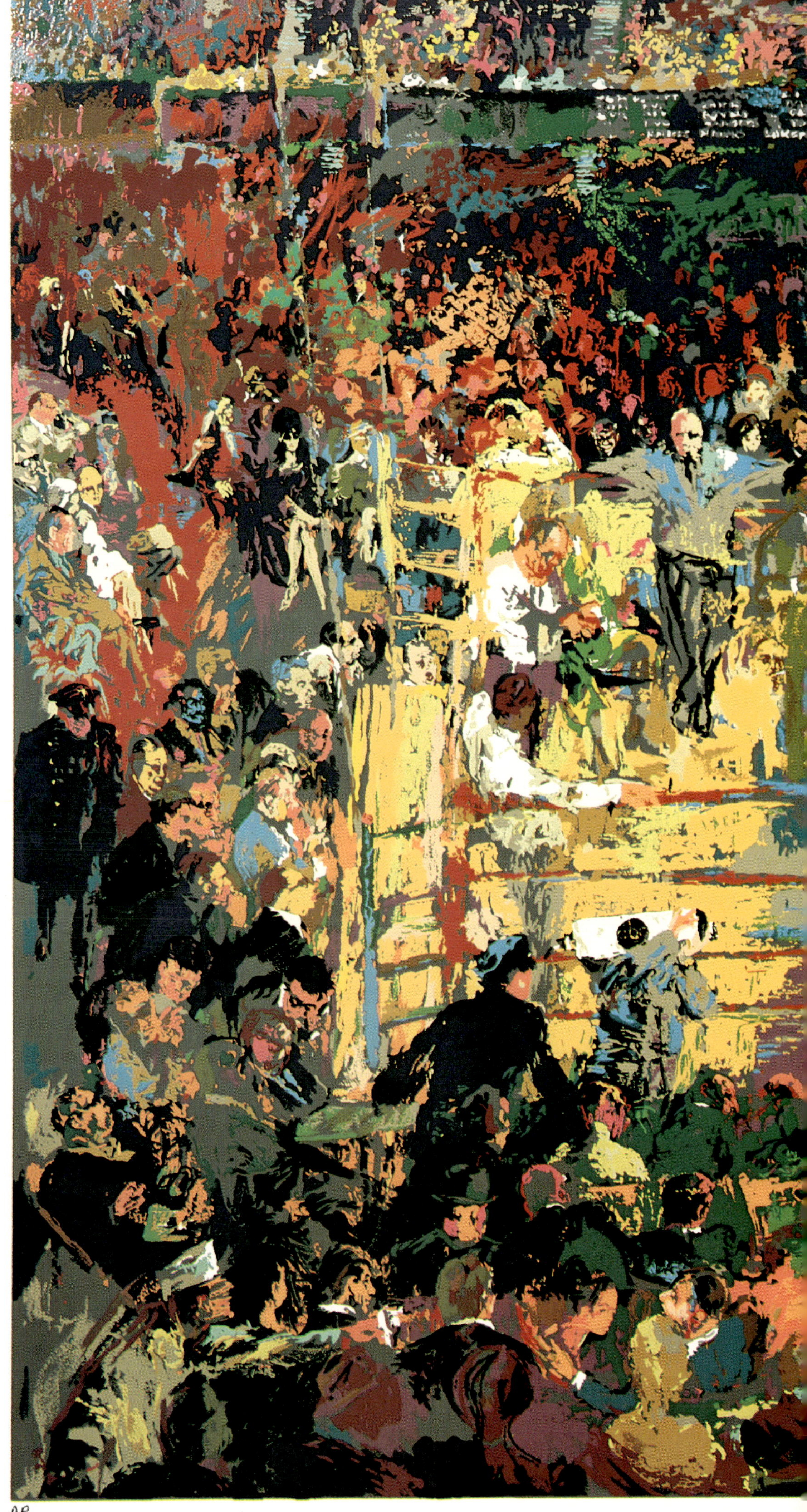

138 Introduction of the Champions at Madison Square Garden
1977
Serigraph
29¼ x 36½ (74.30 x 92.71 cm)
A limited edition of 300, signed and numbered by the artist.

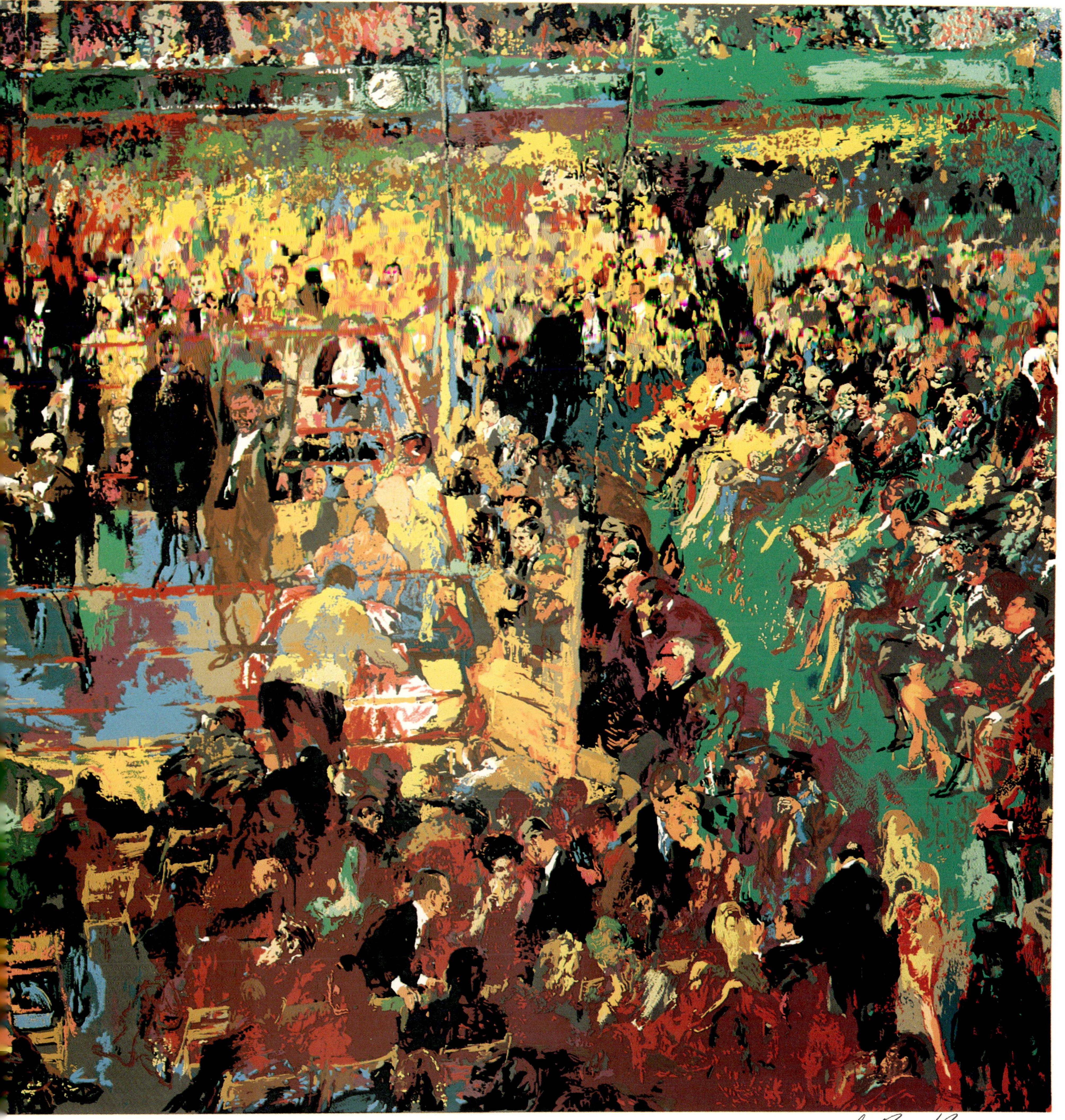

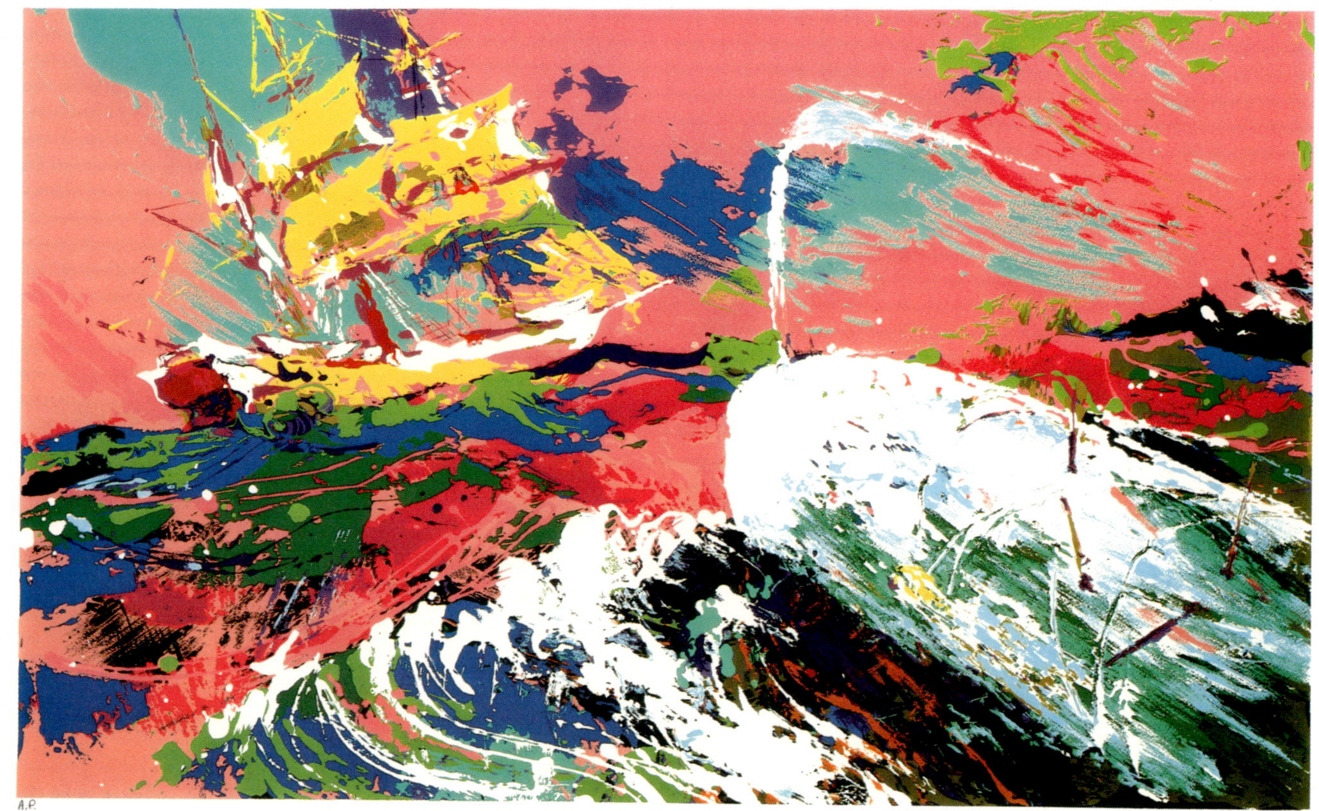

139
**Moby Dick Assaulting
the Pequod**
1977
Serigraph
19 x 30½ (48.26 x 77.47 cm)

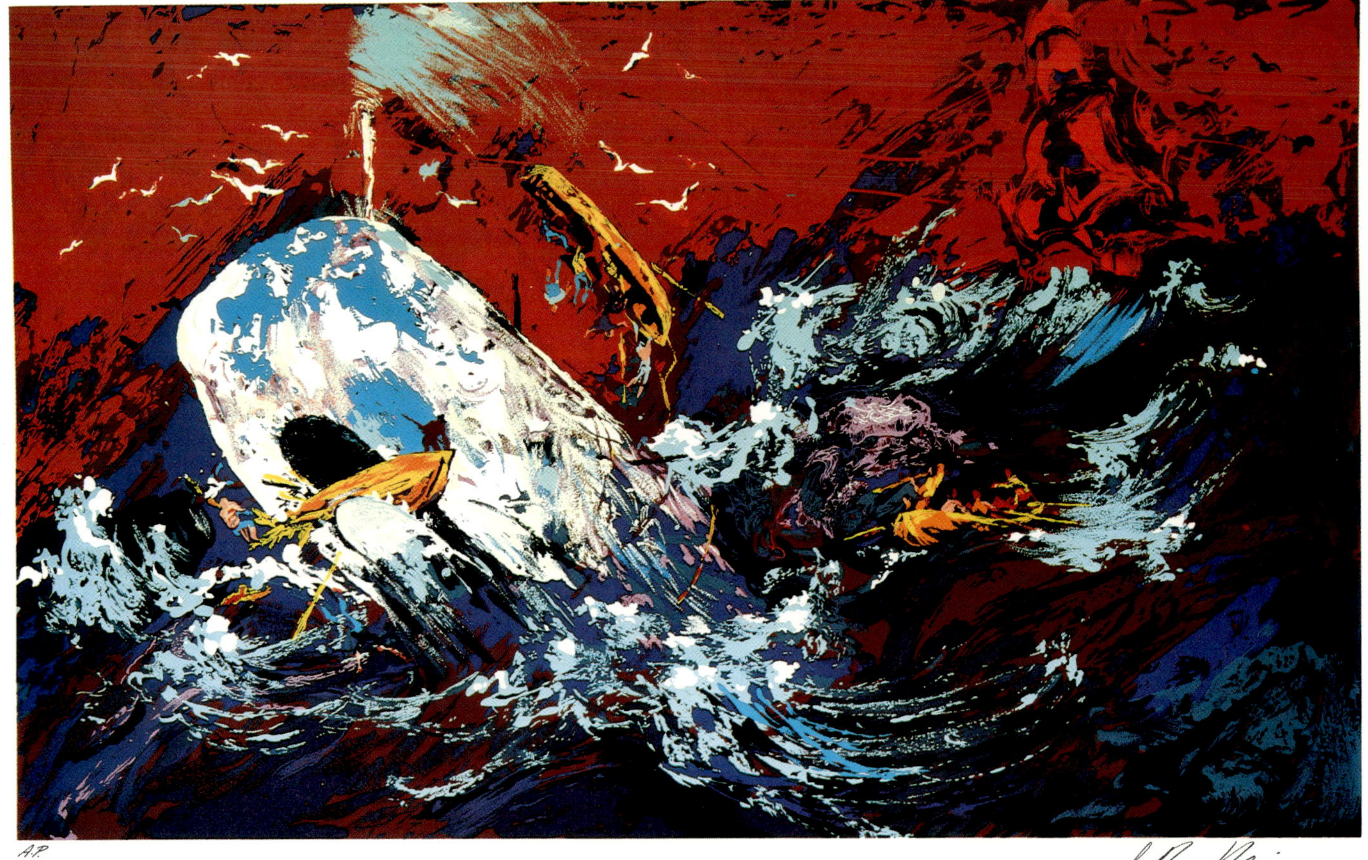

140
Red Sky
1977
Serigraph
19 x 30½ (48.26 x 77.47 cm)

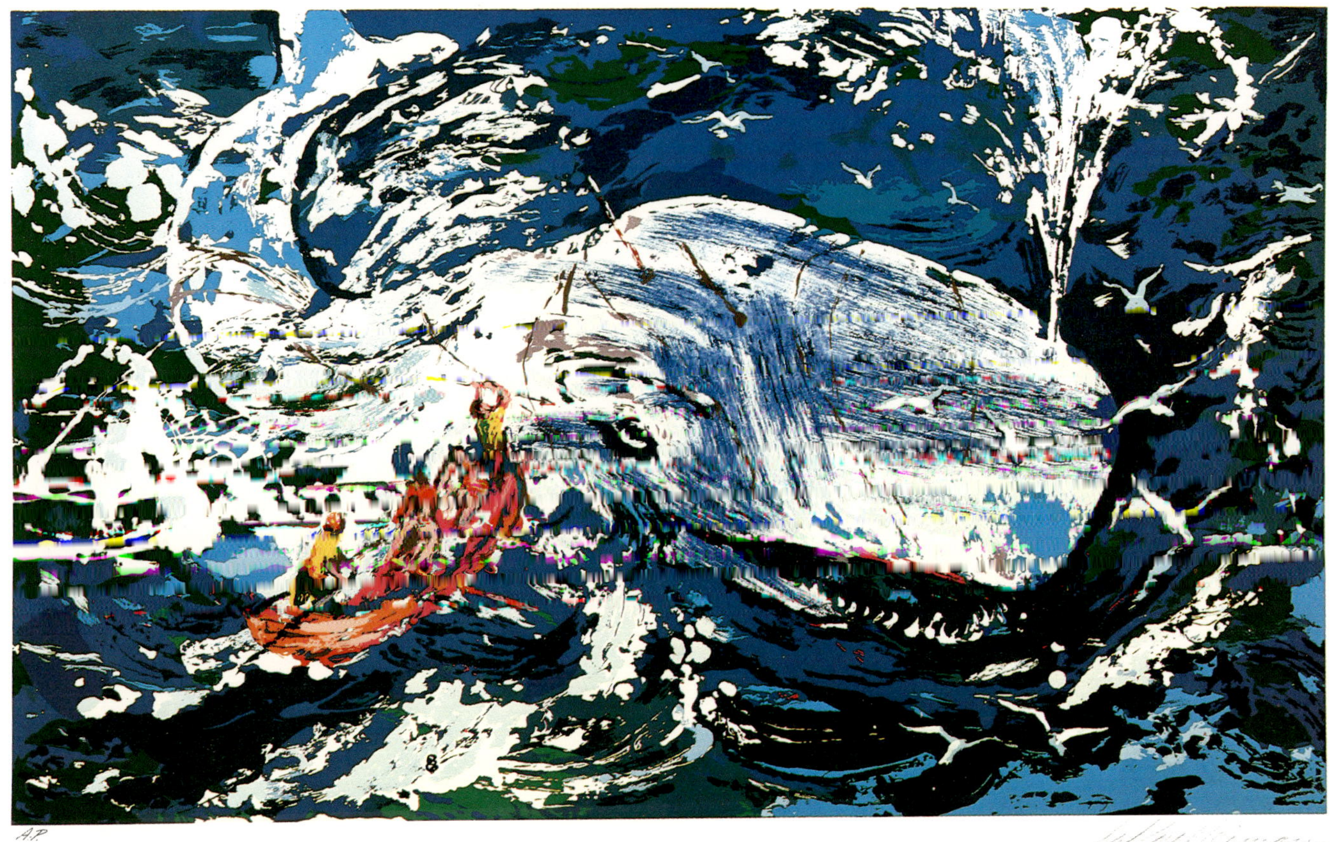

141
Blue Whale
1978
Serigraph
19 x 30½ (48.26 x 77.47 cm)

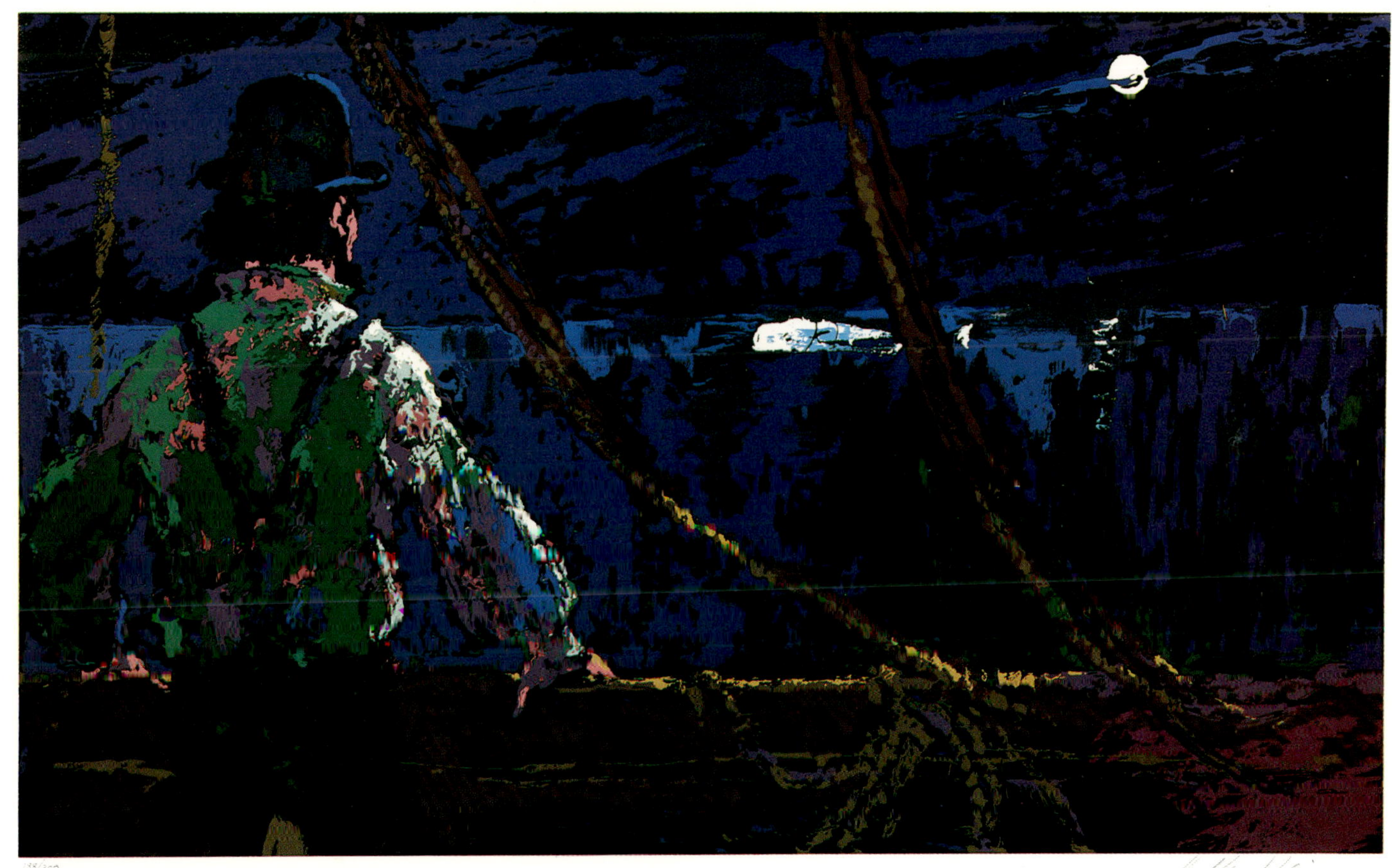

142
Ahab at the Night Watch
1978
Serigraph
19 x 30½ (48.26 x 77.47 cm)

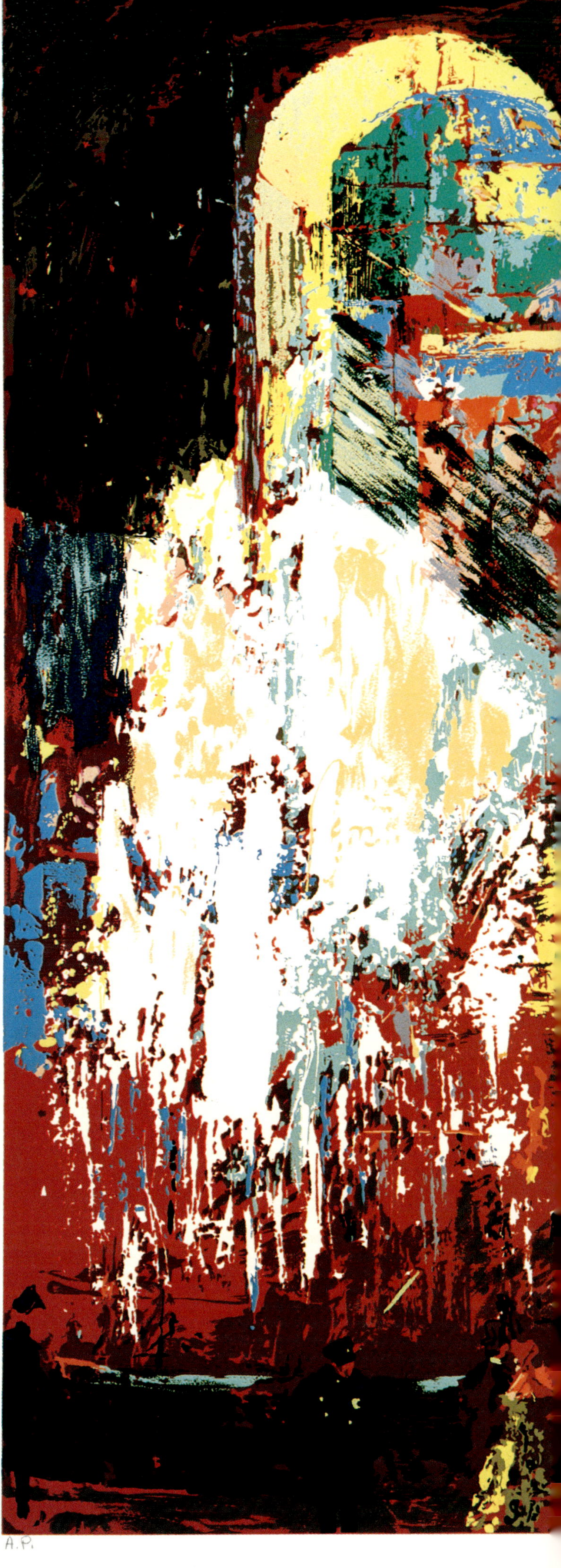

143 Metropolitan Opera
1978
Serigraph
26¼ x 32½ (66.68 x 82.55 cm)
A limited edition of 300, signed and numbered
by the artist.

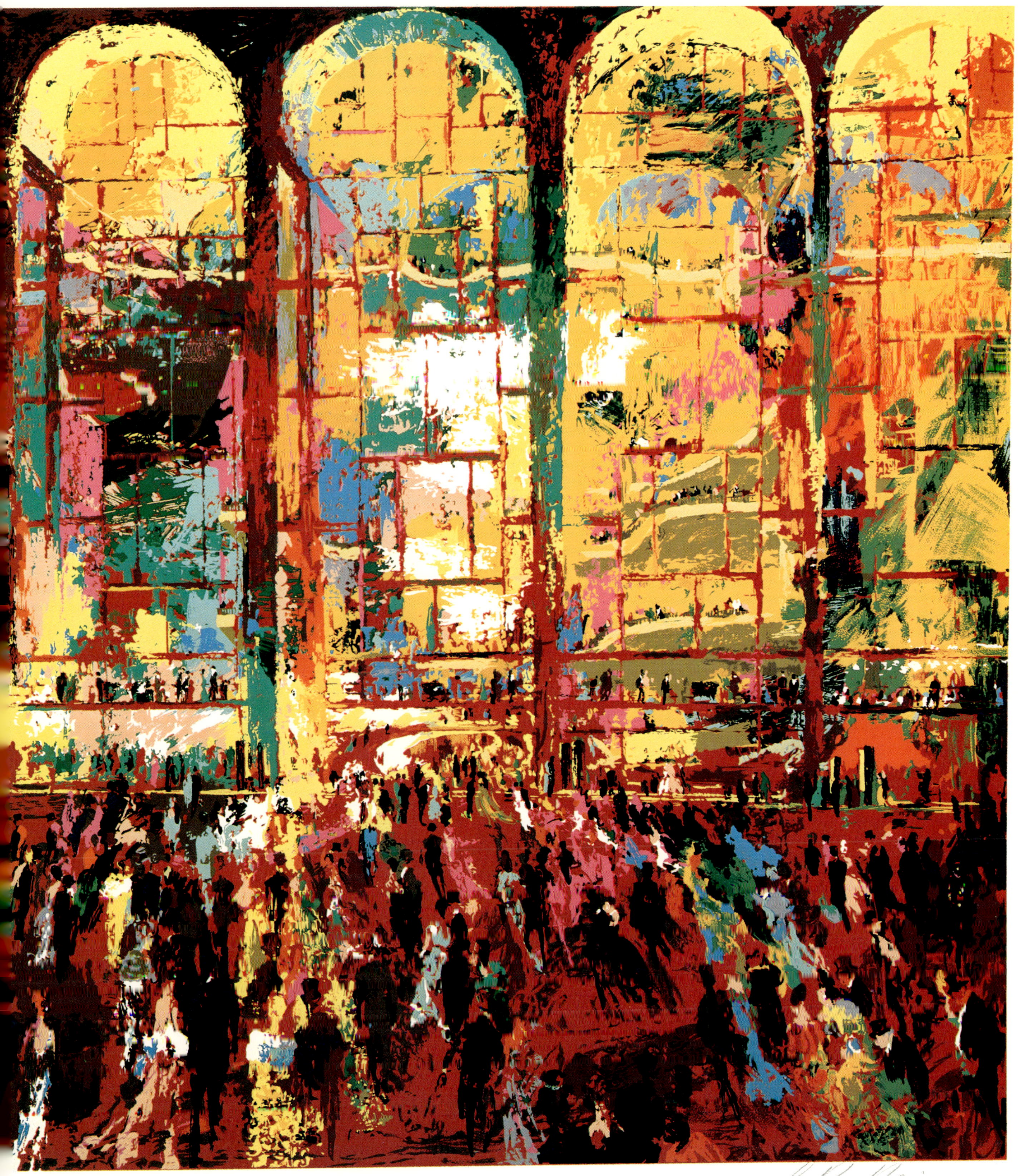

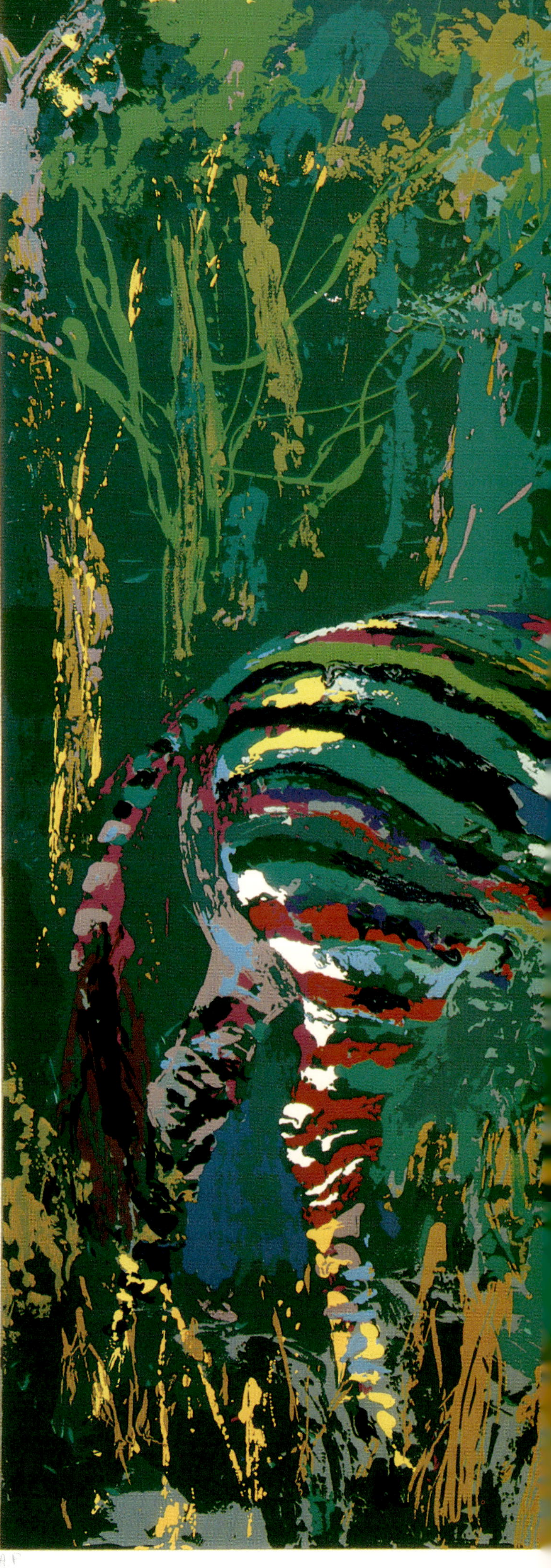

144 Zebra Family

1978
Serigraph
28¼ x 37⅝ (71.76 x 95.57 cm)
A limited edition of 300, signed and numbered
by the artist.

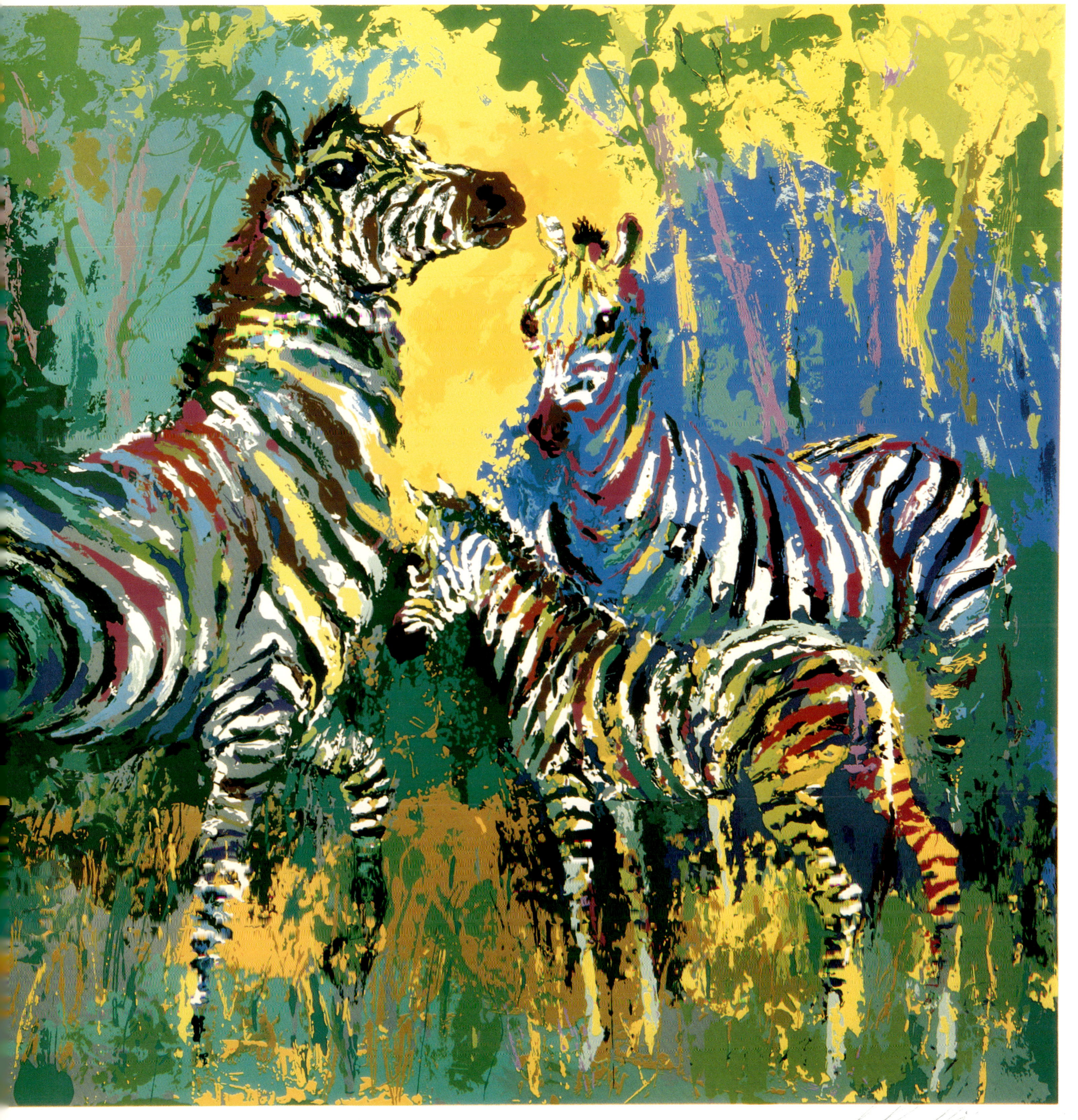

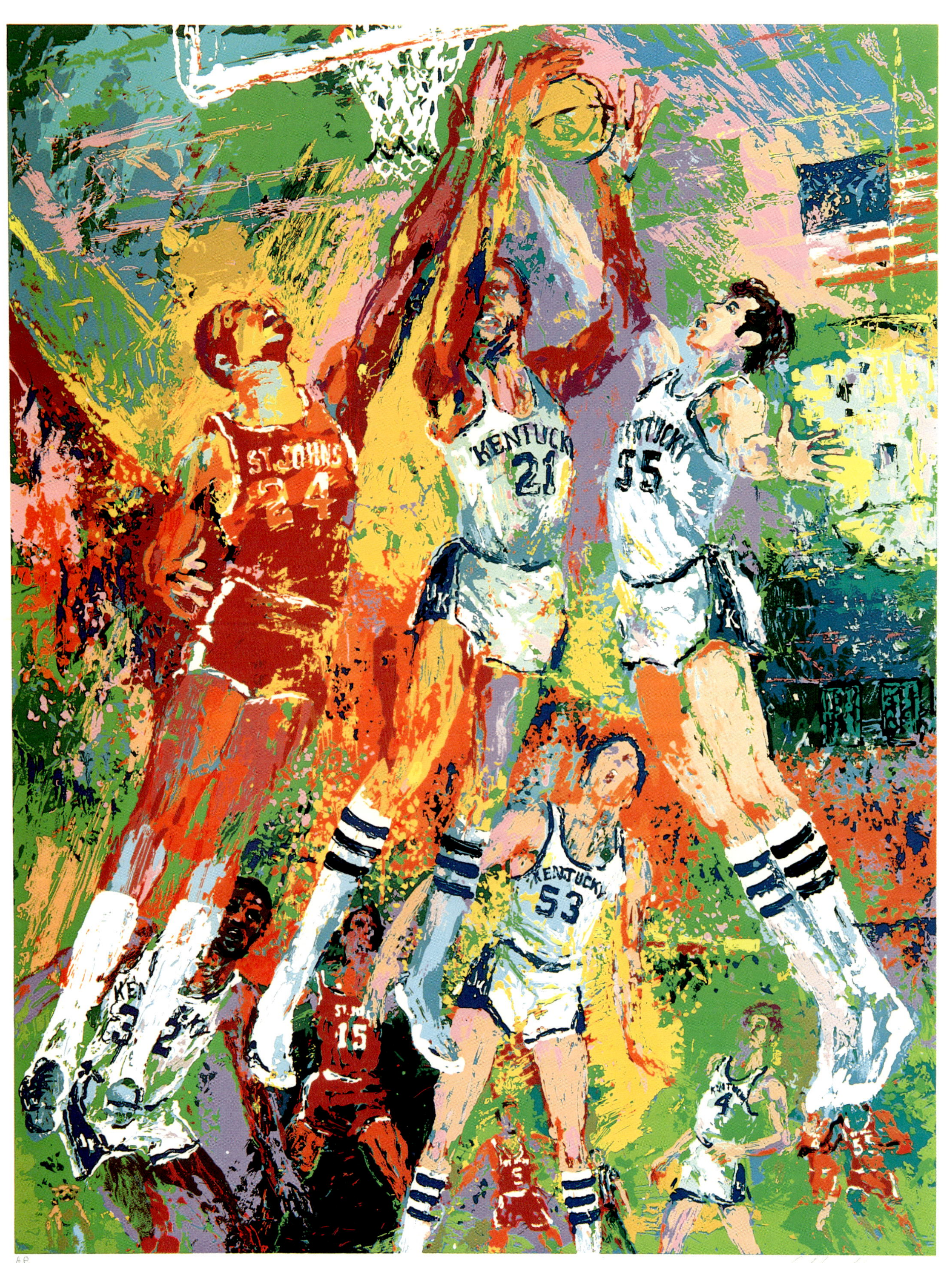# 145 Kentucky Wildcats
1978
Serigraph
36⅜ x 27¼ (92.39 x 69.22 cm)
A limited edition of 300, signed and
numbered by the artist.

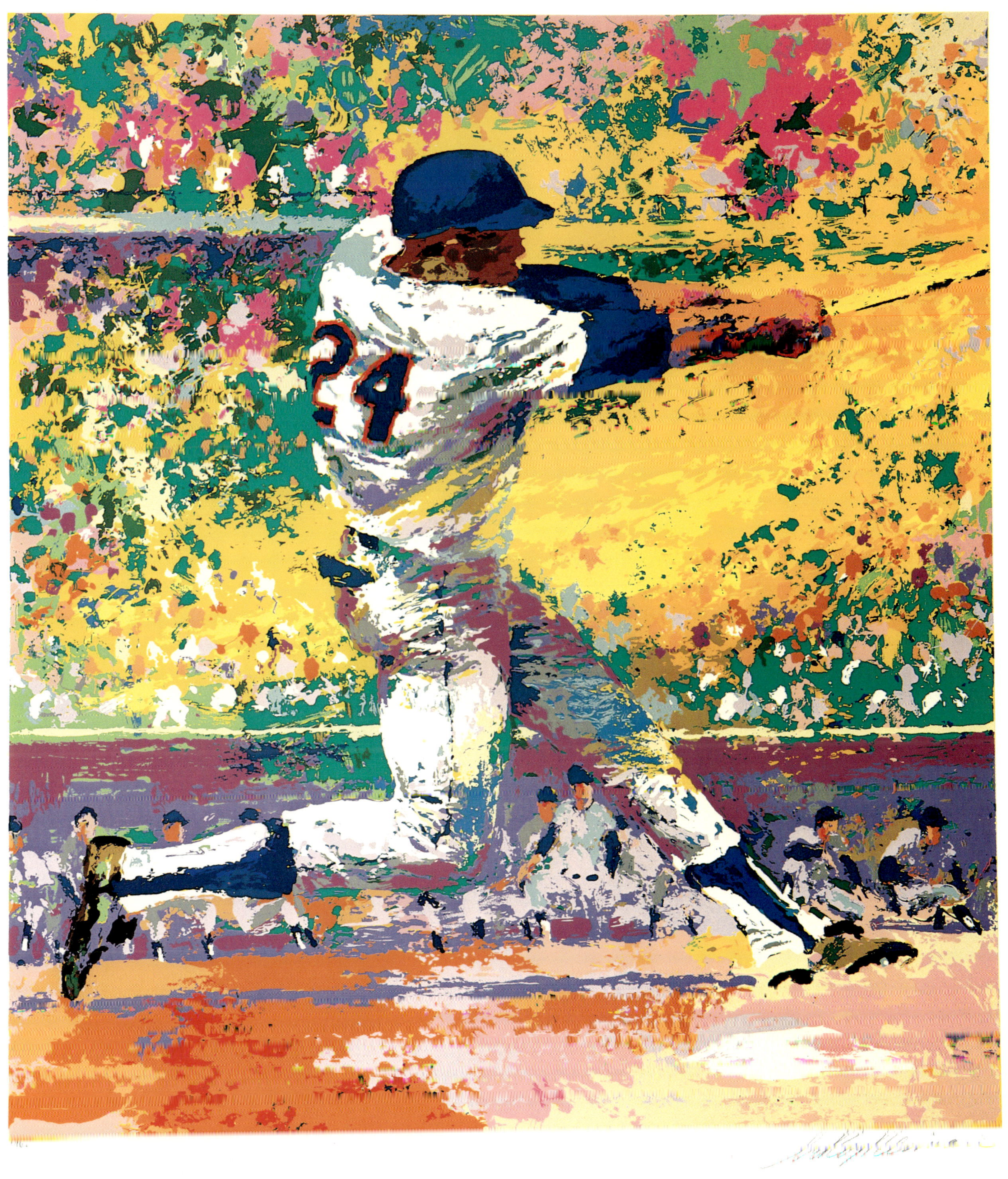

146 Willie Mays
1978
Serigraph
32 x 28 (81.28 x 71.12 cm)
A limited edition of 300, signed and numbered by the artist.

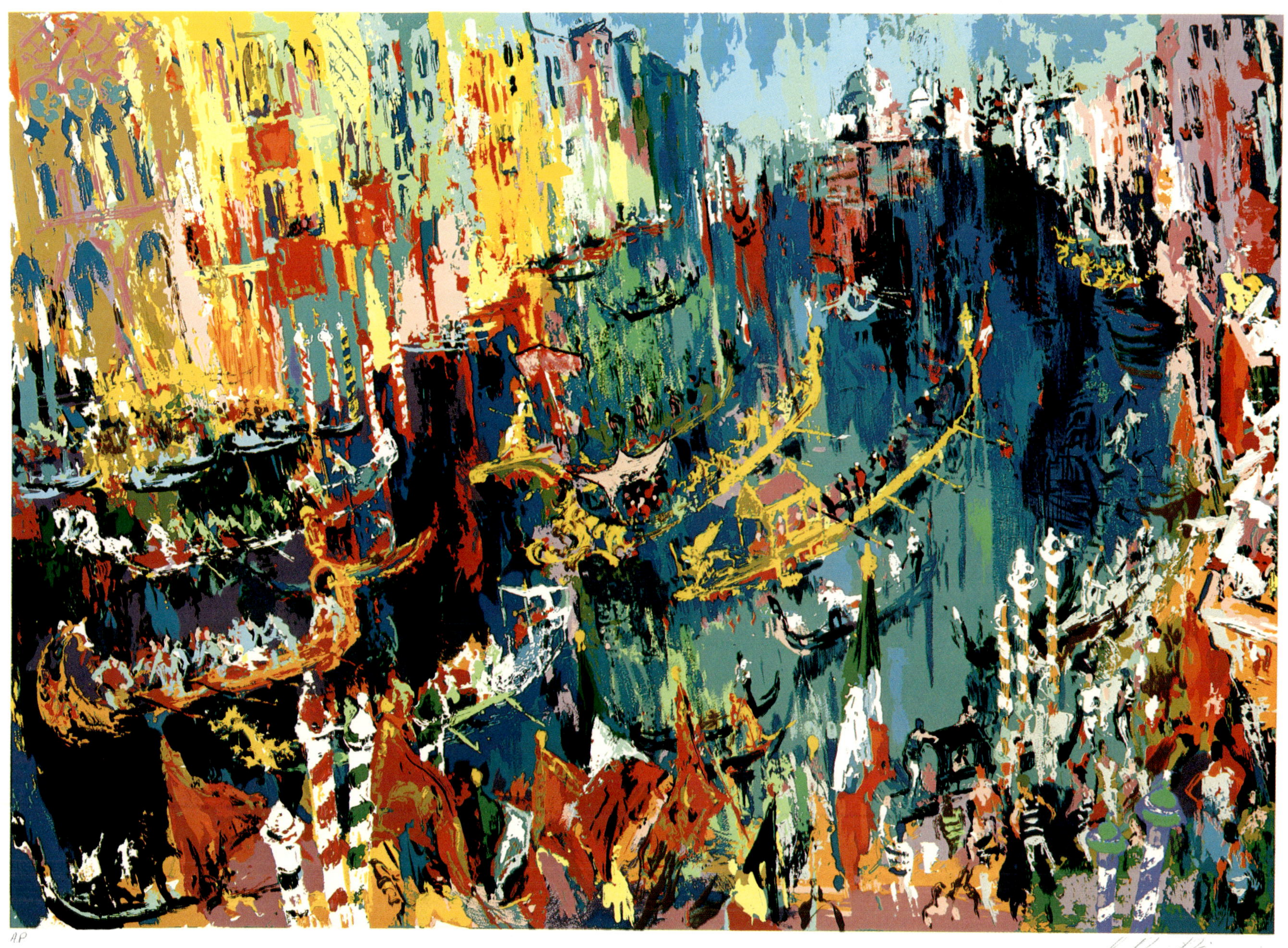

147 Regatta of the Gondoliers

1978
Serigraph
26¼ x 36 (66.68 x 91.44 cm)

A limited edition of 300, signed and numbered
by the artist.

148   Spectator's Fleet-America's Cup
1978
Serigraph
23½ x 35¼ (59.69 x 89.54 cm)
A limited edition of 300, signed and numbered by the artist

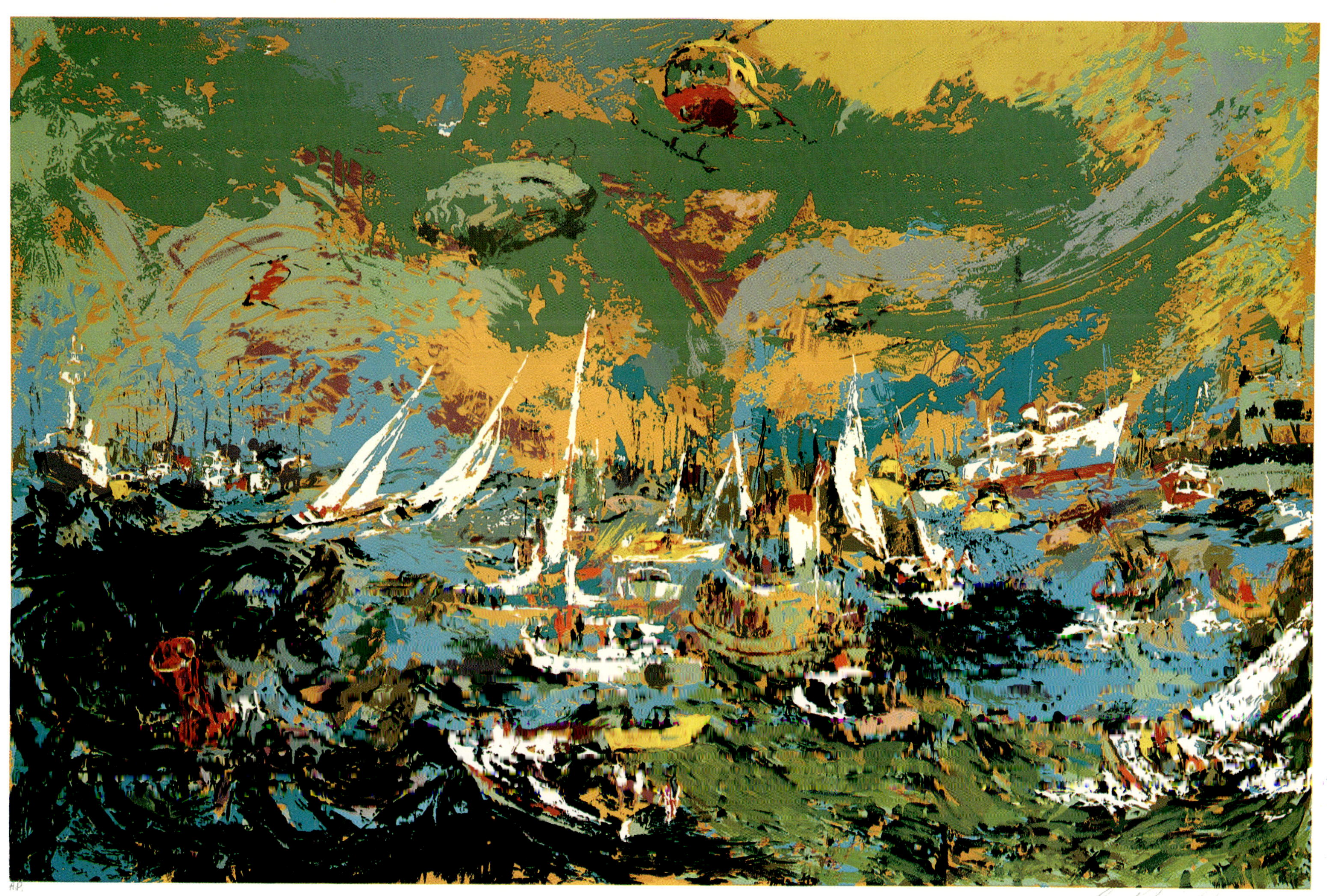

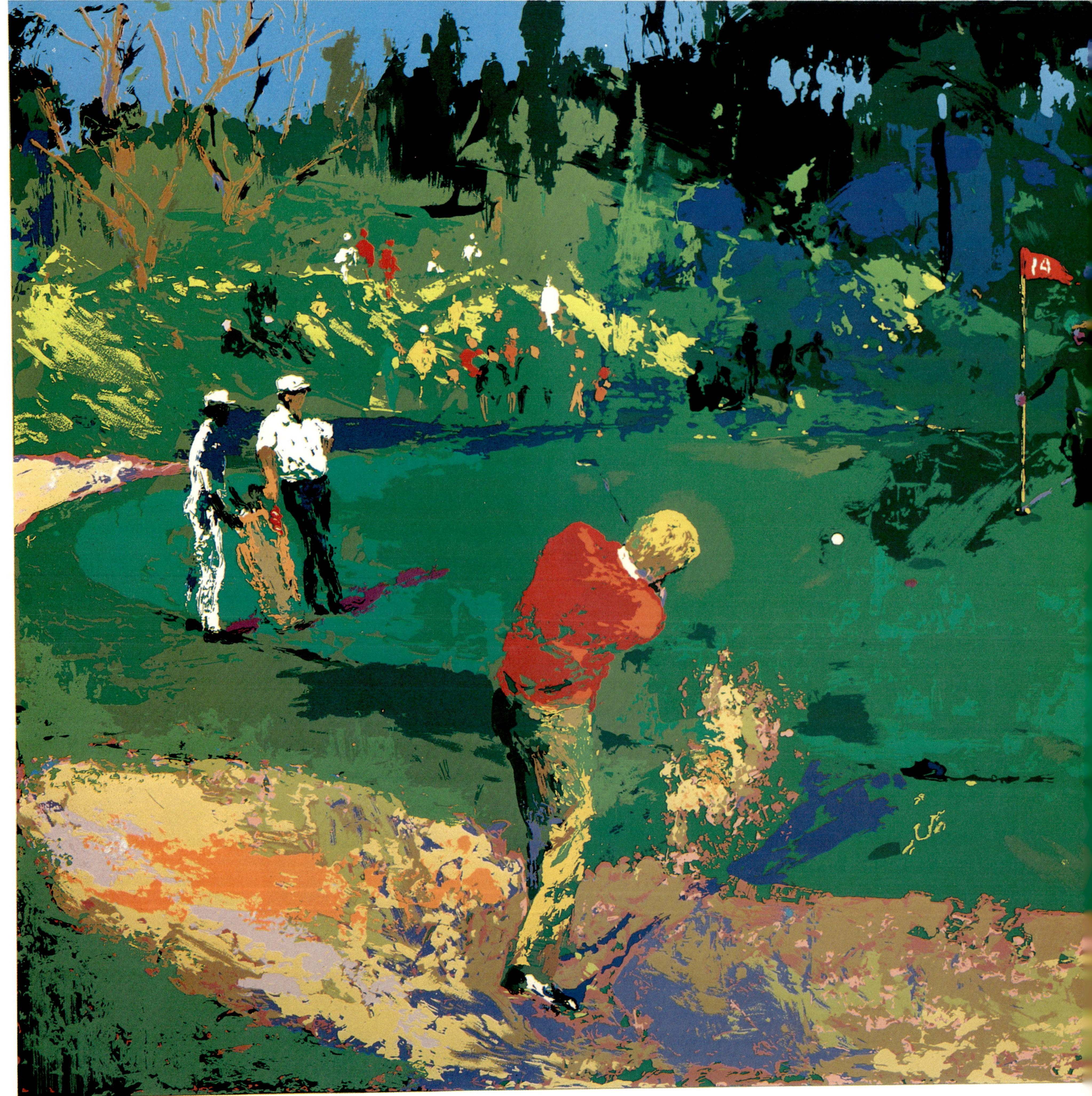

14
A.P.

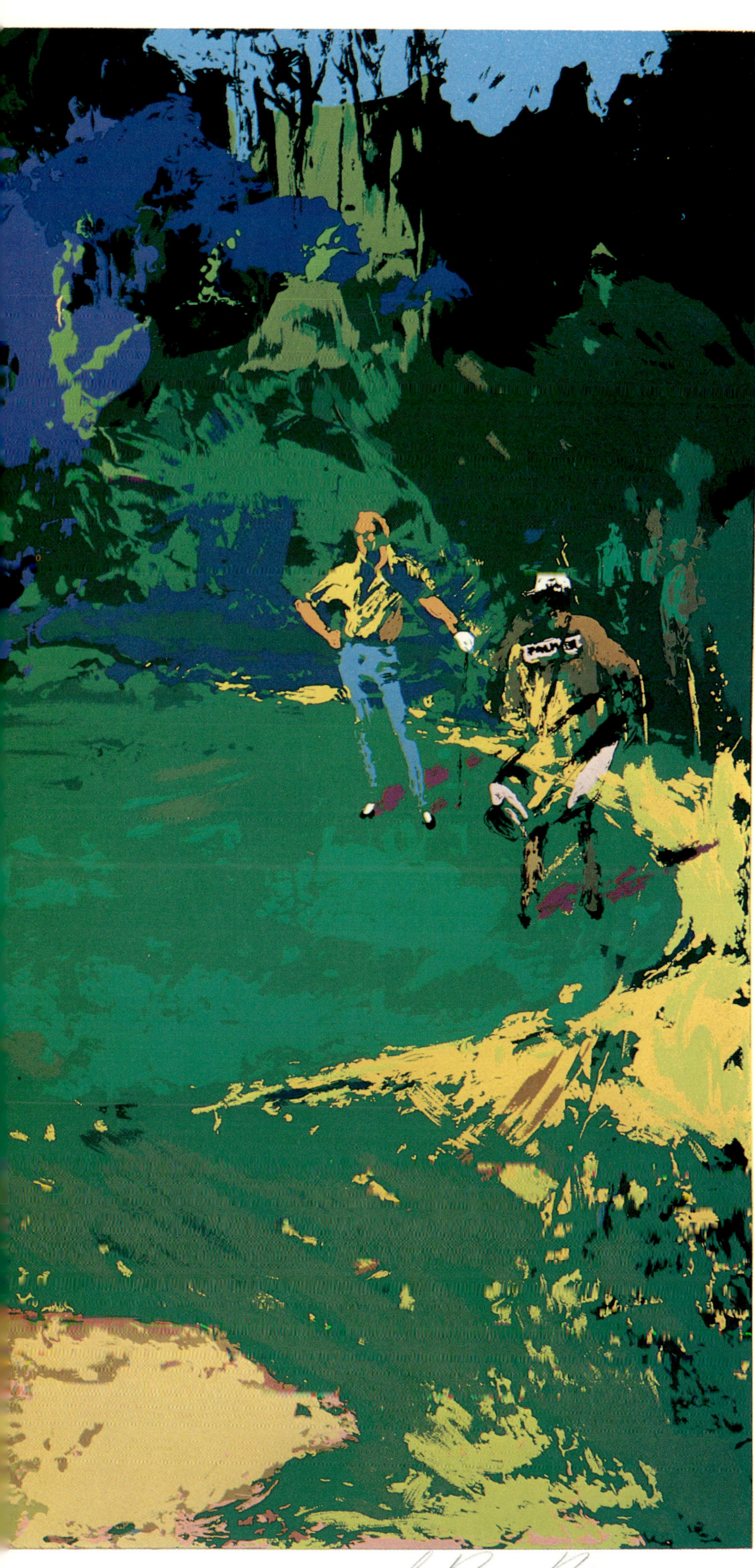

**149   Golf's Threesome
(Trevino, Nicklaus, Palmer)**
1978
Serigraph
23¾ x 35¾ (60.33 x 90.80 cm)
A limited edition of 300, signed and numbered
by the artist.

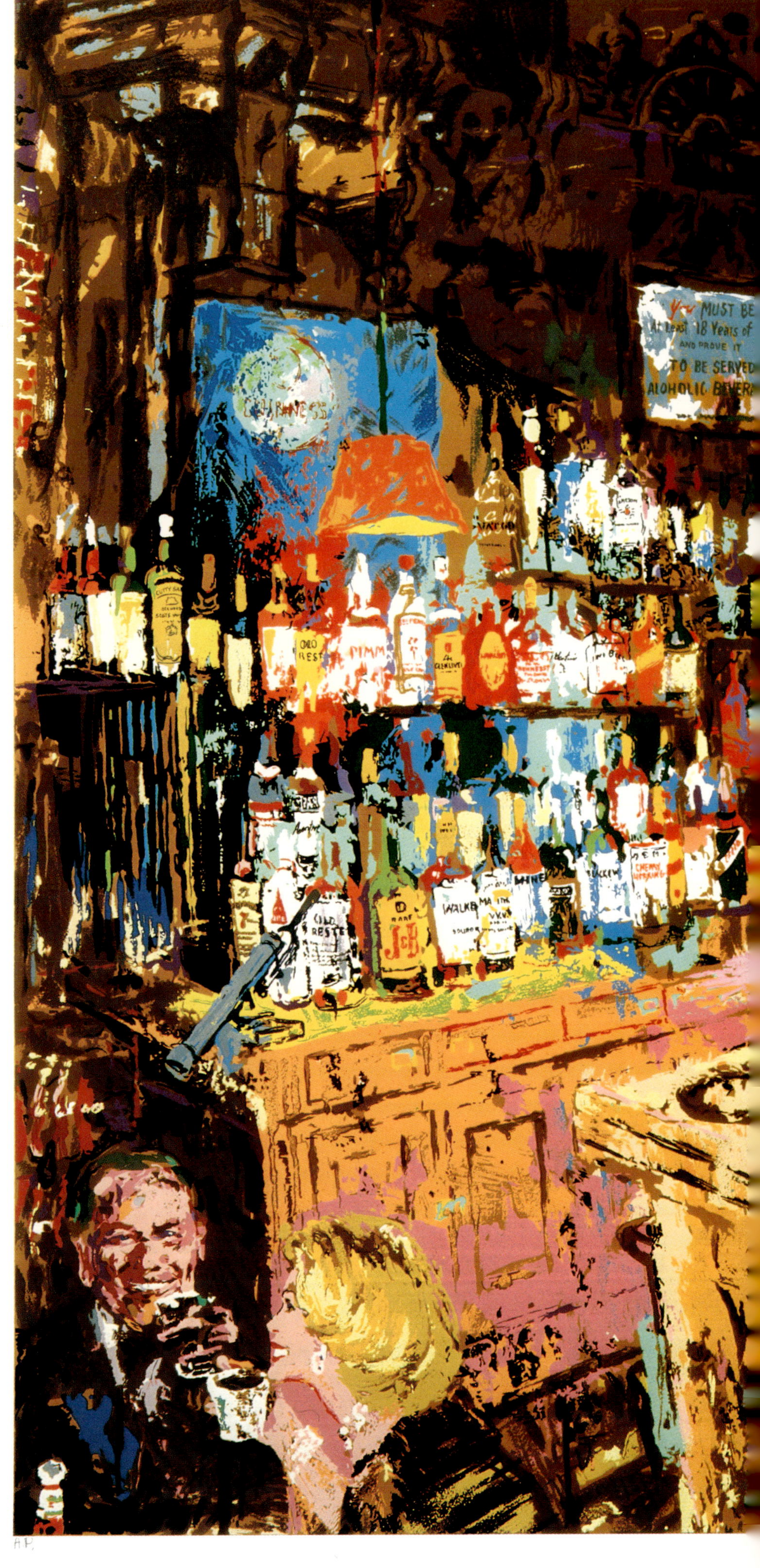

150 P. J. Clarke's
1978
Serigraph
26¼ x 39¼ (66.68 x 99.70 cm)
A limited edition of 300, signed and numbered
by the artist.

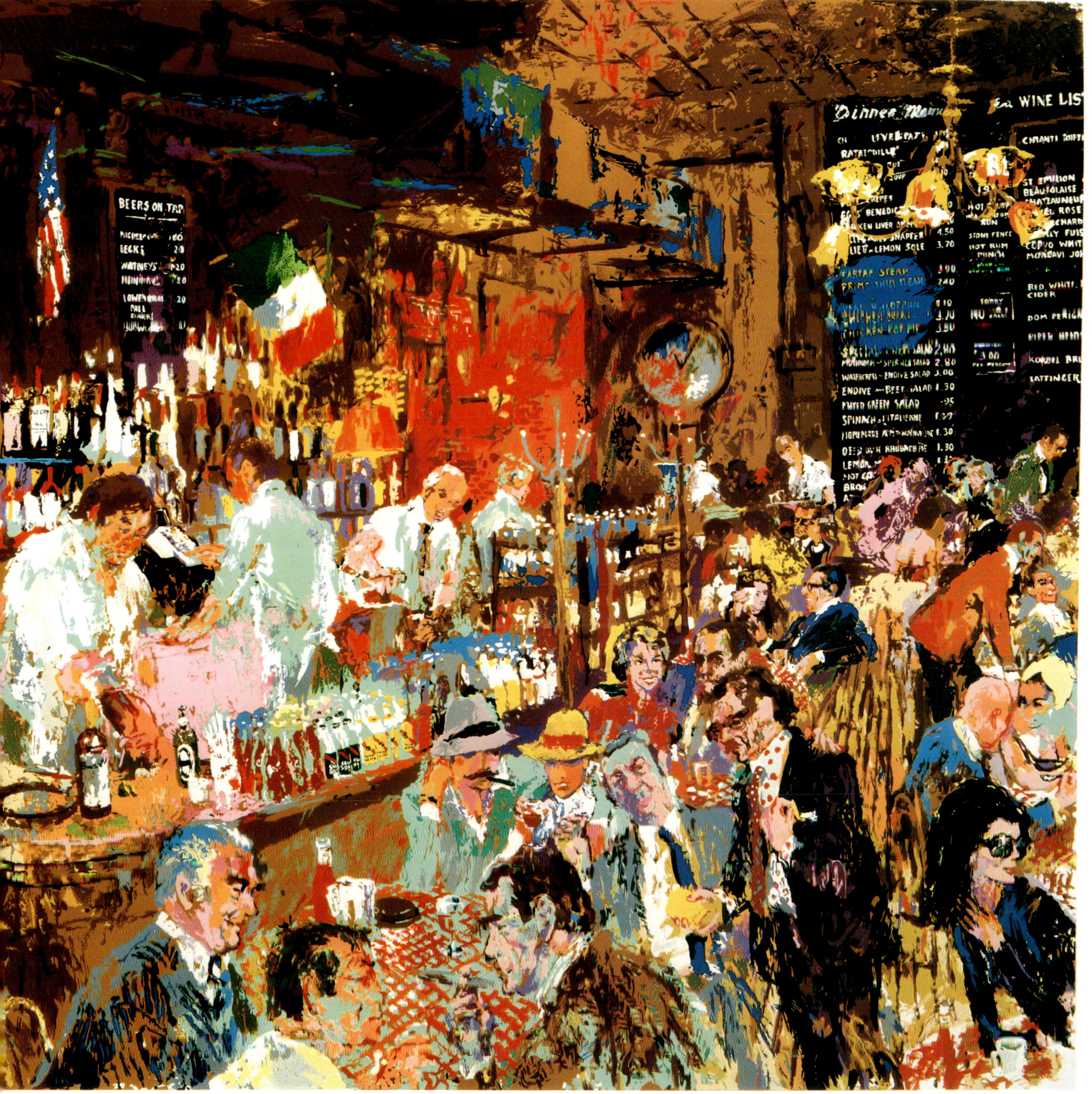
BEERS ON TAP
Dinner Menu
WINE LIST

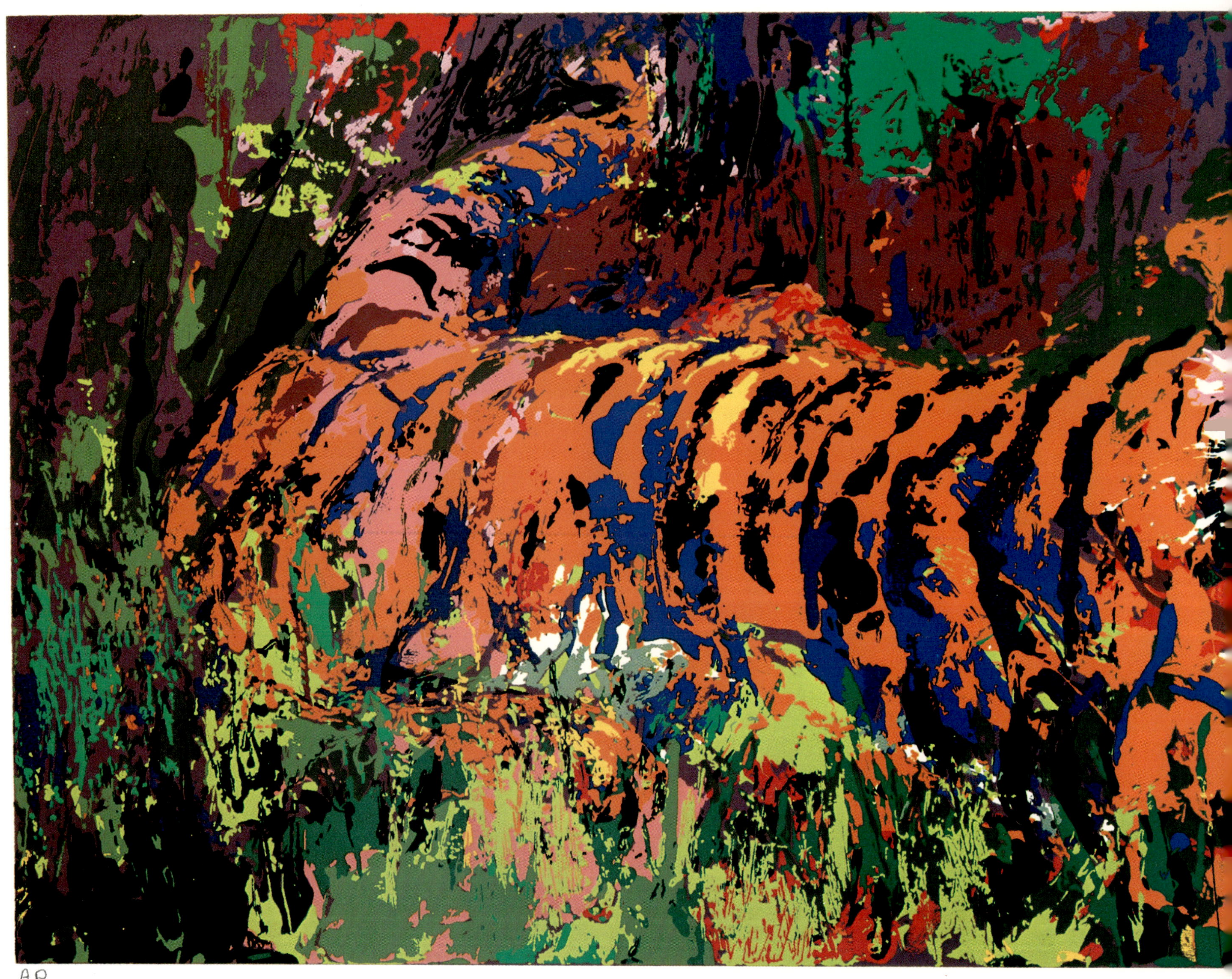

A.P.

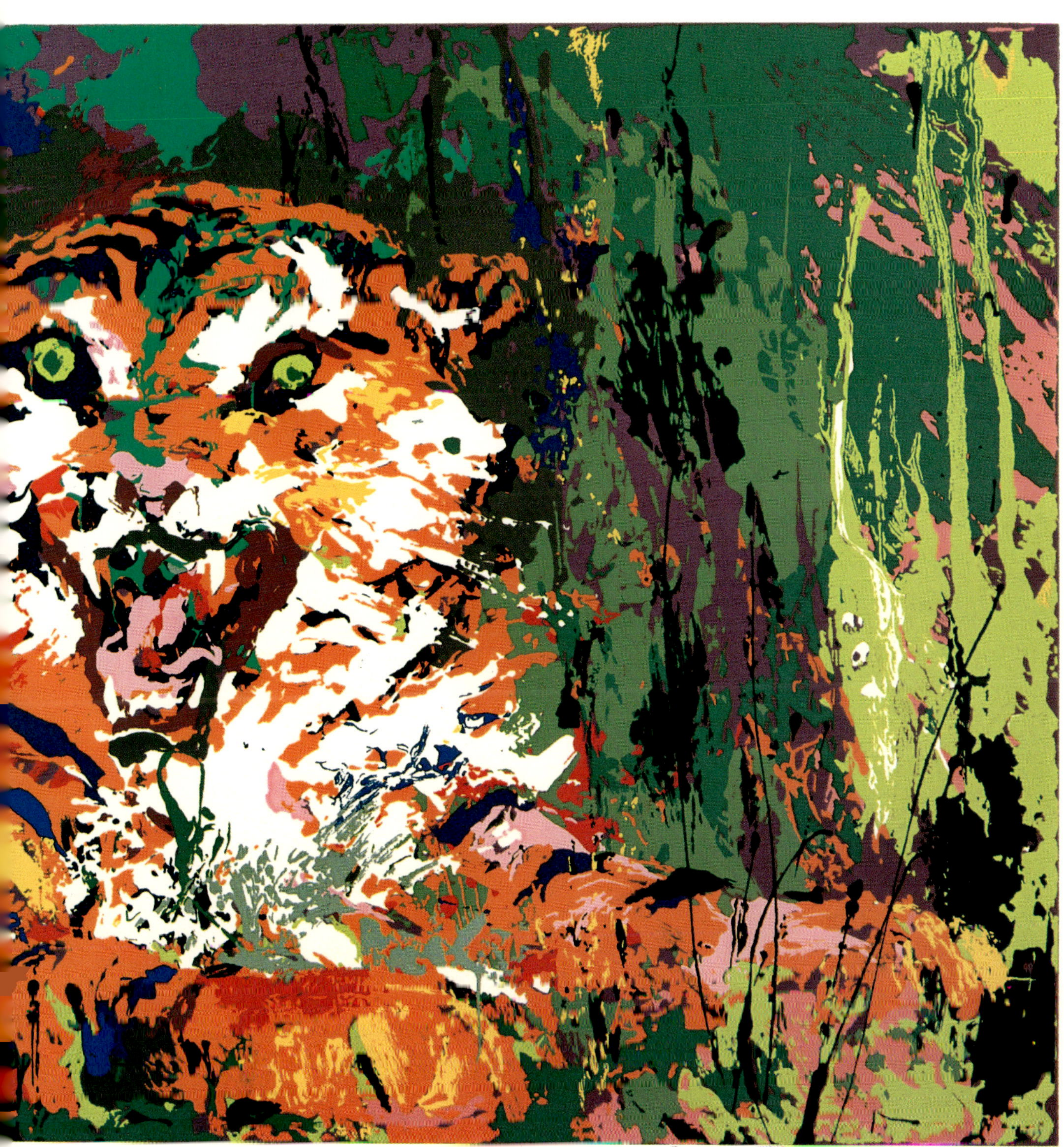

151   Young Tiger
1978
Serigraph
12 x 26¾ (30.48 x 67.95 cm)
A limited edition of 800, signed and numbered
by the artist.

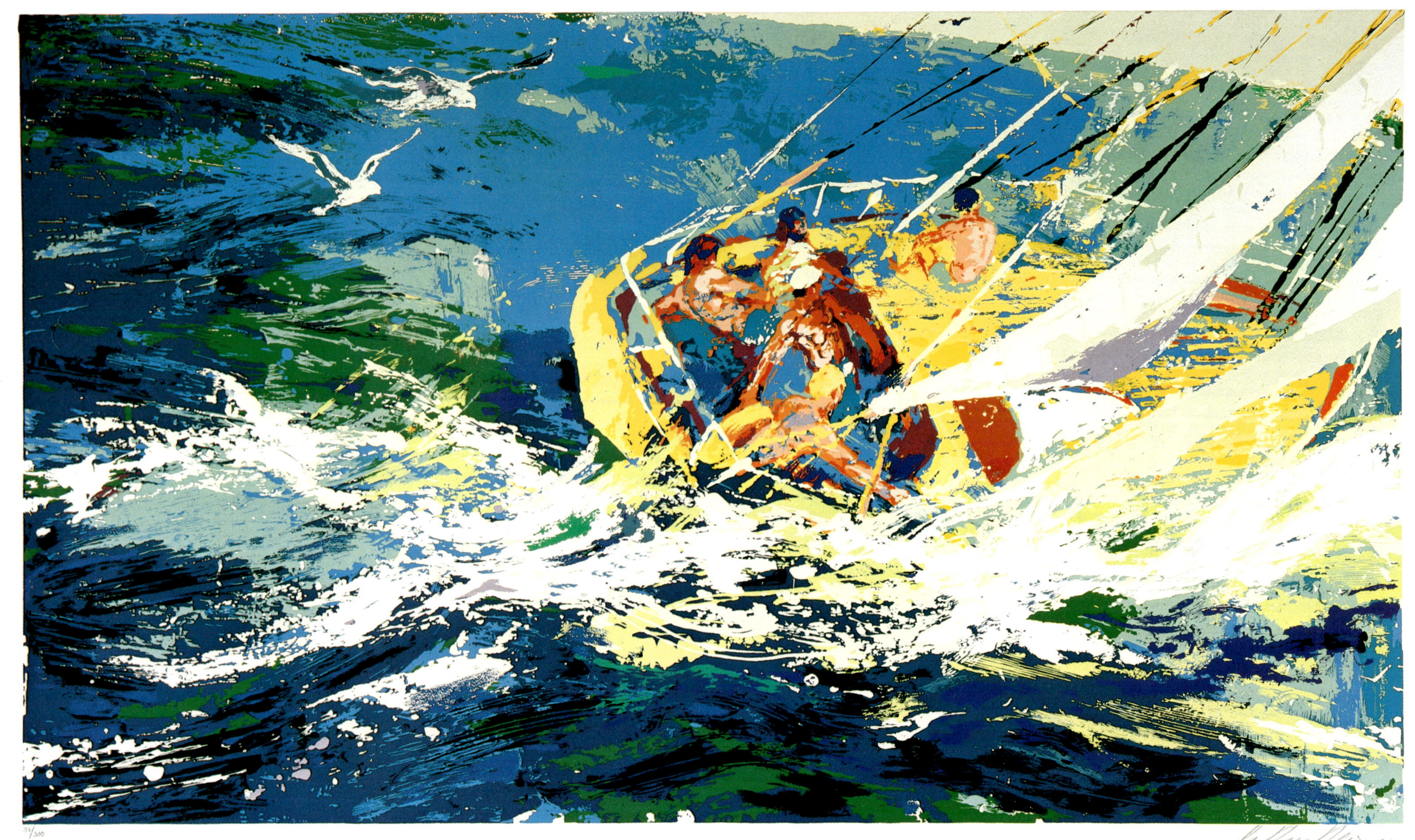

152   Aegean Sailing

1979
Serigraph
22½ x 38 (57.15 x 96.52 cm)
A limited edition of 300, signed and numbered
by the artist.

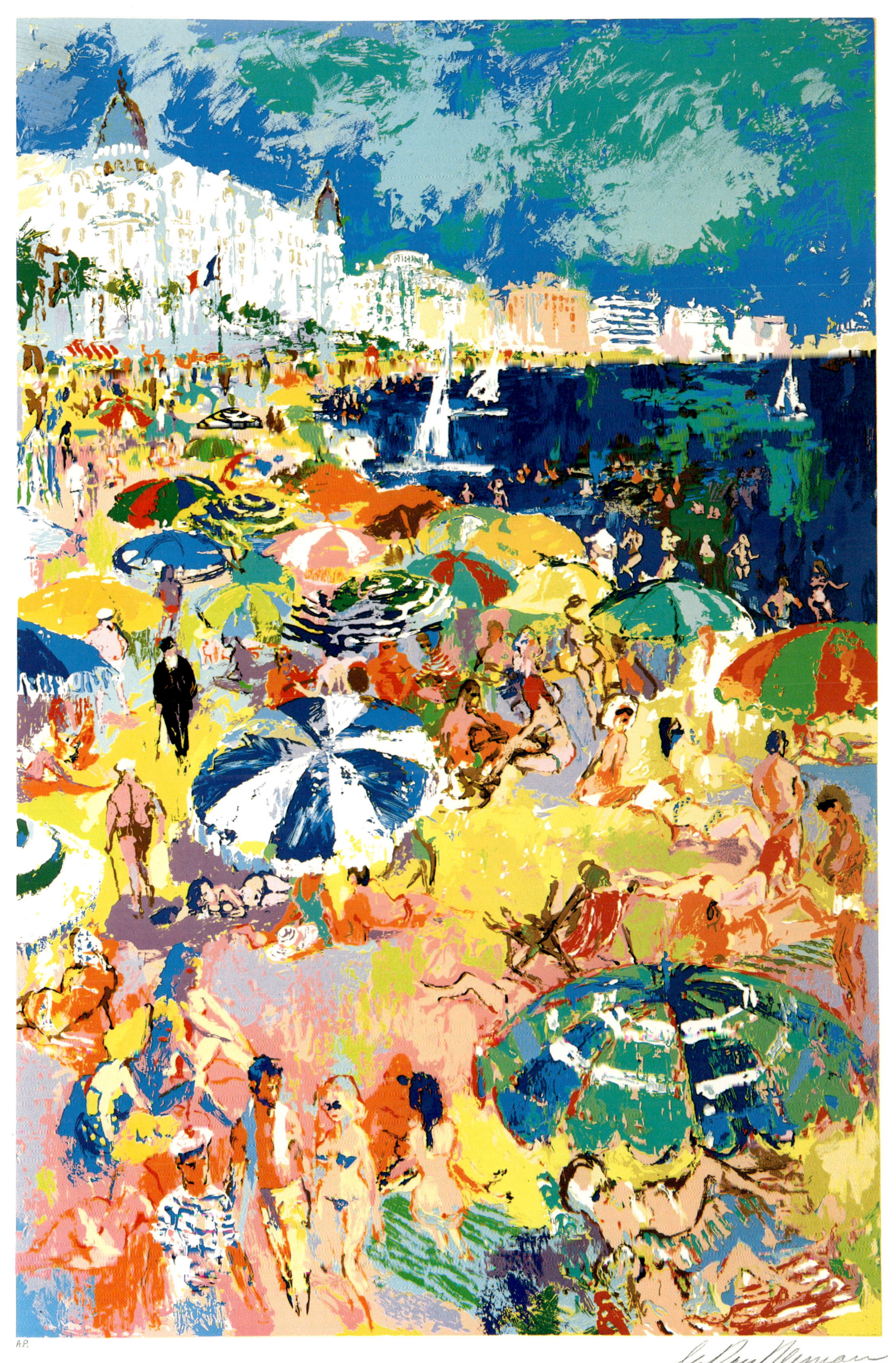

153
The Beach at Cannes
1979
Serigraph
37 x 24 (93.98 x 60.96 cm)
A limited edition of 300, signed
and numbered by the artist.

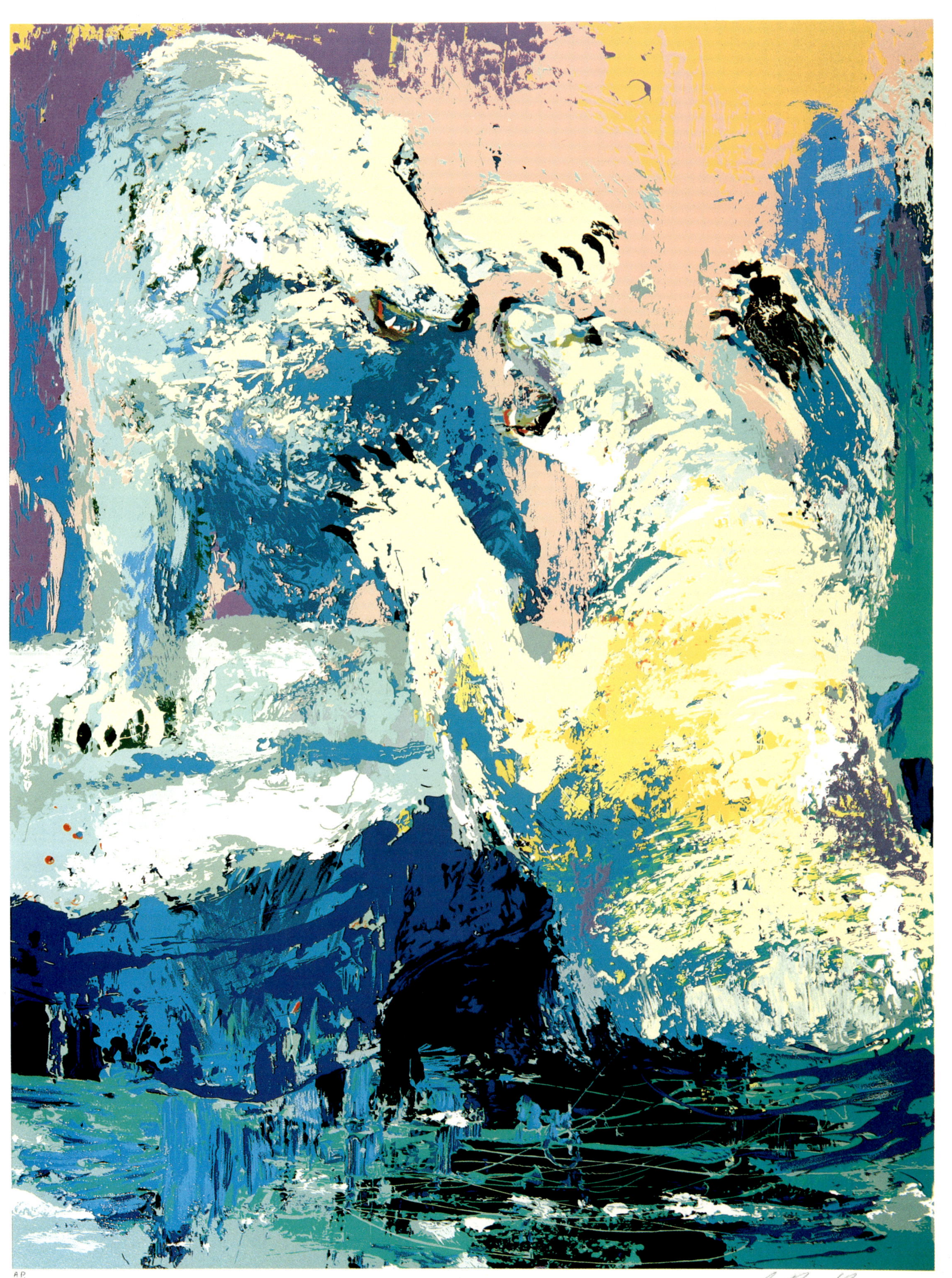

154 **Polar Bears**

1979
Serigraph
38 x 28 (96.52 x 71.12 cm)
A limited edition of 300, signed
and numbered by the artist.

155   American Bald Eagle

1979
Serigraph
28½ x 38 (72.39 x 96.52 cm)
A limited edition of 300, signed and numbered
by the artist.

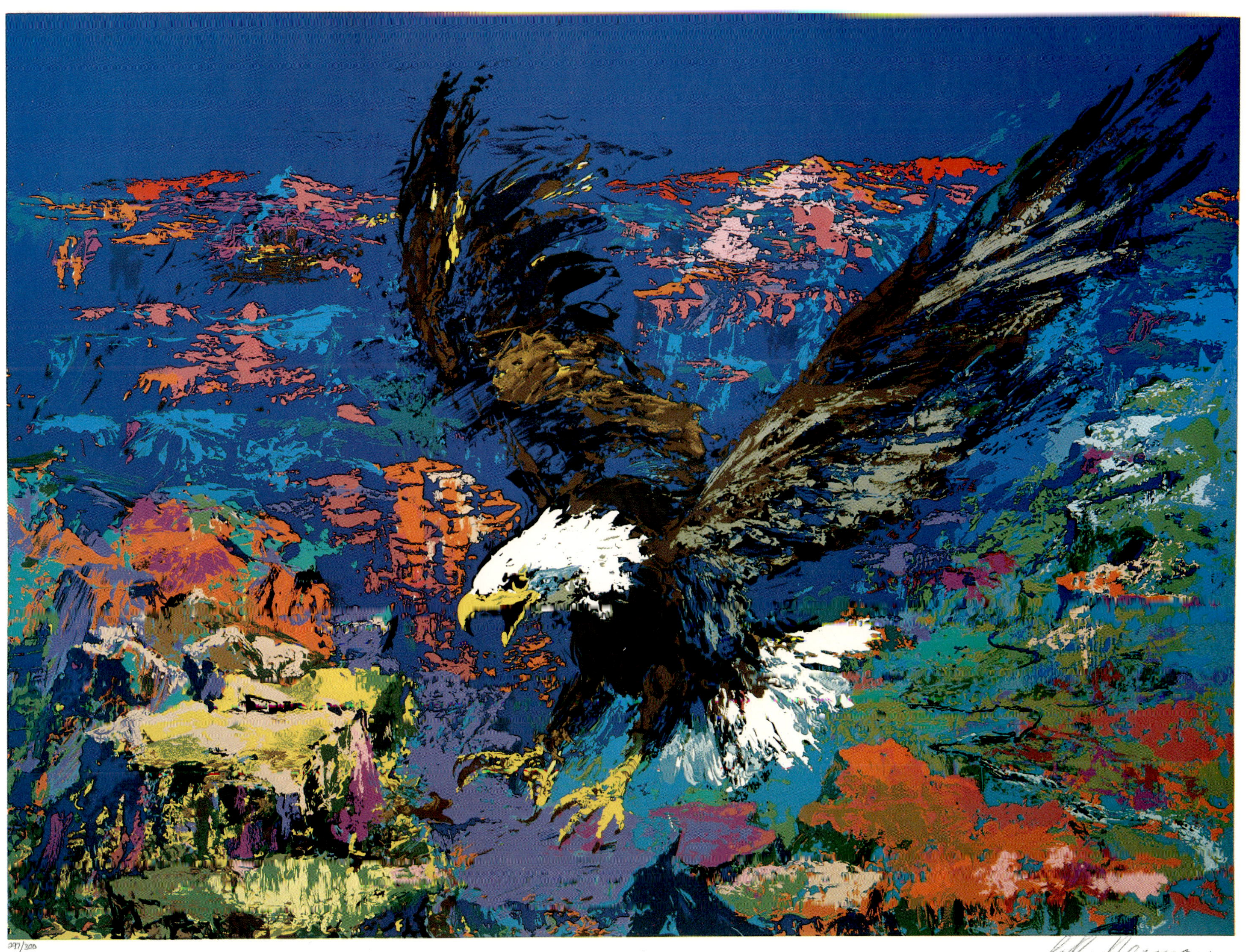

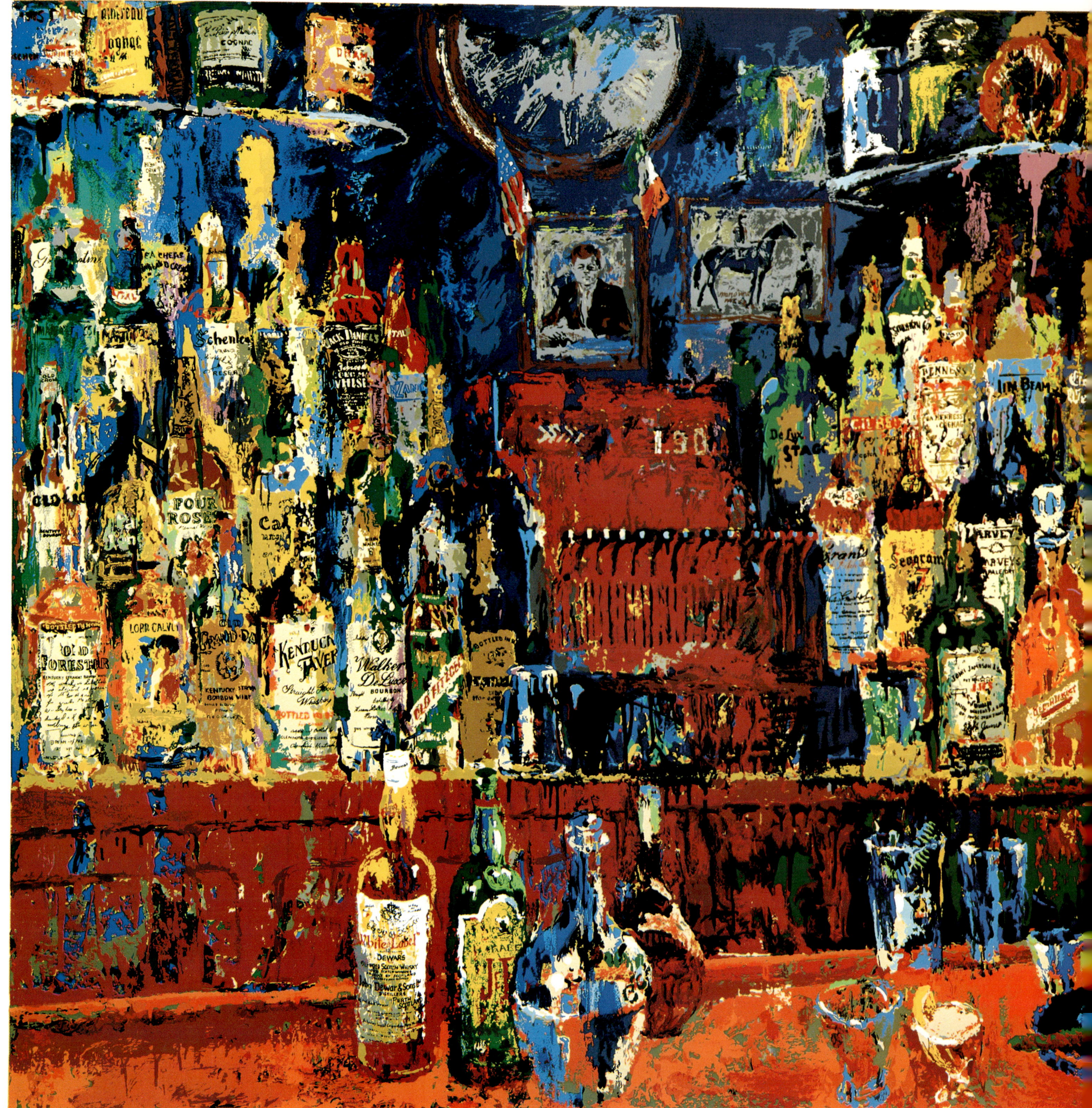
248/300

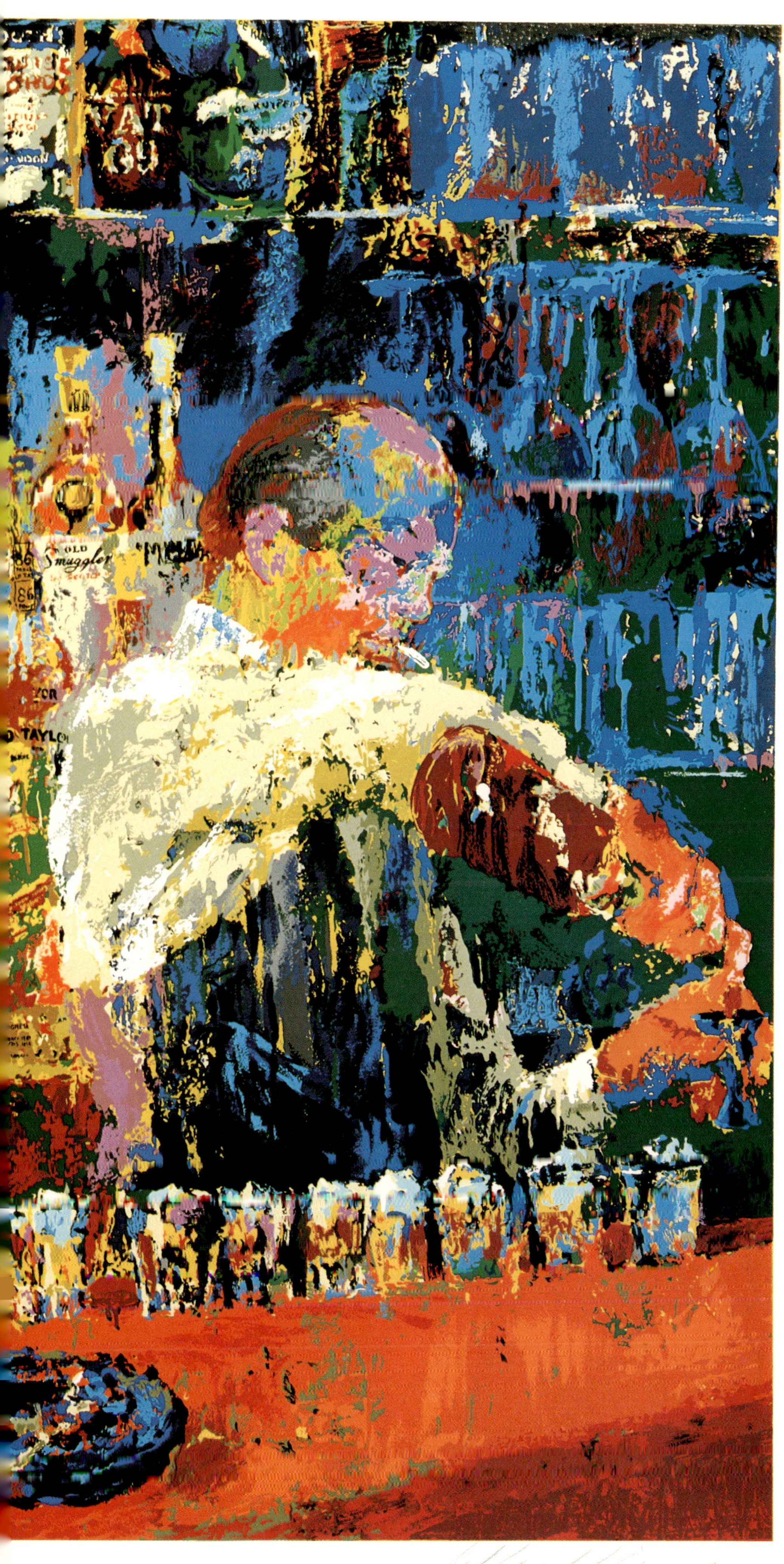

156 Irish-American Bar
1979
Serigraph
26 x 38½ (66.01 x 97.79 cm)
A limited edition of 300, signed and numbered
by the artist.

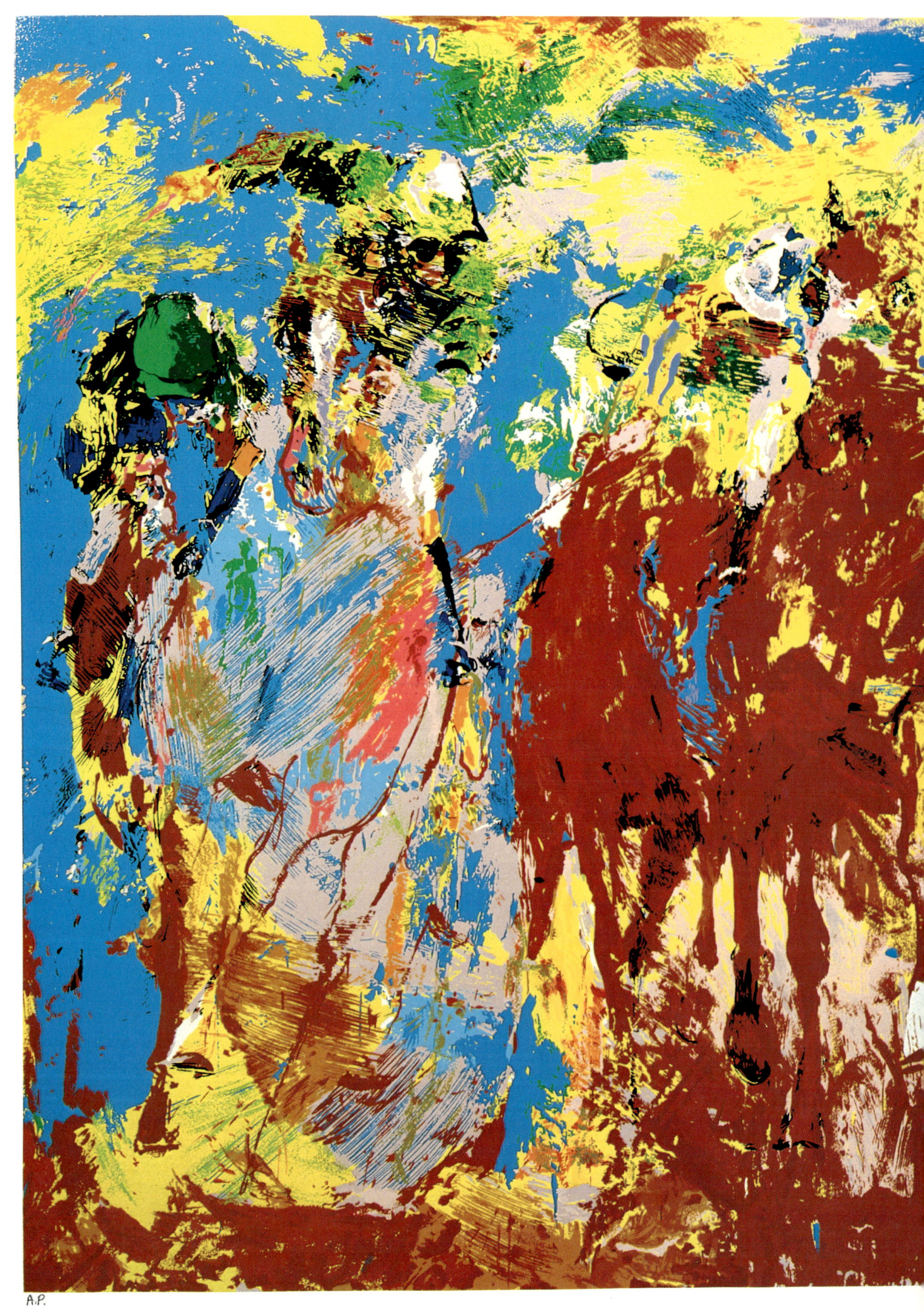

157   Stretch Stampede

1979
Serigraph
30 x 45 (76.2 x 114.3 cm)
A limited edition of 300, signed and numbered
by the artist.

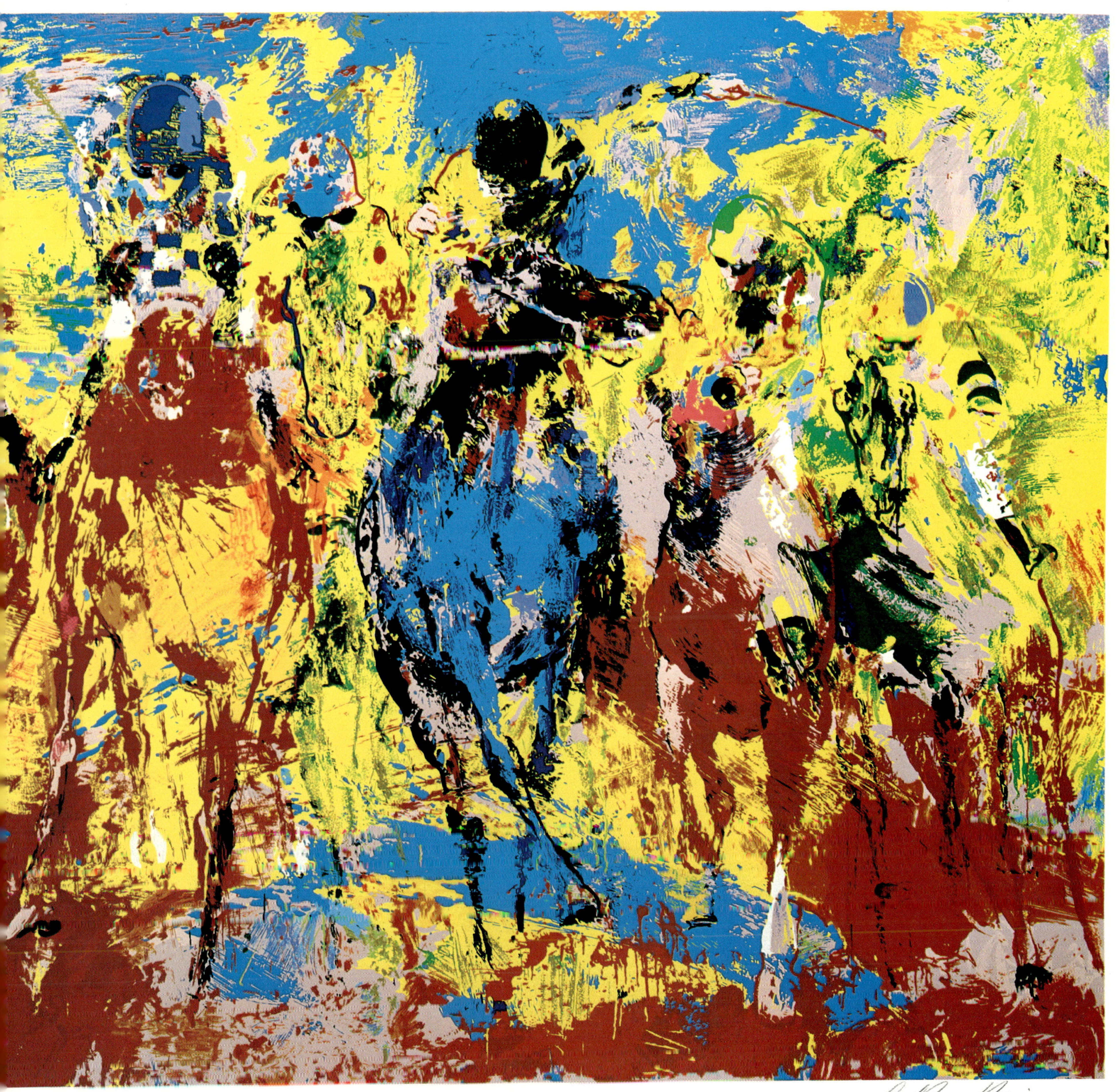

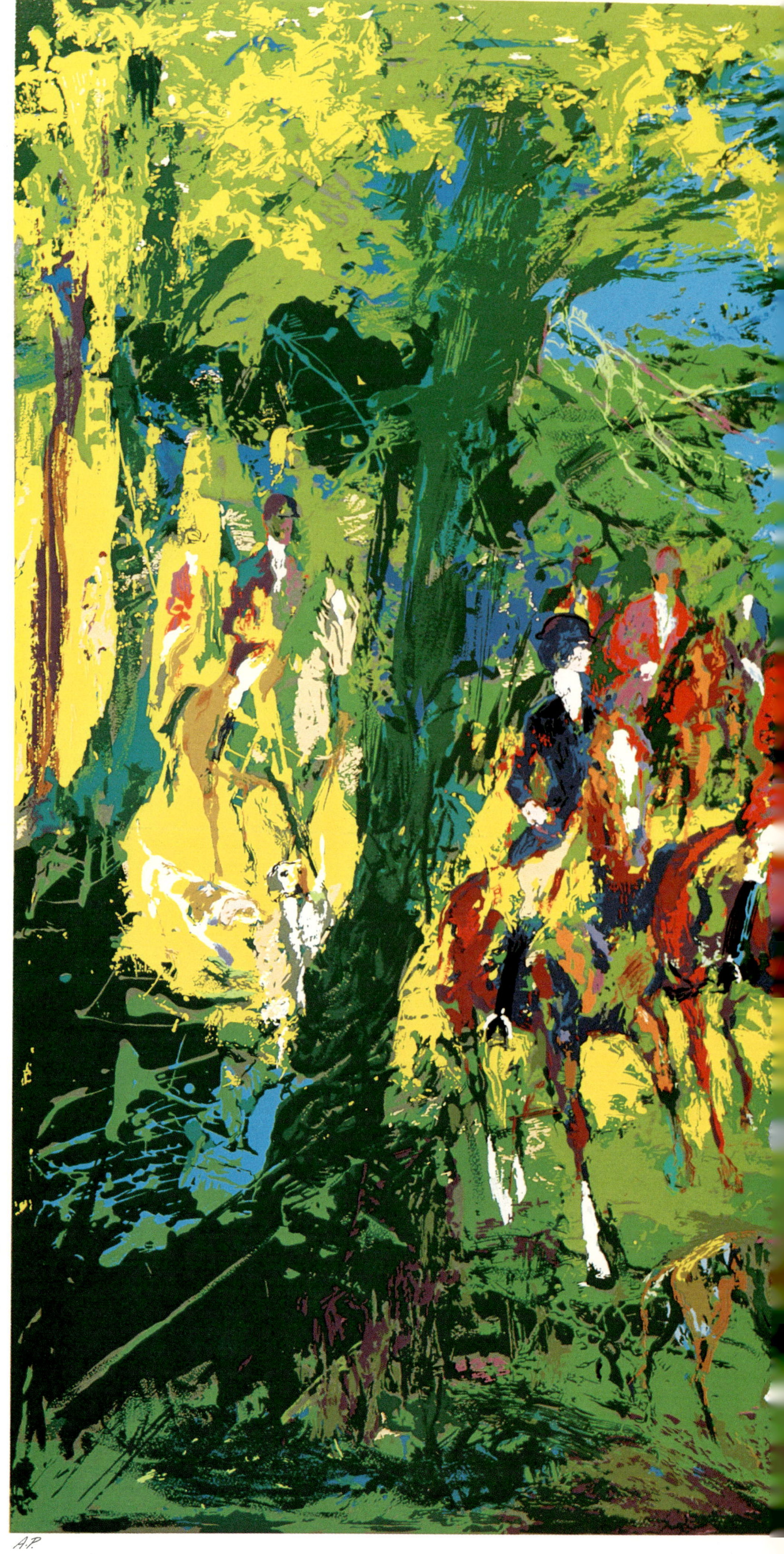# 158   Chateau Hunt

1979
Serigraph
26 x 38½ (66.04 x 97.79 cm)
A limited edition of 300, signed and numbered
by the artist.

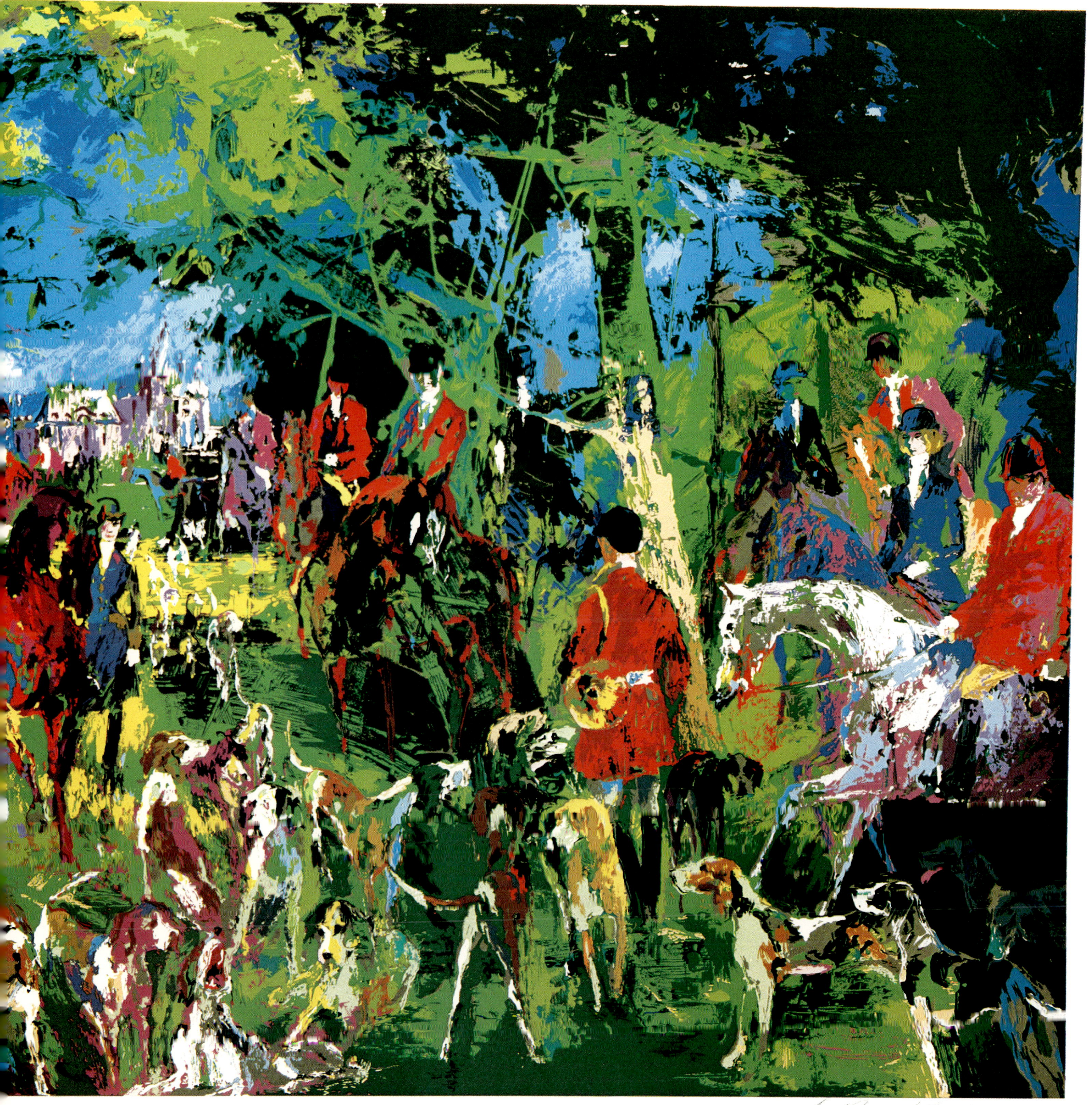

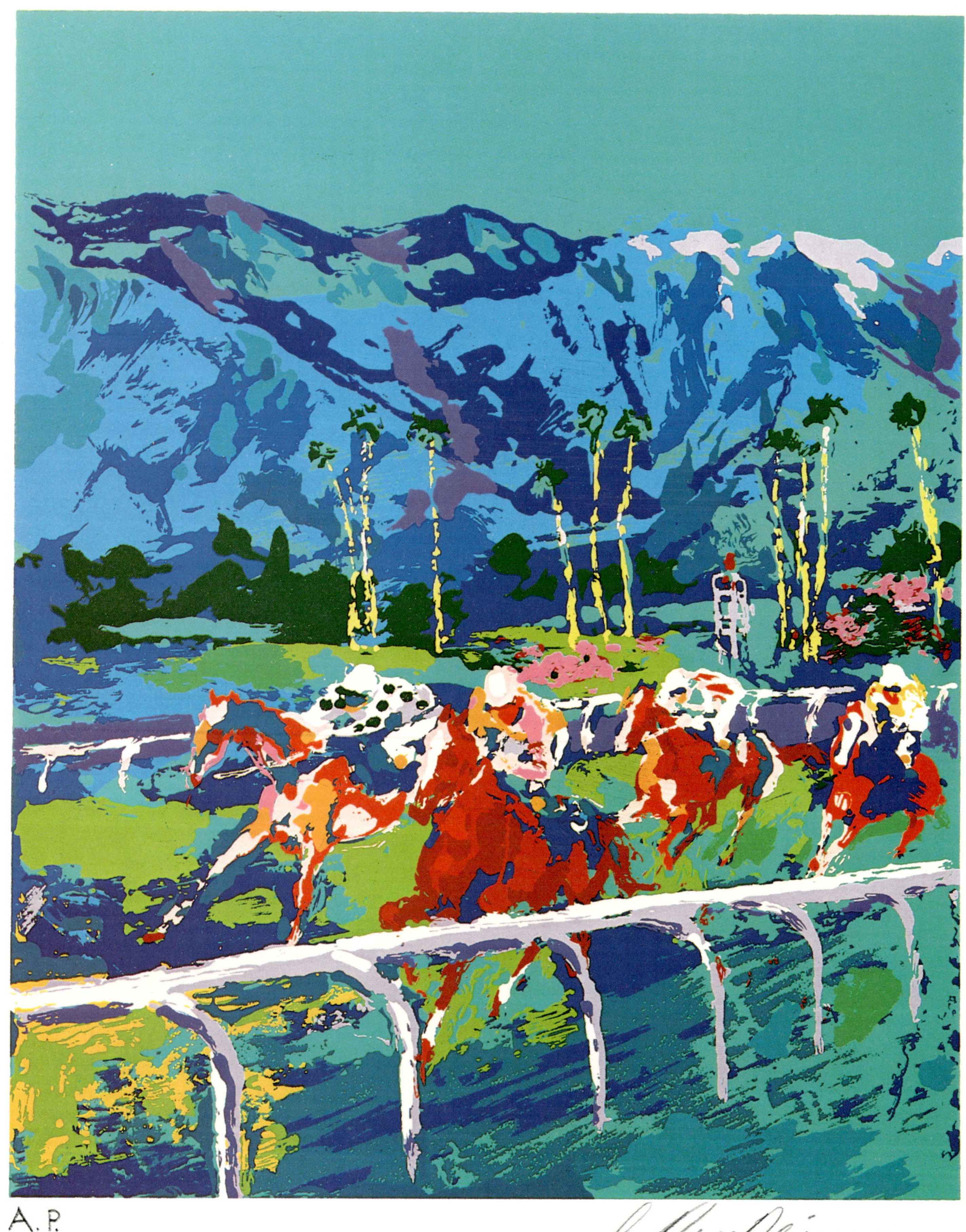

159 Santa Anita

1979
Serigraph
10 x 8 (25.4 x 20.32 cm)
A limited edition of 1200, signed and numbered
by the artist.

1079
Serigraph
21 x 42 (53.34 x 106.68 cm)
A limited edition of 300, signed and numbered
by the artist.

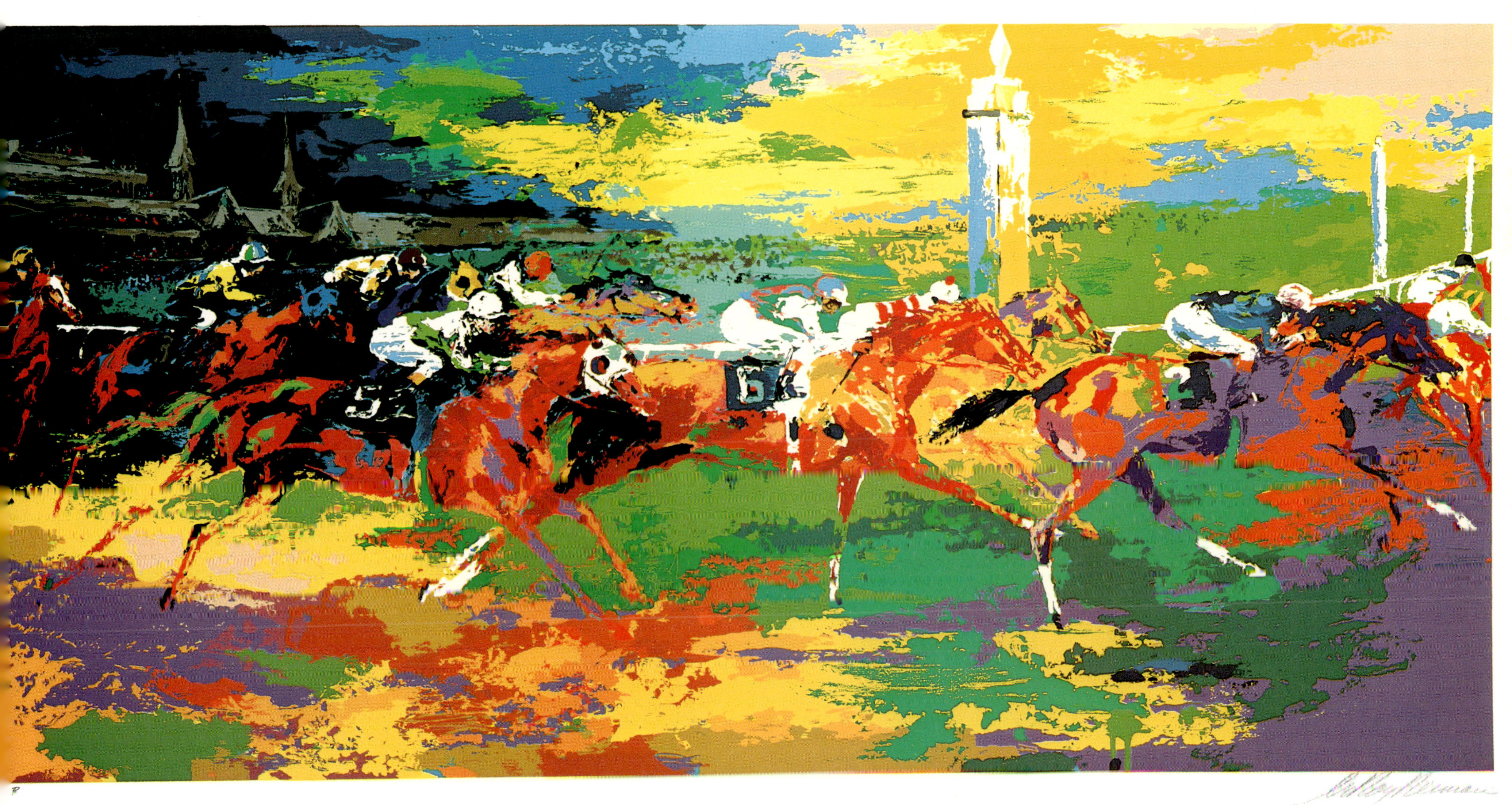

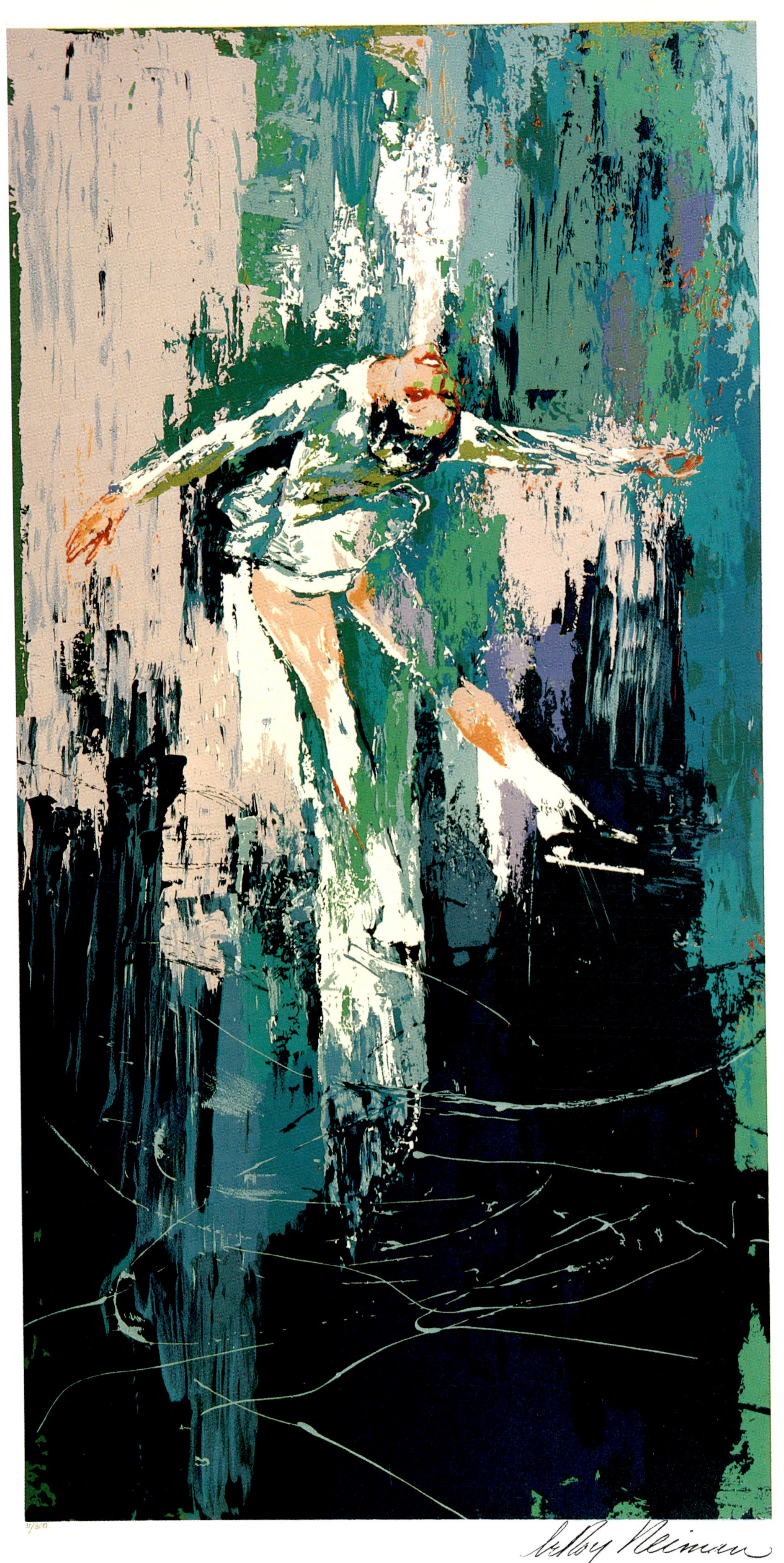

161   Winter Olympic Skating,
Lake Placid, 1980
1978
Serigraph
42 x 21 (106.68 x 53.34 cm)
A limited edition of 300, signed and numbered
by the artist.

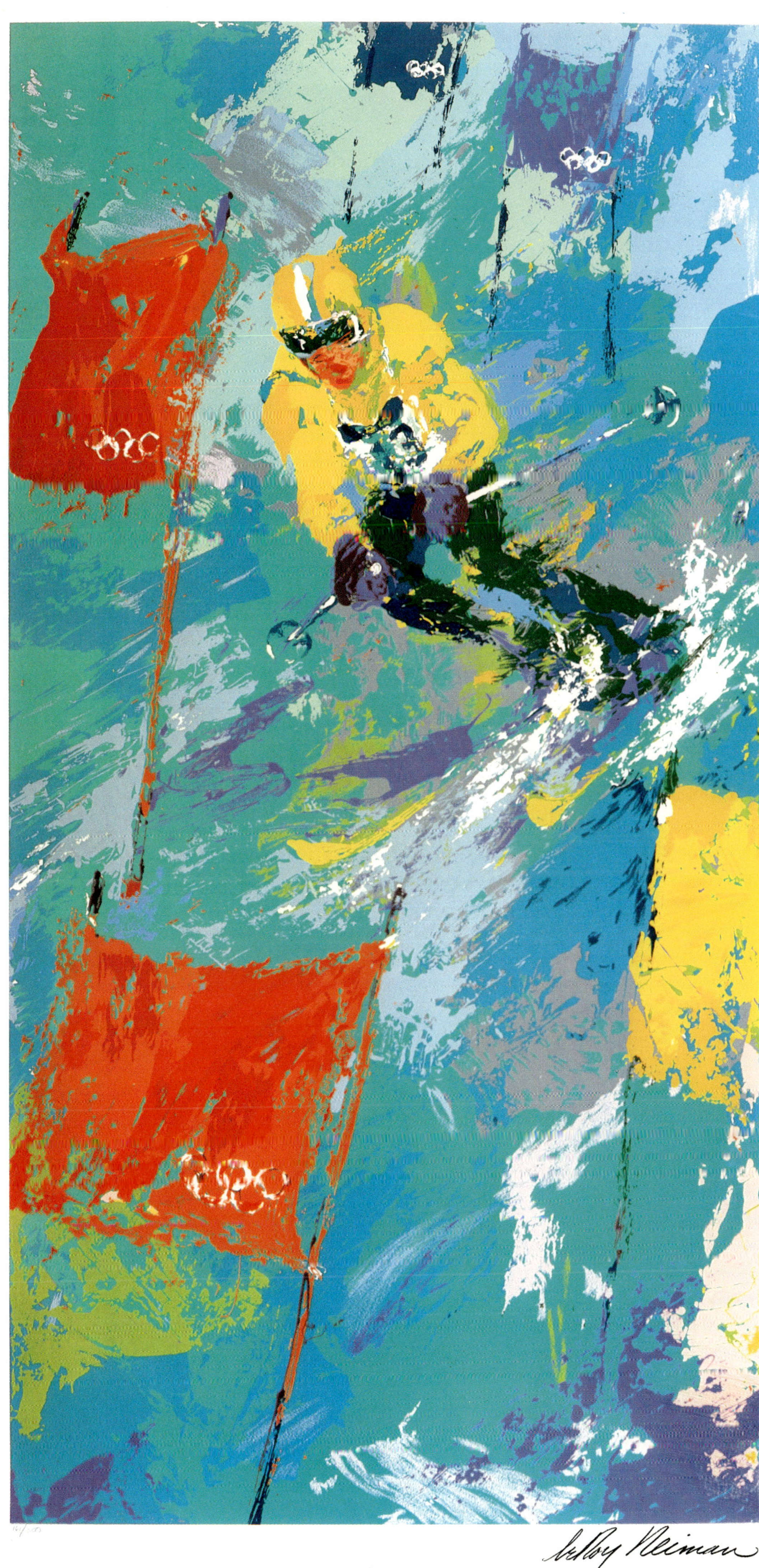

162   Winter Olympic Skiing, Lake Placid, 1980
1979
Serigraph
42 x 21 (106.68 x 53.34 cm)
A limited edition of 300, signed and numbered by the artist.

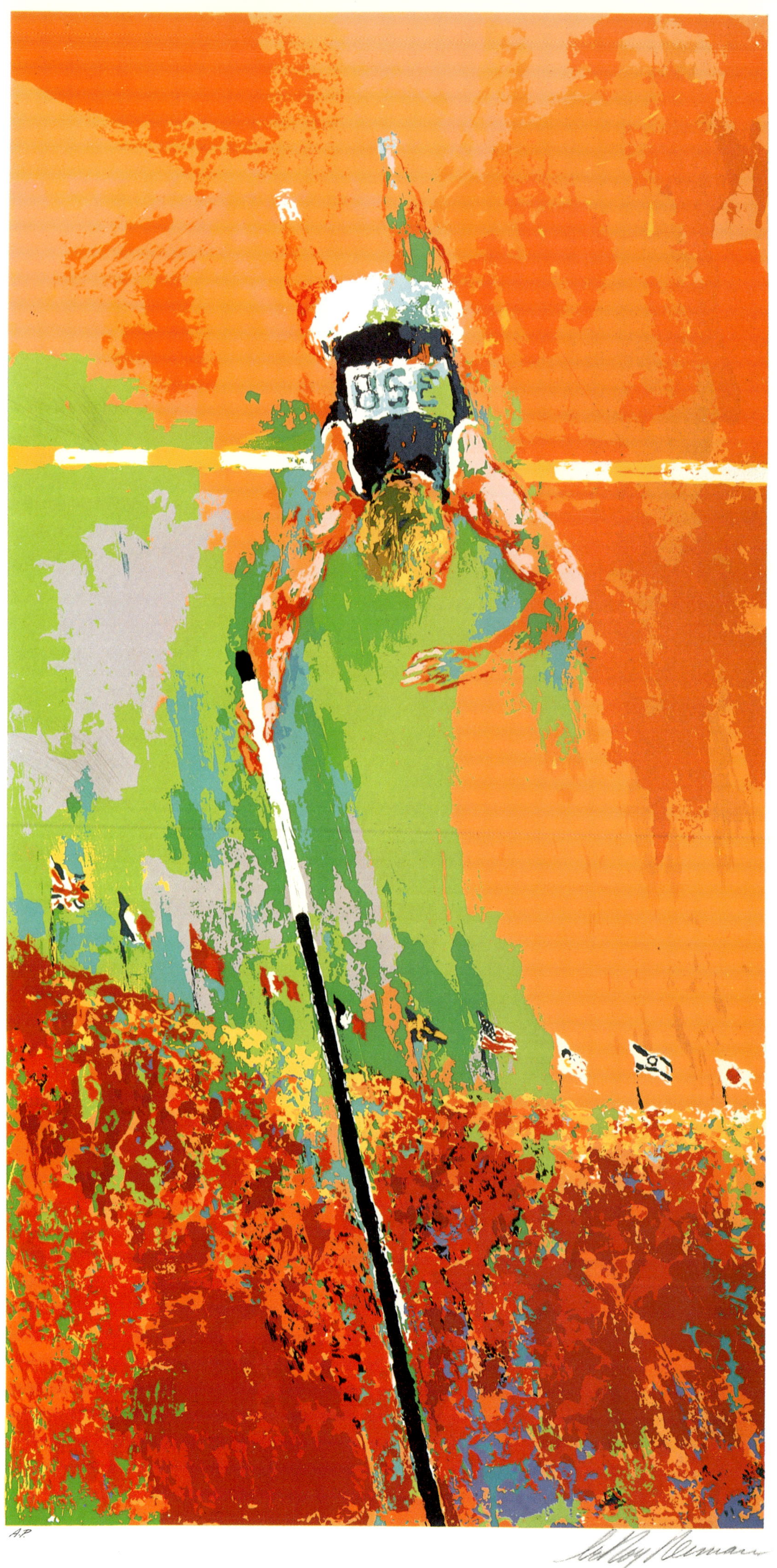

163   Olympic Pole Vaulting, Moscow 1980

1979
Serigraph
42 x 21 (53.34 x 106.68 cm)

A limited edition of 300, signed and numbered by the artist.

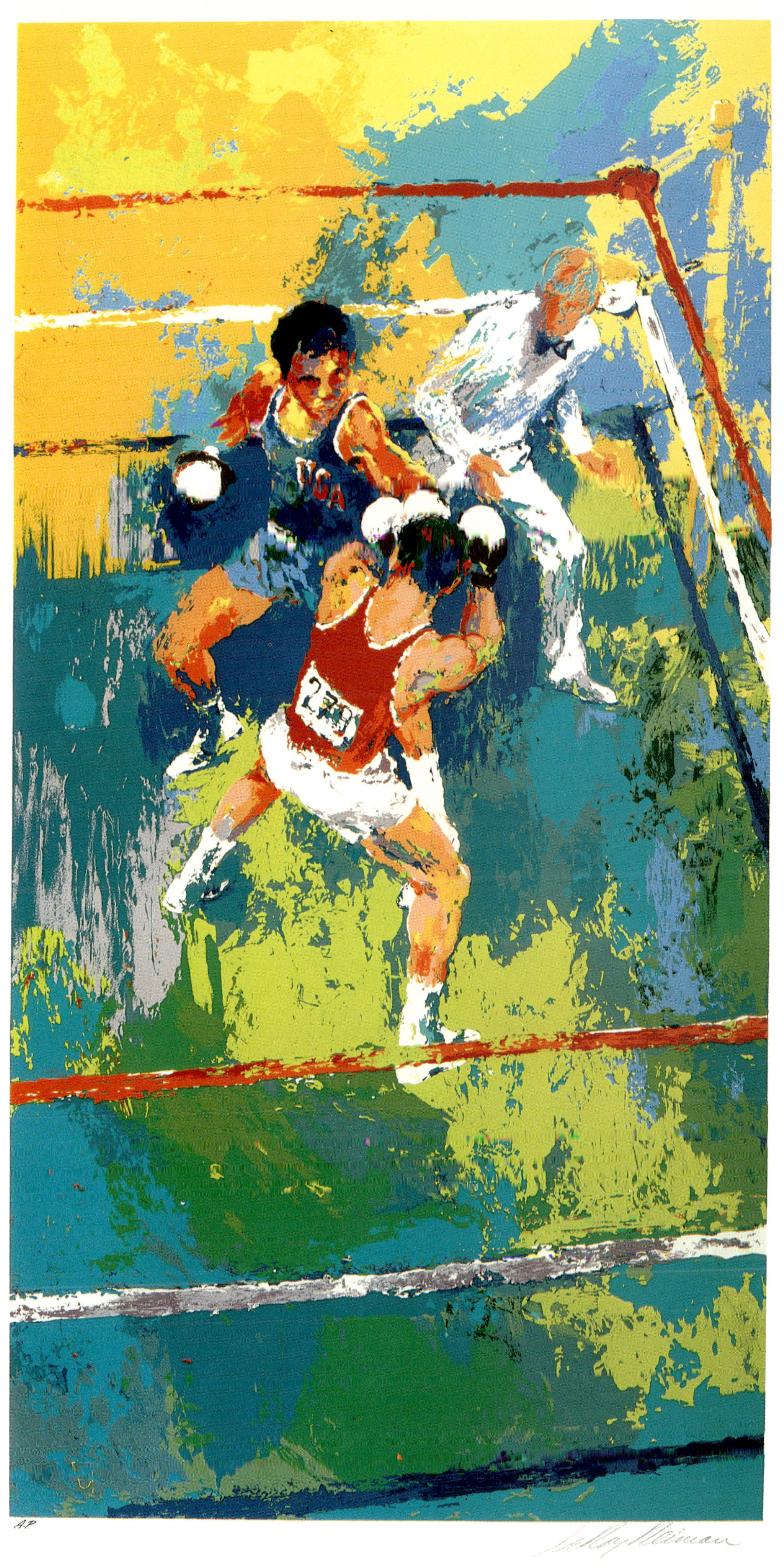

**164   Olympic Boxing
Moscow 1980**
1980
Serigraph
42 x 21 (53.34 x 106.68 cm)
A limited edition of 300,
signed and numbered
by the artist.

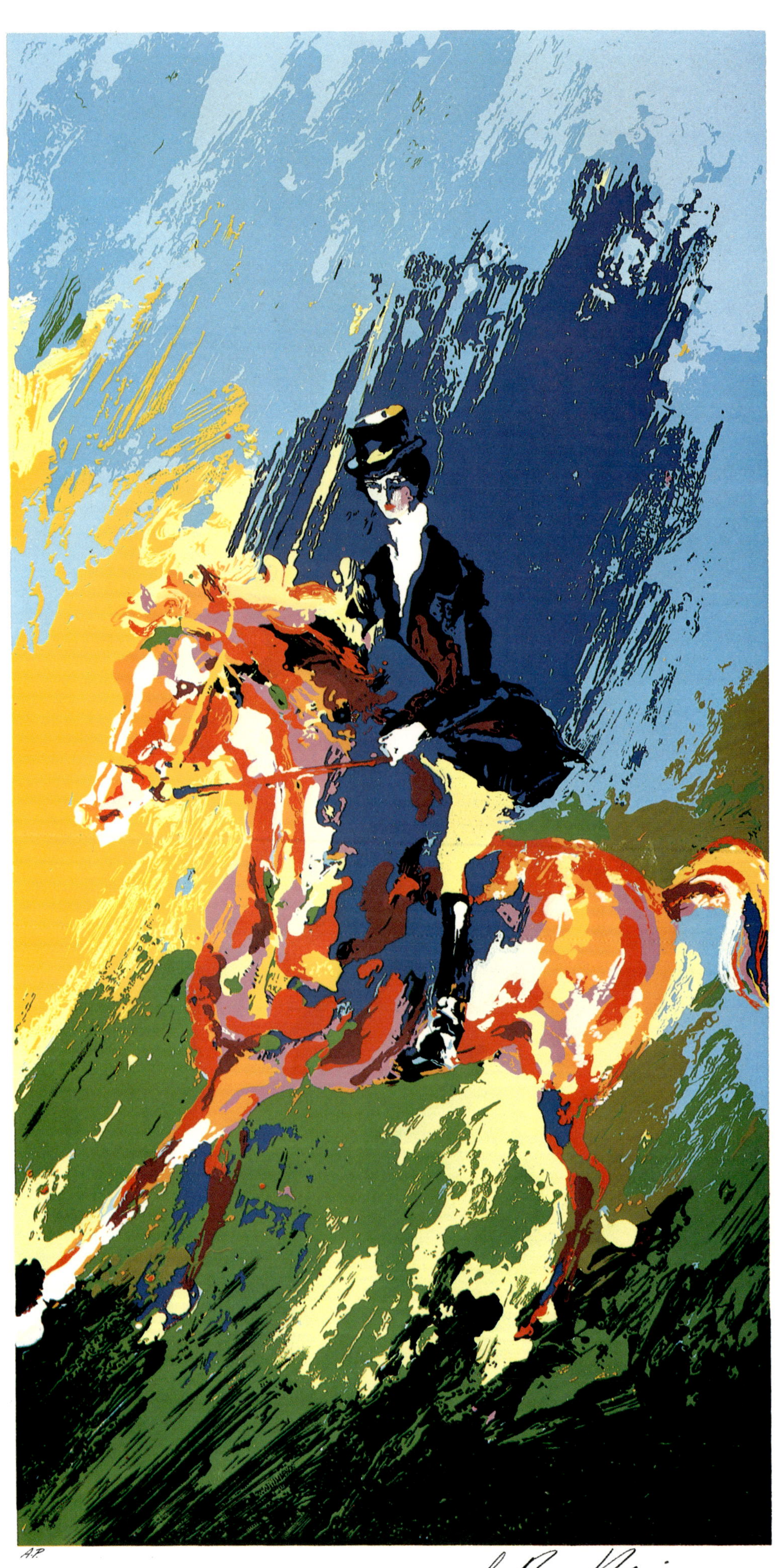

165 The Equestrianne
to be released.
Serigraph
24 x 12 (60.96 x 30.48 cm)
A limited edition of 300, signed and numbered
by the artist.

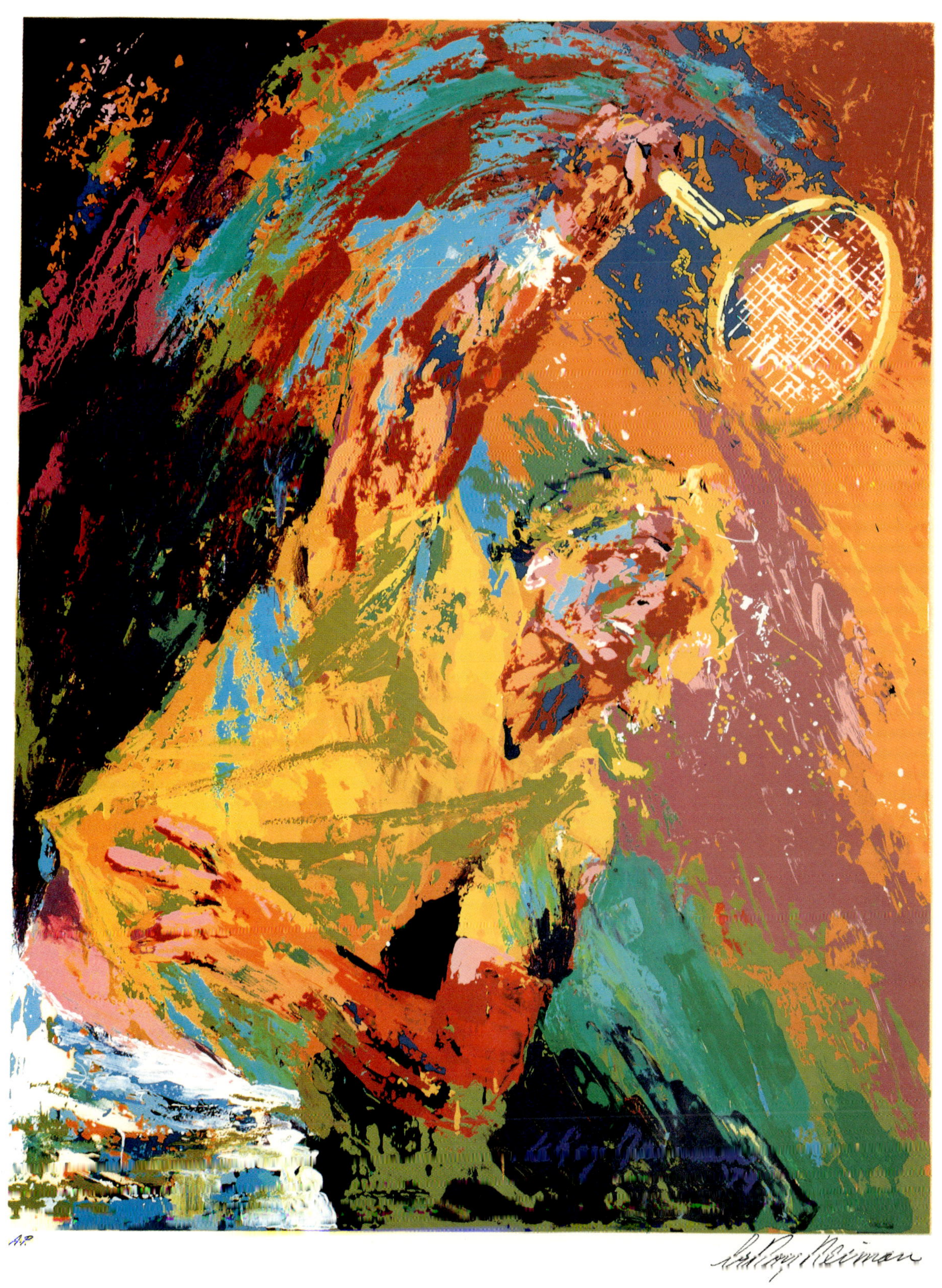

166   Power Serve

to be released
Serigraph
24⅞ x 33 (63.18 x 83.82 cm)

A limited edition of 300, signed and numbered
by the artist.

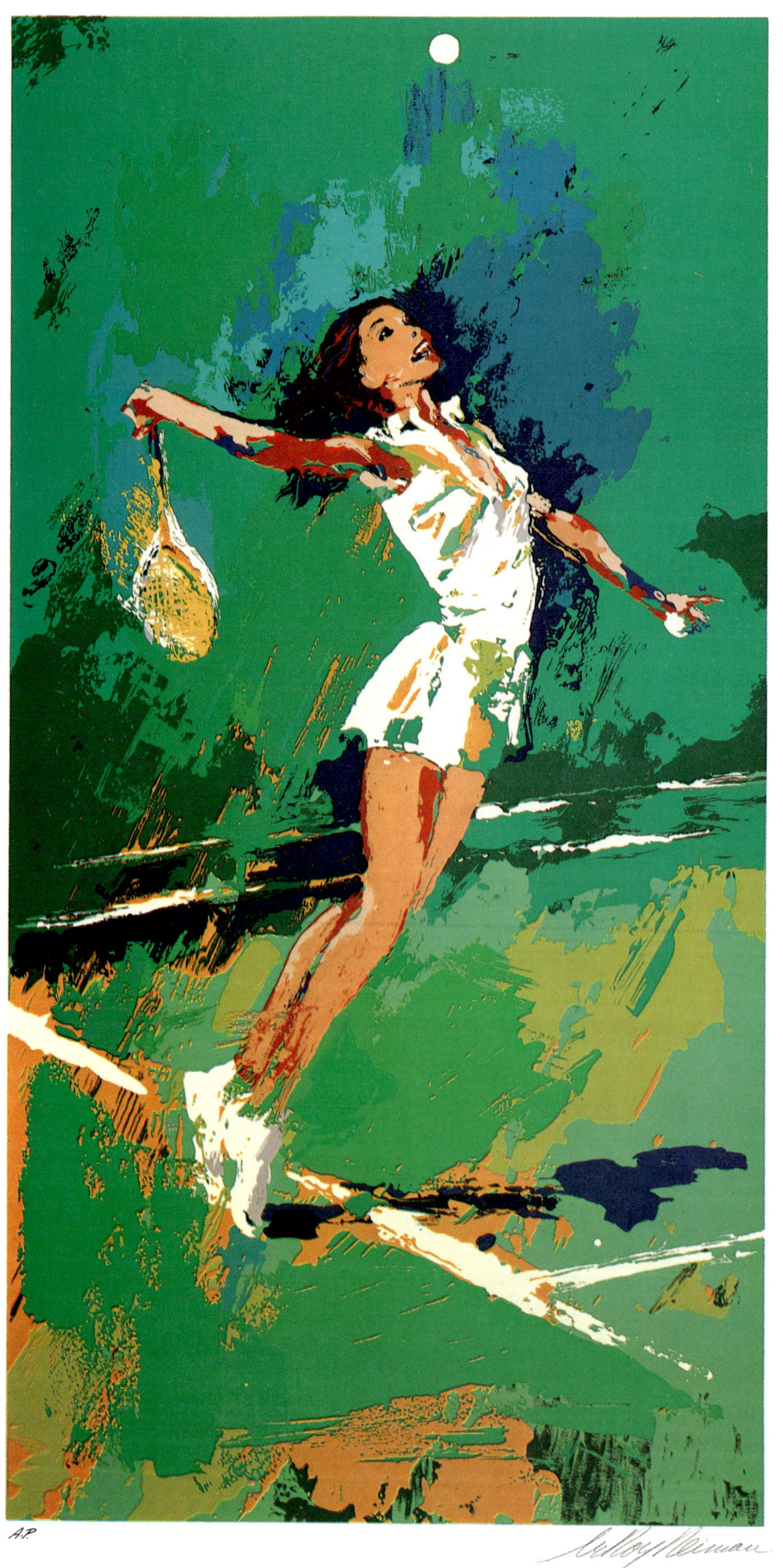

167   Sweet Serve

1980
Serigraph
36 x 18 (91.44 x 45.72 cm)
A limited edition of 300, signed and numbered
by the artist.

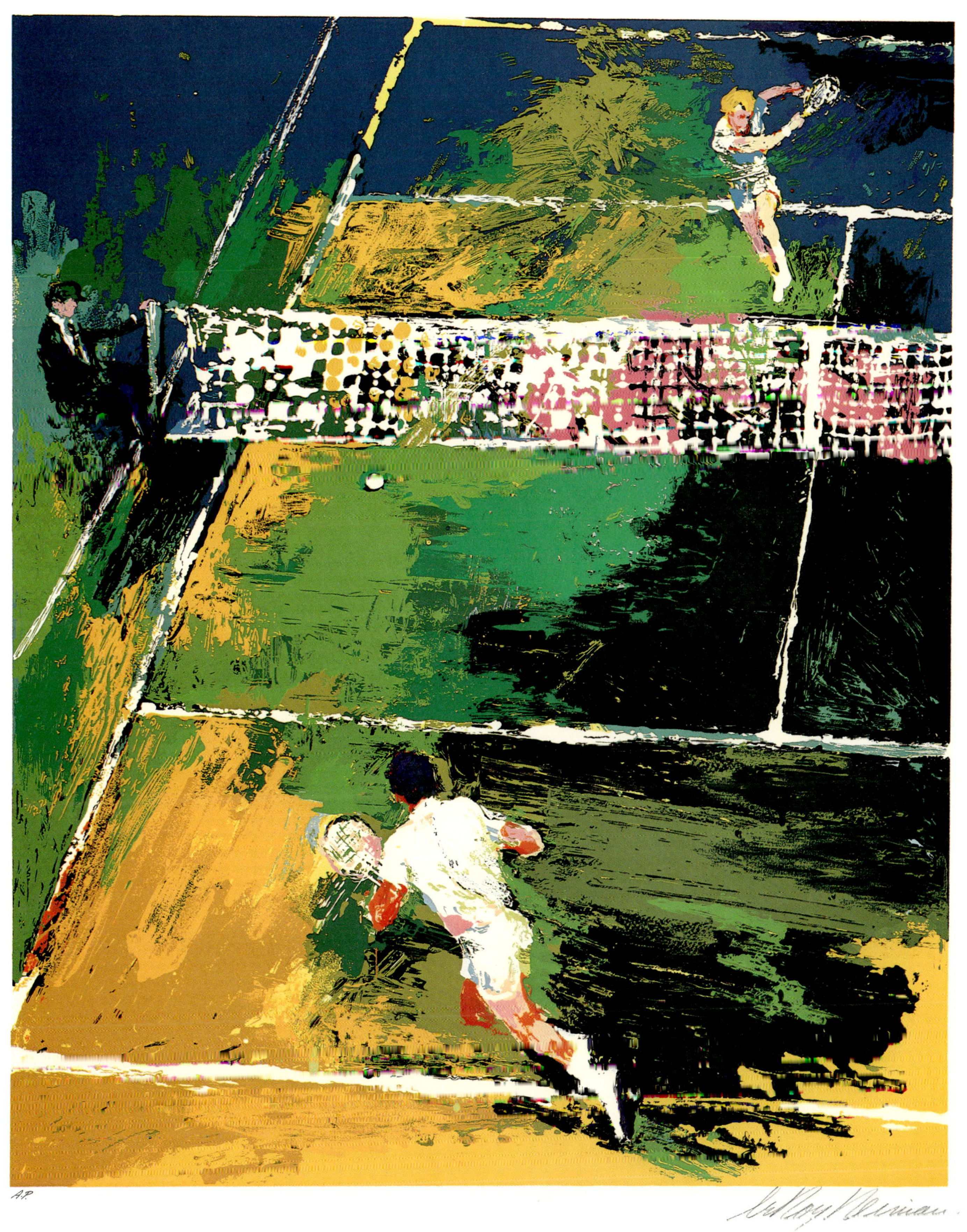

168   Blood Tennis
to be released
Serigraph
28⅞ x 23 (73.34 x 58.42 cm)
A limited edition of 300, signed and numbered by the artist.

169 Indoor Cycling

to be released
Serigraph
13¾ x 14¾ (34.93 x 37.47 cm)
A limited edition of 300, signed and numbered
by the artist.

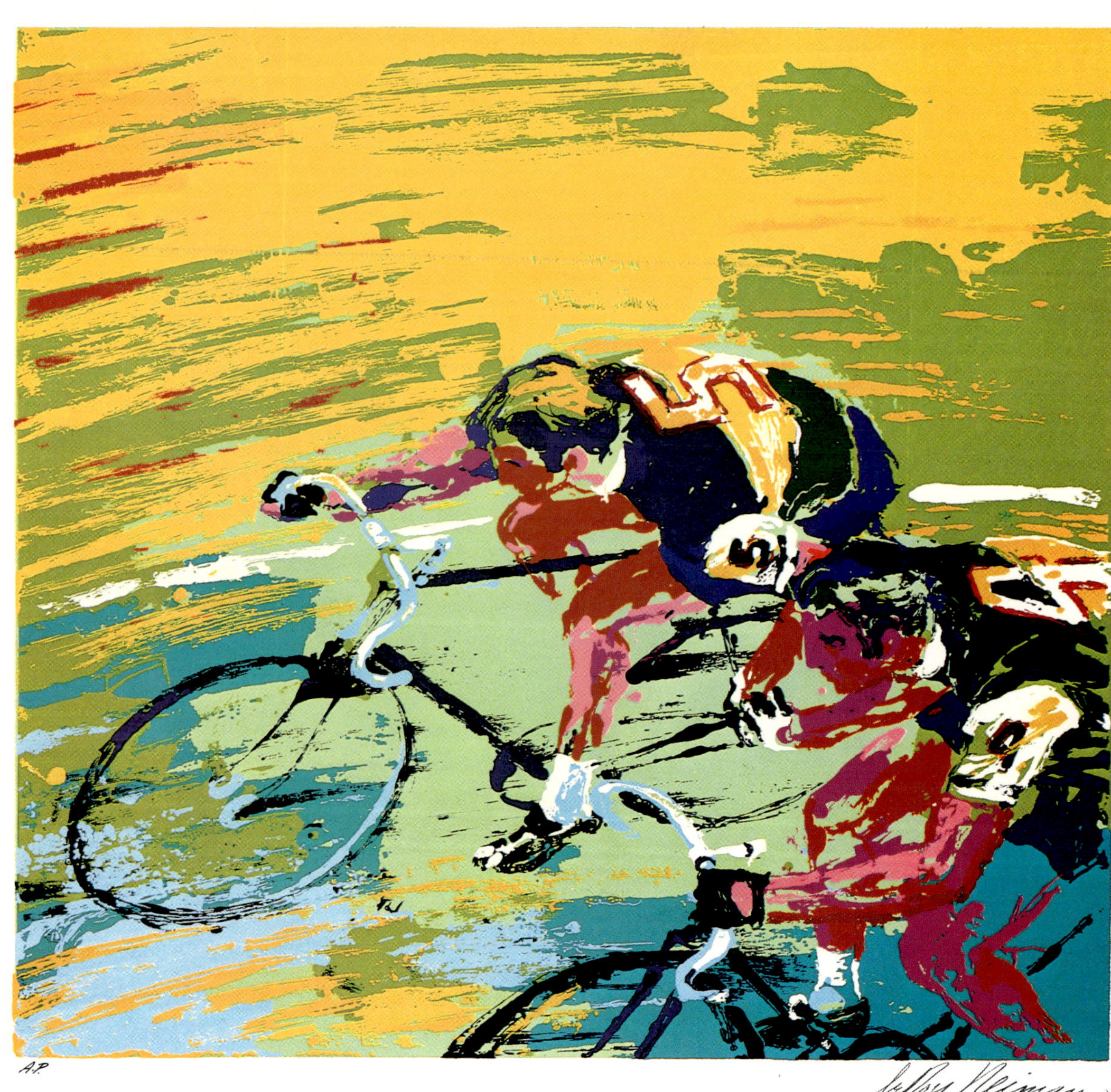

 Sumo
to be released
Serigraph
25 x 38 (63.5 x 96.52 cm)
A limited edition of 300, signed and numbered
by the artist.

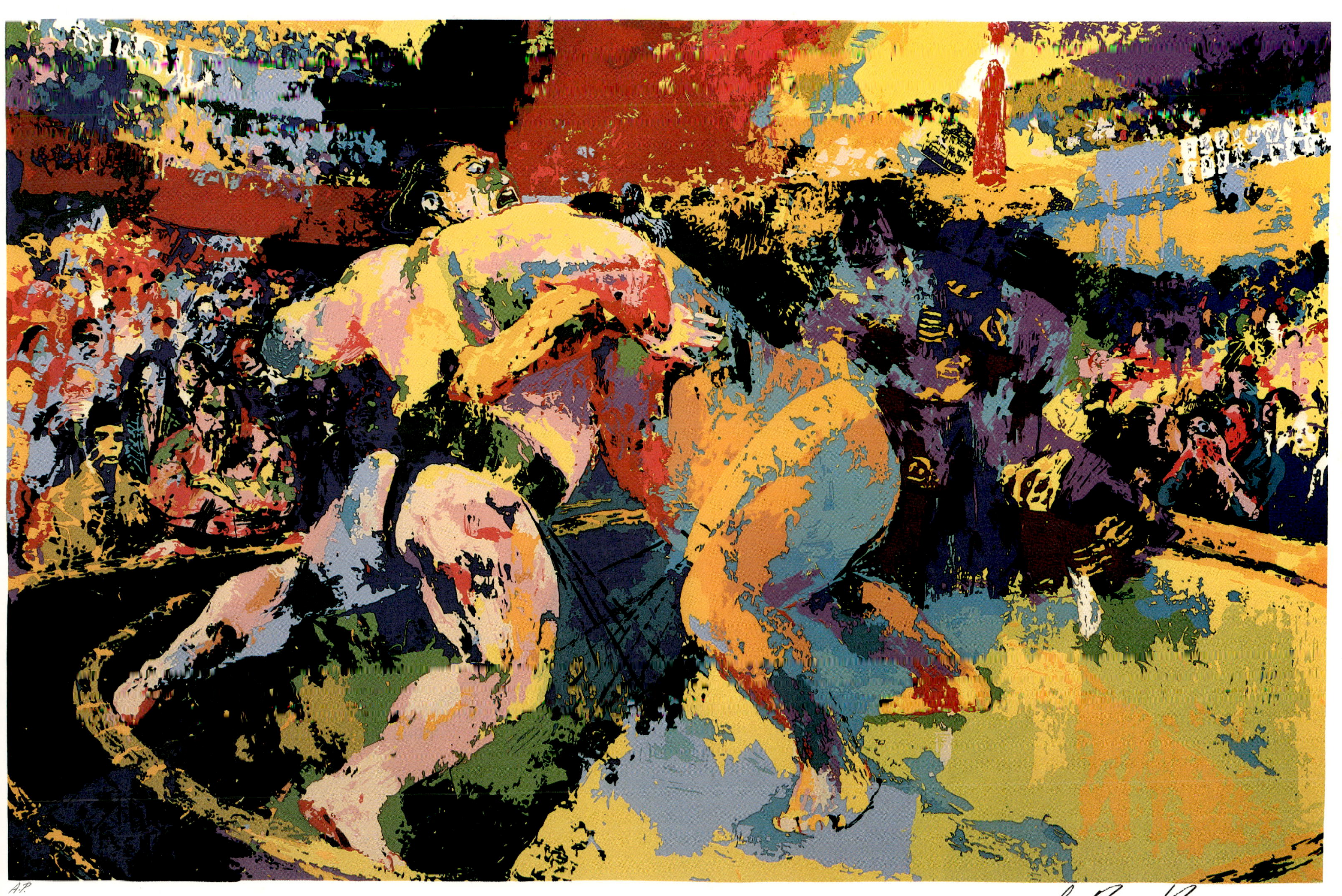

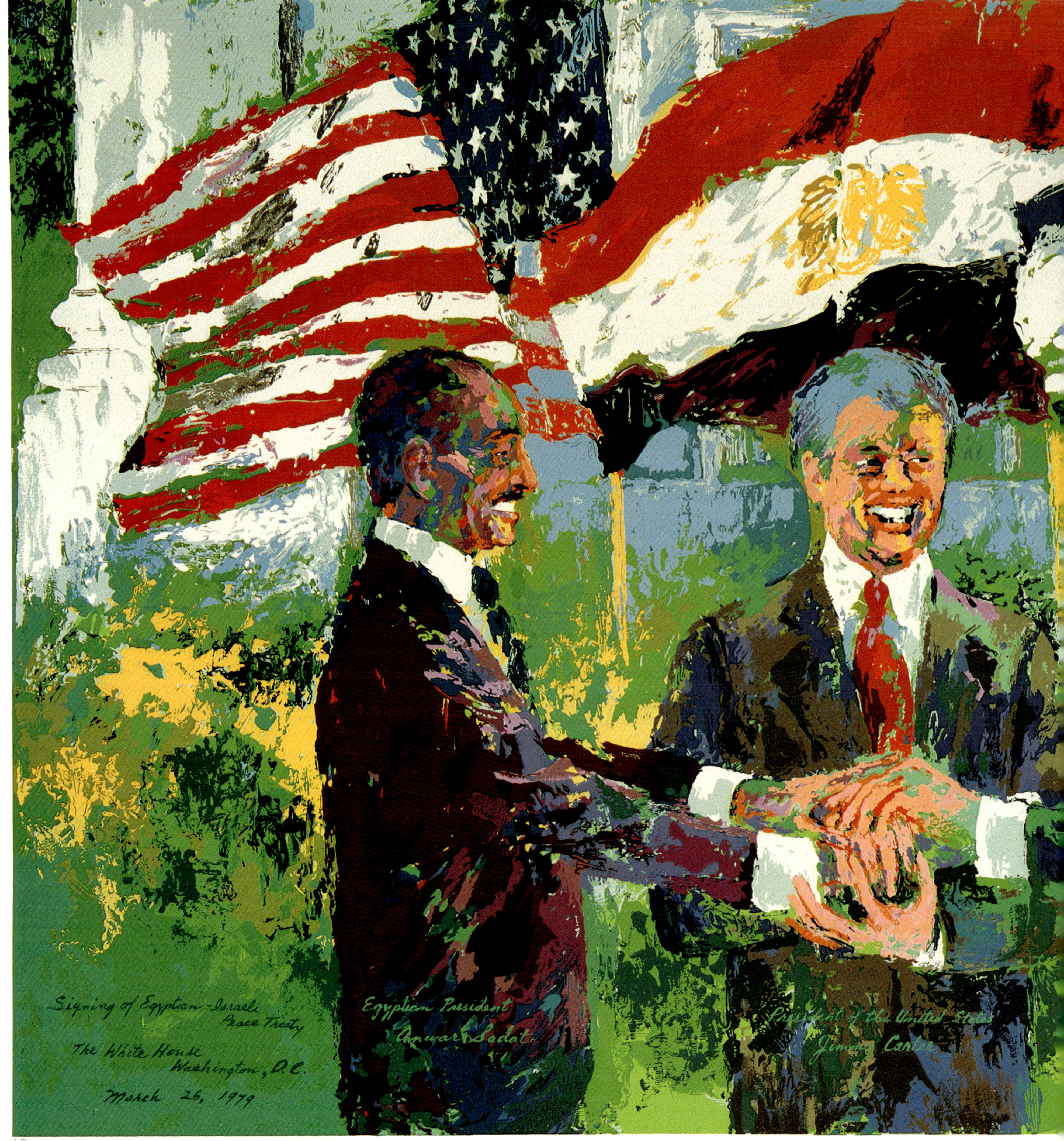
Signing of Egyptian-Israeli
Peace Treaty
The White House
Washington, D.C.
March 26, 1979
Egyptian President
Anwar Sadat
President of the United States
Jimmy Carter
AP

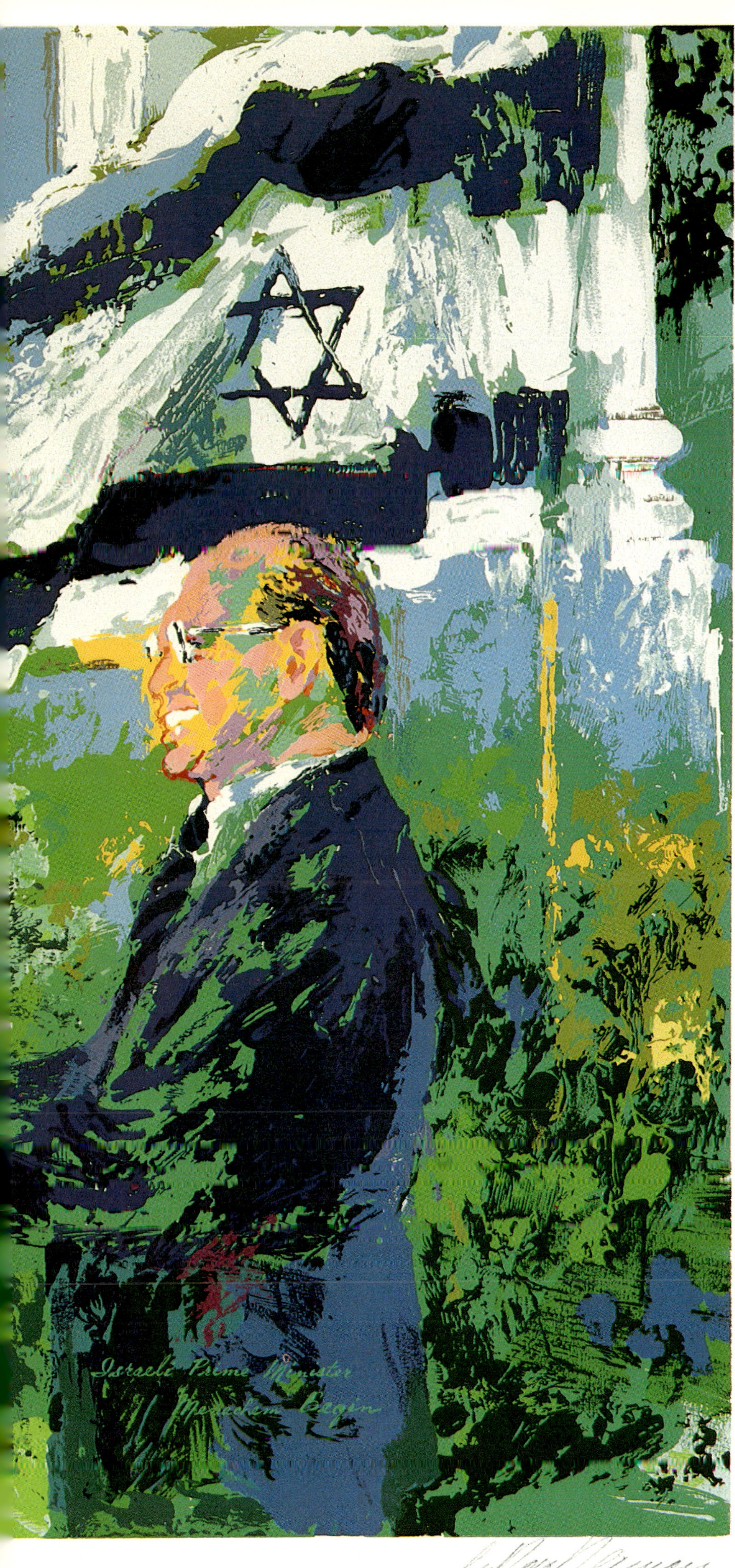

171 **White House Signing of the Egyptian Israeli Peace Treaty.**

1980
Serigraph
26¼ x 38 (66.68 x 96.52 cm)

A limited edition of 300, signed and numbered
by the artist.

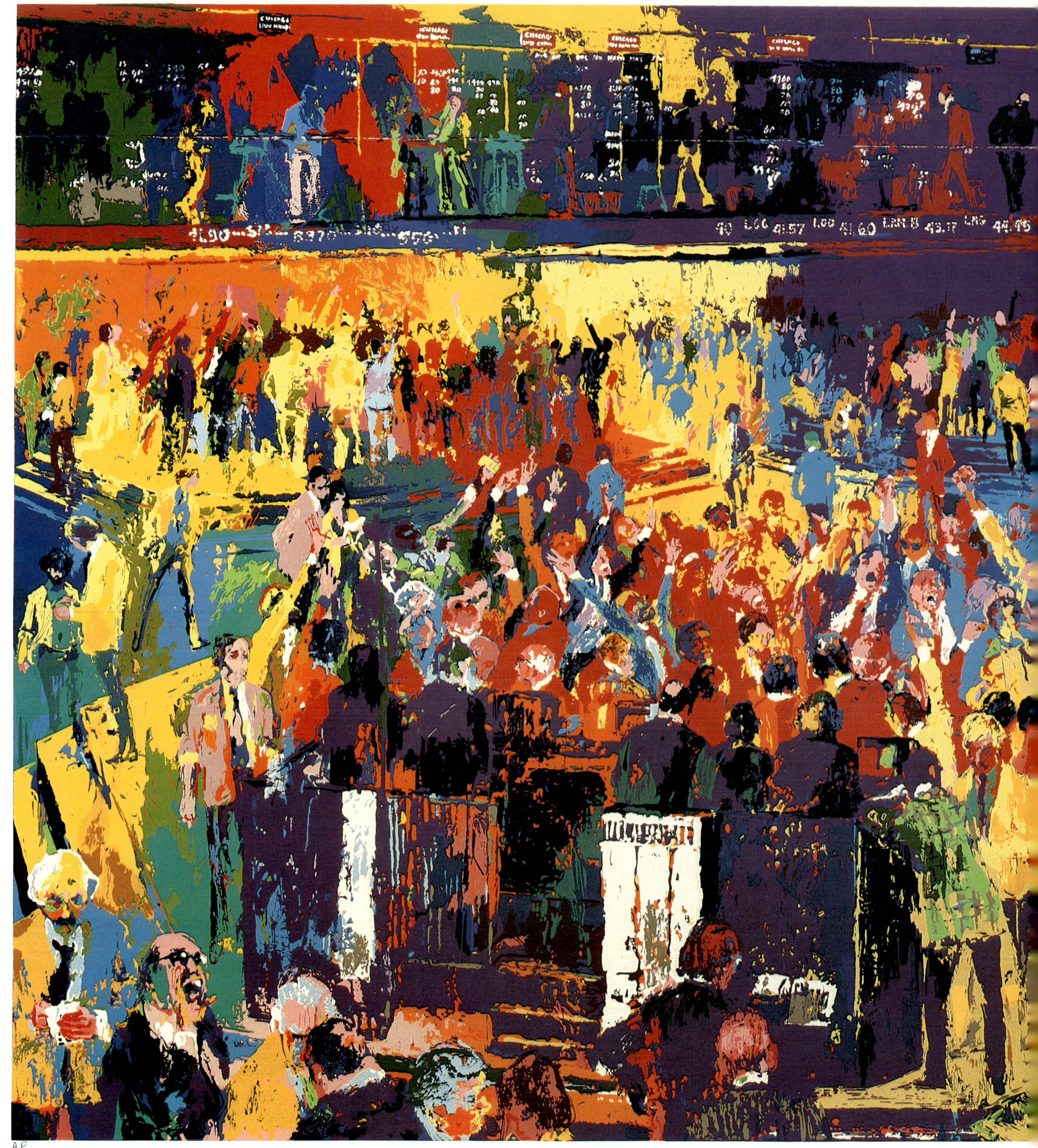

A.P.

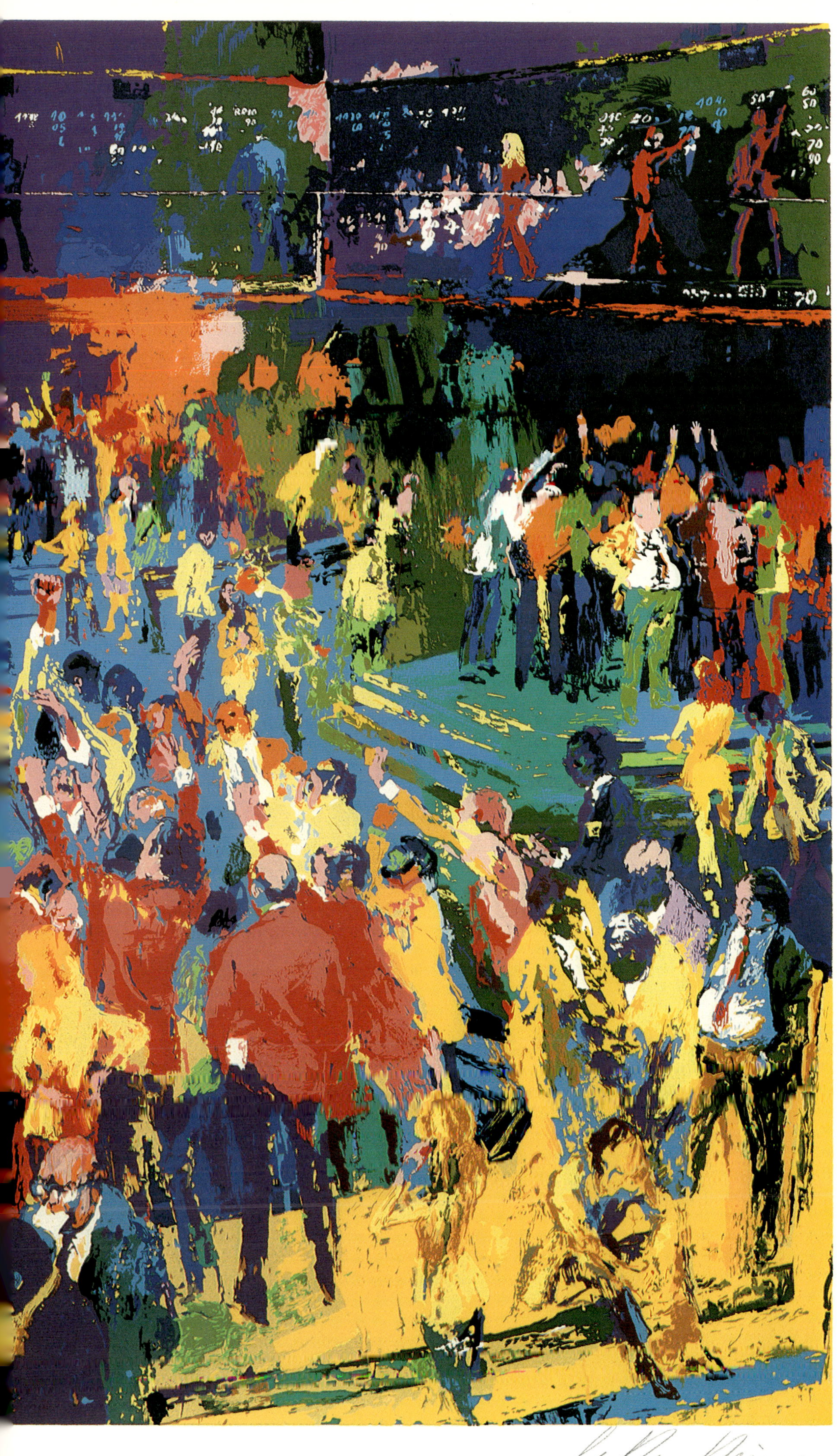

172   Chicago Board of Trade
1980
Serigraph
25⅜ x 38⅛ (64.45 x 96.84 cm)
A limited edition of 300, signed and numbered
by the artist.

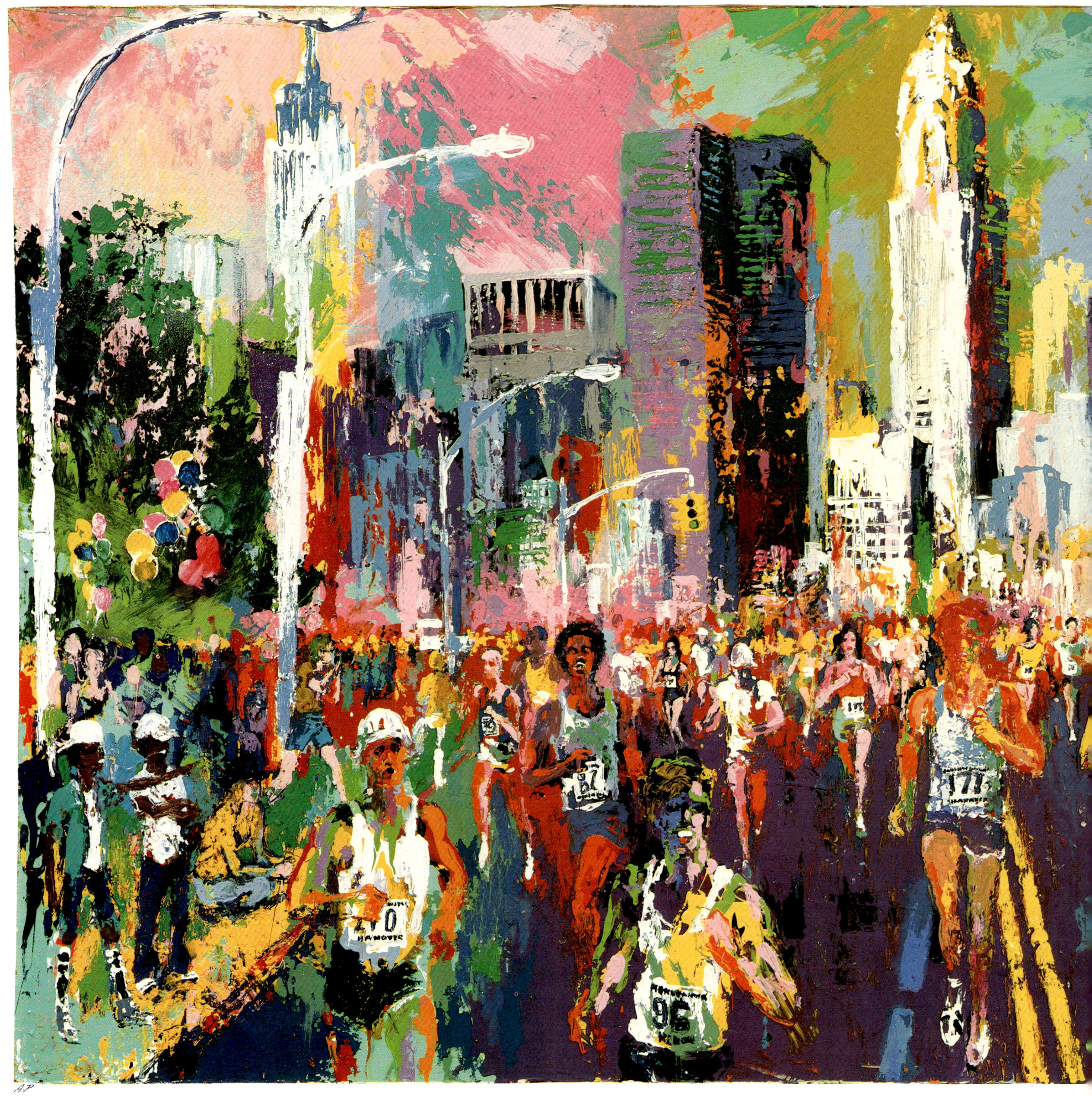

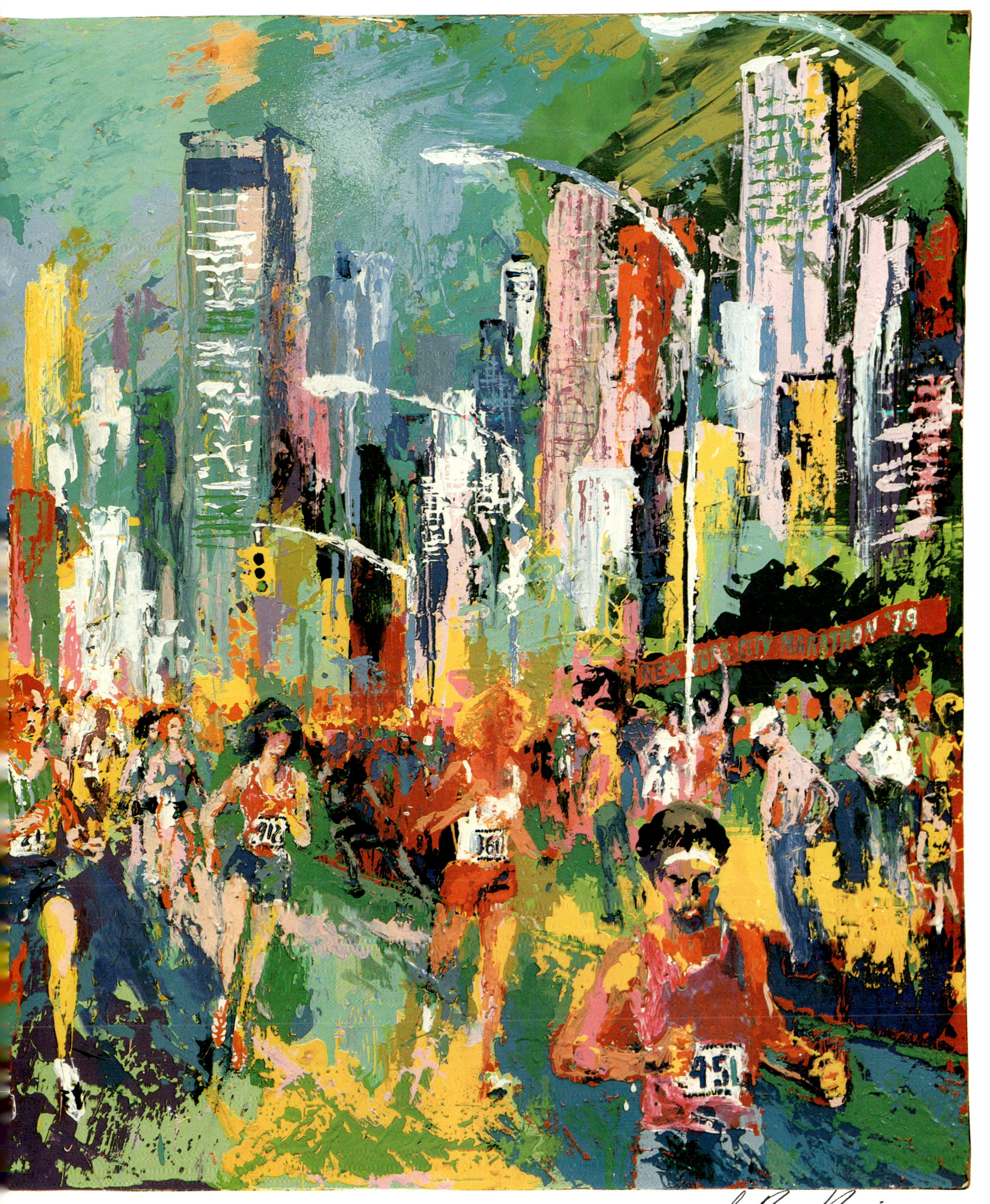

173
New York Marathon
1980
Serigraph
20¾ x 38
(52.71 x 96.52 cm)

A limited edition of 300,
signed and numbered
by the artist.

174   Gorilla Family

1980
Serigraph
28½ x 38 (72.39 x 96.52 cm)

A limited edition of 300, signed and numbered
by the artist.

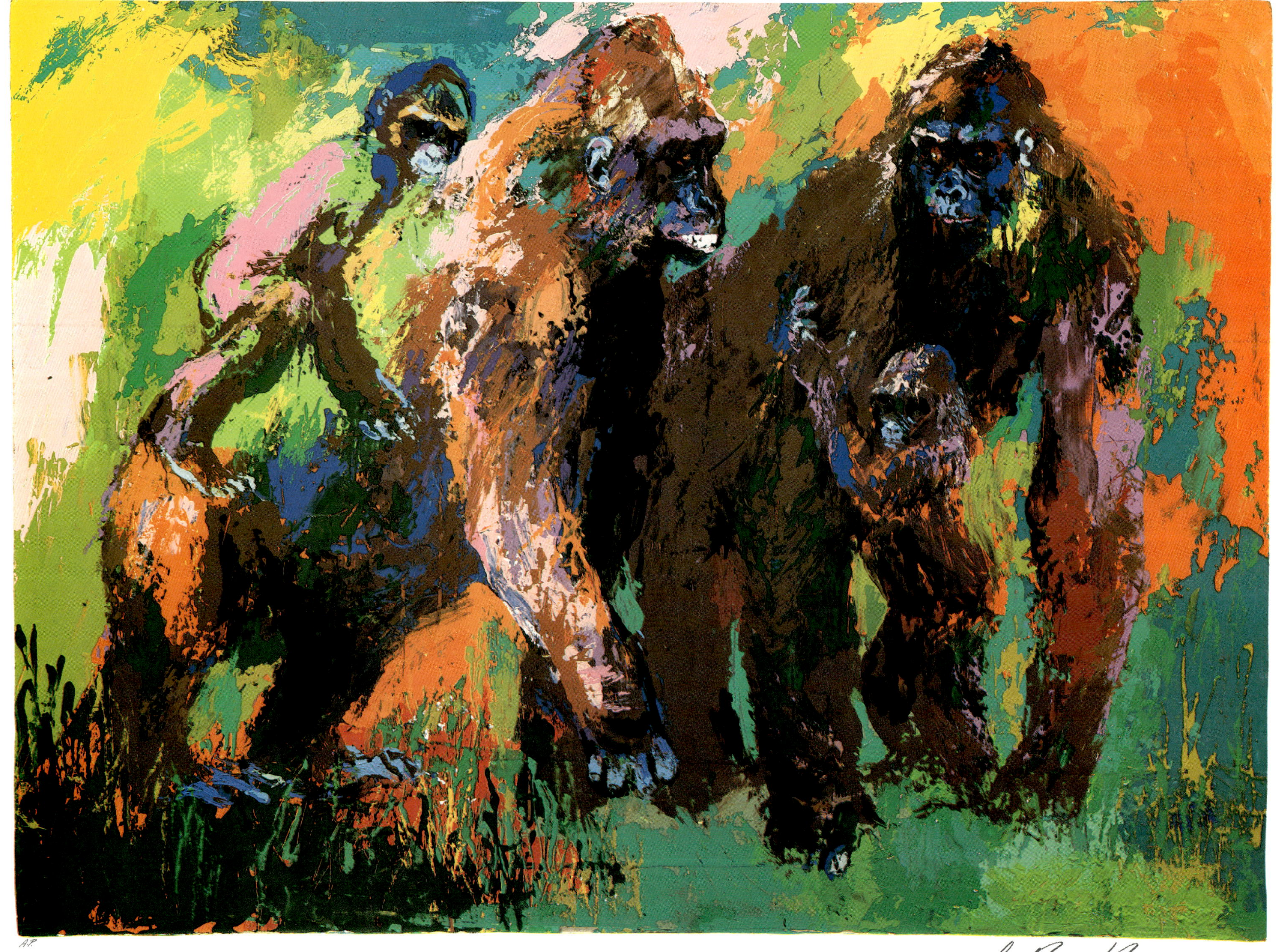

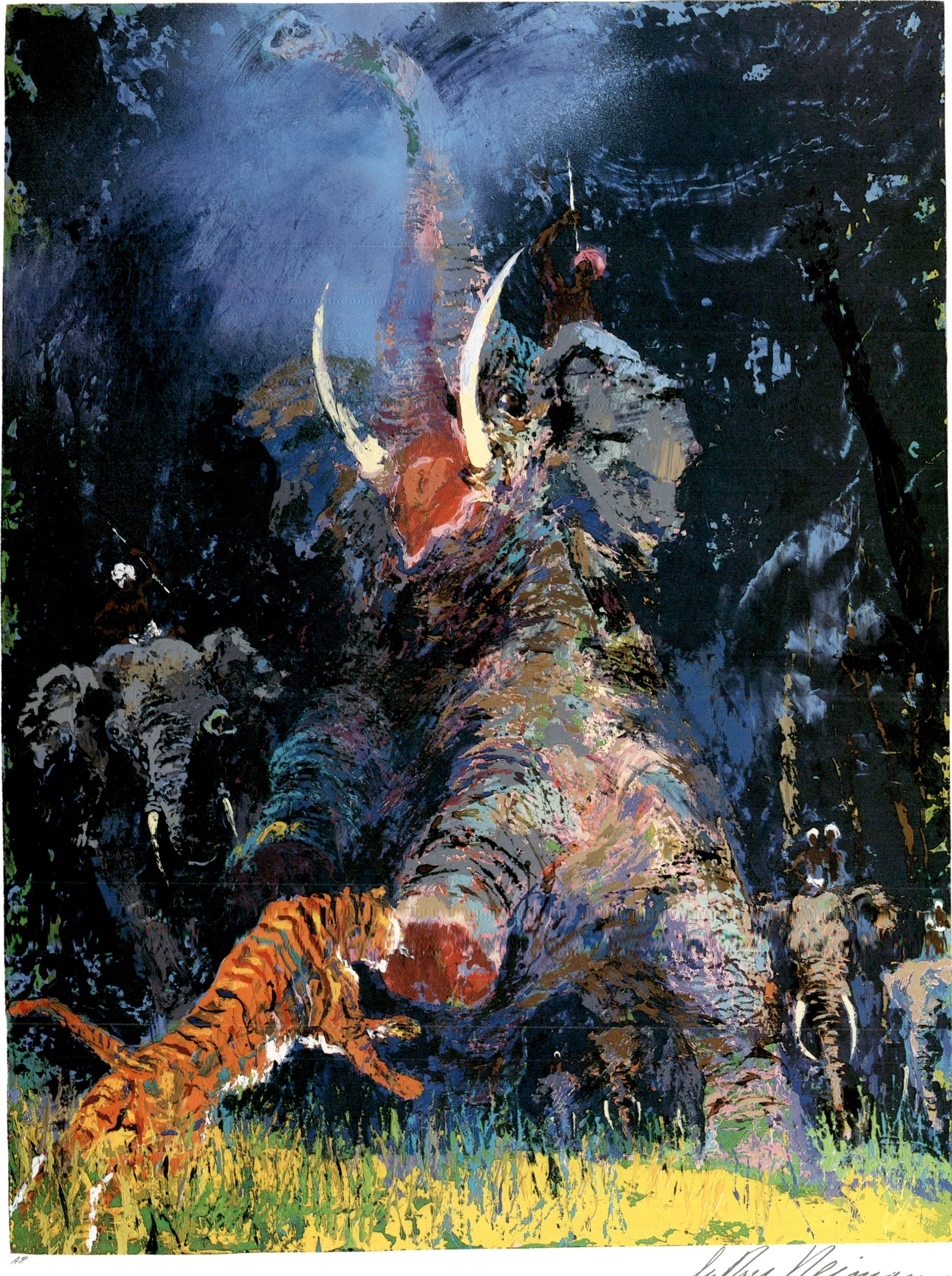

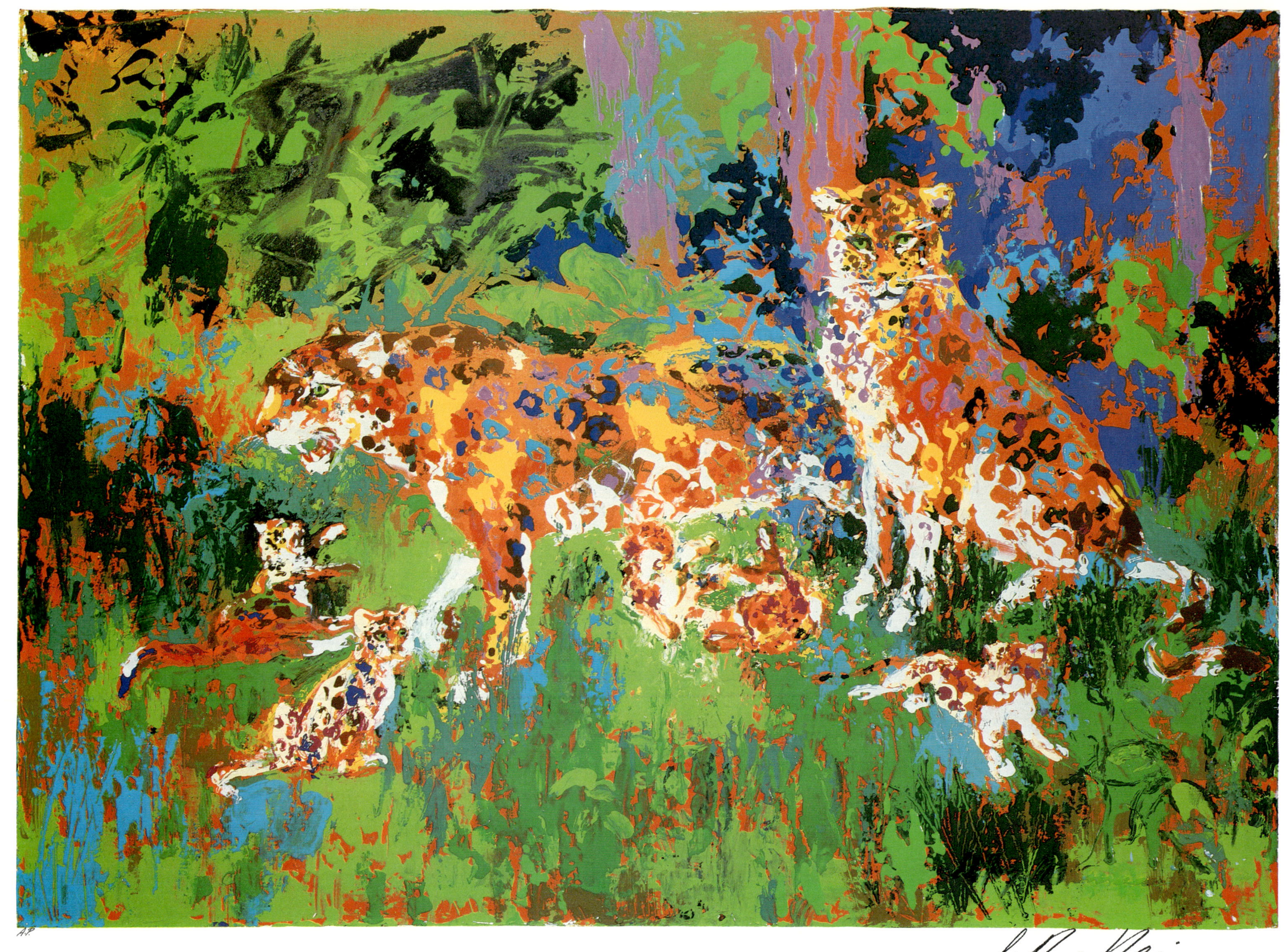

176 Jaquar Family
1980
Serigraph
17 x 23⅛ (43.18 x 58.74 cm)
A limited edition of 300, signed
and numbered by the Artist.

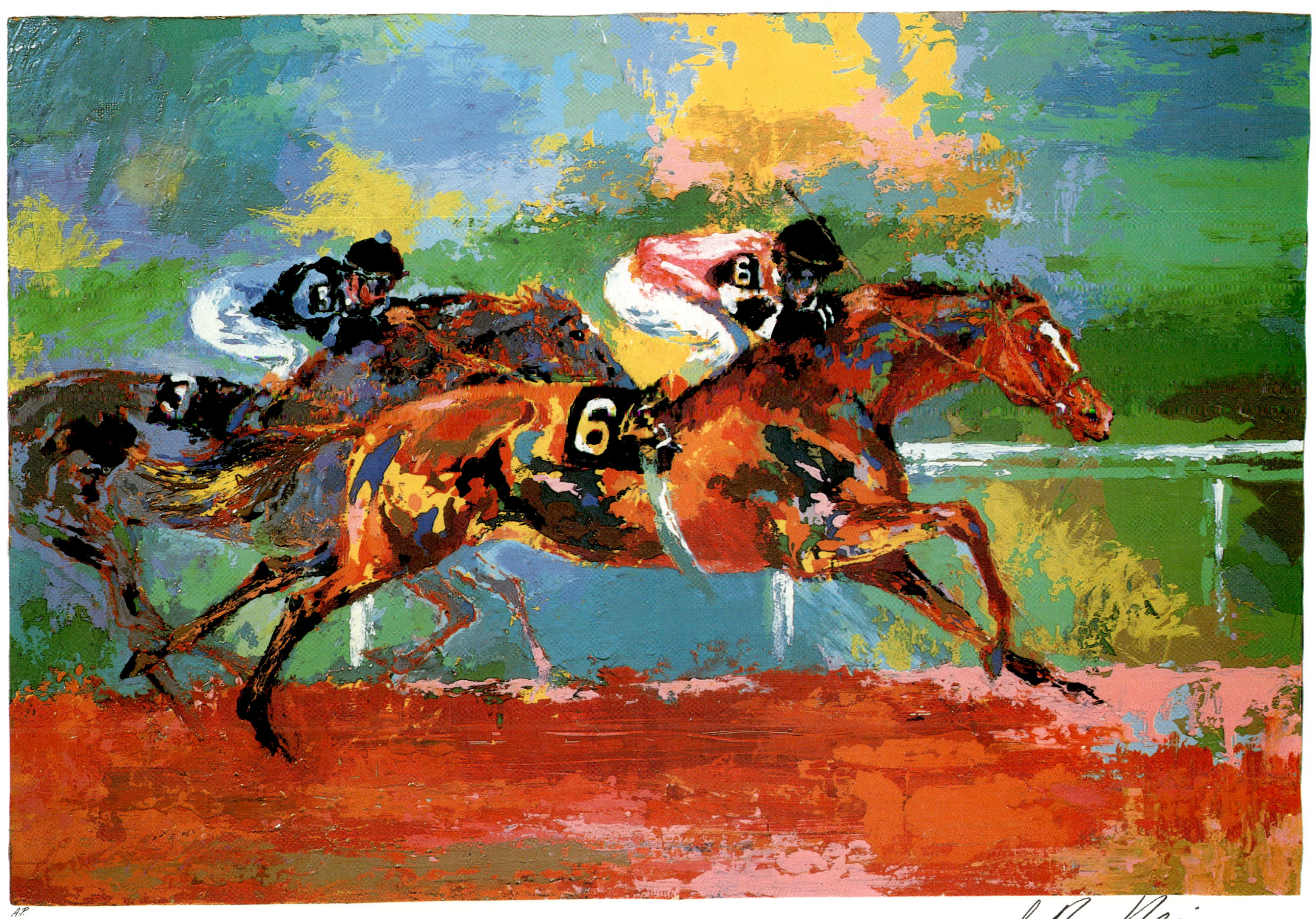

**177   Race of the year
(Affirmed & Spectacular Bid).**

1980
Serigraph
22⅜ x 32¼ (56.83 x 81.92 cm)
A limited edition of 300, signed and numbered
by the artist.

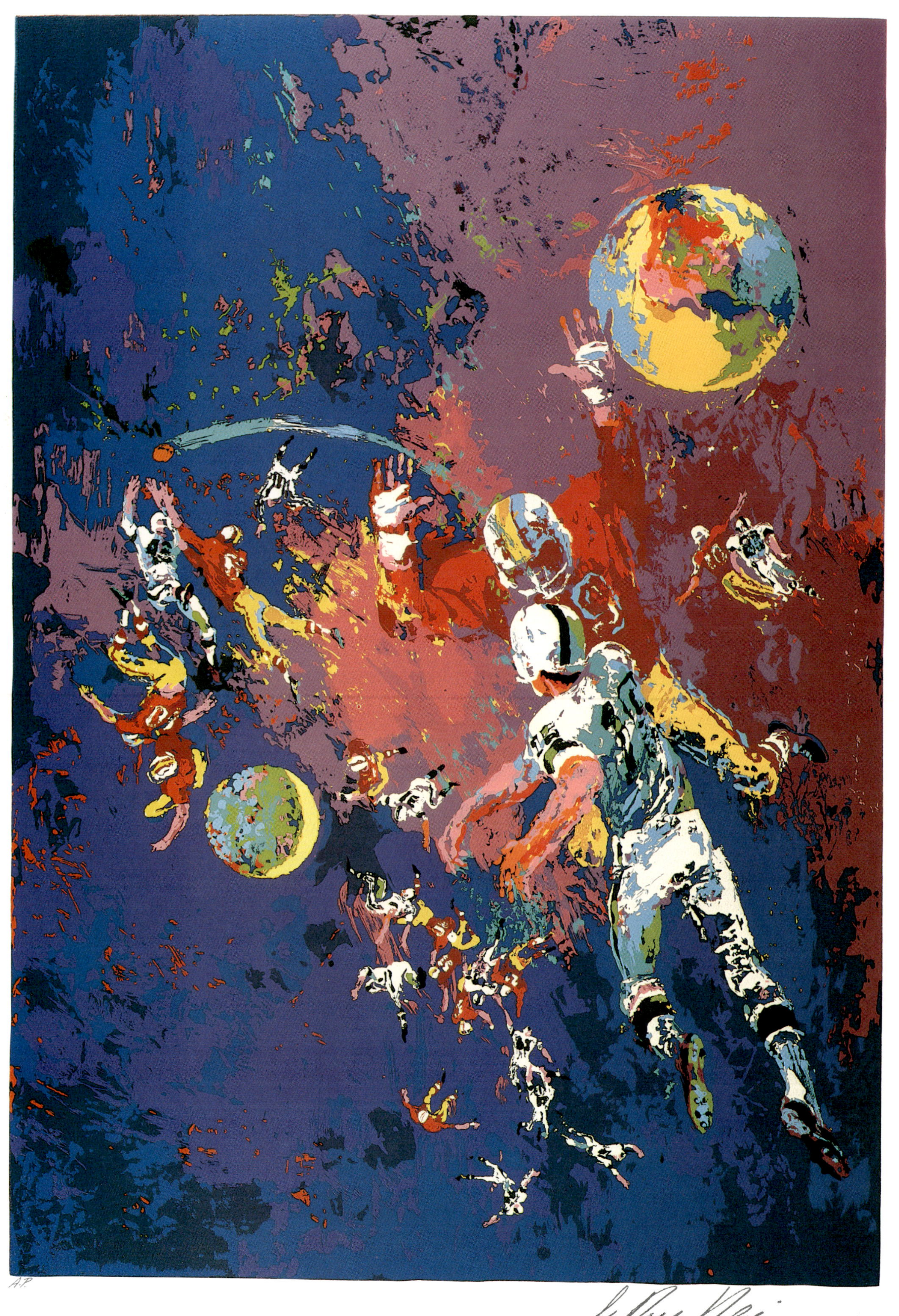

178   Space Football
to be released
Serigraph
35¼ x 24¼ (89.54 x 61.60 cm)
A limited edition of 300, signed and
numbered by the artist.

179   North Seas Sailing

to be released
Serigraph
20 x 27¾ (50.80 x 70.48 cm)
A limited edition of 300, signed and numbered
by the artist.

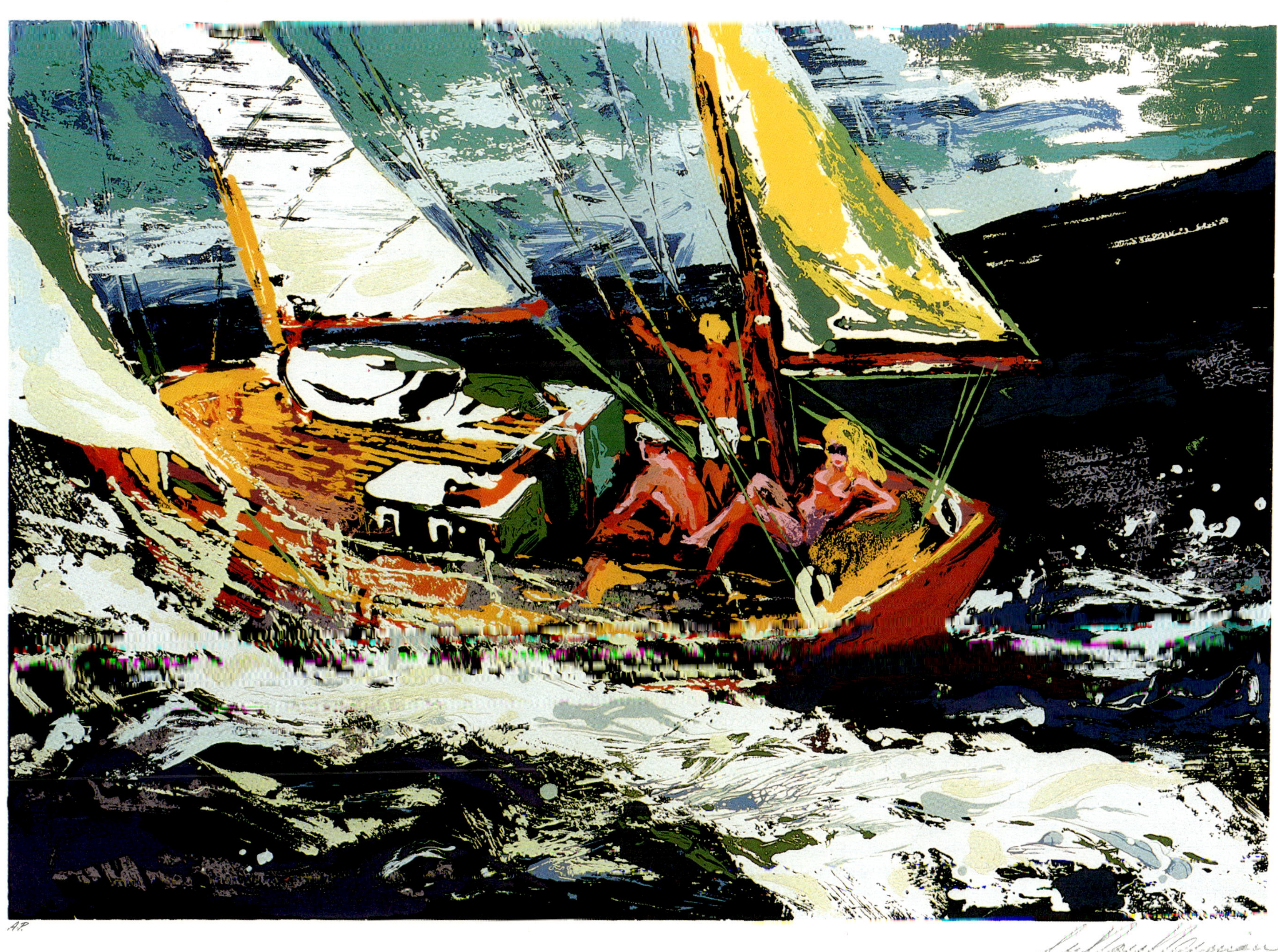

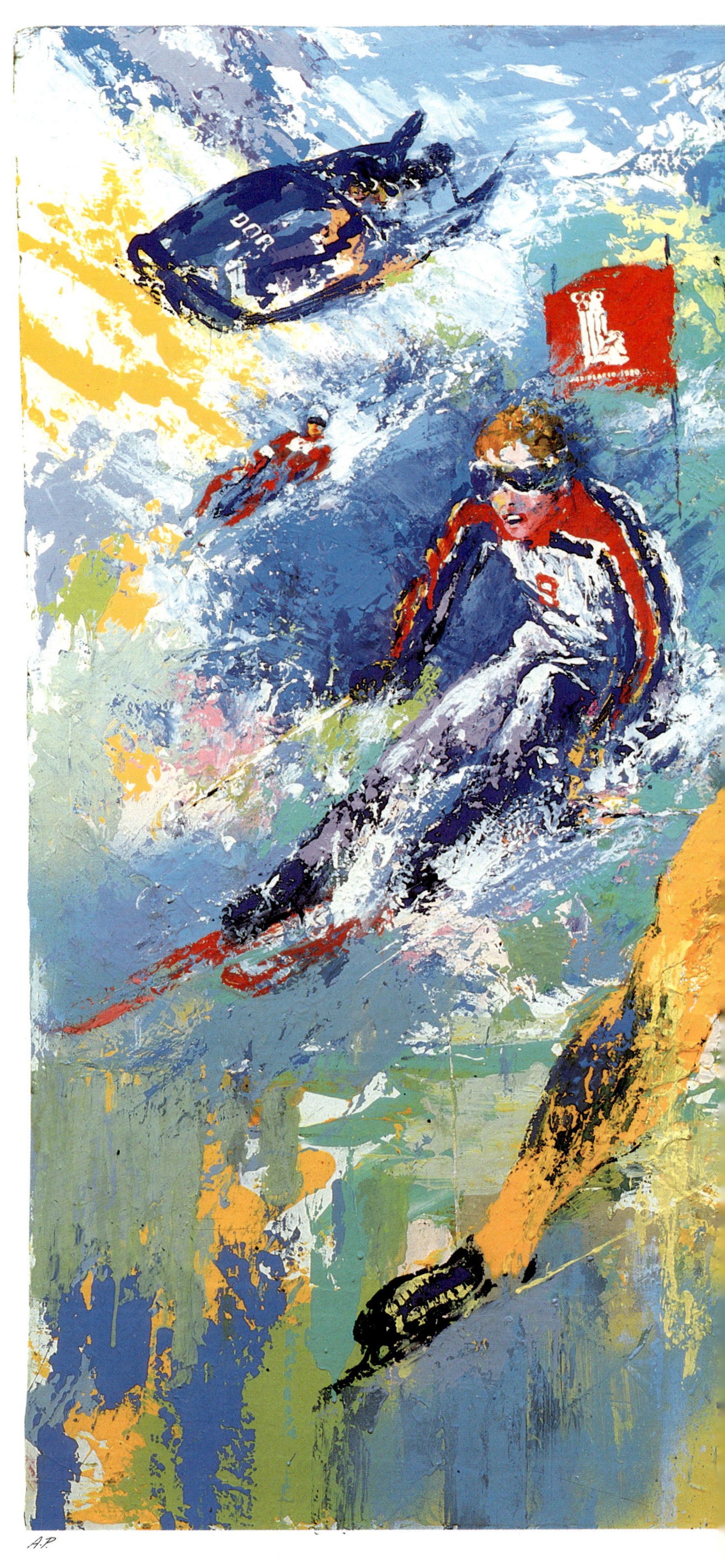

180   Neiman's Lake Placid—1980

1980
Serigraph
32 x 48 (81.28 x 121.92 cm)
A limited edition of 300, signed
and numbered by the artist.

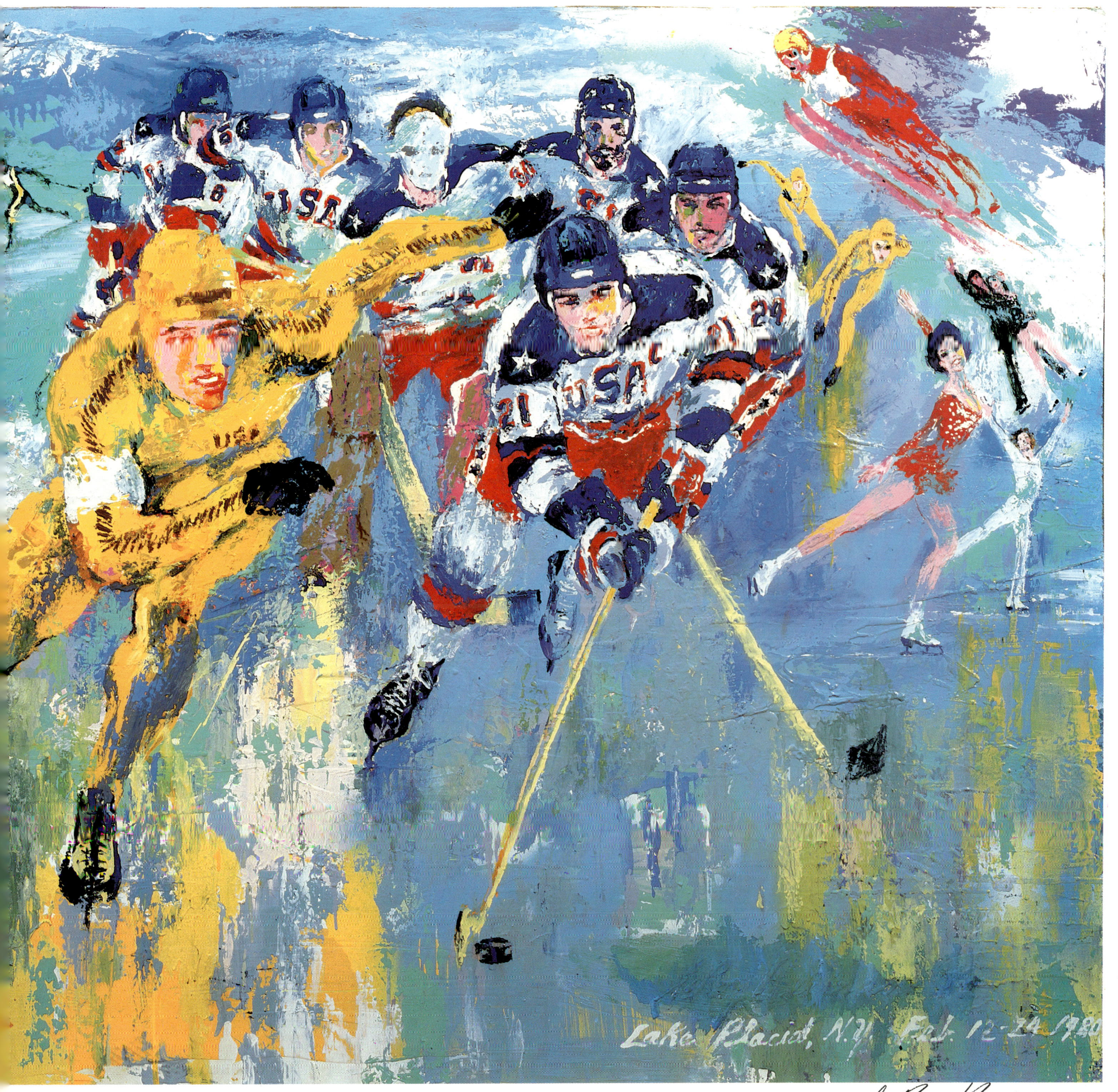

Lake Placid, N.Y. Feb. 12-24 1980
LeRoy Neiman

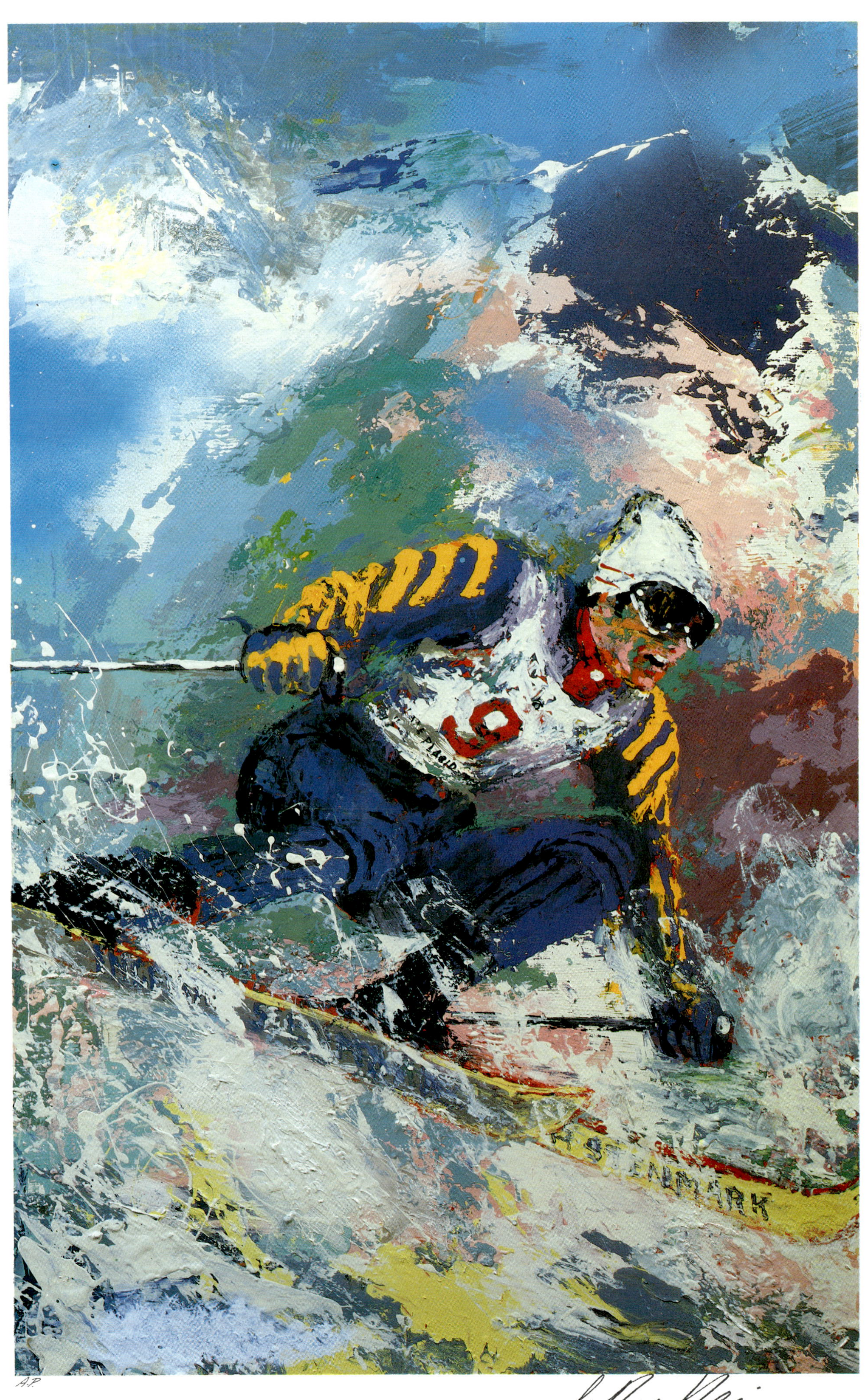

181 Stenmark
1980
Serigraph
38 x 24 (96.52 x 60.96 cm)
A limited edition of 300, signed
and numbered by the Artist.

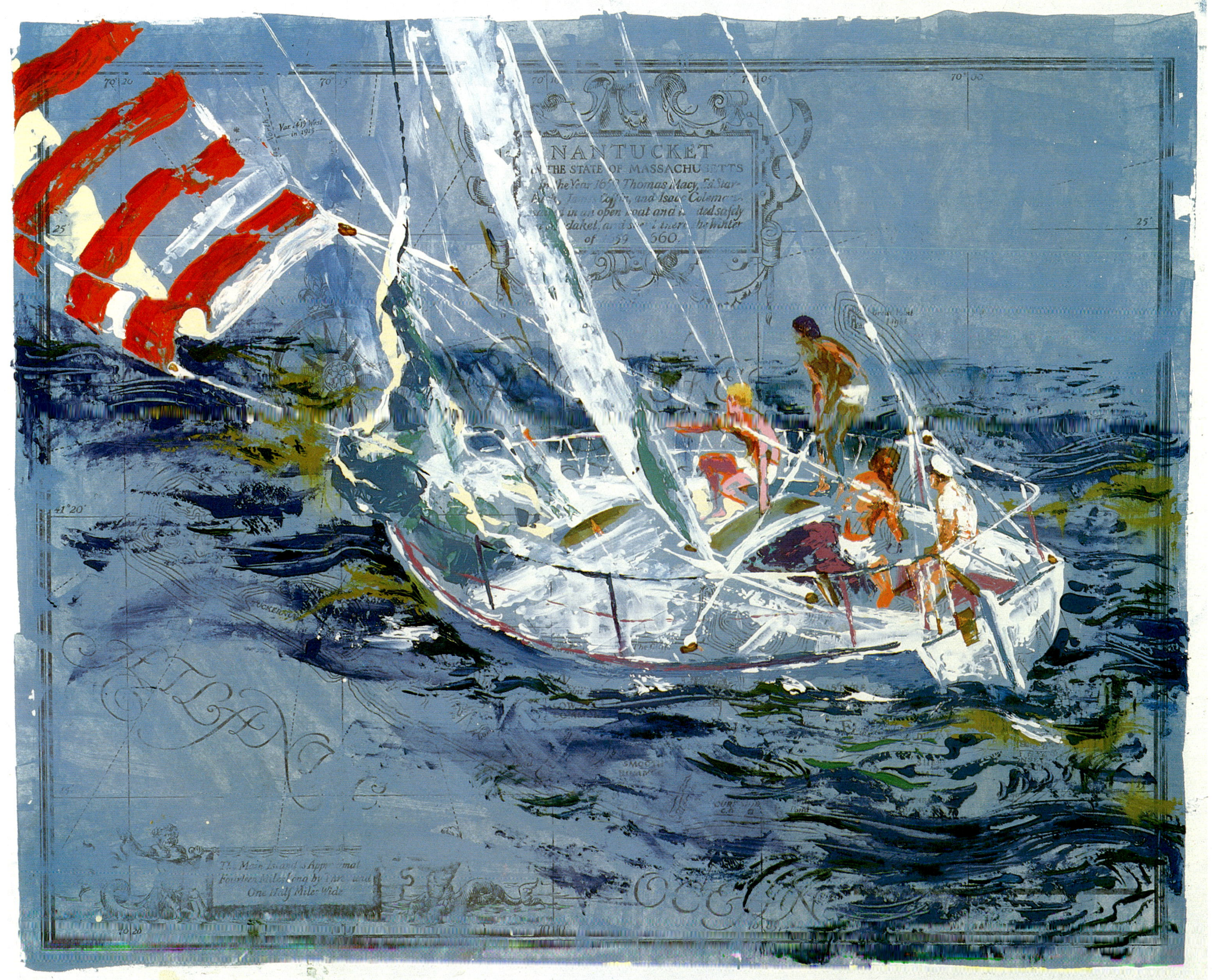

182   Nantucket Sailing
1980
Serigraph
20 x 29 (50.8 x 73.66 cm)
A limited edition of 300, signed
and numbered by the Artist.

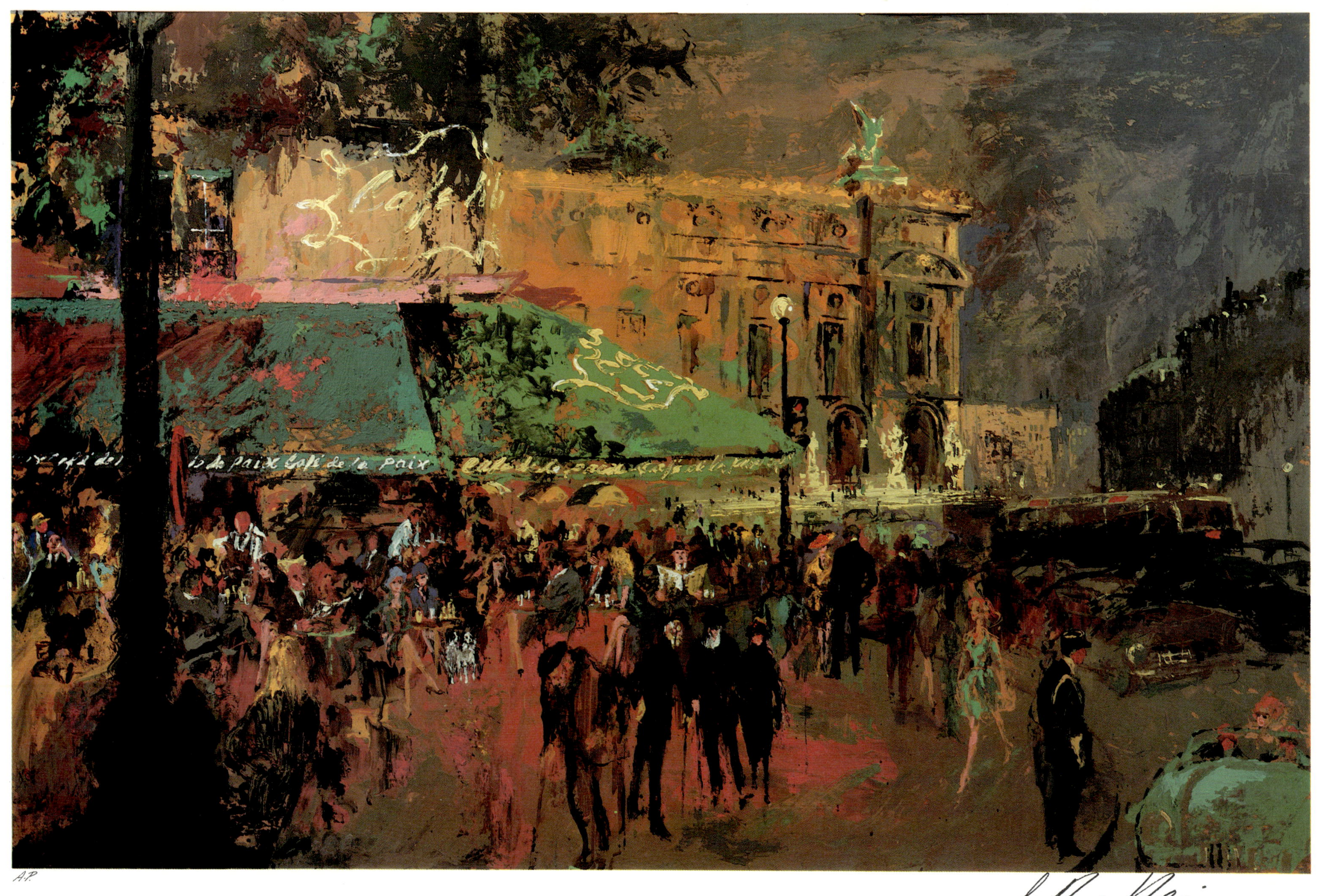

183   Cafe de la Paix

1980
Serigraph
32 x 48 (81.28 x 121.92 cm)

A limited edition of 300, signed and numbered
by the artist.

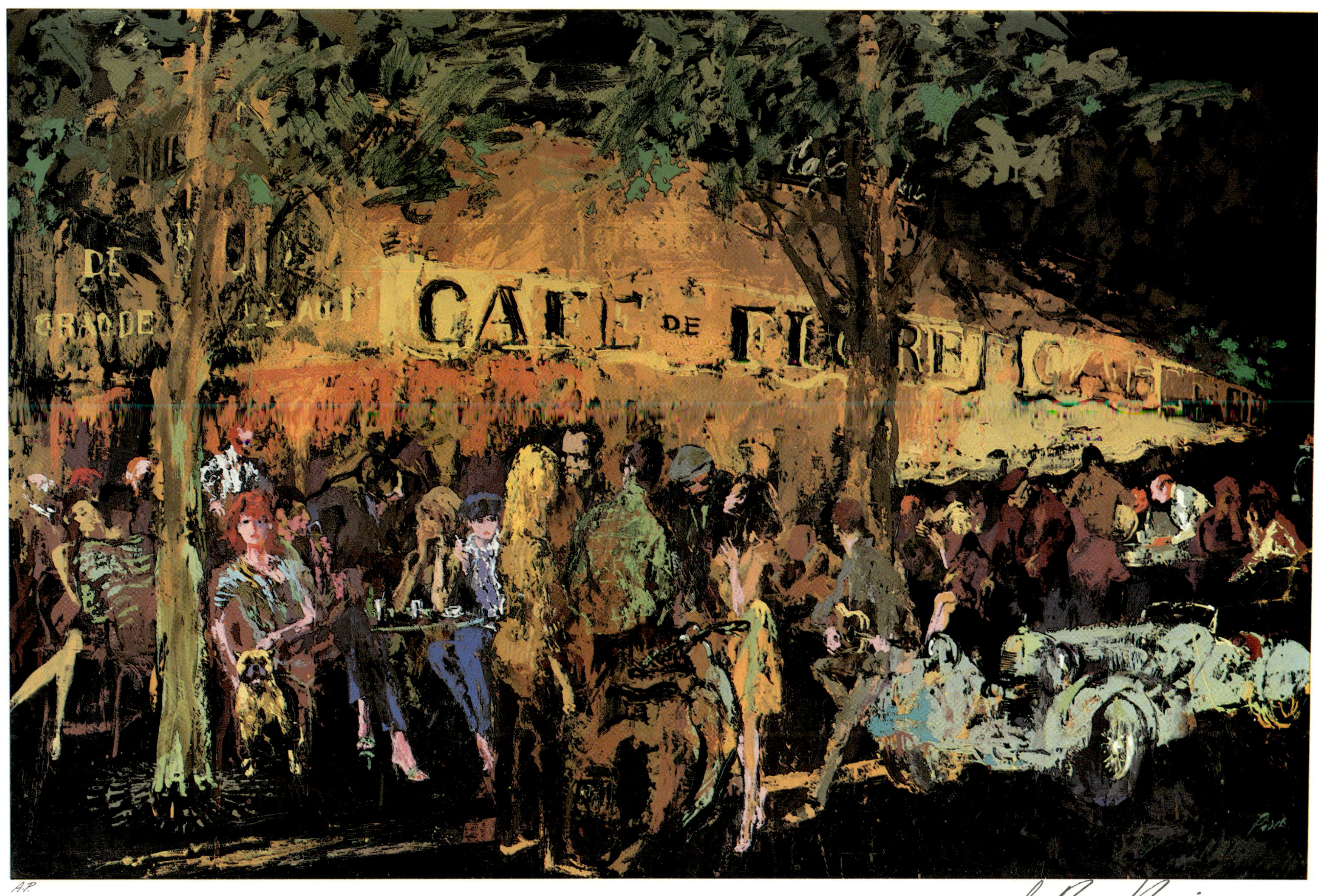

184   Cafe de Flore la nuit
1980
Serigraph
25 x 38 (63.5 x 96.52 cm)

A limited edition of 300, signed and numbered
by the artist.

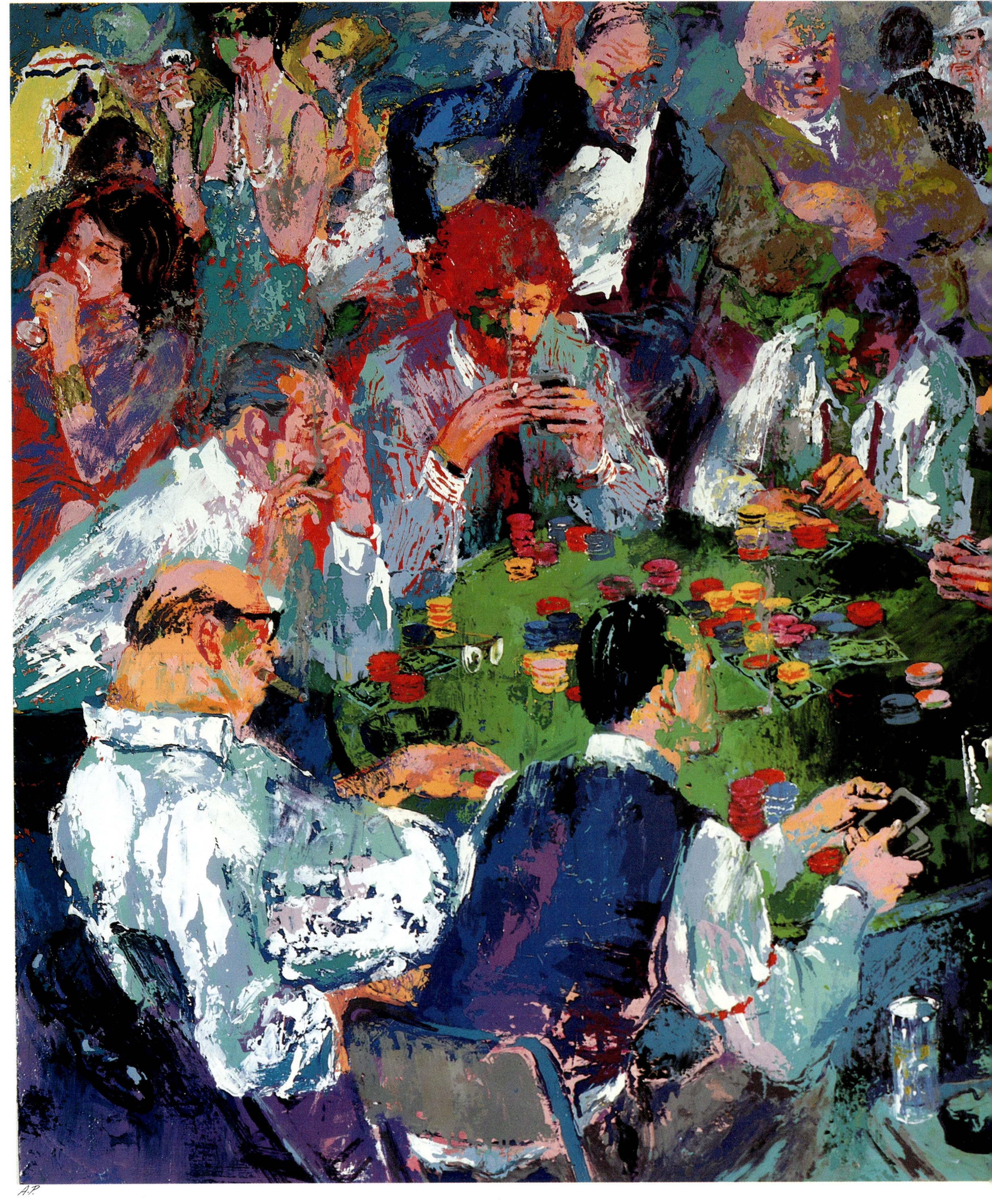

274

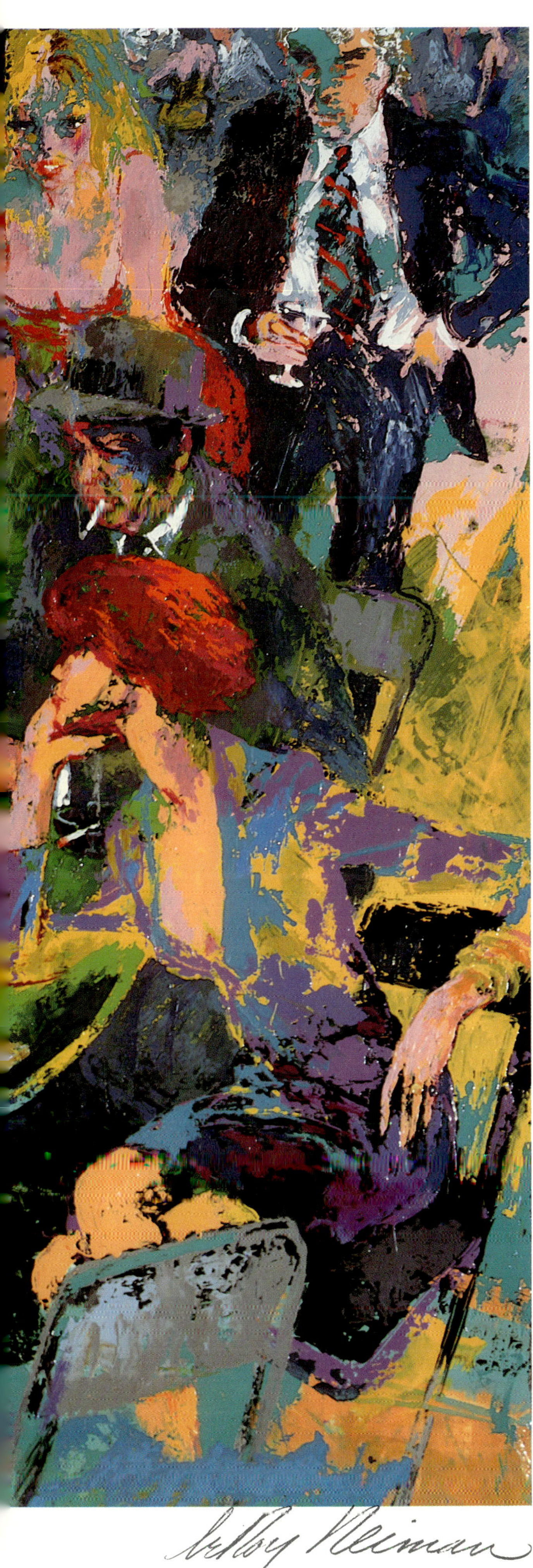

185   Stud Poker

1980
Serigraph
31½ x 38 (80. x 96.52 cm)
A limited edition of 300 signed
and numbered by the artist.

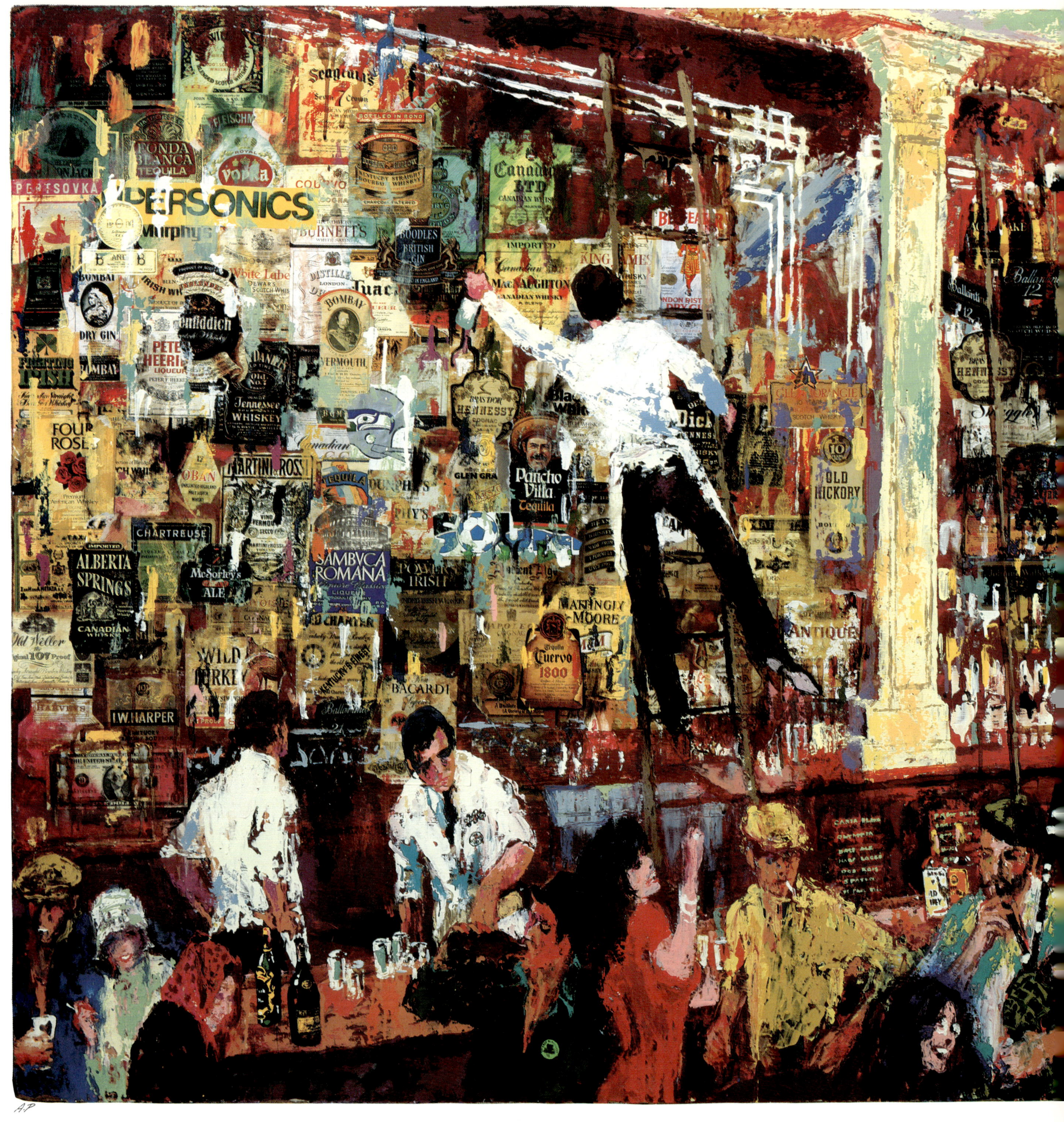

SUPERSONICS

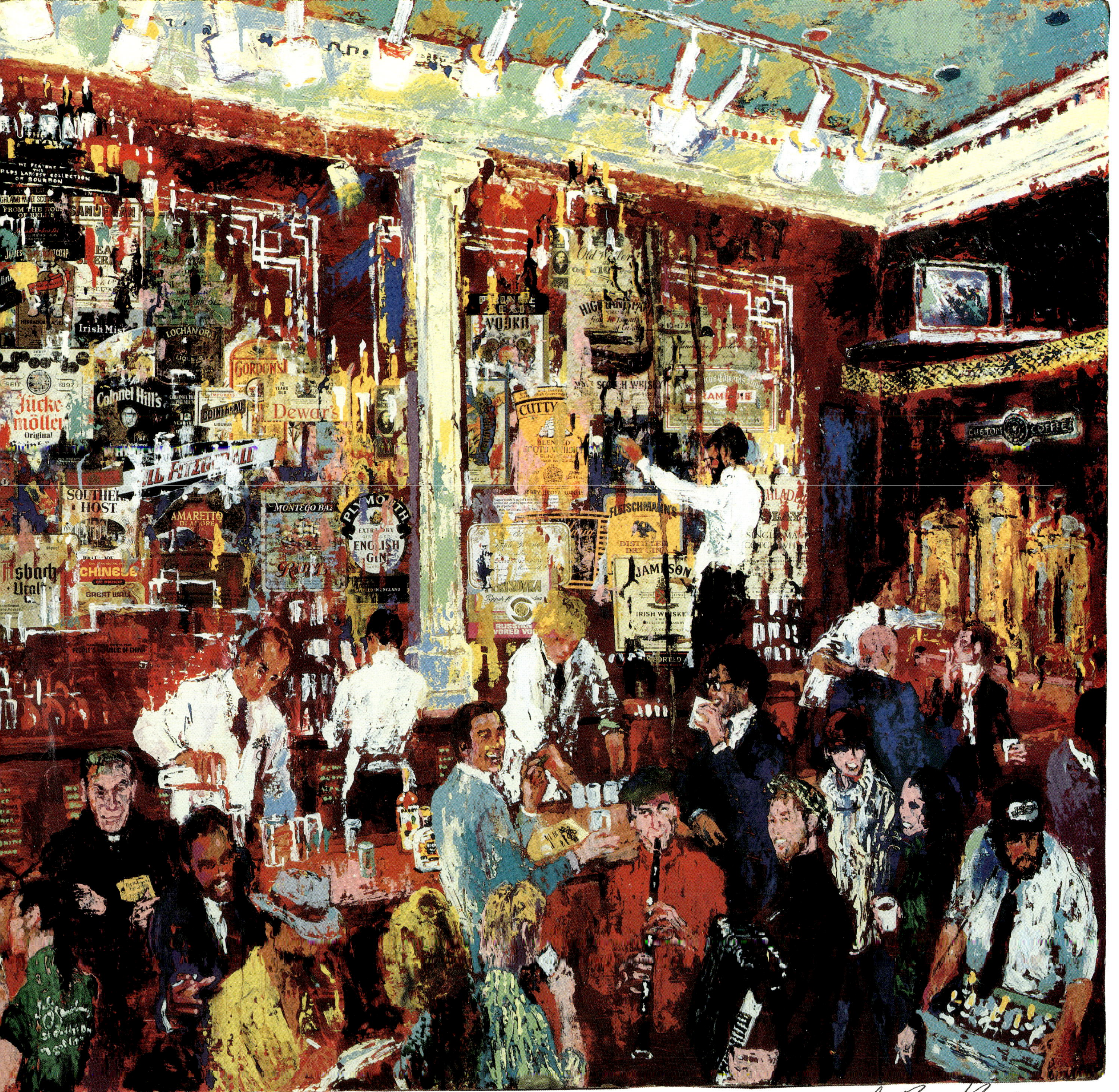

186   F.X. McRory's Whiskey Bar

1980
Serigraph
22⅝ x 45⅛ (57.47 x 114.62 cm)
A limited edition of 300, h.c.-60, signed and numbered by the artist.

The Lithographs & Monoprints

The modern technique of lithography, which began in the late 18th century, became a fine art medium in the 19th century, especially in the hands of Goya, Delacroix, Daumier, and the Post-Impressionists. Neiman admired the work of all those Europeans, as well as the American masters of lithography: Homer, Soyer, Marsh, Bellows, and Shahn.

There are many kinds of lithographic techniques, all of which print in reverse the original image that the artist has made on stone or metal. Neiman began to experiment with these techniques in the 1950s and 60s. During the 1970s, he continued to explore the possibilities of the medium by rendering some of his favorite subjects: women, horses, and the Commedia dell'arte. Some of his color combinations are as simple as black and white. Some are quite complex, such as his recent seven-colored lithograph of Vince Lombardi.

From the beginning Neiman wanted to capture in his prints the dynamic painterly quality of his paintings. The physical properties of the lithograph resisted. So, simultaneously (in the 50s and 60s), Neiman began to explore monoprints, as had Blake, Degas, Gauguin, Picasso, Prendergast, and Tobey.

Neiman's monoprints, like most monoprints, began with an image he made on a sheet of glass. This original image was then pressed on a sheet of paper leaving a unique image (hence the term "mono"). Only five of these "editions of one" have survived from the decade between the "Rouen Cathedral" of the early 1950s and the Hero series of the early 1960s: Napoleon, De Gaulle, and Al Capone. But they are enough to show us how important these explorations were to Neiman. This work gave him a clear idea of the pictorial quality that could be achieved by oil-based multiples. When he was invited to make serigraphic prints in 1970, he capitalized on his experience with monoprints to make images with a similar painterly quality.

F.L.G.

Lithographs

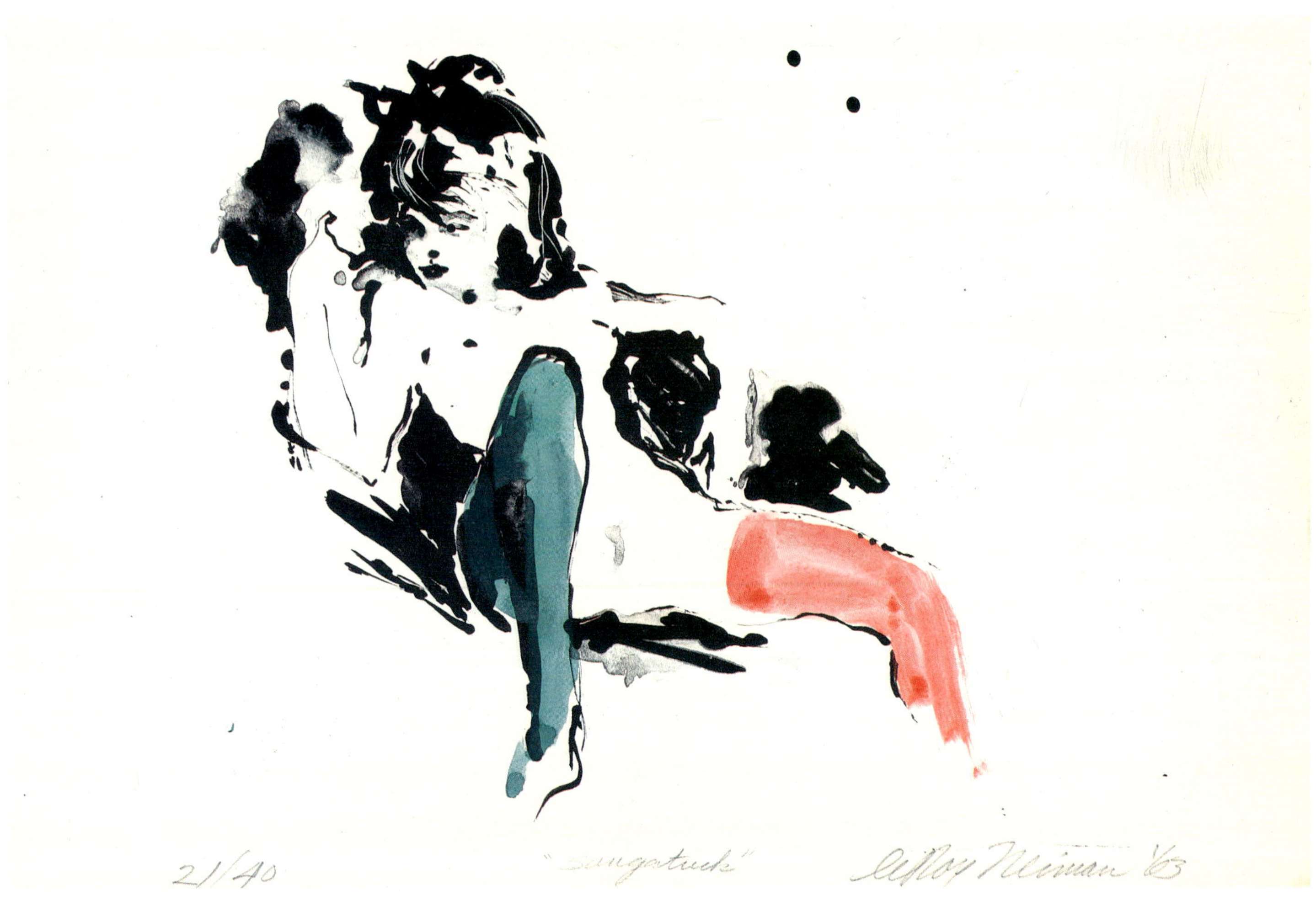

187 Saugatuck (nude)

1963
Handcolored Lithograph
13 x 19¼ (33.02 x 48.89 cm)

**A limited edition of 40, signed and numbered
by the artist.**

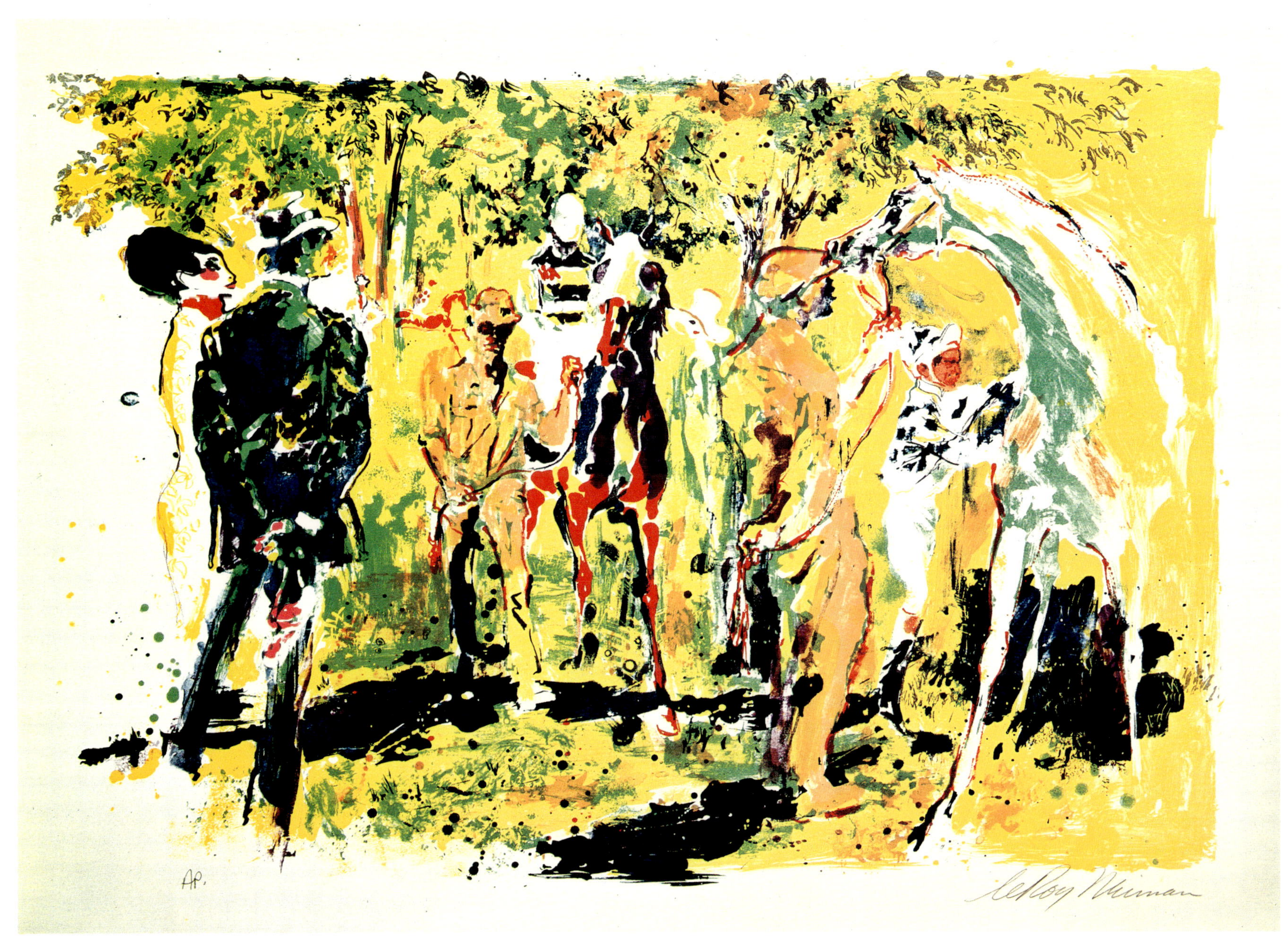

188 Paddock II
1972
Lithograph
19 x 27⅜ (48.26 x 69.53 cm)

A limited edition of 90, signed and
numbered by the artist.

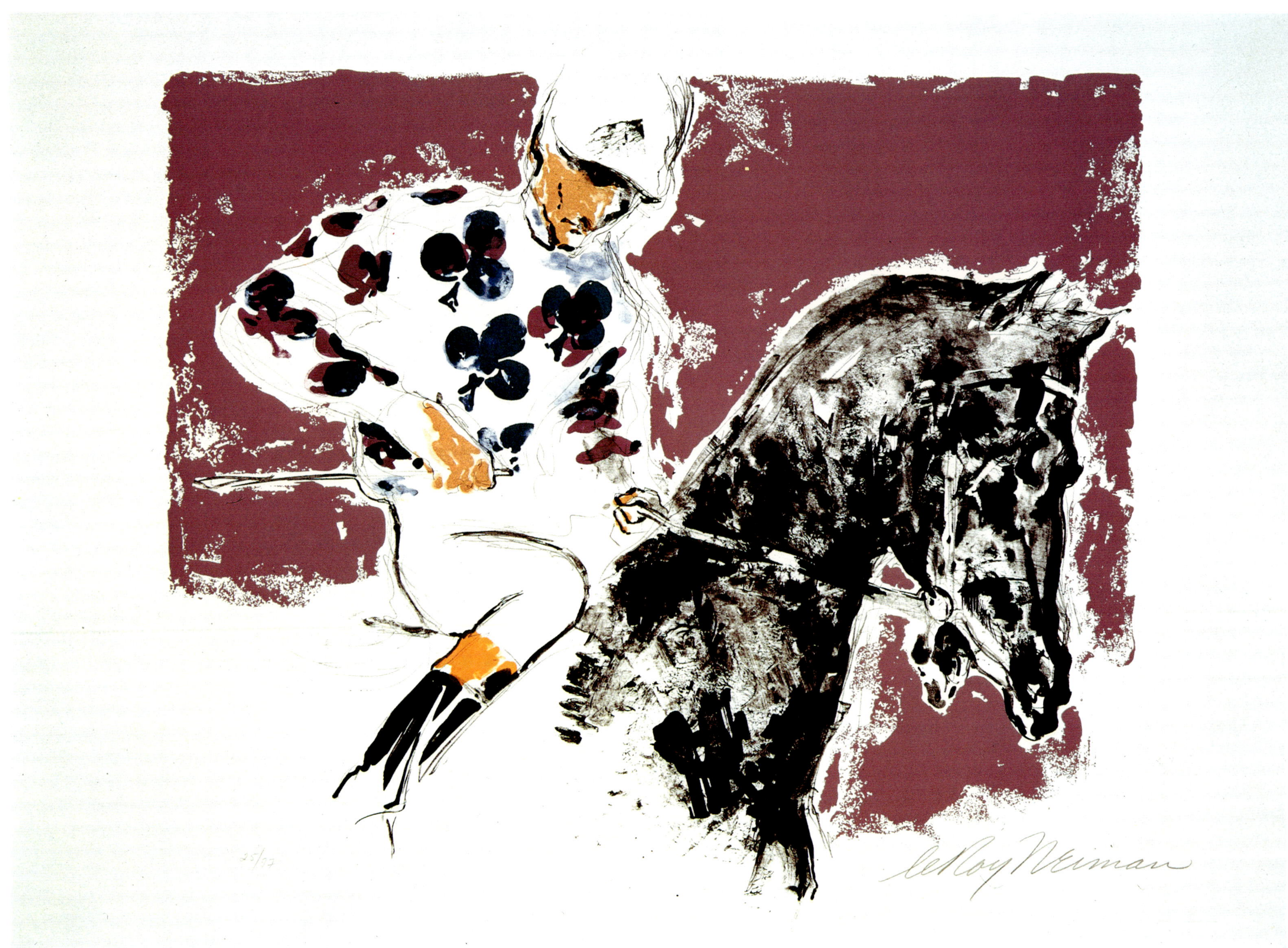

189   Clubs
1972
Lithograph
22 x 29¾ (55.88 x 75.57 cm)
A limited edition of 97, signed
and numbered by the Artist.

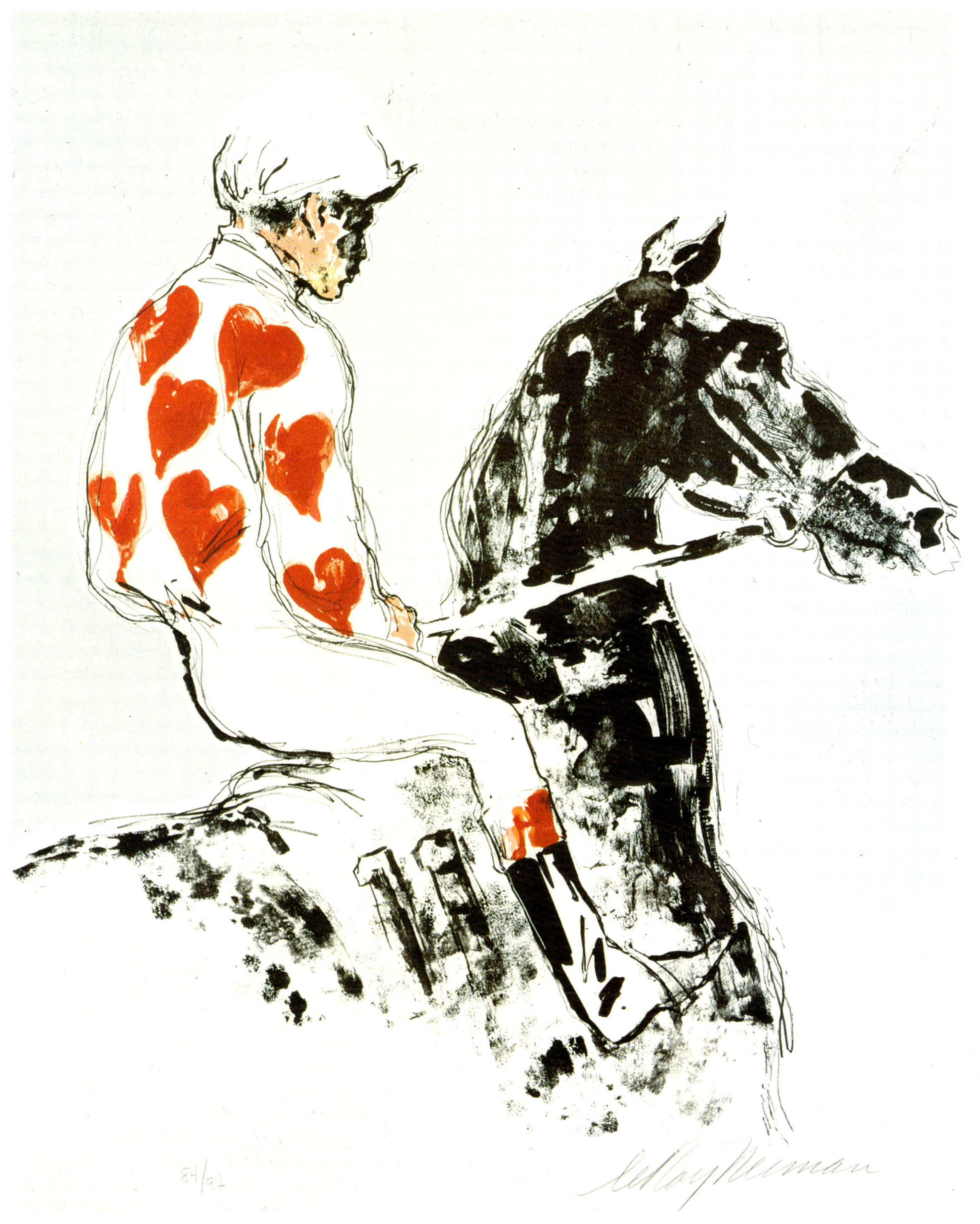

190 Hearts
1972
Lithograph
(29¾ x 22) (75.57 x 55.88 cm)
A limited edition of 97, signed
and numbered by the artist.

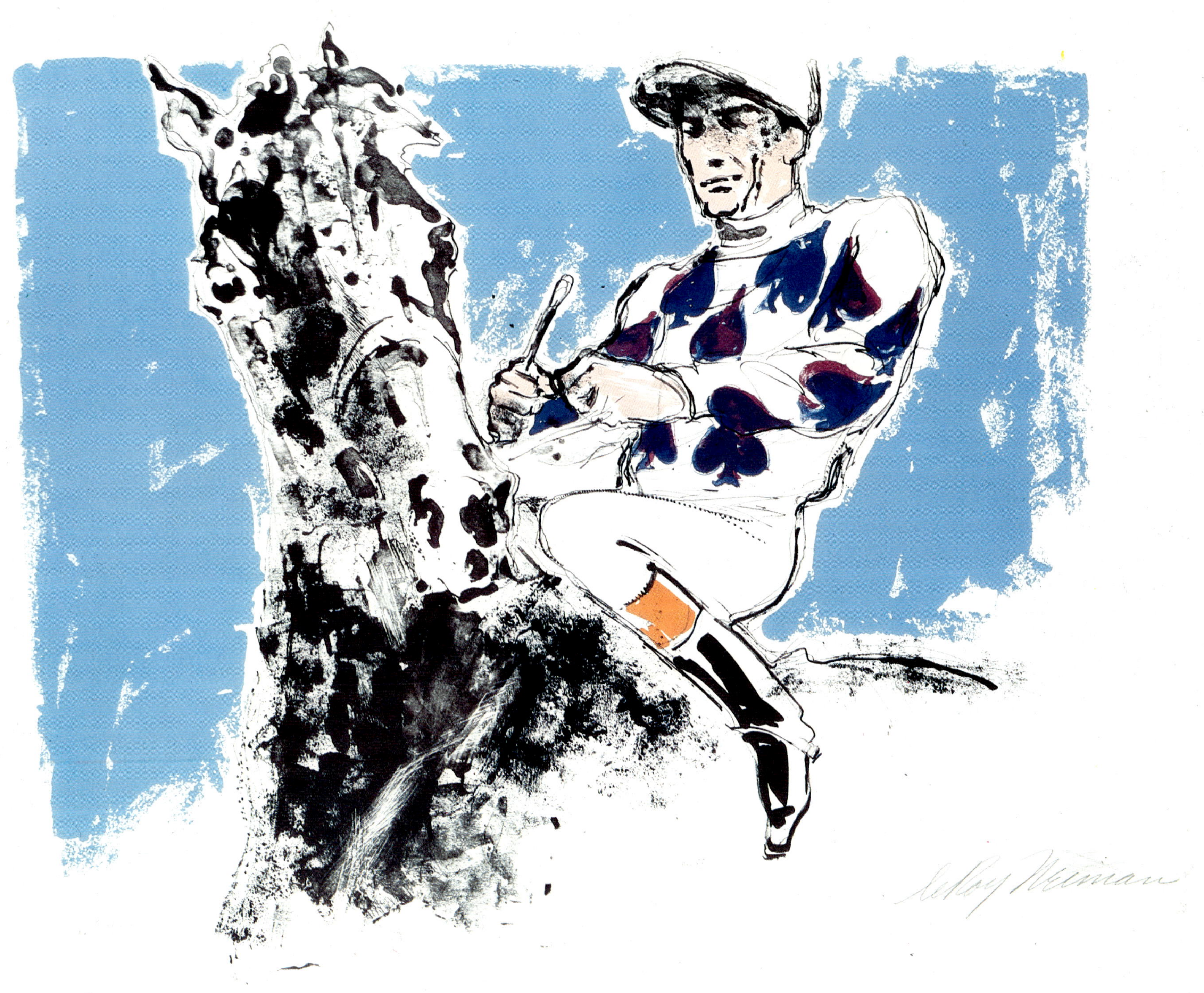

191 Spades
1972
Lithograph
22 x 29¾ (55.88 x 75.57 cm)
A limited edition of 97, signed
and numbered by the Artist.

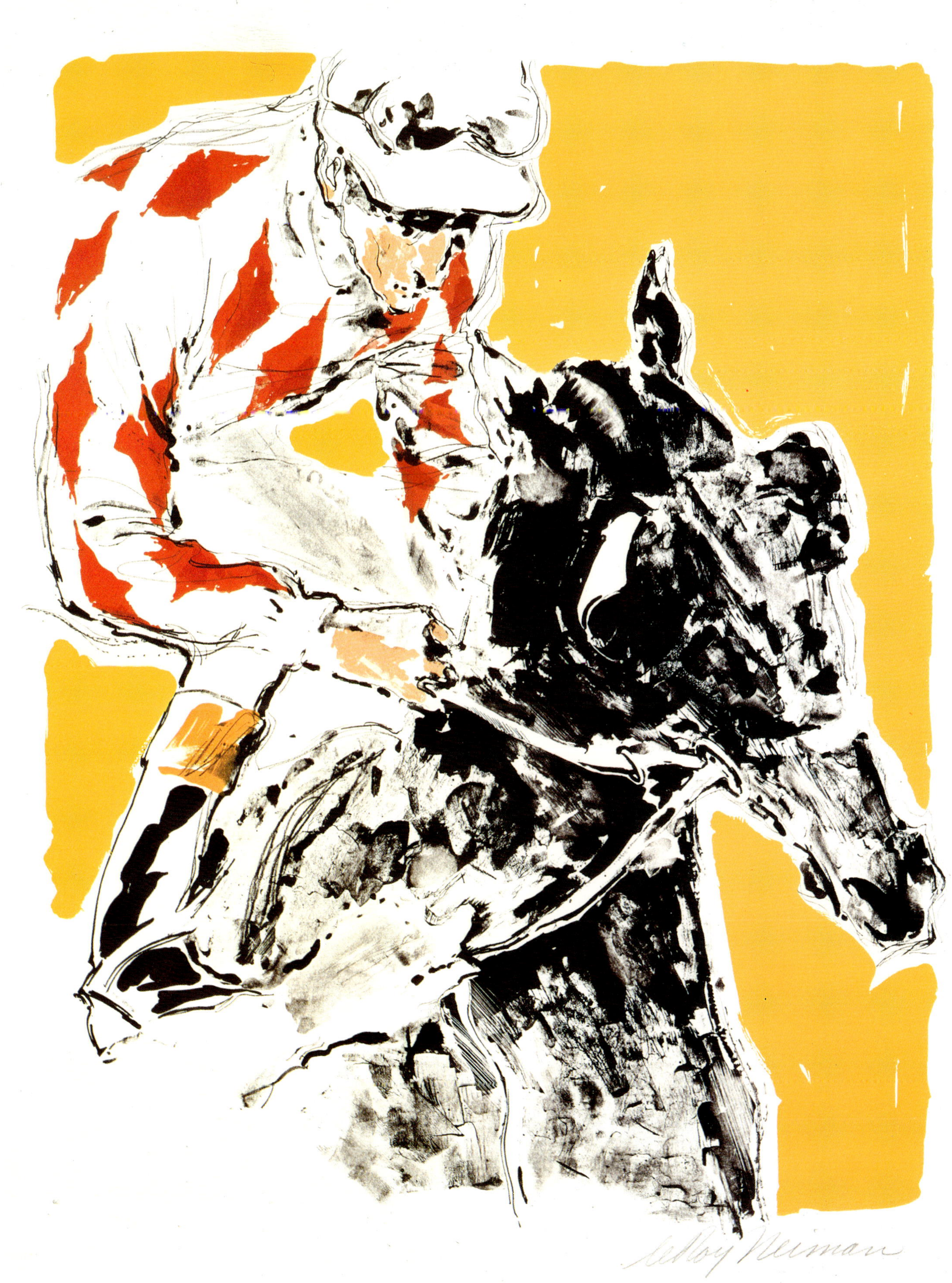

192   Diamonds
1972
Lithograph
29¾ x 22 (75.57 x 55.88 cm)
A limited edition of 97, signed
and numbered by the Artist.

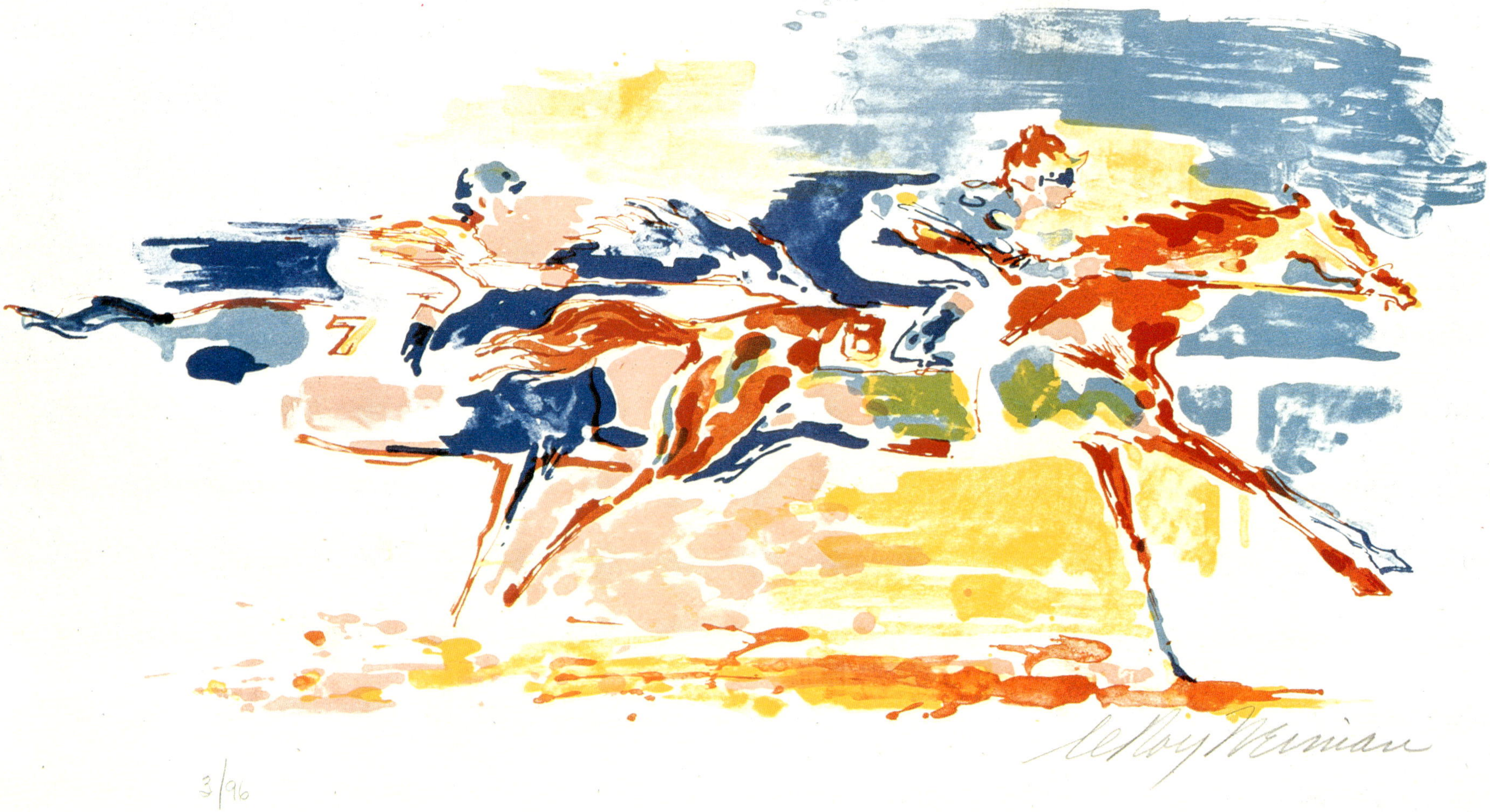

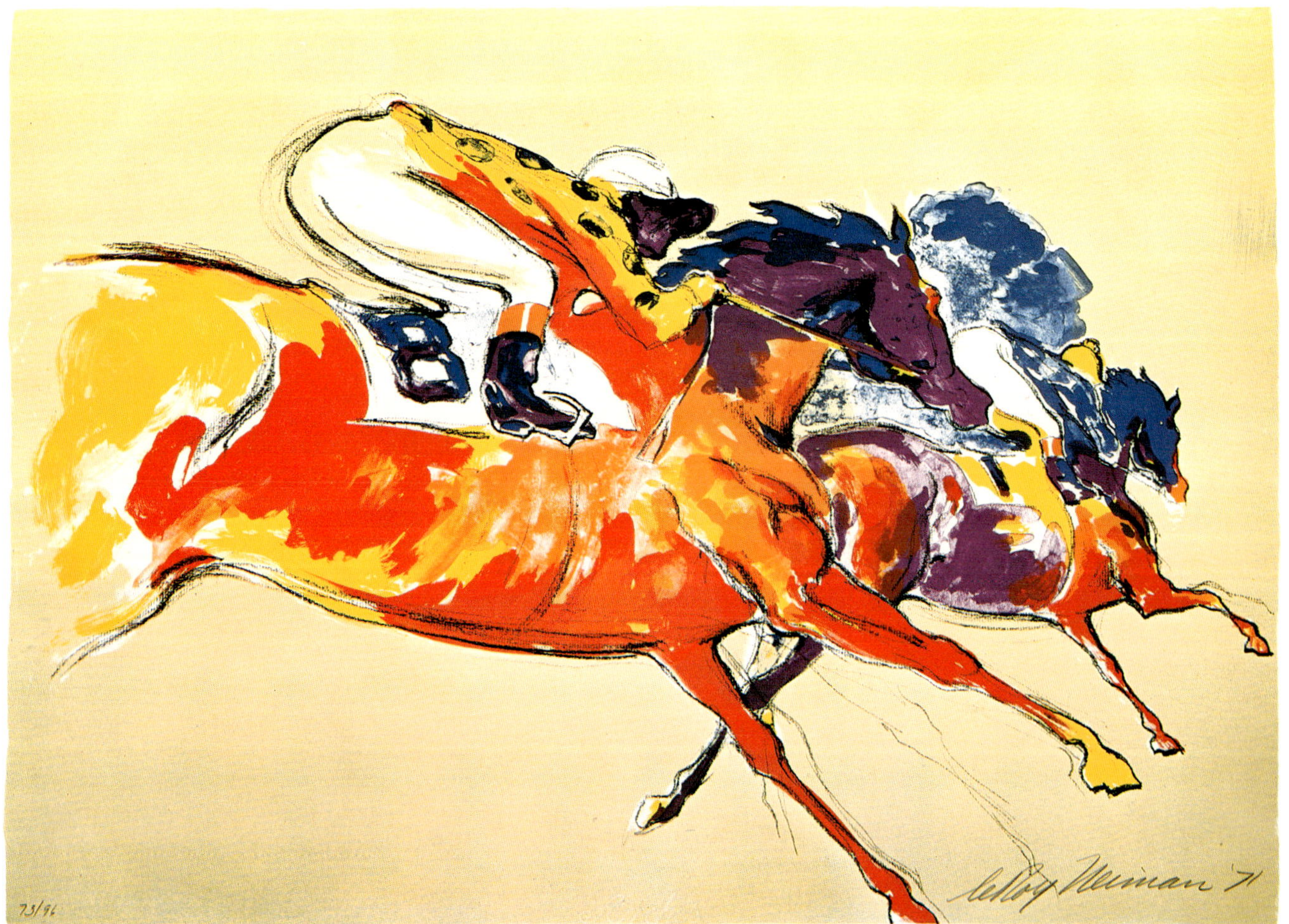

193   Swiss Race
1972
Lithograph
22¾ x 18 (57.79 x 45.72 cm)
A limited edition of 96, signed
and numbered by the artist.

194   Into the Turn
1972
Lithograph
21 x 28⅞ (53.34 x 73.34 cm)
A limited edition of 96, signed
and numbered by the artist.

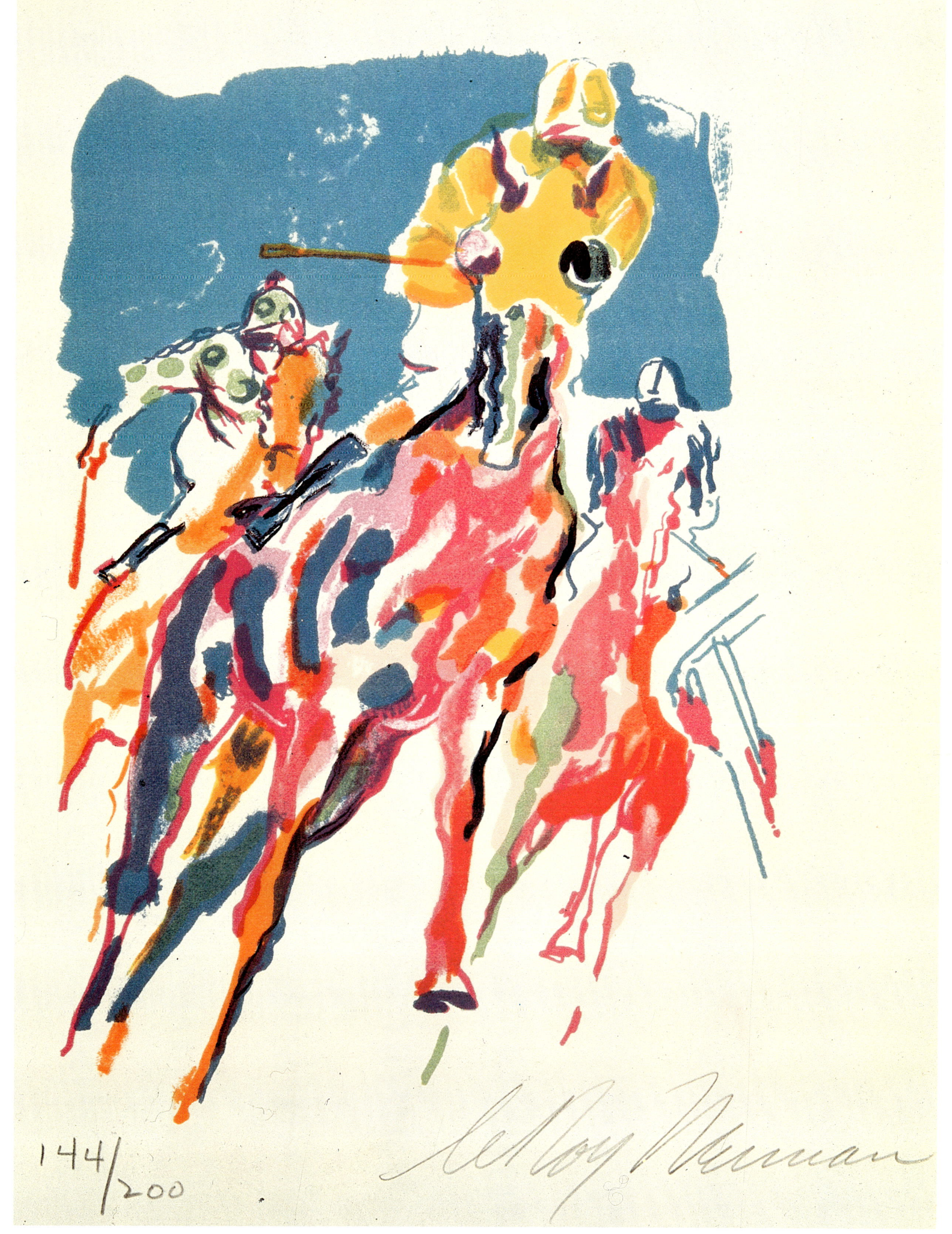

195   Home Stretch
1973
Lithograph
13½ x 11¾
(34.29 x 29.85 cm)
A limited edition of 200,
signed and numbered
by the artist.

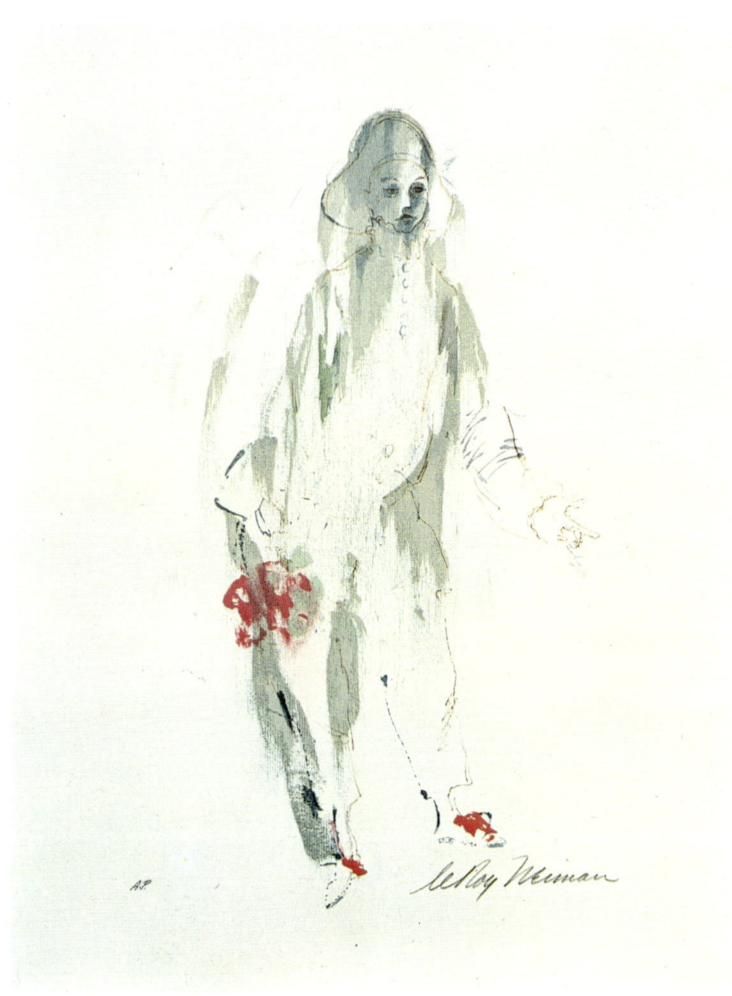

196 Pierrot

1972
Lithograph
21 x 11¼ (53.34 x 28.75 cm)
A limited edition of 200, signed and numbered
by the artist.

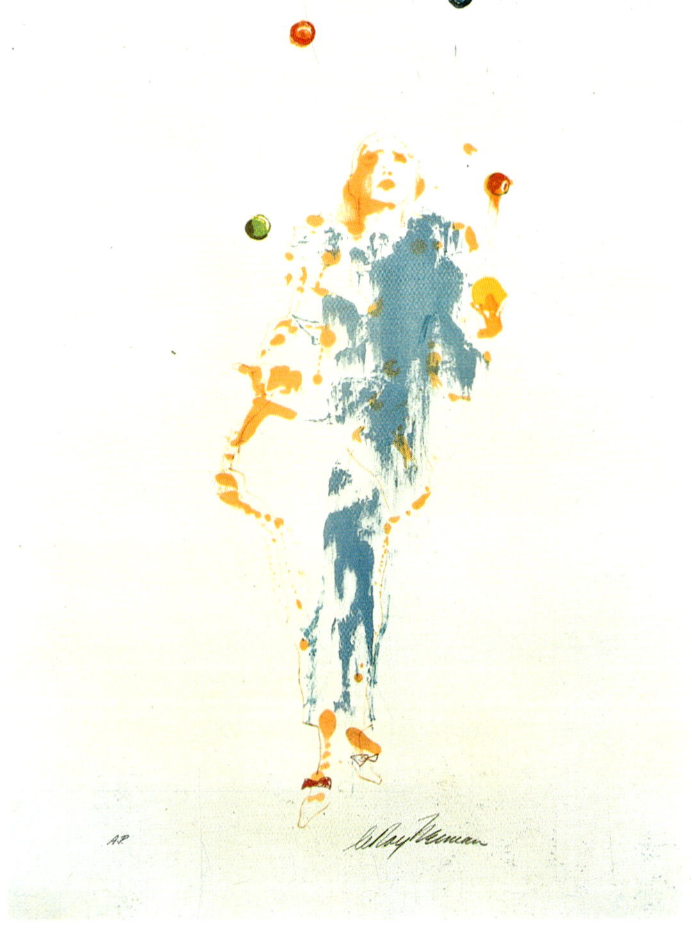

197 Pierrot the Juggler

1972
Lithograph
9 x 25½ (22.86 x 64.77 cm)
A limited edition of 200, signed and numbered
by the artist.

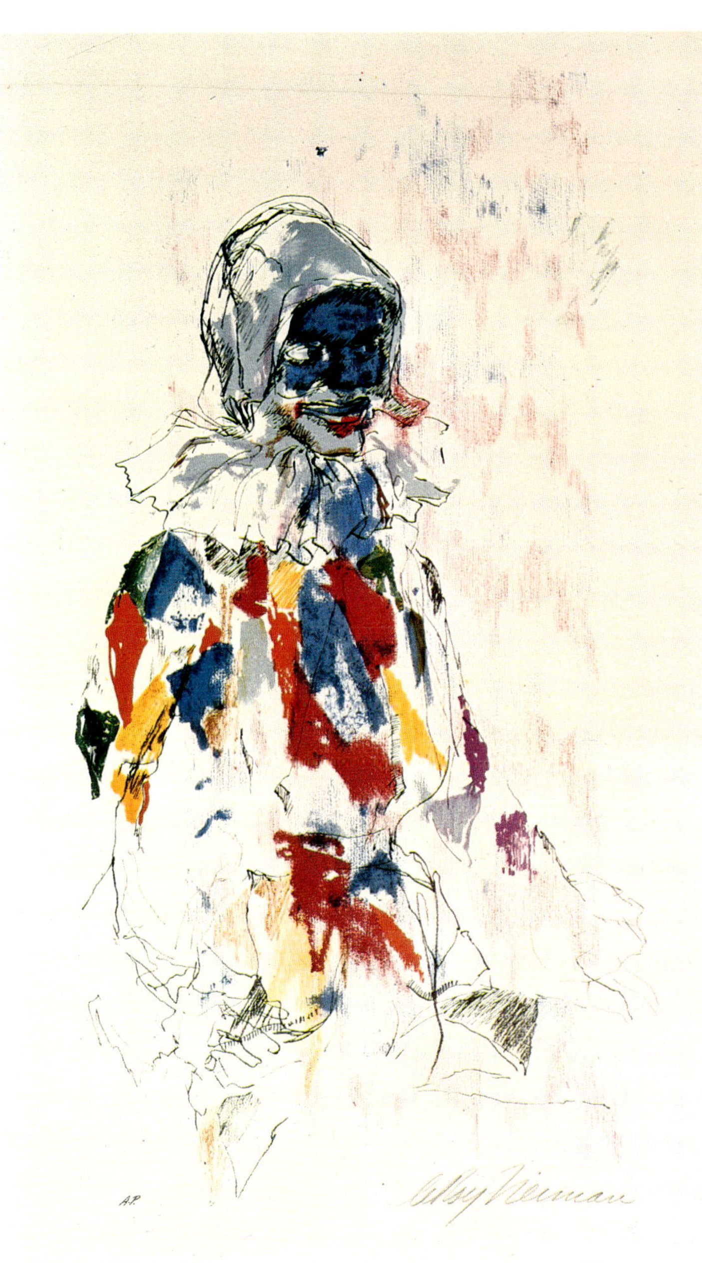

198   Harlequin

1972
Lithograph
24½ x 13½ (62.25 x 34.29 cm)
A limited edition 200, signed and numbered
by the artist.

199   Harlequin with Text

1972
Lithograph
27 x 23¼ (68.58 x 59.05 cm)
A limited edition of 200, signed and numbered
by the artist.

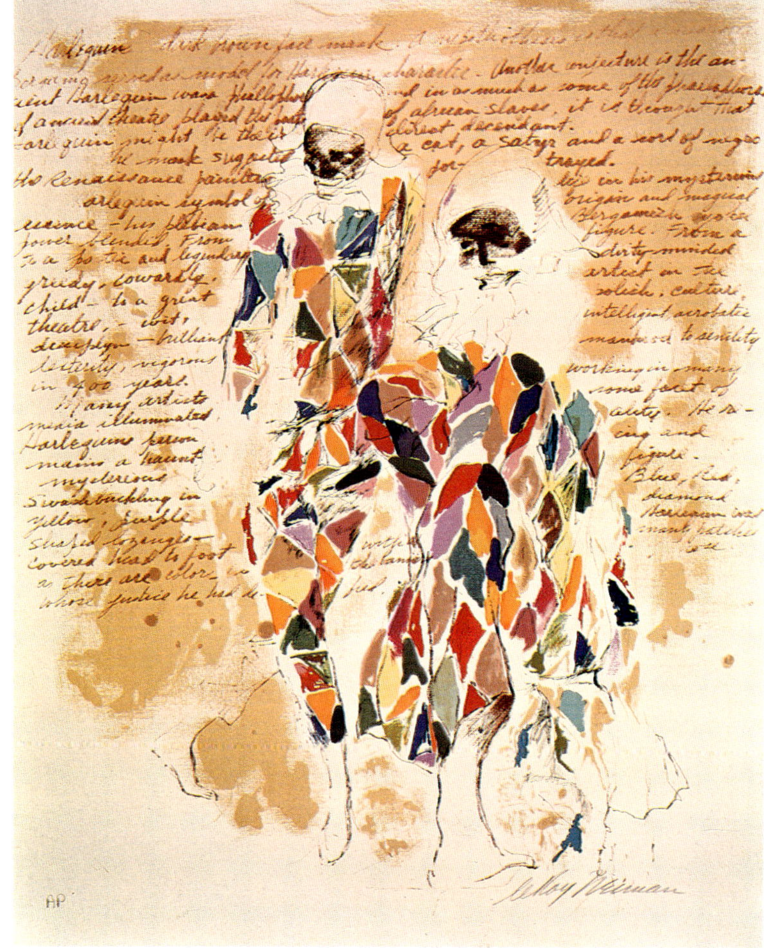

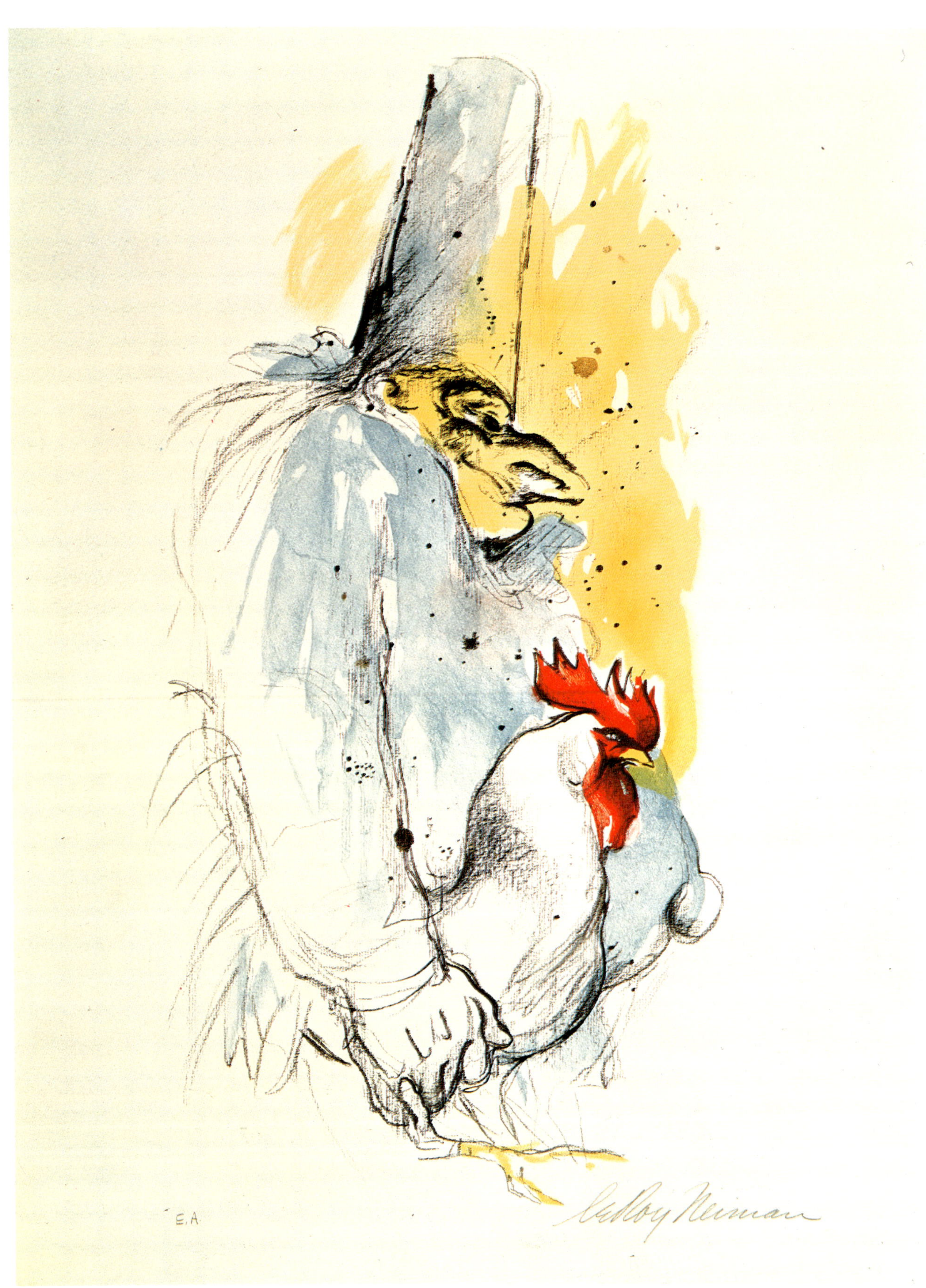

200   Punchinello

1972
Lithograph
26 x 13¼ (66.04 x 33.65 cm)

A limited edition of 200, signed and numbered
by the artist.

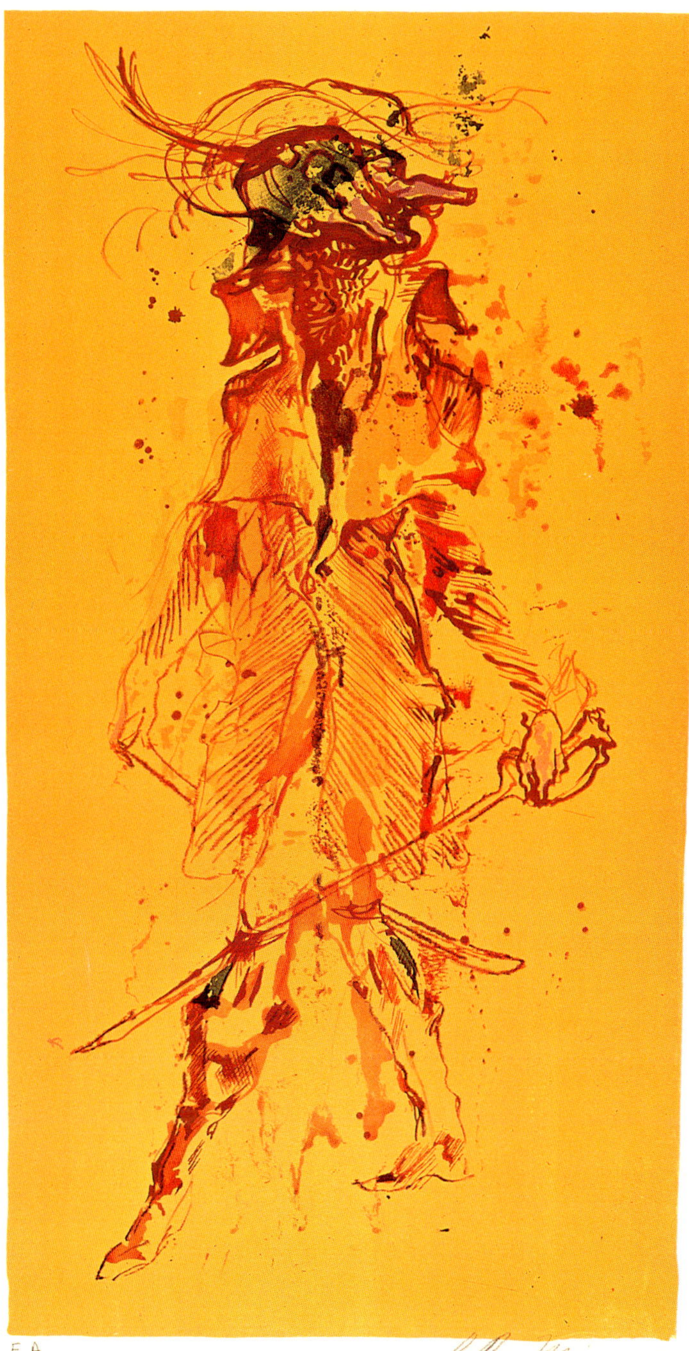

201   The Captain

1972
Lithograph
26⅛ x 13¼ (66.36 x 33.65 cm)

A limited edition of 200, signed and numbered
by the artist.

202   Punchinello with Text

1972
Lithograph
29 x 23½ (73.66 x 59.69 cm)

A limited edition of 200, signed and numbered
by the artist.

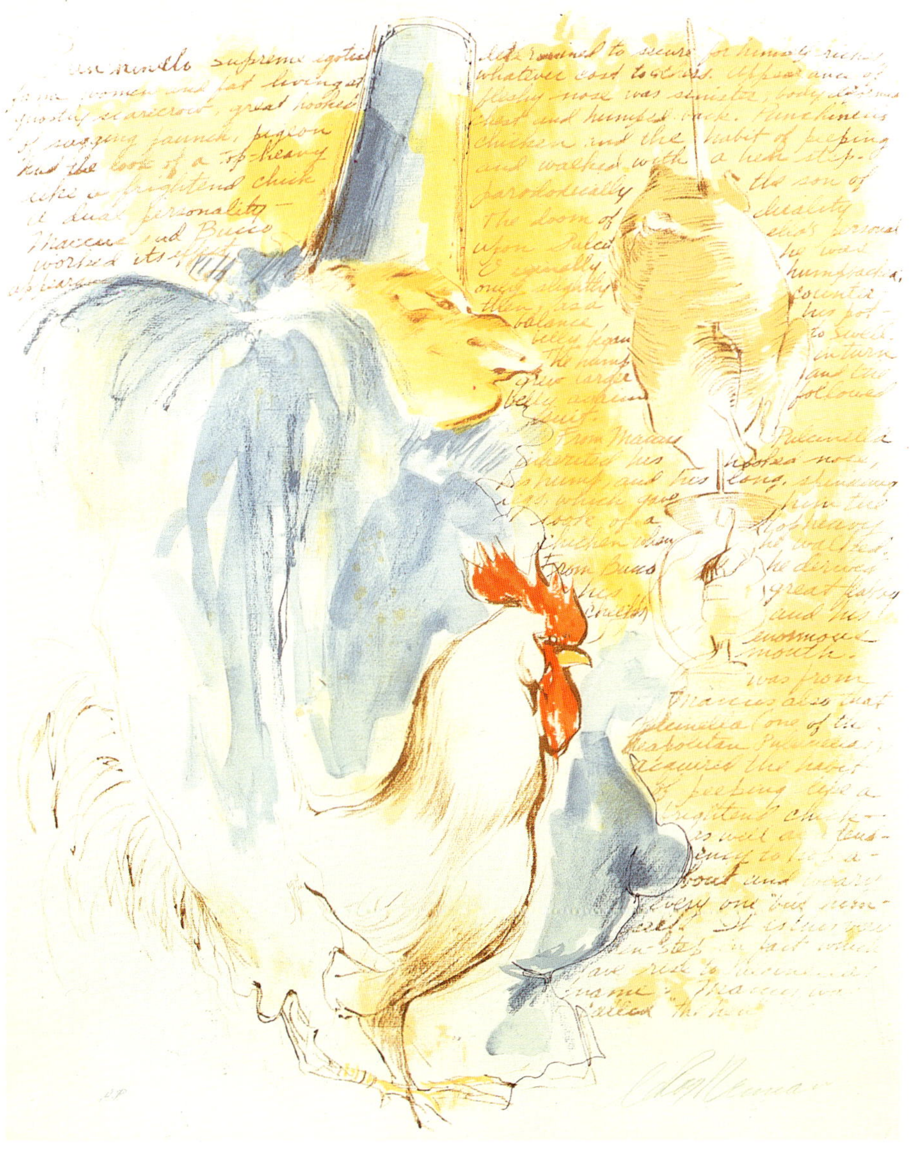

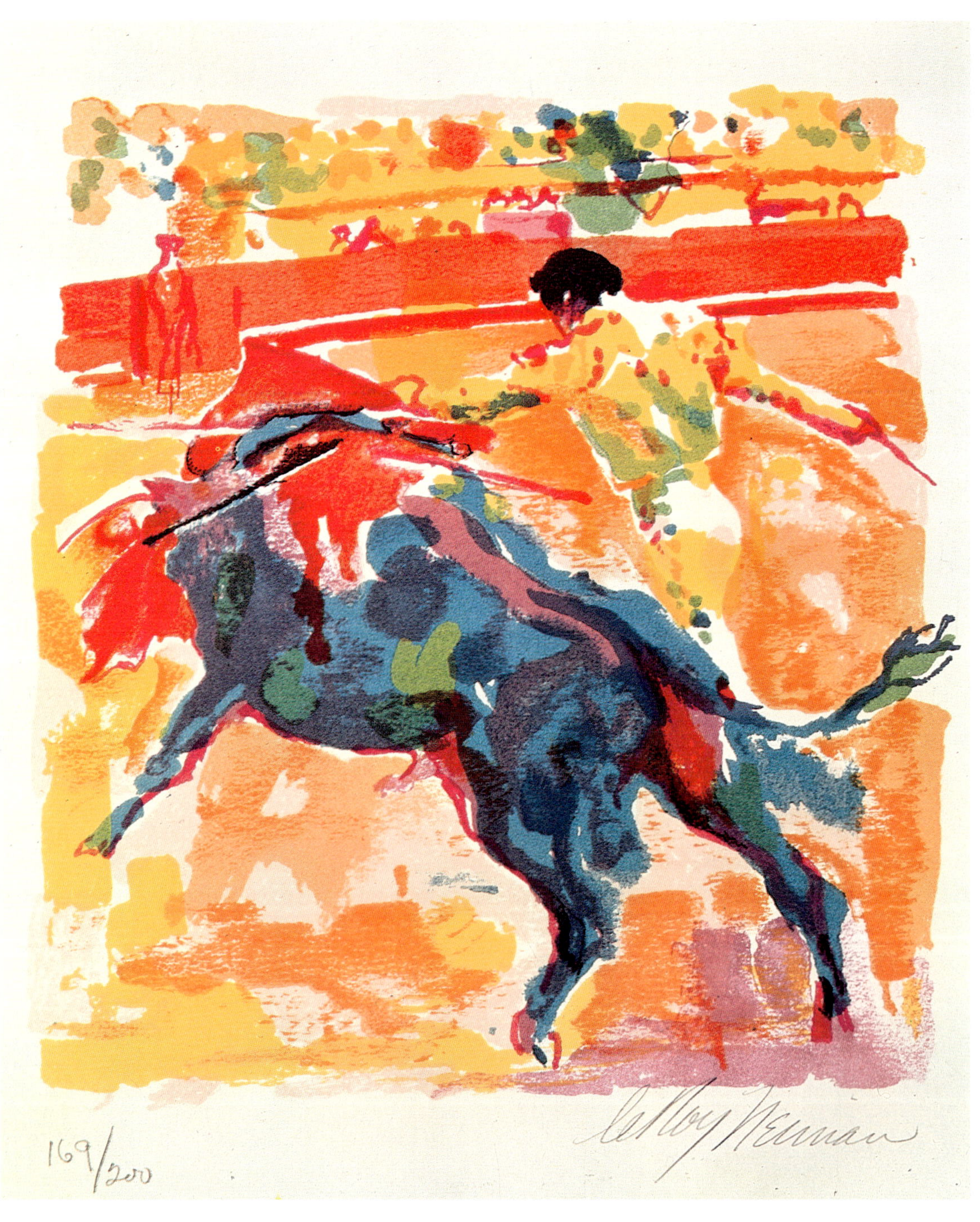# 203 Bullfight

1973
Lithograph
13½ x 11⅞ (34.29 x 30.16 cm)
A limited edition of 200, signed and numbered
by the artist.

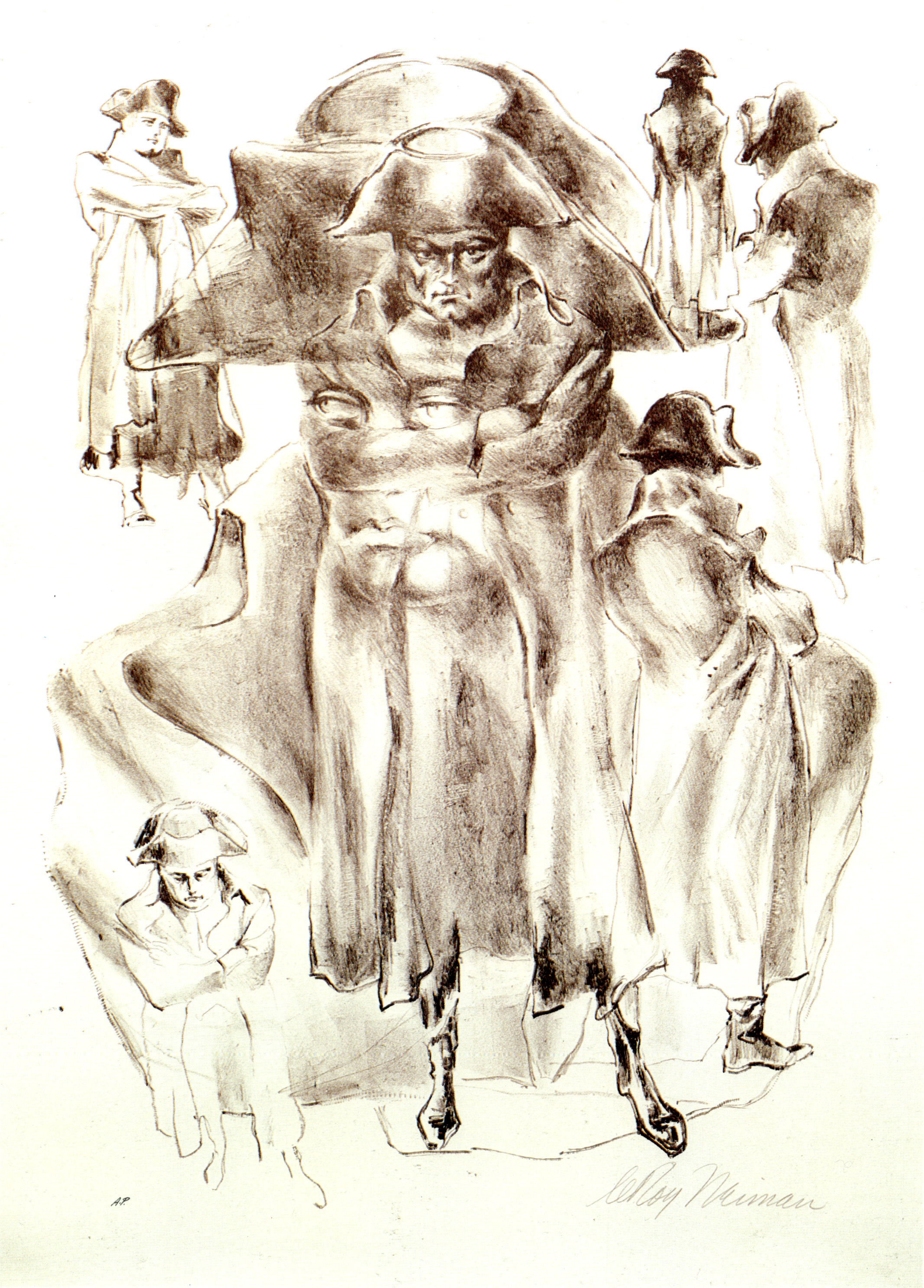

204 Napoleon

1973
Lithograph
35½ x 25 (90.17 x 63.5 cm)
A limited edition of 150, signed and
numbered by the artist.

205 Grooming

1976
Lithograph
First state, Artist's Proof
29⅜ x 41¼ (74.61 x 104.78 cm)
no edition

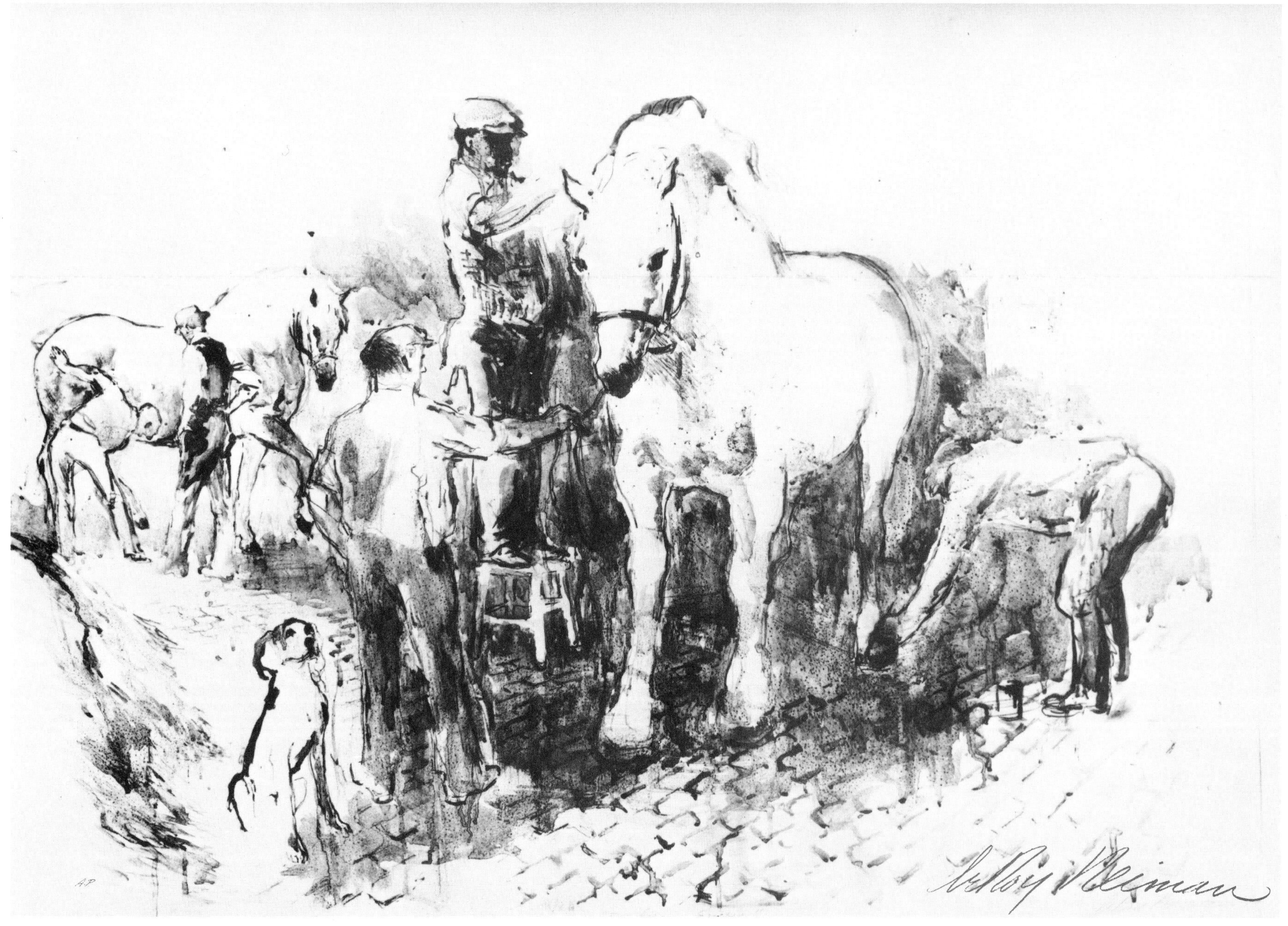

206   Grooming

1976
Handcolored Lithograph
Second state, Artist's Proof
29⅜ x 41¼ (74.61 x 104.78 cm)
no edition

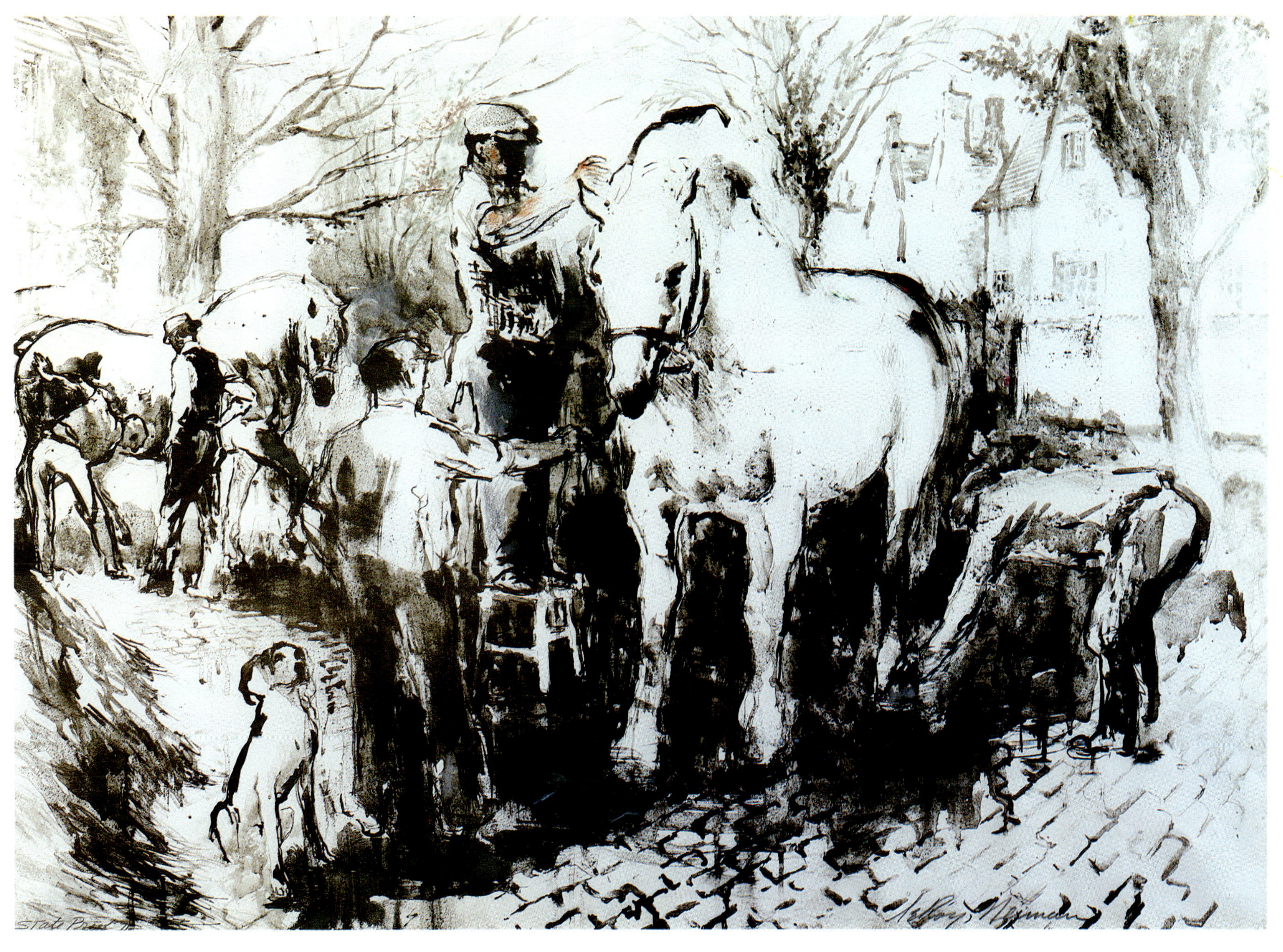

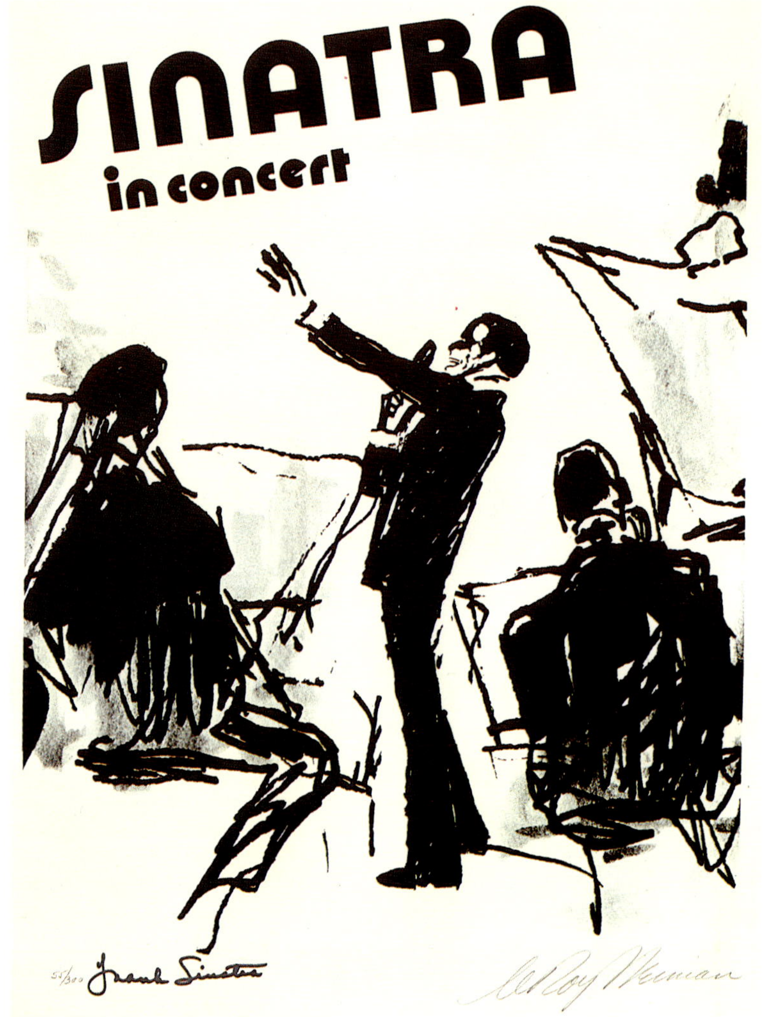

207 Sinatra in Concert

1974
Lithograph
34 x 22½ (86.36 x 57.15 cm)
A limited edition of 300, signed and
numbered by the artist.

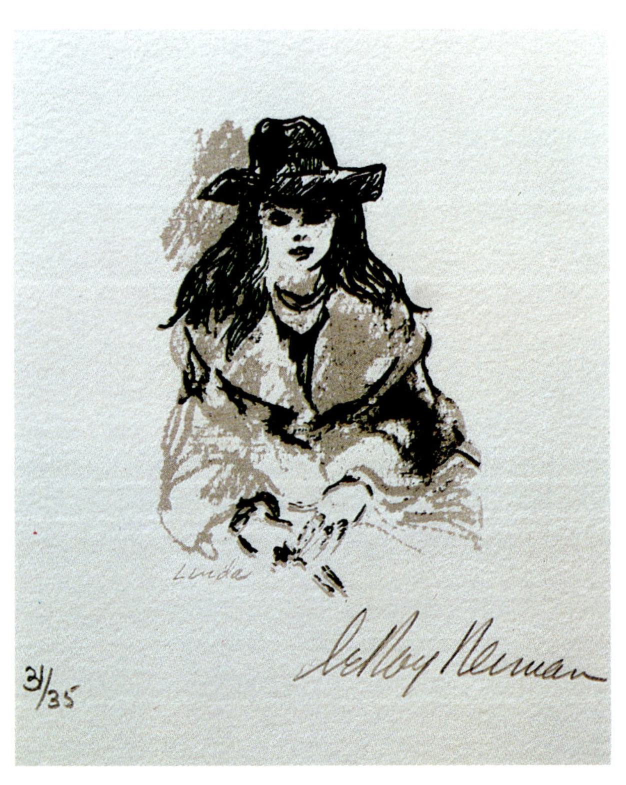

208 Eva

1978
Lithograph
10½ x 11½ (26.67 x 29.21 cm)
A limited edition of 35, signed and numbered
by the artist.

209 Vince Lombardi

to be released
Seven-colored Lithograph
14 x 17 (35.56 x 43.18 cm)
A limited edition of 300, signed and numbered
by the artist.

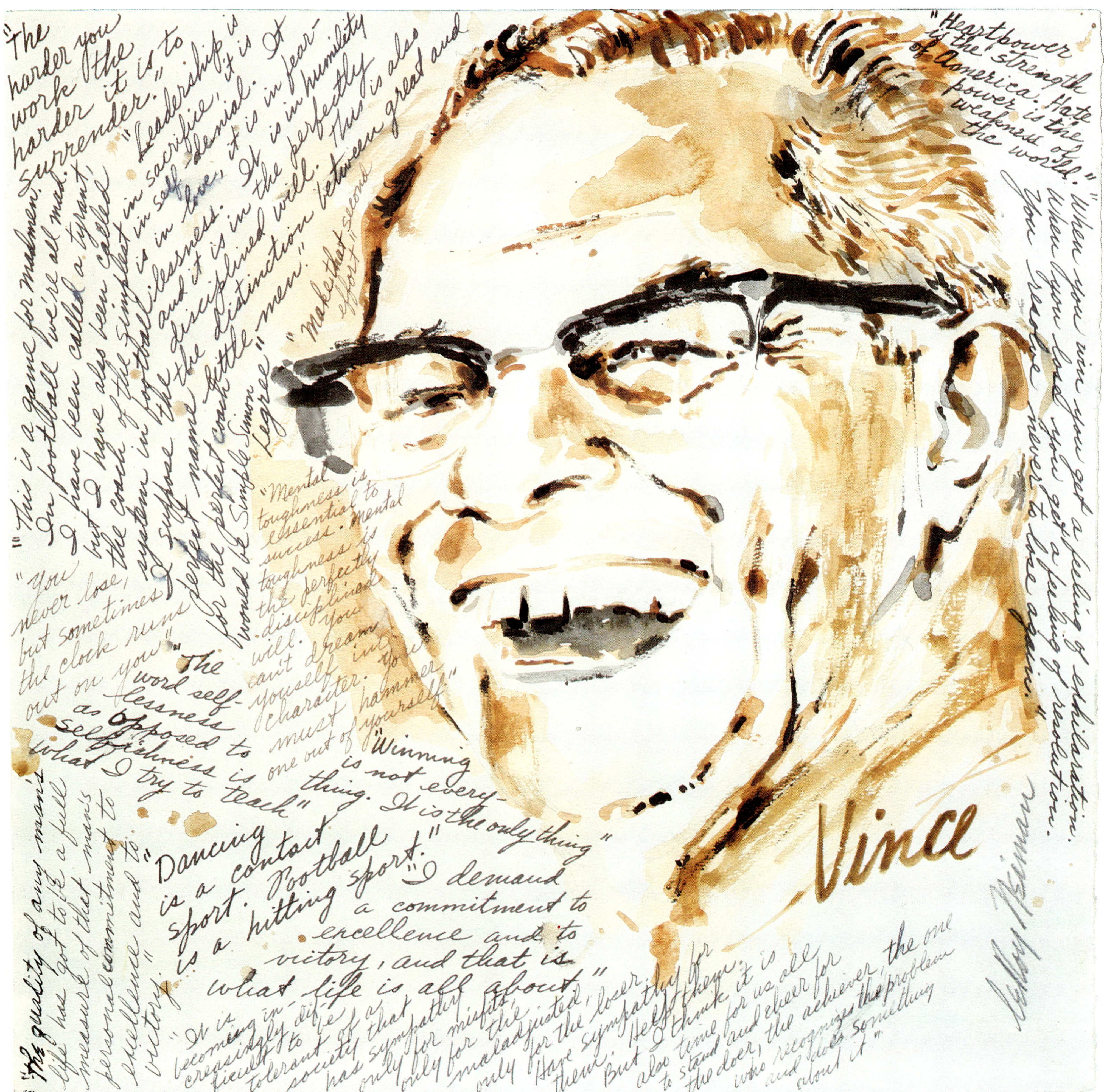

"The harder you work the harder it is to surrender."
"This is a game for madmen. In football we're all mad. I have been called a tyrant, but I have also been called the coach of the simplest system in football."
"Leadership is in sacrifice, it is self-denial. It is in fear, it is in humility, and it is in the perfectly disciplined will. This is also the distinction between great and little men."
"You never lose, but sometimes the clock runs out on you."
"The word self-lessness as opposed to selfishness is one of the perfect examples of what I try to teach."
"Winning is not every-thing. It is the only thing."
"Mental toughness is essential to success. Mental toughness is the perfectly disciplined will. You can't dream yourself into character. You must hammer and forge one out of yourself."
"Dancing is a contact sport. Football is a hitting sport."
"I demand a commitment to excellence and to victory, and that is what life is all about."
"The quality of any man's life is a full measure of that man's personal commitment to excellence and to victory."
"Heartpower is the strength of America. Hate power is the weakness of the world."
"When you win you get a feeling of exhilaration. When you lose you get a feeling of resolution. You resolve never to lose again."
"It is becoming increasingly difficult to be a tolerant society that has sympathy only for misfits, only for the maladjusted, only for the loser. Have sympathy for them. But I think it is also time for us all to stand and cheer for the doer, the achiever, the one who recognizes the problem and does something about it."
Vince

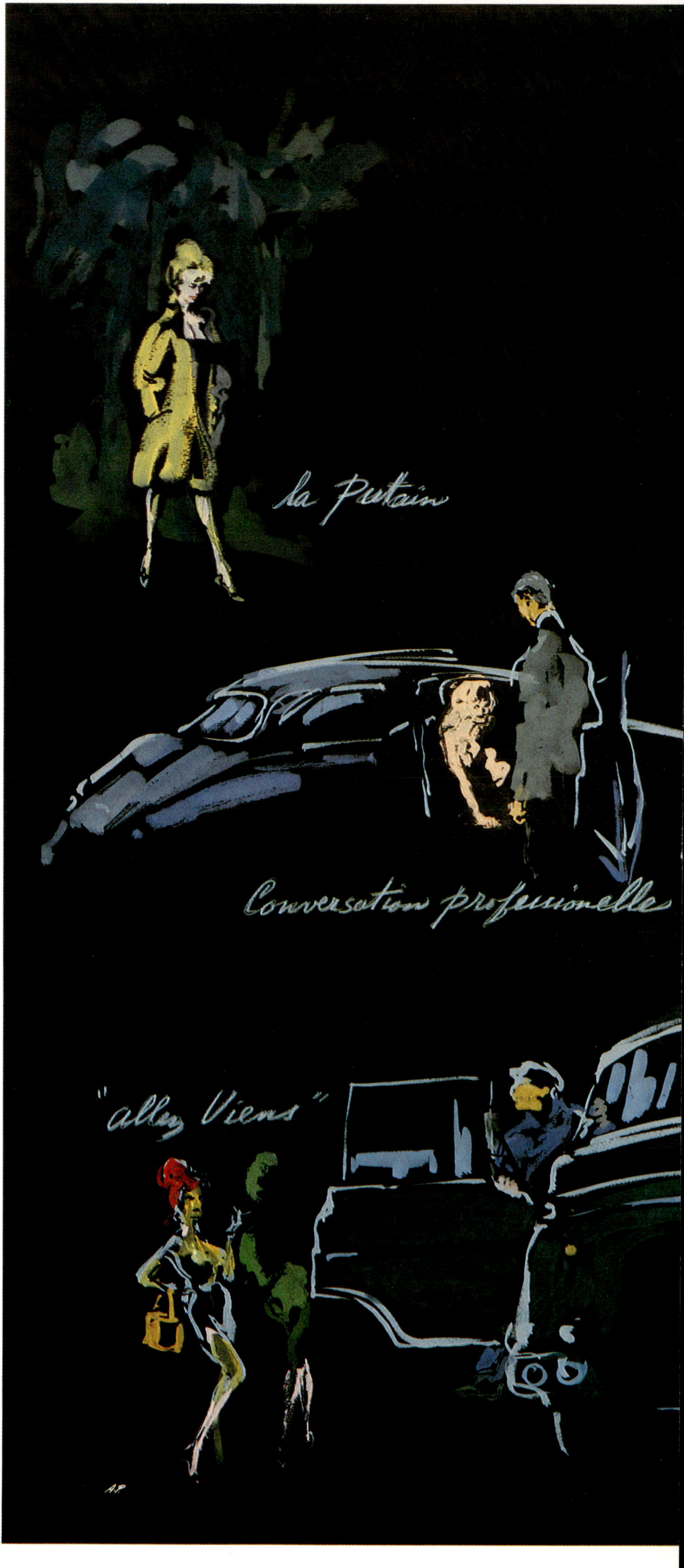

210 Prostituée Française

1980
Lithograph
24 x 36 (60.96 x 91.44 cm)

A limited edition of 300, signed and numbered
by the artist.

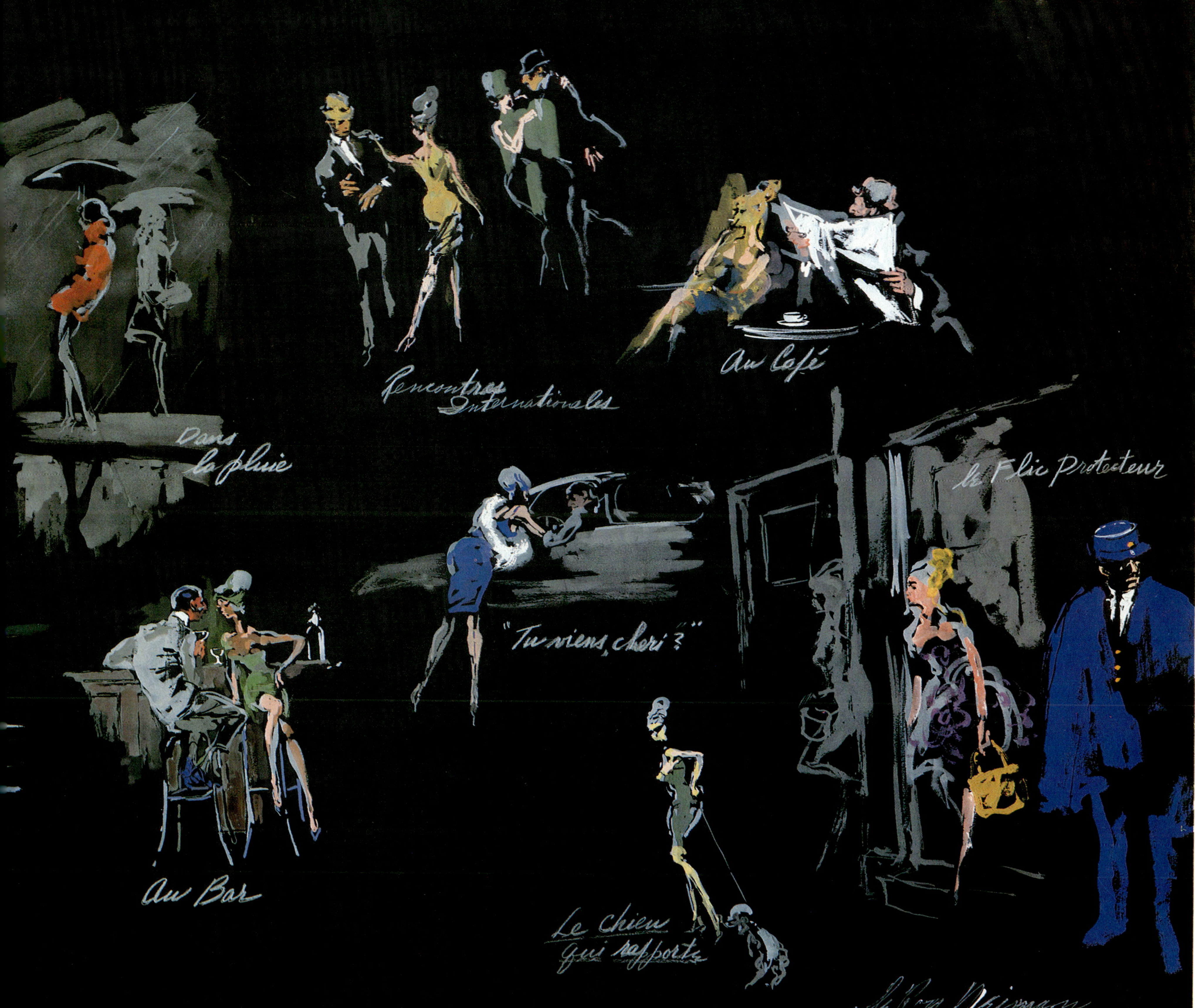

Prostituée Française
Dans la pluie
Rencontres Internationales
Au Café
la Flic Protecteur
"Tu viens, chéri?"
Au Bar
Le Chien qui rapporte
LeRoy Neiman
Paris

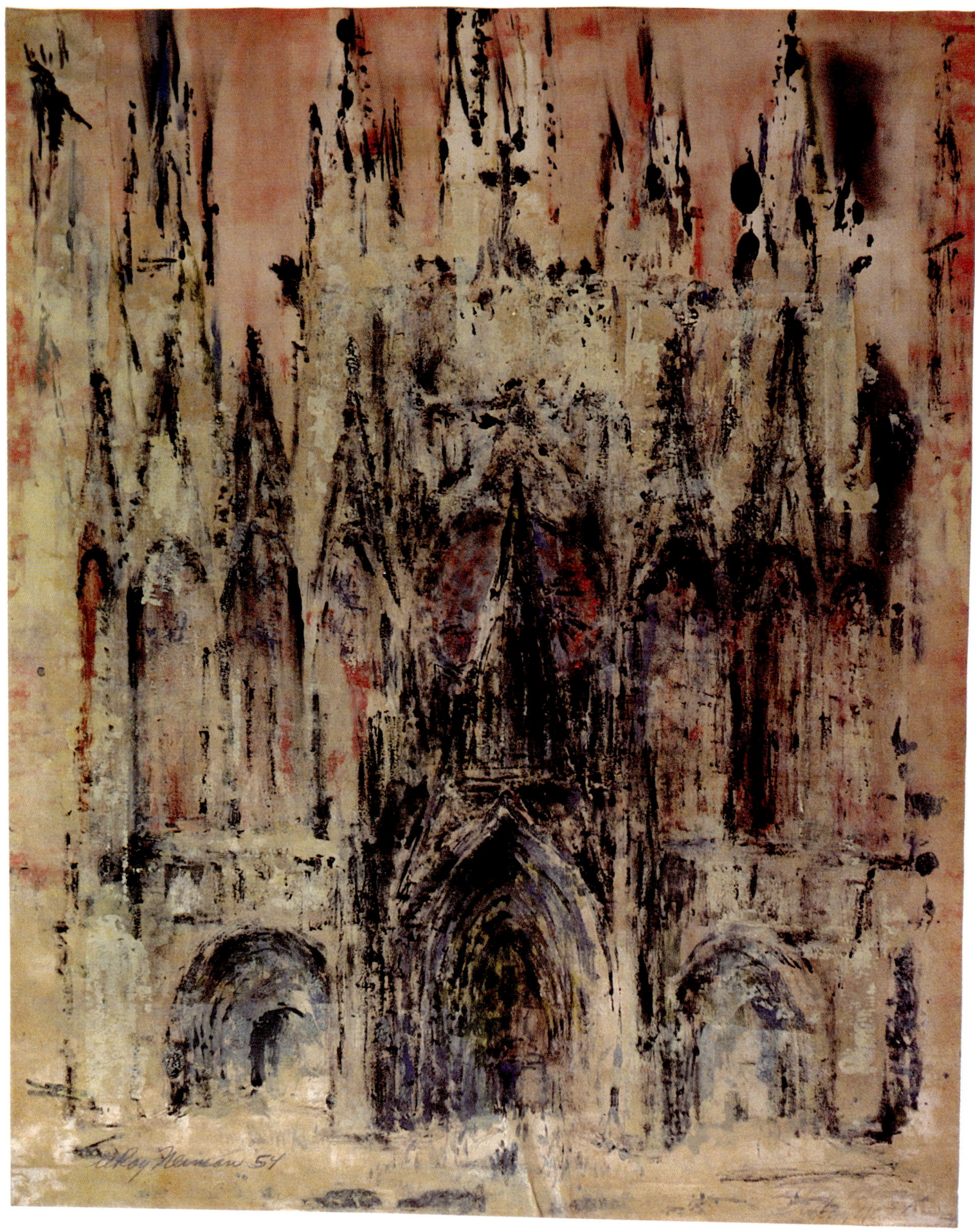

211 Cathedral
1953
Monoprint
24 x 12 (60.96 x 30.48 cm)

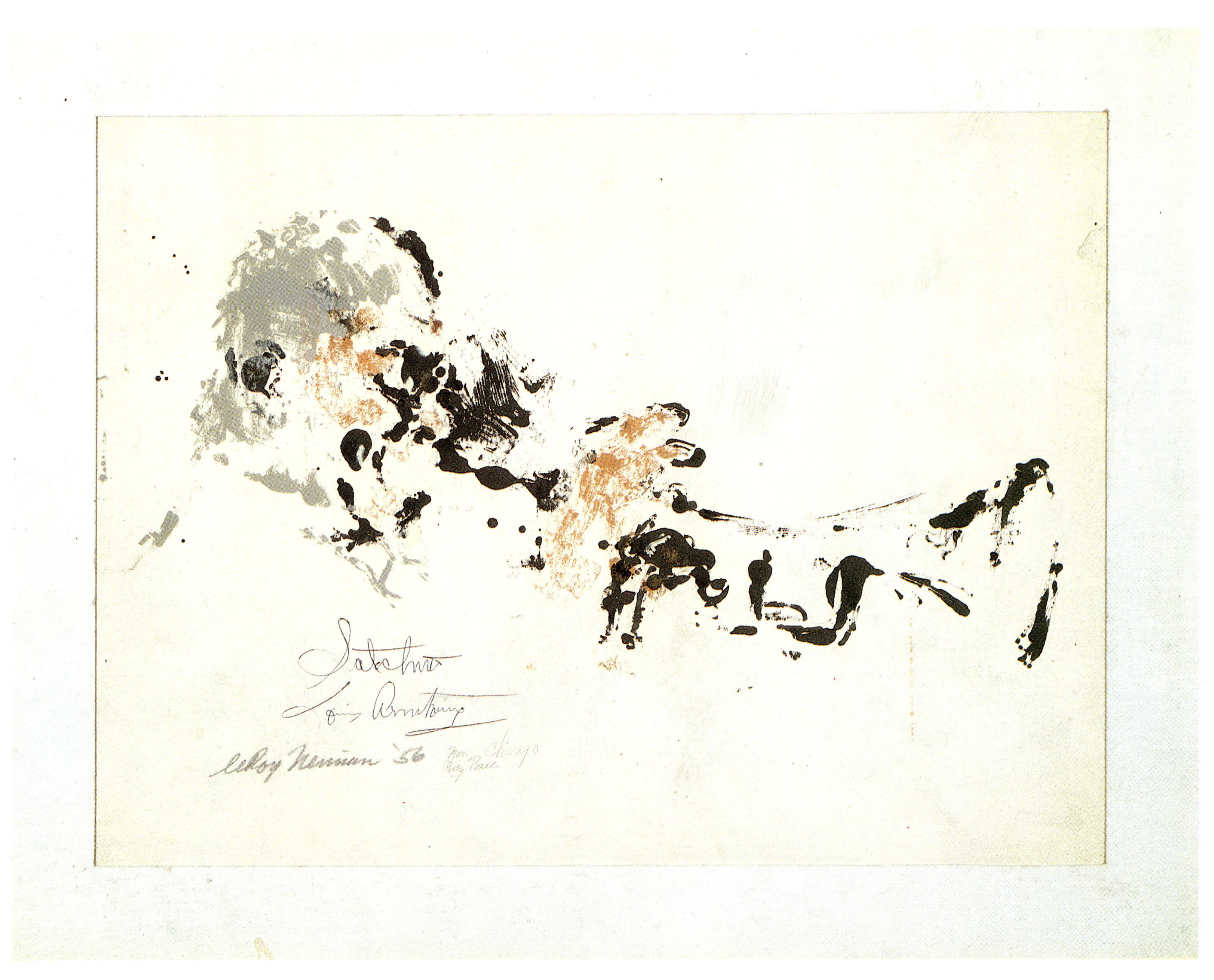

212 Satchmo at Chez Paris
1956
Monoprint
19 x 24 (48.26 x 60.96 cm)

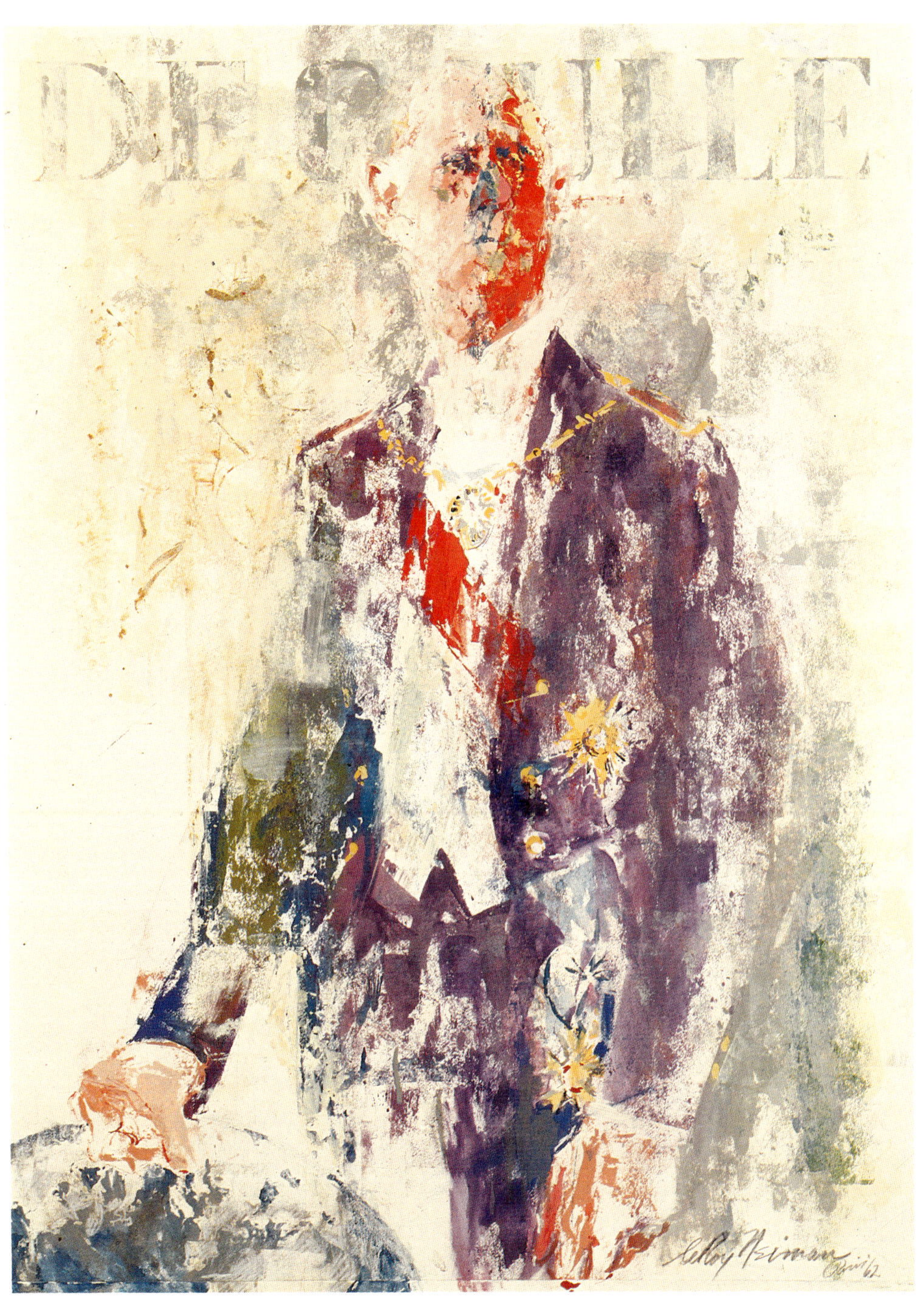

213   DeGaulle
1962
Monoprint
40 x 29¾ (101.6 x 75.56 cm)

214   Al Capone
1965
Monoprint
40 x 29¾ (101.6 x 75.56 cm)

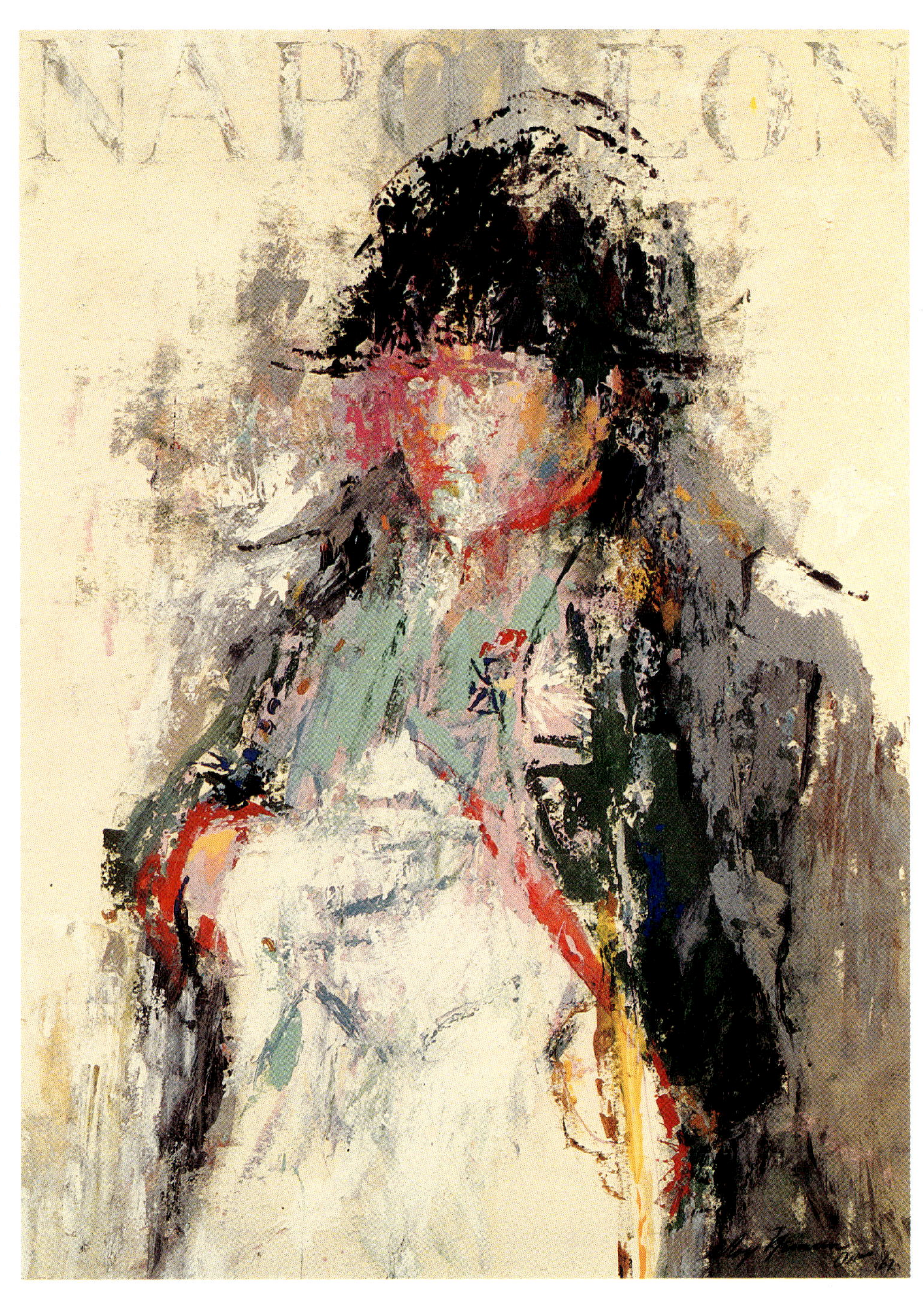

215   Napoleon
1962
Monoprint
40 x 29¾ (101.6 x 75.56 cm).

Etchings

The Etchings of LeRoy Neiman

LeRoy Neiman is at ease with many media. Most of his early years were spent painting and drawing. He explored a number of art-in-multiples techniques, but was not entirely satisfied with the first results.

His tentative experiments with monotypes and lithographs in the 1950s and 60s were followed by his passionate love affair with serigraphs in the 1970s. The technique of serigraphy made his sensuously controlled explosions of color available to a very wide audience. It was not until he had published over a hundred limited editions of serigraphs in an orgy of painterly creativity that he began to feel an attraction for the firm discipline of the etcher's art.

His first etchings were done as learning experiments in Switzerland during 1971. The methodology intrigued him. In 1972, he produced several suites of sports subjects—baseball, skiing, hockey, basketball and boxing. During those early years he worked with various techniques that ranged from aquatint to hand pulled photo-etching. Then he set the etching process aside for a few years.

Late in 1975 he felt the itch to etch again. He bought his own press, and set it up in his New York studio. From that point on, Neiman's etchings started to become deeply personal expressions.

The first suite off the press was a series of nudes, followed by moving studies of people and animals working together in a special kind of natural harmony. The period between 1977 and 1978 marks the mature development of Neiman's work as an etcher.

Since that time all of his etchings have been worked on the various metals in his etching studio. Each image originated as a direct line drawing through a hard ground which was then etched. After the First State proof is pulled, Neiman usually reworks the plate using such techniques as acquatint, dry point, and scraping. Each time the plate is reworked, a state proof is pulled until the artist is satisfied with the image. All of the impressions for each edition are then inked and hand pulled by his printer under Neiman's direction in the etching studio.

Neiman's work as a mature etcher was announced dramatically by his remarkable horse-and-rider series called "Twilight Rider in the Stretch," or simply, "The Stretch." (Catalog no. 282-283).

In these images, the stretch of the horse race expands elastically into that mysterious stretch of space and time.

In the First State, Degas bubbles up through the mud, and the ghost of Ryder hovers in the shadows, as this dark image (half-human and half-animal) races into the night as if he were galloping into the arms of Death.

In the Second State, the entire image has been almost totally transformed. It is as if the plate has been hit by a lightning bolt—as if "The Twilight Rider" has suddenly been *reborn*, at the extreme edge of his journey into Darkness, and is galloping into the Light, energized by an electrifying infusion of raw energy.

Early in 1980, Neiman decided to devote a great deal of time to etching. The results have been quite impressive. His animal studies are joyous celebrations.

"The Game of Life" (Catalog no. 294) is a provocative allegory, and a masterpiece of etching, where representatives from every corner of Planet Earth gather together around the spinning of the roulette wheel.

F.L.G.

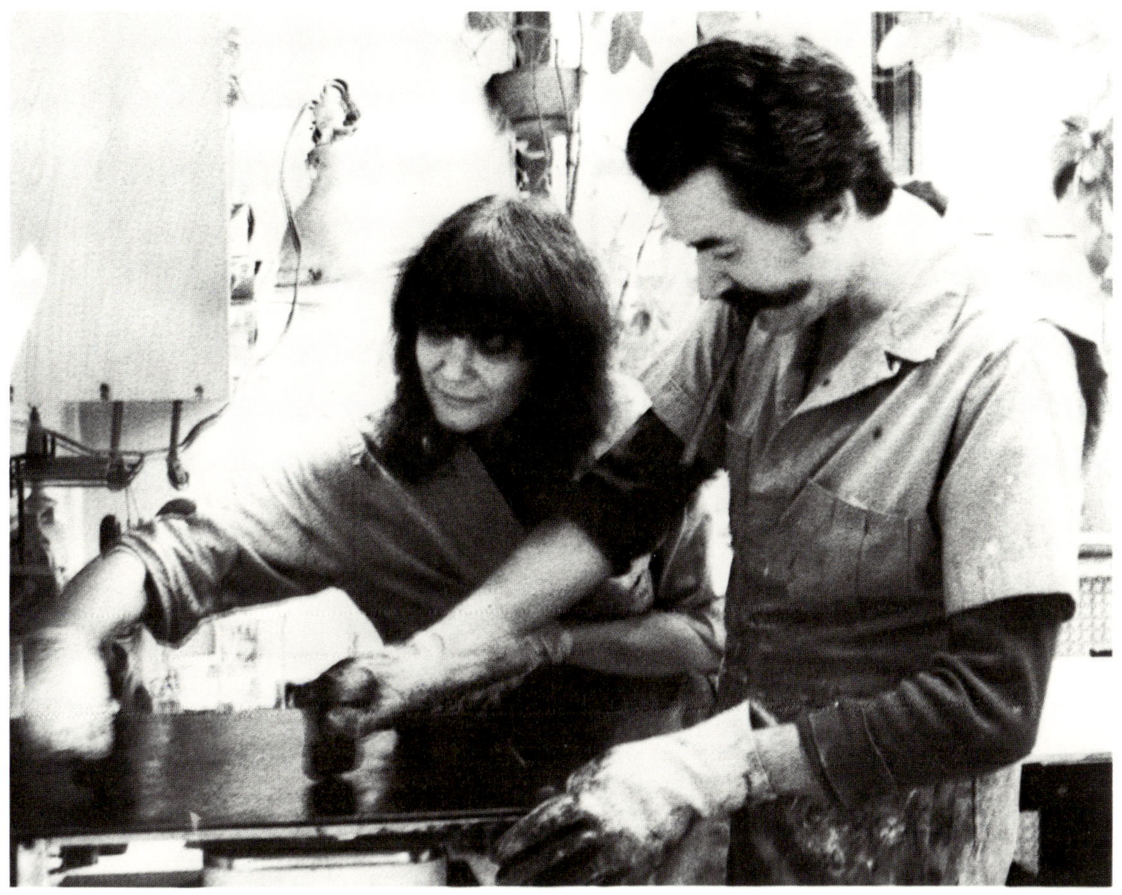

LeRoy Neiman in his private New York Etching Studio, working with his assistant, Madeleine Claude-Jobrack, on his Intaglio Etching Press, a Charles Brand, 32″ x 52″, flat-bed, hand-operated press.

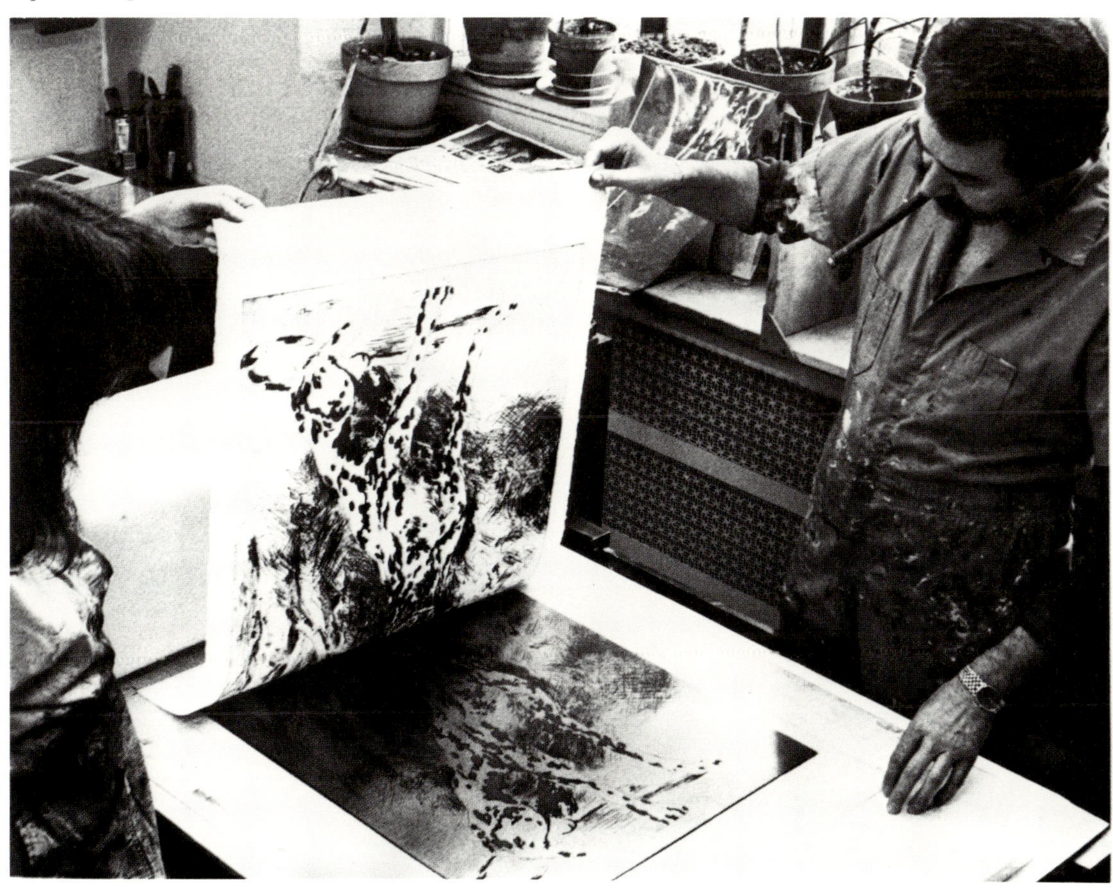

photography by Lisa Jayne Young

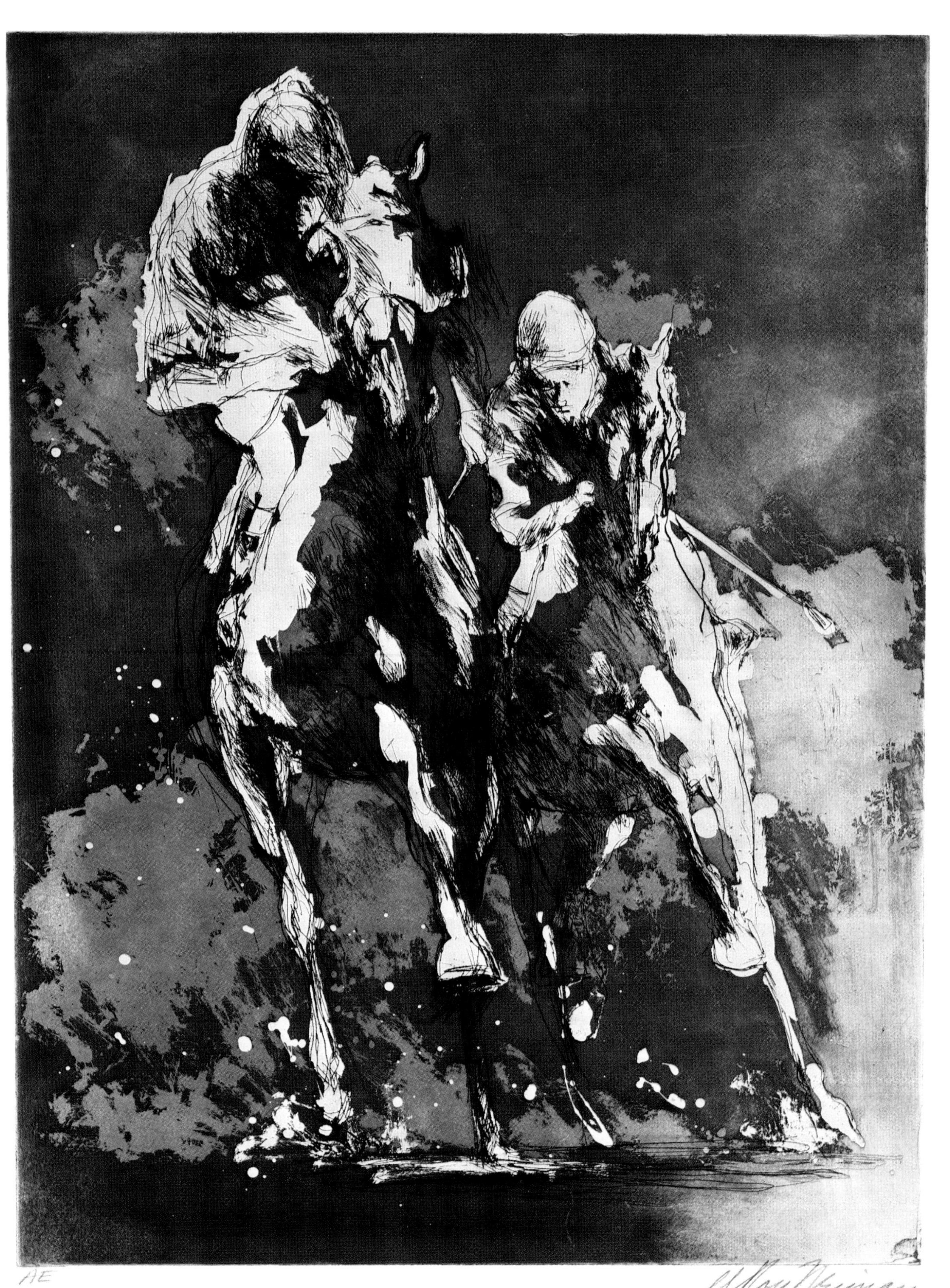

216   The Mudders
1971
Aquatint Etching
20 x 14¾   (51 x 37.50 cm)
No edition

**217   Robert F. Kennedy
Memorial Etching**
197
Twoplate Etching
21 x 16⅞ (53.34 x 42.86 cm
A limited edition of 250, signed an
numbered by the arti

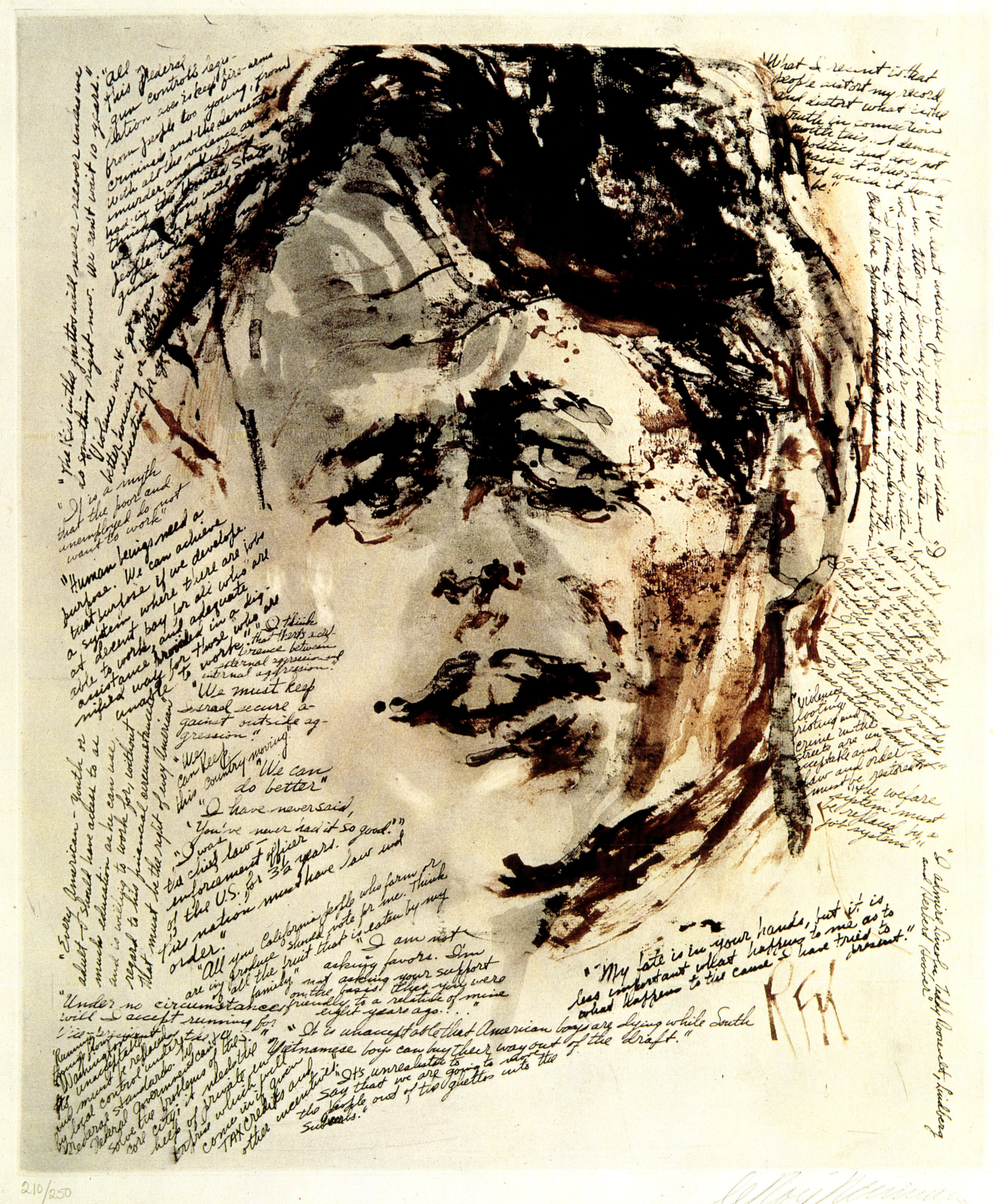
210/250
RFK
"We can do better"
"I have never said, 'You've never had it so good.'"
"My fate is in your hands, but it is less important what happens to me as to what happens to the cause I have tried to present."

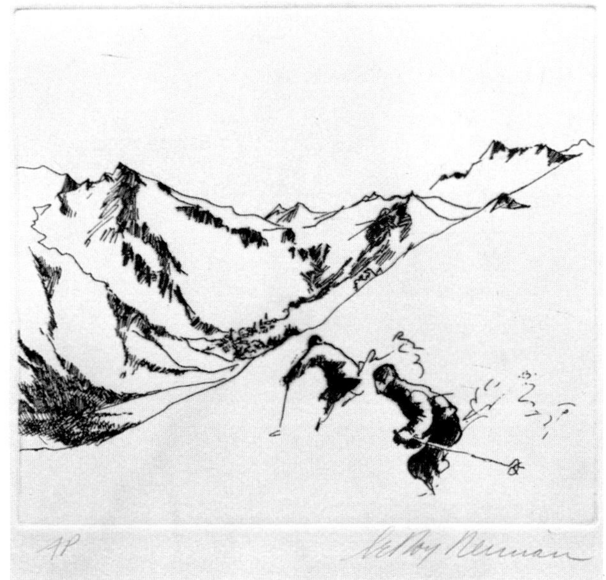

218
Village in the Valley
1972
Etching
7⅜ x 8¼ (18.73 x 20.95 cm)

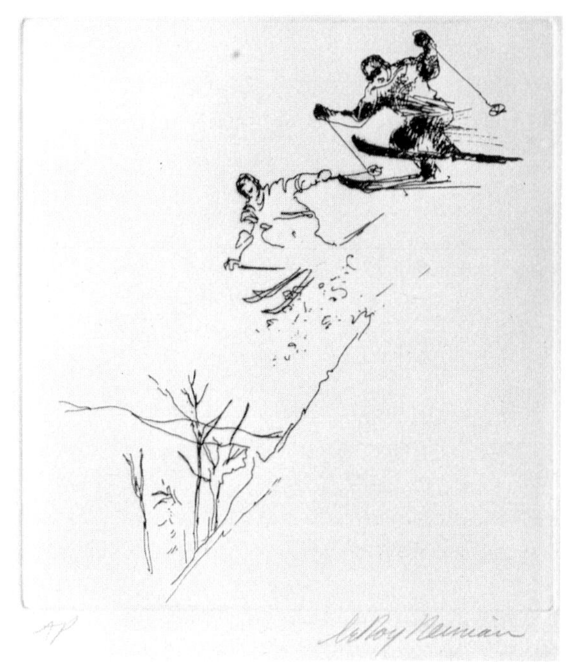

219
Jump
1972
Etching
8¼ x 7⅜ (20.95 x 18.73 cm)

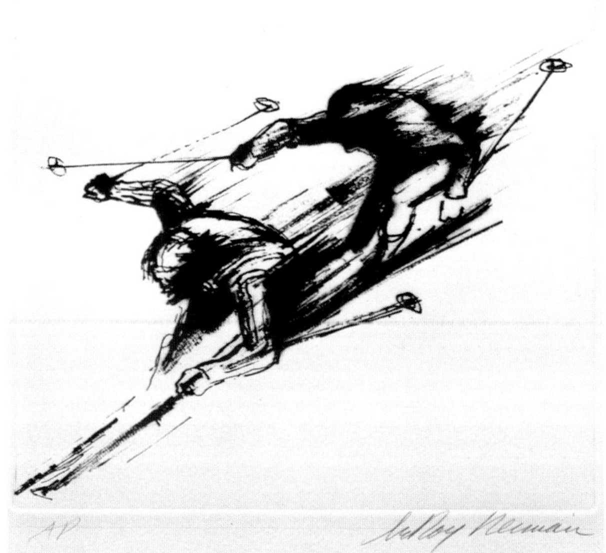

220
Two Racers
1972
Etching
7⅜ x 8¼ (18.73 x 20.95 cm)

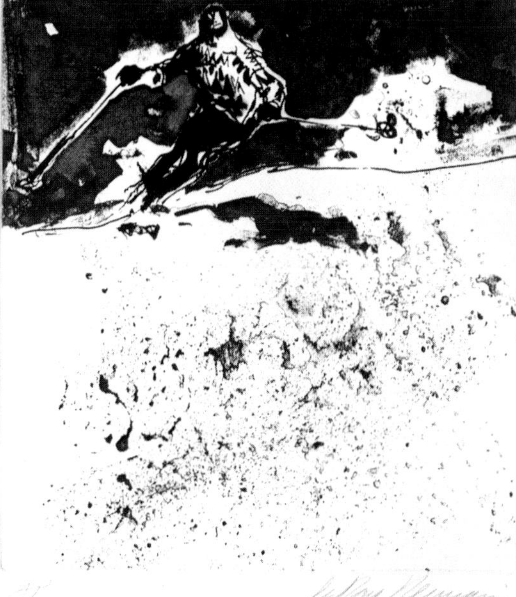

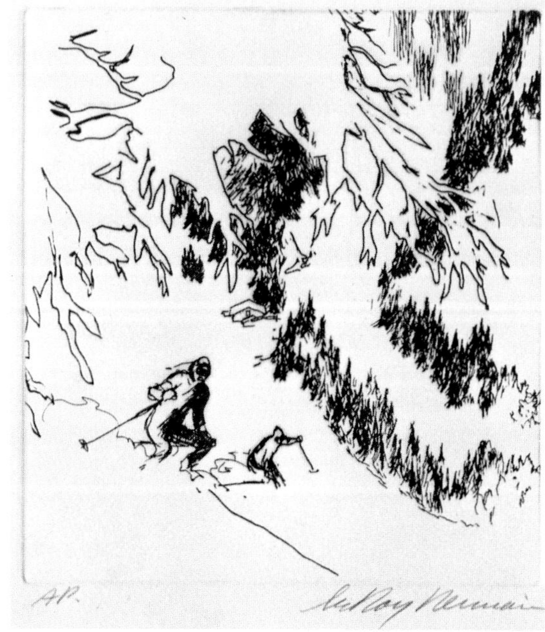

222
House on the Slope
1972
Etching
8¼ x 7⅜ (20.95 x 18.73 cm)

221
Top of the Crest
1972
Etching
8¼ x 7⅜ (20.95 x 18.73 cm)

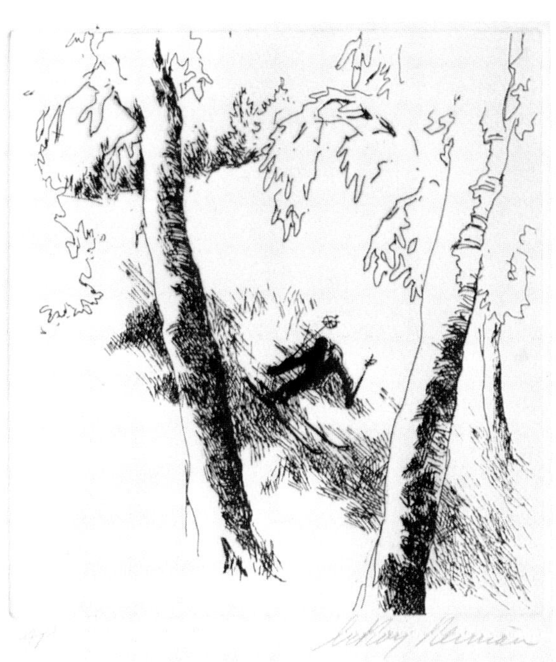

223
Between Trees
1972
Etching
8¼ x 7⅜ (20.95 x 18.73 cm)

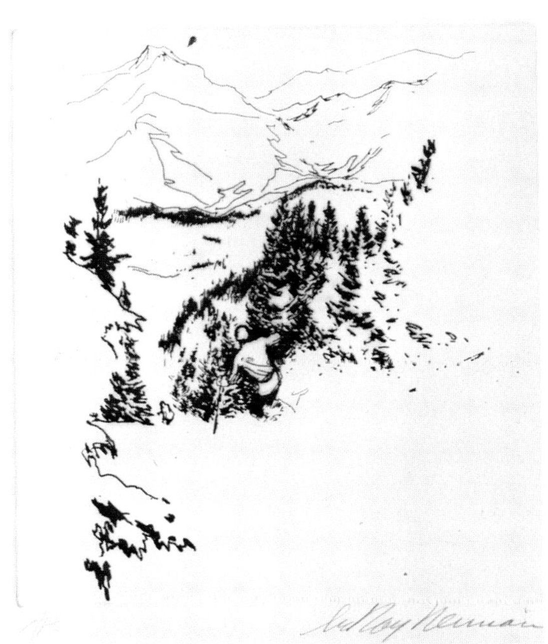

226
Pine Trail
1972
Etching
8¼ x 7⅜ (20.95 x 18.73 cm)

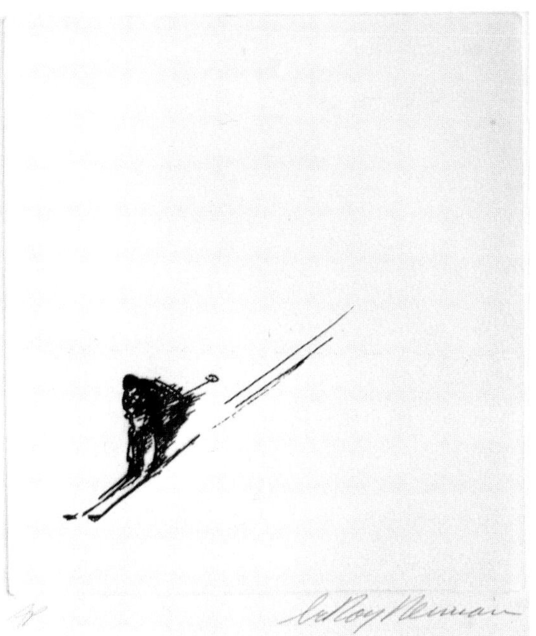

224
Single Skier
1972
Etching
8¼ x 7⅜ (20.95 x 18.73 cm)

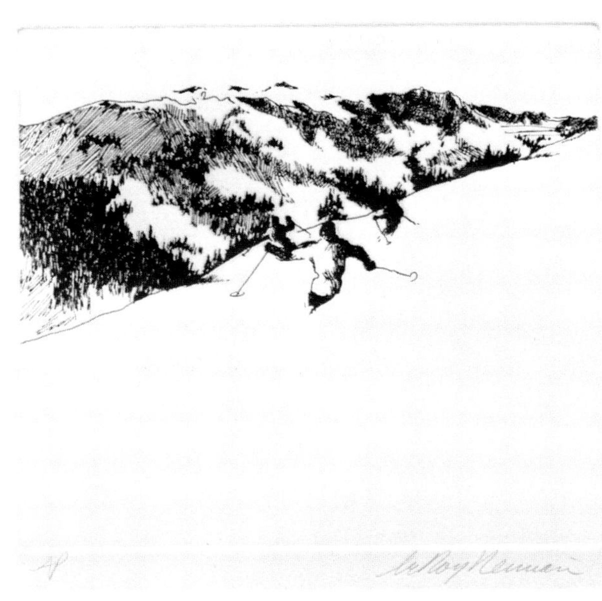

225
Three Skiers
1972
Etching
7⅜ x 8¼ (18.73 x 20.95 cm)

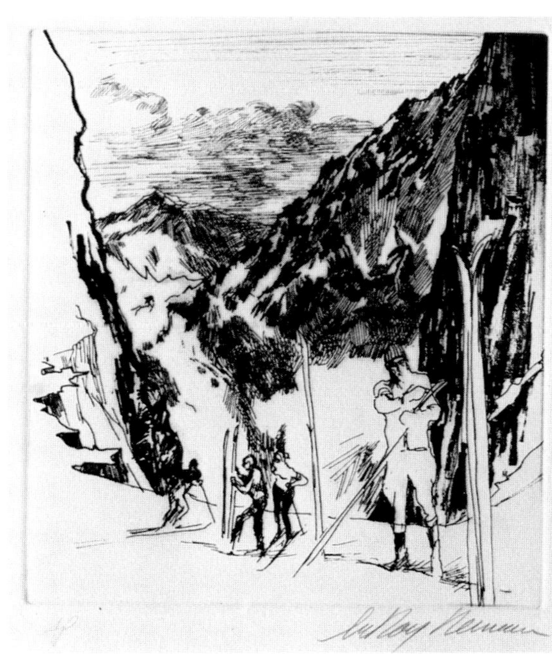

227
Break
1972
Etching
8¼ x 7⅜ (20.95 x 18.73 cm)

HOCKEY SUITE   A limited edition of 150 photo-etchings from original drawings, signed and numbered by the artist.

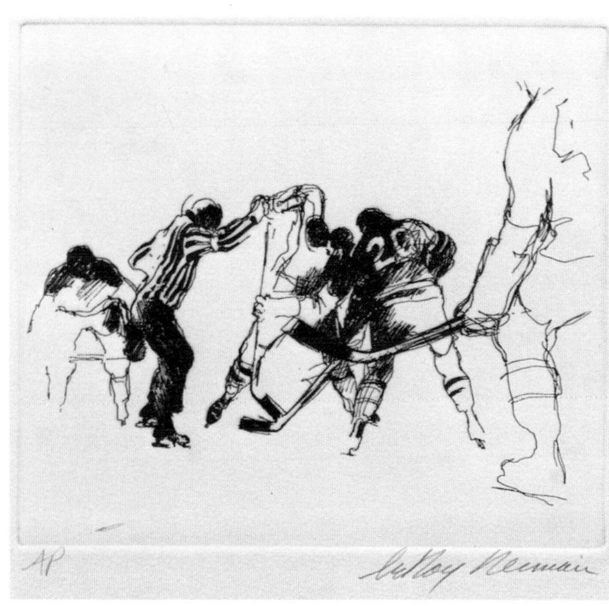

228
Face Off
1972
Etching
7½ x 8¼
(18.73 x 20.95 cm)

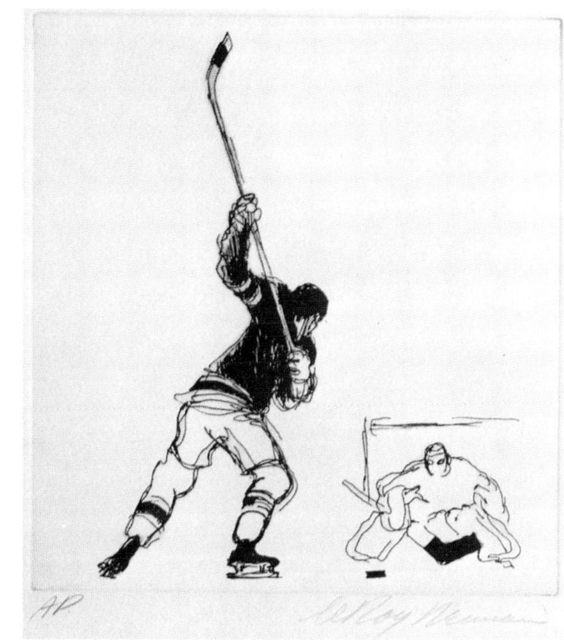

229
Slap Shot
1972
Etching
7⅜ x 8¼
(18.73 x 20.95 cm)

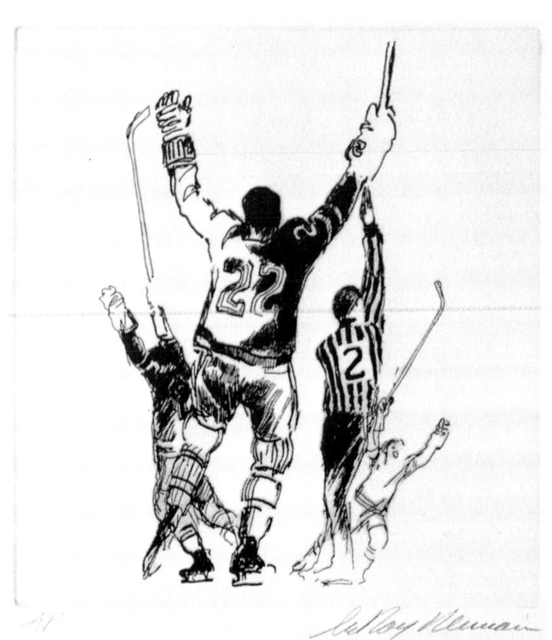

230
Score
1972
Etching
8¼ x 7½
(20.95 x 19.05 cm)

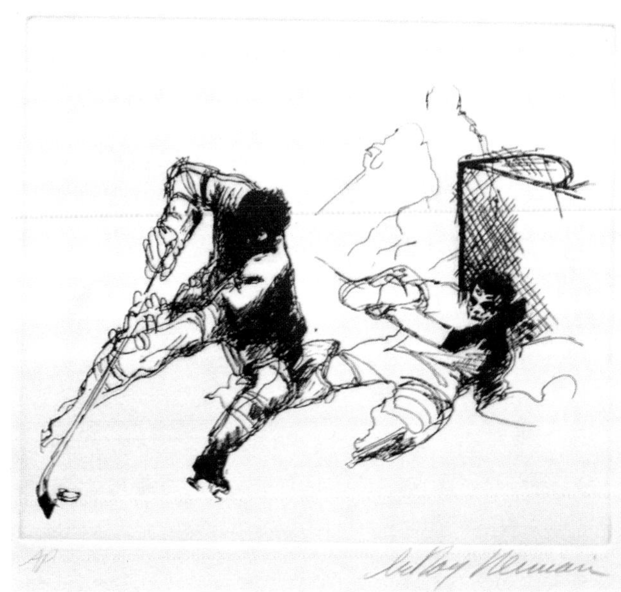

231
1 on 1
1972
Etching
7⅜ x 8¼
(18.73 x 20.95 cm)

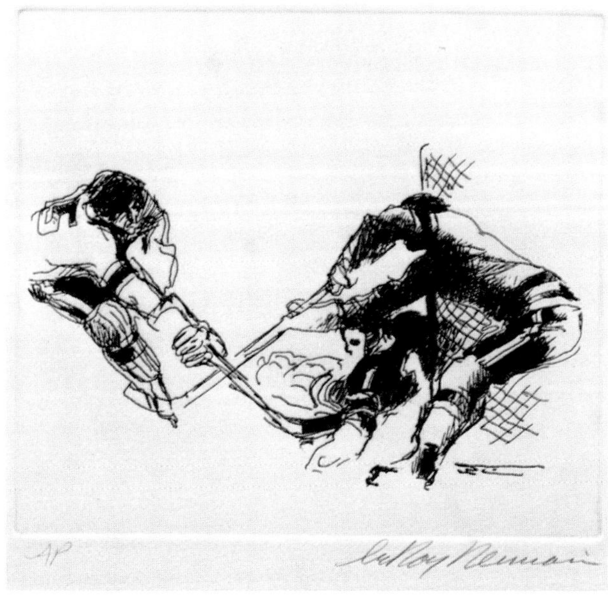

232
Goal
1972
Etching
7½ x 8¼ (19.05 x 20.95 cm)

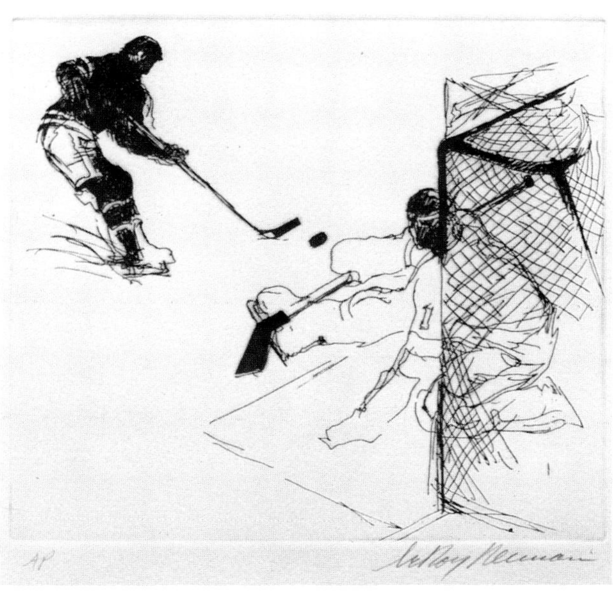

233
Save
1972
Etching
7⅜ x 8¼ (18.73 x 20.95 cm)

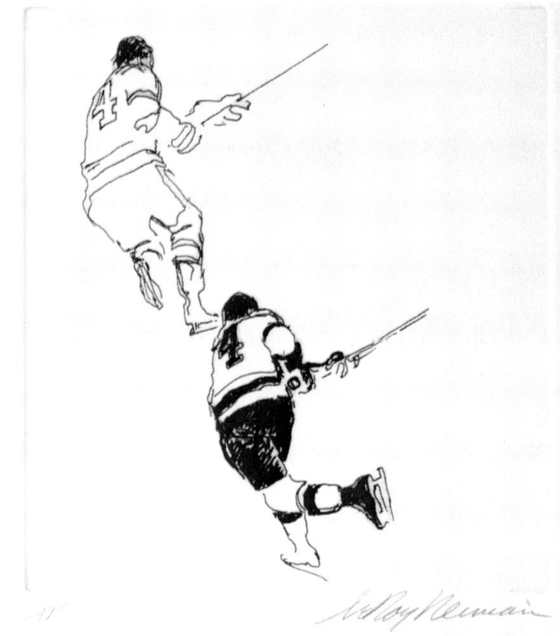

234
Study of # 4
1972
Etching
7½ x 8¼ (19.05 x 20.95 cm)

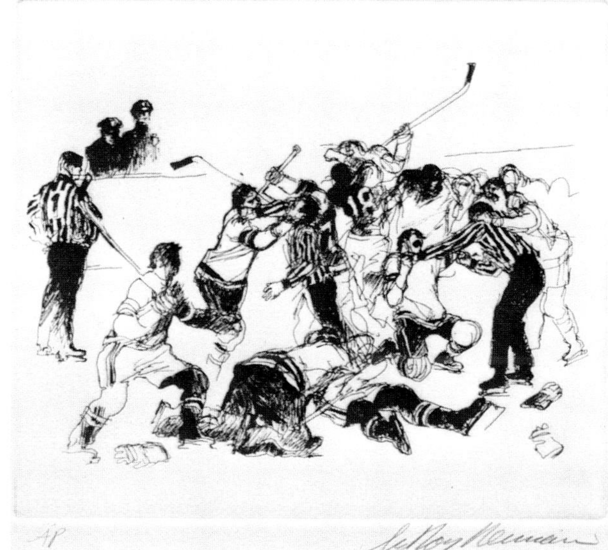

235
Fight with Policemen
1972
Etching
7½ x 8¼ (19.05 x 20.95 cm)

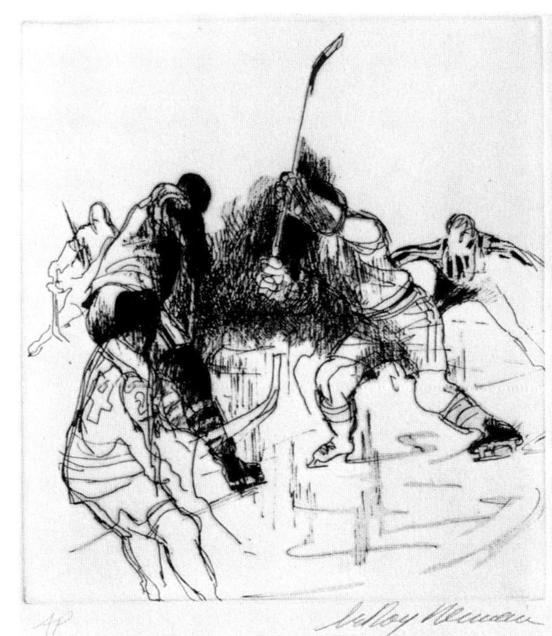

236
High Stick
1972
Etching
8¼ x 7½ (20.95 x 19.05 cm)

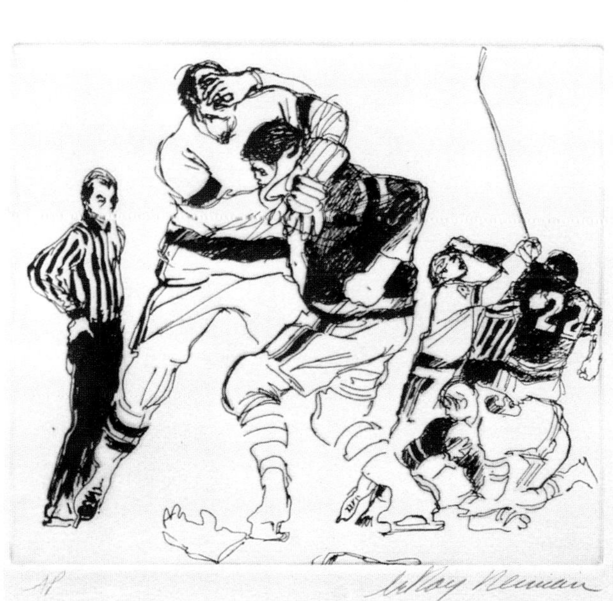

237
Fight
1972
Etching
7½ x 8¼ (19.05 x 20.95 cm)

ALI-FRAZIER SUITE

A limited edition of 150 photo-etchings from original drawings, signed and numbered by the artist.

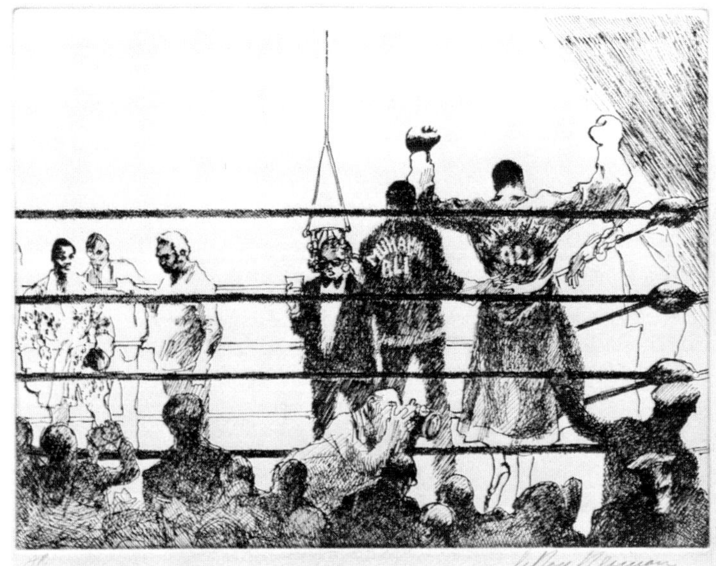

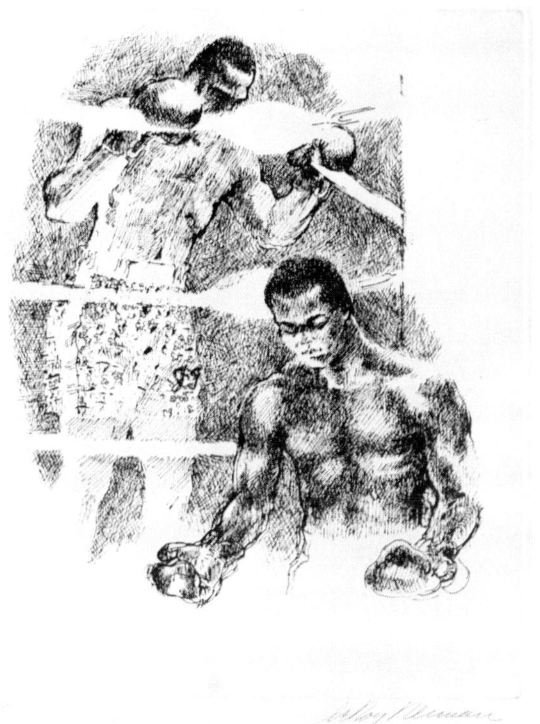

238
The Introduction
1972
Etching
10½ x 13¼ (26.67 x 34.93 cm)

239
Pre-Fight Prayers
1972
Etching
13⅜ x 10⅜ (33.97 x 26.35 cm)

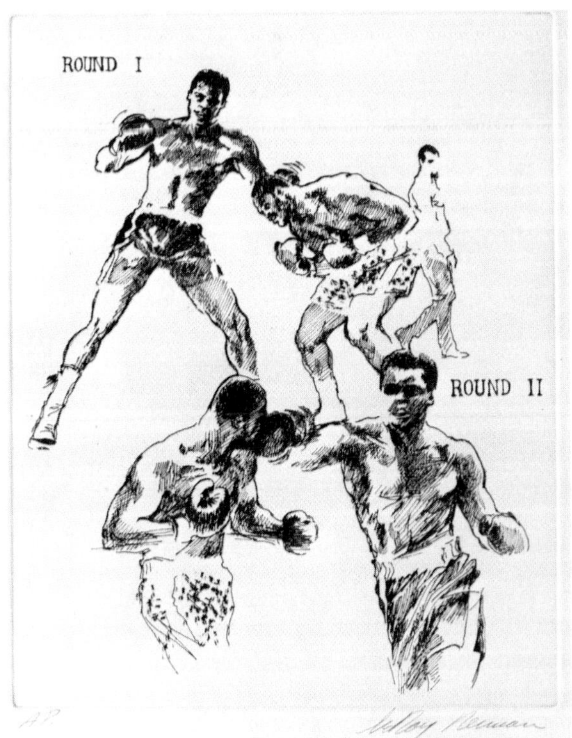

240
Rounds # 1 & 2
1972
Etching
13¼ x 10½ (34.93 x 26.67 cm)

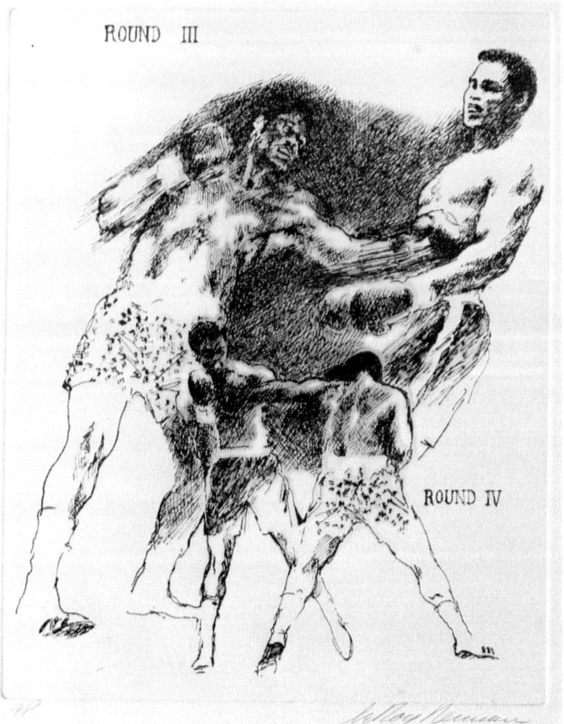

241
Rounds # 3 & 4
1972
Etching
13½ x 10½ (34.93 x 26.67 cm)

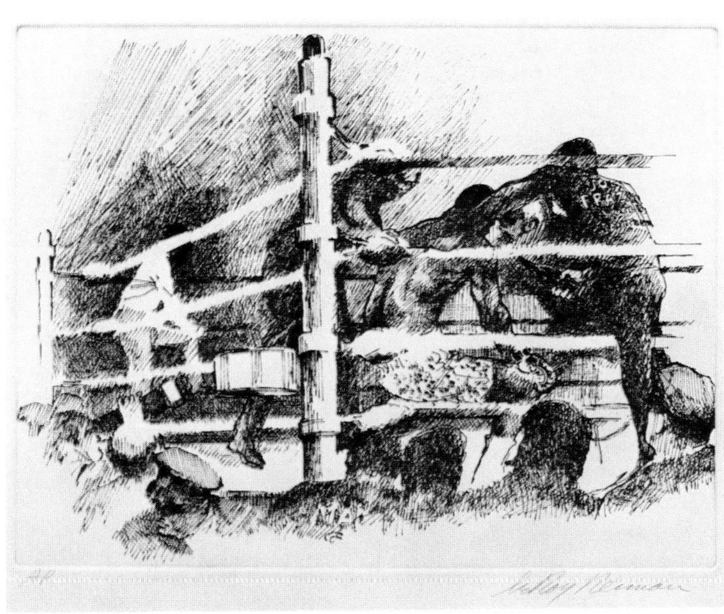

242
Frazier's Corner
1972
Etching
10½ x 13¼ (26.67 x 34.93 cm)

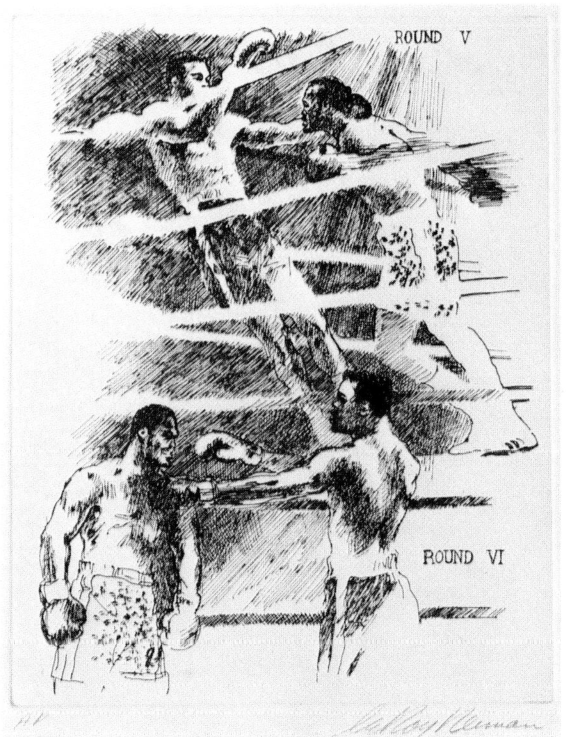

243
Rounds # 5 & 6
1972
Etching
13¼ x 10½ (34.93 x 26.67 cm)

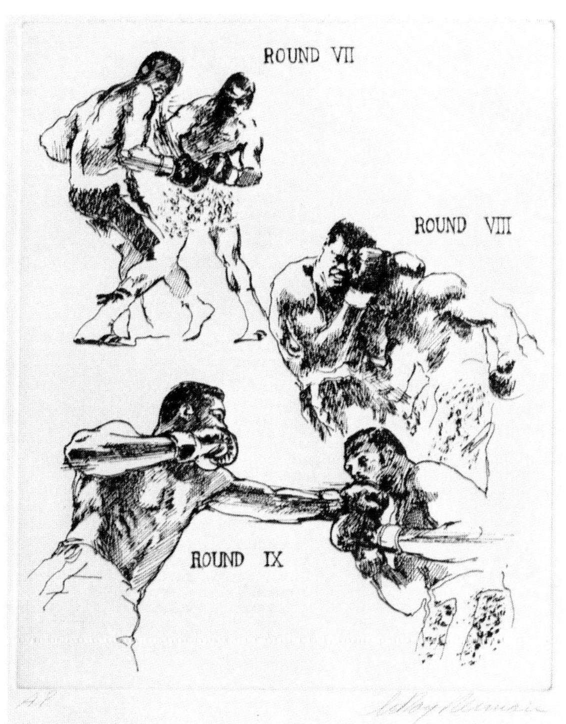

244
Rounds # 7–9
1972
Etching
13¼ x 10½ (33.93 x 26.67 cm)

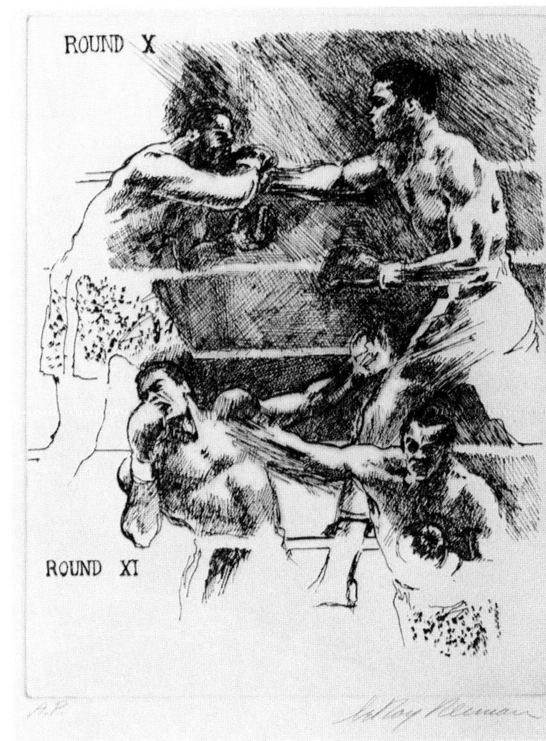

245
Rounds # 10 & 11
1972
Etching
13¼ x 10½ (34.93 x 26.67 cm)

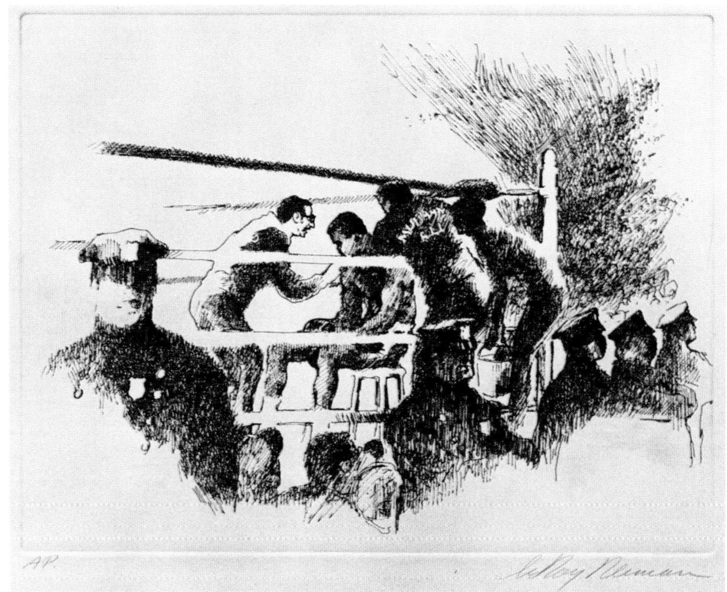

246
Ali's Corner
1972
Etching
10½ x 13¼ (26.67 x 34.93 cm)

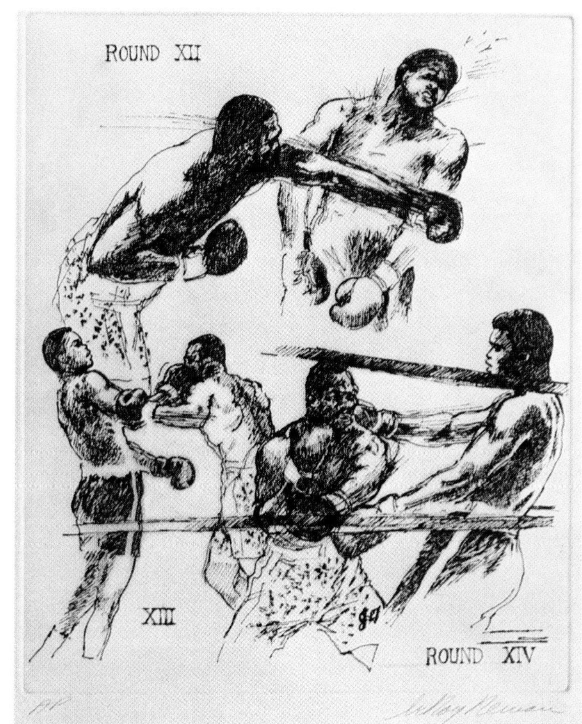

247
Rounds # 12–14
1972
Etching
13¼ x 10½ (34.93 x 26.67 cm)

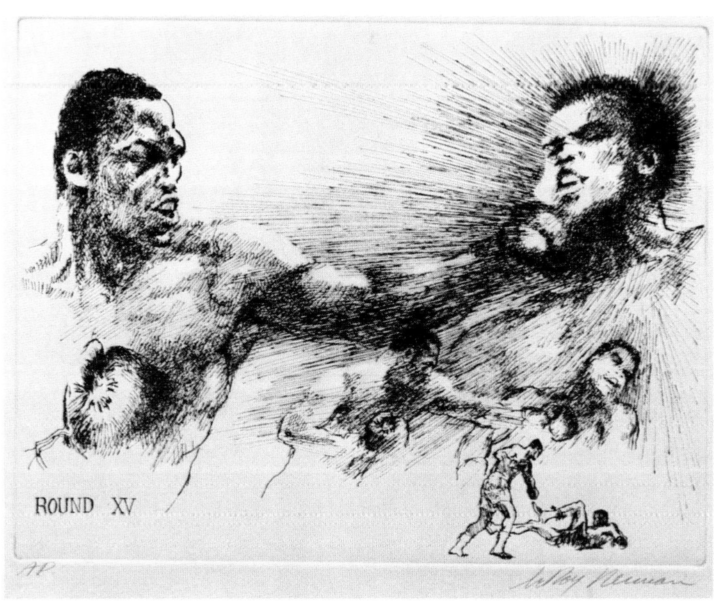

248
Round # 15
1972
Etching
10½ x 13¼ (26.67 x 34.93 cm)

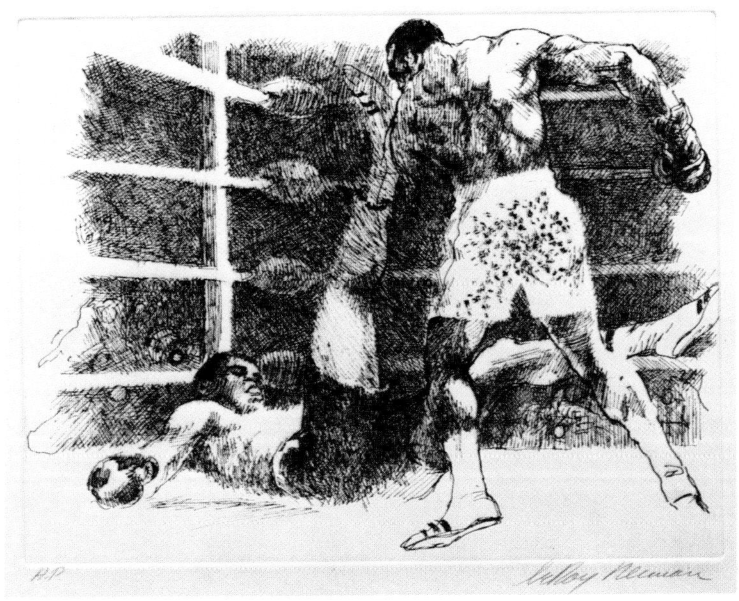

249
Ali Down
1972
Etching
10½ x 13¼ (26.67 x 34.93 cm)

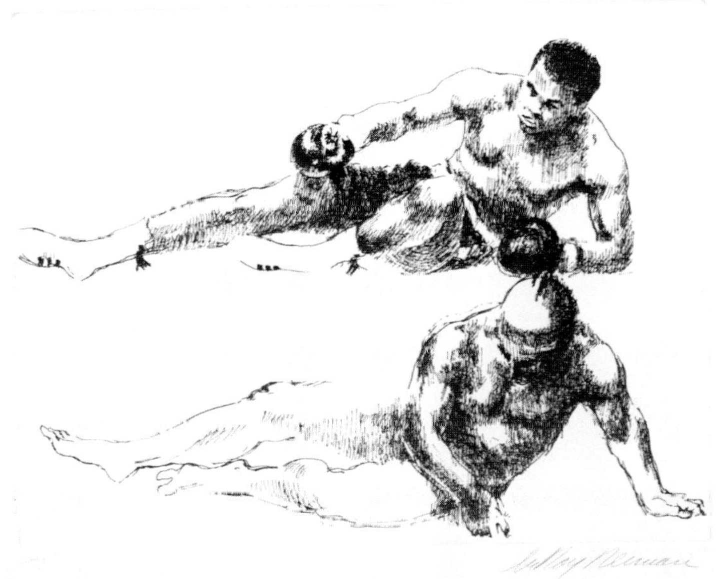

250
Classic Fallen Warrior
1972
Etching
10⅜ x 13⅜ (26.35 x 33.97 cm)

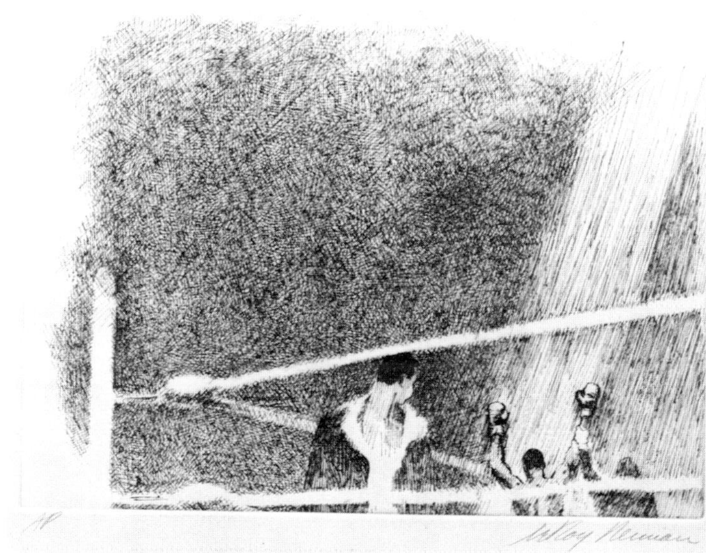

251
The Winner
1972
Etching
10½ x 13¼ (26.67 x 34.93 cm)

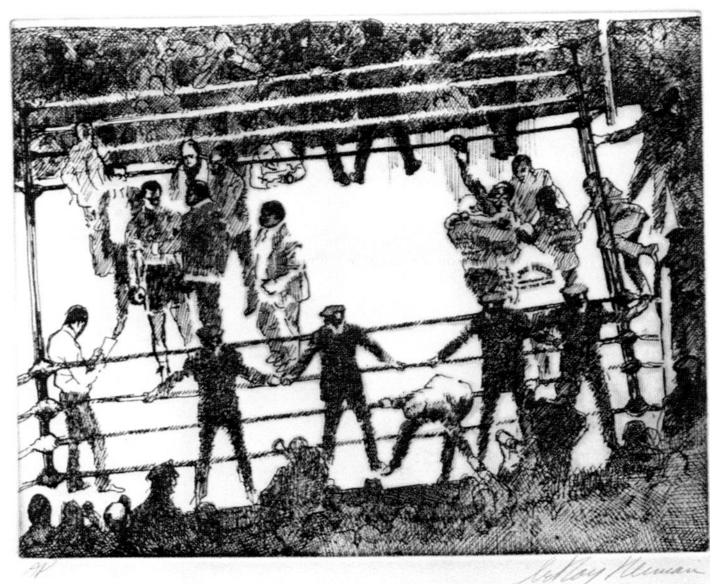

252
After the Fight
1972
Etching
10½ x 13⅜ (26.67 x 34.93 cm)

BASEBALL PLAYER SUITE

A limited edition of 150 photo-etchings from original drawings, signed and numbered by the artist.

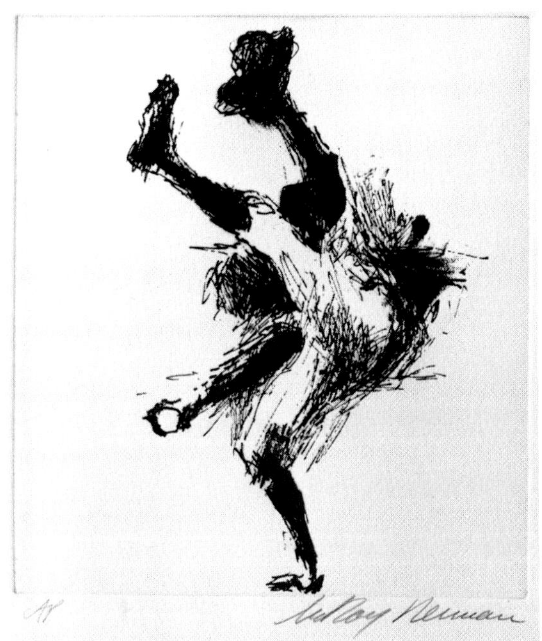

253
Wind Up
1972
Etching
8¼ x 7¼ (20.95 x 18.41 cm)

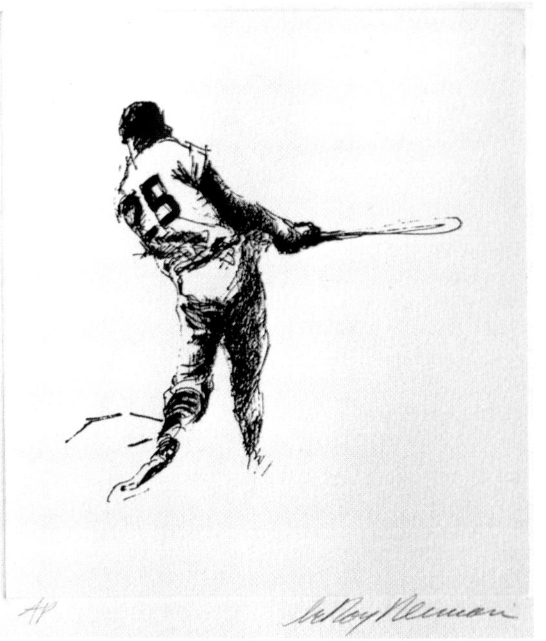

254
The Hit
1972
Etching
8¼ x 7⅜ (20.95 x 18.73 cm)

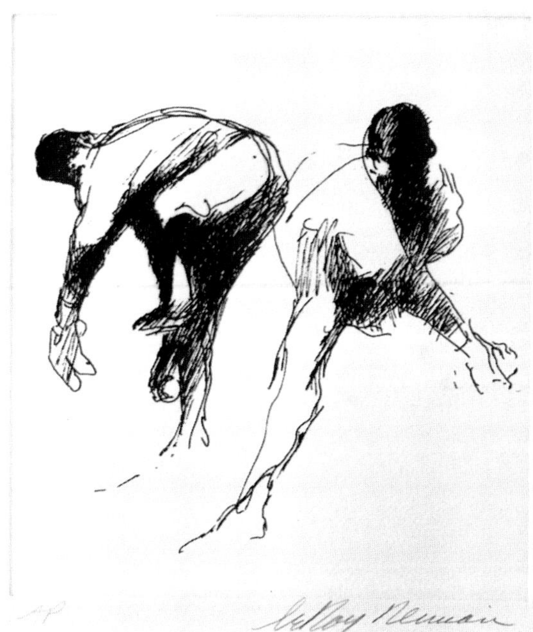

255
The Pitch
1972
Etching
8¼ x 7⅜ (20.95 x 18.73 cm)

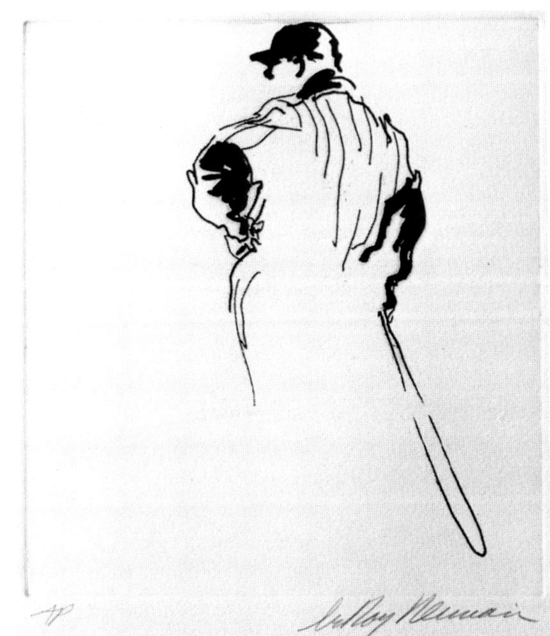

257
Next at Bat
1972
Etching
8¼ x 7⅜ (20.95 x 18.73 cm)

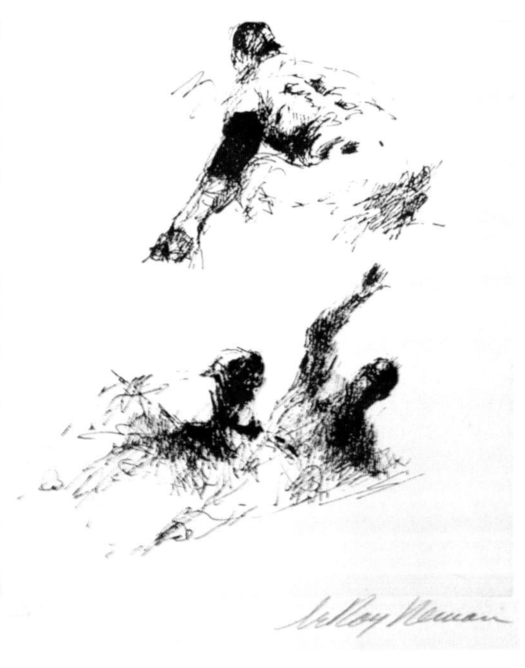

256
Sliding Home
1972
Etching
8¼ x 7¹/₁₆ (20.96 x 18.90 cm)

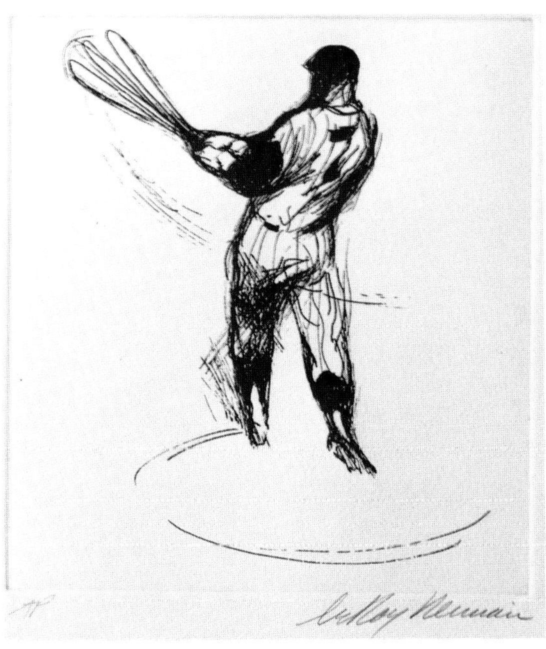

258
Warm up Swings
(Mickey Mantle)
1972
Etching
8¼ x 7⅜ (20.95 x 18.73 cm)

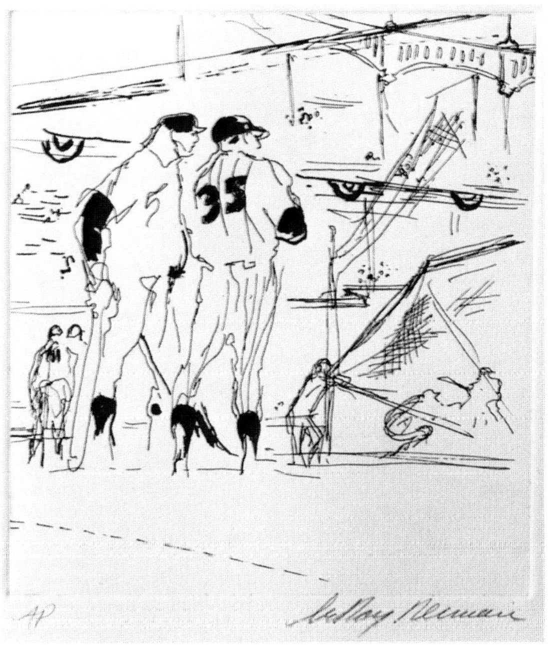

259
Batting Practice
1972
Etching
8¼ x 7⅜ (20.95 x 18.73 cm)

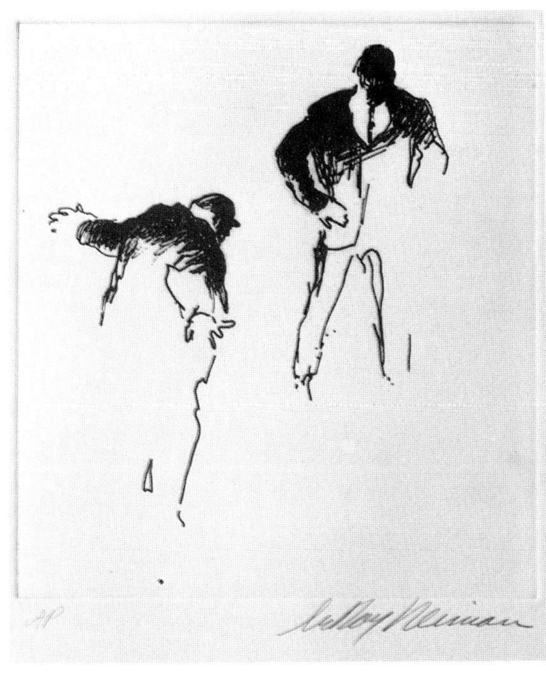

260
The Umps
1972
Etching
8¼ x 7⅜ (20.95 x 18.73 cm)

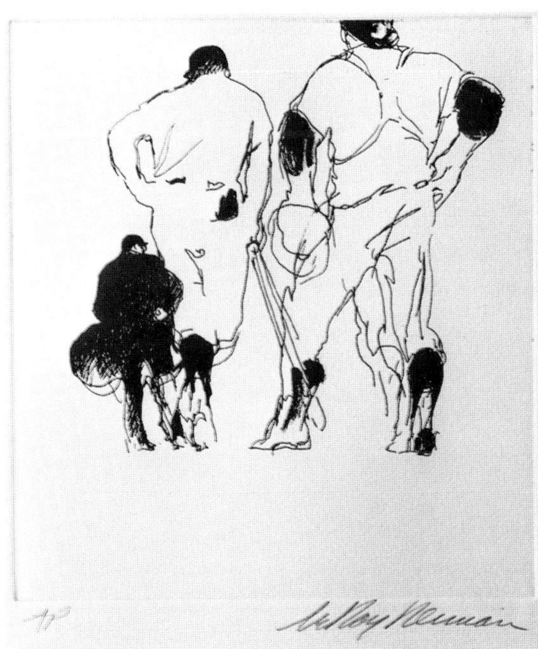

261
Awaiting the Decision
1972
Etching
8¼ x 7⁷/₁₆ (20.96 x 18.90 cm)

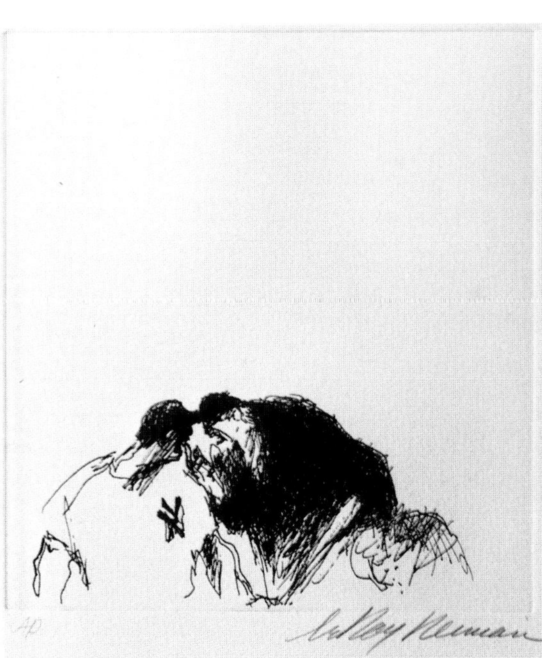

262
The Argument
1972
Etching
8¼ x 7⅜ (20.95 x 18.73 cm)

FOOTBALL SUITE   A limited edition of 150 photo-etchings from original drawings, signed and numbered by the artist.

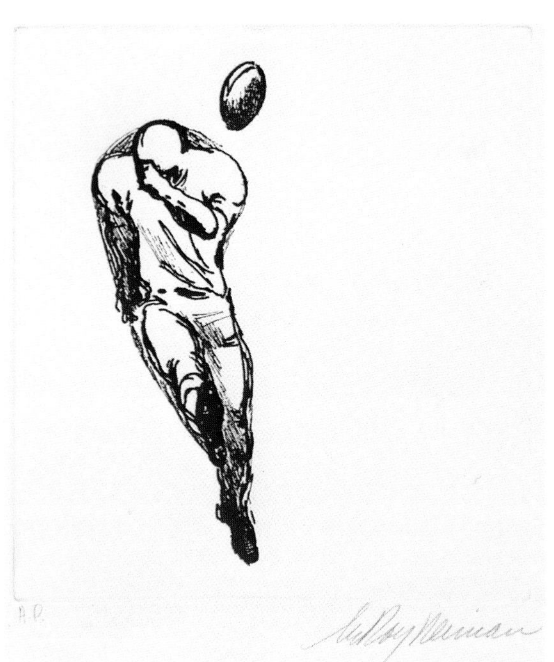

263
Kicker
1972
Etching
8⅜ x 7½ (20.70 x 18.28 cm)

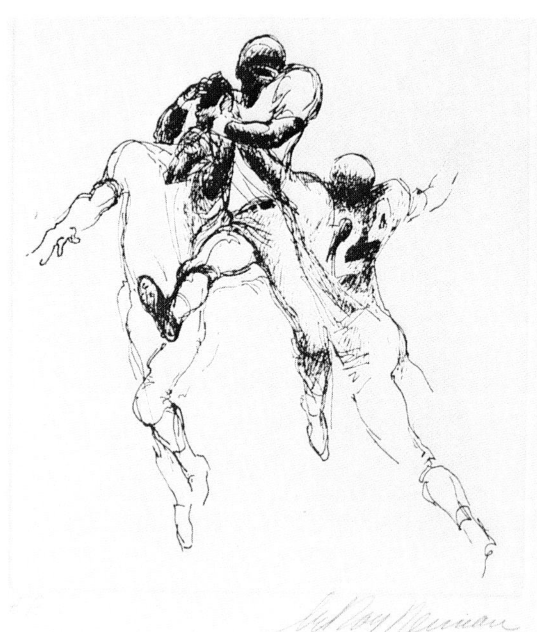

264
Receiver
1972
Etching
8⅜ x 7½ (20.70 x 18.28 cm)

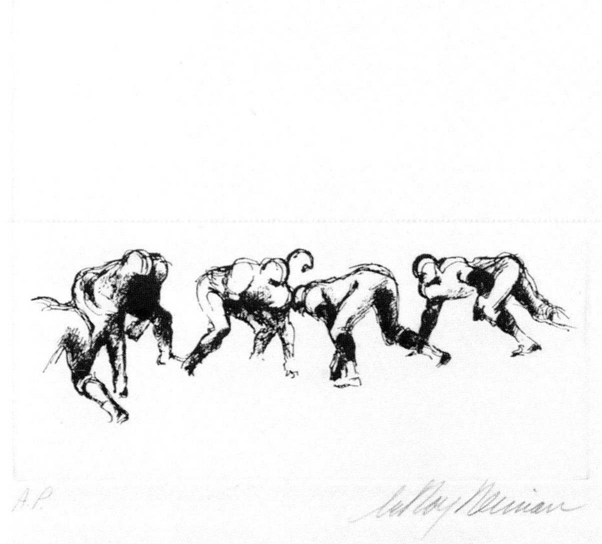

265
The Line
1972
Etching
7½ x 8⅜ (18.28 x 20.70 cm)

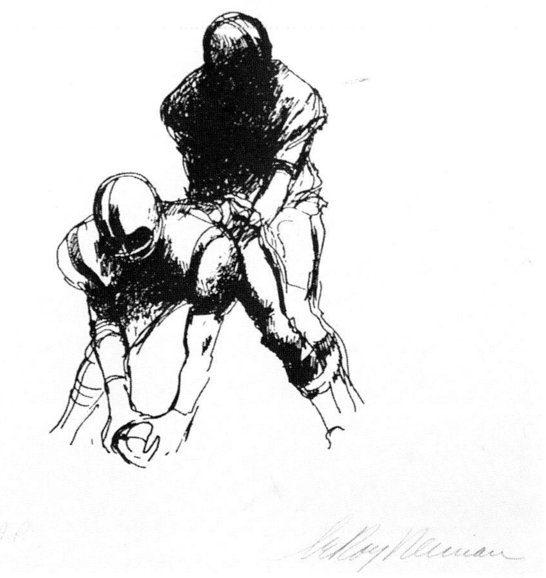

266
Snap
1972
Etching
8⅜ x 7½ (20.70 x 18.28 cm)

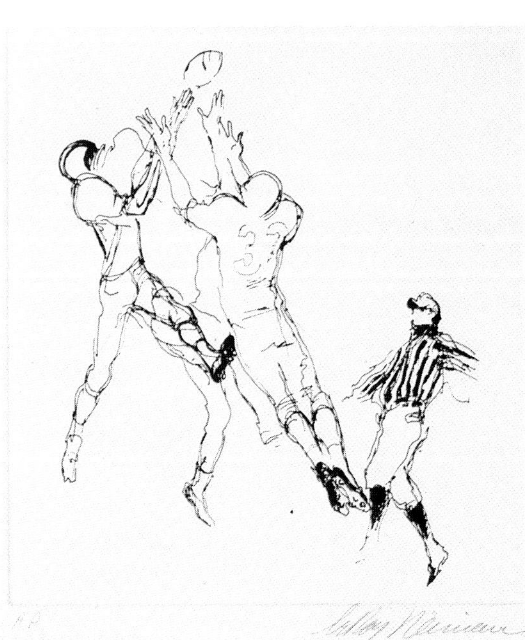

267
The Aerialist
1972
Etching
8⅜ x 7½ (20.70 x 18.28 cm)

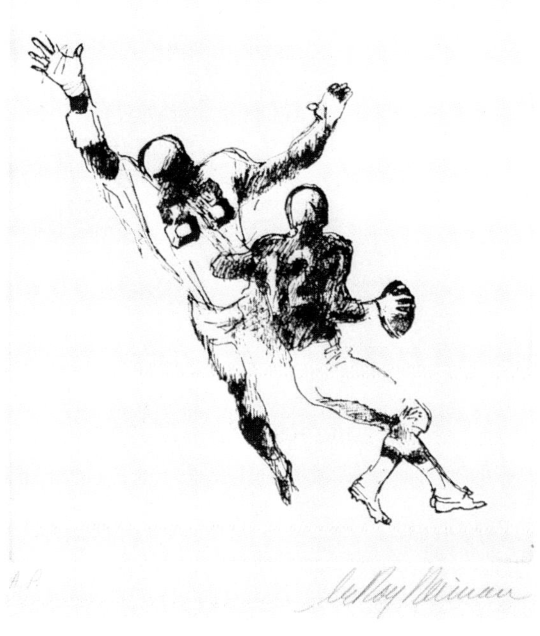

268
Q.B.
1972
Etching
8⅜ x 7½ (20.70 x 18.28 cm)

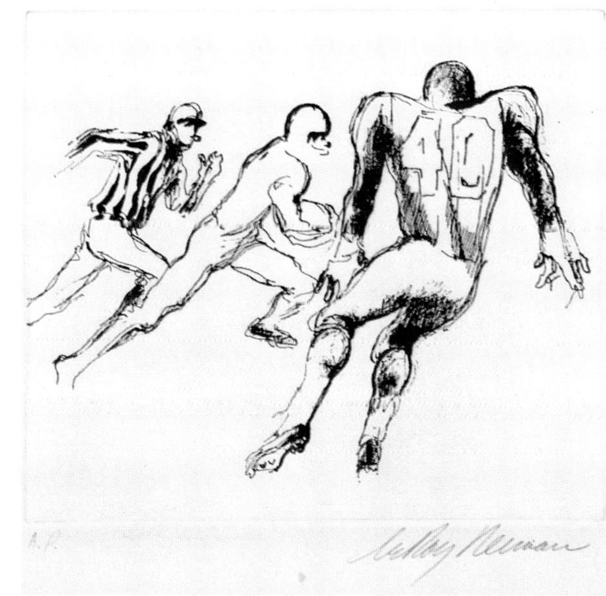

269
Open Runner
1972
Etching
7½ x 8⅜ (18.28 x 20.70 cm)

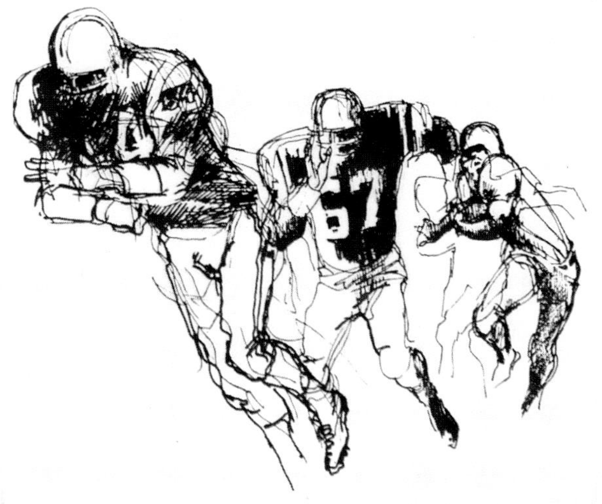

270
Interference
1972
Etching
7½ x 8⅜ (18.28 x 20.70 cm)

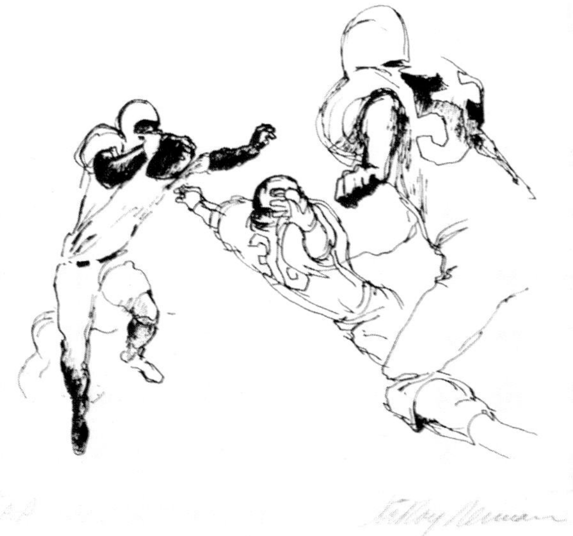

271
Scampering Back
1972
Etching
7½ x 8⅜ (18.28 x 20.70 cm)

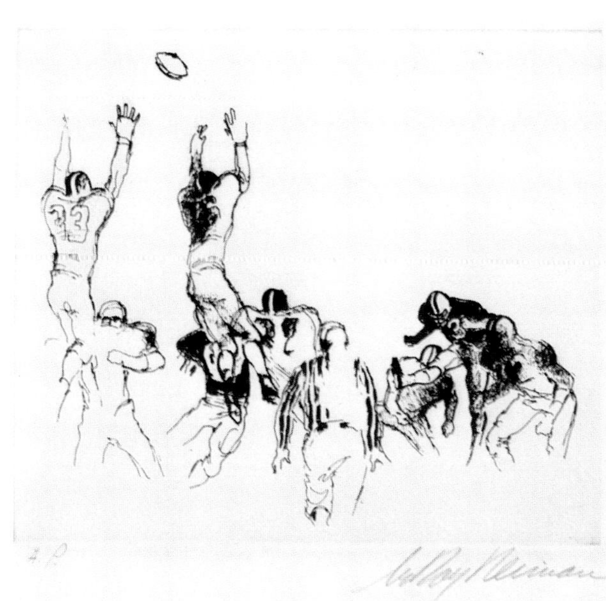

272
Field Goal
1972
Etching
7½ x 8⅜ (18.28 x 20.70 cm)

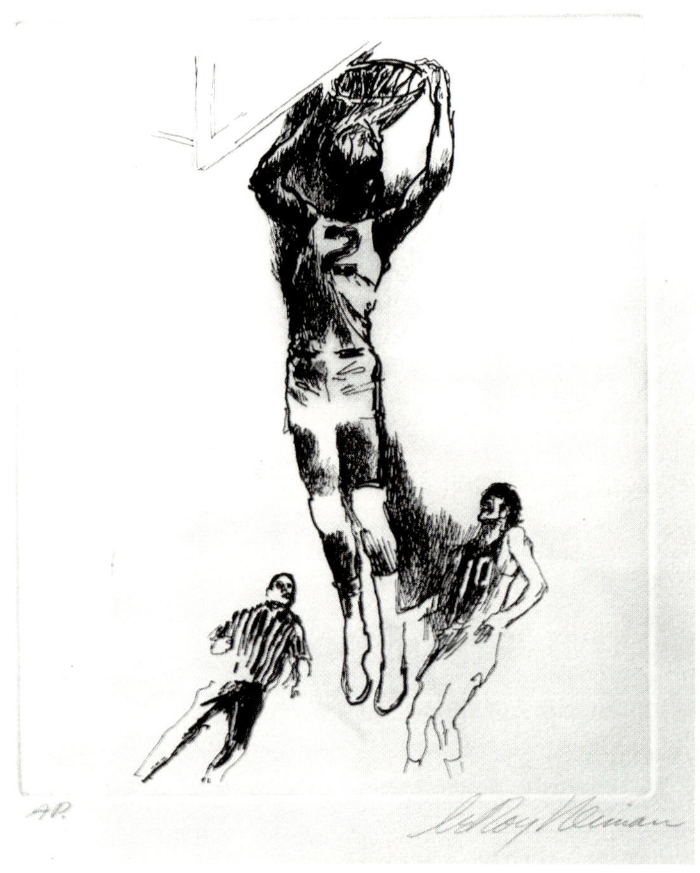

273   Dunking

1972
Etching
11¾ x 9½ (30 x 24 cm)
A limited edition of 5 photo-etchings from original
drawings, signed and numbered by the artist.

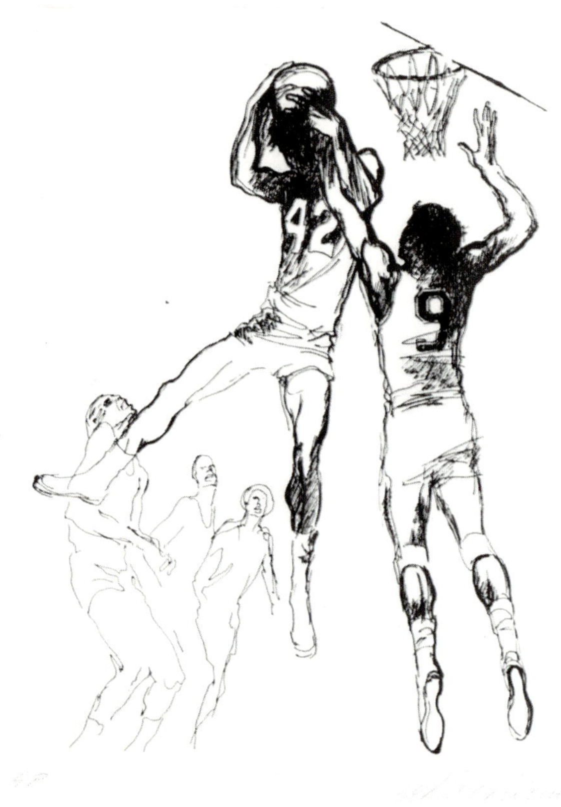

274   Rebound

1972
Etching
11½ x 9 (29.21 x 23 cm)
A limited edition of 5 photo-etchings from original
drawings, signed and numbered by the artist.

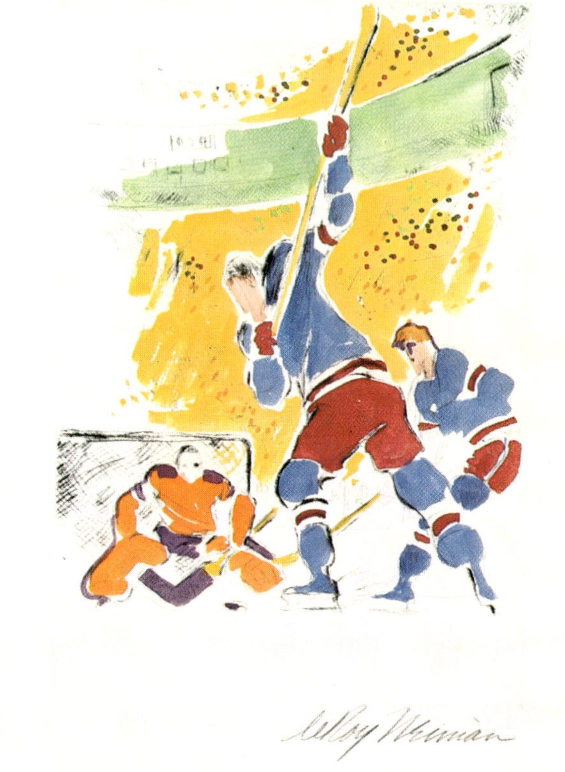

275   Shot on Goal

1972
Etching (hand colored)
9 x 16 (22.86 x 40.64 cm)
A limited edition of 5, signed and numbered
by the artist.

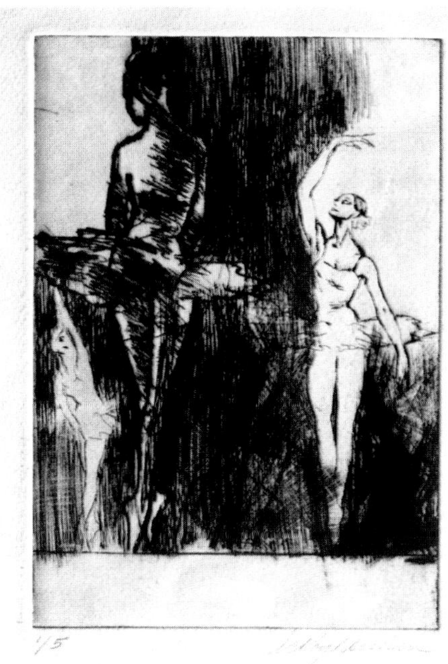

276   On Toe

1975
Etching
8⅞ x 6 (22 x 15.20 cm)
A limited edition of 5, signed and numbered
by the artist.

277   Super Bowl

1976
Etching
Second State
4⅜ x 10⅜ (11 x 26.35 cm)
No edition

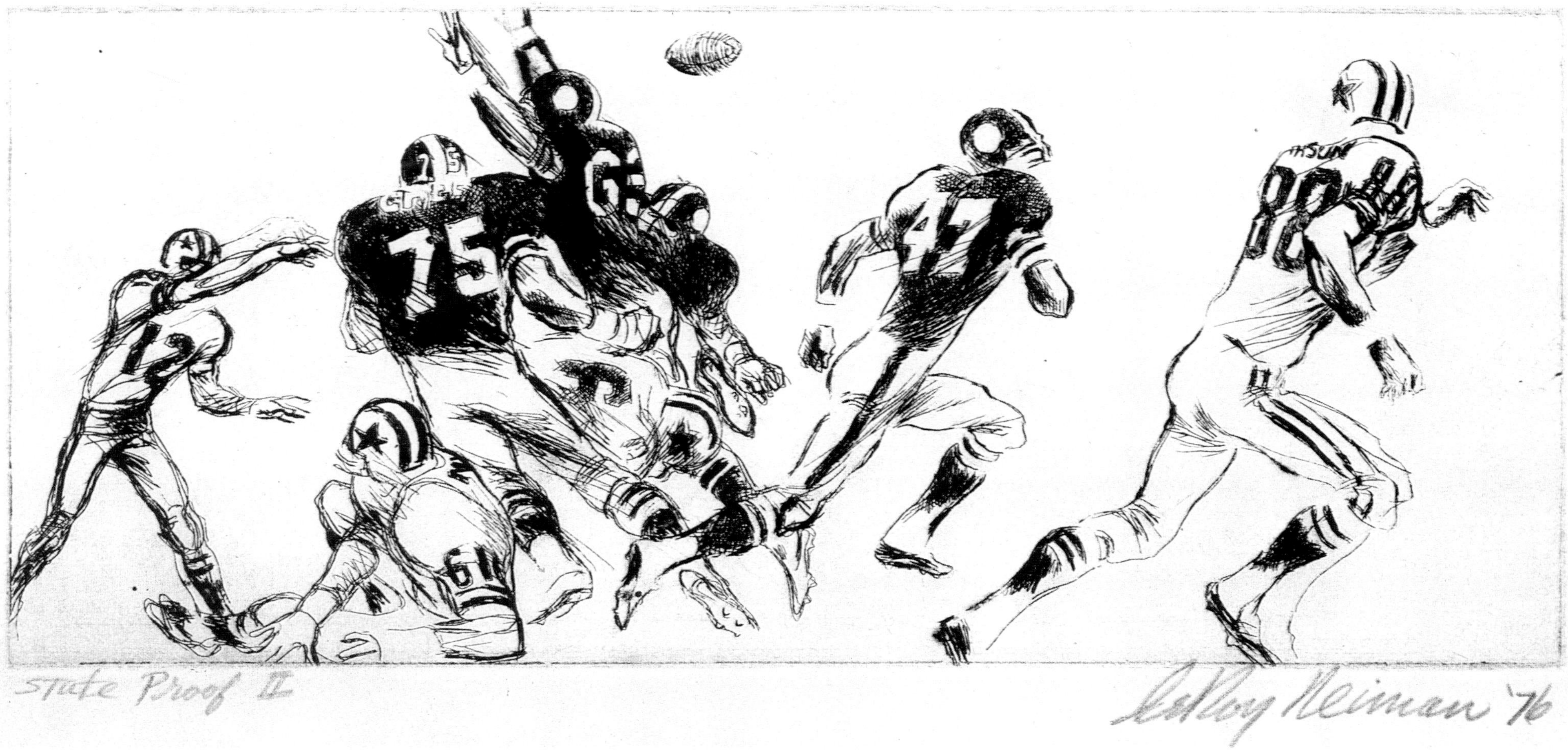

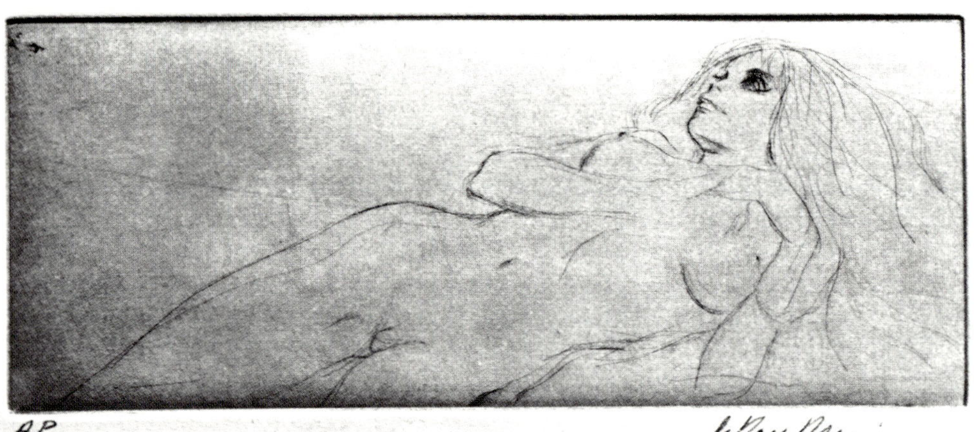

278   Ophelia

Drypoint Etching on Copper
4⅜ x 10½ (11.11 x 26.67 cm)
A limited edition of 10, signed and numbered by the artist.

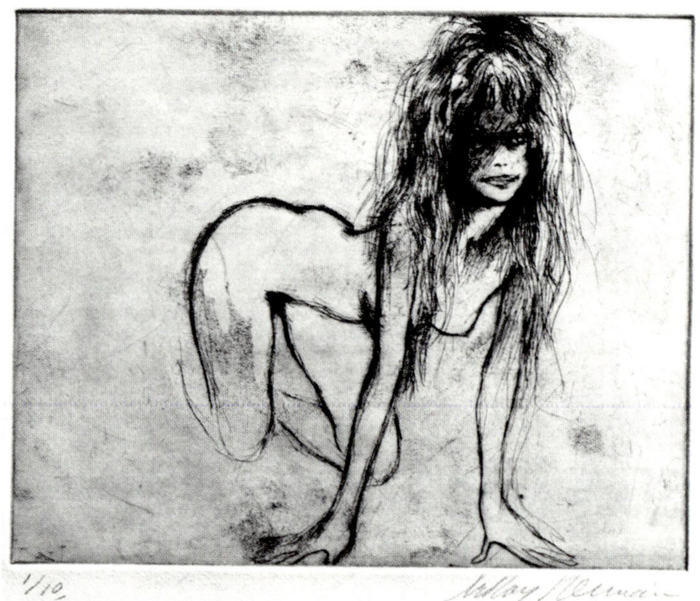

279   Nude on all Fours

1976

Drypoint Etching on Copper
8⅞ x 10¾ (22.54 x 27.30 cm)
A limited edition of 10, signed and numbered by the artist.

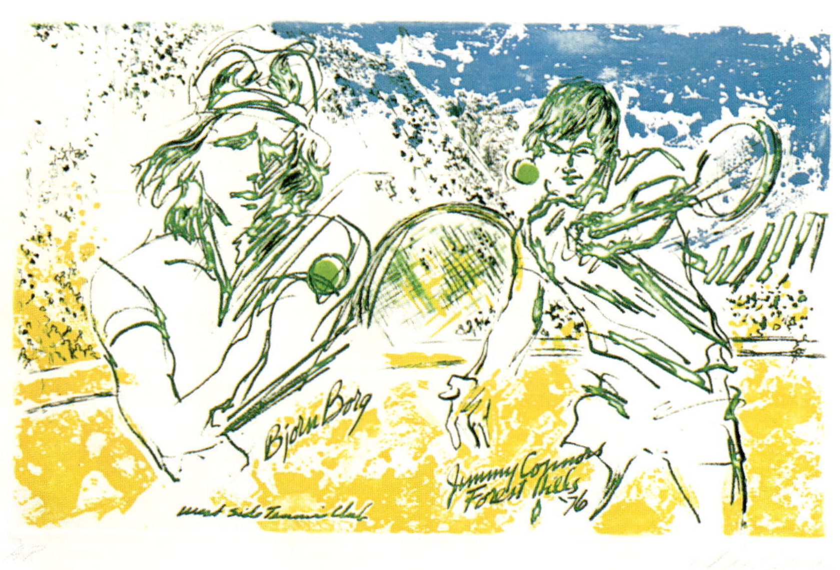

280   Borg/Connors

1977

4 Color Steel Etching with Stencil
13¾ x 21¾ (34.93 x 55.25 cm)
A limited edition of 125, signed and numbered by the artist.

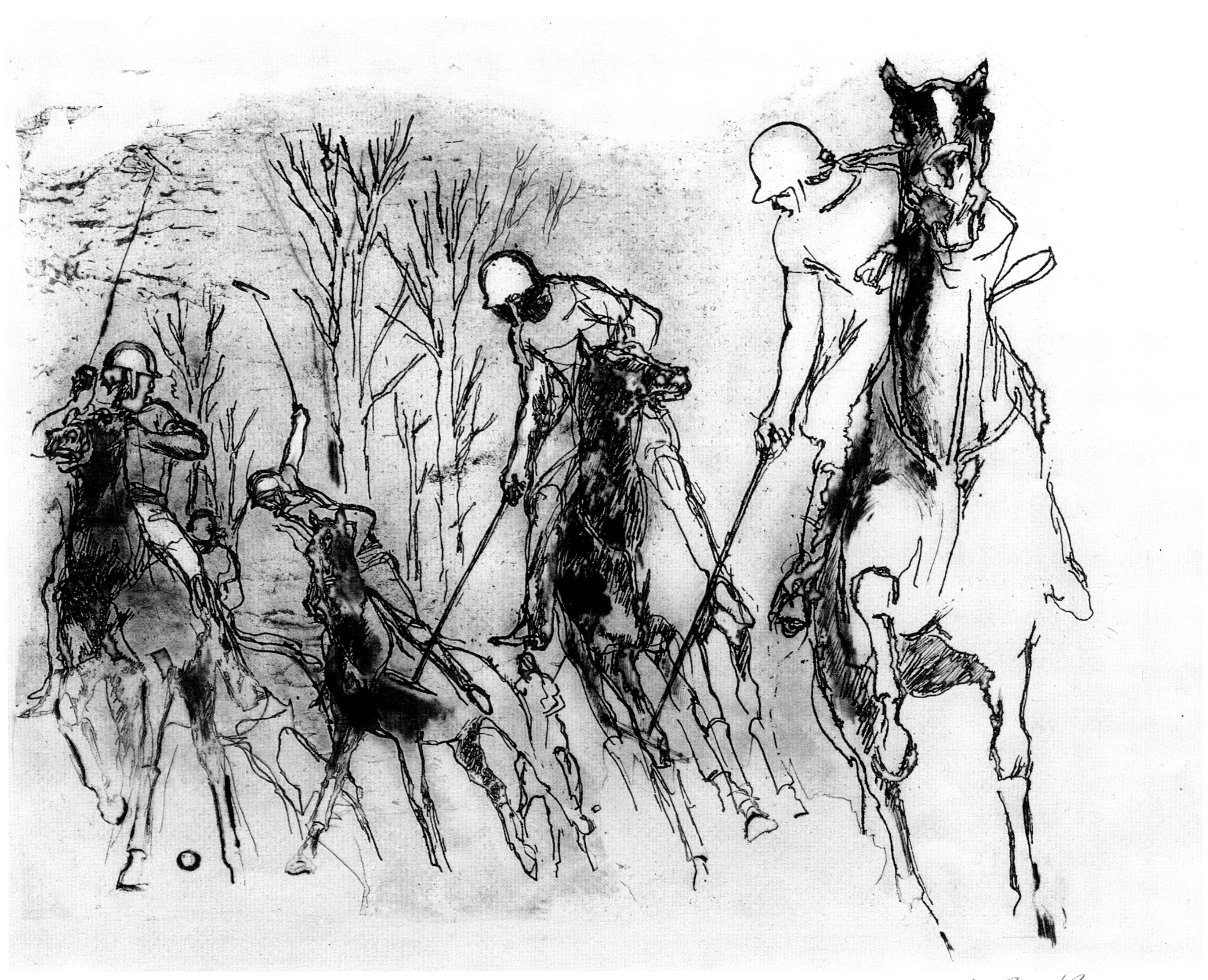

281 Malletmen

1977
Softground etching on Zinc
18 x 24 (45.72 x 60.96 cm)
A limited edition of 100, signed and numbered
by the artist.

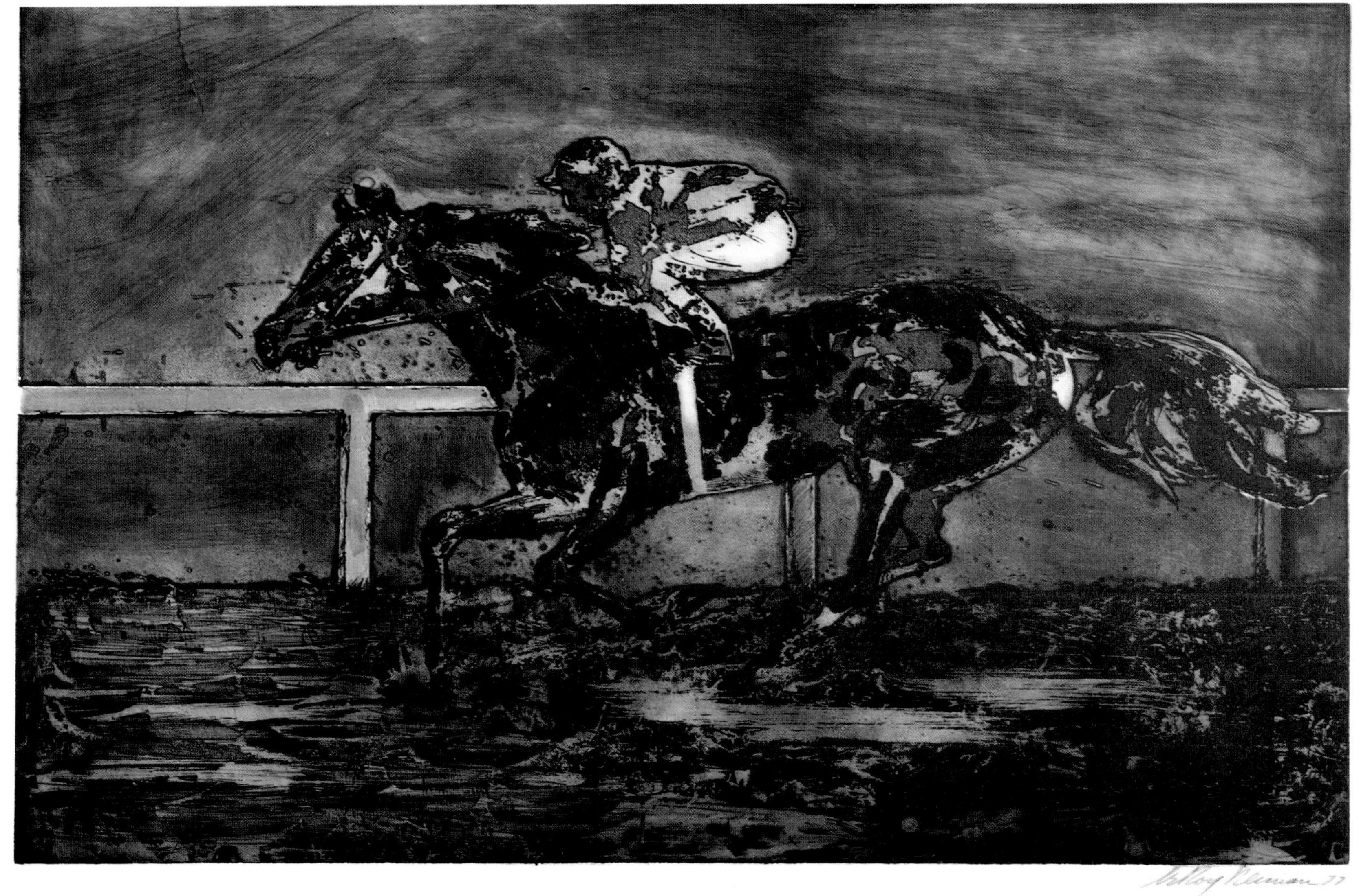

282   The Stretch

1978
Aquatint Etching
First State, Artist's Proof
23⅞ x 35¾ ½ (60.64 x 90.81 cm)
No edition

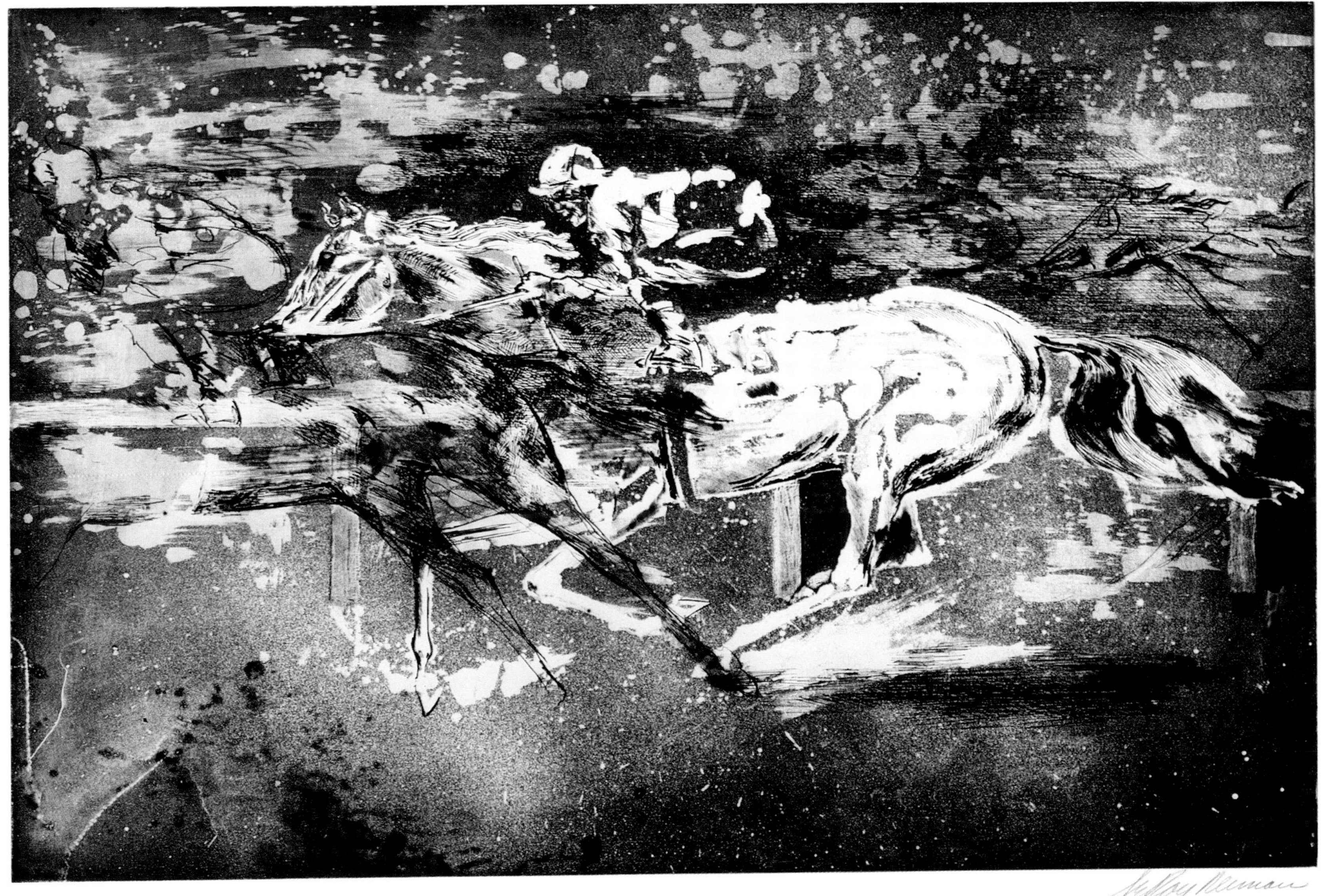

283 The Stretch

1978
Aquatint Etching
Second State, Artist's Proof
23⅞ x 35¾ ½ (60.64 x 90.81 cm)
No edition

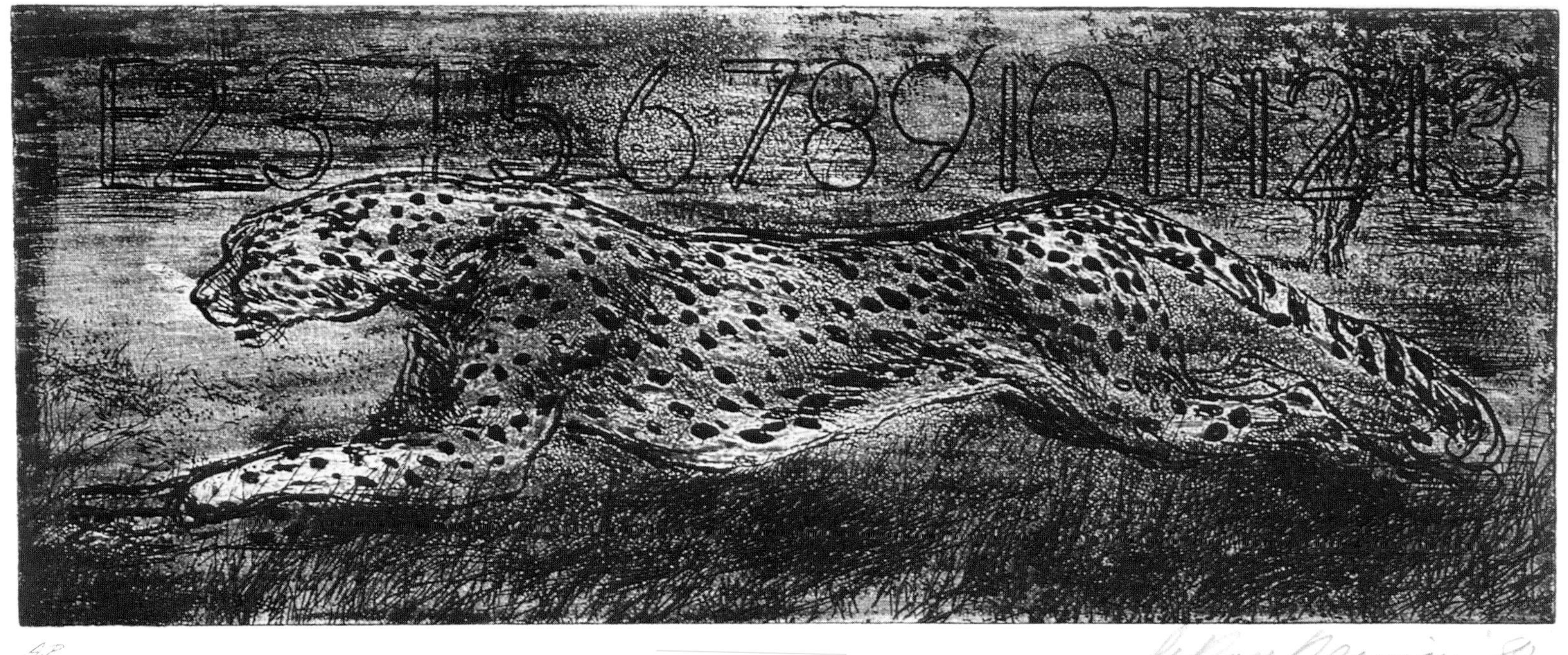

284   Midnight Cheetah

1980
Etching
5⅛ x 12⅝ (13 x 32.06 cm)
A limited edition of 250, signed and numbered
by the artist.

285   Rodeo

1980
Etching (hand-colored)
18½ x 16½ (46.99 x 41.91 cm)
A limited edition of 250, signed and numbered
by the artist.

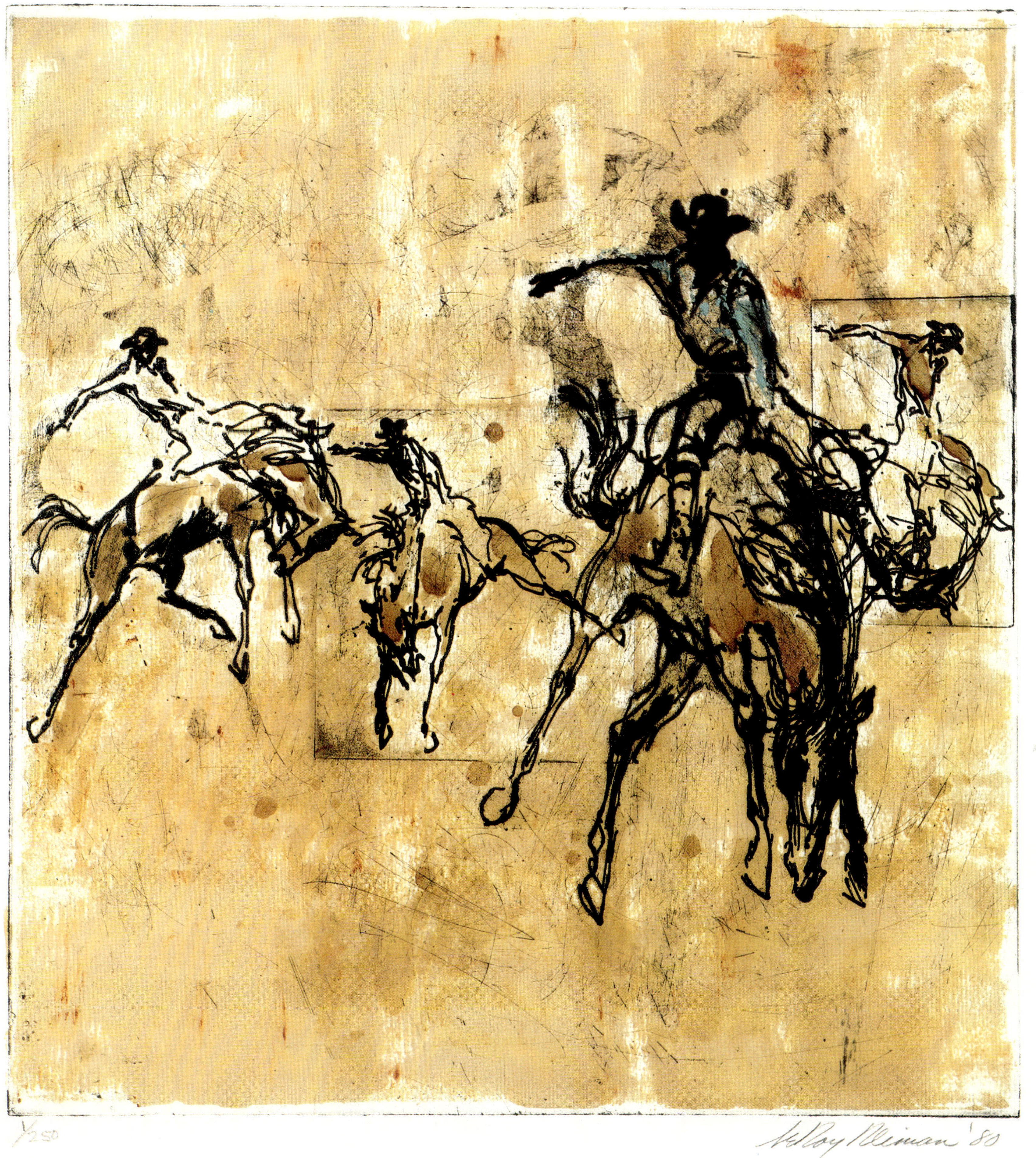

1/250
LeRoy Neiman '80

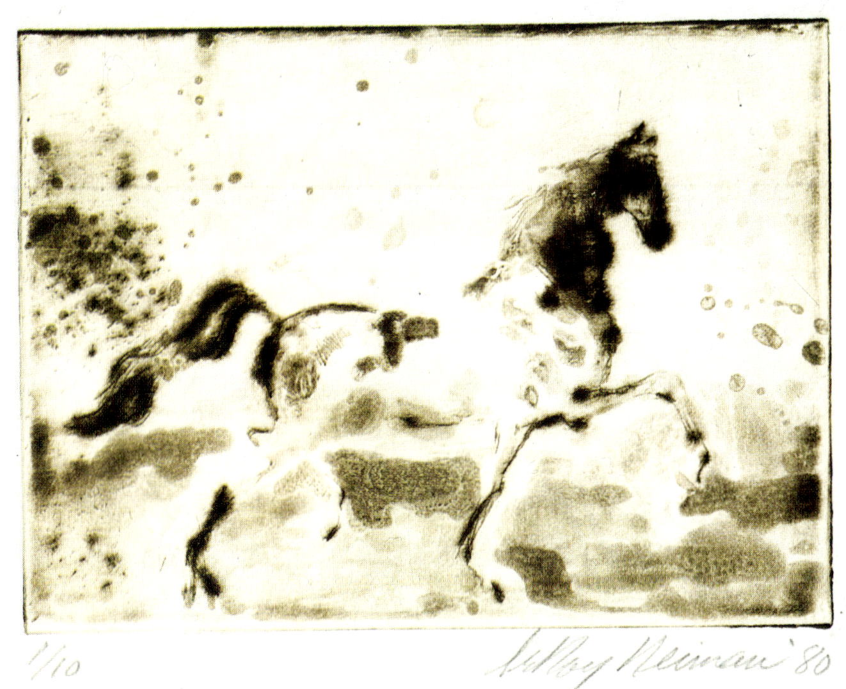

286 Easter Steed
1980
Etching
4 x 5½ (10.16 x 13.97 cm)
A limited edition of 10, signed
and numbered by the artist.

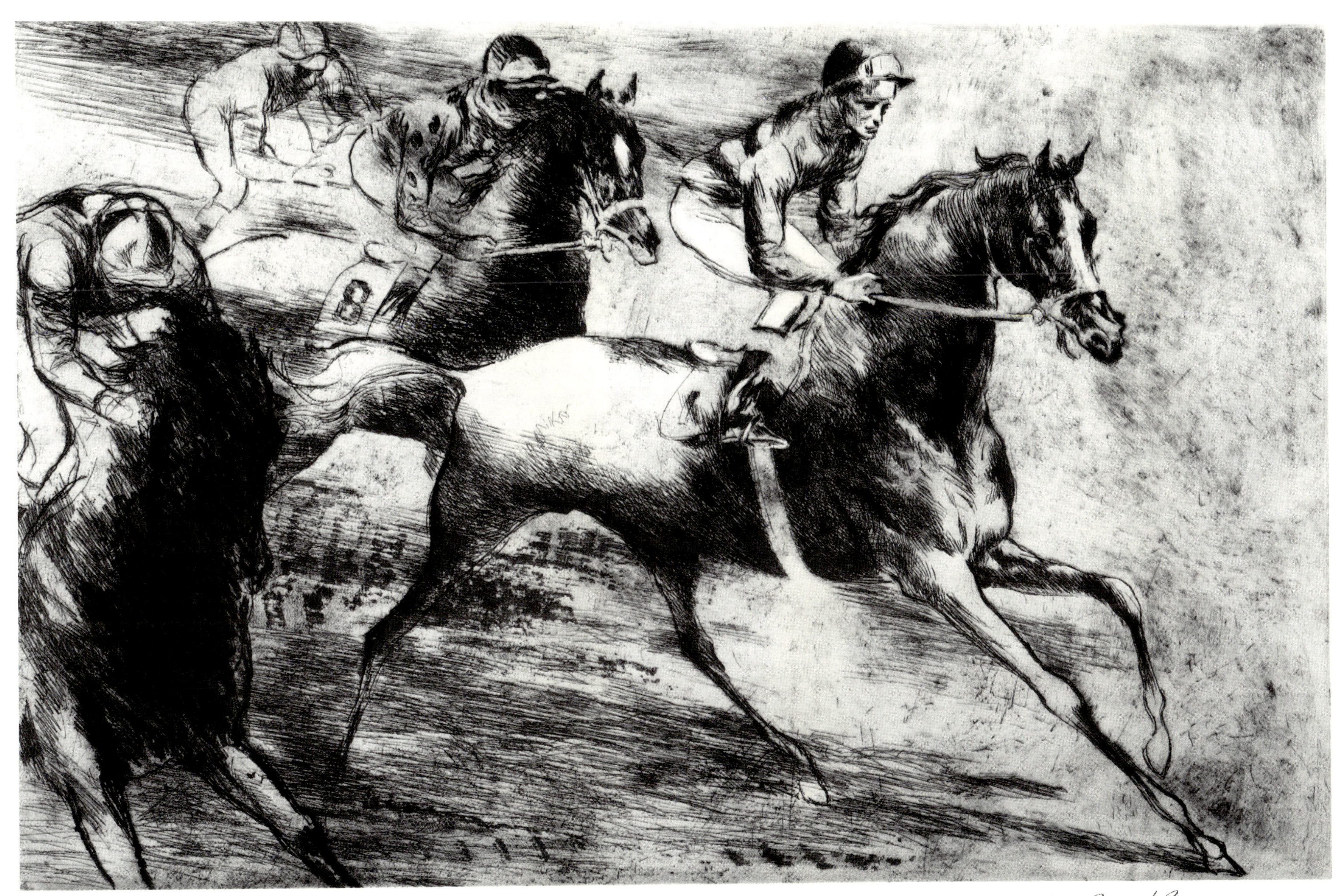

287   Daily Double

1980
Etching
11⅞ x 17⅞ (28.82 x 44.06 cm)
A limited edition of 250, signed
and numbered by the artist.

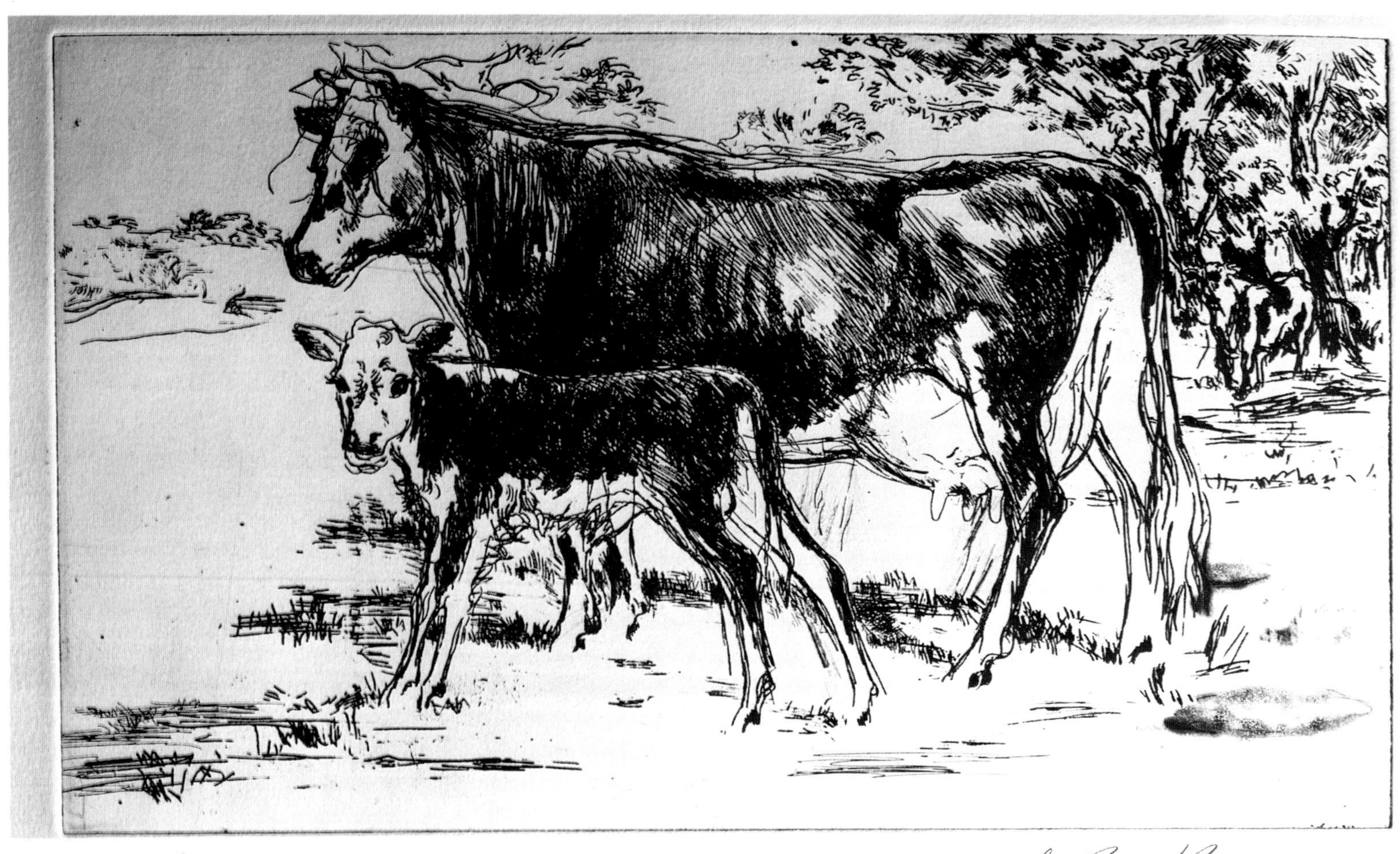

288   Bovine Family

1980
Etching
8⅞ x 14¾ (47.94 x 37.46 cm)
A limited edition of 250, signed
and numbered by the artist.

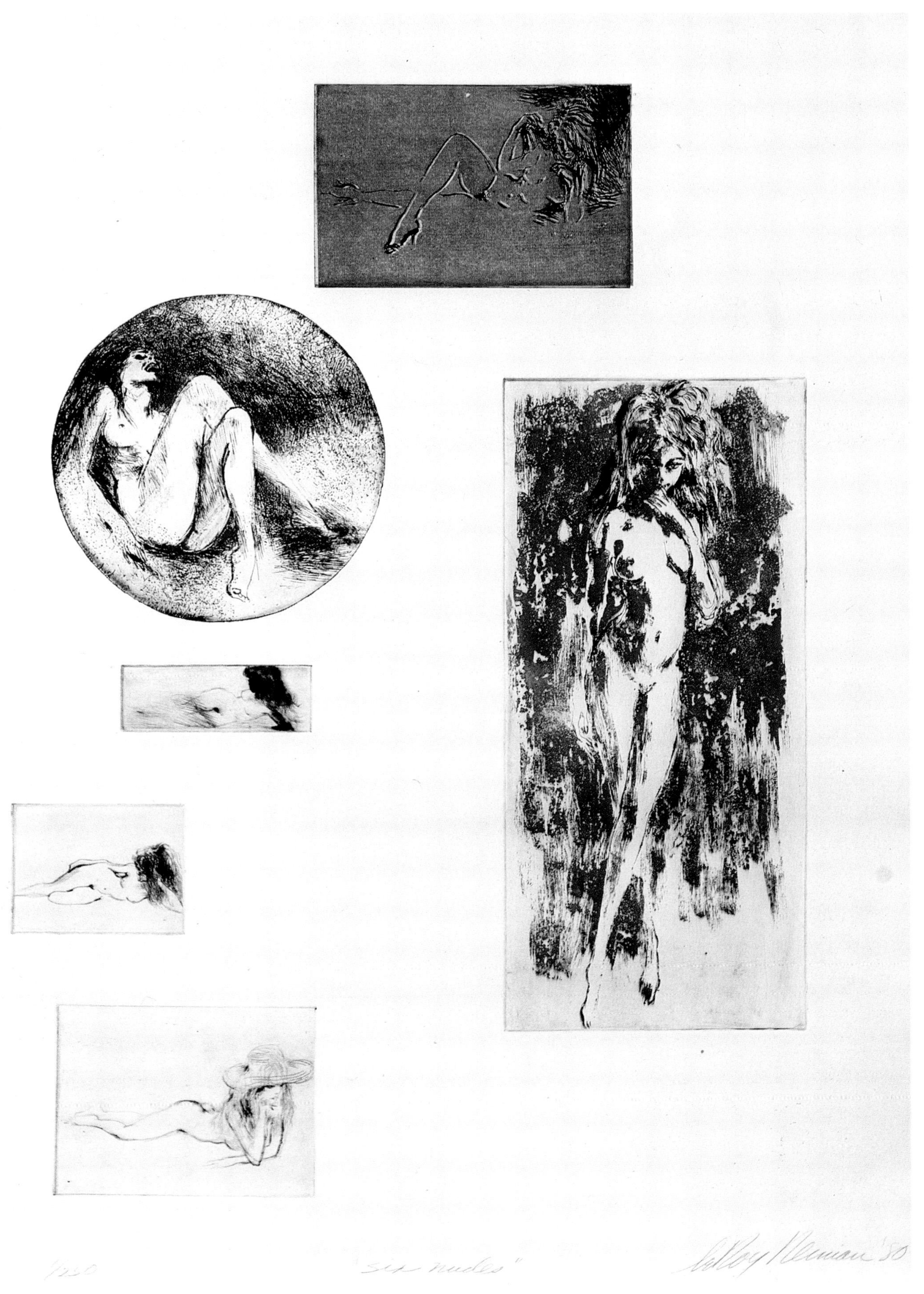

289 Six Nudes

1980
Etching
25½ x 17¾ (64.77 x 44.45 cm)
A limited edition of 250, signed and
numbered by the artist.

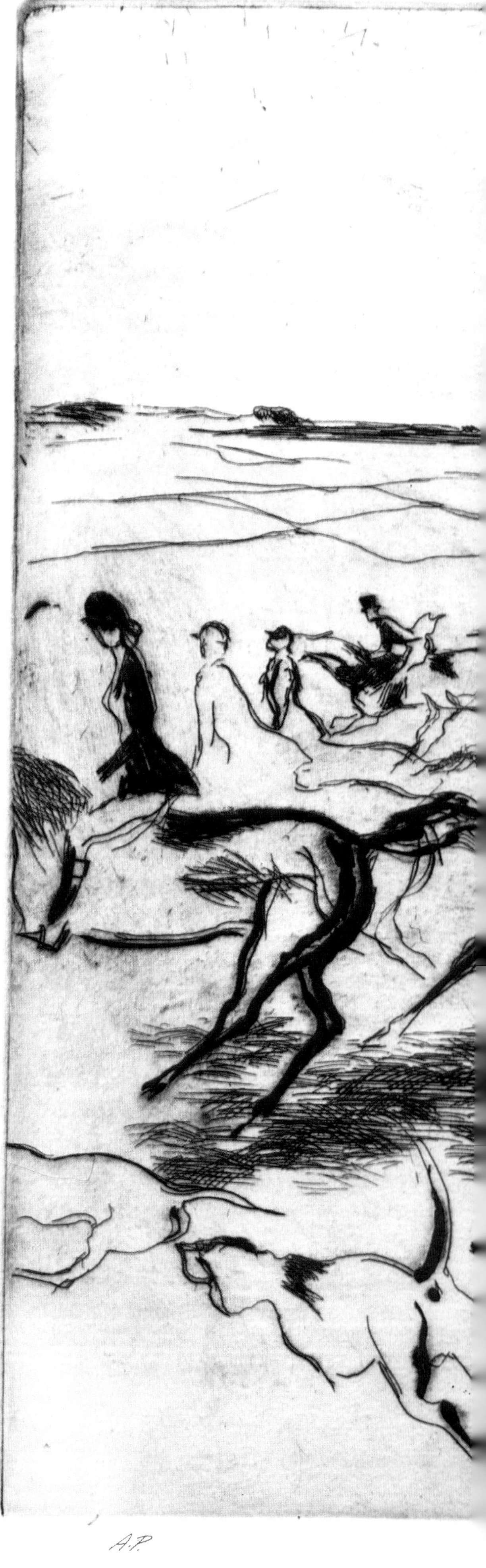

290 Into the Open

1980
Etching
13⅞ x 17⅞ (33.90 x 44.06 cm)

A limited edition of 250, signed
and numbered by the artist.

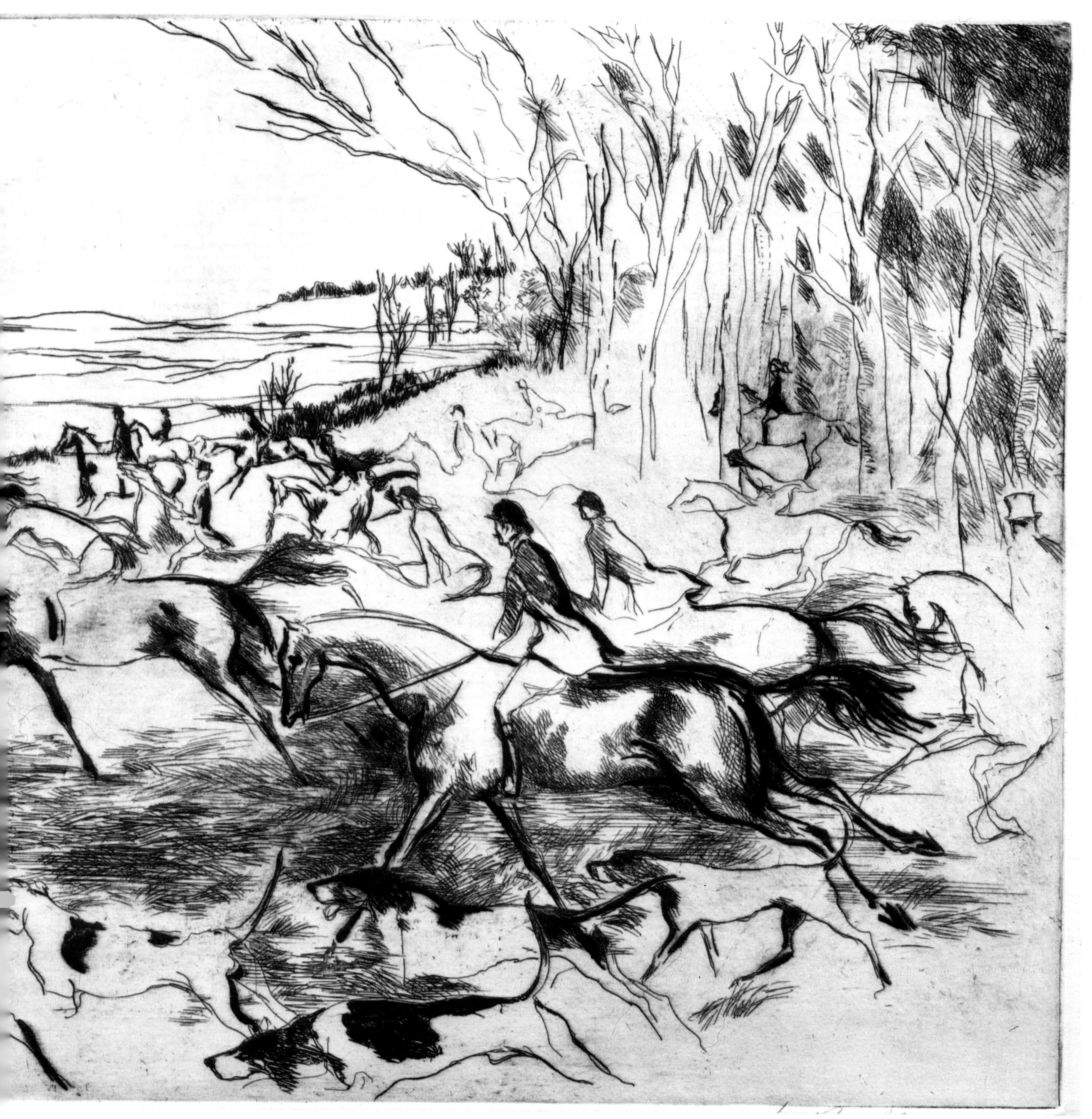

LeRoy Neiman

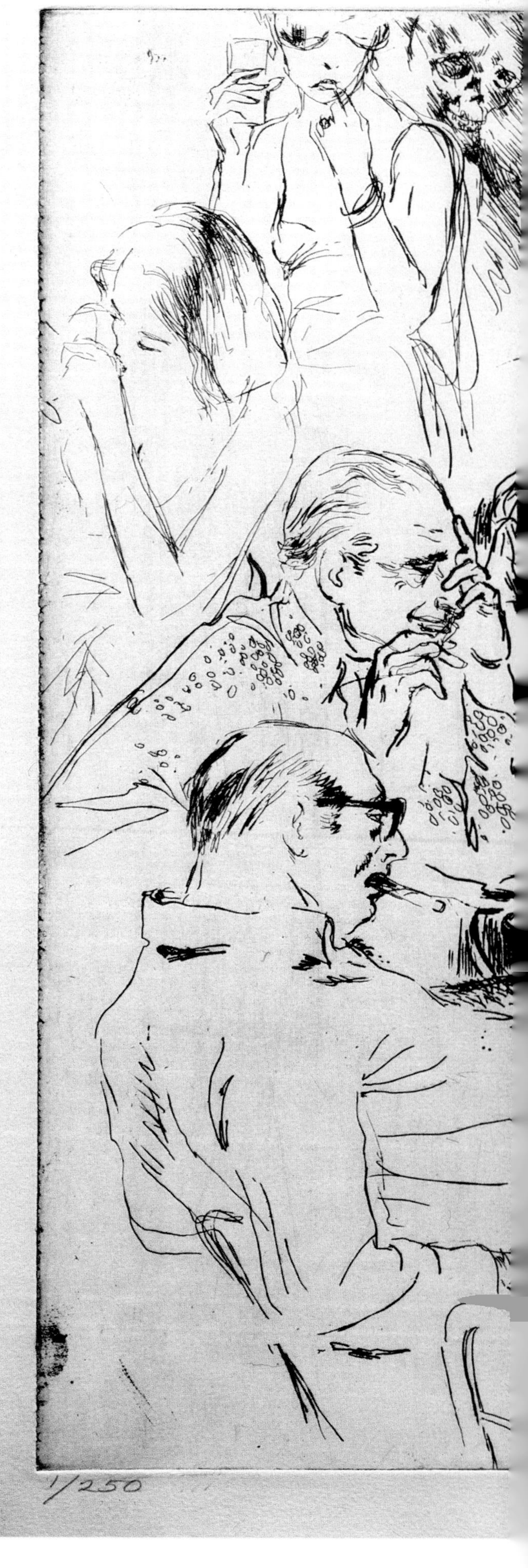

291   Stud Poker

1980
Etching
19¾ x 24½ (43.80 x 52.20)
A limited edition of 250, signed
and numbered by the artist.

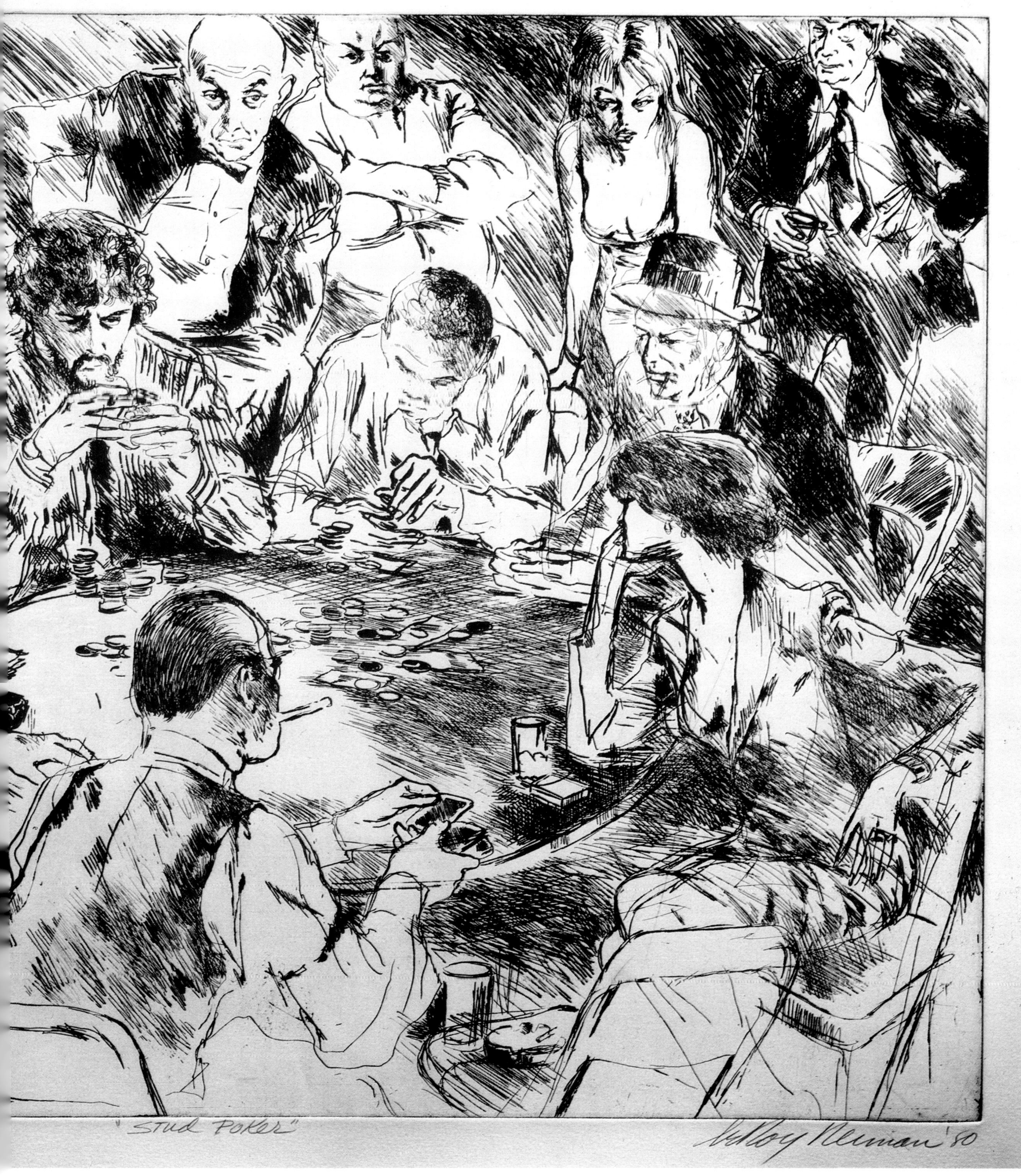

"Stud Poker"
LeRoy Neiman '80

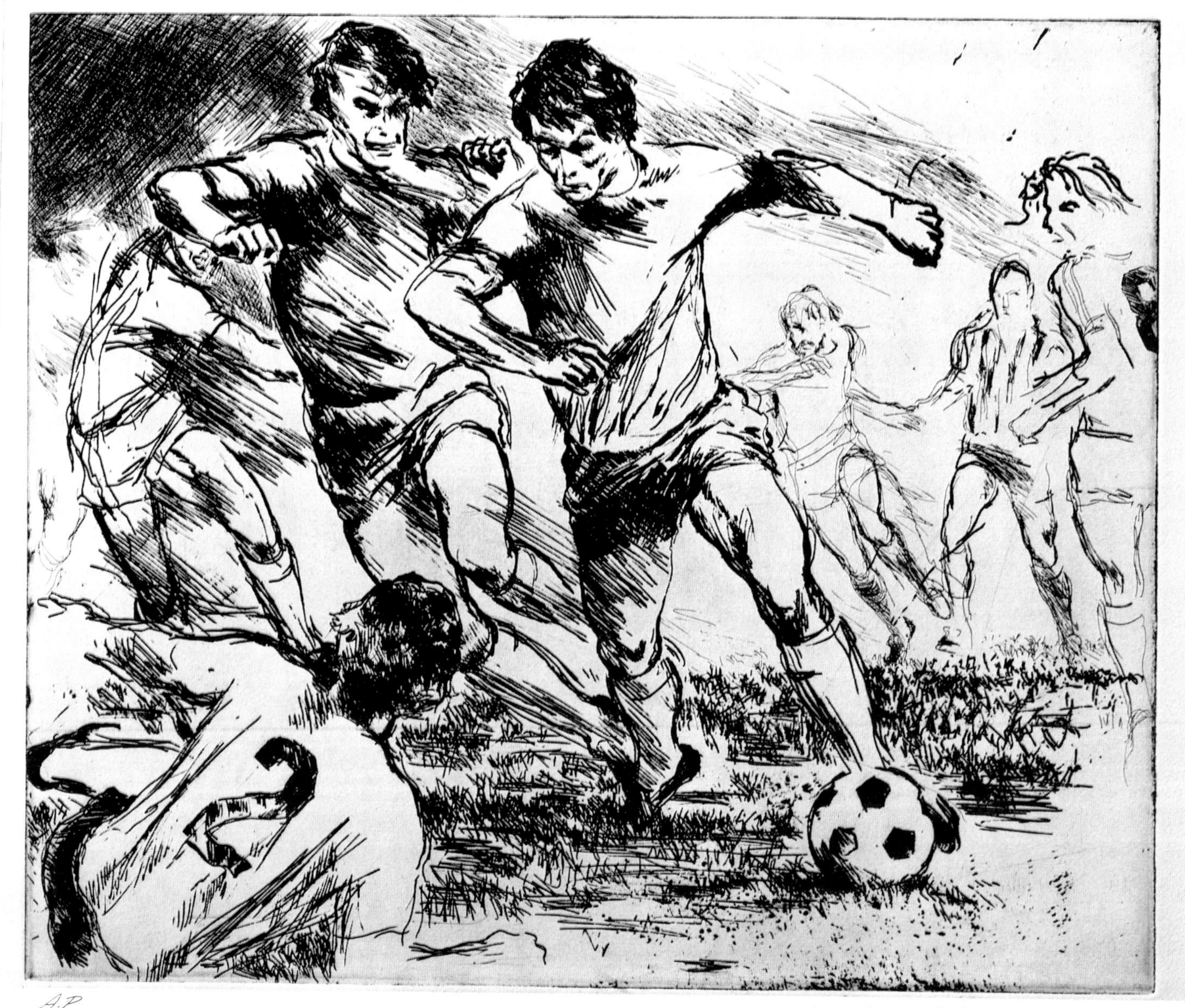

292   Soccer
1980
Etching
12⅞ x 14⅞ (32.70 x 37.78 cm)
A limited edition of 250, signed
and numbered by the artist.

293   Dalmatian
1980
Etching
24½ x 19¾ (52.20 x 43.80 cm)
A limited edition of 250, signed
and numbered by the artist.

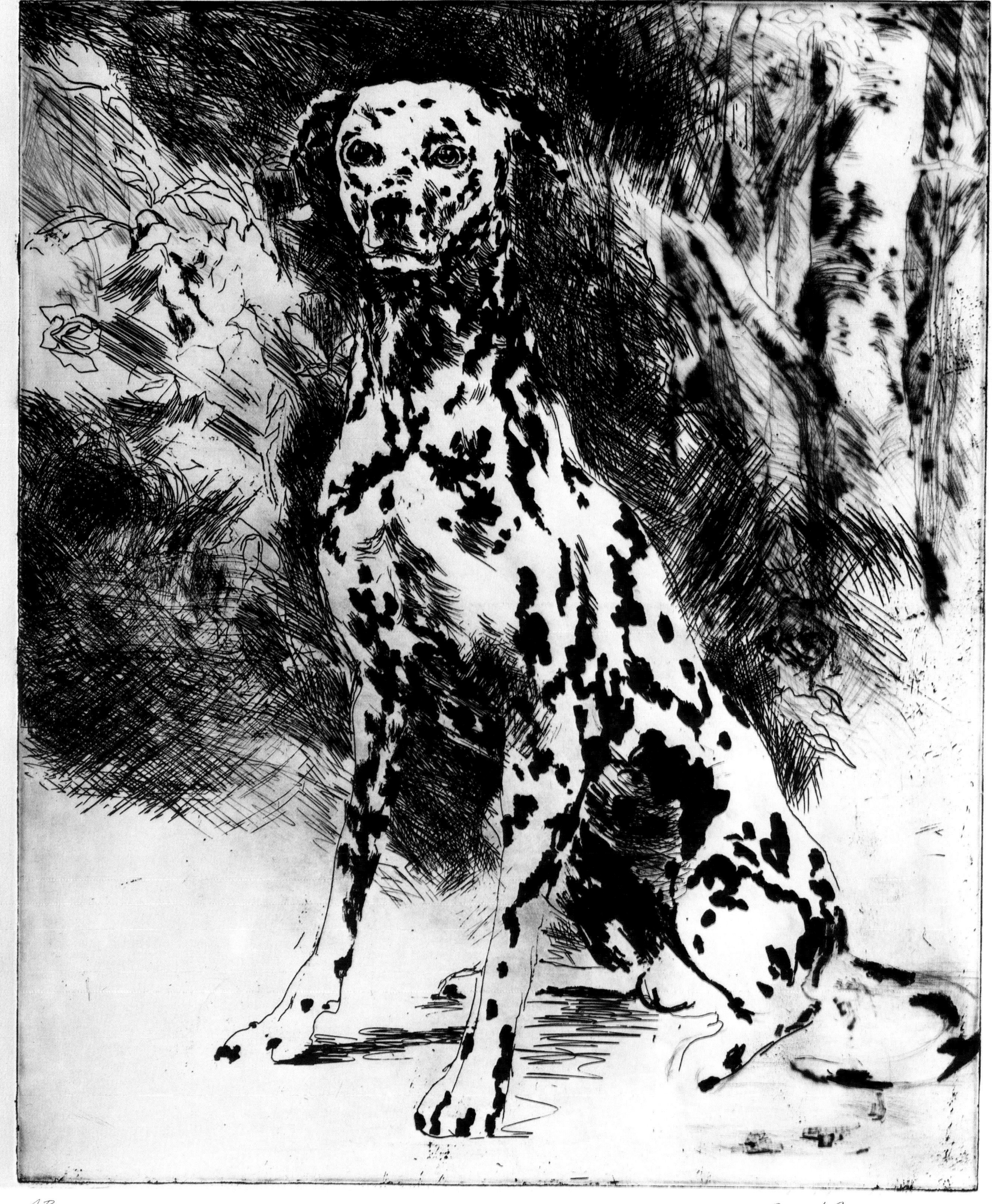

A.P.

LeRoy Neiman

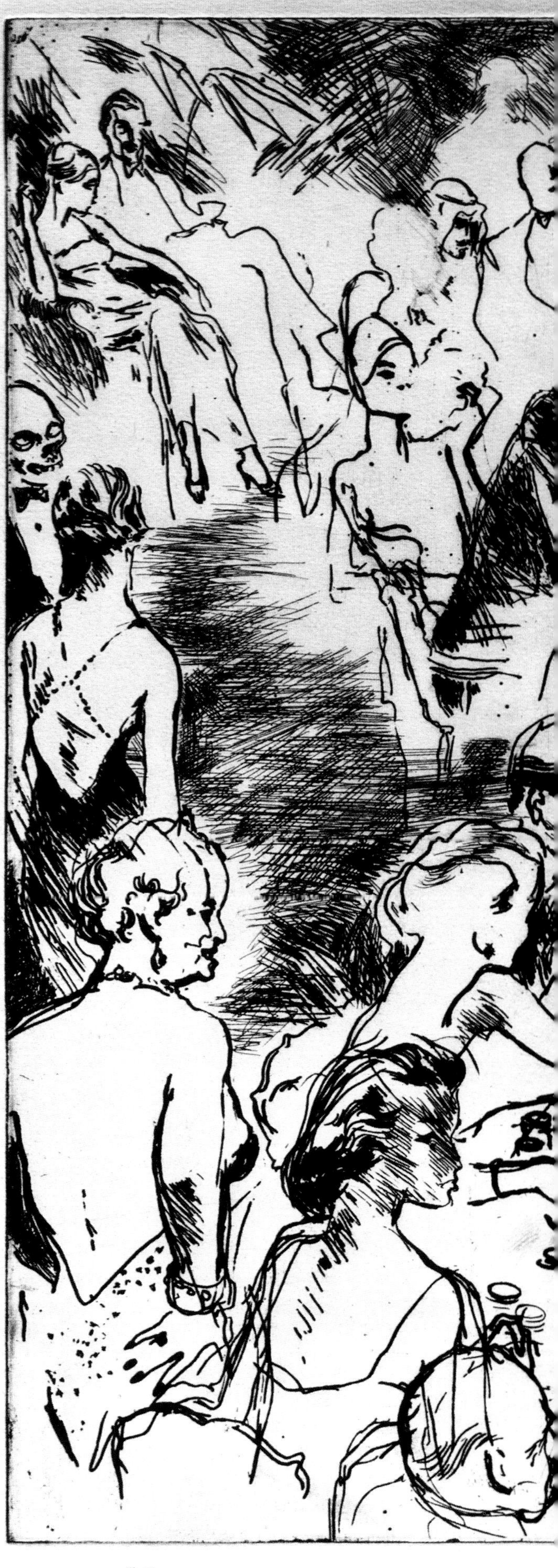

294   The Game of Life

1980
Etching
19¾ x 24½ (43.80 x 52.20 cm)
A limited edition of 250, signed
and numbered by the artist.

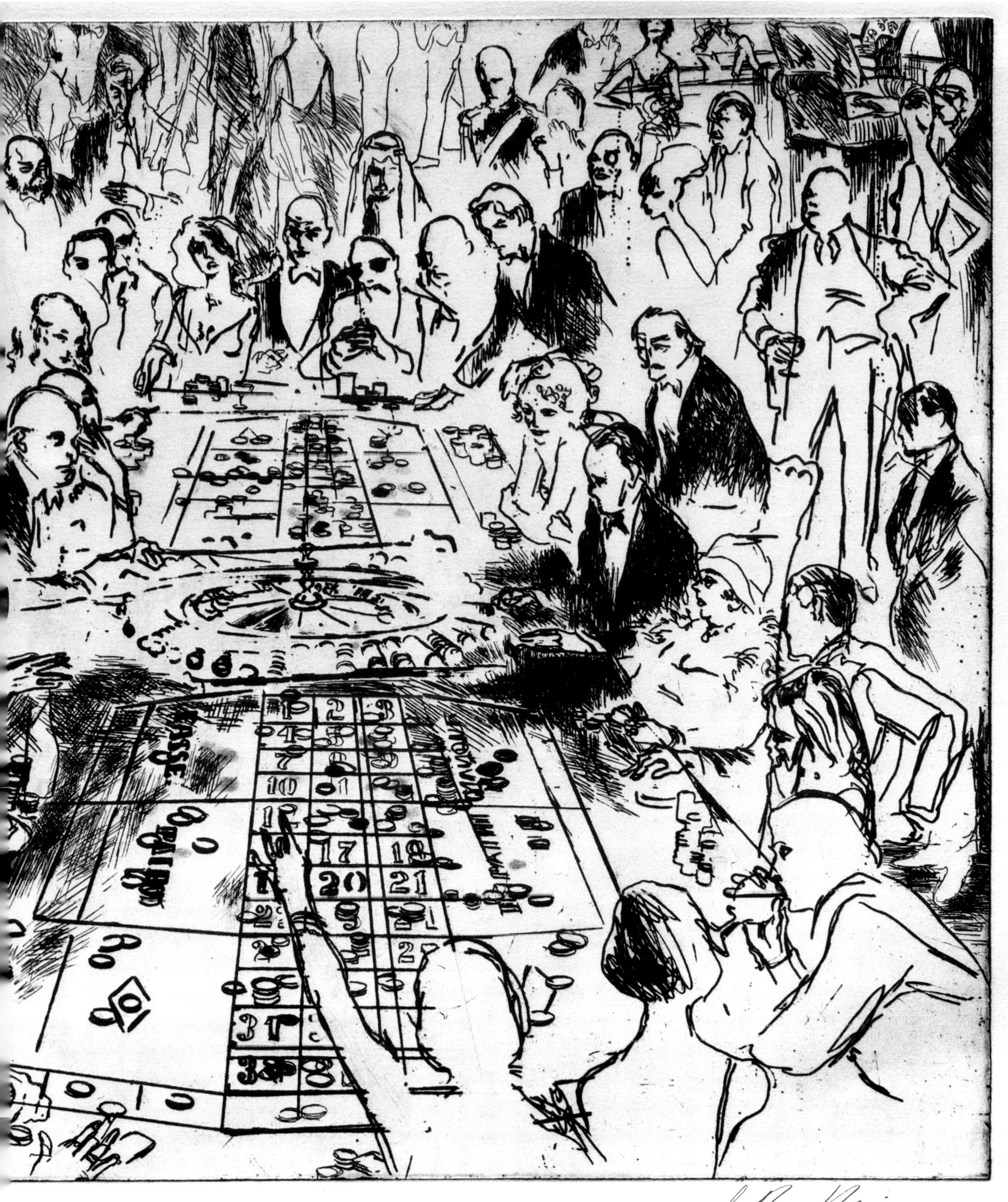

Bibliographic Notes to the Text

1. Neiman made this statement on 25 July 1975. It was first published by Malcolm Lein, then Director of The Minnesota Museum of Art, in the catalogue of the retrospective exhibition he organized of Neiman's work: *LeRoy Neiman Retrospective Exhibition: Paintings, Drawings, Watercolors, Prints, 1949–1975,* Saint Paul, the Minnesota Museum of Art (1975), p.11. Mr. Lein's introductory essay is one of the most sensitive that has been written.

2.   Marochka Anisfeld Chatfield-Taylor (the daughter of Boris Anisfeld) made this statement on 16 October 1979 in conversation with Nicholas Fox Weber who published it in his exhibition catalogue, *Paintings by Boris Anisfeld and a selection of his designs for ballet and opera,* New York, A. M. Adler Fine Arts Inc. (1979), p.8.

3. Conversation with the author, 11 September 1979. This was the first in a series of interviews that continued through March 1980. Those interviews, and other research done during those months, were the foundation for this essay. All of the quotations in the text are from that series of interviews, unless otherwise noted.

4. Conversation with the author, 11 September 1979.

5. The Armory Show took place in New York City in 1913. This exhibition presented both the latest European art, and the latest American art. It is considered one of the most important public events in the history of modern Armerican art. It introduced America to Duchamp, Matisse, and Picasso who would exert enormous influence over American artists for the next 50 years. The details are available in Milton Brown, *The Story of the Armory Show,* Greenwich, NYGS, (1963). Duchamp said at the time that the future of modern art would be in America, and he was right. For those who would like to read a short history of the development of American painting, three are available: James Thomas Flexner, *A Short History of American Painting,* Boston, Houghton Mifflin (1950); F. Lanier Graham, *Three Centuries of American Painting,* New York, Tuttle (1971); Matthew Baigell, *A Concise History of American Painting,* New York, Oxford (1974). Longer books are cited in the bibliographies of these shorter books.

6. Malcolm Lein, *op. cit.,* p.11

7. *Ibid.,* p.12.

8. *Ibid.,* pp.14-25.

9. *Ibid.,* pp.14-25.

10. Andy Warhol was interviewed by Robert Ward who published the results of that interview (along with several other interviews) in his seven-page article on Neiman entitled "Playboy of the Western World," *New Times,* 6 February 1978, p.64. This article also reports how much money Neiman is making.

11. Neiman wrote this letter and conducted his interview with Caxton early in 1961. This quotation is from the article that resulted from their interaction, "LeRoy Neiman: An Exuberant Painter," *American Artist,* April 1961.

12. The first book that Neiman published is entitled *LEROY NEIMAN: ART & LIFE STYLE,* New York, Felicie (1974), 285 pages. The text of this lavishly illustrated book is a chronology of the artist's life and work. In effect the book is something of an autobiography. Neiman's second book is *HORSES,* New York, Abrams (1979), 349 pages. This also was written by the artist and primarily illustrated with the results of his life time study of this subject. Abrams will be publishing a book on Neiman's posters later this year.

13. The psychology of consciousness is still a very young science. The first popular book on right-hemisphere/left-hemisphere research was published in 1972. For the general reader who would like to know more about the subject, a number of books are now available including several in paperback. As a first book there is Betty Edwards, *Drawing on the Right Side of the Brain: A Course in Enhancing Creativity and Artistic Confidence,* Los Angeles, J.P. Tarcher (1979) and Thomas R. Blakeslee, *The Right Brain: A New Understanding of the Unconscious Mind and Its Creative Powers,* New York, Doubleday (1980). More advanced students will profit from a reading of Robert E. Ornstein, *The Mind Field,* New York, Pocket Books (1976); Kenneth R. Pelletier, *Towards a Science of Consciousness,* New York, Dell (1978); Julian Jaynes, *The Origin of Consciousness in the Breakdown of the Bicameral Mind,* Boston, Houghton Mifflin (1976); and Carl Sagan, *The Dragons of Eden,* New York, Random House (1977).

Chronology:

1927 Born June 8 in Saint Paul, Minnesota.

1942–45 Drops out of high school; enlists in the army; serves four years in the European Theatre.

1946 Returns to Saint Paul; picks up high school credits; studies at the Minnesota Museum of Art (then Saint Paul Gallery and School of Art) with Clement Haupers.

1946–50 Student at the School of the Art Institute of Chicago; studies with Boris Anisfeld.

1950–60 Member of the Faculty, School of the Art Institute of Chicago; teaches figure drawing and fashion illustration.

1953 Begins using enamel house paints; first museum purchase (*Idle Boats*) by The Minneapolis Institute of Arts.

1954 Becomes associated with *Playboy Magazine;* illustrates Charles Beaumont story for friend Hugh Hefner.

1955 Instructor of painting at Elmwood Park Art League and North Shore Art League; exhibits in Carnegie International, Pittsburgh.

1956 Included in "New Talent in America in 1956," published in *Art in America,* February, 1956.

1957 Corcoran American Exhibition, oil painting, Washington, D.C.: Instructor at School of the Art Institute Summer Session and Ox-Bow Summer School, Saugatuck, Michigan; teaches landscape painting.

1958 Instructor at Ox-Bow Summer School, Saugatuck, Michigan: starts extensive travels for *Playboy Magazine*–does feature on high life called "Man at His Leisure."

1960–70 Executes hundreds of paintings and two murals for eighteen Playboy Clubs.

1961 Takes studio in Paris with wife Janet; wins gold medal for oil painting at the Salon d'Art Moderne, Paris.

1962 Holds exhibitions in London and Paris.

1963 Returns from Paris, establishes a studio in New York; painting instructor at Arts and Crafts, Inc., Winston-Salem, North Carolina.

1965 Hammer Gallery, holds first one man exhibition in New York, New York: Listed in *The Art Collector's Almanac.*

1966-80 Listed in *Who's Who in American Art.*

1966 Sketches Kentucky Derby; works three months in London painting personalities; paints surfing in California; executes mural for Swedish-Lloyd Ship— S.S. Patricia.

1967 Fascinated with personalities and their environments; sketches and paints Leonard Bernstein, Muhammad Ali, Frank Sinatra, Suzanne Farrell, and many others; covers racing at LeMans, nudist scenes on the Dalmatian Coast of Yugoslavia, the Fiesta at Pamplona, the Dolce Vita of Rome.

1968 Travels to Russia, concentrating on the Kirov and Bolshoi Ballets; artist-in-residence from the bench of the New York Jets Football Team; does critical sketches of the 1968 Democratic Presidential Convention in Chicago.

1969 Teaches painting in the Atlanta Poverty Program; does off-Broadway show art and film credits; covers horse racing at Ascot and Longchamp, camel racing in Morocco.

1970 National Portrait Gallery, The Smithsonian Institution: Travels extensively holding exhibitions and sketching sporting and social events in Dublin, Montreal, Jamaica, Europe, Africa and Greece.

1971 On the move again to Caracas, Monte Carlo, London, Paris and Switzerland; develops interest in printmaking; does two-part TV program on the art of lithography.

1972 Covers Fischer-Spassky world champion chess tournament at Reykjavik, Iceland; and sketches Munich Olympic Games for ABC; covers world series for NBC.

1973 Heavy into sports scene; does Super Bowl art for NBC; sketches the Masters Golf Tournament at Augusta, Georgia; executes special serigraph of Secretariat; sketches Foreman-Frazier fight in Jamaica; has nineteen silkscreens chosen by the Hermitage Museum, Leningrad for its permanent collection.

1974 Has exhibition in Tokyo; covers Stanley Cup hockey playoffs for NBC: draws pre-fight sketches of Ali-Frazier Super Fight II for *The New York Times;* executes 13 illustrations for The Artist's Limited Edition of *Moby Dick;* autobiographical book *LeRoy Neiman: Art and Life Style* is published.

1975 Commissioned to do an oil painting to be reproduced as Saint Paul's official Bicentennial poster; given major retrospective at the Minnesota Museum of Art; flies around world and sketches Ali-Frazier fight in Manila en route.

1976 Listed in *Who's Who in America;* ABC-TV Official Artist at Olympic Games, Montreal; Honorary Doctor of Letters Degree, Franklin Pierce College, New Hampshire; AAU (Amateur Athletic Union), Award of Merit as the "Nation's Outstanding Sports Artist;"

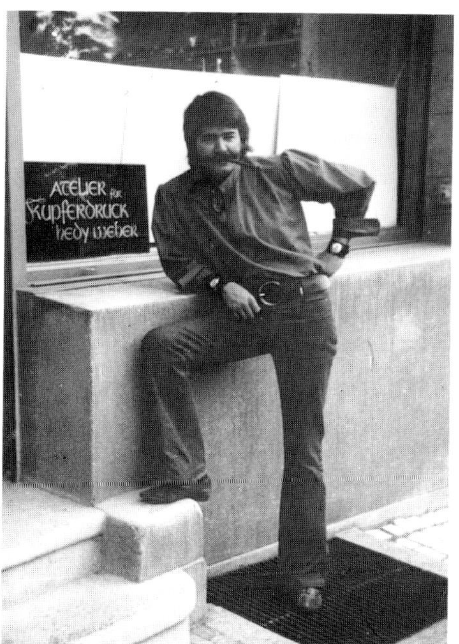

Neiman standing in front of Atelier Weber, Zurich, Switzerland, 1961, where he worked on his first etching.

paints on French Riviera; holds one-man show at Knoedler Gallery in London.

1977 Gold Plate Award, American Academy of Achievement; holds one-man shows in Stockholm and Helsinki.

1978 Appointed an official artist for the 1980 Lake Placid Olympic Games: CBS-TV Computer Artist at the Superbowl, New Orleans

1979 Wall Street Award, "Sports Artist of the Century;" travels to Tokyo to paint the Ginza, Kamakura Buddha, Mount Fuji, to London for Royal Ascot, the Pan-Am games in Puerto Rico for CBS-TV.

1980 Honorary Doctor of Fine Arts, St. John's University, New York; Official Artist of the Democratic National Convention, New York.

Selected Group Exhibitions:

St. Paul and Minneapolis Twin-City Show—
1952, 1953, 1954

Minnesota State Show, St. Paul—1952, 1954

Chicago Artists and Vicinity Show—1954, 1955, 1956,
1957, 1958, 1959, 1960

Carnegie International Exhibition, Pittsburgh—1955

Corcoran American Exhibition,
Washington, D.C.—1957

Chicago Art Institute, American Exhibition,
Chicago—1957, 1960

Collectors' Show, Walker Art Center,
Minneapolis—1957

Toledo Museum, Toledo, Ohio—1957

Traveling Exhibition, USIS, Holland, France, Ger-
many—1957–1959

Musée des Beaux-Arts, Arras, France—1958

Museum of Fine Arts, Rouen, France—1958

Chicago Art Institute, Society of Contemporary
American Art Exhibit, Chicago—1958, 1959, 1960

Ringling Museum American Art Exhibition, Sarasota,
Florida—1959

Des Moines Art Center, Des Moines, Iowa—1960

Butler Institute of American Art, Youngstown,
Ohio—1960

Salon d'Art Moderne, Paris—1961

John Heron Museum of Art, Indianapolis—1964

Galleria Fiorentina d'Arte, Florence—1964

Houston Art Gallery, Houston, Texas—1967, 1974

El Paso Art Museum, El Paso, Texas—1969

Minnesota Museum of Art, St. Paul—1969

Wichita Art Museum, Wichita, Kansas—1969

Delaware Art Center, Wilmington—1970

National Portrait Gallery, Smithsonian Institution,
Washington, D.C.—1970

Otis Art Institute, Los Angeles—1971

Portland Art Museum, Portland, Oregon—1971

Royal College of Art, London—1971

Print International, Basel—1971, 1972, 1973

Koninklijk Museum voor Schone Kunsten,
Antwerp—1972

Gemeenstemuseum, Arnham,
The Netherlands—1972

Kunstverein Munchen, Munich—1972

Musée des Arts Décoratifs, Lausanne,
Switzerland—1972

Central Museum of Art, Tokyo—1973

Umeda Kindai Museum, Osaka—1973

Lowe Museum, University of Miami, Coral Gables,
Florida—1974

Hermitage Museum, Leningrad—1974

Los Angeles Municipal Museum, Los Angeles—1974

Watercolor U.S.A., Springfield Museum, Springfield,
Missouri—1976

Drawings USA 1975, Museum of Art, St. Paul,
National Tour—1976–1977

Hammer Galleries, New York—1978, 1979, 1980

One-Man Exhibitions:

750 Gallery, Chicago—1953

Lincoln College, Lincoln, Illinois—1953

Todes Gallery, Chicago—1957

Chicago Public Library—1958

Oehlschlaeger Gallery, Chicago—1959, 1969

Oehlschlaeger Gallery, Sarasota, Florida—1962

O'Hana Gallery, London—1962

Galerie O. Bosc, Paris—1962

Hammer Gallery, New York—1963, 1965, 1967, 1968,
1970, 1972, 1975, 1976, 1978, 1979

Huntington-Hartford Gallery of Modern Art,
New York—1967

Heath Gallery, Atlanta—1969

Abbey Theatre, Dublin—1970

Far Gallery, New York—1971

Museo de Bellas Artes, Caracas, Venezuela—1972

Indianapolis Museum of Art, Indianapolis—1972

Circle Galleries, New York, Dallas, Chicago,
Los Angeles, San Francisco—1973

Brentano's, Boston, Beverly Hills, New York—1973

Cadaques, Spain—1973

The Saratoga Gallery, Saratoga, New York—1973

University of Illinois, Urbana, Illinois—1973

University of Texas, El Paso—1973

Tobu Gallery, Tokyo—1974

Springfield Museum of Art, Springfield,
Massachusetts—1974

Minnesota Museum of Art, Saint Paul,
Minnesota—1975

Upstairs Gallery, Los Angeles—1975

Knoedler Galleries, London—1976

Fahlnass Konstsalong Gallery, Goteborg,
Sweden—1976

Casagrafica, Helsinki—1977

Galerie Victor Renee, Stockholm—1977

Eastern Illinois University, Charleston, Illinois—1978

Meredith Long Galleries, Houston, Texas—1978

Bowles-Hopkins Gallery, San Francisco—1978

Hermitage Museum, Leningrad, U.S.S.R.

Illinois State Museum, Springfield, Illinois

Indianapolis Museum of Art, Indianapolis, Indiana

Joslyn Museum, Omaha, Nebraska

Memorial Art Gallery, Rochester, New York

Meridian Museum of Art, Meridian, Mississippi

Michigan State University, Kresage Art Center Gallery,
East Lansing, Michigan

Minneapolis Institute of Arts, Minneapolis, Minnesota

Minnesota Museum of Art, St. Paul, Minnesota

Mobile Art Gallery and Museum, Mobile, Alabama

Museo de Bellas Artes, Caracas, Venezuela

National Museum of Sport in Art, New York,
New York

Niagara University, Niagara, New York

Portland Museum of Art, Portland, Maine

Springfield Museum of Art, Springfield, Massachusetts

Tennis Hall of Fame, Newport, Rhode Island

Tuscon Museum of Art, Tuscon, Arizona

Tweed Museum of Art, University of Minnesota,
Duluth, Minnesota

University Art Gallery, Binghamton, New York

University of Illinois, Normal, Illinois

University of Oklahoma, Norman, Oklahoma

University of Oregon, Eugene, Oregon

University of South Florida, Tampa, Florida

University of Texas, Austin, Texas

Utah Museum of Fine Arts, University of Utah,
Salt Lake City, Utah

Vanderbilt University, Nashville, Tennessee

Wichita State University, Wichita, Kansas

Wodham College, Oxford, England

Yuma Fine Arts Association, Yuma, Arizona

The Silkscreen Print, or Serigraph

Excerpted from ART OF THE PRINT by Fritz Eichenberg. Published by Harry N. Abrams, Inc., New York.

Silkscreen is the most recent of the printmaking processes to attain the status of an art form, having suffered in the past from unfavorable association with the commercial uses of the medium. The low regard in which screen prints were held for more than a quarter of the present century is indicated by the coinage of a new name, "serigraphy," attributed to Carl Zigrosser, in order to distinguish art prints from the screen-processed images mass-produced for commerce and industry.

The basic principle of the technique was that of forcing color through the interstices of a silk fabric left open around images cut out of paper and attached to the silk, thus printing the design on a surface laid underneath. In the beginning the stencil was essentially a simple silhouetted design serving to block the passage of color to the printing surface. Later improvements included many radical changes in the basic material of both the resistant stencil and the porous mesh that supports it, as well as chemical sensitizing of the screen fabric to permit the transmission of photographic images.

The stencil process cannot be traced to any one inventor; its antecedents are lost in the remote past. In some of the earliest art periods there appears the "stenciled hand," a motif evolved by prehistoric artists who sprayed color around the spread finders of a human hand on rock surfaces. In primitive societies stencils may also have been used to tatoo the human skin....

In the United States it was the Great Depression of the 1930s and the efforts of the WPA Federal Art Project that prompted a group of artists, headed by Anthony Velonis, to experiment with silkscreen for artistic purposes. In those difficult times the inexpensiveness of the equipment needed for the process offered an important economic advantage over the other print media. The materials were easily assembled, constructed, and operated without heavy investment in copper plates, presses, stones, wood blocks, and the other paraphernalia of the relief, intaglio, or lithographic media....

Not until the late 1950s and early 1960s, however, did serigraphy develop into the generally acclaimed and accepted medium of the so-called avant-garde, producing a plethora of exhibitions and a cross-breeding with other media that breached and finally broke down long-established barriers and definitions....

For the present, the silkscreen process as an art medium has proved its usefulness beyond a doubt. In some respects it has offered to the twentieth century what the first woodcuts did for the fifteenth—a relatively quick, creative way of disseminating ideas and images across the world....

by Fritz Eichenberg